A
# PERAMBULATION
OF
# DARTMOOR

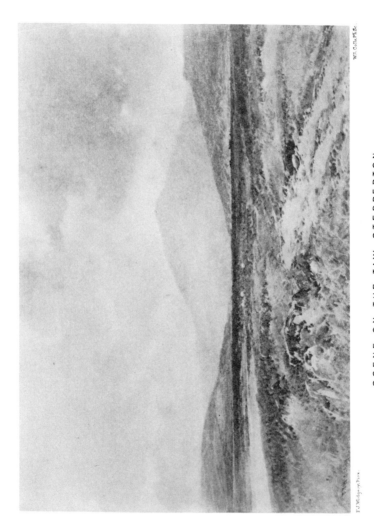

SCENE ON THE TAW, STEPPERTON.

F.J. Widgery, Pinx.

W.T. Goff, Ph.Sc.

# A PERAMBULATION

OF THE

## ANTIENT AND ROYAL

# Forest of Dartmoor

AND THE

## VENVILLE PRECINCTS

OR A

Topographical Survey of their Antiquities and Scenery

BY THE LATE

## Samuel Rowe, M.A.

THIRD EDITION, REVISED AND CORRECTED BY

### J. BROOKING ROWE
F.S.A., F.L.S.

ILLUSTRATED FROM DRAWINGS BY

### F. J. WIDGERY

# DEVON BOOKS

First published 1848
Reprinted 1856
Revised and enlarged 1896
Republished in facsimile 1985

© This edition Devon Books 1985

**British Library Cataloguing in Publication Data**
Rowe, Samuel
    [A perambulation of the antient and Royal Forest of Dartmoor
    and the Venville precincts, or, A topographical survey of their
    antiquities and scenery].
    A perambulation of Dartmoor.
    1. Dartmoor (England)—Description and travel
    I. [A perambulation of the antient and Royal Forest of Dartmoor
    and the Venville precincts, or, A topographical survey of their
    antiquities and scenery]
    II. Title
    914.23′530475      DA670.D2

ISBN 0 86114-773-1

DEVON BOOKS
Official Publishers to the Devon County Council

Devon Books is a Division of A. Wheaton & Co. Ltd,
which represents:
*Editorial and Design*
*Production and Manufacturing*
A. Wheaton & Co. Ltd, Hennock Road, Exeter EX2 8RP
*Sales and Distribution*
Town & Country Books, 24 Priory Avenue, Kingskerswell,
Newton Abbot TQ12 5AQ

*Printed in Great Britain by A. Wheaton & Co. Ltd*

TO

HIS ROYAL HIGHNESS,

# ALBERT, PRINCE OF WALES,

AND

## DUKE OF CORNWALL,

THIS DESCRIPTION OF THE ANTIQUITIES & TOPOGRAPHY
OF HIS FOREST OF DARTMOOR,
DEVON.

*Is humbly dedicated by the gracious permission*

## Of His Royal Highness Prince Albert,

MASTER FORESTER,

AND LORD WARDEN OF THE STANNARIES,

BY HIS LOYAL, FAITHFUL, AND MOST OBEDIENT SERVANT,

### SAMUEL ROWE.

*Vicarage, Crediton, Devon,*
*July 17th, 1848.*

SAMUEL ROWE, born 11 November, 1793.
b.a., Jesus College, Cambridge, 1826.
Curate St. Andrews, Plymouth.
Vicar of St. Budeaux.
Minister of St. Paul's, Stonehouse.
Minister of St. George's, Stonehouse.
m.a., Cambridge, 1833.
Vicar of Crediton.
Died 15 Sept., 1853.

# TABLE OF CONTENTS

# LIST OF ILLUSTRATIONS.

### FULL PAGE PLATES.

### VIGNETTES AND WOODCUTS.

Nun's or Siward's Cross, from the west. Menhir. Prestonbury. Lydford Bridge. Lover's Leap, Holne Chase. Brent Tor. Lydford Castle. Kitt's Steps. Seal of the Stannary Court [see 1. p. 418.] Head of Red Deer. [*Cervus eluphus.*] Ring Ousel. [*Turdus torquatus*]. A Dartmoor Stream. Staghorn Moss. [*Lycopodium Selago.*] Widecombe in the Moor. Piscina, St. Petrock's Church, Lydford. Font, St. Petrock's Church, Lydford. Arch, St. Brigidas' Church, Bridestowe. West Doorway, St. Winifred's Church, Manaton. Font, St. Patrick's Church, South Brent. Tower and Transept, St. Patrick's Church, South Brent. Sundial Stone, Sheepstor Church. Tombstone, St. Peter's Church, St. Peter Tavy. Dartmoor Farmhouse.

Four Sectional Maps of Dartmoor and the surrounding neighbourhood.

# EDITOR'S PREFACE.

THE first edition of this work was published in 1848, and it was soon sold out, and the book is now a scarce one. A second edition, a mere reprint of the first, appeared in a smaller form in 1856, a few copies contained the same illustrations as the larger work, the others had the letter-press with two or three plates only. The second edition is now nearly as scarce as the first, and copies with the full number of illustrations are very seldom indeed met with.

Although since the publication of the Perambulation many guides to the "wild and wondrous region" have appeared, none have been found so useful, none so full of information as this book, and I am informed that for a considerable time past, enquiries for it have been frequent. To meet the evident want, I have ventured to prepare another edition.

I have made many alterations and some additions, but, although entirely dis-agreeing with them, I did not feel at liberty to eliminate altogether the Druidical theories of the author, with which the first edition of the book was saturated. Nor had I any intention of re-writing the book. I was desirous that the Perambulation should be still Samuel Rowe's Perambulation, and that his name should continue to be connected with the best history of the place he loved so much, and to the surpassing interest of which he was one of the first to direct attention. I could not do all that seemed to be necessary in the way of addition and correction, by means of notes, and I have therefore, in many places, altered and extended the text, and have tried to make the reader acquainted with the most recent ideas of students, and to put before them the results of researches made since 1848, in connection with Dartmoor.

The time has not arrived for writing a proper history of the Moor. Many questions have to be settled before this can be undertaken. At the time the work was written there was only one theory as to the origin of the monumental remains of Dartmoor. Since, there have been several. Fifty years ago Pre-historic Archæology was a science unknown, certainly our author was quite ignorant of it. But he tells us that " where history is silent "and monumental evidence is disputable, an ample field is opened " for theory and speculation." And this is so—speculate we may, but it is too soon to dogmatise ; we have not yet sufficient evidence to be positive. There is nothing to support the conclusions of the older antiquaries, that our dolmens, circles and rows were connected with Druidism ; on the other hand, we must know more about them before we can, as Fergusson said, relegate them to the misty haven of pre-historic antiquity. The latest authority, Mr. A. L. Lewis, adduces a considerable amount of evidence in support of his proposition, that the Stone Circles were intended primarily as places of worship or sacrifice, in which case, as he says, it is most likely that the antiquaries of the last century were not so altogether wrong as has since been thought, in pronouncing them to be the temples of our sun and star worshipping ancestors and their priesthood, although there may be, so far, no absolute proof that such was the case.* And Mr. Arthur J. Evans says, that after all perhaps we may find ourselves in Druid company, but we must arrive there by the methods imposed by modern science.† But at present we are only groping our way. Rays of light sometimes strike across our path, and quickly vanish, but they are enough to show, that we are on the right track, and at the same time, that we have much to do before we can reach our journey's end. A hundred years ago the Druidical theory was unhesitatingly accepted, and Stukeley had no difficulty in distinguishing the barrow of an arch-druid, and could with confidence assign a precise date for the rearing of the mighty trilothons of Stonehenge. Then the pendulum swung, and the other extreme was reached. Sir Edward Smirke began to talk about " bearded old mistletoe-cutting humbugs, the

---

*A. H. LEWIS. Stone Circles of Britain. Arch. Journal, vol xlix., pp. 136-154.
†ARTHUR J. EVANS. Stonehenge. Archæological Review, vol. ii., p. 312.

"Druids," and upon this hint others spoke, and asserted that there never were any Druids, and that therefore the monumental relics of Dartmoor could have had nothing to do with sacrifice or worship. To take Grimspound as an instance. Note the various suggestions that have been advanced as to the origin and use of this interesting place. Polwhele states that it was a seat of judicature for the Cantred of Durius ; Samuel Rowe, that it was a Belgic or Saxon Camp; Ormerod considered it a cattle pound, pure and simple; Spence Bate was convinced that it was nothing more than a habitation of tinners, and of no great age ; while now, the work of the Rev. S. Baring-Gould and Mr. Robert Burnard, goes far to show that its construction reaches back into a remote past, and that its antiquity is greater than any former investigator dared to assign to it. This example shows how very necessary it is that we should walk warily, and work on with caution, hoping to solve in time, the riddle that Dartmoor puts to us, and until we can be sure as to the answer, not to make mere guesses at solutions.

I have thought it desirable, as a warning, and to prevent further mistakes, to put this caution clearly, and perhaps strongly. Having done so, I may say that certain conclusions have been arrived at, very difficult to upset, which go far to prove that the megalithic monuments of Dartmoor are the work of the races of the Neolithic and early Bronze periods, peoples altogether distinct from the Celt and early Briton, and by whom they were conquered.

To anticipate criticism in one direction. I have no doubt it will be said that the book is incomplete, and that references to many things and places of interest, are wanting. But I have made no attempt to make the book a perfect one by including in it an account of every relic, thing, and place on Dartmoor. This was not my intention. I have followed the lines of my original, making such additions and alterations as I thought desirable, and which I considered would be of interest to the bulk of my readers. But although it is by no means exhaustive, I hope I have done something to make this new edition, not only a useful guide to the visitor, but that it will not be considered altogether unworthy of the subject by the enthusiast who knows his Dartmoor well.

A sketch map is provided, and four other maps to a larger scale, which pedestrians will find useful. For more convenient

*Editor's Preface.*

use and reference the book has been divided into chapters; the greater part of the work after chapter VIII. is new; the contents of the chapter " Dartmoor Literature," shows how much has been done since the Perambulation was written.

I have to acknowledge very much valuable assistance rendered me by my friends the Rev. S. Baring-Gould and Mr. Robert Burnard; Mr. W. A. E. Ussher, F.G.S., of Her Majesty's Geological Survey, has been good enough to write the chapter on the Geology of the Moor—in the stead of the admirable chapter in the first edition, by the late Dr. Edward Moore, but which the progress of geological knowledge has rendered obsolete— to which Mr. R. N. Worth, F.G.S., has obligingly added some pages on the Petrology, a subject he has made peculiarly his own; Mr. Francis Brent, F.S.A., most kindly furnished me with the the chapter on the Botany, and Mr. Hine gave me the use of the wood blocks from which the illustrations in Chapter XIX. have been printed. To these gentlemen, I return my best thanks. Help from other good and willing friends is referred to and acknowledged in the body of the book.

J. BROOKING ROWE.

*Castle Barbican,*
*Plympton,*
29 *Sept.*, 1895.

# PREFACE TO THE FIRST EDITION.

AN essay on the most prominent objects of antiquarian interest, in the Forest of Dartmoor, was originally read before the Plymouth Institution, in the year 1828, as the result of the united researches of a few members* of that Society, who at different times had pursued their investigations in a district which, although within a few miles of their town, was little known to the neighbourhood and the County in general. The paper drawn up at the request of my esteemed coadjutors, was subsequently published in the Transactions of the Society.† Since that time I have endeavoured to prosecute the investigations thus begun, for the most part with the able assistance of my valued friend the President of the Institution, at such intervals as scanty leisure and few opportunities would permit; hence, abundant materials have been collected for expanding the original essay into the present volume.

The publication has been undertaken with the view of rendering the numerous objects of interest, with which the great moorland district of the west abounds, more generally known and appreciated, in the persuasion that within its limits there is enough to repay, not only the historian and antiquary, but also the scientific investigator, for the task of exploring the mountain-wastes of the Devonshire wilderness. The characteristic tors, capping the hills with their massive granite piles, supply an interesting field of study to the geologist—Wistman's Wood,

---

*Henry Woollcombe (President); Col. Hamilton Smith, F.R.S.; John Prideaux; and the Rev. Samuel Rowe.

†Transactions Plymouth Institution, 1830, p. 179.

primitive and peculiar, affords an unique specimen to the botanist
—and the aboriginal circumvallation of Grimspound, one equally
singular, to the antiquary. It is not difficult to imagine that
relics so remarkable, if situated in a far distant land, would be
sought out, chronicled, and described, for the information of the
learned, and gratification of the curious, whilst in our own country,
objects as fully calculated to illustrate the most antient periods of
British history, as are the extraordinary ruins at Palenque that of
Central America, are overlooked and neglected, as it would seem
for no other reason than their proximity, and facility of access.

The tourist, who ventures to penetrate the Devonshire Highlands, will also find himself greeted with a succession of scenes
of unexpected loveliness and grandeur, especially along the entire
verge of the Moor, many of them rivalling the far-famed scenery
of North Wales, but distinguished by characteristic features of
peculiar beauty. Nor have they been thought unworthy of
admiration by more than one traveller fresh from the charms of
Continental magnificence and sublimity, with whom I have
visited the precincts of Dartmoor. My own opinion may be
attributed to partiality for my native county, and to untravelled
ignorance of

> " The Alps and Apennine,
> The Pyrenean and the River Po ; "

but when it is fortified by the recorded sentiments of strangers,
and by such competent and impartial authority as that of William
Howitt, I feel justified, in specially referring to Devonshire, the
pertinent expostulation which has been made with so much
propriety in reference to Great Britain generally.—

> " Pilgrims of beauty, ye who far away
> " Roam where poetic deserts sadly smile,
> "Oh ! ere ye leave it, view your own fair native Isle."

The testimony of a native of Scotland, a writer of some ten
years ago, in Blackwood's Magazine,* who is evidently well
acquainted with the district he describes, may here be adduced.
" West Devonshire is that large tract of land comprised
" between the Dartmoor mountains, the rivers Tamar and Plym,

---

*Vol. xxxiii., 1833, p. 609.

" and the Plymouth Sound; and illustrious for the number,
" narrowness, and depth of the larger valleys—whose banks
" generally rise into a flat ascent, from the banks of the dividing
" streams—and for many down-like swells and many strangely-
" fractured hills. You may know how dear this district was to us,
" last time we wandered through its delights, when we tell you
" that we often forgot where we were wandering, and believed that
" we were holidaying it in one of the half lowland, half highland
" regions, among the blue bonnets of Auld Scotland. * * *
" Dartmoor—we have nothing like it in Scotland. Our moor of
" Rannoch is a vast flat. * * But Dartmoor is no flat. It is
" indeed an elevated table land; but its undulations are endless:
" there are no separate single masses, nor can it be called moun-
" tainous;* but it is as if a huge mountain had been squeezed
" down, and in the process had split asunder, till the whole was
" one hilly wilderness, showing ever and anon strange half-buried
" shapes striving to uplift themselves towards the sky."

To the same effect, but in a still more enthusiastic strain, is
the panegyric of William Howitt, in his " Rural Life of
" England."†

" If you want sternness and loneliness, you may pass into
" Dartmoor. There are wastes and wilds, crags of granite, views
" into far off districts, and the sound of waters hurrying away over
" their rocky beds, enough to satisfy the largest hungering and
" thirsting after poetical delight. I shall never forget the feelings
" of delicious entrancement with which I approached the outskirts
" of Dartmoor. I found myself amongst the woods near Haytor
" Crags. It was an autumn evening. The sun, near its setting,
" threw its yellow beams among the trees, and lit up the tors on
" the opposite side of the valley into a beautiful glow. Below, the
" deep dark river went sounding on its way with a melancholy
" music; and as I wound up the steep road all beneath the
" gnarled oaks, I ever and anon caught glimpses of the winding
" valley to the left, all beautiful with wild thickets and half
" shrouded faces of rock, and still on high those glowing ruddy
" tors standing in the blue air in their sublime silence. My road
" wound up, and up, the heather and the bilberry on either hand,

---

*Yet he has just called the Dartmoor ridge, " *mountains*," vide supra.

†Vol. ii., p. 378, ed. 1838.

" showing me that cultivation had never disturbed the soil they
" grew in ; and one sole woodlark from the far ascending forest on
" the right, filled the wild solitude with his wild autumnal note.
" At that moment I reached an eminence, and at once saw the
" dark crags of Dartmoor high aloft before me."

Such is the verdict of a popular author, unbiassed by local
partialities, and conversant with the romantic loveliness of the
Rhine, and the stupendous magnificence of the Alps. And such
is the district for which the author thinks himself justified in
venturing to claim a foremost place among the scenes which

" England holds
" within her world of beauty,"

in the hope that the charms of our Devonian highlands will be
more generally known and appreciated, and the interesting monuments of antiquity which they shelter, will be more effectually
protected against the manifold modes of spoliation and destruction
which have arisen from multiplied population, increasing
commercial speculations, and economic improvements. The
venerable relics of past ages (like the antient Britons, retreating
before overpowering numbers) have been pursued from one asylum
to another, until the mountainous districts of the western and south-
western portions of the island afford them their last and only
refuge. But their rocky citadel is no longer secure. Quarries are
opened on the heights of Dartmoor—powder-mills are projected
in the very heart of its solitudes—cultivation is smiting its
corners—steam is marshalling his chariots of iron and coursers of
fire, panting to penetrate its fastness—and the most interesting
vestiges of antiquity are in hourly danger of destruction. An
account of the district which contains them (in a more systematic
form than has yet been attempted) may at least preserve their
memory, or perhaps more happily, may be the means of rescuing
them from the impending assaults of the mason's hammer, and the
excavator's pick, and of perpetuating their existence, by pointing
out their claims to the protection of all who feel becoming interest
in the history of their country and of mankind.

# CHAPTER I.

## INTRODUCTORY.

EXTENT AND BOUNDARIES, ANTIENT PERAMBULATIONS,

AND

NATURAL FEATURES OF DARTMOOR.

DARTMOOR, while it forms in itself the most conspicuous and characteristic feature in the physical geography of the county of Devon, contributes also, in no small degree, to partitioning this important shire into three principal divisions, which, generally speaking, are no less clearly defined by natural boundaries, than distinctly marked by peculiar features. From its extreme northern verge, North Devon* stretches to the Bristol Channel—the Teign sweeps round its eastern extremity within six miles of the Exe, (the well-defined boundary of East Devon) whilst South Devon or the South Hams† includes the fertile tract stretching from the Southern slope of the Moor to the English Channel, and extending east and west from the Teign

---

*The Devonshire tourist will, however, often find himself perplexed to ascertain whether he has reached North Devon or not; but the North has long been proverbially celebrated for the indefiniteness of its whereabouts, and the vagueness of the term is by no means confined to Devonshire :—

    Ask where's the North ? at York 'tis on the Tweed :
    In Scotland at the Orcades :—and there
    In Greenland, Zembla,—or the Lord knows where.
              POPE, *Essay on Man, Epistle II.*

†South Devon is sometimes thus designated, but strictly speaking, the term South Hams is appropriated to a smaller district, and a circle, of which Totnes is the centre, with a radius of twelve or fourteen miles, would perhaps more nearly approach to its generally received limits.

A

to the Tamar.   Thus centrally placed, Dartmoor forms the most prominent and striking feature, not only of the county of Devon (occupying as it does, one-fifth of its entire area) but of the whole Western peninsula.   Yet, though contributing so largely to the beauty of the far-famed Devonshire scenery, and ministering so effectually to the fertility of the soil, until of late years it was comparatively little known even to the inhabitants of the very district which benefits so largely from its proximity.

Dartmoor, the antient and Royal Forest or Chase of that name, has its own specific boundaries, but Dartmoor, in the common acceptation of the word, includes numerous outlying tracts, presenting the same physical features as the forest itself, and in the following description it is intended to include the adjacent land and commons surrounding it, and which partake of the same general character.

Dartmoor and its adjuncts may be thus estimated, as extending about twenty miles from east to west, and twenty-two miles from north to south, and as containing more than 280,000 acres of land. The area of the granite district, coloured pink in the geological map of the Ordnance Survey, which district corresponds fairly with that popularly known as Dartmoor, extends from north to south, twenty-two miles and a half, and from east to west, eighteen miles.   De la Beche* calculates the distance from Butterton Hill in the south to Cosdon Beacon in the north at twenty-two miles,† and observes that " both geographically and geologically, the " elevated land which extends eastward from Cawsand Beacon to " Cranbrook Castle, Buttern Down and Mardon Down, near " Moretonhampstead, ranging round thence by Bridford and " Hennock to High or Hey Tor, forms part of Dartmoor."   From Hey Tor, above Ilsington Church-town, in a south-westerly direction, the boundary takes the line of hills which overlook Ashburton, thence skirting the parishes of Holne, Buckfastleigh, and Brent, it proceeds to its southernmost point at the Western Beacon and Three Barrow Tor above Ivybridge.   Thence, trending to the north-west, it crosses the rivers Erme and Yealm, passes by Cornwood below Pen Beacon and Shell Top, then takes a westerly course in the line of the Hentor Ridge and Shaugh Moor, approaches its westernmost point at Meavy, and thence runs

---

*Report on the Geology of Cornwall, Devon and West Somerset, 1839, p. 5.

†The actual measurement is twenty miles and three-quarters, but neither of these summits are in the extreme limits of the moor,

almost from south to north, by Walkhampton, Sampford Spiney, west of the Tavy, to Peter Tavy, Mary Tavy and Sourton, thence to Okehampton and Belstone, where, at its northernmost point, it reaches Cosdon or Cawsand Beacon, and returns eastwards as above described.

The whole forest of Dartmoor lies within the parish of Lydford, by far the largest parish in the county. We learn from Domesday, that in Edward the Confessor's time, it was of the king's demesne. The entry in the Exeter book is as follows :—" *Rex habet i burgum* " *qui uocatur Lideforda quem tenuit Eduuardus rex ea die qua ipse* " *fuit uiuus et mortuus. Ibi habet rex* xxviii *burgenses infra* " *burgum, et foras* xli, *et isti reddunt per annum* iii *libras ad pensum* " *regi. Et ibi sunt* xl *domus uastatæ postquam Willelmus rex* " *habuit Angliam. Et supra-dicti burgenses habent terram ad* ii " *carrucas foras ciuitatem. Et si expeditio uadit per terram uel per* " *mare reddit tantum de seruitio quantum Totenais reddit uel* " *Barnestapla.*" (Exon Domesday. 87 b.)

Risdon gives the following :—" *Rex habet burgum de Lidford,* " *et burgenses ibidem, tenet vigint' et octo burgenses infra burgum,* " *et* 41, *extra &c. Inter omnes redditus reddant tres libras ad* " *pensum et arsuram, et sunt ibi quadraginta domus vastata* " *prius-quam rex venit in Anglia, et predict. burgenses et manerium* " *de Lidford se extendit per totam villam et parochiam de Lidford,* " *et per totam forrestam de Dartmoor.*"*

In the Domesday entry there is no reference to Dartmoor as a Forest, and Risdon does not give his authority for the addition " et predict' burgenses, etc., etc." but the quotation comes apparently from Hooker's MS. Discourse† from whence, no doubt Risdon copied it with all its errors, but it is not surprising, as observed by the late Sir Edward Smirke, that nothing but the borough is there noticed. " Until the property was granted to a subject in a " subsequent reign, it was in the king's hands, and can have been " liable to pay none of those taxes, which under the names of " hidage, carrucage, etc., were chiefly in view when the Survey " was made." Were it otherwise, an uncultivated tract of land like Dartmoor, would not be likely to find its way into Domesday. It is probable that the Forest was occasionally under grant to members of the Royal family during the 12th century, for we find

---

*Risdon. Survey, p. 221, ed. 1811.

†Devon Assoc. Trans. Vol. VIII, p. 408.

from a charter of John, Earl of Morton, Duke of Cornwall, (and afterwards king) during the life of his brother Richard, that he grants certain immunities to free tenants out of the Regard of the Forest.   The first distinct notice of any transfer of the Castle Manor and Forest by the Crown to a subject, is the grant of Henry III, to his brother Richard, Earl of Cornwall, commonly called King of the Romans, or of Germany.   From that date, the property has been from time to time, under grant from the Crown ; and since 1337, the Forest and its belongings have been permanently annexed to the Duchy of Cornwall, as an appanage of the Prince of Wales.   When there is no heir apparent, the Forest reverts to the custody of the Crown.   Properly therefore, as belonging to a subject, and not to the monarch, Dartmoor is not a Forest but a Chase, but Dartmoor seems to have always had the peculiar privileges of a Forest, and retained such rights, laws and officers as belonged to it when used by the King " for his princely delight " and pleasure," and it is more frequently called *Foresta* than *Chacea*.   In 16 Edward III, we find Dertemore Chase mentioned, and in the preceding reigns, both forest and chase are referred to, and still later *foresta* is used.   The explanation probably is to be found in Coke's statement that " a subject may have a forest by " a special grant of the king."

When Britain was invaded by the Romans, the country was extensively covered with wood.   Cæsar found the people upon the south coast engaged in agricultural pursuits, but inland all appeared to be forest, and he tells us that a town among the Britons is nothing more than a thick wood fortified with a ditch and rampart.*   The extensive tracts of land in different parts of the country called Royal Forests, are so antient, says Coke in his Commentaries upon Littleton's Institutes,† as no record or history doth make any mention of their erections or beginnings.   They were appropriated for animals of the chase with ascertained and well-defined limits, and governed by a code of laws, rigidly, and frequently cruelly, enforced.   When these districts became subject to the Laws of the Forest is unknown, but they were certainly so from very early times,—probably before the date of Canute's *Constitutiones de Foresta.*

Of such a character was Dartmoor down to the time of the

---

*CÆSAR.   Commentaries, Book V, chap. 8.     Forests of England, BROWN.

†COKE, Institutes, IV, 319, quoted by Manwood, Laws Forest, Art. Forests, 5.9. ed. 1741.

Conquest, not necessarily covered with wood in all parts, but there being enough to afford shelter and cover for beasts of the chase, and to serve as a retreat for man escaping from an enemy. The term Forest, as also pointed out by the antiquary whom we have before quoted, does not necessarily imply that there would be more timber or herbage than might be sufficient for food and shelter for the wild animals that ranged over it. Manwood's definition confirms this. " A forest is a certain territorie of woody grounds " and fruitfull pastures, priviledged for wild beasts and fowles of " Forest, Chase and Warren, to rest and abide in the safe " protection of the King, for his princely delight and pleasure, " which territory of ground so priviledged is meered and bounded " with unremoveable marks, meets and boundaries, either knowne " by matter of record or by prescription, etc."*

It is indeed probable, that formerly there existed more wood on Dartmoor than is now to be found, and that the tinners, who certainly were allowed to supply themselves with fuel for the fusion of the ore they obtained, have laid waste the surface, but it is not likely that the granite table-land was ever covered to any extent, with anything entitled to the name of timber. It must not be assumed that diversion was the main object of the appropriation of land as forest. It is very certain that our ancestors (excluding, of course, those who were obliged to be content with humbler fare), relied upon their deer parks, chases and warrens for the supply of their larders. We know that cured venison was an important article of food in royal households, it being salted and packed, and sent from distant parts of the country to the king's larders.†

The ancient woods of Wistman and Piles remain, and there are some antient oaks at Brimps, but at the head of the East Dart, below Great Hey Tor, in Stannon Bottom, and elsewhere branches of trees of considerable size have been found in the bogs. Near Princetown, in an enclosure made by the prison authorities, within a space of ten acres, upwards of twenty cart-loads of wood—oak, willow and alder—were obtained without any trouble.‡ One of the oaks measured seven feet six inches in circumference near the roots.

---

*MANWOOD. Treatise of the Lawes of the Forest, fol. 18, ed. 1615.

†Wardrobe Accounts. 28 Edw. I. Society Antiquaries, London, 1787.

‡*Ex rel.* late Mr. Thomas Kelly, of Yealmpton, who believed that the whole of the great bog in the neighbourhood of Cranmere Pool, was once forest.

Dartmoor is, no doubt, referred to in the Charter of John, while he was Earl of Cornwall, and is mentioned by name in his Charter of May 18, 1203 or 1204, by which all lands in Devonshire, except Dartmoor and Exmoor, are disafforested.

The earliest perambulation of which we have any record was made in pursuance of a writ 13 June, 1240, in the 24th year of the reign of Henry III. "Every forest," says Manwood, "being a "Franches within its selfe, must bee inuironed with marshes, "meeres, and bounderies, round about the same, whereby the "circuit of ground, that is Forest, may be known and discerned "from that which is not Forest."* These "markes, meeres, and bounderies" were to be ascertained by a jury, and upon the construction of the statute, *Carta de Foresta*, 9 Hen. III., it was requisite there should be a writ issued out of Chancery, and by virtue thereof, a verdict upon the oaths of twelve men or more, which were the meets and bounds of the Forest.† We accordingly find that the writ of 13 June, 1240, was directed to the Sheriff of Devon, instructing him to summon a jury of twelve knights to determine by perambulation the boundaries of the Forest of Dartmoor, which, with the Castle of Lidford, had been granted by Henry to his brother Richard, Earl of Cornwall and Poitou. The actual verdict or return to this commission has not been found, but there are several copies, bearing different dates, slightly varying from one another. The twelve jurors were William Brewer, Guy Bretevlye, William Wydeworthy, Hugh Bollay, Richard Gyffard, Odo Treverbyn, Henry, son of Henry, William Trenchard, Phillip Parrer, Nicholas Heanton, William Morleghe, and Durantus son of Botour. They began their perambulation at Cosdon Hill in the north quarter, and proceeded south-eastward skirting the bounds of Throwleigh, Gidleigh, and Chagford, to the point where the North joins the East quarter near Fernworthy. From hence southward the forest boundary runs deep into the moorlands, leaving Moreton six miles to the east, and crossing the road from that town to Two Bridges and Tavistock below King's Oven, *Furnum Regis*, (probably an ancient smelting or blowing house) follows the course of the Wallabrook, until that stream falls into the West Dart, which becomes the boundary as far as Dartmeet. Leaving the West Dart, the line intersects the

---

*MANWOOD, *op cit.* fol. 56.

†NELSON's Manwood, p. 44, ed. 1741.

extensive moors in the south quarter above Holne—proceeding
to the springs of the Avon and thence to the Erme. Passing the
Erme and leaving Yealm Head on the south, the boundary
proceeds northwards to Siward's Cross, enters the west quarter of
the moor, makes for Histworthy *i.e.* North Hessary* Tor, and
from thence mounts to Great Mistor. Thence across the
Walkham and Tavy it goes up the Rattlebrook, passes over the
West Ockment below Yes Tor to the verge of Okehampton
Park, crosses the East Ockment at Halstock below Belstone,
and returns to the starting point at Cosdon.

From a copy of the Perambulation, written on the back of a
map, now in the Albert Memorial Museum, Exeter, the late
Spence Bate†, with much ingenuity, worked out fairly accurately,
the various meets and bounds, but particular reference will be
made to these hereafter.

The Venville or Fenfield districts, and also those wastes‡
anciently known as the " Commons of Devonshire," are mentioned
in the presentment of the jury of the Survey Court for the Forest
made in the sixth year of King James I. 1609. Risdon enumerates
the bounds and limits of the Fenfield men's tenures, beginning
from Podaston Lake, running through Ashburton, and so through
various places specified " to Ashborne, and so from thence to the
"stream of Dart." But it would be difficult, if not impossible,
to identify the names thus enumerated with existing places ; so
that little available information on these points, can be gleaned
from his statement. But a clearer notion of Venville bounds will
be gained by an enumeration of the parishes in Venville, which,
on examination, will be found to lie immediately round the Moor.
Beginning in the north, and proceeding eastward, we find them to
be Belstone, South Tawton, Throwleigh, Gidleigh, Chagford,
North Bovey, Manaton, Widecombe, Holne, Buckfastleigh, Dean

---

*The Devonshire tongue habitually gives "ery" for " worthy," as, for instance,
Woolsery for Woolfardisworthy, Essery for Esworthy, and on the Ordnance Map
are several instances of its adoption, as where Hexworthy, near Dartmeet, appears
as Haxary.

†Transactions Devonshire Association. Vol. V. 1872, p. 511.

‡In the Forest, as well as in the Venville Commons, there have been from ancient
times, certain enclosed lands, called *New-takes*, as appears from accounts rendered
by the officers of the Forest and Manor. The sums paid for these holdings are
entered as *new rents*, and the tenure is called *land bote*. This word in western
rentals means the claim of a copy-hold tenant to a small new-take of manorial
waste or desmesne. Such a custom apparently obtained in other Devonshire
Manors. It is curious to observe that many of these New-takes in the time of
Henry VII, contained no more than a single acre of land. Archæological Journal,
Vol. V. pp. 23, 24.

Prior, South Brent, Shaugh Prior, Meavy, Sheepstor, Walk-
hampton, Sampford Spiney, Whitchurch, Cudliptown, (in Tavi-
stock), Taverton Tything, Peter Tavy, Lydford, Bridestowe,
Sourton.   In addition to these, Burt gives Sampford Courtenay,
Mary Tavy, Lamerton, Okehampton, Ugborough, Cornwood, and
Halford.*

The Venville tenures seems to have originally grown out of
trespasses in the Forest.  By the Survey of 25 Edward I, among
the proceeds of the Forest, are included £4 10s. for fines of the
villagers, and pasturage of cattle.   " In 17 Elizabeth, an account
" was taken of the fines, which had then grown to be fixed rents.
" and they amounted to £4 11s. 4½d.   They are payable at the
" Court Baron, held by the Deputy-Steward of the Forest
" originally at Lydford Castle, but since its being ruinous, at
" Princetown, where homage jurors are sworn in, surrenders
" taken, and grants made to the free and customary tenants."†

The forest is divided into four quarters—east, west, north and
south, in each of which, except the western, is a pound for stray
cattle.   There are some curious remains of feudal customs in the
service which the Venville men above mentioned, render to the
Prince of Wales as Lord of the Forest, and by virtue of which
they hold in Venville under the Duchy.  As tenants of the Prince,
they are liable to the service of driving the moor, after receiving
notice through the Forest Reeve from the Deputy-Auditor, who
fixes the exact time, which is somewhere between new and old
Midsummer day.  The colt drift for the east, south and west, is
under the same precept and warrant.  The tenants also do suit
and homage at the Prince's Courts, and are required to present all
defaults in the Forest and its purlieus.   Their privileges, on the
other hand, are pasturage on the moor at a fixed rate, a right to
take away anything of the forest that may do them good, except
*vert*, (meaning green oak) and venison ; to fish in all waters, and
to dig turf in any place.‡  They are also exempt from tollage in
all fairs and markets throughout England, except London, Totnes

---

*Preface, Carrington's Dartmoor, p. xxxviii.   The valuable Introduction to
Carrington's Poem and Notes, by WILLIAM BURT, should be consulted by all
interested in Dartmoor.   Both the original author and the editor of this edition
of the Perambulation have used this introduction freely.

†BURT, *op cit.* p. xxix.  This is not quite correct, for the court was removed from
Lydford to Prince Town by Sir Thomas Tyrwhitt, and the Castle has become
altogether ruinous since that time.

‡BURT, *op cit.* p. xxx.

and Barnstaple, and the Duchy steward gives them an exemption, under his hand, for all the produce of the Venville estates, and they are free from attachment by any officer, except for the yearly rent of four-pence at Michaelmas. The drifts, at which the Venville men are required to assist, are organised for the purpose of ascertaining what stock is within the bounds, in order that the forest may not be trespassed upon by cattle belonging to those who have no right of pasture there.

The custom of the Duchy authorities is to drive the bullocks and ponies, as before mentioned, in the autumn, on different days in the different quarters, ponies on one day, horned cattle on another, but sometimes there are not more than six drifts in the year. The old customs are not now fully observed. According to antient usage, Mr. W. F. Collier* tells us the drift ought to be exercised in the following way :—A day is fixed without giving any notice to anyone. About two o'clock in the morning a messenger is sent to the moorman of the quarter, ordering him to drive his quarter for colts, who then proceeds, by blowing horns on the tors, to summon the Venville tenants to join in the drift. In the western quarter there was a particular stone, with a hole in it, through which it was customary to blow the horn. "All the " ponies or colts on the quarter, including those on the Commons " of Devon, are then driven from every nook and corner by men " on foot, on horseback, and with dogs, to the usual well-known " place,—in the western quarter it was Merrivale Bridge,—and it " is a curious sight to see herds of these fleet and sure-footed " little animals, in a great state of alarm at the unusual uproar of " hooting, holloaing, and horns sounding, galloping over the " moor all in one direction, giving their tails and manes to the " wind. The movement of ponies on the tors and the noise " proclaim the drift to all the world ; the owners of ponies have been " on the look out as the time of the year approaches, and they pro- " ceed to the drift to claim their property. The driving having been " completed, and the vast number of ponies of all ages, with the " men and the dogs, having been collected together, by this time " in a state of wild confusion, an officer of the Duchy stands " upon a stone,—the old traditional stone in all probability,—and " reads a formidable document with seals attached to it to the " assembly. That ceremony being performed, owners are called

---

*W. F. COLLIER. Venville Rights on Dartmoor, 1887.

"upon to claim their ponies. Venville tenants claim theirs and
"go free, others pay a fine for each animal, but no one is con-
"sidered a trespasser," for this reason that the owners and
occupiers of all lands in Devon (except the men of Totnes and
Barnstaple who were not disafforested when the forest rights were
granted) can have the right, at all events, to pasture and depasture
commonable beasts upon the Commons of Devon, and upon the
Forest upon payment of certain customary fees.  "If an animal
"is not claimed by the owner he is driven to Dunnabridge
"pound, which is the ' Duchy pound.'  If claimed, his owner
"has to pay for poundage and for water, but if unclaimed in a
"given time, he is sold, and the money goes to the Duchy.  The
"horn has not been heard since 1843, and the Duchy now let the
"quarters to the moormen who make as much as they can of
"them."

Besides the Venville rights, there are ancient tenements on
the Moor held by copy of Court Roll, the persons residing on
them being called Customary Tenants, and doing suit and service
at the Court, and bound like the Venville men to assist at the
drifts.  The following is a list of these holdings : three tenements
called Brimps; three, Hexworthy; two, Bellever; five, Dunnabridge; three, Baberry; three, Pizwell; two, Runnage; five,
Huccaby; three, Sherberton, and one each Riddon's, Lower Maze
Pits, Hartaland, Broom Park, Brown Berry, and Prince Hall,
thirty-five in all.*

In the suit of the rector of Lydford, Thomas Bernaford,
against Hext and others, Exch., B. and A. Devon, 1 Anne 43, A.D.
1702, it was proved that there were thirty-five antient tenements
and new takes, and Anthony Torr gave them with their tenants.
Their names were Rennidge and Warner, three tenements,
Piswell, ; one, Hastiland, ; one, Riddam, ; three, Barbary ; three,
Brimpston; four, Huccaby or lying in Huccaby; one, Dury or
lying there ; three tenements, Hexworthy ; three, Sherborne or
lying there, ; five, Dunabridge or lying there ; one, Brownberry ;
one, Princehall ; one, Bellaford ; two, Bellaford, one lying in
Bellaford, and the other in called Lake.  These were all ancient
forest tenancies, but Anthony Torr says, that there were divers
new-takes which he gives as follows : two, Bradrings, ; Stannon,
Eyremerrypit, Laster Hole, Bellaford Combe, Winford, Laughter

---

*Vide BURT, *op. cit.* p, xxxi.

Combe, Broad Oak, Cock's Lake, Dead Lake, Swancombe Head, Swancombe, three called Holeshead, and Swancombe Ford.*

The bounds of the Royal Forest and the adjacent commons and moorlands, comprehend the district which forms the subject of the present volume, under the general name of Dartmoor, so called, probably from one of the principal of those numerous streams, of which it is the prolific parent. The whole of this large tract of land rises conspicuously above the surrounding country. Its appearance is singularly characteristic and picturesque, on whatever side it may be approached from the adjacent lowlands. The bard of Dartmoor, Noel Thomas Carrington,† with the eye of an accurate observer, and with the feeling of a genuine poet, describes as one of its prominent characteristics, the belt,

" Of hills, mysterious, shadowy "

by which it is encircled, as with a natural rampart, whilst it is moated by deep valleys, which wind round its base and are replenished by streams pouring down from the heights in every direction.

This primæval circumvallation comprehends within its stupendous enclosure, an elevated table-land, which is not strictly a plain, but a series of hemispherical swellings or undulations gradually overtopping each other, and here and there interrupted by deep depressions, yet without forming what may be properly called distinct mountains. " To a person standing on some lofty " point of the Moor, it wears the appearance of an irregular " broken waste, which may best be compared to the long rolling " waves of a tempestuous ocean, fixed into solidity by some " instantaneous and powerful impulse."‡ It is thus, with much

---

*Publications Dart, Pres : Assoc. Vol. I. pp. 89-90.

†CARRINGTON, whose poem entitled " Dartmoor " is so frequently quoted in this volume was the son of an artisan in the Dockyard at Devonport, then Plymouth Dock, who also kept a small shop. The boy, finding his apprenticeship in the yard uncongenial, ran away and entered himself on board a man-of-war, and was present at the Battle off Cape St. Vincent, in Feb. 1797. Some verses written by the lad on the occasion, came under the notice of the captain, who, being interested in the lad, befriended him, gave him his discharge and sent him home. He then resolved to be a teacher and eventually settled down in his native place as a schoolmaster, where he remained until within six months of his death, which took place at Bath in 1830. His principal poems are " Dartmoor " " The Banks of Tamar " and " My Native Village." With regard to the first, in 1824 the Royal Society of Literature offered a premium for the best poem on Dartmoor, and Carrington decided to compete, but the premium was awarded to Mrs. Hemans, long before he knew the time for sending in the poems had arrived, and " Dartmoor " was, under the advice of Mr. William Burt, the secretary of the Plymouth Chamber of Commerce, published with notes written by the latter, in 1826. It immediately obtained a more than local success, and in six weeks another edition was called for.

‡BURT, op cit. p. 102.

graphic accuracy, that the author of the Notes to Carrington's Dartmoor, paraphrases Gilpin's compendious description of the Moorland district of Devon, when he says, " Dartmoor spreads " like the ocean after a storm, heaving in large swells."    Even at a distance, it wears this billowy aspect, which in every zone, according to Humboldt, is the characteristic of primitive chains.

The late John Prideaux faithfully sketches the geological features of the southern quarter of the moor, which, as he justly remarks, will apply to the whole.    It is entirely mountainous, the highest hills being on the borders, where some of them attain the height of nearly 2000 feet.*   The valleys run in various directions, but have a tendency, upon the whole, to the north and south line. The hills rise often steep, sometimes precipitous,—their sides clothed with long grass except where rushes or moss indicate subjacent bogs, and they are often strewed with loose blocks of granite, from fifty or more tons, down to the size of a flag-stone. A crag called a *Tor* usually projects at the summit of the hill, having a very striking appearance of stratification, the fissures being sometimes horizontal ; more commonly a little inclined. This stratified character is not less general in the quarries, where although there are none of those marked divisions indicative of intermissions, in the original depositions of the rock, the stone always comes out in beds.    The dip is different in different hills, but seems to have a prevailing tendency towards east and south.†

The principal rivers which have their source in the north table land of Dartmoor are :—

The Dart, formed of the East Dart with numerous nameless tributaries flowing under Hartland Hill to Post Bridge, and of the West Dart receiving the Cowsick, Blackabrook, Cherrybrook, and other small streams.    The two branches unite at Dartmeet Bridge ; receive the Webburn near Holne Chase, and flowing by Buckfastleigh and Totnes, the Dart finally reaches the sea at Dartmouth, after a course of about forty miles.

The Teign, which is the next river northwards, also consists of two main branches.    The north Teign rises near Sittaford

---

*Cosdon Beacon, 1799 feet above the sea-level, was generally considered the highest point on Dartmoor until De la Beche published his Report on the Geology of Cornwall, Devon, and West Somerset, wherein he estimates Yes Tor at 2050 feet, and Amicombe Hill at 2000.    But the new Ordnance Survey makes the High Willhays Bench Mark 2039 feet, and Yes Tor 2029ft. 6in.

†PRIDEAUX.  Transactions Plymouth Institution, 1830, p. 20.  See chapter IX.

Tor, north of the Grey Wethers' Circle; takes an easterly course towards Gidley Common, where it receives the Wallabrook; and being joined near Chagford by the South Teign, which also rises near the Grey Wethers, the united stream passes under Chagford, Fingle, Clifford, and Dunsford bridges, amidst some of the most picturesque and striking scenery, and bounding the moorland district to the eastward, proceeds by a southerly course towards Chudleigh and Teigngrace, where it receives the Bovey; and, taking a tributary from Newton, disembogues itself into the sea at Teignmouth.

The Taw rises near Cranmere Pool; and taking a northerly direction flows below Cosdon Hill and Belstone, and leaves the Moor at Sticklepath. In its northward progress, it gives the name to South and North Tawton, and being joined by the Yeo, near Eggesford, by the Little Dart, near Chulmleigh, and the Mole from Southmolton, flows into the Bristol Channel in Barnstaple Bay.

The West Ockment or Okement taking its source near Cranmere Pool, flows below Yes Tor to Okehampton, and there is joined by the East Ockment, from the glen below Belstone and Okehampton Park, it takes a northward course through the centre of the county, and falls into the Torridge near Meeth.

The Lyd rises in the hollow below Branscomb Loaf, flows south by Doe Tor, forces its passage through the rocky chasm at Skit's Hole, thence through the celebrated ravine of Lydford and beneath its romantic bridge, towards Maristow, where it receives the Lewwater, and being increased by the Thrushel Brook, renders its tributary waters to the Tamar, near Lifton.

The Tavy rises about a mile westward from Cranmere Pool below Great Kneeset Tor, flows north of Fur Tor and Watern Oak, above Tavy Cleave it is joined by the Rattlebrook which comes from the north, down a deep valley below Amicombe Hill, leaves the moor by a fine mountain gorge between Gertor or Great Tor, and Stannon Hill, flows amidst a succession of picturesque scenery to Tavistock, and receiving the Walkham at Screeche's Ford, passes under Denham Bridge through the richly-wooded dales of Buckland Abbey and Maristow, to join the Tamar at Beer Ferrers, where the noble estuary presents all the appearance of an inland lake of singular beauty.

The Walkham, incorrectly called in the old one inch Ordnance Map, Wallacombe, rises in a swamp below Lints Tor, and taking a southerly course leaves Great Mistor on the left, flows under Merivale Bridge and Huckworthy Bridge by Walkhampton, to which probably it gives name, and thence through Horrabridge to its junction with the Tavy.

The rivers rising in the swampy table land of the south are :—

The Plym, rising near Eylesburrow, flows westward below Trowlesworthy Tor to Cadaford Bridge, Dewerstone, and Shaugh Bridge, where it receives the Mew, or West Plym, from Meavy and Sheepstor. The augmented stream continues its course through Bickleigh Vale, receiving the Tory Brook at Long Bridge, thence to the estuary of the Lary, and falls into the sea at Plymouth, to which famous port, as well as to the borough of Plympton, and the parishes of Plympton St. Mary and Plymstock, it is supposed to give name.

The Yealm rises in the boggy table-land south of Shaver-combe Head, and flows in a direct course to Cornwood. At Lee Mill Bridge it is crossed by the great Plymouth road, passes Yealmpton, to which it gives name, and meets the sea in a lovely estuary, completely landlocked by the heights of Wembury, Newton Ferrers, and Revelstoke, so as to form, at full tide, two lakes of singular beauty.

The Erme, or Arme, takes its rise south of Cater's Beam about a mile and a half from Plym Head. It passes Harford church in its way to Ivybridge, flows by Ermington, to which it gives name, and falls into Bigbury Bay, at Mothecombe.

The Avon, Aven, or Aune (which seems to have been the antient appellation) has its source on the highest part of the southern table-land, north of Cater's Beam, near Peter's Bound-stone. Thence it flows southward, to Brent, Avon Bridge, and Diptford, leaves Modbury on the right, and flowing by Loddiswell, gives name to Aveton, or Auton Gifford, where it expands into an estuary, and falls into Bigbury Bay, near Burr Island.

De la Beche concisely describes Dartmoor as " an elevated " mass of land, of an irregular form, broken into numerous minor " hills, many crowned by groups of picturesque rocks, provincially " termed tors,* and for the most part presenting a wild mixture of

---

*Like most other provincial terms, *tor* is a relic of the ancient language of the country, preserved in the vernacular of the common people. It is found in both dialects of the antient British tongues : Cornish, *tor*; Welsh, *twr*; as well as in the Gaelic, *tor*—a tower, heap or pile. In addition to these it is traced by Bosworth (Anglo-Saxon Dict. *in voc.*) to the Dutch *toren*, Old German, *turre turen*, "heath, bog, rocks and rapid streams." Such are the general features of this singular district, which from its stern and frowning aspect, as viewed from the surrounding lowlands, and as contrasted with their smiling pleasantness, has been long branded by traditional prejudice with an ill name. From generation to generation it has been proverbial as the chosen spot, where bleak skies and brooding storms maintain undisputed and undisturbed, "their antient solitary reign," causing Dartmoor to be regarded through the entire neighbourhood, as the very fatherland\* of the whole family of rains, from a mist to a waterspout. Its lofty tors may often be discerned glittering with an Alpine scapular of snow, amidst surrounding verdure ; and frequently when Spring is smiling among the coombs of the South Hams, "Winter lingers" and "chills the lap of May" along the bleak expanse of the Moor.

This proverbial barrenness of soil,† and inclemency of climate, may account for the slight and cursory notice which historians and topographers have, until late years, thought fit to bestow upon the great Moorland district of Devonshire. Even the indefatigable Risdon contents himself (and appears to think he has satisfied all reasonable inquirers thereby) with enumerating "three remarkable things"‡ within the precincts of Dartmoor ; and from his time to the present day, the opinion seems to have generally prevailed, that a tract so wild and barren, could afford little to encourage research into its past history, or to repay investigation into its present condition. But wild as it is, it is not "all barren." The native rudeness and untamed simplicity of these upland solitudes, become subjects of the deepest interest to those who find pleasure in contemplating nature in her sterner moods and more austere aspects ; while they secure to the antiquary means of investigating

---

Danish, *taarn*, (which is almost Devonian, as our Moormen pronounce the word *tar*, and not *tor*), Swedish, *torn*, &c. So that it is found in all the cognate Teutonic dialects, as well as in the Celtic ; to which however, Lye traces its primary derivation. " Originem habet in lingua Celtica qua mor.s dicebatur *Thor* : quæ Syris et Chaldeis ' efferebatur *Thur*. Radicem hujus conservant Cambri in verbo *dwyre* surgere etc. Inde etiam nomina montium et monticolarum apud varias gentes ; *ex gra*, Dyr. Atlas lingua Mauritaniæ, Taurus mons Asiæ. Tauri montes Sarmatiæ. Taurini gentes Alpinæ. Turinum caput Pe-de-montii *etc.* Thuringi vel Toringi montani monticolæ.

\**Nimborum Patria. Virgil.*

†The soil of the Moor can scarcely be regarded as barren. The difficulty of cultivation is mainly due to the climate, especially to the wet west and south-westerly winds. See Chapter x.

‡Crockern Tor, Childe of Plymstock's Tomb, Wistman's Wood, Risdon, ed. 1811, p. 223.

the earliest history of the island which he would vainly seek in more favoured districts, where cultivation has obliterated the venerable memorials of primitive times.

Finding among the wild uplands of Devon, the most unquestionable vestiges of a period of our history of which so little that is authentic has come down to us, we are scarcely disposed to join in the lament which the sterility of Dartmoor has called forth. As the guardians of many an antique memorial, which in more accessible and attractive spots, would have long since experienced a fate, unhappily but too common, the tors and wilds of the antient Forest of the West, find favour in the sight of those who feel that other wants besides those of the body, are legitimate objects for the consideration of an intellectual, not to say an immortal, being. And without any affected or morbid deprecation of the peaceful triumphs of the ploughshare, nay, with the sincerest wish that every acre of waste which can be made to bring forth " green herb " for the service of man " may be reclaimed, until that period arrives, one may be pardoned for regarding with pleasure, the wilds of Dartmoor in their primitive state, and may be permitted to rejoice that there are myriads of acres equally unproductive and far less picturesque, which may justly be required to be subjected to the dominion of agriculture, before their " free and unhous'd condition is put in circumscription and confine."

That there are tracts on the Moor, which may be cultivated with success, we do not for one moment question ; and that much credit is due to those enterprising individuals, who have from time to time engaged in extensive, and to some degree, successful attempts to reclaim considerable portions of the waste, we are free to admit. All honour to the cultivator " who makes two blades of " grass grow where one only grew before," and, if it should really come to a question of the production of a sufficient quantity of food for the teeming population of a nation, all other considerations must give way, just as in seasons of great public peril, a siege or an invasion, the monuments of antiquity, the " gorgeous palaces " and even the " solemn temples " would be levelled, rather than that they should stand to impede the defenders, or to advantage the enemy. But that which would be praiseworthy patriotism in such an extreme case, would in a less manifest emergency be reckless spoliation, such as has been too often perpetrated upon the venerable relics of Dartmoor, without the pretence of a plea of the urgent necessities of the community. One may contemplate

with satisfaction, such judicious and well-planned efforts, as may
be seen in the vale of Cowsick, near Two Bridges, at Archeton, and
on a much larger scale at Prince Town, the result of prison labour ;
but it is melancholy to witness the abortive attempts that have
been sometimes made on the bleak hillside, where, after a rock-
pillar has been demolished for a gate-post, or a cromlech
overthrown for a foot-bridge, or a kistvaen destroyed for a
new-take wall, the injudicious attempt has been abandoned as
hopeless, after irreparable mischief has been done.    Even
Carrington's honeyed strains fail in inducing us to sympathise with
his satisfaction when exercising the powers of poetic vaticination,
" rapt into future times," he views with delight

> " The dauntless grasp
> Of Industry assail yon mighty Tors
> Of the dread wilderness."

nor shall we, like him, kindle with misplaced indignation, and
demand,

> " Shalt thou alone
> Dartmoor ! in this fair land where all beside
> Is life and beauty, sleep the sleep of death,
> And shame the map of England ? "

Rather would we subscribe to the opinion expressed by a
writer, who, in speaking of the present state of the Moor, observes,
" perhaps it serves as it is, the gracious purposes of Providence."*
On this subject alone, we cannot applaud the sentiments of the
honoured bard of Dartmoor, as much as admire the attractive
forms in which he has embodied them,—here our mountain
minstrel seems to have struck the only jarring chord in the whole
compass of the wild harp of the desert.

Those who have climbed the bleak summits of Dartmoor, and
threaded the granite labyrinths which perplex their acclivities,
must be persuaded that profitable agricultural efforts must be
confined to the lower grounds, and every attempt to carry
cultivation up to the rugged eminences of the tors, can only issue
in loss and disappointment.    Besides, who will venture to affirm,
if Dartmoor could be ploughed to its very crest, and a scanty and
precarious crop reaped from corn patches, two thousand feet above
the sea-level, that there would be no counter-balance to the dearly-
bought benefit ?    How much of health is now wafted from the

---

mountain's brow over the circumjacent towns and villages? How much of beauty and refreshment is poured down from the perennial fountains of the misty moor upon the smiling lowlands of the South Hams,—of West and Central Devon? Carrington appropriately describes Dartmoor as the "source of half the beauty of Devon's austral meads," and while he mourns over its native barrenness, he justly celebrates its importance to the whole surrounding region, in the bountiful economy of Him who " sendeth His springs into the rivers which run among the hills."

> " For other fields
> Thy bounty flows eternal.  From thy sides
> Devonia's rivers flow ; a thousand brooks
> Roll o'er thy rugged slopes ; 'tis but to cheer
> Yon Austral meads unrivall'd, fair, as aught
> That bards have sung, or fancy has conceived,
> 'Mid all her rich imaginings."

Would the same fertility and the same loveliness then be produced, if there were no condensing apparatus set up in Nature's wondrous laboratory, amidst the wilds of Dartmoor?  The primal paradise of Eden was not perfect without the " river which went " out to water the garden, and was thence parted into four heads." —*Genesis* ii, 10.  Would Devon challenge the envied designation of the garden of England, if the Urn of Cranmere were broken and dry?  Where would be the characteristic amenities of the Land of Promise, those striking features which mark Devonshire as the Canaan of the West—"a good land, a land of brooks of " water, of fountains that spring out of valleys and hills ; a land of " wheat and barley, of milk and honey ; a land whose stones are " iron, and out of whose hills thou mayest dig brass."—*Deut.* viii, 7,8,9 ; where, but for Dartmoor, to which must be attributed, mainly, the fact that this inspired description may be applied to Devon, without figure, accommodation, or vain glory?  Since then the poet traces so much of the beauty of the lowlands, to the rugged steeps of the central wilderness, and philosophers regard Dartmoor as the source of much of the fertility of the surrounding region, the admirers of its wild simplicity may be pardoned for hoping that other means may be found for rendering its wide expanse productive, without impairing its solitary grandeur, or of destroying its venerable memorials of aboriginal antiquity.  Nor is this hope visionary.  It was the deliberate opinion of one of the most enterprising of the modern experimentalists on Dartmoor, the late Mr. George Frean, of Plymouth, as it has been since by others of equal authority, that the pasturing of cattle on the uplands, connected with judicious cultivation in more sheltered spots, is likely to be the most profitable husbandry, and best adapted to the circumstances of the soil and climate.* And it is curious to observe that this method, if carried into effect, will probably be little more than a recurrence to the practice of our forefathers.

Rich in pre-historic remains, Dartmoor also, in later times, as an antient Stannary district, and a Royal Forest or Chase, urges many claims to our attention, whilst in its present state, as a field of scientific research, a region of picturesque and romantic scenery, and an asylum of old-world customs and language, it can scarcely fail to excite the interest, not only of those whom local partialities might be supposed to influence, but of all others who hold, with the great English moralist that " whatever withdraws " us from the power of the senses,—whatever makes the past, the " distant, and the future, predominate over the present, advances " us in the dignity of thinking beings."

To an object so important, the wild uplands of Dartmoor are calculated to minister, and that in no ordinary degree. Who, with a particle of sensibility can climb its tor-crowned steeps, traverse its rock-strewn ravines, or penetrate its tractless morasses, without an irresistible impression that every object around belongs to a period of unrecorded antiquity? And who, when thus surrounded by the silent yet eloquent memorials of the mysterious past will not acknowledge their influence in " withdrawing him from the power of the senses," and in carrying forward his thoughts to the still more mysterious future? He wanders in a desert encircled with primeval mountains, and beholds nature piling all around in fantastic and mimic masonry, huge masses of granite, as if to mock the mightest efforts of human art. Vast and gloomy castles appear to frown defiance from the beetling crags around. But no mortal hand ever laid their adamantine foundations, or reared their dizzy towers. Nature is the engineer that fortified the heights thousands of years ago,—hers are the massive walls,—hers the mighty bastions,—hers the granite glacis, scarped down to the roaring torrent below—hers the hand that reared those stupendous citadels which fable might have garrisoned with demigods, and beleaguered with Titans; whilst in the recumbent mass that

---

*See Chapter x. Agriculture.

guards the approach, imagination, with scarcely an effort, might discern an archetype of the mystic Sphynx* in kindred prophyry, of proportions far more colossal, and of date far more antient, than that which still looks forth in serene and lonely grandeur over the sands of the Memphian desert.

There are numerous tracts of the moor, where, around the whole expanse, the eye cannot light upon a single feature that is not pristine, intact, and natural.  The entire scene in spots, such as that beyond Tavy Head, at the foot of Fur Tor, is of this untamed and primeval character.  Not a trace of man's presence or occupancy is to be detected.  Even the half-wild cattle which range the other parts of the moor at pleasure, seem to shun the swampy steppes of the central wilderness.  It is only on the spot that the graphic accuracy and poetic beauty of Carrington's description can be appreciated, when with master hand he sketches the characteristic features of a scene, which seems to transport you in a moment from the richly cultivated and thickly-peopled provinces of England, to some unexplored and desert tract, in the remotest regions of the globe.

> " Devonia's dreary Alps ! And now I feel
> The influence of that impressive calm
> That rests upon them.   Nothing that has life
> Is visible ; no solitary flock
> At wide will, ranging through the silent moors,
> Breaks the deep-felt monotony ; and all
> Is motionless, save where the giant shades
> Flung by the passing cloud, glide slowly o'er
> The grey and gloomy wild."

The desert expanse has come down to us rude and inviolate from primeval times.   The tors pile their fantastic masses against the sky, as they first " frowned in the uncertain dawn of time," the granite wrecks of some original convulsion still lie scattered " in most admired disorder."   The roar of " many an antient river " foaming along its rock-bound channel, breaks upon the still silence of the waste, as it did hundreds of ages ago.   All bears the impress of unaltered duration and undisturbed solitude.

And if from a period, whose chronology reaches far beyond the epochs of cycles, lustrums, and olympiads, we come down to the

---

* In the road from Two Bridges to Tavistock, Dr. Berger and his friend Mr. Necker, were both struck, at once, with the resemblance of a granite rock—Vixen Tor—to the Egyptian Sphynx, in a mutilated state.—CARRINGTON'S Dartmoor. Notes, p. 193.

era of monumental antiquity, all is still antique, mysterious, and venerable. The simple and time-worn memorials of unchronicled ages, rear their hoary forms amidst the sombre solitudes of the moor. The mossy cairn surmounted by its primitive unwrought pillar, carries the thoughts back to a period which out-dates the Pyramids and Babylon,—a period when the Mesopotamian patriarchs erected their monumental column, as the witness and memorial of the earliest treaties in the history of man. The columnar masses which mark out the sacred enclosure formed by our Pagan forefathers, stand in rough and native simplicity, untouched by the workman's tool. Walls, which fortified the towns of the aboriginal inhabitants, and bridges, which spanned the swollen torrents of the desert, yet remain, of ruder and more primitive construction than the cyclopean architecture of far-famed Mycenae. And desolate as Dartmoor is, with thousands of acres now destitute even of a turf-cutter's cabin, considerable vestiges of antient dwellings may still be traced in various parts of the Forest and its precincts.

" E'en here,
Man, rude untutor'd man, has liv'd, and left
Rude traces of existence."

# CHAPTER II.

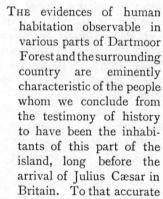

THE evidences of human habitation observable in various parts of Dartmoor Forest and the surrounding country are eminently characteristic of the people whom we conclude from the testimony of history to have been the inhabitants of this part of the island, long before the arrival of Julius Cæsar in Britain. To that accurate observer and faithful commentator on what he saw, we are indebted for a brief but important notice of the inhabitants of the country he invaded. *"Britanniæ pars "interior ab iis incolitur, quos natos in insnla ipsa memoria "proditum dicunt: maritima pars ab iis, qui prædæ ac belli inferendi "causa ex Belgis transierant ; et bello illato, ibi remanserunt, atque "agros colere ceperunt."†* How strikingly does this prove that man is the same in every age, and that similar circumstances issue in the same results. More than two thousand years ago, the Belgian adventurers having crossed the Channel and landed on the coast of Britain, were enabled, doubtless by the power of numbers, or superior civilization, to make good their footing along the maritime parts, and to drive back the original dwellers to the less inviting, but more secure districts of the interior, just as the English settlers and their transatlantic descendants, established

---

*This Chapter must be read with caution.  See the two concluding paragraphs.

†*The interior of Britain is inhabited by people, who are reported by tradition to have been indigenous in the island.   The maritime parts are possessed by invaders who came over from the country of the Belgæ, allured by the hope of booty, and having made war upon the Britons, established themselves in the country, and began to cultivate the land.—Cæsar Bell. Gall. b. v. c. 5.*

themselves on the coasts of America, and thrust back the aboriginal Red-men into the forests and savannahs of the North American continent. Thus before the Roman period of our history, we find two distinct classes, perhaps two distinct races of inhabitants, on the southern coast of England, the origin of one, not doubtful, as they were universally acknowledged to have passed over from the country of the Belgæ, and to have settled in those maritime tracts which lay opposite to the coast of Gaul, and in parts of which (Hampshire) their name long remained, and marked an important division of the country. Whence the earlier settlers who were supposed to have been the aboriginal inhabitants of the island, came, is not so apparent. Cæsar gives no information on a subject which has caused no little controversy among antiquaries. Whitaker maintains that Britain was peopled from Gaul, about one thousand years before the Christian era, and, that the Belgæ, whom Cæsar mentions, followed more than six hundred years after. We are not aware whether there is any better authority for this, than Richard of Cirencester, who records, under the date Anno Mundi M.M.M. "*Circa hæc tempora cultam et habitatam* "*primum, Britanniam arbitrantur nonnulli, cum illam salutarent* "*Græci, Phœnices que mercatores.*" If Richard be the only voucher for this exposition, as it appears to be, of Cæsar's text, those who are acquainted with the doubts which were formerly raised as to the sources of the monk's information, and who now are told on undoubted authority that his work is a forgery, will not be inclined to overrate its importance. Polwhele, our western antiquary, contends that the aborigines mentioned by Cæsar, did not come from Gaul, but that they arrived by sea, from the eastern parts of Asia, Armenia as he supposes, and voyaging by the Straits of Gibraltar, at length reached the westernmost coasts of Britain. Having settled in Cornwall and Devon, in after-times they were visited in succession by Phenician and Greek traders, who made the distant and perilous voyage in search of tin, for which metal, the Cassiterides were already famous at this early period of history. In support of his favourite theory, he goes so far as to trace vestiges of these aboriginal settlers in the name of one of our Dartmoor rivers, and in that of a parish on its banks. Ermington, is doubtless, still generally pronounced Armeton, by the common people, and this our enthusiastic antiquary regards as evidence that the Asiatic navigators might have debarked at the mouth of the Erme (Arme) in Bigbury Bay, and named the country which was to be their future habitation in memory of the land they had left. If they did so, their Danmonian descendants, some three thousand years after, imitated their example when they emigrated from the mouth of the Plym to an island in the Pacific and founded a new Plymouth at the Antipodes.

But the hypothesis of Asiatic colonization rests on far better support than this questionable etymology. The emigration of bodies of people, in every age, has been attended with one universally accompanying circumstance,—the importation of their religious opinions and rites into the country of their adoption. That there is a striking similarity between the religious opinions and sacred rites of the Druids, and those of the eastern nations, none acquainted with the testimony of antient authors on the subject will venture to question. From the undeniable evidence which Holy Writ affords, we know how popular and universally prevalent was the worship of the heavenly bodies among the nations of the east, and with what frantic eagerness and perverse obstinacy, even the well-instructed Hebrews recurred again and again to idolatrous practices, which the Holy One of Israel had expressly forbidden on the pain of his hottest displeasure, and had punished with the severest vengeance times out of number. Still "they tempted " and displeased the most High God," and " burned incense unto " Baal, to the sun, to the moon, and to the planets, and to all the "hosts of heaven."—2 *Kings, xxiii.,* 5. And this worship the Israelities derived from "the nations round about," for so early as the times of Job, it was the pardonable boast of that upright man, that he had not been carried away by the general prevalence of idolatry in the land of Uz, "his heart had not been enticed, nor " his mouth kissed his hand if he beheld the sun when it shined, "or the moon walking in her brightness."—*Job, xxxi.,* 26-27. The Baal or Bel of the Canaanities and the Phœnicians was evidently the same deity whom Diodorus describes as the object of worship, in a northern island over against the Celtæ of Gaul. They had a large grove and a temple of a round form, to which the priests resorted to sing the praises of Apollo*—*Diod. Sic. b. iii.*

But whilst the Druids, in the time of Cæsar, ministered to the popular propensities by sanctioning the worship of idols and, perhaps, the use of images, there are just reasons for the belief that these, with other practices, were the result of their inter-

---

*BORLASE asserts that the old British appellation of the Scilly Islands was *Sulleh* or *Sylleh*, signifying rocks consecrated to the sun.—Ant. Corn. II., c. 19.

course with the Phenicians, who seem also to have introduced
the worship of their favorite goddess Astarte, or Bali Sama, *i.e.*,
the queen of heaven.† Their earlier and purer practice seems to
have been much more nearly allied to the Sabæan creed—the
worship of the sun under the form of fire—and abhorrence of
every kind of image of the invisible God. They also appear to
have scrupulously abstained from using any tool in the construction of their temples and altars,—a practice utterly unknown to
classical antients, and which seems again to point to an eastern
origin, and even to a traditionary acquaintance with the express
ordinance of the Almighty, for the guidance of the Israelites in
this particular. (*Ex.* xx., 25.) But the Druids had their hill
altars,—and sacred groves,—in exact correspondence again,
with those idolatrous practices of the east with which Holy Writ
has made us familiar; and, what is worthy of remark, the favourite
tree with the primitive British priesthood, for this purpose, was
the oak, the very tree which is specified by the prophet Isaiah, as
connected with the worst atrocities of paganism, in the practice of
his idolatrous countrymen, whom he accuses of "inflaming
themselves with idols among the oaks [*margin*] slaying the
children in the valleys under the clifts of the rocks."—(*Is.* lvii., 5.
margin.) The Druids, like the Chaldeans, cultivated the science
of astronomy (doubtless in connection with astrology) and were
great observers of the motions of the heavenly bodies. *Hi terræ*
*mundique magnitudinem et formam motus cœli ac siderum, ac quod*
*Di velint scire profitentur.*—Pomp: Mela. lib. ii, c. 2. But the
most remarkable point of similarity is the belief in the transmi-
gration of souls which the Druids are believed to have held in
common with the Gymnosophists of antient India. Taliessin, the
Welsh bard affirms that he has experienced, in his own person,
the changes of the metempsychosis:—"I have died, I have
"revived; a second time was I formed,—I have been a blue
"salmon; I have been a dog; I have been a stag; I have been

---

† The Rev. Vernon Harcourt asserts that the Phenicians introduced the worship
of Baal or Fire, five hundred years before the Christian era, among the aboriginal
inhabitants of Ireland, whom he calls Momonii, and whom he describes as Arkites.
"There are two places," observes this author, "called Magh Turey, one in the
"north, the other in the south, and at both, not long before the Christian era, that is
"about the time when the Arkites received a strong reinforcement by a Scythian
"swarm from the north, called Tuath de Doinan, a battle was fought between the
"Belgæ, the worshippers of Bel or Baal on the one side, and the Danans *i.e.* the
"Danai, the Dionusans, the Arkites, and the Caledonian or Deucaledonian, Diluvian
"tribes on the other.—Doct. Deluge, Vol. i., 487.

"a roebuck on the mountains; I have been a cock; I have been "Aedd; returning to my former state, I am now Taliessin.* All these facts† may fairly be brought to support the hypothesis of an oriental colonization of the south-western parts of England previously to the immigration of the Belgæ from Gaul, B.C. 350.‡ It may, however, be objected, that although an earlier peopling of Britain than this might have taken place, it does not then necessarily follow that the settlers might not have crossed the narrow seas from the continent, at a remoter period, for instance A.M. 3000, as Whitaker supposes. To this it is answered that few, if any, traces of similar religious doctrines are observable across the continent, in a direction which a wave of population from the east would have taken, had it reached the shores of Britain, in one flow, or by successive undulations. Druidism had taken no root among the German nations, and in Gaul, where it flourished in the latter times of the Roman republic, it was not indigenous. Cæsar expressly records that the Druidical discipline was discovered in Britain and transmitted thence to Gaul. *Disciplina in Britannia reperta, atque in Galliam translata esse existimatur.*—Cæsar. Bell. Gall. lib. vi., c. 13. The Rev. V. Harcourt, in his elaborate and valuable researches into the vestiges of the Scripture doctrine of the Noachic deluge among the heathen nations of antiquity, traces them in their traditions, mythology, and worship, as well as in the etymology of the names of persons and places. He adduces a mass of remarkable testimony to prove that the Arkite worship (which he believes Druidism to have been in its purer and more antient form) prevailed from India and China in the east, to Britain in the west. In proceeding with an account of the existing monumental relics of Dartmoor, which we do in the next chapter, it will be curious to remark in how many particulars they appear to bear out the theory which this learned author has brought forward.

After much hesitation, we have decided to allow the foregoing speculations to remain much as they appeared in the former editions of this work, but it must be observed, firstly, that there is

---

*DAVIES. Mythology of the Druids, p. 573.

†Pliny was evidently struck with the same similarity. *Britannia hodieque eam attonite celebrat tantis ceremoniis, ut dedisse Persis videri possit.* PLINY, lib. *xxx.*

‡DIOGENES LAERTIUS says the Druids and Gymnosophists of India were similar. Proem, 4-5, ed. He. Stephens, 1594.

no proof whatever that Druidical worship prevailed at any time upon Dartmoor; and secondly, that the Eastern origin of the antient people of Britain, arguments for which our author thus adduced, was supposed to be well established until recently. The investigations of Latham, and of German and French scholars, have now altogether upset this oriental theory, and it is upon linguistic grounds as well as for other reasons, that it is now supposed that the origin of these very early settlers in Britain, must be sought for in Mid-Europe, and not in the far East. And what applies to Britain, applies to Dartmoor, for there is no reason to believe that Dartmoor was different from the rest of the country. " It is plain that the civilization which we find in Europe at the " beginning of the historic period, was gradually evolved during " a vast period of time, and was not introduced cataclysmically, by " the immigration of a new race."[*]

Traces of Neolithic man, as well as of those men who succeeded him, are to be found, as in other parts of our island, on Dartmoor, as evidenced by recent most important investigations, to which reference will be made in succeeding chapters of this work. It is unnecessary to occupy space with any of the results of enquiries as to these pre-historic people, to whose history so much research and learning has of late years been devoted. The evidence obtained from barrows, and hut circles, and the camps of which so many are found on the borders, is of the greatest interest, although it is too early to be dogmatic as to the theories which this evidence supports. It will be sufficient to say here, that the Neolithic people reached Britain from the Continent, and being a little stronger and more enterprising, and with better weapons than those possessed by the people they found here, drove before them the Paleolithic men, who had no power to make resistance. With their stone axes, they made a clearing in the woods in which to place their settlements. They brought with them domestic animals, sheep and goats, dogs and pigs. They grew corn and manufactured a rude kind of pottery. Each tribe lived in a state of war with its neighbours. These few words (although Dartmoor has not so far, given us so many examples of the life history of these people as are here mentioned) will enable us to understand much of what has hitherto been a mystery to some who have essayed to write upon Dartmoor matters.

---

[*]ISAAC TAYLOR. The Origin of the Aryans, 1890, p. 132.

# CHAPTER III.

OF the Antiquities of Dartmoor, none are more conspicuous than the so-called Sacred Circles. We have no example approaching either in vastness or extent to the massive proportions of Stonehenge, but there are not wanting specimens equally decisive in character, although inferior in magnitude. For the construction of these circles the region supplied ample and appropriate material. The accidents of nature have more to do with the decision of matters of this kind, than we are usually free to allow. The colossal architecture of Egypt had its birth in the granite quarries of that peculiar country; the bituminous plains of Babylon, suggested the employment of brick in the construction of the vast edifices of that "lady of the kingdoms." The granite tors of Devon and Cornwall in like manner, furnished materials for the erection of circles, cromlechs, and rows, abundant in supply, and suitable in form and quality;—as to form, sublime from their very simplicity and vastness; and as to durability, imperishable as the hills from which they were taken, rude and untouched by the workman's tool, as when dislodged by some primeval convulsion of nature from their original position.

The rude simplicity and complete absence of all preparation in the materials of the Dartmoor circles, mark their high antiquity, and in this respect, invest them with an interest superior to the majestic but artificial trilithons of Stonehenge. The circle was evidently a rude patriarchal temple, thinks Sir R. C. Hoare. "That they were erected for the double purpose of religious and "civil assemblies may be admitted without controversy" says he in his Antiquities of Wilts.*

Our Danmonian Circles are apparently of the same description as the fine inclosure at Abury in Wiltshire, and are similar in the size, form and character of the stones of which they are constructed. Although the mighty columns of Stonehenge are connected by horizontal imposts, in no instance does there appear the least vestige of any provision for a roof. On Dartmoor, the stones which form the circle, are for the most part, insufficient in height for any such purpose, nor in any instance, have the uprights ever been furnished with imposts. The size of the area would also have precluded any attempt at covering it with a roof. It is therefore clear that the uses of the enclosures of Stonehenge, Abury, Stanton Moor, Stennis and elsewhere, and of those on Dartmoor, are identical, and if the purposes for which the first were erected could be discovered, the clue to the objects of the last mentioned would be obtained.*

It was a favourite idea of the old antiquaries, to consider these circles Druidical erections, and they called them Sacred Circles, and connected them with the avenues near, and concluded that they were Dracontian temples, in which serpent worship was practised, and from their circular form, as indicating solar worship. Really all that can be said at present with any certainty about them, is that they were connected with burial, and probably with worship and sacrifice.†

These remains approach, in all cases, more or less to the circular form. They are of various dimensions and are constructed of granite blocks of irregular shape, and by no means uniform in size. Taking a general view of monuments of this class in our island, some antiquaries have fixed the number of stones as ranging from twelve to twenty-seven; it is stated also that they are more

---

*Vol. II., p. 118 ; Lond. 1812.

*R. N. WORTH. Notes and Gleanings. Vol. III., p. 109.

†Vide Stone Circles of Britain. A. L. LEWIS, Arch: Journal, Vol XLIX. p. 136. Heth and Moab, C. R. CONDER, 1883. See also a very valuable and important paper by ARTHUR J. EVANS, on Stonehenge, in Archæological Review, Vol II, p. 312.

frequently found of the former number than any other. This number is still preserved in the inner circle at Abury. This conjecture, however, seems to be much at variance with conclusions drawn from an examination of Dartmoor specimens. In some instances the number has been found to be twenty-seven, but circles consisting of twenty-five, fifteen, twelve, eleven, and even ten, have also been observed, the height of the stones above the surface, ranging from seven feet and a half, to eighteen inches. In the latter cases they have probably been mutilated. The circumference varies from thirty-six feet to three hundred and sixty feet, which is the size of the Grey Wethers, below Sittaford Tor, the largest on the Moor. It would seem possible to distinguish two kinds of circles, one surrounding a place of burial, the other enclosing a larger area in which no trace of an interment has been found. Sometimes these circles, are, as at Merivale Bridge, Drizzlecombe, Erme Pound, and elsewhere, found in connection with avenues; at the Grey Wethers, (some of the stones of which have been apparently worked so as to form square heads) there are two circles whose circumferences almost touch each other, and one example has been observed, containing two concentric circles, and one on Castor, a sepulchral one, with four. These stone rings which we continue to call Sacred Circles for want of a better name, must not be confounded with the Hut circles, or the Pounds, the former of which are so numerous on the Moor. The stones of which the Sacred Circles are composed, are in all cases set up at intervals of greater or less extent, whereas the latter clearly indicate a totally different purpose, the stones being set as closely together as their rugged and unwrought form will permit.

The most noticeable of the Dartmoor Circles, are those of Scorhill, The Grey Wethers, Froggy Mead, and Trowlesworthy, the two first being the most important, and the last discovered, in 1894, a very fine one on Langstone Moor, the stones of which have been recently re-erected.

ROWS.  The Stone Avenues, Rows, Alignments, or Paral-lelithons, have been as productive of Druidical speculations as the Circle. These the older antiquaries liked to call Avenues. They did not know that many of them on Dartmoor were single lines only, not double, nor did they know, or imagine, that an avenue could be composed of more than two rows of stones. It was in the year 1827, that the author, in company with Col. Hamilton Smith and others, examined the avenues near Merivale Bridge. Before this time, little notice had been taken of this class of remains, and they had been scarcely mentioned by our local topographers and antiquaries. Polwhele, who in the most systematic and elaborate manner classifies and enumerates every remnant of antiquity on Dartmoor, mentions the avenue only in an incidental and cursory manner, in his minute account of the Drewsteignton Cromlech, which he says " is placed on an elevated " spot, overlooking a sacred way, and *two rows of pillars, which* "*mark this processional*" road of the Druids. Lysons in his History of the County, makes no mention of anything of the kind, although the existence of this curious conformation of stones was well known to the inhabitants of Tavistock and the neighbourhood, under the popular name of the Plague Market. Rows—for as suggested by Mr. R. N. Worth, this is a much better name than any other—are very numerous on Dartmoor, more so than anywhere else. Examples of these are found in other parts of Great Britain, and in other countries, although as far as the magnitude and number of the stones is concerned, there is nothing elsewhere like the rows in Brittany—those of Kermario, Menec, and Erderven.

On Dartmoor these avenues occur always in connection with other relics, and most commonly with the circle. Mr. Lukis indeed considers it probable that all of them were originally connected with burial mounds, and he says that out of the twenty-four he examined, fourteen were still connected with or attached to cairns. Of the examples of circles and cairns with single lines may be mentioned that on Staldon Moor, south-east of Erme Pound. Here we have a circle of about fifty-two feet in diameter, and in a direction from it almost due north, is a line of stones which have been traced by the late Rev. W. C. Lukis for a distance of eleven thousand two hundred and thirty nine feet. On Hingston Hill, east of Down Tor, is a cairn surrounded by a circle and a single line of stones, which are visible to the extent of eleven hundred and seventy three feet ; on Hartor, east of Blackdown is a cairn with an excavation in the centre, and a single line of stones, which has been partially destroyed by a stream-work, is traceable for about two hundred feet, and lastly the curious collection of stone monuments on Glazebrook Moor, where we find two cairns, with a third a little west of the line, and a single line of stones four hundred and eighty six feet long, besides other remarkable lines to be presently referred to. Of circles and cairns with lines, may be mentioned that east of Cosdon Beacon, on South Tawton common, where there is a triple row of stones starting from sepulchral circles at the west end, and with kistvaens and tumuli west of the circles, and also that at Assycombe, where there is a double row running east and west for four hundred and thirty feet, starting from a sepulchral circle at the eastern end. Another, at the foot of Hartor near the cairn with the single line before mentioned, an avenue runs from the cairn almost due west for four hundred and fifty feet.

There are also examples of Rows consisting of four and five lines, and the very remarkable one on the moor between the streams of the East and West Glazebrook, outside Glazecombe Moor Wall, which Mr. Lukis with infinite patience and trouble investigated, and pronounced to be of thirteen rows, extending for about three hundred and thirty feet. Here, there is a line of stones leading to a cairn, and then to a stream, as before mentioned. By the side of the most distant cairn, is a larger one, and from this in a south-westerly direction, run the thirteen lines referred to. Particular features which may have their bearing on the intentions of those who erected these circles and avenues, may be noticed in connection with these remains as the result of an examination of the principal specimens to be found on Dartmoor. They are never serpentine, although not always quite straight, one example is very slightly curvilinear for a short distance. The stones comprising them are from two to four feet high, and appear to have been chosen with a view to some degree of uniformity, and they are placed at irregular distances, but generally about three feet and a half apart. The terminating blocks are in most cases of larger size than the others, some are of great size, as for example those at Drizzlecombe, in the Plym Valley, and the parallel lines stand about four feet and a half asunder. The general direction of the avenues, appears to be from a circle to a neighbouring stream, and in several instances there seems to be preference given to a leaning east and west. But the Staldon Moor row, with its circle 59ft. 9in. in diameter at one end, and the cairn 27ft. in diameter at the other end, and exclusive of these, as before mentioned, measuring two miles and a quarter long, crosses the Erme river. Had the straight line been followed, an obstruction in the precipitous bank of the river would have been met with, so the builders of this great monument deviated eastward, to where the bank was more sloping and the water more shallow. Here the stream was crossed and gradually tending towards the west, the Row finally reached the cairn at the north end. Mr. Hansford Worth has traced this the whole length, as did Mr. Lukis.*

Some of these alignments commence, and sometimes end, with a menhir of greater or lesser size. At Drizzlecombe there is a cairn which is connected by a row, two hundred and sixty feet long, with an upright stone seventeen feet nine inches in length, formerly prone, but once more erect, and standing thirteen feet six inches above the ground. Near Headland, on what is known as Challacombe or Chillacombe Down, is an avenue to which attention was first drawn by Prideaux fifty or more years ago. He only mentions lines, and does not give the number, but Mr. Baring-Gould considers there were originally eight rows, three of which are perfect, and the others now represented by a few stones only. These lines run from N.N.W. to S.S.E. for five hundred and twenty eight feet, and end in a menhir eight feet six inches high, and are of a varying width to five feet. It is safe to assume that all these circles and rows are memorials of the dead and connected with burial, but beyond this we cannot at present go.

In chapter xviii., we are enabled to give a list of the known existing Stone Rows on Dartmoor, and in the list of plans prepared by the late Rev. W. C. Lukis, in the same chapter, will be found those measured by him. Mr. R. N. Worth has given much attention to these remains and has recorded the results of his investigations in three papers printed in the Transactions of the Devonshire Association, 1892-3-4, and to these we must refer our readers for a full account of the Dartmoor Rows, and of the speculations with regard to them, some of which are ludicrous.

Among the relics of antiquity, authors have enumer-
ROCK IDOLS. ated the Logan Stone and Rock Idol. Of the latter of these, not to be confounded with the Rock Pillar or Menhir, Dartmoor can boast many remarkable specimens. Moulded as they are, as Carrington soothly sings,

> " Into a thousand shapes
> Of beauty and of grandeur,"

few are the tors which would not attract attention, and inspire awe, if pointed out for the purpose of worship to an

---

*Trans. Plym. Inst. Vol. xi., p. 181.

Ç

ignorant and superstitious people. But there is no evidence
that such adoration was ever offered by our aboriginal forefathers, although Borlase has ventured to particularize and
classify these stone deities. To give any accurate notice of
objects of this class, would be scarcely less than to enumerate
the principal tors on the moor; or rather it would be impossible to discriminate, in a classification, in which the
judgment would have far less exercise than the imagination.
Some have thought, that a so-called rock-basin on any tor, or
pile of rocks, is decisive of its mythological character. Polwhele,
who is by no means over cautious in admitting the claims of
various objects to Druidical honours, judiciously restrains his
fancy in this particular, and truly enough observes, that " we are
afraid to fix on a Druid Idol, lest the neighbouring mass should
have the same pretensions to adoration, and all the stones upon
the hills and in the vallies, should start up into divinities."* Yet
he thinks "the principal rocks on Dartmoor might have been
British idols," and is inclined to concede to Blackstone† and
Whitstone, near Moreton, the honour of canonization. And
when we gaze upon such a mass as Vixen Tor, grand and huge,
as it towers above the vale of Walkham, or view such a singular
pile as Bowerman's Nose, on Heighen or Hayne Down, we
scarcely err in concluding that if the Druids had their Rock Idols,
these must have ranked high in their granite mythology. Bowerman's Nose may have been utilized as an idol, but its formation is
due to the granite rock having fallen away along the lines of
parting.

LOGAN STONES. The Logan Stone seems to have formed an important
and characteristic feature in the mystic apparatus of
Druidism, but there are only one or two specimens
now known to exist in Devonshire, and even these have almost, if
not entirely, lost the quality which originally gave them fame and
distinction. The celebrated Drewsteignton Logan Stone might
be repeatedly passed by, without exciting more curiosity or
attention than any other huge granite mass, standing aloft in the
bed of the river. And it is impossible to traverse the moor in any
direction without observing many a similar rock, which once
might have been a Logan Stone, or might have been easily made

---

*Historical Views of Devonshire, p. 53.
†Blackystone and Heltor, as they are commonly called in the neighbourhood.

Logan Stone Rippon Tor.

*to logg*, that is, vibrate—so fantastical and singular are the positions in which such superincumbent masses are continually found, balanced on another rock below, so nicely as to admit of the immense bulk being moved, by the application of no more force than the strength of a man's hand. Such curiously adjusted masses, seem not to have been unknown to the antients. Pliny, observes Polwhele,* hath evidently the Logan Stone in view, when he tells us that at Harpassa, a town of Asia, was a rock of a wonderful nature, "Lay one finger on it, and it will stir; but thrust at it with your whole body and it will not move." But the most curious mention of the Logan by the antients, is that of Apollonius Rhodius; from which it would appear that such rocking stones were sometimes artificial, and raised as funeral monuments, in connection too, with tumuli or barrows.

"In sea-girt Tenos, he the brothers slew,
And o'er their graves in heapy hillocks threw
The crumbling mould; then with two columns crowned
Erected high, the Death devoted ground;
And one still moves, (how marvellous the tale)
With every motion of the northern gale."

*Fawkes' Argonaut, b.* iv.

In Wales, such stones are called Maen Sigl, the Shaking Stone, a term equivalent to the Logan or Logging Stone of Devon and Cornwall. Our vernacular probably still retains the word; and "*a great logging thing*" familiarly and popularly describes any large mass in vibratory motion.

The purposes to which the Logan Stone was supposed to be applied by the Druids, have given rise to no little antiquarian controversy. According to Toland, "the Druids made the people "believe that they alone could move these stones, and by a miracle "only; by which pretended power they condemned or acquitted "the accused, and often brought criminals to confess what could "in no other way be extorted from them." Borlase having observed rock basins on the Logan Stones in Cornwall, conjectures, that by means of these basins, the Druids made the Logan subservient to their judicial purposes, and applied it as an ordeal to convict or acquit a culprit, by filling or emptying the basin, and by this displacement of the centre of gravity, rendered the mass immovable, or the contrary, at pleasure. This ingenious conjecture of the

---

*Hist. View Dev., p. 56. Juxta Harpasa, oppidum Asiæ, cautes stat horrenda, uno digito mobilis; eadem, si toto corpore impellatur, resistens.—PLIN. lib. ii.

antiquary has been thus felicitously rendered subservient to poetical purposes by Mason :—

　　　　　　　　　" Behold yon huge
　　　" And unhewn sphere of living adamant,
　　　" Which poised by magic, rests its central weight
　　　" On yonder pointed rock.　Firm as it seems,
　　　" Such is its strange and virtuous property,
　　　" It moves obsequious to the gentlest touch
　　　" Of him whose heart is pure ; but to a traitor,
　　　" Tho' ev'n a giant's powers nerved his arm,
　　　" It stands as fixed as Snowdon."

Fosbrooke considers the Logan or Rocking stone as the " stone of power," referred to so frequently in the poems of Ossian, according to which authority it appears that the bards walked round the stone singing, and made it move as an oracle of the fate of battle.　" He called the grey-haired Snivan, that sang round " the circle of Loda, when *the stone of power* heard his voice, and " battle turned in the field of the valiant."

That stones so placed as to form Logan Stones is the effect of natural circumstances, there can be no doubt.　Norden's explanation may apply to many, if not to all the examples.　" It is to be " imagined that theis stones were thus lefte at the general floude " when the earth was washed awaye, and the massie stones " remained, as are mightie rocks uncovered, standing upon loftie " hills."

ROCK BASINS.　Like many other disputed points of antiquarian interest, where no contemporary authority or external evidence can be adduced on either side, the Rock Basins have afforded a fruitful source of controversy.　Whilst some have strenuously advocated their claims to the venerable character of Druidical relics, " others at this doctrine rail," and attribute their formation to the action of the weather, and to the facility with which the component particles of granite disintegrate under certain circumstances.　That numberless hollows on granite masses have been thus naturally formed, no observer of the natural phenomena of Dartmoor will for a moment question.　A typical specimen, is that on the top of Great Mis Tor, one of the loftiest hills on the moor.　This basin is in a singularly perfect state, in form a circle, three feet in diameter, and eight inches deep.　Its sides are regularly formed, rising straight from the bottom which is flat, a spout or lip is formed in its northern edge.   It might be most characteristically described as a pan, excavated in granite, and accordingly Mis Tor Pan is its popular designation, " a rocke " called Mistorr pan," say the perambulators of 1609.   On Castor Rock is another fine specimen, two feet seven inches deep, and seven feet six inches in diameter across the top, narrowing to two feet at the bottom.

The frequent occurrence of Rock Basins on the surface of Logan Stones, induced Dr. Borlase to conclude that they were intended to regulate the motion of the Logan Stone.   The same author supposes them to have been used for libations of blood, wine, honey or oil, and describes some, as large enough to receive the head and part of a human body.   Fosbrooke unhesitatingly pronounces Rock Basins to be " cavities cut in the surface of a rock " supposed for reservoirs, to preserve the rain or dew in its original " purity, for the religious uses of the Druid."*   Polwhele observes " with respect to the uses of these basins, I think we may easily con- " jecture that they were contrived by the Druids as receptacles of " water, for the purpose of external purifications, by washing and " sprinkling.   The rites of water lustration and ablution were too " frequent among the Asiatics, not to be known to the Druids, who " resembled the Eastern nations in all their religious ceremonies, " fashions and customs. . . . . . . From such basins the officiating " Druid might sanctify the congregation with a more sacred " lustration than usual.   In this water he might mix his mistletoe " or infuse his oak leaves, for a medicinal or incantorial potion."*

We learn from Vernon Harcourt that the connection, or rather the identity of Druidism with Arkite worship, may be satisfactorily traced in this remarkable relic of antiquity, the Rock Basin.   In the opinion of the Druids, or of their predecessors in the Arkite priesthood, water was deemed so essential to the mysteries of regeneration, that they took great pains to secure a supply of it in the best way they could, and for this purpose they excavated basins upon the surface of the rocks in their high places to contain it.   The same author notes a curious circumstance, related by an oriental traveller, " There are three large troughs or rock basins, " really cut out on the flat surface of a granite rock at Axum, in " Abyssinia, out of which, tradition says, that a great snake, the

---

*Encyc. of Ant. Vol. ii., ed. 1843, p. 778.

*POLWHELE.  Historical Views of Devonshire.  Vol. i., p. 59.

"presiding genius of the flood, who resided in the hollow of the "mountain, used to eat."*

Such are the theories of the older antiquaries as to the origin and use of Rock Basins. But geologists take another view. In an exhaustive Memoir on Rock Basins in the granite of the Dartmoor District, contained in the Quarterly Journal of the Geological Society, the late George Waring Ormerod entered fully into the history of these hollows. In this, and other memoirs, he stated that the granite of Dartmoor consisted of three belts reaching across the Moor. The first is a crystalline belt, in the northern part, in which very few basins are found; a belt of coarse grained laminated granite that occupied the central portion, in which most of the basins are found; and a belt of a variable nature to the south in which very few basins occur. The characteristics of the Rock Basins observed in various parts of Dartmoor, may be noted as follows: situation, commonly on the highest spot of the loftiest pile of the tor, very often near the edge of the block in which they are hollowed; in many instances with a lip or channel, to convey the water from the basin; the bottom flat; sides, perpendicular; form, for the most part circular. The diameters of thirty-five perfect basins examined by Ormerod, varied from eleven by ten inches to forty-two inches by fifty-four inches, and the depths from two inches to nine inches. He examined thirty-six basins besides these, that were not perfect, and he knew of eleven others that he had not been able to examine. In addition to these, there are four others, that far exceed the average size, viz., those at Hell Tor, Cas Tor, Ingstone, and Bell Tor. Sir Henry De la Beche, Dr. McCullock and Mr. Ormerod had no doubt but that these hollows were caused by atmospheric action upon the rock, aided by the spheroidal structure of the granite.† The opinion of Ormerod is generally accepted, but Sir J. Gardner Wilkinson combatted his reasoning, and, while admitting that the greater number of Rock Basins were natural, thought that some were formed by human agency.‡

---

*Doctrine of Deluge, Vol. II., pp. 505-6.

†Quart. Journ. Geol. Society, Vol XV., part 1, February 1859.

‡Journal Brit. Arch. Assoc., Vol XVI., 1860, p. 101.

CROMLECHS OR DOLMENS. The Cromlech, or Dolmen as it should be called, is perhaps the most curious relic of our aboriginal ancestors, and the precincts of Dartmoor can boast one of the finest in the kingdom, and the only perfect specimen in Devonshire. Sir R. C. Hoare observes that cromlechs had long been confounded with kistvaens, but that he had strong reason for supposing they were raised for different purposes. The true cromlech, as distinguished from the kistvaen, generally consists of three rude unwrought stones, artificially fixed in the ground, and supporting a fourth of an irregular tabular form, as a canopy, in most cases at the height of several feet from the ground ; whereas the kistvaen consists of four, five or more slabs, forming a kind of rude stone coffin or sarcophagus, fixed in the ground with a cover stone, for the reception of corpses. Instances occur of four, and even six supporters to the impost in cromlechs ; but three is the more usual number. It is singular that Dr. Borlase should never have found more than three supporters, as the Trevethy Stone, near St. Cleer, in his own county, has seven. He supposes three to have been chosen in preference to a larger number, as not requiring so much nicety in bringing the impost to bear. The masses of which cromlechs are composed, are rude and unwrought, and appear to have been placed in their present position, rough from their native bed,—and untouched, except by the winter storm. The term, cromlech, is of doubtful import, and the researches of antiquaries into its etymology have thrown little light on the purposes for which these primitive monuments were originally designed. Rowlands *(Mona Antiqua Restaurata)* derives the name cromlech from the Hebrew *Carem luach*, which he renders a *devoted stone* or altar. Sir R. C. Hoare traces the etymology to the British words *crom, bending*, or *bowed*, and *llec*, a *broad, flat stone*. Dr. Borlase hazards the conjecture that the word means the *crooked stone*, the impost or quoit being generally of a gibbous or curved form. And with regard to the particular specimen at Drewsteignton, Polwhele is of opinion that the name of the farm on which it stands, may be regarded as favouring this etymology, as he thinks Shilston is no more than a corruption of Shilfeston* (by which term the estate is described in antient deeds,) which " signifies the shelf-stone, or shelving stone."† One of the

---

* *Hist. Views Dev.*, p. 76.

† In Gaelic, *Crom* means crooked, or bent, and *leac* a broad, flat stone. The name of Shovelstone also applies to a rock in Widecombe and is one of the boundary points between the Manors of Widecombe Town (Mrs. Drake's), and Dunstone, (the

characteristics of the cromlech is its shelving cover-stone, or quoit as it is more commonly called ; and by those who contend that these curious monuments were gigantic altars,*—raised for the celebration of the bloody rites of Druidism,—this form is supposed to have been adopted to afford the assembled votaries a fuller view of the devoted victim and sacrificing priest, and to allow the blood to run off readily.  But whilst standing by the altar, is a position familiar to all, as the universally prevailing practice among all nations where sacrifices have formed part of the worship of the people, the idea of a priest standing upon it is altogether foreign to our notions, and would doubtless appear to be abhorrent to the feelings of the Druids, who seem to have been most scrupulous in inculcating peculiar reverence for places and objects consecrated to the purposes of religion.  Such an elevation as that of the Drew-steignton cromlech, could never have been reached, except by the help of a ladder or steps.  A Cyclopean staircase of granite blocks might have given access to the surface, but no traces of such an accommodation have ever been found in any of the numerous existing examples.  For these and other reasons, we may justly question the hypothesis, which would discover a colossal altar in these remarkable monuments of aboriginal antiquity, and would conclude that this was their original destination.  Still they might have been the scene of religious rites, although the cromlech itself was not intended to form an altar, but rather a shrine, or perhaps the tomb of some distinguished personage.

Sir R. C. Hoare considers the absence of human remains in a particular instance, as evidence in favour of the cromlech having been intended for an altar ; but Dr. Borlase remarks " as the whole " frame of the cromlech shows itself to be unfit for an altar of " burnt offerings, so I think it points out evidently to us, several " reasons to conclude that it is a sepulchral monument," though he allows that in his researches, he never found bones or urns to support his hypothesis.

---

late Mr. Robert Dymond's).   It is worthy of remark, that in our genuine Devonshire vernacular, the word *shelf* is still pronounced *shil*, and thus far supports Polwhele's notion.   Moreover the Anglo-Saxon *scilfe* is not only a *shelf*, but also an *abacus*, a *roof* or *covering*, as rendered by Bosworth, (*Anglo-Sax. Dict.* in voc. *abacus scamnum, tabulatam, tectum,*) terms which describe with singular accuracy, the cromlech at Shilston. in the parish of Drewsteignton.

*OLAUS WORMIUS appears to support this hypothesis.   " Ararum structura apud " nos est varia.   Maxima ex parte congesto ex terra constant tumulo, in cujus " summitate, tria ingentia saxa, quartum, illudque majus, latius ac planius, " sustinent, fulciunt ac sustentant, ut instar mensæ tribus fu eris innixæ emineat."

Fosbrooke quotes Hollinshed in support of the altar hypothesis, but although the old chronicler speaks of an altar, it by no means follows that the altar he mentions, must be a cromlech. "Cromlechs "are further designated as altars, by Hollinshed, . . . . where, "after mentioning places compassed about with huge stones, round "like a ring," he adds, "but towards the south was one mightie "stone, farre greater than all the rest, pitched up in manner of an "altar, whereon their priests might make their sacrifices in honour "of their gods."* A mighty stone (standing singly) might be "pitched up in manner of an altar" without supporters beneath, (for this would destroy its altar-like character, and constitute it a table, *instar mensæ*, as Olaus Wormius has it) and there are thousands of large stones on Dartmoor which only require to be raised to form altars,† and closely approaching to the pedestal or truncated form, so generally preferred among the nations of classical antiquity, for this essential and prominent feature in the arrangement of their temples. Another hypothesis regards the cromlech as a sanctuary or sacred cell, a place of occasional retreat for a Druid, and intimately connected with Arkite cere-monies, probably representing the ark itself.

Borlase and Polwhele, (from their acquaintance with the examples in Cornwall and Devon) conclude that cromlechs were chiefly intended as sepulchral monuments, raised only to persons of eminence and distinction, although this might not prevent their being used for other purposes. That very curious specimen, the Cromlech of St. Cleer, in Cornwall, is popularly called the Trevethy‡ Stone, and if this is rightly rendered the *house* or *place of graves*, it would appear that some evidences of antient burials had been found within its area. At least we are certain that human remains have been discovered beneath the massive canopy of the cromlech, in various instances, although Sir R. C. Hoare adduces an example, mentioned above, in which a cromlech occurs, surrounded by five kistvaens, all which contained bones ; yet none

---

*FOSBROOKE. Encyc. Antiq., *ed.* 1843, p. 775.

†"The huge piles of stones erected from time immemorial, in several parts of Ireland, with immense coverings, raised in due order, are doubtless of Pagan times. Some think them Druidical altars. They have the generic name of *Leaba na Feine*. (Feine in Gaelic means Fingalians or Fenians.) These words signify the beds of the *Phœni* or *Carthaginians*." FOSBROKE. Encyc. Antiq. *ed.* 1843, p. 513. From this etymology, it may however, be inferred that these erections were burying places rather than altars.

‡NORDEN, however, calls it Trethenie, *Casa Gigantis*; but Trevethy or Trethevy is the name by which it is still known in the neighbourhood.

were found under the cromlech itself: but then it must be borne
in mind that the learned Wiltshire antiquary, as he himself allows,
never had an opportunity of examining a cromlech, his own county
not offering the same advantages as are presented to the Danmonian investigator in the fine specimens which remain in
Cornwall and Devon. Polwhele pronounces that the Drewsteignton Cromlech "was the sepulchre of a chief Druid, or of
"some prince, the favourite of the Druid order. Hence the crom-
"lech acquired a peculiar degree of holiness; and sacrifices were
"performed in view of it to the manes of the dead."* That
religious ceremonies were celebrated at or near these singular
erections, may be inferred from the designations which some of
them have traditionally obtained. Fosbroke mentions that the
Cromlech, near Marecross, in Glamorganshire, is still called the
*old Church* among the common people.

Yet another theory, that of William Chapple, who in his
incomplete work, "*Description and Exegesis of the Drewsteignton
Cromlech,*" etc., 1778, satisfied himself from various careful
measurements and other conclusions arrived at, that it "could not
"be primarily intended either as a religious structure or a sepulchral
"monument, but was partly designed for sciatherical purposes,
"and in general, as the apparatus of an ASTRONOMICAL OBSER-
VATORY."† Chapple infers that one thousand two hundred years
have elapsed since the Drewsteignton Cromlech was erected. He
computes the super-incumbent quoit to contain two hundred and
sixteen cubic feet, and calculates its weight at sixteen tons and
sixteen pounds. When we consider that this huge mass of granite
rock, was, until its fall in 1862, as hereinafter mentioned,
supported at the height of nearly seven feet from the ground, and
had preserved its position for perhaps twenty centuries; we should
be unjust in forming a low estimate of the mechanical skill of the
people who could construct such a massive and durable fabric.

But among all these speculations, fanciful and wild, and even
ridiculous, as some are, no reference has been made to the
probability, if not certainty, that this Cromlech was, like so many
of the Brittany Dolmens, originally in the centre of a mound of
earth, and not free standing. The Trevethy Stone was formerly
covered by a mound, and although as far as we know, no
remains of interments have been found in or near it, or under or

*Hist. View Dev.*, p. 94.
†*Op. Cit.* p. 138.

about the Drewsteignton Cromlech, the latter presents so acceptable
a spot for treasure seekers, situated as it is in the midst of a cultivated field, that their non-discovery does not militate against the
opinion, that this structure was also of a sepulchral character.
This cromlech has been supposed to be the only one on Dartmoor,
and consequently, from being so perfect, has attracted much notice,
but really there are three others on the Moor, but unfortunately all
in a ruined condition. The first is at Merivale Bridge; the
second on Shuffle Down; and the third on Shaugh Common.

The Kistvaen, Cistvaen, Cist or Stone Chest, has
KISTVAENS. been thought to differ from the Cromlech only in size,
but its formation is essentially different. By the
term Kistvaen, is commonly understood, stones placed edgewise,
enclosing a small space of ground, and covered with a similar
stone. " Of this relic of British antiquity," says Sir R. C. Hoare,
" I am enabled to speak with certainty, if, by its form and name,
" it did not speak for itself; it is composed of several stones, set
" upright, with a large one incumbent, thus forming a stone coffin
" or chest, in which the ashes or bones of the deceased were
" deposited."* Sometimes it is found on the summit of a cairn, as
at Molfra, Cornwall, but we have observed no example of this
description in Devonshire. Sometimes it is embedded in the cairn,
and one of this kind remains on the highest part of Cosdon Hill.
One we noticed near a trackway, below Rippon Tor, within the
inclosure of one of the hut circles, or foundations of aboriginal
habitations, and which would therefore not appear to be designed
for sepulture. We observed and measured a fine specimen, about
a furlong south of Hound Tor, within a circular enclosure, (constructed of slabs closely set) about twenty-two feet in diameter.
The kistvaen itself is formed of four stones,—one of the lateral
slabs remains almost upright in its original position ; it is not less
than six feet one inch long, one foot in average thickness, and
fifteen inches wide. At the south end, the head or foot-stone
remains erect, two feet three inches broad, and thus giving the
breadth of this aboriginal sarcophagus. The other side and end
stones are thrown down. Of late years this kistvaen has been
much mutilated and some of the stone removed. Kistvaens are
sometimes found in connection with the sacred circle, and with
cairns, as above described; but they are more usually observed

---

*Antiq. Wilts., vol. ii., p. 115.

simply placed, i.e., independently of any other relic.  In the centre is frequently seen a circular excavation, from which, in most cases, there is good reason for supposing a cinerary urn to have been removed, as in many instances both urns and bones have been found within these primitive depositories.  It is thought by some that Kistvaens were used only for the deposit of the burnt ashes of the deceased, but examples with complete skeletons in them have been found.  Kistvaens, in barrows, with sepulchral remains, according to Sir R. C. Hoare, are usually found in barrows at the broad or eastern end.  Our Dartmoor kistvaens number about fifty.  They, without exception, says Mr. Robert Burnard "lie "longitudinally north and south, or with variations east and west "of these points, the object evidently being that the remains "should face the sun."*  They have been long associated in the minds of the inhabitants of the moor with treasure and they call them Money Pits, Money Boxes and Gold Crocks.  Mr. Burnard gives an illustration of one of the smallest examined which is locally known as the Crock of Gold.  It is near Princetown, leading from Tor-Royal to Swincombe, and from its dimensions, it probably contained the burnt remains of the body.

The Tolment or Holed Stone, as the word in Cornish
TOLMENS. implies, of which we have several examples on
Dartmoor, is found in Cornwall, in Ireland, and according to Fosbrooke, in the East Indies.  This antiquary describes the tolmen as a perforated stone for drawing children through, and adults also; and adds that "two brass pins were "carefully laid across each other on the top edge of this stone for oracular purposes."‡  Whether the holes in the Dartmoor Stones or any of them, are artificial, or the result of natural causes, there is no doubt but that tolmens have played their part in the superstitious observances of by-gone times.  With reference to the great tolmen at Constantine, near Penryn, Gilbert observes that it seems probable that the aperture was an instrument of superstitious "juggle and applied to the purposes of purification, "or penance, or for the removal of bodily disorders."§  Borlase on the other hand regards the tolmen as a rock idol,—"there is

---

*Trans. Devon Assoc., vol. xxii., pp. 200-207.
†*Tol* in Gaelic means *hole*.
‡Encyc. Antiq. p, 75.
§Hist. Survey of Cornwall, 1817, vol. i., p. 177.

" another kind of stone deity which has never been taken notice of
" by any other author that I have heard of, its common name in
" Cornwall and Scilly is Tolmen, or the Hole of Stone, literally
" *the Stone of the Hole.*" Besides the celebrated specimen at
Constantine, he mentions one at St. Mary's Island, Scilly, on the
Salakee Downs and the other on the little isle of Northwithee.
All these however, are huge masses resting upon natural rocks
below, and leaving apertures beneath ; but near Lanyon is one of
the same description as the Teign Tolmen, (as we would venture
to designate it) though incomparably less curious. It is described
by Gilbert as one of " three erect stones on a triangular plane."
The tolmen " is thin, flat, and fixed in the ground on its edge ; it
" has a hole in the middle near two feet in diameter, from whence
" it is called *Men-an-tol*, that is, the holed stone." This evidently
however, is artificially set up, whereas our Men-an-tol in the Teign,
—described in Chapter IV—seems to have been placed in the bed
of the river by natural agency.

Mr. Harcourt unhesitatingly connects the tolmen with some
recondite mysteries of Arkite worship, since, as he finds them in
connexion with other Arkite monuments on Brimham Moor, near
Pately Bridge, Yorkshire, he concludes they can leave no doubt of
the religious system to which they belonged. The description
given of these monuments by a writer in the Archæologia, would
lead them generally to be classed as Druidical relics, strictly
speaking, even if it be granted that Druidism is a more recent
form of Arkite superstition. This account is quoted by Mr.
Harcourt, and may be adduced in proof of the opinion above
advanced—that the holed stone of the Teign is a Druidical
monument of the tolmen class. Among other relics, three tolmens
are described. " One of them with an aperture through which a
" man might pass, and a rock-basin at each entrance ; in another,
" the passage was three feet and a half across, and contained a
" rock-basin three feet in diameter. The excavation in the third
" is little more than three feet square at the entrance, and runs in
" a straight direction no more than six feet ; but on the right hand
" side, a round hole, two feet only in diameter, is perforated quite
" through the rock to the length of sixteen feet ;—and, from this
" form, it has obtained the name of the Great Cannon. A road
" has been made over a bed of rock on purpose to reach it, and the
" whole rock is ninety-six feet in circumference." Lastly, he
describes an assemblage of rocks which seem to have been a chosen

spot for religious ceremonies; "here," says he, "we find rock "idols, altars, circular holes, evidently cut in the sides of rocks, "and passages between, for some sacred mysterious purpose."*

There is no Dartmoor cromlech with a hole in any of the stones composing it, but many foreign examples have them, and as before mentioned, also in Cornwall. The hole in the capstone of the Trevethy Cromlech, is a well-known example and there are many others. "They have been made by piercing the stones "from opposite sides and then slightly enlarging and smoothing "the aperture."† Wherever Stone Monuments are found, holed stones are found also. They were set up, no doubt, to provide an instrument by which solemn promises, vows and oaths were taken, and St. Wilfred's Needle at Ripon, and the wedding ring, which the Church enjoins, are survivals of more antient practices. Many of them, however, were formed to serve as a rude but sufficiently effective arrangement for hanging a gate, or supporting a bar to form a fence. Others, no doubt, not so originally intended, are made to do duty for these purposes.

In the lane leading to Cholwich Town Farm, is a cross used as a gate post, in the back of which is a round hole three inches in diameter and three inches and a half deep. In a wall, in a lane near Teigncomb hamlet, is a stone, in which near the top is a round hole four inches in diameter and four inches and a half deep, and there are others of a similar kind which Mr. Lukis considered as true holed stones, but which may have been merely gate-posts, the holes having been made to receive the hanging part of the gate. Like those next to be mentioned, they should rather be called cupped stones, the holes having been made, it is said, to receive food for the dead, and not running through from side to side of the stone. Near French-bere Farm are two stones, almost circular, about four feet across:—one with a hole, six and a half inches in diameter and seven and a quarter inches deep, the hole in the other, smaller and shallower, and a similar stone is to be seen in a wall, in a lane at Teigncomb, near the upright-stone mentioned above, and there is another in the lane leading from Chagford towards the Prince Town Road. In the same lane is to be seen a circular stone about three feet three inches in diameter, and about six inches in thickness, with the perforation running quite through, and in the Teigncomb lane before referred to, in a

---

*Doct. Deluge, vol. ii., p. 509.

†REV. W. C. LUKIS. Proc. Soc. Ant. Ter. ii., Vol. vii., p. 289

wall, is a stone lying on its side, four and a half feet long by ten inches thick, in which is a hole of an hour-glass shape, four and a half inches in diameter on the outside, diminishing to three inches in the centre, and again swelling out to nearly five inches on the other side. All these are good examples of the tolmen. But many stones with a socket cut in them to serve useful purposes, have been taken for tolmens.

We have occupied some space in this account of Holed Stones, more particularly as Mr. W. C. Lukis thought them of consider- able interest, and connected with traditions and the folk-lore* of this and other countries.

BARROWS. The Barrow, Tumulus or Cairn, is too well known as a primitive monumental mound, to require any lengthened description. Where stones were not abundant, the soil heaped together, at once protected the remains of the dead, and formed their monument. But where stones of convenient size abounded, as on Dartmoor, the monuments of the departed were raised by an accumulation of stones, all of a size to be easily carried by a man, since we learn that every person in the army or community or town, brought one stone to the cairn, as the Roman soldiers were each accustomed to bring a helmet full of earth to the tumulus, and thus formed the cairn or carnedd, which Sir R. C. Hoare observes, resembles the barrow both in shape and purport, but differs in its materials and situation. Most of the Dartmoor barrows consist of heaps of stone or mounds of earth, and they contain a small chamber or chest of stone. In these have been found vessels of baked clay which had contained the burnt remains. In some, flint implements have been found, and in one, an amber ornament and a bronze dagger. On the new Ordnance maps, barrows and cairns are marked as " tumuli." Some authors distinguish between cairn and carnedd, regarding the latter as a place of sacrifice, the former, of burial. But Sir R. C. Hoare pronounces that several have been opened without any appearance of sepulchral remains being detected, and thence concludes that many cairns, or artificial aggregation of stones, are merely heaps of memorial, raised for the purpose of commem- orating some remarkable event or transaction. The venerable and unerring records of Divine history afford a well-known

---

*See Proc. Soc. Ant. Ser. ii., vol. viii., pp. 289-480 ; also Strange Survivals and Superstitions. REV. S. BARING-GOULD. Article. Holes, p. 252.

example of the existence of this custom in the earliest ages of the world, when Jacob raised a heap of stones in attestation of the compact of reconciliation and amity between himself and his father-in-law, Laban ; and in the terms employed, and the ceremonies resorted to, it is not a little curious and instructive, to trace the indications of the several purposes to which similar monuments were alike applied by the Mesopotamian patriarchs, and by our Celtic fore-fathers. In this highly interesting record, we have preserved even some minute details of the process of forming the monumental erection, after the conflicting parties had adjusted the preliminaries of the compact. " Now therefore," said Laban, " come thou, let us make a covenant, I and thou, and " let it be for a witness between me and thee." The effect of the appeal made to the domestic charities and kindliest feelings of our nature, are seen in the construction of that kind of simple but significant monument, which was no doubt the recognized symbol and memorial of similar transactions. Jacob, as the chief of his clan or household, first chooses a columnar stone, Maen or Rock Pillar, such as are frequently seen on Dartmoor, and then calls upon his family and followers to collect other stones of a form suitable for the construction of a cairn or barrow. " And Jacob " took a stone and set it up for a pillar, and Jacob said unto his " brethren, gather stones : and they took stones and made an heap " and they did eat there upon the heap." We find that the word here rendered heap* properly means any round accumulation, the Hebrew root implying, in its primary sense, something rolled into a spherical form. Hence commentators have imagined that the stones thus collected might have formed a circular mound, with a single stone erect in the centre, and that it was upon this rudely constructed inclosure the people sat, when " they did eat there " upon the heap," whilst the central pillar might have been an altar, of which arrangement there are many examples, especially when the surrounding enclosure is a sacred or columnar circle. But the patriarchal monument which we are now examining, was more probably a simple cairn or round stone barrow, with a rock pillar elevated in the centre ; and, as all the family and retainers seem to have been called upon to carry stones to the heap, it appears to have been intended to impress upon their memory, the transaction in which they had been engaged, and thus to constitute them all so many witnesses of the

---

*Gal. *acervus, cumulus, in rotundum, aggestus,* SIMONIS, *Lex. Heb.* in voc,

covenant into which their chiefs had entered. That this cairn was primarily designed to attest and perpetuate the treaty of reconciliation and amity, we are expressly told, and the names which the patriarchs respectively gave it—each in his proper tongue, leave no room for doubt on this point. Laban called it Jegar Sahadutha; but Jacob called it Galeed, both importing the same thing, the heap of witness. But Laban appears to have added a further designation, which indicates another use to which these cairns were applied. It was also called Mizpah—i.e., a beacon or watch-tower; for he said, " The Lord watch between me and thee, " when we are absent one from another." Placed on some of the loftiest peaks of Dartmoor, the cairns were doubtless used as most suitable watch-towers; and when alarm was necessary, the flaming pile raised upon them would be a conspicuous signal to the whole surrounding country. A beacon kindled upon the cairn on the top of Cosdon, often perhaps, roused the warriors of North Devon, whilst it would be also seen from Hey Tor, and thus spread the alarm through East Devon and the South Hams. The mountain retains the name of Cosdon Beacon to this day. Furthermore, the mound raised by the patriarchs on this memorable occasion, probably answered the purpose of a landmark or boundary.—" And " Laban said to Jacob, This heap be witness, and this pillar be " witness, that I will not pass over this heap to thee, and that thou " shalt not pass over this heap unto me, to do me harm." Such were the purposes, among others, to which these primitive monuments appear to have been applied; nor can we doubt that the counterpart of the Heap of Witness, piled up some four thousand years ago in the wilds of Syria, is to be found in many of the cairns and barrows of our British ancestors.

Many of the cairns on Dartmoor, as those which gave name to Three Barrow Tor, at the southern extremity, are popularly but incorrectly called barrows, the simple and descriptive designation of the latter being conveyed in the words, *Sepulchrum cespes erigit*, a monument formed of the sod, whereas the cairn is constructed of stones, whence, in the rocky wilds of Devonshire, where these materials are abundant, the cairn is frequent, while the true sod barrow is of comparatively rare occurrence. On the other hand, in a more champaign region, such as the Wiltshire downs, the barrow, in every shape, is found to prevail. Of the four principal

D

kinds* which Sir R. Hoare enumerates, we have numerous specimens of the first kind, the Long Barrow, on the moorland heights
of Devon.   These are thought by this learned author to have been
clearly alluded to by the celebrated Danish antiquary, Olaus
Wormius, when describing royal barrows, in the form of a large
ship, *(Regii tumuli ad magnitudinem et figuram carinæ navis)*—
it would seem, keel upwards.   Mr. Harcourt points out this form
as identifying this kind of monumental relic with that traditionary
knowledge of the deluge, and veneration for the ark, which
prevailed so extensively among the antient nations of the world—
" It is not difficult to account for the reversed position of the ship;
" for when the first wanderers over the ocean desired to have a
" place of worship, to which they might repair in bad weather,
" with the least possible deviation from their antient usages, it
" would naturally occur to them, that by hauling their ships on
" shore and turning their keel upwards, they would obtain at once
" an object of religious reverence and a shelter from the storm."†
But whatever might have given rise to the form, and to whatever
other purposes the barrow or cairn might have been applied, its
sepulchral character will not admit of question; although Sir R.
C. Hoare thinks it wonderful that such gigantic mounds should
have been raised for the deposit of a few human bodies, but in
this remark he seems to betray the want of his usual acumen, as
it is evident on very slight reflection that magnitude was the only
means by which monuments of such simple materials could be
rendered conspicuous, distinctive, or permanent.   But our Wiltshire antiquary admits that some cairns have been proved
sepulchral, and as to barrows there can be no doubt, though both,
as we have already seen, may have been applied to other purposes.
And with regard to their size being disproportioned to their object
as monumental erections—in proof of what has been advanced
above, we have an account of the opening of a Cairn on Haldon
by the Rev. John Swete, of Oxton, in the centre of which was
found a single cinerary urn, though the cairn was more than two
hundred feet in circumference.‡   We may therefore believe

---

*1—Long Barrow ; 2—round or bowl-shaped ; 3—bell-shaped ; 4—Druids' Barrow.
The three latter forms are scarcely likely to occur where stone barrows or cairns
prevail, as in Devonshire.   Mr. R. N. Worth, contrary to the opinion of our author,
considers that the tumuli of Dartmoor, whether Barrow or Cairn, are wholly of the
round or bowl-shape, as distinguished from the long.

†*Doct. Del.*, vol. ii., p. 272.

‡Essays by a Society of Gentlemen at Exeter, 1796, p. 106.

Rock Pillar at Merivale.

Silbury to have been a colossal monument (as well as a hill altar) especially as this Wiltshire wonder, vast as it is, shrinks into comparative insignificance when contrasted with the tumulus of Ninus, near the city of Nineveh, which, according to Ctesias, was nine furlongs in height and ten in breadth.

This method of burial was continued down to the Saxon era. Thus in Caernarvonshire, Bedn Gwortigern, still preserves the memory of Vortigern—a large Carnedd or stone barrow. Whitaker* quotes Adamnan's Life of Columba,† to show that it continued a century later, as the burial of a person is thus expressly described, *socii congesto lapidem acervo sepelierunt.*

MENHIRS. A simpler commemorative monument is the Rock pillar, or rude stone obelisk—similar, probably to that pillar which Jacob erected on the above occasion, and still more like that which he had previously set up at Bethel, to commemorate the precious manifestation of his Divine presence, which the God of his fathers had vouchsafed, and the promise to his countless posterity of that whole land on which he lay a forlorn and houseless wanderer. In the former case, where the pillar stood only as the witness to former transactions between man and man, we have no mention of any ceremonial or dedication. But the pillar, which was raised to transmit to future generations the remembrance of the heavenly vision of the Most High, appears to have been dedicated by the patriarch as marking a spot consecrated by the manifestation of the Almighty Presence, and regarded by him as none other than the House of God and the Gate of Heaven. The sacred historian writes, that Jacob took the stone that he had put for his pillow, and set it up for a pillar, and put oil upon it. "This passage," says Burder, "evinces of how great antiquity is the custom of considering "stones in a sacred light, as well as the anointing them with "consecrated oil." And in speaking of blocks of stone, still worshipped in Hindostan and other eastern countries, the same author observes, "that it is very remarkable that one of the "principal ceremonies incumbent upon the priests of these stone "deities, according to Tavernier, is to anoint them daily with "odoriferous oils. From this conduct of Jacob, and this Hebrew "appellative (*Bethel*) the learned Bochart, with great ingenuity

---

*Hist. Manchester, ii., p. 140.

†*Lib.* i., c. 33.

"and reason, insists that the name and veneration of the sacred "stones called *Bactyli*, so celebrated in all pagan antiquity, were " derived." Thus, the setting up of a stone by this holy person, in grateful memory of the celestial vision, probably became the occasion of idolatry in succeeding ages to these shapeless masses of unhewn stone, of which so many astonishing remains are scattered up and down the Asiatic and European world.\* Many such are to be found on Dartmoor, and were probably designed for similar purposes. A striking specimen appears amidst the relics near Merivale Bridge, on the Walkham, in the Western quarter. Tapering in form, it presents, in a shaft of unwrought granite, twelve feet high and eight in girth, at the base, a rude type of the architectural obelisk, and may be regarded as a characteristic illustration of the designation by which monuments of this kind are described by antiquaries—*Maen Hir*—the *Long Upright Stone*. The Bair Down Man, near two Bridges, and the fine Menhirs at Drizzlecombe are also typical examples. When thus found, in connection with other relics, a variety of purposes to which these columns might have been applied, suggest themselves to the mind ;† but that the primary objects were those of burial memorials, or the commemoration of remarkable or important events there seems little reason to doubt. But it may also be observed, that although our Dartmoor Menhirs cannot compare in magnitude with those to be found in Brittany, it is difficult to suppose that the objects which the people who erected them had in view were different; and that if the *Pierre du Champ Dolant* at Dol, was the scene of certain rites, it is probable the upright stones of Merivale and Drizzlecombe were resorted to for the same purpose.

---

\*BURDER, *Orient. Cust.* vol. i., p. 40.—*Lond.* 1827. But MR. HARCOURT, in noticing the vast numbers of such relics in various parts of the world, attributes them to a much earlier origin ; and regards them as so many undoubted memorials of the Deluge, in a variety of forms ; symbolizing " The highest peak of the Diluvian Mountain," i.e. one of the columnar or pyramidal crags of Mount Ararat.

†SIR R. C. HOARE states that no example occurs in Wiltshire " but they are to be found in other parts of our island, in Ireland and in Wales. Ant. Wilts, vol. ii., p. 114. The Devils' Arrows in Yorkshire and the rock pillars at Trelech, in Monmouthshire, are cited as examples, but the authority seems to have been ignorant of the existence of our fine Devonshire specimens, which, standing as they do, are more decidedly monumental than the former, which are found in connection with others.

# CHAPTER IV.

## HUTS, FORTS, ROADS, &c.

IMPERFECT but undoubted relics of the dwellings of the antient inhabitants are found in profusion in almost every part of Dartmoor. It is worthy of remark how, until very recently, little attention has been paid by topographers and historians to these curious and unquestionable vestiges of the early population of our island. The observations of Sir R. C. Hoare in reference to Wiltshire, will, for the most part apply with equal if not with greater pertinence, to Devonshire. " It is some-" what singular " he remarks " that the discovery of our British " settlements should not have been made previous to my own " researches, and that they had escaped the notice of Aubrey, " Stukeley and every subsequent writer on our national antiquities. " Their eyes seem to have been dazzled with the splendour of an " Abury and a Stonehenge, and to have noticed only the tumuli of " the Britons, without turning a thought towards the residences " of the living, to whose memory these sepulchral mounds were " raised at their decease." So the Drewsteignton Cromlech and the Logan stone are the theme of every topographer, but the hundreds of ruined dwellings scattered over the highlands of Devonshire appear, for the most part, to have escaped observation, or to have been deemed unworthy of attention.

HUTS AND HUT CIRCLES. The hut, known as the bee-hive, on Dartmoor, as elsewhere, was constructed by its builder setting up on end stones in two circles, one within the other, and filling up the space between with turf, and placing stones upon the upright ones. This walling, if it may be so called, was drawn together as it was raised, the stones being selected as flat as possible, until a dome-shaped roof was formed, at the top was a hole for light and for the escape of smoke, and on one side of the hut a doorway was formed with two upright stones and another resting upon them to form a lintel. The only perfect one of this character—and that one of the smallest—is situated on the bank of a little stream which falls into the Erme. This is about six feet long, four feet wide and three feet high, and was probably, a tool house, the kind of construction mentioned would be that used in the smaller huts only. The larger dwellings, instead of having stones above the upright blocks, had turves for the roof, and in them is frequently found in the middle of the floor a heap of stones, sometimes described as a fireplace, but which Mr. C. Spence Bate thought was the spot on which an upright pole was fixed for the purpose of supporting the roof. In still larger dwellings the roof required some other kind of support, and it is probable that the turf roof in these was kept up by wooden beams or rafters, one end of each supported upon the external walls, the other meeting the rest in the middle, and the whole fastened together. The smaller bee-hive hut has sometimes been found to have been built into the walls of the larger hut circle, in which case, apparently, it would be not used for habitation, but as a store-house. And these dwellings, of various sizes, are sometimes found in groups enclosed with a circular rampart.

These ruined abodes of our rude fore-fathers, are more numerous along the declivities on the skirts of the moor, and on the hill-sides in the interior, which slope down to the water-courses, than in other parts. The principal groups of houses, villages or towns, are invariably found in such situations. For miles in the heathy table-land round Cranmere Pool, we have only been able to find a single insulated dwelling, while on the slopes of almost all the vallies, especially those fronting to the south and west, they are of frequent occurrence. The large village near Merivale Bridge has a western aspect, and is situated on the side of the hill gently rising from the banks of the Walkham; Grimspound with its cyclopean circumvallation, is built on the western declivity of Hameldon, with a spring rising on the eastern side of the inclosure, and Langstone with its numerous hut circles, with one group of huts protected by an enclosing wall, lies open to the southern sun. But in whatever situations the rude dwellings of the primitive inhabitants are

found, whether inclosed within walls as at Grimspound, or in
unwalled villages as at Merivale—they are all apparently similar
n design—and all, with only one ascertained exception—on the
Erme—in the same completely ruined condition, with nothing but
the foundations and the door jambs remaining.    These Hut
Circles as they are generally called, to distinguish them from the
so-called Sacred Circles (from which they differ essentially) are all
circular in plan,  and consist of granite blocks, set firmly in the
ground on their edge, and placed closely together (instead of at
wide intervals as in the Sacred  Circle) so as to form a secure
foundation for the super-structure, whether it were constructed
of stone and turf, wattle—*Junctæ cortice virgæ*—or other material.
To adopt the language of Whitaker, in describing the houses
of  the  Lancashire Britons,  "they  were  great  round  cabins
" built principally of timber on foundations of stone, and roofed
" with a sloping covering of reeds."    It would however appear
that where stone was abundant, as on Dartmoor, the cabins, in
some instances at least, were constructed entirely of stone, as the
same author remarks of the  remains of British buildings in
Anglesea and Wilts.    In this kind of masonry, the interstices
were filled with turf or earth, as, according to Whitaker, was the
practice in the Western Isles of Scotland, who might have found
modern examples of the same kind of building in England, since
this rough-and-ready method of erecting walls seems to have been
handed down from the earliest times, and prevails among our
Dartmoor peasants to this day.

The Danmonian huts have their counterparts in the Shealings
of the Orkneys some of which are of this form, and are constructed
of stone and turf; others have a base of stone, consisting of two
circles one within the other, with a roofing of fir poles converging
to a point, and thatched with branches or heather.    Both kinds
appear to have existed on Dartmoor; and the vestiges which still
remain sufficiently accord with the descriptions given by Diodorus
Siculus and Strabo, of the habitations of the Britons of their times,
to induce the belief that they had received the accounts from some
of those enterprising mariners, who had seen the buildings in their
trading voyages to the isles of tin.

The ruined basement, which constitutes the hut circle consists,
in the majority of examples, of a single course of stones, but in
some instances a double circle is observed.    These stones stand
generally from eighteen inches to thirty inches above the surface.

The door jambs also of stone, are, in most cases, higher placed, nearly at right angles to the outline of the circle; in a very considerable proportion of examples, the door faces the south. These dwellings measure from twelve to thirty feet in diameter, the most usual size being about twenty six feet, though some occur of much larger dimensions, and these were, perhaps, appropriated to the chieftain of the clan. Cæsar describes the houses of the Britons as similar to the dwellings of the Gauls, lighted only from the door, and on this, Fosbrooke remarks that his account was perfectly correct, from the representation of the British cabins on the Antonine column where they appear as circular buildings, with sloping or domical roofs, having an opening at the top for the emission of smoke. The Britons of the interior were a pastoral people, as we may safely conclude from Cæsar's account of their mode of subsistence ; "*Interiores plerique "frumenta non serunt, sed lacte et carne vivunt.*" The nomadic life and habits evidently implied by this brief but comprehensive description, their inattention to tillage, and their subsisting upon milk and flesh, would be quite in keeping with the nature of the wild uncultivated tracts of Dartmoor.* Hence we may infer that the Britons had out-buildings and inclosures for the folding of their cattle, and that, therefore, some of the ruined foundations which have been described above, are the remains of buildings raised for purposes of this kind, and, as in our times, in most cases, adjoining the habitations of the owners of the flocks and herds. But it is also very probable that some of these hut dwellings will prove to be the temporary habitation of the tin miners and smelters remains whose workings are so very apparent in various parts of the moor.

C. Spence Bate noticed in the valley below Shell Top a chambered dwelling, which he mistakenly called a cairn. This, besides the rounded end of the passage, which is about five feet wide, contains four chambers. It is so far the only observed hut cluster on Dartmoor, and has been described by Mr. R. N. Worth.†

---

*Like the Nomads of the antient times, and the more modern Tartars our Britons resided upon the hills, sheltered by huts from the inclemency of the weather, and subsisting on the produce of their cattle, and the venison, which the woods supplied in abundance. The numerous remains we have discovered in each district of our county, sufficiently prove the original residence of the Britons to have existed upon the hills; but in later times, when civilized by the Romans, they probably began to clear the vallies from woods, and to seek more sheltered situations in the vales, and in the vicinity of rivers.—*Antiq. Wilts.*, vol. ii., p. 106.

†Trans. Devon Assoc. vol. xxii., p. 237.

Besides these huts, which are of a circular shape, others occur, rectangular in form.   These, where they are not ruined blowing houses, are no doubt more modern than the others mentioned, and are the remains of the dwellings of miners.

The ruins of the hut dwellings on Dartmoor are now undergoing a very careful examination.   The pick and the shovel for the first time have been called to aid in the attempt to discover some of the secrets of the Moor.   The investigations recently undertaken by the Rev. S. Baring-Gould and Mr. Robert Burnard, and commenced at Grimspound, Broadun, Broadun Ring, Tavy Cleave and Langstone Moor, and which are now being extended by them and those associated with them in the work, in other directions, are leading to the establishment of facts of the greatest importance. So far as these explorations have gone, the presence of a considerable neolithic population on Dartmoor has been apparently established.   We say apparently, as, comparatively speaking, only a very small number of the hut dwellings on Dartmoor have been explored, and it is absolutely necessary that these investigations should be pursued with care, and that there should be no jumping to conclusions upon what may prove insufficient data.   There is very much yet to be learnt from Dartmoor, and it is very probable that the work now in progress will result in discoveries of much value.   To refer more particularly to the characteristic features of these dwellings.   In the first place, like other houses of a similar kind, these had roofs formed by poles fastened into the walls, which were drawn together at the top and fastened by thongs of hide, and covered with turves, or rushes, or dried grass, or all three, with a hole somewhere to allow the smoke to escape.   Nothing remains of sufficient height to show whether there was a window, but it is not likely there was any.   The stone walling of the foundation, rose probably as high as the jambs of the doorway, which is ordinarily on the south or south-west side, and on the jambs rests a lintel.   The hut contains the hearth, which is either against the wall, on the side opposite the door, or in the middle of the house, and is a large flat stone with marks of fire upon it.   There is also frequently, another flat stone embedded in the ground, the use of which is only matter of conjecture, it may have been an anvil, or a stone for killing small animals upon.   Generally on the right hand side of the entrance is a raised mass of stone, upon which it is supposed the bed of fern and leaves was placed, and one of the

Grimspound huts has a bed for two, there being a division in the centre formed of stones set on edge. But the most remarkable feature has yet to be mentioned, and it is one which gives us a most interesting insight into the customs of these early inhabitants of our moor. In the floor of every hut so far examined, is a hole lined with stones about nine inches deep. These holes were the cooking places of the natives. They are always full of charcoal ashes, and as so far, not a single scrap of pottery of any kind has been found, it is evident that the food was placed in these holes, with heated stones, after the manner of the Assinneboins, a tribe of North American Indians, visited by Catlin. When these Indians " kill meat, a hole is dug in the ground about the size of " a common pot, and a piece of raw hide of the animal, as taken " from the back, is put over the hole, and then pressed down with " the hands close around the sides, and filled with water. The " meat to be boiled, is then put in this hole or pot of water ; and " in a fire, which is built near by, several large stones are heated " to a red heat, which are successively dipped and held in the " water until the meat is boiled. The custom is a very awkward " and tedious one, and used only as an ingenious mode of boiling " their meat, by a tribe who was too rude and ignorant to construct " a vessel or pot." At the time Catlin saw these people, the custom, except at public festivals, had fallen into disuse, they having been taught, by being brought into contact with their more civilized neighbours, the method of manufacturing good and serviceable earthen pots.* There is an account too of the Fena, a primitive Irish race, whose custom it was to dig holes in the ground, and after heating round stones, put them in the bottom of the pits, and over them the meat to be cooked, and then another layer of hot stones and covering the whole over, allowed them to remain until the meat was dressed. These rounded stones have been found not only at Grimspound, but at Broadun. These old dwellers on the Moor were evidently low in the scale, even of Neolithic people, they had no pottery, no iron, no hand-mills for grinding corn. Clothed in skins and mainly dependent upon the chase for their sustenance, with weapons of flint and bone, and scrapers of flint for dressing the skins, the lot of these men must often have been a hard one ; although, once within their huts, the door closed with a hide,

---

*Letters and Notes on the Manners, &c., of the North American Indians. Vol. i., p. 54, 1841.

and a supply of food secured, their refuges were no doubt found snug, and, so far as the wants of the occupants were concerned, comfortable ones, certainly quite as much so as those " old black " houses " of the islands of Lewis and Harris in the Hebrides, in which, as Dr. Mitchell says, so many thousands of people have been born, have lived, and have died.*

POUNDS.

Those curious enclosures popularly called Pounds by the moormen, which occur in so many places, are traditionally supposed to have been constructed for the protection of cattle. That they were intended to protect the inhabitants as well as their cattle, on any sudden emergency, there can be no doubt, although it would appear that the most perfect of them—Grimspound—was designed as the fortification of a permanent settlement, rather than as a temporary stronghold, to which, as we learn from Cæsar, the Belgic Celts were accustomed to retreat with their families, flocks and herds, on the approach of danger. The enclosures are either low walls of stones piled rudely together in a ridge-like form, or belts of huge granite blocks placed erect in the ground. Their general form is circular, but some examples are elliptical. Remains of habitations are in most cases found in these primitive entrenchments, so that we may justly conclude that they were originally constructed for purposes of retreat, security and defence.

A fine specimen occurs on the commons, west of Castor Rock, adjoining a moorland road which forms the boundary between the parishes of Chagford and Gidleigh, where the Roundy Pound, as it is called by the moormen, exhibits the foundations of a house within the inclosure, which itself forms a kind of courtyard round the dwelling, with the jambs at the entrance still erect.

Grimspound is by far the finest and most important of all the relics of this class. Viewed from Hooknor Tor, which commands its entire area, it presents to the spectator an object of singular curiosity and interest. Its situation is on the N.W. slope of Hameldon, on the borders of the parishes of Manaton, North Bovey, and Widecombe. The wall is formed of moorstone blocks, rudely piled up, but so large as not to be easily displaced: it is double, a space, probably a passage with entrances to it from the interior face, running between the two walls, but it may be only the space left to be filled up with earth which has

---

*The Past in the Present, p. 49.

now been washed away. The base of this rampart covers in some parts a surface of twenty feet in breadth, but the average height of a section taken at any point would not exceed six feet. With the exception of openings on the east and west sides through which the road run, the inclosure is perfect, surrounding an area of about four acres. The original entrance is on the south-east, the wall here being from ten to twelve feet thick, composed of enormous stones; the width of the entrance is seven feet, it is paved, and has three steps in its thickness. The vestiges of antient habitations within this primitive entrenchment are numerous, as already observed, and occupy the whole area, leaving only one vacant spot at the upper or north end, which might have been a place for driving cattle into, or a kind of forum, or place of public concourse, for the inhabitants. There are twenty-four hut circles within the enclosure, and their examination shows that ten of these were dwellings, and that the rest were used as store houses or cattle pens. One is double, and has a tall upright stone set against the wall, making it more conspicuous than the rest. A spring rising on the eastern side, and, skilfully conducted for some distance below the wall, supplied the inhabitants with pure water; and the whole presents a more complete specimen of an antient settlement, provided with means of protracted defence, than will perhaps be found in any other part of the island. A road which leads from Manaton to Headland Warren runs through the inclosure.[*]

Dunnabridge Pound between Two Bridges and Dartmeet is another large enclosure, measuring, according to Ormerod, one hundred and ten paces from north to south, and from east to west one hundred and seventeen paces. The height of the wall where perfect is nearly six feet, the base being three feet, diminishing at the top to two feet and a half and having a double facing. It is probable this is nothing more and was never any other than it is now, a moor pound.

Of another kind of enclosure, or circumvallation as it may be called, we know but one existing specimen which was observed by us first in the year 1828. It was situated in a small pasture field about a furlong south-east of Manaton Church,

---

[*]Since the above was written, the First Report of the Dartmoor Exploration Committee (Grimspound) has been published in the Transactions of the Devonshire Association, vol. xxvi., 1894, and to this we must refer our readers for further details as to these most interesting and important investigations.

and conjectured by Col. Hamilton Smith to have given the original name to the parish, Maen-y-dun, the Fort or inclosure, of Erect Stones. This appeared to be a description of primitive circumvallation unknown to, or at least altogether unnoticed by antiquaries. The following description applied to its state when first visited, the hand of the destroyer played havoc with it soon after. It was elliptical in form, and in an exceedingly perfect condition. The masses of which the fence was constructed, were from four to six feet high, placed in a double row and set closely together. One stone, however, was so large that it filled the whole breadth, being six feet wide by five feet thick. The diameters of the elliptical area were one hundred and thirty-eight feet by one hundred. There were no vestiges of any monumental relic within the inclosure or near it, and the most cursory observer would instantly remark that its character was totally different from the Pounds, and still more so from the Columnar or Sacred circle. As it was situated on comparatively low ground, where pasturage must have been abundant, it was probably erected for the protection of cattle. But we have been informed by a gentleman who knew it well, that it was, in his opinion, a sacred circle, and one of the finest on the moor. Whatever the character of this may have been, it was ruthlessly destroyed in 1849, by the Rev. William Paul Wood, who carried off a part of the stones, to build a wall, and used the rest in dividing two fields.

TRACKWAYS. Wherever there are communities having settled habitations, however simple and uncultivated the people, we justly expect to find some traces of the means of communication between village and village, or one settlement and another. Nor is Dartmoor without numerous examples of this kind, affording proofs, in addition to those already advanced, of its having been inhabited in remote times. Trackways, under which designation those roads or causeways which cross the moor in various directions are generally known, were no doubt often made to serve the purpose of boundary lines. Sir R. C. Hoare describing those which he had examined in Wiltshire, observes " The lines of communication between one village and " another, were by means of trackways, not paved or formed, but " following the natural ridge of the country, by which they have " gained the additional name of Ridgeways, which some of them " still retain." Such an ancient trackway was the Abbot's Way, between the Cistercian Abbeys of Buckfast and Buckland. Branching from it was another to Tavistock Abbey. These are not paved roads, but are formed simply by the constant traffic which in time formed the hard pathway. But in a country where stone was so abundant, as in the Devonshire highlands, it is probable we should find other roads of a more substantial character. Here we find them constructed of stones (too large to be easily displaced) irregularly laid down on the surface, and thus forming a rude but efficient causeway, the general breadth of which is about five or six feet, but which, in one example (near Three Barrow Tor) we found to be fifteen feet, though much obscured by the encroaching vegetation.

The most extensive and important trackway which has come under our notice, is one which is supposed to traverse the forest in a line bearing east and west from Hameldon to Great Mistor. Considerable portions of the line can be traced in a direction corresponding to these points, but a large extent of it rests rather upon the testimony of tradition than upon the evidence of existing remains. The oral topographers of the uplands* recognize this trackway as the equator of the moorland region, all above it being considered the north, and all below it the south country, a circumstance which, though it affords good evidence of the antiquity of this relic, might be supposed to give it the character of a boundary rather than of a road, but which will have less weight in this scale when we consider how frequently antient roads are found to form boundaries between parishes, manors, and other divisions of country.† This trackway may be observed in high preservation, coming down the northern slope of Chittaford Down towards the banks of the East Dart. Here it can be traced for a considerable distance, and is visible due west through Hollocombe, and up the opposite hill to Lower White Tor, down the common, towards the Dart, it bends towards the north-east, but in the level near Post Bridge it takes a direction southward. With some difficulty it may be detected through the boggy meadows below Hartland Farm. The peat-cutters are reported to come upon it below the surface in some places; nor is it at all

---

*On the authority of the late Rev. J. M. Mason.*

†A case which seems completely in point, occurs near the town of Plympton, where an old road that crosses the crest of the hill in a remarkably straight direction, is still called the Ridge Lane, and which for a considerable distance divides the parish of Brixton from the two Plymptons, St. Mary and St. Maurice or Plympton Earl.

unlikely that the encroachments of the vegetation, which in some instances are only partial, should in others have extended over the whole breadth of the trackway, and thus have obliterated all traces of it in the lower grounds. This trackway has been commented on by Mr. R. N. Worth and Mr. R. Burnard ; by the latter it has been most carefully traced and surveyed. The conclusion which these gentlemen have arrived at, upon evidence which it is impossible to resist, is that it formed a portion of the great Fosseway,* the British road which the Romans found and utilised. Mr. Burnard traced it for eighteen miles from the eastern side of Haytree Down beyond Hameldon, in one direction, nearly to Tavistock in the other. In its perfect state it seems to have been about ten feet wide, and it was formed of stone from two feet to two feet six inches deep.

The trackways have no characteristic which would lead us to refer their construction to the Roman period of British history, nor have we documentary evidence that any of their roads ran through Danmonium in a direction corresponding to that of the Dartmoor trackways. In none of these trackways or roads are there any marks of modern construction, as fences or bounds ; the remains of the oldest cattle fences on the Moor, being so strikingly different, as to be evident to every observer of common penetration.

TRACKLINES.　　Greatly similar in construction are the Tracklines or Boundary Banks, which are invariably observed in connection with aboriginal dwellings and sepulchral remains. They are numerous in every part of the moorlands, and like the same kind of primitive fosse which Sir R. C. Hoare describes as of frequent occurrence " throughout the " downy district " of Wiltshire, " were originally thrown up for " the double purpose of defence and communication," serving for bounds and pathways, and connecting and enclosing dwellings. The most striking specimen is perhaps that which is presented on the south-eastern slope of Torrhill, near the road from Ashburton to Moreton, below Rippon Tor. Here are evident marks of regularity of design, and the tracklines intersect each other in such numbers that nearly the whole hill-side is partitioned into squares, conveying, in a remarkable manner, a lively idea of an aboriginal rural settlement, as there are remains of many antient habitations, within their respective enclosures. It would be too

---

*Trans. Dev. Assoc. vol. xvii. p. 351 ; vol. xxi., pp. 431-436.

much to pronounce that we have evidence of a different fashion
prevailing in these constructions in different parts of the Moor,
but on the south side of Heytor, in the neighbourhood of Torrhill,
they are observed in rectangular outlines, while on Cosdon, they
are in curves ; on Archeton Hill, and below Wistman's Wood in
various irregular forms; and near Littleford Tor one occurs
connecting two ruined dwellings in a line, which forms the
segment of a circle.

With regard to these lines, however, further examination does
not confirm the above opinions.     Mr. R. N. Worth considers
" that they appear, as a rule, to represent enclosures exterior to the
" immediate surroundings of the huts, and to belong to a more
" recent date than the so called pounds.   Carefully traced, the
" majority will be found equivalent to the remains of hedges,
" walling the little fields taken out from the moor for the purpose
" of pasturing or protecting stock, or raising hay in the immediate
" vicinity of huts or villages when the moorland farming had
" began to advance beyond its primitive original.   Probably they
" are among the most modern of the moorland antiquities.   They
" are certainly among the least mysterious."*

BRIDGES.           In a region such as Dartmoor, intersected by rivers
and brooks in all directions, and these streams so
peculiarly liable to be swollen by summer torrents,
and by the thawing of the accumulated snows in winter, the
progress of the trackways would be continually interrupted by
these natural and formidable obstacles.   In some instances they
may be found pointing to a ford, as would appear to be the case
with the grand central road below Chittaford Down ; but as the
East Dart would frequently become impassable at that ford, the
necessities of the case would task the ingenuity of the earliest
inhabitants in contriving the erection of a bridge.   Happily the
materials, which lay at hand, when such a necessity arose to a
primitive people, were of a more durable kind than the felled tree,
which in more wooded districts forms a ready and not incon-
venient bridge.   Vast slabs of granite afforded the means of
constructing solid piers by being merely laid one upon another,
yet stable enough without cement or other adventitious appliances,
to breast the impetuous rush of the moorland torrents.   The
necessity of arching was obviated by massive imposts of a tabular

* Notes and Gleanings, vol. iii., p. 60.

Leather Tor Bridge.

form laid horizontally from pier to pier. Some of these are formed of a single stone, and would then probably come under the vernacular denomination *clam*, a term also frequently applied to a bridge formed of a plank or single tree, although we have noticed a distinction sometimes made, the wooden bridge being called a clapper, and a stone bridge a clam.

Adjoining Post Bridge (a modern county bridge over the East Dart, traversed by the Tavistock and Moreton road) stands one of these venerable and characteristic relics of probably very early times, presenting a truly interesting specimen of primitive architecture. The piers are two, and these with the abutments form three sufficient openings for the waterway. Its construction though rude, is of the most durable kind. No structure of ordinary stability could have withstood the fury of the vehement Dart in his most turbulent moods for so many centuries. The piers consist of six layers of granite slabs above the foundation. The superincumbent stones are singularly adapted for the purpose to which they are applied. The centre opening is narrower than the side openings ; the imposts here were two, one of these was thrown down many years since in an attempt to form a duck-pond, and it remained in the bed of the river for a long time. It has now however been restored to its original position, and the bridge is again perfect. The stones are about fifteen feet long, and six wide, and thus a roadway was made over which, even the scythed chariot of the Danmonian warrior might pass the river in safety. There are other specimens of what has been called the Cyclopean bridge, in various parts of the moor, those at Two Bridges, Okery Bridge and Dartmeet may be mentioned, but this is by far the largest and most interesting. Mr. Bray in enumerating other local antiquities, bears the testimony of an observant traveller to the uncommon character of these curious structures. " It is not unlikely that they are unique " in their construction ; at least I can say that though I " have visited in England, South Wales, and Brittany, many " places celebrated for Celtic remains, I have never yet seen " anything like our antient Dartmoor bridges." Nor are there any such examples to our knowledge in North Wales or in Westmoreland or Cumberland, but at Tar Steps between Hawkridge and Winsford in our county, there is a bridge over the Barle, of similar construction, with nineteen openings, the total length being one hundred and fifty feet. There is nothing necess-

E

arily indicating extreme antiquity in these bridges. The form is such as the material at hand lends itself to, and for the purposes for which these bridges were made, as long as foot passengers and pack-horses only used them, man, a hundred years ago, would raise a similar structure to his predecessors many centuries before. Mr. Burnard, in his survey before mentioned, shows that the bridge at Post Bridge could not have been a part of the Great Central Trackway, but of the old packhorse road from Plymouth to Moreton Hampstead and Ashburton, the Trackway crossing the East Dart by a ford, a considerable distance above this bridge.

CAMPS. The Camps, or earth-works, which are found on the skirts of the moorlands, may be regarded as forming a connecting link between the aboriginal period of British history, and the succeeding eras of Roman and Saxon dominion, since the same positions, from their national capabilities, would be occupied in many cases by the different invaders or defenders of the country in succession. Prestonbury on the Teign, near Drewsteignton, and Henbury on the Dart, near Buckfastleigh, are both hill forts, so strikingly characteristic of the Celtic method of castramentation, that we can scarcely err in attributing their original construction to the Britons. We learn from Cæsar that our warlike progenitors, when repulsed by the Romans, betook themselves into strongholds, chosen, it would appear, with great discernment for their natural advantages, and strengthened by art with so much skill, as to deserve the commendation of a commander so well versed in military affairs as the conqueror of Gaul. He describes such a stronghold as excellently fortified by nature and art. A favourite position according to the same authority, was a peninsulated hill, moated naturally, to a greater or less extent, by a river, and fortified, on the most accessible side, by a ditch and rampart drawn across the neck of land. Such was the fortress of the Aduatici, in Gaul, described by Cæsar. "The Gaer-Dykes, or Coxall Hill, where "Caractacus was finally defeated, is a similar position," says Fosbrooke, "on the point of a hill accessible only one way." The same author observes, that "the British camps in general, occupy "the summits of hills of a ridge-like form, and commanding "passes." This is precisely the description of Prestonbury, which is a Celtic hill fortress, evidently of high antiquity, and of a most interesting description, whether we consider its construction, or the situation it occupies. This characteristic specimen of the primitive fortifications of the Danmonian highlands, occupies the extreme point of a ridge-like hill, which forms the northern bank of the Teign, to the extent of about a mile between Fingle and Clifford bridges. Immediately above the former, it rises from the brink of the river in the form of a bold headland, fully commanding the low ground beneath, from its precipitous character. The hollow between Prestonbury, and the acclivity which rises towards Drewsteignton Church, has evidently the appearance of a pass from the champaign country to the uplands by the ford, which doubtless existed before the erection of the oldest bridge, at or near where the picturesque arches of Fingle now span the rapid current of the Teign. Thus situated, Prestonbury was admirably calculated for a watch-tower, as well as a fortress, and the strength of its entrenchments seems to indicate the importance attached to the position. The extremity of this inland promontory is the highest ground of the ridge, which on the south side is scarped down by nature in a precipitous rocky glacis to the river's brink. Nature having, therefore, so amply provided for the security of the fortress on this side, less was demanded from the resources of art, so that a rampart without any ditch, rising immediately from the precipice, was evidently thought sufficient. But on the north, where there is a much gentler declivity landwards, the rampart is of a far more formidable appearance, forming an entrenchment in some parts, eight yards in height. The circumference of the circumvallation taken along the crest of the vallum, is five hundred and twenty yards, and this part of the entrenchment, which may be considered as a kind of keep, was defended by two parallel outworks, constructed on the ridge of the hill. The ground declines slightly from the eastern side of the keep, and at sixty yards distance, the first of the outworks occurs—a rampart and a ditch crossing the ridge saddle-wise, and dying away in the precipice on the south. The next entrenchment is thrown up at the distance of one hundred and twenty yards, here the vallum is loftier and the fosse deeper. Beyond this line of entrenchment, the ground rises, till at the distance of about a furlong east of the keep, or principal work, it is lofty enough to command the fortified portion of the hill already described. At this point therefore, we find fortifications erected to guard the approaches, where the ridge gradually slopes eastward, and where easy access might be otherwise obtained by the enemy. But when the whole of the neck of land was thus fortified, ample means were afforded for preventing surprise, and for maintaining a protracted defence if necessary.

Here, then, on the northern verge of our moorland region may be observed a curious and interesting specimen of those strongholds, to which the Celtic tribes were accustomed to retreat in cases of danger; for although such a post as this would scarcely fail to be garrisoned by the troops of the successive occupants or invaders of the country, and might undergo some alterations in the lapse of centuries, yet, enough of the primary features remain to enable the antiquary to trace the original fortifying of this remarkable hill, to our warlike Danmonian progenitors.

The monuments of antiquity which have been thus far enumerated, indicate a rude and simple state of society, and may be reasonably traced to the requirements of a primitive people, suggested probably, in some degree by the nature and abundance of the materials supplied by the surrounding district. The memorial of some compact between two reconciled tribes would probably be needed, and the neighbouring tor would alike furnish materials for another Jegar Sahadutha (*Gen.* xxxi., 47)—the heap of witness—as well as for a memorial pillar, or for a conspicuous and durable landmark to define the limits of adjoining pasture grounds. Their villages would require defence from hostile attack, or protection from the beasts of prey, with which the rocky slopes and swampy thickets of the Forest abounded, and the unwrought boulders of moorstone would readily form the cyclopean fortification of Grimspound. Their religion demanded open shrines—and a circle of rude granite obelisks guarded the primitive sanctuary from all profane intrusion. Or if we look beyond natural circumstances, and should conclude that there would appear to be more of premeditation and design in the choice of their materials, and in the forms employed, it might thence be inferred that the notions which led to their erection were not of indigenous growth, but were brought from other lands by the original settlers. Since, also, points of resemblance have been observed between these monuments and such as are found in eastern countries, or are known to have existed there in the earliest ages, for purposes which are recorded, although they do not establish the hypothesis of the colonization of Britain from the east, they certainly favour an opinion which is also countenanced by tradition, and which, no less than eight centuries since had assumed a shape sufficiently definite to be preserved in one of the most valuable documents of mediæval times—the Saxon Chronicle—which states that "the first inhabitants of this "country were Britons, who having come from Armenia, estab- "lished themselves in the southern parts of Britain." The legendary fable of the voyage of Brutus, from the Mediterranean to the shores of Devonshire, his landing at Totnes, and overthrow of his gigantic antagonists at Plymouth, however unworthy of credit as to details, deserves consideration, as indicating some substantial truths, just as shadows, however distorted and exaggerated, are proofs of an actual substance. And if there is any just foundation for the ingenious theories of Vernon Harcourt, that the Albion of Aristotle (De Mundo, c. 3.) Britain, was one of the Isles of the Blessed, of antiquity; the *macaron nesos* of Lycophron (according to Tzetzes), that the celebrated Atlantis may be more reasonably sought for in the British Isles than elsewhere—that it was here that the slumbers of the Titanian Kronos were guarded by the hundred-handed Briarchus, as reported by Plato; that the island which was the abode of Neptune, was Britain,* and that the Hesperides, to which Hercules travelled to fetch the golden apples for Juno, were also the same islands, since Apollodorus expressly says that the Hesperian apples were not in Libya, but at the Atlas, among the Hyperboreans†—then shall we conclude that there is more cause for believing that there existed a much earlier communication by sea, between our islands and the eastern shores of the Mediterranean, than has been generally supposed, and that this may have partly arisen from the circumstance of the original colonization of the British isles having taken place by a voyage through the Straits of Gibraltar.

The expedition of Brutus is alleged to have been undertaken

---

*We question whether the composer of the once popular sea-song, ever imagined that he could boast such high authority as the celebrated Athenian philosopher, for regarding our island as the contemplated residence of the god of ocean.

"Daddy Neptune one day unto Freedom did say—
If e'er I should live upon dry land,
The spot I should hit on would be little Britain,
'Tis such a snug, tight little island."

†*Doct. of Deluge*, vol. ii., pp. 150-152.

about the year 1100, B.C., and in the first century after the Trojan war, from which period, Britain is supposed to have taken its name from that successful invader. These legendary tales may preserve the memorial of a real descent by some foreign chief, about the time in question, and appear to intimate that the invaders had to encounter the opposition of a fierce and warlike people. Hence these traditionary legends evidently assume that this island must have been peopled (it may be presumed) for some ages anterior to the reported landing of the Trojan adventurers in the estuary of the Dart, and their conflicts at the mouth of the Plym—both Dartmoor rivers, and therefore identifying these legends with the *venue* of this treatise. But it is far more probable that the truth of these fables will be found in a Tyrian expedition, rather than in a Trojan, when impartial history,* regarding the claimants with equal eye, *(Tros, Tyriusve, nullo discrimine)* steps in to decide the rival claims, since we are assured that the enterprising traders of Phenicia had brought tin by sea from some western country, before the time of Homer, and that it is not more probable that Brutus, a great-grandson of Æneas, ever made an expedition to Totnes, and gave his name to Britain, than that he founded the city of Tours, in Gaul, as gravely asserted by Geoffrey of Monmouth. Much less fanciful is the etymology which would derive the original designation of our island, with the writers Bochart, Sammes, and others, from two Phenician words—*Barat-anac*, the land of tin, translated in after-times by the Greeks, Cassiterides ; since it is so far supported by historical evidence, as we learn from classical writers that the Phenicians‡ were the earliest traders upon record to the tin countries beyond the pillars of Hercules, in the Hyperborean ocean.

We learn with what jealous vigilance the Phenician voyagers guarded the lucrative monopoly of the tin trade. The account of the patriotic shipmaster, who ran his vessel aground to prevent his course from being traced by a Roman galley, and his reimbursement by his grateful countrymen, is well known. It is also recorded that

---

*" I am not for wholly rejecting," says Bishop Nicolson, "all that is contained in that history, believing there is somewhat of truth in it, under a mighty heap of monkish forgeries."—*English Historical Library.* p. 37.

‡Bishop Nicolson contemptuously dismisses the speculations of Sammes about " the Phenicians his only darlings," but subsequent researches of others have shown that opinions which have been entertained from the times of Nennius, and were advocated by Bochart, are not to be summarily disposed of, without investigation, as the baseless reveries of an enthusiastic, but ill-informed antiquary.

the Greeks of Marseilles, who had long been anxious to obtain a share in this traffic, were at last successful in their attempts to discover the Cassiterides, which became known to them B.C. 330. But Herodotus, more than a century before, whilst he confesses his ignorance of the precise situation of the Cassiterides, mentions tin, without any question, as the product of the extreme regions of Western Europe, with which he was unacquainted.* Tin was one of the commodities in the fairs of Tyre, enumerated by the prophet Ezekiel (B.C. 595) and was known to the Jews in the time when Isaiah prophesied (B.C. 760.) If therefore tin was generally recognised by the common consent of antiquity as a product of the Cassiterides, and an import of the Phenicians, we are carried back to the age of Homer, who mentions the metal as forming an ingredient in the manufacture of armour in those early ages of the world. But if, with the apprehension of an anachronism in this particular, we hesitate to go back to the siege of the Troy (1190, to 1200 B.C.) there can be no difficulty in admitting that a voyage from the Levant to Britain, might have been accomplished at so remote a period as about one thousand years before the Christian era. The historian Heeren fixes the flourishing period of Tyre and the Phenician States, from 1000, to 332, B.C., nor does it seem without the bounds of probability to suppose that their enterprising navigators possessed, even in those early times, the means, as they doubtless had the desire, of extending their policy of foreign colonization, even to the remote isles of Britain. A prominent feature in that policy was the forming of their mercantile settlements on islands and peninsulas. We know that they pushed their discoveries, by coasting Africa in a southern course, after passing the Pillars of Hercules. There does not therefore appear any sufficient reason for questioning the probability of their having (as early as the reign of David or Solomon) voyaged northwards along the coasts of Spain and Gaul, until they reached the islands of Baratanac, the country of tin.

The period of our history, characterized by the Camps we have referred to, may therefore be regarded as commencing before the arrival of the Phenician mariners, and as extending over the time when the tin trade was carried on by them, and subsequently by the Phocæan-Greeks from Marseilles, previously to the invasion of the Romans. Among those relics, examples of two kinds of

---

*" Neither am I acquainted with the Cassiterides Island, from whence tin comes to us." HERODOTUS. *Thalia.* vol. iii., p. 115. Gronov.

fortresses have been mentioned.    That of Prestonbury evidences
more artificial preparation, and considerable advance in knowledge
than the simpler circumvallation of Grimspound, and it may
with great propriety be assigned to a period when the art of
defensive warfare had been improved by intercourse with the
classical nations.    But proofs of the presence of these adventurous
navigators may be traced with far more certainty in the vestiges
of works—more congenial to the commercial spirit of the merchant
princes of Tyre and Sidon, and more germane to the views with
which they dispatched their argosies to brave the terrors of the
Hyperborean ocean—in the remains of primitive mining operations
which are still to be found in various parts of the moor.

Polwhele remarks that the parishes of Manaton, Kingsteignton
and Teigngrace, present examples of these antient works, which
the inhabitants attribute to that period when wolves and winged
serpents were no strangers to the hills or vallies.    The two latter
lie beyond our moorland district towards the estuary of the Teign,
but the former is one of the border parishes of the forest, and
contains many of the remains in question, which, although it is
impossible to assign them any date, with even an approach to
historical certainty, have been generally conjectured to be the
relics of British operations, under the direction of Phenician
traders.    Speaking of these primitive stream-works, Polwhele
goes on to observe that " the Bovey Heathfield hath been worked
" in the same manner.    And indeed all the vallies from the
" Heathfield to Dartmoor bear the traces of shoding and stream-
" ing, which I doubt not was British or Phenician."  *Not only in
Manaton, but in the parishes of Chagford, Walkhampton,
Sheepstor, and Lydford, (the Forest) may be noticed many
similar remains, all in situations favourable for the peculiar
operations of streaming.    And without controverting the opinions
of our zealous antiquary, that some of these may present veritable
examples of forsaken mines of the British and Phenician period,
we cannot suppose that of all the vestiges of these antient works,
none are to be assigned to a later age.    The nature of the case
would rather suggest the inference, that as mining operations
have been carried on in our country from very early times downwards, so the existing relics, if discrimination were possible,
would be attributable to different adventurers, and to successive
ages and generations.    Leaving those speculations, therefore, in

---

*POLWHELE.   *Hist. Views of Devonshire.* p. 110.

the obscurity and uncertainty wherein time has enveloped them, and which can never be dispelled, let us proceed to collect the few scattered rays of light which antient history casts upon the mining operations and commercial transactions of the period in question, as far as they come within the plan of the present work.

Britain had long been regarded as isolated from the rest of mankind, no less by its remote and insular position, than by the fierce and intractable character of its inhabitants—*toto divisos orbe Britannos*. The jealous policy of the Phenicians would doubtless be directed to foster this opinion as much as possible, to which they themselves had probably first given currency, from the desire of preserving in all its integrity, their much-valued monopoly of the British commerce. Hence, as we have seen in the case of Herodotus, little was known by antient authors on the subject of the Cassiterides, beyond the fact of their existence amidst the fabled horrors of the Hyperborean sea. But after the Greeks of Marseilles had succeeded in obtaining a knowledge of the country, and a share in its valuable trade, the philosophers and historians of antiquity had the means of acquiring some information on a subject of no little interest, which, at no distant period, were further enlarged by the invasion of Cæsar. The late General Simcoe, as recorded by Polwhele, accurately applies Cæsar's notice of the metallic productions of Britain, to Devonshire and Dartmoor. "When Cæsar, speaking of Britain, says, *Nascitur* "*ibi plumbum album in Mediterraneis regionibus, in maritimis* "*ferrum, sed ejus exigua est copia*, he elucidates our western "history. To Cæsar it appeared that tin came from the inner "country."* Under the general appellation of the midland, or rather, perhaps, inland parts, Dartmoor must have been included, as well as the metalliferous districts of Cornwall, since we have abundant testimony, as already shown, that the south-western angle of Britain was the principal scene of antient mining operations. But Cæsar, relying on hearsay evidence, collected probably in Kent, had been evidently misled as to the exact situation of the principal tin mines, some of which, even in our moorland district, were too near to the coast to be correctly described as existing in

---

*" The original road by which this tin was conveyed should be an object of your investigation ; and probably you will find it carried over fords, and forming towns in its progress between Dartmoor, and where SIR R. WORSLEY now traces it to have entered the Isle of Wight. On these fords, too, you will probably find a Roman settlement, and not impossibly, account for Crockern Tor, Chagford, &c., having been formerly places of eminence."—Gen. SIMCOE to REV. R. POLWHELE. *Hist. Views of Devonshire*, p. 110.

the interior. With regard to iron, his observations are borne out by the presence of that valuable metal at Shaugh Bridge, on the southern verge of the moor, within six miles of the sea.

The Greek historian, Diodorus Siculus, who flourished about 40 B.C., enters more into detail and has recorded some particulars of antient mining operations, and the tin trade carried on in the southern parts of Britain, of the most interesting character. He incidentially notices that the soil of the tin country was rocky, but had soft veins of earth running through it, whence the metal was extracted. He also describes the principal tin mart, in a celebrated passage which has exercised the ingenuity, and divided the opinions, of successive commentators and antiquaries. Describing the smelting of tin by the Britons, he says, " When " they have cast it into ingots, they carry it into an adjacent " island, which is called Iktis. For when it is low water the " intervening space is left dry, and they carry into that island great " quantities of tin, in wagons." Henry, the historian, as well as Whitaker, misled probably by the name, hastily conclude Iktis to be the Isle of Wight, without considering the insuperable difficulties which this hypothesis presents.* And since, among other speculations as to the real position of this island, Polwhele has assigned it a site which would constitute it the emporium of the aboriginal Dartmoor stannaries, his exposition of the curious and interesting passage of Diodorus, as far as it bears upon our local antiquities, deserves consideration.

After disposing of the arguments of Whitaker,† Borlase, and

---

*If the antient Vectis was the island meant by Diodorus, the improbable postulate is indispensable that the massive metal must have been brought to the shores of Hampshire, opposite to the Isle of Wight, from the South of Devon and the extremities of Cornwall (Belerium) either by land or by sea. If by land, the vehicles, as well as the roads of our aboriginal ancestors, must have been in a state of advancement for which few would be prepared to give them credit. If by sea, the argument requires that these antient traders should have shipped their tin on the coasts of Danmonium, and then steered up the Channel to some port of the Belgic Britons, opposite to the Isle of Wight, on the coast of Hampshire, where they landed their cargo, as it would seem, for the mere pleasure of having it transported across the strait, in wagons, (when the channel became dry—if ever it did—at the ebbing of the tide) instead of adopting the more obvious and direct method of landing the tin immediately on the island, even if they did not make directly for the coast of Gaul, from their original port, which would more probably have been the course adopted.

*BORLASE confesses himself at a loss to decide the situation of Iktis, but supposes it to have been the largest of the Scilly Isles, and identical with the Mictis of PLINY. PRYCE discovers it in the Black Rock in Falmouth Harbour ; POLWHELE claims the honour for St. Nicholas' Island, in Plymouth Sound ; HAWKINS in his " Tin Trade of Cornwall," pronounces that it is St. Michael's Mount, in which he is followed by Dr. BARHAM, DE LA BECHE, and others, and C. SPENCE BATE suggests Mount Batten as complying with the required conditions.

Pryce, in favour of the Isle of Wight, Scilly, and Falmouth, Polwhele enters into an elaborate and ingenious disquisition to prove that the much-controverted situation of Iktis, is to be found in Plymouth Sound. Without referring to the extraneous points, it will suffice to advert to those bearing upon our subject. The same objections which militate against the adoption of the Isle of Wight as the stannary emporium of the south-west, lie in a great degree against Scilly, or even the Black Rock Islet, at Falmouth, with relation to Devonshire; whereas the geographical position of Plymouth Sound, at the mouth of two navigable rivers, running down from the heart of the tin districts of Devon, and those of East Cornwall, would offer facilities, common to both counties, which no other place presents. We can also comprehend the sending of tin from the western districts, to an emporium higher up the Channel, which had already become (as is highly probable) an exporting place for its own neighbourhood; but we can hardly imagine it probable, that tin from Dartmoor and Hingston Down, would be sent so far west as Falmouth, and still less as Scilly, to be shipped for Brittany, in its way to Marseilles. The position of Plymouth, with reference to the parts where the metal was raised, as well as to the country for which it was to be shipped, is thus far favourable to the claims of St. Nicolas' or Drake's Island, but there is one objection to this theory which has been overlooked by its advocate. Diodorus intimates that the metalliferous district which he describes is in the neighbourhood of the promontory Belerium. If by this, we are to understand the Land's End, as is generally supposed, we should be scarcely justified in allowing the expression so wide a scope, as to embrace Plymouth Sound; unless we should conclude that this is another instance in which the imperfect geographical knowledge of the Greeks cannot be relied upon. It might then be supposed that the Belerium being a striking object to the navigators, and some tin mines being observed by the Greek traders in its neighbourhood, in such a general description as that of our historian, other mining districts, though at a considerable distance, might possibly be included. And whilst we should infer from natural circumstances, that the products of the stannary districts on both sides of the Tamar would be exported from the mouth of that river, we are fortunately in possession of unquestionable historical evidence, that this noble and convenient roadstead was known to the Greeks, at the period under consideration, by the appellation of *Tamarou ekbole* the

*Tamari Ostia* of the Romans, and thus far might have been the scene of the famous emporium of Diodorus.

But should we advance a step farther with Polwhele and fix upon St. Nicolas' Island* as the very spot, an obstacle of great local importance, which appears to have escaped his notice, immediately presents itself. He supposes that the isthmus, over which, at the ebb, the tin wagons passed, lay between the island and Mount Edgcumbe; and that in the reef of sunken rocks, known to this day as the Bridge, may be found the remains of a neck of land once passable at low water, but since swept away by by the action of the waves. That the sea has encroached upon the land in many parts of our island, is a fact too well known to admit of dispute; but in Plymouth Sound, the converse appears to have taken place, from sundry fragments of raised beach which have been laid open under the Hoe, opposite St. Nicolas' Island, and from the well-established historical fact, that, in past ages, the tide flowed up from Millbay over the marshy plain between Plymouth and Stonehouse, so that the channel between the island and the mainland was probably much deeper 2000 years since than it is now, and the possibility of the existence of an isthmus, over which wagons could pass at low water, scarcely imaginable. But even if such a means of communication had existed, the slightest acquaintance with local circumstances would immediately show that this islet must have been most inconveniently situated for the purposes in question. The tin wagons from Dartmoor could never reach it without first crossing the wide estuary of the Tamar; and those from Hingston Down,† and the Cornish side of the river, in general would have to approach the peninsula of Mount Edgcumbe by a circuitous and

---

*RISDON is of opinion that this island may have been mentioned under the name of Tamarweorth, upwards of a thousand years ago. "In the Saxon's Heptarchy, this harbour (Plymouth) was called Tamarweorth (as is to be read in the life of St. Indractus) if St. Nicolas' Island be not meant thereby; for Weorth. in Saxon, is a river island." LELAND describes this islet, as "lying at the mouthes of the Tamar and Plym rivers," but gives no intimation of its possessing, in his time, any of the peculiar characteristics of the Iktis of DIODORUS.

†That this district was the scene of antient mining operations, may be gathered from a popular tradition current in the time of CAREW, no less than from the evidence afforded by the present appearance of this conspicuous hill. "From Plymouth Haven," writes the old Cornish Chronicler, "Hengsten Downe presenteth his waste head and sides to our sight. This name it borroweth of *Hengst*, which, in the Saxon, signifieth a *horse*, and to such daintie beasts, it yieldeth fittest pasture. The countrie people have a bye-word, that

"Hengsten Down well ywrought
Is worth London town, dear bought,"

Which grewe from a store of tynne, in former times there digged up "—
CAREW'S *Survey of Cornwall, p.* 272.

incommodious route.   But although these objections appear fatal
to the claims of St. Nicolas, in particular, they do not in the least
apply to Plymouth Sound in general ; and, taking into consideration the acknowledged retrocession of the sea from this coast we
may perhaps look, with better success, for such an island as
Diodorus describes, to the site of Plymouth itself.   Feeling
persuaded that the advantages of such a port as must have existed
at the mouths of the Plym and Tamar, could not have been overlooked, either by the Phenicians or Massilian Greeks, we think
it must be conceded, that in all probability, the ore raised in the
neighbourhood would be sent down to that point on the Plymouth
coasts which at that period was the most favourable for embarka-
tion.   And if the sea has receded from the inlets and creeks of the
harbour to the extent that some have imagined,* an island
answering to all the conditions required, might be found in
Plymouth Hoe, and in the parts adjoining, separated at full tide
from the rising ground, north of the present town, but connected
with it at low water by the dorsal tract, which, amidst the chances
and changes of twenty centuries, still exists in the direction of
Old Town, sloping on one side to the Frankfort marshes and
Millbay, and on the other, to Sutton Pool.   Or if it should be
deemed that we have no sufficient data for concluding that the
water ever reached so high a level, as must necessarily be presumed, if the Hoe were originally an island, there can be no
reasonable doubt that the corresponding hill on the opposite side
of Catwater, was once insulated by the union of the waters of the
Lary with Sutton Pool, and that Catdown would probably then,
at low tide, be approachable by an isthmus, not unlikely lying in
the same direction as the old lane leading from Tothill to Catdown.
The same rise of tide which in old times flooded the Plymouth
marshes and brought the sea to Frankfort Gate, would abundantly
suffice to cover the comparatively low ground between the Lary
and Sutton Pool.   Thus, if the reference to Belerium could be

---

*Modern geologists assert. that in past ages the shores of the English Channel
have been raised forty or fifty feet ; and if, according to FORCHAMMER, the disrup-
tion of England from the Continent occurred not more than 2,500 or 3,000 years
ago, we can readily imagine that vast changes must have taken place, along the
whole line of the coast, from the Land's End to the Nore, even if we had not direct
testimony to the fact.

†If the term Cassiterides included all the tin country of the western peninsula,
might not *Belerium* have been the Greek appellation for the Roman *Jugum
Ocrinum* (the mountainous ridge reaching from Dartmoor to the Land's End,) and
the name of the promontory, in which it terminates, put by synecdoche, for the
whole chain?   Were this hypothesis tenable, " the dwellers below the promontory

satisfactorily explained,† an island would be found, in all other respects, answering with singular exactness, to the description of Diodorus, and most conveniently situated for the Danmonian miners to bring their metal from the interior, for shipment to Gaul, for Marseilles, or in earlier times, for the Levant direct, by the Straits of Gibraltar.

But whether the claims of Plymouth to the disputed honours of Iktis be allowed or not, it can scarcely be questioned that transactions, similar to those described by the Greek historian, from the very force of circumstances, must have taken place at some part of the shores of Plymouth Harbour. The contrary supposition, that with every facility for exporting the metal, raised almost on the very coast,* the traders should have conveyed the ponderous commodity by wagons to some distant port, is too absurd to be admitted. If the Dartmoor miners, then, had not the identical Iktis at the mouth of their rivers, and in sight of their southernmost hills, they had doubtless a similar emporium on their shores, and the interesting description of the maritime Britons may be fairly applied to the Danmonians of the neighbourhood of *Tamari Ostia* as well as to the other trading inhabitants of the Cassiterides. "The inhabitants of that part of Britain, below the "promontory called Belerium, are exceedingly hospitable *(fond of* "strangers)* and on account of their intercourse with foreign "merchants, are more civilised in their habits of life."†

With reference to the existence of some kind of emporium on

---

called Belerium" of DIODORUS, might be fairly interpreted as describing the inhabitants of the mining districts of the south coasts of Devon and Cornwall. Or, since the informants of DIODORUS probably made the Land's End first, in their voyage, they might have termed the country eastward, the coast "below Belerium," if so, the term might have included, as above, all the maritime inhabitants of the stannary districts of Danmonium.

*The tidal waters of the Plym are known to have flowed, in former times, over a great part of the Saltram marshes, close to Plympton St. Mary Churchyard, and even as far as the ditches of Plympton Castle, *usque ad castrum*, as an old document tells us, so that the mining ground, near Hemerdon, Newnham, and Boringdon Park, was much nearer to the estuary than at present.

†It is not impossible that the precincts of Dartmoor may have supplied materials for the Dockyards of Greek naval architects, two thousand years ago. POLWHELE has noticed a circumstance which is worth observing. "That famous ship which was built at Syracuse under the direction of ARCHIMEDES, is at once a proof of the proficiency of the Greeks in the maritime arts, and of their connexion with Britain. According to ATHENÆUS, the ship had three masts, of which the second and third were easily procured; but it was long before a tree for the mainmast could be found. At length a proper tree was discovered in the mountains of Britain, and brought down to the sea coast by a famous mechanic, PHILEAS TAUROMENITES. This is a curious fact. And the mountains of Britain, I conceive, were the mountains of Danmonium. In other parts of the island the Greeks had very slight connexions. It was with Danmonium they traded, etc., etc."—*Hist. Views of Devon*, p. 145.

the coast, at a convenient distance from the mining districts of Danmonium, it may be further observed that the place known to the Greeks by the name of Tamara, had obtained sufficient celebrity in antient times, to be mentioned by Ptolemy, among the few places which his scanty information enabled him to enumerate on the Danmonian shores. This could scarcely have arisen from any other cause than the natural advantages of Plymouth Sound—its contiguity to the stannary region, and the consequent growth of an emporium for the staple commodity of the country, at some convenient spot, in the parts adjacent. Had there been no direct evidence of the existence of such a port, nature would have indicated, that as a roadstead like Plymouth Sound, and such harbours as Hamoaze and Catwater, could not have escaped the notice of the Phenician and Greek traders, so the circumstance of their resorting there for purposes of traffic, would naturally lead to the gradual rise of some kind of port, of greater or less consequence. But having the testimony of Ptolemy to the existence of a town in the neighbourhood of the Tamar, it is no longer matter of conjecture or inference, but an historical fact that such a place near the coast of Danmonium, was known to the Greeks and other classical nations, in the age of Ptolemy, and in all probability long before. Nor is it less certain that, with the sole exception of Isca, (Exeter) we can fix the situation of Tamara with more accuracy than any other of the Danmonian towns and places enumerated by Ptolemy. Its name identifies it with the banks of the Tamar, and most probably with the immediate neighbourhood of the estuary, since this author mentions both Tamar Mouth and Tamara. Guided by the landmarks of nature, and the evidence of etymology, many antiquaries have agreed that the antient Tamara is to be sought for in the modern Tamerton ; a conclusion at which those who are best acquainted with local circumstances will scarcely fail also to arrive, although others, with Horsley, have supposed it to be Saltash. Dr. Borlase, referring to Ptolemy, says, " The third " city is Tamara, in which the name of the river Tamar is too " strong to be questioned, and Tamerton, on the eastern bank of " the river, lies almost opposite to Saltash, and must have been " the place." Polwhele, venturing, on very slender and questionable authority, to divide antient Danmonium into *cantreds* (which he says gave rise to *hundreds*) finds the principal town of the cantred of Tamara in Tamerton or Plymouth. Without adopting this author's fanciful opinions on the subject of these supposed cantreds, we may conclude that there was a district of some extent, known by the name of Tamara, comprehending, perhaps, the tract of country bounded by the Tamar, the Dartmoor Hills, the Plym, and Plymouth Sound; and that within these boundaries, at the village of King's Tamerton, in the parish of St. Budeaux, the true site of the Tamara of the antients will probably be found, opposite to Saltash, on the Roman road to the ferry, and from its commanding situation, in full view of the estuary of the Tamar, and therefore a situation likely to be fixed upon by the Danmonian Britons, or the Phenician traders.

Since Diodorus describes Britain as a populous island, we may justly conclude that this description must have applied to that part of the country, concerning which he had received the most accurate information, viz., the metalliferous districts. Hence we infer that the south of Devon, before the Roman era of our history, was inhabited by a numerous population;—that on the coast, at the mouths of the rivers flowing down from the hilly country, where the staple commodity of the island was raised, there would be smelting establishments, and ports for the shipment of the metal by foreign merchants;—that the maritime inhabitants, from their intercourse with these traders, became comparatively civilized, and probably adopted many foreign practices and opinions, whilst the dwellers of the interior retained their nomadic habits, and preserved their primitive superstitions, amidst the Forest wilds and rugged steeps of Dartmoor, as Carrington soothly sings:—

> " These silent vales have swarm'd with human life,
> These hills have echo'd to the hunter's voice—
> Here rang the chase—the battle burn'd—the notes
> Of Sylvan joy at high festivities
> Awoke the soul to gladness!  Dear to him,
> His native hill—in simple garb attired,
> The mountaineer here rov'd.

>                        'Tis said that here
> The Druid wander'd.  Haply have these hills,
> With shouts ferocious, and the mingled shriek,

Resounded, when to Jupiter upflam'd,
The human hecatomb.   The franctic seer
Here built his Sacred Circle; for he lov'd
To worship on the mountain's breast sublime—
The earth his altar, and the bending heav'n
His canopy magnificent.   The rocks
That crest the grove-crown'd hill, he scooped **to hold**
The Lustral waters; and to wond'ring crowds
And ignorant, with guileful hand he rock'd
The yielding Logan."

F

# CHAPTER V.

HAVING in the preceding chapters taken a compendious view of the several relics which may be regarded as so many monuments, reflecting the few and flickering beams which history casts upon the obscure period to which they may with most probability be justly assigned ; and having shown that they are eminently characteristic of the peoples who must have occupied this part of England before it was subjugated by the Romans, we now proceed to a topographical survey of the interesting district, whose very wildness and inaccessible character has insured their preservation, amidst the chances and changes of twenty centuries—the venerable, and often the only, witnesses of the unrecorded events of aboriginal times.

In pursuit of this object, let us take the antient Perambulators of Henry III. (1240) for our guides, following their course, as before referred to,* as closely as the imperfect vestiges which can still be traced will permit, and while with them we make the Perambulation from east to west, and "beat the bounds," let us endeavour to lead the contemplative wanderer to those objects of antiquarian interest and natural beauty most worthy of his examination within the bounds, metes, and precincts of the antient and Royal Forest of Dartmoor.

The Perambulators began their circuit at Hoga de Cossdonne, and thence in an easterly direction to a Little Hill, which they say is called Little Hundetorre. These two hills are the great one of Cosdon and the little one of Hundetorre, which is identified with Shelstone. The former is spelt in various ways, but the name given in the Ordnance map is now generally adopted, and Cawsand Beacon, once supposed to be the highest point, was a suitable place for the king's men to commence their work. They started probably from somewhere in the immediate neighbourhood of Stickle Path. This picturesque village is on what was the great mail-road from Exeter to Okehampton, and into Cornwall, which road sweeps round the very base of Cosdon Hill. Here will be found accommodation such as may well content the moorland tourist bent on exploring the "wild and wondrous "region" extending beyond the eminence which towers so majestically above the village nestling among the thickets that fringe the rocky channel of the Taw, here issuing forth into the champaign country, from a noble mountain gorge. The Hoga, the point from which the Perambulators set out, must have been sufficiently near to Cosdon, to authorize our making Stickle Path the starting point of our Forest perambulation.

Proceeding along the high road up the ascent from whence the village derives its name,† at its western extremity, we notice on the left hand, hard by the wayside, and on the verge of a rocky common, the shaft of an antient cross, formed of the durable granite from the neighbouring mountain. It stands nearly six

---

*Ante. p. 6.

†Stickle-Path, the *steep road* from Sticele (Saxon) steep and path. In the Devonshire vernacular, we still retain the Saxon word; a *stickle* roof is a high pitched roof.

feet high, is about eleven inches in thickness, and has its sides
rudely sculptured in curves, lines, and crosses, with little regularity of design, but which, having been much defaced by the
weather or by violence, are scarcely discernible, unless the sun
shines full upon the shaft.*   Adjoining the cross, a path winds
away into the upland gorge, formed by Cosdon on one side and
the Belstone hills on the other.   Looking down upon the windings
of the Taw, with the mill and the cottages peering through the
trees on its banks, we are strongly reminded of some of the softer
features of Welsh scenery in similar situations.   A rugged path
through broken ground, high above the river's western bank, leads
to Taw Marsh,† a plain of considerable extent, and remarkably
level, dotted with huge masses of granite, and surrounded by
lofty eminences, with all the features and incidents characteristic
of the peculiar scenery of the moor.   Here is one of the spots
where the evidences of some mighty convulsion of nature strike
the beholder with astonishment, and carry irresistible conviction
to the mind.   The characteristic tors of Belstone, cresting the
rocky hills on the west, their sides sloping down to the marshy
level through which the Taw winds its way, are strewn with
blocks and slabs of granite, forming those aggregations of stone
which are known to the moormen by the name of Clatters,‡ a
term expressive of their confused appearance.   Among those may
be noticed, near the river's brink, a stone of so unusual a size, and
so singularly shaped, that it has been supposed by some to have
been artificially reduced to its present figure; but a slight examination is sufficient to prove that Nature alone has formed its rude
outline, like a mimic gnomon of colossal proportions, and planted
it firmly in the ground as if to mark the progress of the silent
hours of the desert.   Down through the rugged and precipitous
glen on the south, comes the Taw, white with foam, and hastening
to soothe his ruffled waters in the level channel of the plain below.
Here, in Taw Marsh, the philosophic observer may detect evidences of the existence of groves and woods, which once appear

---

*MR. CROSSING considers this an inscribed stone and not the shaft of a cross.
The Crosses of Dartmoor and its Borders have received much careful investigation
in two works by Mr. W. Crossing, published in 1887 and 1892.

†DR. ARTHUR B. PROWSE has carefully examined Taw Marsh and its surroundings,
and has described other interesting remains in the neighbourhood, besides those
mentioned here.   *Vide* Trans. Devon Assoc., vol. xxii., 1890, p. 185.

‡The *Clatter* or Clitter is sometimes erroneously confounded with the *Tor*; but
the latter is the natural rock, cresting the hill, while the Clatter is the collection of
stones, apparently hurled promiscuously together, along its declivity.

to have clothed the vallies and acclivities of the moor to a far greater extent than at present. Deep in the antiseptic soil, here, and in similar situations, whence the peat has been removed, branches, trunks, and roots of trees, chiefly oak and birch, have been frequently found, which on exposure to the air, speedily acquire great hardness. The birch, as is well known, delights in the moorland soil, nor is there any just reason for questioning that the trees thus exhumed, once flourished on the spot where they were afterwards submerged in the morass, having probably been gradually undermined by the saturation of the ground with excessive moisture.

Leaving these speculations, and the boggy level which has given rise to them, let us take advantage of the natural stepping-stones which during the summer may be found in the wider parts of its channel, to cross the Taw, and scale the steep of Cosdon which rises abruptly from the eastern bank. Advancing up the ascent, we shall soon look back upon Belstone Church; and taking its tower for a landmark, shall find the advantage of making for the beacon on the summit of the mountain by shaping our upward course in a south-easterly direction. We shall thus also come upon one of those antient paved ways, in a state of good preservation, principally exhibiting the characteristics of the *trackway*, described in Chapter IV., but partaking somewhat of the character of the *tracklines* also. The direction of this antient roadway, or boundary, or both, is from the valley and inclosed country N.E. by E. It can be traced to the extent of four hundred and seventy yards, and it terminates towards the west in another line of similar character, which runs off in an acute angle.

As we ascend, our attention will be attracted by other monumental relics. Scarcely fifty yards from the trackway, a cairn, much dilapidated, and diminished by the removal of many of the stones, will be noticed. But when we have nearly reached the object of our toilsome ascent—" the windy summit huge and high,"—we shall find a cairn of a peculiarly interesting description at no great distance from the highest point of the hill. Unlike those monumental erections in general which are merely extemporaneous agglomerations of stones, inartificially heaped up in the form into which they would almost necessarily fall, this cairn betokens much more preparation and design in its construction. The pile is inclosed by a ring of slab stones closely set, leaning outwards, apparently by design, and some of them not less than three feet in height.   About sixty yards S.W. of the last, will be observed another cairn, of which the materials are unusually large.   Surrounded by the stones of which the cairn is composed, is a kistvaen, about seven feet square.   The sides of the kistvaen are formed of slabs in the usual way, and two of them remain erect, and perfectly forming one of the angles of the sarcophagus. The others are more or less inclined or prostrate, and some appear to have been removed.   Seventy yards W.S.W. of the above, within the area of a circular inclosure, similar to that observed near Hound Tor, formed of slabs set closely together, and fifty-four feet in diameter, is a dilapidated kistvaen eight feet square, and apparently exhibiting traces of an inner coffin, or sarcophagus, the coverstone of which is not more than two feet and a half broad.   One of these kistvaens may probably be *Cosdon House*, of which the moormen speak as existing somewhere on Cosdon Beacon.

Somewhat more than a hundred yards N.E. by N. from the kistvaen last described, is a circular inclosure totally different from the former, as the stones of which it is composed are small and pebbly, and irregularly heaped together, forming a sort of miniature *Pound*, and, with the exception of a small portion of the circumference, in a remarkably perfect condition.   The area inclosed by it is boggy ground, although it is very nearly on the highest part of the mountain on which Cosdon Beacon stands, at an elevation of 1,799 feet above the level of the sea.

This far-famed beacon bears south east from Belstone Church, and was long thought to occupy the loftiest spot in Devonshire and consequently in the south of England.*   But recent observations have proved that this is not so, as we shall see further on, but Cosdon apparently has the advantage, from its rising immediately, without any intervening high ground, from the lowland country at its base.   From this circumstance, it has more the appearance of a true mountain than any other of the Dartmoor Hills, though Mistor, seen from the gorge of the Walkham, cannot be regarded as a rival of mean pretensions.

The cairn on the summit, is about ninety yards in circumference, and appears to have been opened in two distinct places, where there are hollows of considerable size; but for what purposes these hollows have been dug, does not appear, unless

---

*It is perhaps not generally known that the Dartmoor hills are the loftiest South of Cader Idris and Snowdon, Skiddaw, Helvellyn, and Ingleborough.

with the view of forming a kind of hearth for the reception of the fuel of which the beacon-fire was made. Few places could have been chosen more admirably adapted for the purpose of rousing the whole neighbourhood than this, where the eye can sweep three-fourths of the entire horizon, and look forth upon the greatest part of North Devon, with large portions of the Western and Eastern districts of the county, and some of the loftier points of Cornwall, Somerset, and Dorset. Exmoor looms large and distinct in the north, and it is said that the Bristol Channel can be seen on a clear day, which is perfectly possible, while there is no doubt that the English Channel, off Teignmouth, is distinctly visible. Imagine, then, the bale fire kindled on this commanding eminence. Heytor, which rises full in view against the south-eastern sky, would instantly catch the intelligence, and repeat the signal to Buckland Beacon, above Ashburton, whence it would be as speedily communicated to Brent. Brent would report to its neighbour the Eastern Beacon, which would repeat the signal to the Western, above Ivybridge. Pen Beacon, in full view of Plymouth Sound, would alarm the coast, and send the fiery despatch around the Western Quarter and through the central moorlands by Eylesburrow, Bellever, and Mistor, till Amicombe and Yes Tor caught the intelligence on the north-west, and sent it by Kit Hill, Treninnow,* Caradon, and Rowtor, through the whole Cornish peninsula. In the north the flaming telegraph would be discernible from the entrenchments on Mockham Down, the southern outposts of Exmoor, and from thence would be rapidly communicated to Dunkery Beacon, and the loftiest hills in Somersetshire.

Let us not leave this lofty and solitary spot without observing how exactly it illustrates the allusion of the prophet Isaiah (xxx., 17)—"left as a beacon upon the top of a mountain, and as "an ensign on an hill"—nor shall we fail to reflect how widely this ready and natural mode of conveying intelligence has pre-vailed in various countries, and in all ages of the world. Beacons were not only used to spread the alarm of an approaching enemy,† and to rouse the population for the defence of the country, but were resorted to for despatching other tidings of importance. Among the Jews, notice was given of the appearance of the new

---

*Treninnow Beacon, above Whitsand Bay.

†Beacon fires are mentioned as having being kindled upon the towers of Bethulia, on the invasion of Judæa by the Assyrians under Holofernes.—JUDITH vii., 5.

moon, by firing beacons set up for that purpose.   The same mode
of telegraphic communication was practised by the Greeks, as the
intelligence of the taking of Troy, according to Æschylus, was
thus conveyed to Clytemnestra.

Reluctantly leaving the beacon and the noble panorama it
commands, we proceed down the south-western declivity, and
nearly opposite Belstone Tor, shall observe a group of circular
basements, the remains of aboriginal dwellings, nine in number,
partly within and partly without an inclosure of similar construction, three hundred and forty yards in circumference.   Still lower
down the declivity a trackway may be traced leading from the
valley of the Taw, in a south westerly direction.

To mount the summit of Cosdon and regain the valley on the
opposite side will not be a difficult task for a vigorous pedestrian,
and may be accomplished, with due allowance for detention by
the antiquities and the prospect, in about two hours.   The top
can also be reached from the Sticklepath side on horseback, by
those who may prefer the aid of a moor pony for that purpose.

Towards Throwleigh on the eastern side the descent is gradual
and easy, and in this direction our perambulation now proceeds.
Crossing a stream which flows down from the little tarn, described in the old one inch ordnance map as Raybarrow Pool, we
shall soon reach Clannaborough Common, between the inclosed
lands of Throwleigh and Shellstone Hill, and about one mile west
of Throwleigh church.   Here, was formerly to be seen, one
of the most remarkable specimens of aboriginal architecture
to be found on the Moor.   We are confident that it had never
been described by antiquaries, until we printed our account of it,
although in some respects it is even more curious than Grimspound.
It was called a Pound by the moormen, but from the small area
inclosed and the description of walling, it appears to have been
erected for purposes different from those contemplated in the
cyclopean structures popularly comprehended under the general
designation of Pounds.   Much more regularity of design, and
exactness of construction than we have noticed in any other
instance was exhibited in the wall, yet it was evidently of aboriginal
character.   This wall remained in an unusually perfect state, and
the stones of which it was formed, instead of being thrown together
as in the vast amphitheatre of Grimspound and in other similar
enclosures, were laid in courses in several parts of the wall where
they were of comparatively small size ; while in others, huge blocks

occupied the whole height of the wall, standing from two feet and a half to four feet above the ground. The average thickness of the wall thus formed was above seven feet, and on the western side it was built against the slope of the hill. The area was remarkably free from ruins, and appeared to have been hollowed out. We are afraid not a vestige of this remains. It was perfect when the first edition of this work was printed. In immediate connexion with it, was a trackline running down the hill eastward. Ruinated dwellings and other antient remains abound in its immediate neighbourhood. Among the rest, half a furlong south of the former, is another circle of similar character, but of smaller dimensions, twenty-four feet and a half in diameter, much more dilapidated, and having its area strewn with ruins  All the surrounding objects convey the idea of an aboriginal settlement, and the situation is precisely such as our British progenitors are known to have chosen in other parts of the moor. Here, as in many other instances, regard seems to have been had to the supply of water. The streamlet from Raybarrow flows, at a short distance in its course, towards Pain's Bridge; and, still nearer, a tributary of the Teign rises immediately below Shellstone Tor. Both these streams wind their devious way towards Chagford, to unite with the Teign, in its southward progress, while within a few yards of the former, a brook takes its rise from the roots of the Cosdon, and joins the Taw in its course to the Bristol Channel in the north. Shilston Tor or Shellstone Hill was identified by C. Spence Bate, as the "Parvum Hogam," and not Hound Tor, the latter tor being west of Cosdon and not east, and two miles, and not one, as the place sought for should be, distant from it.

One of the tributaries of the Teign, just referred to, may possibly be the Wotesbrook, described in the Perambulation as falling into that river. Or it may be the stream which we shall observe in our progress over Endsworthy Hill, flowing in the hollow below towards Wallabrook, but this we are unable to ascertain. Above, on Shellstone and Endsworthy Hills, are cairns or barrows, placed, like most other monuments of this description, on the crest of the eminences. Nearly due west from Endsworthy, Steepelton Tor and Hound Tor rise above the course of the Taw, but will scarcely offer attractions enough to draw us so far away from the interesting object which we begin to discern, after we cross Buttern Hill and descend the slope of Scorhill Down. This

is the sacred circle of Scorhill, and is by far the finest example of
this rude kind of relic in Devonshire ; and although unnoticed by
antiquaries or topographers, may successfully dispute the palm
with many that have acquired historical celebrity, such as the
circle at Castle Rigg, near Keswick, or that at Rollright, in
Oxfordshire.   Scorhill* Circle stands near the tor of that name
on the downs west of Gidleigh Park, and at a short distance
above the Wallabrook, at its confluence with the North Teign.
The rugged and angular appearance of the massive stones of
which this rude hypaethral temple is constructed, forms a striking
contrast to the Grey Wethers—the Sacred Circle below Sittaford
Tor, which are of a squarer and more truncated form.   The two
principal columnar masses in this granite peristyle stand at nearly
opposite points of the circle ; the highest, which in its widest part
is about thirty inches, rising nearly eight feet from the surface and
the other standing upwards of six feet.   The lowest are about
three feet high ; eight stones lie on the ground and twenty-four of
these time worn obelisks still maintain their erect position, and
twenty stones would be required to fill up the vacancies.   The
circle is ninety feet in diameter.   There is no appearance of any
central column or altar, and the whole of the inclosure has
evidently been industriously cleared of stones, as the surrounding
common without the area of the circle is abundantly strewed with
the usual moorstone.   Such then is the finest and most complete
specimen of a sacred circle in the county, and few spots could
have been chosen more in accordance with our notions of the
requirements of that singular system of worship, which, as we
learn from undoubted contemporary testimony was carried to such
a pitch of perfection in Britain that the Gauls who wished to be
initiated into its most recondite mysteries repaired to this island
for instruction,† as to the general university of the Druidical
communion.

Our course now leads to the Wallabrook, which flows at the
foot of Scorhill Down.   The means of crossing is afforded by one
of the primitive bridges, of which we have so many examples on
the Moor, consisting of a single slab of ponderous granite, fifteen
feet long, nearly three wide, and twenty inches thick.   Pro-

---

*Query Scaur, q.d. Scaurhill.   Scor in Gaelic means a sharp rugged peak.

†Disciplina in Britannia reperta, atque inde in Galliam translata esse existimatur.
Et nunc qui diligentiùs eam rem cognoscere volunt, plerumqus illò,discendi caussa,
proficiscuntur.   CÆSAR. Bell. Gall., lib. vi., 13.

Wallabrook Clapper Bridge.

ceeding westwards, we shall cross the swampy flat, between the Wallabrook and North Teign, and mount Watern Hill to examine the singular tor which forms so conspicuous an object on the northern extremity of the ridge. Watern Tor is one of the many remarkable natural conformations of the granite rock which will repay a more particular examination. It consists of a series of piles, rising from the ridge of the hill, the stratification of which presents the appearance of laminar masses in a horizontal position. The two piles at the N.N.E. extremity, in one part near the top, approach so closely, as to appear to unite when seen from some points of view, leaving a large oval aperture in the tor, through which, the moormen say, a man can ride on horseback. But on a closer examination, it will be observed that there is an interval of at least one foot wide in the narrowest part; and in the widest, the piles stand about eight feet apart, leaving ample room for man and horse to pass through. This aperture appears to have given rise to the name of Thirlstone,* by which this part of the tor is known. The lesser of the two piles, if viewed apart from the rest of the tor, is not unlike the far-famed Cheeswring, on the Cornish moors, but the courses (to borrow a term from masonry) are thinner. Its elevation is about twenty feet above the grassy surface of the hill. Had all rock basins been merely natural formations, we think many would have been found on Watern Tor, but not one example is to be found.

Following the ridge of the hill at the southern extremity, we shall observe a large barrow or cairn of the ordinary description. Other similar cairns will be noticed on the opposite hill near Wild Tor, and on the higher hills above Taw Head, towards which we shall now bend our course, bearing due west from the cairn on Watern Hill. Watern Tor being a well known object, may serve the tourist as a landmark in his search for Cranmere Pool, which hides itself almost as successfully from the Dartmoor explorer, as the Nile concealed his fountains from the antients. From the cairn at the eastern end of Watern Hill above mentioned, we descend to the Wallabrook (here, only a small rivulet near its source,) and proceeding westward to White Horse Hill, which is a track of high heathy land, undistinguished by tors, ridges or bold features, but probably taking its name from large patches of the granite floor of the mountain having been laid bare and

---

*Thirlstone—*thirl, dirl*, or *drill*-stone; the perforated stone.

whitened by exposure, presenting probably, at a distance, the rude outline of a horse.  In this immediate neighbourhood, quantities of turf are cut for fuel, and somewhat beyond the farthest point of the turf-cutters operations,* the approach to Cranmere may be made on horseback without difficulty.  The tourist will find himself on the borders of the vast expanse of boggy tableland, which characterizes the remotest and most inaccessible parts of the moorland wilderness.  If he has penetrated thus far by the aid of a Dartmoor pony, he will find it prudent to take advantage of the rude hut which the turf-cutters have raised in this wild spot, for temporary shelter against " the war of elements," to leave his horse, and pursue his wearisome way on foot towards Cran-mere Pool.  The way in itself is toilsome, as you are continually plunging into the plashy soil ; or, to avoid getting knee-deep in the bogs, are constrained to leap from tuft to tuft of the firmer patches of rushy ground.  Nor is there anything in the surround-ing scenery to cheer the wanderer who requires a succession of new and attractive objects to animate him in his progress.  Here the image of " a waste and howling wilderness " is fully realized.  Glance where it may, the same slightly undulating, but unvarying surface of heath, common, and morass, presents itself to the eye.  Scarcely even a granite block on the plain, or a tor on the higher ground, " breaks the deep-felt monotony " of the scene.  Yet in this very monotony there is a charm, for it gives birth to a feeling that you are now in the domains of primæval Nature, and that this is one of the few spots where no indication of man's presence or occupancy are to be traced.  The few sounds that, at long intervals, disturb the brooding silence of the desert—the plaintive cry of the curlew, or the whirring rustle of the heath-fowl, roused by the explorer's unexpected tread—the sighing wind, suddenly wrapping him perhaps in a mist-wreath, or the feeble tinklings of the infant streamlets—for we are now amidst the fountains of the Dartmoor rivers—are all characteristic of the scene ; and wild, remote, and solitary as it is, this central morass is thus associated with the richest, most populous, and loveliest spots of our fair and fertile Devon.  Hence, then, in imagination, we follow the mountain-born streams, along their devious course to the distant ocean, through green pastures and wavy cornfields—by the noisy mill and the plenteous farm—now lingering by the fragrant-

---

*The Moor-men call the spots where peat is cut for fuel, *turve*, i.e., turf, *ties*.

CRANMERE POOL.

blossomed orchard, and now sweeping by the golden furze-clad hill; now flashing in sunshine along the enamelled meadows, and now darkling beneath deep "o'erarching groves;" at one time mirroring the simple cottages and grey steeple of the sequestered village, and anon where the tidal waters have widened into a lake and deepened into a harbour, bearing on their ample bosom, the riches of commerce, and the terrors of war—reflecting the bristling masts of the crowded port—or the guarded battlements of the frowning citadel. All these are present to the mind's eye ; and whilst by contrast with the visible objects around, they render the desert still more waste and lonely, they will not fail to remind us of the justice of the poet's acknowledgment of the obligations of the smiling lowlands to Dartmoor, as " the source of half their " beauty."

Accordingly Carrington has sung the " Urn of Cranmere " in strains of harmonious eulogy.

" What time the lib'ral mountain-flood has fill'd
The Urn of Cranmere, and the moisten'd moor
Pours to the dales the largess of the heavens !
O let me wander, then, while freshness breathes,
Along the grateful meads, and list the voice,
Dartmoor—exhaustless Dartmoor—of thy streams,
Thou land of streams !"

But Cranmere Pool itself, is not, as it is sometimes supposed, the source of the numerous streams which pour down from the reservoir which nature has established in this lofty but humid region. Taw Head is half a mile distant eastward ; the sources of the Tavy are under Great Kneeset, a mile to the south-west ; Dart Head about the same distance south ; and the springs of the Teign still farther in a south-easterly direction. Ockment alone flows from Cranmere Pool, which was the largest piece of water in Dartmoor or its precincts, where we can boast of nothing like the mountain tarns of Wales and Cumberland. It is exceedingly difficult to find without a guide, and when the indefatigable tourist has reached the object of his toilsome walk he may perhaps scarcely think that the deep dark-looking hollow before him, imperfectly filled with water, with the heap of stones, has repaid him for the trouble he has taken to penetrate the watery fastnesses of the moor. The pool was formerly of an oblong form, and at its brink was about 220 yards in circumference and with an average depth of five feet. The bank some fifty years ago was apparently dug through on the northern side and the result is that for a considerable time past it has been and is now nearly dry, a mere hollow in the bog, but the outline of its former extent is clearly to be seen.  In this direction the springs of the Ockment find an outlet, and flow below Links Tor and Amicombe Hill towards Okehampton.

We shall find nothing to detain us in the Cranmere morasses, from whence these variously wandering streams take their rise, after we have satisfied our curiosity with the inspection of what remains of the Pool, and shall therefore return to the White Horse Hill.  Proceeding eastward we shall notice some vestiges of antient mining operations above the course of the North Teign, which we shall cross by a primitive Cyclopean bridge of three openings, in a state of high preservation.  In character it is similar to Post Bridge but on a smaller scale.  The piers are built of rough unwrought granite masses; and the roadway over is rather less than seven feet wide, formed of slabs of the same durable material.  The length of the bridge is twenty-seven feet and eight feet wide.  Opinions differ as to whether it is of antient or recent erection.  Mr. R. Burnard says the latter unhesitatingly. Passing over the hill through extensive turf-ties towards Sittaford Tor, we reach the circles popularly known by the name of the Grey Wethers.  The circumference of these circles almost touch each other.  They were, in the opinion of the late G. W. Ormerod, originally apparently constructed of thirty-two stones each, some of these are still erect.  The largest has been displaced and lies on the ground.  It is a slab four feet nine inches wide, less than a foot thick, and must have originally stood about five feet high.  The north circle is in diameter one hundred feet and the south one hundred and five feet.*

Returning eastward, and leaving the North Teign on the left, within two miles from Grey Wethers, we shall reach Frogymead Hill, adjoining Fernworthy.  Here is another circle of a similar description but of smaller dimensions.  Its diameter is sixty-three feet.  Twenty-six stones now remain about three feet apart, still preserving their original position, but one has recently fallen.  Mr. Ormerod thought that originally there were thirty-one stones. The highest stands four feet from the ground.

---

*These have been carefully examined and planned by Mr. ROBERT BURNARD, and full descriptions and measurements will be found in the second volume of his " Dartmoor Pictorial Records," *pp.* 49, 54.

STONE AVENUE ON THE TEIGN.

Passing the enclosed lands, and reaching the other side of the little stream which flows into the South Teign, above the river itself upon Thornworthy Down, the cairn, opened by Mr. Samuel H. Slade in 1879, may be visited. It contained two kistvaens, the smaller of which was removed to, and is now in the Museum of the Torquay Natural History Society. A flint knife and a flint scraper, and two other flints were found, and also fragments of an earthenware vessel, one of the very few instances of pottery being found upon Dartmoor.*

Proceeding northward, about a mile and a half from Frogy-mead, we shall explore a cluster of remarkable relics, beginning with the Gidleigh Rock Pillar, called in the Ordnance Map, Long Stone. The letters D.G. inscribed on one face, and D.C. on another, denoting the division between the parishes of Gidleigh, Chagford, and Dartmoor Forest, show that this primitive obelisk has been used as a boundary stone in modern times ; but that it is a fine specimen of the genuine Menhir of antiquity, there can be no reasonable doubt. It stands on the slope of a hill, about a mile S.W. of Castor Rock, and is evidently in connexion with the avenues and circles, referred to in a former chapter of this work. The stone measures twelve feet in height, and is at the base, three feet by two feet.

The avenues, although presenting the same general features with those at Merivale, are in far less perfect preservation. If any of these parallelithons deserve the name of *Cursus*, which has been sometimes applied to them, from the supposition that they were designed as race courses by our British forefathers, the Longstone Avenue certainly could not have been one. The ground is ill-adapted for the purposes of a hippodrome ; while on the other hand, the construction and arrangements indicate to the believer its character as a *Via Sacra* or *processional* road of Druidical worship, according to the Arkite ceremonial. Beginning on the acclivity above Longstone Maen, the avenue passes over the hill towards the Teign in the direction of the great Sacred Circle on Scorhill Down, above described. The Teign flows at the distance of about one mile from the Pillar, and this row, one hundred and fifty four yards long, terminates in full view of another, near at hand, which runs down the declivity towards the river. At its southern extremity, is a dilapidated cairn, the only example observed in the immediate neighbourhood. The avenue

*W. PENGELLY. Trans. Devon Assoc. Vol. xxii., 1880, p. 365.

instead of being perfectly straight, as at Merivale and Stanlake, in the West Quarter, is in some parts slightly curvilinear. This is the only indication of an ophite feature which we have been able to detect in any of the Danmonian avenues, and it is so slightly serpentine, as scarcely to warrant the belief, indulged in by some, that the vestiges of a Dracontium or Serpent Temple may here be traced. The avenue appears suddenly to stop one hundred and ten yards from the kistvaen. From its second commencement it runs nearly direct, and almost parallel to another at a short distance down the declivity eastward. These two avenues can be traced about one hundred and forty yards, the eastern having its commencement at two large stones lying on the ground on the north side of three concentric circles. There are ten stones in the outer circles, six in the middle circle, and eight in the third. The diameters are, outer circle twenty-six feet, middle circle twenty feet, and third circle three feet. This avenue runs down the hill, becoming more and more imperfect until it disappears for a considerable interval.*
There is however apparently a distinct termination later on, in two erect stones, which stand apart, although evidently in the same line. Great havoc was made with these monuments, when the walls of Thornworthy New-take were erected. At the same time what is supposed to have been a Dolmen, known as the "Three Boys," was destroyed, two of the great stones having been removed. The impost was lost long before.

Taking Castor Rock for our landmark we shall now bend our steps northwards, and on the western acclivity of the hill from which that conspicuous tor rises, we shall notice an interesting specimen of the hut circle or ruined habitation, surrounded by an external inclosure. By the moormen it is well known as the Roundy Pound, and is situated near a moorland road which forms the boundary between the parishes of Chagford and Gidleigh. This consists of an external enclosure in the form of a spherical triangle, with an inner circle nearly adjoining the north west side of the outer enclosure. The walls were probably built of upright rough masonry, those of the inner circle have had care paid them in their erection, and the door jambs still remain. The inner circle is thirty-five feet in diameter and the wall about five feet thick. The area between this circle and the outer enclosure, now a confused heap of stones, was divided into six compartments by

*G. W. ORMEROD. Rude stone remains on the Easterly side of Dartmoor. 1876. p. 9.

narrow walls extending from the inner circle to the outer enclosure. Here is a small hut circle ten feet in diameter at the north angle of the outer enclosure, and a small triangular enclosure adjoins the remains of the outer wall of the western side. The late Mr. Ormerod has[*] described the foundations of other remains situate about a hundred yards to the south of the Roundy Pound, consisting of small enclosures and two huts which he has named the Square Pound. There are no other huts within a hundred yards of these pounds. At Bovey Combe Head there is an enclosure greatly resembling the Roundy Pound, which Mr. Ormerod describes.[†]

Castor Rock rises high above Chagford, and, standing on one of the outposts of Dartmoor, forms a conspicuous object from a large tract of North Devon, and consequently commands a varied and extensive prospect. From Cosdon in the N.W., to Mardon in the E., the eye ranges round a grand amphitheatre of moor and mountain. Besides Cosdon Beacon, Yes Tor, Watern Tor, White Horse Hill, Warren Tor, Heytor, and East Down above Manadon, are all conspicuous eminences. Haldon, the Blackdown hills, and Exmoor, bound the view in the distant horizon. Chagford "tower and town" are seen on the slope below Middledown in front, with the rocky dells and sylvan wilds of Gidleigh on one side, and the glades and groves of Whiddon Park on the other.

On Castor, besides five other smaller ones, is one of the finest, so called rock basins, on the moor, it is seven feet six inches in diameter at the top, four feet two inches, half-way down, and two feet at the bottom, and is two feet seven inches in depth. This basin was discovered by Mr. Ormerod, in 1856, it having been completely concealed by heather and it is now surrounded by iron rails to prevent accidents to cattle. On Middletor, a singular rock on the same common, is another very perfect specimen of the Rock Basin, almost circular in form, and about six inches deep. One side of this tor overhangs at least ten feet, and forms a massive granite canopy, under which the cattle frequently are seen to take shelter. Descending the hill towards Chagford, we pass over Teigncombe Down, where many hut circles, tracklines and other antient vestiges will be noticed. Teigncombe Common lane, through which our course now leads, may be noticed as a

---

[*]ORMEROD. *Op. cit.* p. 11.

[†]*Op. cit.* p. 11.

G

curiosity.   Of all the approaches to the moor, by which turf,
furze, etc., are conveyed to the neighbouring farms and villages,
and cattle driven, this is certainly the most extraordinary.   It is
difficult to conceive anything bearing the name of a road less
suited to the purpose than Teigncombe Common lane, which is
nothing more than a gulley between two hedges.   The steep floor
is bare granite, strewn with boulders and stones of the same
material, many of them deposited there by the force of the
torrents rushing from the hills.   In former years all the turf for
the supply of the immediate neighbourhood was brought down
this lane on packhorses, but since carts have come into general use,
it is now only traversed by the sure-footed moor pony, or by
cattle pasturing on the common above.

In our downward progress, we follow the course of the South
Teign, through broken ground and little verdant crofts, so characteristic of the moorland borders, to Yeo Bridge, passing through
the little hamlet of Teigncombe, where was formerly a chapel, the
ruins of which are still to be seen, served from the mother Church
of Chagford.   Here the banks rise into steep cliffs, and form
richly wooded dells, at the bottom of which, the stream hurries
along, foaming over the rocky masses of which the channel is
formed.   Just below Lee Bridge, is the junction of the North and
South Teign, whose united waters run from thence towards Holy
Street, through the deep and rugged glen which bounds Gidleigh
Park on the south.   Scarcely half a mile above Holy Street, a tor
rises near the river's brink on the south side, called by the
country people the Puckie, Puckle, or Puggie Stone, and celebrated for the large rock-basin, or pan (as it is popularly called)
on its summit.   The antiquary, trusting to local report, will be
disappointed when, after having succeeded in scaling the rock, he
finds that the characteristics of the genuine rock-basin, as herein-
before described, are not sufficiently clear to enable him to
pronounce that this is not one of the examples attributable
exclusively to the operation of natural agencies.   Although of
large size, it is not of the usual circular form, nor do its sides
display any decisive indications of artificial adaptation.*   But if

---

*The author was shown, at the old house at Holy Street, by the late Mr. Nicholas
Clampit, a semi-circular stone which appears originally to have formed half of a
circle of eighteen inches diameter.   There had evidently been a hole perforated in
the centre, about two inches in diameter, and the appearance of the stone altogether
was that of a part of the upper stone of an antient quern or hand-mill.   It had been
dug out of a swampy spot on Holy Street Farm, which Mr. Clampit was engaged in

A TOLMEN.

disappointed in the main object of his research, the explorer will be repaid for his escalade, by the commanding view he will have gained of the wild-wood glen, down which the Teign rushes, foaming along its rock-bound channel, in all the youthful vigour of a mountain-born torrent. And if, on his descent from the crest of the Puckie Rock, he will brave the difficulties of the rugged glen before him, and thread his adventurous path up the course of the North Teign, he will skirt the fine woodland scenery of Gidleigh Park, until he emerges upon the moor, amidst the countless granite masses which strew the steep sides of the declivity, or have been precipitated into the channel of the river, checking the force of the headlong current for a moment, and forming a succession of miniature cascades. Among these, let us pause to remark a singular mass, lying near the right or northern bank of the river, as we ascend the stream, which, had there been no other object of attraction, would repay the antiquary for his walk up this sequestered and romantic glen.

This granite mass, approaching to an irregular rectangular form on its north side, is embedded in the channel of the Teign, and rests on two subjacent rocks, at an angle of about twenty-five degrees. The outline of the stone, above the surface, measures about thirty feet, and near the southern edge is a large and deep perforation, of a form so regular, that at first view, it will scarcely fail to convey the idea of artificial preparation, but a closer inspection will probably lead to the conclusion that natural circumstances, within the range of possibility, may have concurred to produce this singular conformation, although, on the other hand, it is far from improbable, that advantage might have been taken of some favourable accident of nature, and as in the case of the Logan stone, art had perfected the operations of nature, and this remarkable cavity had thus been adapted to the rites of Druidism, for lustration or some other religious ceremonial, which is the tradition connected with this stone by the legendary chroniclers

---

draining. There were several others of a similar description, and one, a perfect circle. with a hole in the centre, taken from the spot at some considerable depth below the surface. If not parts of the antient hand-mills referred to in Holy Writ (Isa. xlvii., 2—Jer. xxiii., 10—Matt. xxiii., 41, etc.) universally used among the nations of the east, and doubtless known to the Phenicians, and to our aboriginal ancestors, I am at a loss to conjecture for what purpose such stones could have been intended. If they really are parts of primitive querns, or hand-mills, then have we in our moorland district, not only numerous remains of the dwellings of the original inhabitants, but a curious specimen of their domestic utensils. The hole is exactly similar to that described by Fosbrooke, as made in the upper mill-stone of the antients, for pouring in the corn. (*Encyc. Antiq.*, p. 308). He remarks that specimens are quite common, and refers to one figured in Montfaucon,

of the moor. But its present condition (as it has no bottom) precludes the possibility of its having been used as a rock basin, except in some extraordinary flood, when the waters of the river might rise above the under surface of the block, and partially fill the cavity so as to admit of its being appropriated to the purposes of a font or lustral vessel. It presents the appearance of a cylindrical trough, hollowed out in the granite, just three feet in diameter at the top, about two feet ten inches at bottom, and two feet eight inches in depth, with a convexity in the middle like a barrel. The outer side, towards the centre of the stream, is partially broken away, thus rendering the cylinder imperfect in that direction, leaving a curved breach in the southern face of the mass, about two feet high, and thus adding to the singular appearance of this curious relic, whether seen from the northern or southern bank of the river. When this breach might· have taken place, and whether in past ages the bottom and side might not have been perfect, can, of course, be only matter of conjecture. Under these circumstances, or on the supposition that the river might occasionally rise sufficiently high to fill the cavity, its being employed for lustral purposes is perfectly imaginable. To this, or some other Druidical ceremonial, it is traditionally supposed to have been appropriated ; and while this primitive font was so used for adults, the legends of the moor relate that a smaller one (which is supposed to have been destroyed) was resorted to for children. Without therefore pronouncing that this was never "a rock" which the Druid "scoop'd to hold the lustral waters," the antiquary will not fail to have suggested to his mind another kind of aboriginal relic, from an inspection of this curious memorial of by-gone ages. From its present aspect, he will probably conclude that it should rather be pronounced a Tolmen ;* and if it really belong to this class of relics, the interest with which we shall regard it, will be much increased, as it is the only known specimen in Devonshire. It has hitherto escaped the notice of topographers and antiquaries ; and while the Cromlech, the Logan-stone, and Grimspound are popularly known, and have been described in county histories and topographical and antiquarian works, this singular relic, unique in its character, and obscure in its destination, is known only to the oral topographers of the moor.

The accompanying circumstances of the tolmen in the Teign

---

*Vide Chap. iii., p. 44.

are strikingly similar.   The sacred circle stands at a short distance on Scorhill Down.   On Middletor, near Castor Rock, on the other side of the Teign, as we have mentioned, is a fine rock-basin.   Not far south-west, is placed the Longstone-pillar, already described, in immediate connexion with the cursus, or paral-lelithons, on the slope of the hill below Batworthy.   Here then, as at Brimham Moor, we find an assemblage of relics, "which "seems to indicate a chosen spot for religious ceremonies;" and here, as in the Yorkshire example, we find the Tolmen in imme-diate connexion with other monuments of primitive character and incontestable antiquity.   Should the tourist, instead of proceeding up the glen from Holy Street, visit the tolmen, from Longstone and the avenues, he will find it by following the course of the Teign downwards, at forty yards from the spot where the Walla-brook falls into that river, immediately opposite a new-take wall, which separates Batworthy from the Moor, and which terminates on the southern bank, in front of the holed part of the stone.

We have remarked that the assemblage of relics at this spot, seems to designate it as a place, dedicated in past ages, to the celebration of religious ceremonies, the general nature of which it is not difficult to conjecture, although it may not be easy to assign to the different monuments, the particular ceremonies for which they were originally designed.   But the observation may be justly extended to a much wider scope, than the immediate precincts of the Teign Tolmen.   The whole neighbourhood is rich in pre-historic remains, and if the antiquary wished to establish himself at a point where, as from a centre, he could, within a moderate circumference, have the means of inspecting a specimen of the several monuments of Danmonian antiquity ; he could fix on no place more advantageously situated for the accomplishment of his wishes, than the pleasant little town of Chagford, where he will find comfortable accommodation at respectable inns, and be placed within reach of those various objects of antiquarian interest and picturesque beauty, with which the neighbourhood abounds.

Chagford itself, as an antient Stannary and market town, built on a pleasing acclivity, backed by the lofty eminence of Middledown, with its jagged crest—a preminent outpost of the granite range—with the moor stretching away indefinitely in the distance, and the diversified vale of the Teign directly in front, is well worthy of a visit.   It presents some of the most interesting characteristics of our moorland border towns. There is an air of picturesque informality in its general appearance. Many of the houses are of moorstone, grey, antient looking, substantial; some with projecting porches and parvis-room over, and granite mullioned windows, while a perennial stream, fresh from the neighbouring hills, and clear as that which flowed from the Blandusian font, speeds vivaciously along the principal street, through a clean moorstone channel. The church, substantially built of native granite, with its sturdy steeple of the same durable material—embattled porch with granite-groined vault, springing from low columns, with Norman-looking capitals—appropriately forms the central and principal object, among the simple buildings of this quiet, retired border-town. The quaint little market-place is in perfect keeping with the accompanying features of the scene. Standing apart from any great thoroughfare, the echoes of the Chagford hills are never awakened by the "twanging horn," nor its streets roused by the rattle of the stage-coach or royal mail. At the door of the Three Crowns, a postchaise is still, nearly at the close of the nineteenth century, enough of a phenomenon, to collect a group of rustic gazers. The carriage-road from Moreton to Okehampton and the north of Devon, passes over Rushford Bridge, about a mile from the town; but the roads and lanes leading to the adjacent parishes, hamlets, farms, and commons, are, for the most part, so steep and rugged, as to be ill-adapted for any vehicles, where springs form an integral requisite in the construction. Accordingly, the methods of conveyance and transit partake of the olden times, and are characteristic alike of the country and the inhabitants. Breasting a formidable ascent on the south, the road to Ashburton is much better adapted to the packhorse of the last century, than to the carts or wagons of the present day; while the upland track—which the western traveller, to his no small wonder, is admonished, by a timely finger post, to follow, as the road to Tavistock—scales a precipitous hill, and would have been far more suited to the wary paces of the palfrey of the abbot of the religious house of that antient town in by-gone days, than to the poles and springs of the Broughams and Britschkas of modern times. Instead of the convenient market-car of the lowlands, we therefore observe, without surprise, that panniers maintain the ascendancy with the rustic dames of the neighbourhood, and the phenomenon of a double horse, with saddle and pad, or even the antiquarian curiosity of a pillion, might recently, and perhaps may still be met with in the rugged and narrow by-ways of a district where rural manners and old-world customs still linger, and find an asylum which modern fashions render every day more precarious and untenable. Among the patriarchs of the hills, the straight-breasted blue coat (the relic and memorial of the 'prentice suit, or the wedding garments) made before the revolutionary innovation of lappels had been imported from republican France, may still be seen with (but a much rarer occurrence), the shoe fastened with buckle and strap, a memorial of the days of "their hot youth when George the "Third was king." In the market and at church the observant eye will trace also among the elder women the vestiges of the fashions of their youth in the carefully preserved red cloak, with its graceful and convenient hood—the respectable looking matronly silk bonnet, edged with black lace, and set off by the becoming mob cap of past generations. On a rainy day, the costume of such a matron will be characteristically completed by the umbrella, with which she protects her head-gear from the impending shower. The faded green cotton material; the stout stick, with a few faint vestiges of original paint, the ring at the top; the substantial whalebone ribs, enough to furnish forth a dozen of the flimsy productions of modern bazaars; the absence of crook and ferule (and every similar contrivance to make the umbrella perform the additional duty of a walking stick) all characterize this as a specimen of original construction, and point to a time when the appearance of this useful invention at a Devonshire church, would cause a general sensation in the congregation, and furnish more than a nine days' wonder to the whole neighbourhood.

Many agricultural implements, which have quite disappeared in the more level districts, will still be found in the homesteads of the hilly country. In such a place as Chagford, the cooper, or rough carpenter, will still find a demand for the pack-saddle, with its accompanying furniture of crooks, crubs, or dung-pots. Before the general introduction of carts, these rough and ready contrivances were found of great utility in the various operations of husbandry, and still prove exceedingly convenient in situations almost, or altogether, inaccessible to wheel carriages. The long crooks are used for the carriage of corn, in sheaf, from the harvest field to the mowstead or barn—for the removal of furze, browse, faggot-wood, and other light materials. The writer of one of the happiest effusions of the local muse, with fidelity to nature, equal to Cowper or Crabbe, has introduced the figure of a Devonshire pack-horse, bending under the " swagging load " of the high-piled crooks, as an emblem of Care, toiling along the narrow and rugged path of life.   *" Care pushes by them, o'erladen with crooks."* This line will be found in " The Devonshire Lane " by the Rev. John Marriott.*   While we can readily imagine that the identical lane which furnished the excellent author with his original sketch, may be found in the neighbourhood of Broadclyst, and while we could fancy that one bowery lane in particular, leading towards Poltimore, might have sat for the picture, yet there are so many of our moorland border-lanes which exhibit an exact family like-ness, that every feature of a scene so faithfully depicted, and so felicitously applied, may be traced in numerous instances, especially in the environs of Chagford, Moreton, Ashburton, and Plympton.

> "In a Devonshire lane, as I trotted along
> T'other day, much in want of a subject for song,
> Thinks I to myself I have hit on a strain,
> Sure marriage is much like a Devonshire lane.
>
> " In the first place 'tis long, and when once you are in it,
> It holds you as fast as a cage does a linnet ;
> For howe'er rough and dirty the road may be found,
> Drive forward you must, there is no turning round.
>
> " But though 'tis so long, it is not very wide,
> For two are the most that together can ride ;
> And e'en then 'tis a chance but they get in a pother,
> And jostle and cross and run foul of each other.
>
> " Oft poverty greets them with mendicant looks,
> And care pushes by them, o'erladen with crooks ;
> And strife's grazing wheels try between them to pass,
> And stubbornness blocks up the way on her ass.
>
> " Then the banks are so high, to the left hand and right,
> That they shut up the beauties around them from sight ;
> And hence you'll allow 'tis an inference plain,
> That marriage is just like a Devonshire lane.

---

*The Rev. JOHN MARRIOTT was not a native of this county, but of Leicestershire. He was Rector of Church Lawford with Newnham Chapelry, in the county of Warwick, but illness in his family, compelled him to live in Devonshire.  Having no cure of souls, he was always ready to assist the clergy at Exeter and Broadclyst. He died 31st March, 1835.  Another poem of his entitled " A Devonshire Sketch " will be found in Everett's " Devonshire Scenery." p. 232.

"But thinks I, too, these banks within which we are pent,
With bud, blossom, and berry are richly besprent;
And the conjugal fence, which forbids us to roam,
Looks lovely when deck'd with the comforts of home.

"In the rock's gloomy crevice the bright holly grows;
The ivy waves fresh o'er the withering rose,
And the evergreen love of a virtuous wife,
Sooths the roughness of care—cheers the winter of life.

"Then long be the journey, and narrow the way,
I'll rejoice that I've seldom a turnpike to pay;
And whate'er others say, be the last to complain,
Though marriage is just like a Devonshire lane."

The force and point of the imagery must be lost to those who have never seen (and as in an instance which came under our own knowledge never heard of) this unique specimen of provincial agricultural machinery. The *crooks* are formed of two poles, about ten feet long, bent when green into the required curve, and when dried in that shape are connected by horizontal bars. A pair of crooks thus completed is slung over the packsaddle; one "swinging on each side to make the balance true." The short crooks or *crubs* are slung in a similar manner. These are of stouter fabric and angular shape, and are used for carrying logs of wood, and other heavier materials. The *dung-pots*, as the name implies, were also much in use in past times for the removal of dung and other manure from the farm yard to the fallows or ploughlands. The *slide*, or sledge, may also still occasionally be seen in the hay or cornfields sometimes without, and in other cases mounted on low wheels, rudely but substantially formed of thick plank, such as might have brought the antient Roman's harvest load to the barn, some twenty centuries ago.*

The primitive contrivance for hanging the gates of the moor-land crofts and commons, may also be seen in this neighbourhood. No iron hinge of any kind, nor gate-post is employed. An oblong moorstone block, in which a socket is drilled, is built into the wall, from which it projects sufficiently to receive the back stanchion of the gate, while a corresponding socket is sunk in a similar stone fixed in the ground below, unless a natural rock should be found *in*

---

*Tardaque Eleusinæ matris volventia plaustra.—Virg. *Georg.* i, 163. These, the Delphin annotator supposes to have had wheels *without spokes*, Plaustra quorum rotæ non erant radiatæ, sed instar tympanorum, e solidis tabulis.

*situ*, suitable for the purpose, which is frequently the case.   The gate thus secured, swings freely, swivel-like in these sockets, and thus, from materials on the spot, without the assistance of iron, a simple, durable, and efficient hinge is formed by the rural engineer.   These contrivances are found in all districts where stone is plentiful, and they are constantly met with in Brittany.   Enthusiasts discover in them Tolmens, and Holed stones, with mysterious attributes.   See chapter iii. and ante, p. 46.

The *flail*,* with its monotonous strokes, still resounds from the barn-doors of all our smaller farms, where economy or attachment to old usages has prevented the introduction of the modern threshing machine.   Still more rarely is the old method of winnowing resorted to ; but in a few instances the *windstow* may yet be seen, where the process is accomplished by simple manual labour—the grain being subjected to the action of the wind, on some elevated spot, and passed through sieves, shaken by the hand, until " clean provender " is produced, like that which was " winnowed with the shovel and with the fan,"† on the hills of Judæa of old.   In this primitive process, the memory of the method of separating the grain from the chaff, so common in our county (before the introduction of the winnowing machine), is still preserved.

When we construct our roads of iron, it may be justly said that we live in an iron age.   Ploughs, harrows and drags, wholly of iron, have superseded the timber framework of those implements to a great extent; but the old wooden plough may yet be seen on some farms, little, if at all, changed in its material parts, from that which the Romans might have taught our rude forefathers to use, when they subjected the western angle of their island to their sway, and induced them to become husbandmen, even if they had not been previously brought to add this useful occupation to their

---

*In Devonshire, the hand threshing instrument is not known by the name of flail. Our vernacular retains the old Saxon word *Therscol*, by metathesis *Threshel ;* and, as in *Dring* for *Thring*, the aspirate *th* changed into *d*, makes it dreshel ; so *thorpe* a village, in Saxon, becomes *dorp*, in Dutch.   In the Lancashire dialect they have the same word, *Threshel*, (identical with ours) instead of *flail*.

†Is. xxxii.. 24.   Our winnowing sieve answers to the shovel here mentioned, and to the fan, (MATT. iii., 12,) which, as SHAW (quoted by Burder, Oriental Customs, vol iv., p. 298) observes is too cumbersome a machine to be thought of, for it is represented as being carried in the hand (" whose fan is in his hand.")   Burder further remarks, " that the Greek word from the verb to spit, spit out, properly " signifies a shovel, whence corn is thrown or spit out as it were, against the wind, to " separate it from the chaff.   That this is the true sense of the word, and not a *fan* " *or van*, is evident from Homer Iliad, xiii., v. 588, where the same Greek word is " used in the same sense and connexion."

more antient one of shepherds and herdsmen.  The antiquary versed in classic lore, will observe with interest, the striking similarity between Virgil's description of the plough, in the reign of Augustus, and that which may still be seen in Devonshire, after a lapse of eighteen centuries.

" Continuo in sylvis magna vi flexa domatur
" In burim et curvi formam accipit ulmus aratri.
" Huic ab stirpe pedes temo protentus in octo,
" Binae aures duplici aptantur dentalia dorso.
" Caeditur et tilia ante jugo levis, altaque fagus,
" Stivaque, quae currus a tergo torqueat imos."
—Virg. Georg., lib. i., 169.

The *buris*, or beam (though not always made of elm) has still a slight curvature.  The *ear* of the ploughshare, by which the sod is turned off from the furrow—the *stiva*, handle (or *haul*, vernacular) by which the plough is guided—and the yoke (where oxen are employed, as is still sometimes the case in Devonshire) formed of the light alder, instead of the lime, or linden tree, which is not so common with us as in Italy—all exhibit a remarkable accordance with Virgil's description, and prove the tenacity with which antient usages maintain their ground among the sons of the soil.  The goad, still in use for guiding, and urging on a yoke of oxen, carries us back even to more remote periods still, although the weapon which Shamgar (Judges iii., 31) wielded with such deadly effect against the Philistines, must have been of a more formidable description than those used by our ploughboys to incite the slow but patient ox to his useful toil.  It would appear, from observations made by travellers in the east, that the antient ox-goad combined in one instrument, the goad properly so-called, used by the ploughboy in driving the oxen, and the implement known to our husbandmen as the *paddle* shovel, for removing the mould which clogs the ploughshare and coulter.  The observations of one of our older travellers, so satisfactorily illustrate the passage above cited from Holy Writ, and so directly connect our old-fashioned husbandry with the practice of eastern nations, tenaciously perpetuated from the earliest ages, as to become peculiarly interesting.  " It is observable " says Mr. Maundrell, " that in ploughing, they use goads of an extraordinary size. " Upon measuring several, I found them about eight feet long, " and at the bigger end, six inches in circumference.  They were " armed at the lesser end with a sharp prickle, for driving the

"oxen, and at the other end, with a small spade or paddle of iron,
"strong and massy, for cleansing the plough from the clay that
"encumbers it in working. May we not, from hence, conjecture
"that it was with such a goad, as one of these, that Shamgar
"made that prodigious slaughter related to him. I am confident
"that whoever should see one of these instruments, would judge
"it to be a weapon not less fit, perhaps fitter, than a sword for
"such an execution. Goads of this sort I saw always used
"hereabouts and also in Syria ; and the reason is because the
"same single person both drives the oxen, and also holds and
"manages the plough, which makes it necessary to use such a
"goad as is above described, to avoid the encumbrance of two
"instruments."* The goads used by our ploughboys are generally
about the same length, with a similar *prickle* fixed in the smaller
end of the pole or stick, which, however, is of slighter make,
being used only for driving the oxen, while the paddle-shovel
stick (and it is to be noticed that Maundrell uses our provincial
term), would just correspond in size with that which our traveller
noticed as still used in the country of the heroic Hebrew, who,
like another Tell, roused, perhaps by some crowning act of
wanton outrage, from his peaceful occupation, to withstand "the
"fury of the oppressor," found an extemporaneous and efficient
weapon *(furor arma ministrat)* in that implement, which, probably, the jealous policy of the Philistines might allow the
oppressed Israelites to sharpen, as in the disastrous reign of Saul,
when "they had a file for the mattock, and for the coulters, and
"for the axes, and to sharpen the goads." (I Sam. xiii., 21.)

"Not rural sights alone but rural sounds," as the poet of the
country—Cowper—so smoothly sings, "delight" those whose minds
are not so absorbed by one particular pursuit as to render them
insensible to every other object of interest and gratification. The
plaintive strain, or peculiar kind of recitative which the ploughboy
chants to his team, as he directs or urges them onwards, is both
"musical and melancholy ;" especially when it comes wafted up the
hill by the fitful winds of autumn, or the gusty breezes of spring. It
is probably a custom of considerable antiquity, and its singularity in
keeping with the slow and measured pace and pensive looks of the
oxen—their necks bent earthward by the yoke, but patient of
toilsome march through the furrows all the livelong day. A team

---

*MAUNDRELL. A Journey from Aleppo to Jerusalem.

of four or six fine oxen forms one of the most pleasing accidents of an agricultural landscape ; but one looks with almost Levitical repugnance at the ill-assorted combinations which sometimes present themselves, by the harnessing of bullocks in the same team with the horse or the ass (Deut. xxii., 10.)*

While in the midst of scenes and sounds like these, the valetudinarian may successfully " woo Hygeia on the mountain's " brow,"—the artist may richly replenish his sketch-book—the botanist store his herbarium with specimens of moorland flora†— and the geologist fortify his theories of volcanic protrusion, or aqueous deposits, from phenomena presented in the abrupt hills and deeply-scoop'd valleys around ;—the antiquary, with whose pursuits this work is more immediately concerned, will find himself most advantageously stationed at Chagford for visiting such monumental relics as the columnar circle on Scorhill Down—the tolmen—the stone avenues with the Longtone Maen—the Roundy Pound, Castor Rock—hut circles, on Teigncombe Down—the rock-basins, on Middletor, and the Puckie Stone, as well as those near Sandypark—the Drewsteignton cromlech—the Logan-stone, in the Teign, near Whiddon Park—Cranbrook Castle on the heights immediately above, and Prestonbury, near Fingle Bridge. All these, and many more antiquarian objects of minor importance, lie within a circle of which Chagford is the centre, with a radius of not more than three miles, so that a pedestrian may, without difficulty reach them all, " albeit unus'd," it may be, to moorland explorations.   But many a zealous investigator would not find it a task too arduous to extend his perambulations (even without the aid of a moor-pony or vehicle) from hence to the Grey Wethers circle, to the avenue and circle near Fernworthy, to the pounds on Shellstone hill, to Cranmere Pool, or even to the top of Cosdon. Nor let the explorer of our upland wilds be deterred from the excursions thus indicated, by calculating his powers of locomotion from the result of his pedestrian efforts along a muddy lane, or a dusty highway.   With the springy turf at his feet, and with the mountain air above and around him he will find his step acquiring

---

*Agricultural progress has extended to Dartmoor and the levelling down process has affected the former simplicity of the dwellers herein, both in manners and costume.   We shall look in vain now for many implements and some customs and peculiarities of dress which were common when the first edition of this work was published.

†The bright green and Glomuliferous Parmelia (*Parmelia glomalifera*) and the Resupinate Nephroma (*Nephromia resupinata*) will be found on the rocks and trees in the immediate neighbourhood.—(See chapter xvii.)

unwonted elasticity and vigour, and will be enabled to accomplish, without undue fatigue, over the free and breezy moorlands, a distance which would present a toilsome, if not an impracticable task, in the beaten and confined thoroughfares below.  We shall however now proceed to visit, in succession, those objects which have not already been noticed, or which from their importance, demand a more detailed account than has been given in the introductory chapters.

Among these, the Drewsteignton cromlech holds a pre-eminent place.*   It has been noticed that the character and position of the abacus may probably be traced in the name of the adjoining farm.  But without relying too much on the controverted evidence of etymology, the name of the parish is much more important, since it has been confidently appealed to as intimately connected with and directly relating to, the aboriginal relics with which the environs abound.   Polwhele's enthusiasm has led him to regard these relics, viewed in connexion with the name, and with local circumstances, as pointing to the very metropolis of Druidism in the West—the seat of the regal, or arch-druidical court.   That such courts existed in countries where the Druidical religion prevailed, there can be no doubt in the minds of those who are acquainted with Cæsar's clear and circumstantial account of the nature and extent of the authority, exercised by that powerful priesthood in Gaul.†  Nor can we hesitate in coming to the conclusion that similar authority was wielded in Britain, whence, as it has been already observed, the Gauls derived their knowledge of Druidical system.   But whilst the existence of such courts in Britain will hardly be disputed, the precise spots where they may have been held must ever remain a subject of pure conjecture.   Monumental relics are the only guides in the absence of historic testimony.   Presumption, therefore, is in favour of a spot where an unusual congeries of Druidical relics still exists—

---

*For the reasons given in the preface here and throughout the book, many of these Druidical speculations are allowed to stand as in the former editions.

†Writing of the order of men called Druids, CÆSAR shows that their authority extended to the most important questions of litigation, ecclesiastical and secular. If any recusant opposed their decision, the ghostly terrors of excommunication were resorted to, for the purpose of enforcing the sentence of these absolute judges :—nor were the decrees which were issued from the solemn groves of the central Carnutes, less formidable than the interdicts which in after ages, were fulminated from the Vatican.   " Nam fere de omnibus controversiis, publicis privatisque constituunt ; et si quod est admissum facinus ; si cæde facta si de hæreditate, si de finibus controversia est, idem decernunt; præmia pænasque constituunt."   CÆSAR, Bell. Gall., lib. vi., 13.

DREWSTEIGNTON CROMLECH.

and such a spot is certainly found in the immediate neighbourhood of the Drewsteignton cromlech—where the conditions requisite to make out a case *(prima facie)* are probably less equivocal than in Anglesea, where Rowland and others have traced vestiges of the seat of an Archdruid. Our Devonshire cromlech is incomparably more striking and curious than that at Plas Newydd, on the Menai Strait ; nor is that accompanied by such an assemblage of relics, as enriches the neighbourhood of Drewsteignton. With all due allowance for local predilection, and for the sanguine conclusions of the antiquary, whose wish is confessedly often " father to his " thought," the following observations of Polwhele, with reference to this point, may not be deemed altogether unworthy of consideration. " If we confine ourselves within the limits of Devon " and Cornwall, and fix an archidruidical seat in the west, I should " imagine that Drewsteignton would be the most eligible spot. " The very name of *Drewsteignton* instantly determines its " original appropriation to the Druids. And that this *'town of the* " *Druids, upon the river Teign,'* was the favourite resort of the " Druids, is evident from a great variety of Druidical remains in " the neighbourhood of the town . . . . The only remaining " cromlech in Devonshire marks this spot as more peculiarly the " seat of the Druids. And the Archdruid perhaps could not have " chosen a more convenient place for his annual assembly."

After controverting the opinion entertained by Westcote, Risdon, and Prince, that the prefix of Drew is derived from Drogo, who held lands in the Parish, in the reigns of Henry II., and Richard I., Chapple—to whose treatise on the Cromlech, reference has been previously made, proceeds to trace the origin of the name, to the occupancy of the Druids, more than a thousand years before.* " As we find it called Tegn' Dru or Drues- " Teignton, in other antient records, it seems to me most probable " it was thus distinguished, as having been before the Roman " Conquest, the residence of a principal Druid. For, that some " considerable one governed here, and had great numbers under

---

*This theory of Chapple, aroused the ire of Sir Edward Smirke, and he wrote to Mr. Pitman Jones, falling foul of Druids altogether, calling them bearded old mistletoe-cutting humbugs, whose assistance was always invoked to set two stones on end, or to bore a hole in a boulder. " Indeed their whole time must have been " spent in hauling about lumps of granite, and their habitual residence must have " been upon the tops of moors and wastes, where neither oaks nor mistletoe are " ever likely to have flourished." This little outburst of Sir Edward's, set the example, and induced some recent writers on the Moor, to rush to the other extreme, to deny that there ever were any Druids. There is not, however, the slightest evidence of Druids or Druidism in connection with Dartmoor.

"his command, may fairly be inferred, from this stupendous
"monument of their labour and skill.   And that its present name
"was formed from Druid's Teignton, has been the opinion of
"most persons who have seen its cromlech, and judged it to be a
"Druidical structure, though uncertain for what purposes it was
"erected.   Hence also, Drewston,* the name of a farm there, had
"probably its origin, having been perhaps once the seat of some
"Druid or Druids, and as such, called by the Saxons, Drewston,
"from some such name of the like signification, given it by the
"Britons.   And the like, may be observed of another Drewston,
"situate in the adjoining parish of Chagford, but on the other side
"of the Teign."†

Should the tourist regard these etymological and antiquarian
speculations as of any validity, they will increase the interest with
which he will proceed to visit the cromlech and its associated relics.
Who can affirm that this was not the place, or one of the places,
to which these Gauls resorted, whose anxiety for a more perfect
initiation into the mysteries of Druidical lore, would lead them to
Britain, to inbibe draughts of instruction at the fountain head?‡
Without, however, venturing to fix the precise spot, it is scarcely
within the bounds of probability that no such establishment
existed in or about Dartmoor, where so many Druidical vestiges
abound; and if this be granted, I know no situation where, from
existing circumstances, it might be sought for with greater
promise of success, than in the neighbourhood of the Drewsteignton
cromlech, unless the neighbourhood of Wistman's Wood might
dispute the claim, and challenge for itself the honours of the
*gorseddau* and Druidical college.   With what additional interest
will the explorer look down from the Puckie Stone upon the oaken
groves which overshadow the channel of the Teign, when he
thinks that in the same spot, and beneath former generations of
similar oaks, the Druid might have celebrated his dark and blood-
stained rites, or instructed those who, perhaps, from the remotest
parts of Gaul, had repaired hither to consult the hierophants of
their mystic creed!   And as he threads his way down the romantic
glen, towards Holy-street, a deeper horror will envelope those

---

*Drewsteignton is also frequently abbreviated to Drewstone by the country
people.   It is also sometimes called Teignton, without the prefix.

†CHAPPLE'S uncompleted work, "Description and Exegesis of the Drewsteignton
"Cromlech."   1779.   p. 30.

‡CÆSAR, *Bell. Gall.*, lib vi., 13.

venerable woods. Association will not fail to enhance the interest of the scene, rich as it is in intrinsic charms. And few spots can boast natural features more striking and lovely, while the works of man, where they interpose, are so harmonious in their character, as to be in perfect keeping with the works of nature. The mill, at Holy-street—the substantial dwelling-house hard by with high pitched roof and gables, mullioned windows and low-browed doorways, all of enduring moorstone, its quaint terraced garden, trim with ever-green hedges, its enclosed paved court, with a crystal streamlet running through to join the river below—all suggestive of old hereditary occupancy and rural quiet—and all felicitiously harmonizing with the sequestered and sylvan character of the surrounding scenery.

If the opinions of some antiquaries are to be credited, in passing from Holy Street homestead along the margin of the Teign, we are treading the Via Sacra of the Druids, which, it is conjectured, might have led from hence to the Cromlech itself, about two miles distant. The name of Holy Street is too signifi-cant to be lightly passed over ; and whatever may be said of many other etymological speculations, we believe it is generally held as an established canon in archæology, that the word *street* applied to roads in different parts of the country, may be regarded as conclusive evidence of the existence of some antient paved high-way in or near the spot. Such was probably the road passing along this romantic woodland glen, where it expands into a vale at the foot of the acclivity, on which the town of Chagford is built. Whether the Holy Street lane is to be pronounced the Via Sacra, or processional road of the Druids, leading (it may be) from the Cromlech to the Tolmen and Sacred Circle, or not, it would seem impossible to emerge from the narrow lane (by which we came down from Teigncombe Common, to the South Teign and the Puckie Stone) as it winds by Holy Street house, and pass into the sylvan glade, which then opens before you, without feeling, that few spots more likely to have been dedicated to the purposes of the Druidical consecrated grove, could be found in the whole island. Even now the venerable oaks towering aloft from the grassy floor, strewn with moss-grown rocks, and spreading a deep religious shade around, can scarcely fail to suggest thoughts of our barbarian forefathers, congregated at the summons of the mighty priesthood, in such a scene as this, "inflaming themselves with idols, among the oaks," (Is. lvii., 5).

H

But when, in addition to the oaken grove, on the level—the moss-covered rocks, and the darkly flowing river—all the surrounding eminences rose, thickly garnitured with primeval woods, it seems morally certain, that a scene so characteristic and appropriate, could not have been overlooked by the Druids, in a district where, as we have already seen, such unequivocal traces of their ritual still remain.

We will now proceed along the valley towards Chagford Bridge, since, if there is attention to be given to the etymological inferences drawn from the name of Holy-street, the Via Sacra could scarcely have taken any other direction, than that indicated by the course of the river.    But before taking a final leave of Holy-street, let us remind those whose predilections may lead them to regard these antiquarian speculations with the indifference, if not with the scornful scepticism, of an Ochiltree, that the feature of natural loveliness in this dale are so manifold and striking, that they will not fail to repay the " pilgrims of beauty " for a visit to this sylvan shrine, on the verge of the moorlands, especially if they should make their pilgrimage after the early frosts have tinged the oaken grove with the varied hues of autumn.    Nor will the botanist, in his return from lichen hunting among the rocks on Teigncombe Common, or the woods in Gidleigh Park, fail to observe, in the clear and rapid mill-leat by the road side, the luxuriant water plants, mantling the stones deep in the stream—green as an emerald, and thick and wavy as the tresses of Sabrina's hair, when evoked from her " coral paven bed," by the potent spell of the Miltonian muse.

Having reached Chagford Bridge, we shall find our way along a pathway on the north bank of the Teign, until we reach Rushford Bridge, where the road from Moreton to Okehampton crosses the river.    Turning to the left, at Rushford Barton, we mount the woody ridge which rises at the back of Sandy-park. On the summit we shall find a number of tors and boulders scattered along a strip of verdant turf, which seems to have given rise to the name of the " Bowling-green," by which it is (or was) known among the neighbouring peasantry, while the convivial designation of "the punchbowl " was given to a rock-basin on one of the masses which crest the hill.    Descending on the other side we shall soon regain the road, and after proceeding northwards about a mile, shall reach the Cromlech, which will be found in a small level field belonging to a farm called Shilston, adjoining

the road, which here proceeds eastward to Drewsteignton church-
town, from which the Cromlech is distant about a mile and a
quarter, and from whence it can be most conveniently approached
by visitors from the east and north. Chapple describes its
situation as " nearly in the middle of the county of Devon, being
" within two miles and a half of the centre of its circumscribing
" circle. From which circumstance, by the bye, ' continues this
" author,' we might infer the fitness of the place for a Druidical
" assize, supposing (what however we can at this distance of time
" have no certainty of) that the present limits of this county were
" then also, nearly, the boundaries of a distinct province of
" Druidical government, in this western part of Britain."

This venerable monument is popularly known by the name
of the Spinsters' Rock ; the origin of which appellation is thus
accounted for by the same writer who learnt it as the traditions of
the neighbourhood—" their common saying is, that it was erected
" by Three Spinsters, one morning before their breakfast. These
" *Spinsters* tho' the appellation among lawyers is peculiar to
" Maiden Women, but seems to be originally derived from the
" common Employment of young girls in former ages, the
" Inhabitants represent, as having been not only Spinsters in the
" former Sense, but also Spinners by Occupation. For according
" to their account, they did it after finishing their usual Work, and
" *going home with their Pad*, as the phrase here is; that
" is carrying home their pad of Yarn to the Yarn-jobber, to be
" paid for spinning it : And on their return, observing such heavy
" materials unapplied to any Use, and being strong Wenches,
" (Giantesses we may presume, such as *Gulliver's Glumdalclitch*,
" or the Blouzes of *Patagonia*,) as an Evidence of their Strength
" and Industry, and to shame the Men who, either from Weakness
" or Laziness, had desisted from the Attempt, they jointly under-
" took this task, and rais'd the unwieldy Stones to the Height and
" Position in which they still remain. This is the Tale, which
" they say has been handed down to them from Generation to
" Generation : and thence they tell us, this romantic Structure had
" its name."* Nor is the memory of this legendary fable extinct
at the present day. Whilst, however, Mr. Chapple records the
tradition, he by no means acquiesces in the derivation of the term,
but appends a conjecture of his own, " taking for granted that the

*CHAPPLE. "Description and Exegesis of the Drewsteignton Cromlech," pp. 98,
99.

" original Name of this *cromlech* was expressive of the Use for
" which it was design'd . . . . Why then might not the
" Astronomical *Druids* give it some Celtic Appellation significant
" of that Use ; such as *Lle Yspiennwr rhongca*, (in the *British*
" Dialect of the *Celtic*,) The *place* of the *open* or *hollow Observatory?*
" or possibly *Yspienddyn Ser rongca—The open Star-gazing*
" *Place.*"*

Without venturing to pronounce between the rival claims of
these "astronomical Druids," and the stalwart spinsters of
traditionary fame, it may be worth while to look a little further
into the bearings of the legend.   Shrouded under the wild
extravagance of the popular fable, there may lie some mythic
notion of antient and wide-spreading prevalence—or even some
historical truth of revelation, however perverted.   May we not
therefore, possibly, detect in the legend of these three fabulous
spinners, the terrible Valkyriur, of the dark mythology of
our northern ancestors.†   Or if the statement of a writer,
quoted by Polwhele, be correct, the tradition with regard to the
builders of the cromlech, varies, and that in some cases, he found
its erection attributed to three young men, instead of young
women.   "But," continues this writer, commenting on Mr.
Chapple's observations, "the tradition goes farther and says that
" not only the three pillars were erected in memory of the three
" young ones, but that the flat stone which covers them, was
" placed there in memory of their father, or mother, according as
" you supposed the young ones to be male or female, and that

---

*CHAPPLE.   *Op. cit.* p. 104.

†The Fatal Sisters, the choosers of the slain, whose dread office in the wild and
gloomy mythology of the Norsemen, to "weave the warp and weave the woof"
of Destiny, is thus celebrated in the lyric strains of the English Pindar :—

" Glittering lances are the loom,
    Where the dusky warp we strain,
Weaving many a soldier's doom,
    Orkney's woe and Randver's bane.

" See the grisly texture grow,
    ('Tis of human entrails made)
And the weights that play below,
    Each a gasping warrior's head.

" Shafts for shuttles, dipt in gore,
    Shoot the trembling cords along ;
Sword, that once a monarch bore,
    Keep the tissue close and strong.

" Mista, black terrific maid,
    Sangrida and Hilda, see,
Join the wayward work to aid—
    'Tis the woof of victory."
                              —THOMAS GRAY, *The Fatal Sisters.*

"each of these, both young and old, fetched these stones down
"from the highest parts of the mountain of Dartmoor, where, for
"some reason or other, they had thought fit to take up their
"residence.  Perhaps the expression, Lle Y'spinnwr, which the
"author seems to think a *spying* or *surveying* place, might give
"rise to the idea of spinners, and thus turn into three *ladies*.
"But you will, perhaps, guess why I incline to suppose these
"stones might be erected, among other reasons, in memory of
"*an old man* and his *three sons*, who descended from an exceeding
"high mountain, on a certain occasion."*

What was the occasion alluded to by this writer, it is not
difficult to divine ; and if Druidism is indeed no more than a
corruption of a religion, diffused throughout the world in the
earliest ages, by the descendants of the three diluvian patriarchs,
after the division of the world in the time of Peleg (*Genesis* x., 25)
then will this conjecture, as to the legend of the cromlech, be
found of more importance than might at first appear.  This
opinion will also derive strength from the fact, that an examination of the situation and circumstances in which the cromlech is
placed, has led to the conclusion that there are other relics
immediately adjacent to the cromlech, which are strongly indicative of Arkite worship.

All these poetical theories must be abandoned.  There can be
little doubt but that the Cromlech, or Dolmen as it should be
called, was similar to others in Wales and Brittany, and was
primarily, a place of burial, standing by itself, or being a central
chamber, approached by a covered way.  In either case it would
have been covered with a mound of earth, which has now by the
forces of nature and the hand of man, been destroyed.

The satellites which Polwhele mentions as attending the
Drewsteignton cromlech—"two rows of pillars marking out the
"processional road of the Druids, and several columnar circles,"
and "rock idols at the end of the down, that frown with more
"than usual majesty," will now be sought for in vain.  But on
the north side of the road by which the cromlech field is bounded,
there were objects highly worthy of examination, generally overlooked, and now altogether lost, and probably unknown to many,
whose interest was absorbed in the celebrated Spinsters' Rock.
Very fortunately the late Rev. William Gray, in 1838, with his
brother, visited the Cromlech and its surroundings, and carefully

*POLWHELE. *Historical Views of Devonshire.* p. 79.

examined and mapped the remains referred to on the north side of the road bounding the Cromlech field.   He says that there are two concentric circles of stones, the inner circle having entrances facing the cardinal points, that to the north being sixty-five paces in length and five paces broad.   The outer circle, besides these, has avenues diverging towards the N.E., S.E., S.W., and N.W., and a smaller circle seems to intersect the larger, of which the avenue eastward is very evident.   Mr. Gray measured the remains and made a plan of them on the spot, which plan he completely finished the same night at Okehampton.   In 1872, Mr. Gray mentioned the fruit of his visit so many years before, and the results to the late R. J. King, who communicated them to G. W. Ormerod, which resulted in a memoir by the latter, printed in the Archæological Journal.*   These most remarkable remains seems to have been carted away from time to time for building purposes, and the last of them disappeared in 1865, when the few remaining, were used as materials in the erection of a new farm house in the neighbourhood.

On Friday, 31st January, 1862, the Drewsteignton Cromlech fell.  G. W. Ormerod soon visited the spot, and wrote, " The southerly and easterly stones had given way, and the first " had fallen leaning against the northerly stone, the two others " were under it ; judging by the small depth of soil on the ground, " it is a wonder it did not fall before."   The fallen Cromlech was re-erected in November of the same year, at the cost of Mrs. Bragg, of Furlong, under the superintendence of the rector of the parish, the Rev. William Ponsford.   A full account of this restoration will be found in the memoir above referred to.†

Bradford, or Bradmere Pool, a few hundred yards north of the cromlech, is now generally supposed to be the site of an antient tin mine.   With less regularity of outline in its banks, it would approach more closely to the appearance of a mountain tarn, than any piece of water in our western moorlands.   It covers an area of about three acres; of a rectangular form, about forty yards wide, and not less than one hundred and eighty long, is said to be seventy-five feet deep, and is surrounded on all sides by trees. There seems to have been a provision for draining this piece of water, should occasion require.   On the south side, the bank rises

---

*Journal of Royal Archælogical Institute, 1872, vol. xxix., pp. 348-350.

†Arch. Journal, vol. xxix., pp. 346-348.   See also Trans. Dev. Assoc. Vol. iv. 1871, pp. 409-411, and vol. v., 1872, pp. 73-74.

steeply from the brink of the pool, and forms apparently the slope
of an earthwork, where the vestiges of a ditch or moat can
be traced, surrounding a mound of an elliptical form, measuring
on the top, one hundred feet, by one hundred and thirty feet.
There are too many indications of regularity and design, to admit
of the supposition that this mound is nothing more than the upcast
of an abandoned mine : but if it should be thought that the
traces of entrenchment are not sufficiently decisive to warrant its
being regarded as having been constructed for the purposes of
defence ; there is yet another hypothesis, which would assign its
erection to the earliest periods of history, and connect it with the
artificial formation of the adjoining sheet of water, and the
legendary erection of the cromlech, as notice above.

We have before us the MSS. notes of Col. Hamilton Smith,
on these relics, after a visit to the spot, in which he marks
the appearances which presented themselves to our notice, and
records the conclusion to which he had arrived from a personal
inspection.   " The sheet of water, or dub, embracing a part of
" the sacred hill, and probably a sacred grove, having on one side
" an oblique communication with the water, by a gradual ascent,
" occurs in other places, particularly in two similar monuments
" of Celtic origin, among the Savern hills and the Vogesian
" mountains, where altars, sacred inclosures, and consecrated
" pools of great depth, occur, as here.   Forests surround them, as
" was no doubt the case, also, at Shilston.   As for the sloping
" ditch, forming a road, it may have served for the covered coracle,
" containing the novice in his mystic regeneration, and second
" birth, to be drawn up from the waters to the mimic Ararat of
" Gwidd-nau."

"Worship on high places," says Mr. Harcourt, "imitations or
" at least memorials of Ararat—was a characteristic feature of the
" diluvian rites," and the same author has adduced a number of
instances to show, that where natural hills or mountains contiguous
to, or peninsulated by, water, did not occur, that the memory of
the diluvian mountain would be preserved in artificial mounts and
pools, such as Col. Smith supposes those at Shilston to have been ;
where, as it has been shewn, the artificial piece of water, *Dub*,[*]
is in immediate connection with an artificial mound.   The reasons
for this he traces to a traditionary recollection of the altar built
upon Mount Ararat, by Noah, and to a supposed injunction of

---

[*] " *Dub*, in Chaldee, is to flow."—*Doct. Del.*, vol. ii., p. 417.

that patriarch to his descendants to construct their altars in such
situations as would preserve the memory of that awful catastrophe,
and that the cause of the deluge was the impiety of mankind.
" Thus every high place devoted to religion would become a sign
" or emblem of Ararat. . . . . All indeed, who retained any
"reverence for the patriarchal precept, would avoid a long residence
"upon extensive plains, because it would deprive them of their
"hill altars.   When, therefore, the rebels of Shinar, in opposition
"to the Divine will, determined not to be dispersed, their leaders
"could not devise a more politic plan for keeping them contentedly
"in the plain, than by building an artificial mountain to be their
"place of worship, that the name of the Lord might dwell there."*
Our author further shows, from a variety of evidence, that
" the mountain was honoured, first, as the throne of the avenging
" deity, and, secondly, as the sanctuary of peace, which was
" first disclosed by the retiring flood.   At the same time," he
continues, " there is distinctly visible an idolatrous disposition to
" transfer the glory of the Creator to the creature, either to the
" mountain or the man, which extended itself even to the remotest
"islands scattered in the Pacific Ocean, and must, therefore, be
" admitted to exhibit, in the strongest light, the indelible per-
"manence of its character, and the antiquity of its origin."
" Those," says the missionary Ellis, " who were initiated into
" the company of Areois, invoked the Mouna Tabu, or sacred
" mountain, which it further appears is exactly like one of the
" mountains or mounds which were held sacred by the Celts, for it
" is conical and situated near a lake, and what is most material
" to this enquiry, the natives have a tradition which shows at
"once, the reason of its being Tabu, or sacred.   The Sandwichers,"
says the missionary, " believe that the Creator destroyed the
" earth by an inundation that covered the whole earth except
" Mount Roa, in Owhyhee, or Hawaii, on the top of which one
" single pair had the good fortune to save themselves."†
If, therefore, it should be questioned whether the evidence of
the existence of such a sacred mound and lake‡ at Bradford Pool,

---

*Doct. Del., vol. i., p. 149.

†Doct. Del., vol. i, p. 378.

‡Among the legends of the neighbourhood, may be mentioned one, which relates
that there is a passage lined with large stones (high enough for a man to walk
upright) from this lake to the Teign, near the Logan Stone. . This seems to point to
a covered way connected probably with the Cromlech, the *allee couverte* of the
Brittany dolmens.

as are above described, is sufficiently conclusive, it must be admitted that the spread tradition of the deluge, in connexion with consecrated mountains may justly be alleged as an argument in its favour. If the memory of that "overwhelming flood" is preserved at the antipodes in our own times, it can scarcely be imagined that it had not reached our Celtic ancestors, two or three thousand years ago, by means of their intercourse with the Phenicians, even if it had not been brought hither by aboriginal settlers from the east. In that curious specimen of our antient native literature, the Welsh Triads, we accordingly find an express mention of the deluge, in the account of the bursting forth of the lake Llion, by which the face of the earth was over-whelmed, and all mankind drowned, with the exception of a single pair, who escaped in a boat, and subsequently re-peopled the island of Britain.

The tradition of the deluge being thus manifestly familiar to the primitive inhabitants of our island, it is far from improbable that indications of its existence would be found in their religious rites and monumental relics. And if, as some antiquaries contend, cromlechs are Arkite cells, not only is plausibility added to the conjecture, which interprets the legend of the erection of the Drewsteignton cromlech, by three young men and their father, who came down from the heights of Dartmoor, as origina-ting in an obscured and perverted tradition of Noah and his three sons,—but the probability of an Arkite character pervading the accompanying archæological relics is increased in proportion.

In 1871, a bronze palstave was found at Drewsteignton, five and a half inches in length, and weighing fifteen ounces. It had no side loop or ear, A portion of a bronze *cake*, whatever that may be, was said to have been found with it.

We shall now proceed eastward, by the Drewsteignton road, to Stone Cross, the origin of which appellation we shall have no difficulty in tracing to the far-famed crom-lech. Turning out of that road, at the cross, we shall take the right-hand lane, and passing by Stone Farm and Parford, shall reach Sandypark at the crossing of the roads to Okehampton and Moreton, Chagford and Exeter. Here at the wayside inn, the stranger may obtain directions for finding his way to the Logan-stone, should the route now indicated be insufficient for that purpose, which, however, will scarcely be the case. The

Moreton road from Sandypark will lead us directly to the bridge
over the Teign, within a furlong from the inn.   We shall not cross
the bridge, but shall follow a beaten path on the left, down the
river, along the northern bank.   Following the course of the
stream, as it winds through the meadows, we shall soon reach
that point where a rock-crested headland rises abruptly above the
little lateral vale of Coombe, on one side, and the wooded steps of
Whiddon Park press forward to narrow the valley, on the other.
Scarcely a quarter of a mile from this point, by keeping close to the
river's brink, on the north side, we shall discover the Logan-stone.
Should the explorer inadvertently follow a more accessible track,
which winds along the side of the hill, at a short distance above
the river, he may pass the Logan-stone without noticing it,
among the numerous masses of granite with which the channel of
the Teign is profusely strewed; but by making his own path close
to the brink, he will not fail to find the object of his search,
rising boldly out of the bed of the river, near the northern bank.
It is an irregular pentagonal mass, the sides of which are
of the following dimensions.   Eastern, five feet four inches
in width; northern, seven feet eight inches; north-west, six
feet four inches; south-east, five feet four inches; and the
southern, towards the river, ten feet six inches.   It is about
seven feet and a half in height at its western corner.   This
huge mass rests on a single rock, and still *loggs* perceptibly,
but very slightly, by the application of a man's strength; but
the motion must have been greater in former times, especially
in those early ages when possibly its nicely-adjusted equipoise
was rendered subservient to the purposes of Druidical or other
delusion.

Proceeding down the river we shall be greeted with some of
the most striking vale scenery in the west of England.   The
course is a continuous succession of graceful curves; the banks
on the south, or Moreton side, clothed with wood and heather,
as high as the eye can reach, and on the Drewsteignton slope
presenting abrupt and bare declivities occasionally interspersed
with craggy projections, beetling above our rugged, but romantic
pathway.   In one particular spot, high in the abrupt declivity,
two bold cliffs will be observed, jutting out from the hill, like the
ramparts of a redoubt, guarding the narrow pass below.   Lower
down, the northern bank becomes wooded and the path, proceeding
through a tangled copse, at length emerges upon the Drewsteignton

E.T. Widgery. Pinx.

W.L.Colls. Ph. Sc.

FINGLE BRIDGE.

and Moreton road at Fingle Bridge.* Here let us pause on its
narrow roadway—just wide enough for a single cart—to gaze
from its grey moorstone parapet, on a scene, the general features
of which may be recorded by the pen, but of whose particular
features of loveliness, the pencil alone can convey an adequate
idea. Three deeply-scooped valleys, converging to one point—
two or three little strips of greenest meadow-sward, occupying
all the narrow level at the foot of the encircling hills—the fortified
headland of Prestonbury, rising bold and precipitous, its rigid
angular outline strikingly contrasted with the graceful undulations
of the woody slopes which confront its southern glacis—the mill
at their base embowered in foliage, and the river, clear and
vigorous, giving animation to the scene without marring its
sylvan seclusion,—all combine to form a scene of surpassing
loveliness, which it is a disgrace for any Devonians not to have
visited, before they set out in search of the picturesque, to Wales
or Cumberland, or the highlands, and, still more, before they
make their continental peregrinations,

> " Or by the lazy Scheld, or wandering Po ;
> Or onward, where the rude Carinthian boor
> Against the houseless stranger shuts his door."†

---

*Some topographers, misled by sound, or anxious to impart an Ossianic character
to the spot, have spelt this word, Fingall. Mr. Shortt derives Fingle from *Fyn*,
Cornish, a boundary, and *Gelli*, hazel. But oak is the characteristic tree of this
moorland boundary, and not hazel. May not *Gill*, the well-known designation of a
water-fall among the Cambrian Celts, form part of the original word which would
then be *Fingill* ? *Fingill* would mean the White Waterfall.

†GOLDSMITH, The Traveller.

# CHAPTER VI.

### The Perambulation Continued, Fingle Bridge to Ashburton.

PROCEEDING from Fingle Bridge, we shall now mount the adjacent hill towards Moreton, by a steep mountain road, at whose narrowness and ruggedness we shall not for one moment repine, since it retains enough of primitive simplicity, and freedom from modern improvement, to make the supposition perfectly credible, that it is the identical track by which our aboriginal forefathers maintained a communication between Prestonbury fort and the champaign country beyond, and Cranbrook Castle on the crown of the hill above, and the moorlands of the interior.  So steep is the ascent, that it can only be accomplished by a succession of zigzags; and these, at the several angles, present the most favourable points for commanding the romantic scenery of the vale of the Teign below. At one of these elbows, about half a mile up the hill, the view is so striking that it will amply repay those who perhaps generally content themselves with the more accessible beauties of Fingle Bridge for the trouble of the ascent.  The road passes through oak copse, which shuts out all but glimpses of the surrounding scenery, until you reach this point, when a scene of singular loveliness bursts upon the sight.  We look down upon the wooded glen, through which the Teign winds its devious course from Chagford to Fingle Bridge.  Five projections of hills fold in behind one another, the last on the right bank, being the craggy ridge above the Logan-stone, and on the left, the wooded declivity of Whiddon Park.  Imagine the morning to be still, and partially overcast (and to be seen in perfection we should reach our point before the sun has passed the meridian) such a sky as we often have in August and September, when the lazy clouds, pacing slowly along, throw one part of the landscape into dark shadow, while the other remains in uninterrupted sunshine.  The narrow vale of the Teign seen from this spot, thus enveloped in shade, seems to sink deeper down into gloom and pleasing mystery. Beyond its western gorge, in the middle distance, cornfields, pastures, groves, cottages, and farmsteads, are glowing beneath the sunbeams in distinct and characteristic colours, while Cosdon from these peculiar " skiey influences," borrows more than his natural elevation, and towers, in purple majesty, high in the distant west.

At the angle of the next zigzag, we look down upon Prestonbury, and enjoy a favourable opportunity for obtaining a bird's eye view of the fortifications of this remarkable headland ; and shall be better able to estimate the wisdom of our British ancestors, in fortifying this important position, which, as has been already observed, seems intended to command a border pass from the champaign country, north and east, by the ford, or bridge (which, probably of cyclopean construction, existed even in the earliest ages) into the moorland district, then the favourite habitation of the hardy Danmonian Britons.

Emerging from the copse, the road still winds upward through a common, richly embroidered with the purple heather, golden furze, and green whortle.  Arrived at the top, a grass path turns off from the beaten road over the common to the left, by following which we shall soon find ourselves within the area of another of these hill-forts, of which there was an evident chain guarding the moorland frontier.  Cranbrook Castle occupies the highest ground of all the neighbouring forts; and whilst it would be chosen for the purposes of defence, it seems impossible to observe how it commands the whole of the vale of Chagford, the country round Drewsteignton, together with a vast tract of Dartmoor, south and west, and a considerable extent in north and east Devon, without concluding that it would be also used as a *speculum*, or watch-tower, and that an alarm would be often given from this height by the kindling of the beacon-fire.

Mr. Shortt describes Cranbrook Castle as "consisting of a "vallum, or agger of moorstone, without cement, about seven "acres in extent."  Lysons mentions it "as an irregular encamp- "ment, containing about six or seven acres, with a double ditch "on the south, a single ditch on the west, and none on the north "and east."  It is six hundred and sixty-six paces within the rampart, the inner slope of which, on the south side, is about twenty-one feet, the outer forty-two feet in height.  It is quite clear that the north side (towards the deep vale of the Teign) was never so strongly fortified as the southern and western sides, where the hill is much more accessible.  No one can visit this interesting monument of antient days, without grieving to observe the wanton spoliation to which it has been exposed by reckless ignorance and parochial parsimony.  We perceive, with indigna- tion and regret, that the rampart has been resorted to (and that in a country where stone is found at every step in redundant profusion) as a convenient quarry for road material.  In one spot, on the west, we found the vallum, or rampart, had been dug up to the very foundations.  Our lamented friend and antiquarian coadjutor, the late Henry Woollcombe, of Plymouth, first called attention to this gratuitous spoliation, and in 1840, Mr. Shortt brought it under the notice of the late Col. Fulford, whose regard for the venerable relics of antiquity, we rejoice to say, immediately led to securing this interesting relic from total destruction. W. P. Shortt in his "*Collectanea Curiosa*," (*p.* 26) gives the following account:—" The composition of the vallum, or agger, "is chiefly moorstone, loosely piled together, of no great height, "in some parts grauwacke or shillet.  Part of both have been

" broken into small fragments, as material for the adjacent roads,
" and ready for removal.  I took the first opportunity of remon-
" strating in the proper quarter, against this vandalic piece of
" profanation, which is of a piece with that which, in other parts
" of the kingdom has fast obliterated the traces of many noble and
" venerable works of antiquity, . . . . and hope to save the noble
" camp from future devastation, by the mediation of a trustee of
" the property, the public-spirited representative of the antient
" house of Fulford."   " The agger of granite at Cranbrook, may
" have been British," continues Mr, Shortt, " and the shape on
" the north-east and south-west, which is not entirely circular,
" may perhaps lead some to suppose it was an *aestivum*, or summer
" camp of the Romans."  But Mr. Woollcombe, in his manuscript,
containing the results of his examination of more than fourscore
of these antient hill-forts in Devon,* unhesitatingly pronounces it
to have been a British settlement.   " Cranbrook Castle, near
" Moreton," he writes, " is situated in that parish.  It is con-
" structed on the brow of a hill, above the Teign, commanding
" most extensive views on every side ;  to the north, seeing hills,
" which I conclude must be in the neighbourhood of Barnstaple,
" Coddon Hill and that range ; to the south, seeing the barrier of
" Dartmoor.  On this side, Cosdon is magnificent ; and many
" tors adorn the scene, especially Heytor, in the south-east
" quarter.  Towards Exeter the view is uncommonly rich, as it
" is likewise westward, though not equally so.  This castle is
" evidently the remains of a British town of large dimensions,
" being surrounded by a single rampart only, and one ditch on the
" outside.  The vallum has been composed of stones principally,
" but many have been dug up to make fences, yet still enough
" remains to attest the antiquity of the structure."  On revisiting
Cranbrook, Mr. Woollcombe made a more particular examination of the ditch and found it double, on the south, as before
stated.

Returning by a grassy path to the Moreton road, we shall
soon reach a weather-beaten granite guide-post, at a crossway.
Turning to the right, we shall follow the old Exeter and Chagford
road, down the hill, as it skirts Whiddon Park, and thus completing our circuit, return to Chagford to prepare for our next
excursion.

Having mounted the hill immediately above the town, and

---

*This manuscript is now in the Library of the Devon and Exeter Institution.

examined the rock-basins on Middledown, we shall proceed by the Tavistock road, towards the moor, in the direction of Jesson. Near this place, the road passes through a moor-gate, where the place of gate-posts is supplied by two natural masses of granite rock. On the top of that on the right, are three rock-basins, one of which is very perfect and well-defined. On the opposite rock, there are some cavities, evidently of natural formation, presenting a marked contrast to the artificial appearance of the former.

Pursuing our course in a westerly direction, we shall enter upon the commons, towards Broadmoor mires and Bushdown Heath, one of the spots where a few black grouse still find shelter in the heathery cover. Here the hills begin to swell boldly from the lowlands, and numerous springs trickle from the bogs to render their tribute to the neighbouring Teign. The scene which here presents itself, might have formed the original of the moorland border picture, so graphically sketched by the truthful pencil of Walter Scott. "A few birches and oaks still feathered the "narrow ravine, or occupied, in dwarf clusters, the hollow plains "of the moor. But these were gradually disappearing, and a "wide and waste country lay before them, swelling into bare hills "of dark heath, intersected by deep gullies, being the passages by "which torrents forced their currents in winter; and during "summer, the disproportionate channels for diminished rivulets "that winded their puny way among heaps of stone and "gravel, the effects and tokens of their wintry fury, like so many "spendthrifts, dwindled down by the consequences of former "excesses and extravagance."—*Old Mortality*, chap. xv. Many of these streams, such as Shute Lake, are tributaries of the South Teign, towards which we shall now bend our course for the sake of visiting the Grey Wethers, by this route, should the tourist prefer it to the excursion along the North Teign, already pointed out. Passing between Loughten Tor on the left, and Fernworthy on the right, we shall follow the principal stream of the South Teign, in a westerly direction, and having traced it to its source, within a mile of Sittaford Tor, shall be in a position to command a full view of these remarkable circles. Seen from this spot, we shall readily trace the popular designation to the appearance, which at a distance, these time-worn masses would present to the moorland shepherds, of a flock of sheep, pasturing on the common. But the more poetic eye, will rather here realize the image of a group of overthrown Titans, as "bodied forth" by the bard, who might almost be supposed to have sketched, on this spot, the grand and gloomy imagery of one of the most striking scenes of his " Hyperion."—

> " One here, one there,
> Lay, vast and edgeways, like a dismal cirque
> Of Druid stones, upon a forlorn moor,
> When the chill rain begins at shut of eve,
> In dull November, and their chancel-vault,
> The heav'n itself, is blinded throughout night."
>
> —KEATS, Hyperion.

These circles have been already referred to in the preceding chapters (pp. 30, 94) nor shall we find anything at Sittaford Tor sufficiently attractive to induce us to extend our excursion in that direction. We shall therefore retrace our steps along the eastern bank of the south Teign. Here the moormen will point out to us the dark green spikes of the Sparrow-grass, which they affirm to be of the most deleterious quality, if eaten by bullocks before Midsummer, but perfectly harmless and nutritious for cattle, after that season of the year.* Continuing by a moorland cart-track, in the same direction, we shall soon pass Mevil, near which is the moor-gate bounding the parishes of Lydford and Chagford. Following this track, with the Teign on the left, flowing below Thornworthy Tor, we shall cross Tawton Common, where are some faint vestiges of tracklines, and a hut circle of the ordinary description, about thirty feet in diameter. From hence we may vary our route by following the lane nearest to the Teign, through Gully Hole, instead of taking the road which passes immediately below Middledown to Chagford.

Bidding farewell to Chagford, we shall proceed by the high road to Moreton Hampstead, our next station, passing Wick Green—a name in which will probably be traced vestiges of an antient *Vicus*—and Drewston,† the place referred to by Chapple, quoted above, as indicating, together with Drewsteignton, the former haunts of the Druids. Moreton is situated on the turn-pike road from Exeter to Plymouth and Tavistock, and is the market and post-town of a considerable district. In the situation of Moreton, and the objects by which it is surrounded, we shall

---

*We have not been able to ascertain what species of grass is here referred to, or indeed, to verify this observation in any way.

†FOSBROOKE derives the similar name of Drewson, a village in Pembrokeshire, from a Druidical circle formerly there. *Ency. Antiq.* p. 508,

I

not fail to observe evidence sufficient to convince us that the true orthography of the name is Moortown, and to none of our border-towns could the appellation be so properly applied, encompassed as it is by a noble amphitheatre of hills and moorlands, at a greater or less distance in every direction. Moreton is a clean-looking, cheerful little town, built on a gently-rising knoll. The streets are irregular, and many of the houses are of that antient and substantial character which marks the neighbourhood of the moor. The sunken cross, leaning against an old pollard elm, in the principal street—the open arcade of circular-headed arches (a relic of the early part of the seventeenth century) in front of the old poor-house, and the church, with its lofty granite tower, will all be noticed as characteristic and interesting features in the scene. From the brow of the knoll on which the church is built, one can scarcely look forth on the surrounding eminence without being forcibly reminded of the hills which stand round about Jerusalem, as beautifully described by the sacred lyrist in Psalm cxxv. And while our thoughts are thus directed to Him, whose omnipresent power stands round about His people, the rock-idol, which rises darkling from yonder rugged steep, and Heytor, with its rock-basins, looming huge and grand in the southern horizon, carries the thoughts back to "the vanities" of our heathen forefathers, and to the sad spectacles which their blood-stained altars presented, in contrast with the pure and peaceful shrines of our Christian England, consecrated to the service of "the True God, and Jesus "Christ whom he hath sent."

Let us now proceed to examine the relics, which can be conveniently visited from Moreton as a central point. Taking a northward direction, the ground we traverse will be adjacent to that which we passed in our excursion to Cranbrook Castle. Leaving the town by the old road to Exeter, we shall mount a steep ascent, and, at about the distance of a mile and a half, shall diverge to the right, across the common, to examine the antiquarian relics on Mardon Down. But before leaving the road, let us pause to cast a glance at the landscape which stretches away to the south, as we shall never see Heytor to greater advantage than from this point. The view of Moreton and the surrounding country is also very interesting. Mounting the northern slope of Mardon, we shall notice some aboriginal relics. Among these, the most conspicuous is a circle, thirty yards in circumference, with nine stones remaining erect in their original position, one of which stands two feet and a half above the surface, and is of similar form with the jambs of hut circles, in other parts. The collection of small stones in the area, would rather convey the notion of a dilapidated cairn from which the greater part of the stones had been removed. Near the circle are some tracklines, two of which intersect each other. Mounting the hill and bearing towards the south, in search of the Giant's Grave, on the S.E. side of Mardon, we shall notice the remains of a cairn, which seems to be the relic so designated. The Rev. W. Ponsford told the author, and Mr. Shortt says, that the tumulus of the giant, on Mardon, was unfortunately stripped of its granite to repair the roads, and the place of sepulture was nearly obliterated. Turning northwards again, and following a moorland track over the common, we shall leave Butterdon Down high on the left, and return by the old road from Moreton to Clifford Bridge, passing Pinmoor (more correctly perhaps Penmoor) in our way to Wooston Castle. Near a finger-post, where a road branches off to Chagford in the direction of Cranbrook Castle, we shall diverge to the left over a common, overgrown with heath and furze, which slopes northwards in the direction of the Teign. The ground has evidently been much disturbed, and it is traditionally reported in the neighbourhood that the appearances here presented are vestiges of antient mining operations, but some of them look much more like fortifications, in connexion probably with Wooston Castle, which we shall now proceed to examine, as it is immediately in front, rising boldly above the wooded glen of the Teign.

Wooston Castle is by far the most curious and interesting specimen of antient castrametation, in the whole of our moorland region. Mr. Shortt pronounces it to be a British camp, and justly conjectures it, with Cranbrook and Prestonbury, to "have been one of a chain of forts on the Teign." The camp itself is an earthwork of an irregular oval form, but there are subsidiary entrenchments and other works, in immediate connexion with it, of an exceedingly interesting description. The site itself is worthy of remark, as occupying much lower ground than the hill which ascends immediately behind it on the south. But in relation to the valley of the Teign, it rises high above a precipitous, wooded cliff. It would appear, therefore, that the greatest danger was apprehended from the north, where, probably in the lowlands, tribes of different manners and hostile dispositions were seated, against whose incursions the Danmonian highlanders found it necessary to guard their frontier. The camp occupies a platform, or ledge, on the side of the furzy hill, above described. On the north and west sides, the rampart follows, for the most part, the natural outline of the ground, which sinks deeply down towards the river. The rampart, or vallum, is accordingly very inconsiderable, where the ground itself rendered the camp impregnable. On the north, west, and part of the east side, the rampart is unprovided with a fosse, but on the southern side there is a deep ditch, and a rampart at least ten or twelve yards in average height, from the bottom of the trench to the crest of the vallum. The line of circumvallation on the south and west sides can be distinctly traced to an extent of two hundred and forty yards. The late Henry Woollcombe gives the following description of the subsidary earthworks. " About two hundred feet up the hill, " towards the south, where the castle was very defenceless, another " considerable rampart was made, with a deep ditch on the outer " side. On the eastern side of the castle, and immediately " communicating with it, is a covered way, which descends to the " river, and might afford shelter for access to the fortress. But " from whence it communicates with the camp, it proceeds up " the hill for some distance beyond the second rampart, and " terminates in a mound,* which, apparently, may have been used " as a fire-beacon, as from hence may be seen Prestonbury and " Cranbrook Castle on one side, and Holcombe and Perridge† " on the other, and an immense extent to the northward. Higher " up the hill, adjoining the road to Moreton, another piece of " rampart occurs, totally unconnected with the castle. This has " much the appearance of the banks raised by the Romans for " their roads, but it is an isolated piece, which I could trace no " further. It is true the ground adjoining is cultivated, and, " therefore, its continuation may have been obliterated."— *Fortified Hills in Devon, MSS.* The notion of the fire-beacon on the south, in connection with the principal work, removes a difficulty which occurred to us when we observed that from the castle itself so few of the neighbouring hill-forts could be seen. Neither Cranbrook nor Cotley are in view from that point, but

---

*A deep trackway, or ditch, appears to lead into the work from the upper part of the hill, and there is, besides, a small crescent-shaped redoubt, or outwork, above the camp, and facing to the west. SHORTT. *Collectanea*, p. 28.

†Better known by the name of Cotley, on the crown of a conical Hill, in the N.E. corner of the parish of Dunsford, commanding a fine view of Exeter and the vale of the Teign. The adjoining field is still called Castle Field.

since these and others can be commanded from some spot within
the entrenchment, the choice of this situation for a fortified post
is more intelligible ; yet should we be far from concluding that a
work of such extent was ever constructed for the purposes of a
beacon only, as appears to have been sometimes supposed, from
Mr. Shortt's pertinent remarks on the subject. " The shape and
" defensive lines of Wooston and its adjacent colossal brethren,
" must put an end to the hypothesis of their being mere beacons,
" on which no such labour was needed to be lavished ; nor were
" they the Gorseddau, or British courts, seats of judgment and
" Gorseddadleu, convened in the open air, on the tops of hills, for
" the same ostensible reason, any more than astronomical observa-
" tories of Druidism."

Taking advantage of the covered way, above described by
Woollcombe, by which our ancestors resorted to the river for
water or other purposes ; at the interval of twenty centuries, we
shall follow their footsteps through brakes and thickets, down to
the south bank of the Teign, where it forms a sharp bend
immediately beneath the natural glacis of the castle. From hence
we shall make our way, by a beaten path—where occasional
difficulties will scarcely do more than increase the interest of the
walk along this sequestered dell—until we reach Clifford Bridge,
where the old road from Moreton and Chagford passes eastward
to Exeter and Crediton.

The scenery here, though not so bold and romantic as at
Fingle, is varied, pleasing, and characteristic. The river glides
away in a graceful sweep below thickly-wooded acclivities on the
right bank towards Dunsford. The country on the eastern side,
though inclosed and cultivated, rises scarcely less boldly, and from
several points commands highly-interesting views of the course of
the Teign, as it flows down through its woodland gorge from the
western moorlands. Prestonbury, with its bold angular headland,
scarped down to the river's brink, forms a prominent object in
front of the deep, wooded glen beyond, while the giant bulk of
Cosdon shuts in the scene in the distant west.

Crossing Clifford Bridge we shall diverge from the Moreton
road, and follow a pleasing rural lane on the right hand, which at
first, skirts along the eastern bank of the river, but soon striking
into the inclosed country, leads us through the charmingly-situated
village of Dunsford to Dunsford Bridge, where the features of
natural beauty, though of similar character, are more striking than

those at Clifford. We now find ourselves on the direct road from Exeter to Moreton, and, as we mount the hill, looking down a precipitous slope to the river on the right, shall notice the peculiar characteristics of the scenery of the upper Teign, in the steep cliffy banks of reddish gray rock, shouldering back the course of the river—the protruding banks being bare and rocky, and the corresponding recessions on the opposite side being, for the most part, woody. These characteristics prevail along the course of the Teign, in a greater or less degree, from Whiddon Park to Dunsford Bridge. Many patches of the shelving bank on the north side, studded with groups of low brushwood, with the gray debris of the rock scattered between, will recall, on a small scale, the appearance of Fairfield Hill, above Rydal Mount, Westmorland, as seen from the top of Loughrigg, on the opposite side of Rydal Water.

Still following the turnpike, we shall observe a wild brow rising on the left above the road, called Woodhill, where huge boulder masses project from among the furze and heather; the first characteristic and unequivocal indications of our approach to the great granitic district of Devon from the east. We shall continue to follow the road until we reach the top of the hill, at the crossway, where a finger-post points out a road to Crediton on the right, and a lane on the left leads to Blackystone. By taking the latter road, and proceeding eastward, we shall soon discern this remarkable tor, rising in sombre majesty from the common. It consists principally of two huge masses of natural rock, the upper, crowning its colossal supporter, with an immense granite cap. This tor, like its twin-brother, Whitestone (or Heltor, as it is more generally called), forms a conspicuous object to the whole country round, and as far south as the mail road, near Bickington, it may be seen peering over the edge of Peppern Down. Leaving Blackystone by the road which winds round its base, we shall proceed somewhat to the north, and, at about the distance of a mile, shall reach Heltor, which occupies a more commanding position than even Blackystone, as the hill on which it stands rises abruptly from the vale of the Teign. Hence it is discernible from a greater distance to the north and east, than its giant brother is to the south. Viewed from Dunsford and the immediate neighbourhood, it wears the appearance of some antient castle-keep, draperied with ivy, and built to defend the pass below. On a closer examination, it is found to consist of two distinct, but

closely adjacent piles, on the top of which are rock-basins; three
on the northern pile, and three on the southern. One of these is
considerably larger than the others. They are all of irregular
forms; the larger about three feet in diameter. Thus, on the
eastern confines of the moor, Heltor and Blackystone are stationed
at the gates of the wilderness; the Teign, which flows hard by,
forming the natural boundary of the Dartmoor district; and the
former of these remarkable tors, rises, as we have seen, immediately
above the southern bank of that river.

Heltor stands about a mile north of Bridford Church.
Proceeding to that village, and going along the road to Exeter,
about a quarter of a mile, we shall observe in a field on the right,
adjoining the lane, a conglomeration of stones, looking like the
remains of a dilapidated cairn. In this heap of small stones, two
tabular masses, appearing originally to have formed the side
stones of a large kistvaen, are placed in a parallel position, the
largest, six feet wide, three feet above the surface, and about
eighteen inches in average thickness.

Proceeding southward from Bridford, we shall mount the hill
which rises in front of the village, to visit Skat Tor, remarkable
for its singular conformation. The south front is graduated into
a series of rude seats or steps, leading to a broad platform, on
which is placed a mass of rock, with a smaller one at the side, as
if it might have been the result of art. We do not find that Skat
Tor ever enjoyed the reputation of a logan-stone; but if so, this
curious appearance would, in all probability, be satisfactorily
explained. Skat Tor occupies a commanding situation above the
vale of the Teign, between Bridford and Christow.

Retracing our steps by Blackystone to the Moreton turnpike,
we shall pass near a farm, called Moor Barton, in the parish of
Moreton, where, at no distant time, there existed a cairn, which
was destroyed by the occupier, in carrying into effect some agricultural improvements on the estate. The tumulus, Mr. Shortt
says, " was nine landyards round, in which a sort of rude kistvaen,
" of six great stones, was found, with a spear-head of copper, the
" two pegs, or screws, which fastened it to its staff; a glass British
" bead, and a small amulet of soft stone—memorials of some chief
" —calcined bones, ashes, &c."*—The spear-head, glass bead,
&c., which were taken from the kistvaen, were for some time in
the possession of the Rev. Mr. Carrington, late vicar of Bridford,

---

*SHORTT. *Collectanea*, p. 29.

and are important in the chain of evidence by which the occupancy of this part of the island in remote ages is established.

Following the turnpike as it winds down the hill towards Moreton, one of the finest of our moorland border landscapes expands before us. The greater portion of the amphitheatre which sweeps round the town, is seen from a most favourable point of view. The huge dorsal ridge of Hameldon stretches far across the western horizon, while along the Bovey vale, southward, the eye looks down a long-drawn vista, where the picturesque forms of the ground, and the rich variety of foliage irresistibly attract the attention, and make us resolve to obtain a nearer view of the individual features of this charming scene, assured that they will lose nothing of their attractions on a closer inspection.

Our next excursion will therefore lead us by the Bovey and Newton road to Lustleigh, which we shall reach (within five miles), by diverging to the right. Lustleigh Church is placed on the pleasant slope of one of our deepest Devonshire coombs,* where the most pleasing features of village scenery are happily combined, whilst not a single uncongenial object intrudes to mar the keeping of the harmonious whole. A clear vigorous stream, ripples cheerily down the dell—to turn the busy mill at the end of the hamlet; graceful shelving acclivities partitioned by varied foliage into green crofts, or blooming garden grounds, substantial farm-steads, and whitewashed cottages, peep from among the orchards, or are nestled under sheltering trees. Boulder rocks, with thicket and copse interspersed, protrude from the soil, on the higher ground, while the far-famed Lustleigh Cleave with its granite barrier, fences in the vale from the storms of the neighbouring moor. The combination of rural scenery of this particular class, thus presented in this sequestered spot is certainly not surpassed, if equalled, in any other part of Devonshire.

Passing from the church up a steep bridle road, to a nearer examination of the Cleave, we shall find it to be a genuine moorland clatter, where amidst the wilderness of granite masses, it will be difficult to detect the particular block which is said to be a logan-stone, but where many are so placed that they might be easily made to logg, and some may have thus moved, without strictly claiming the honour of the antient logan. But if we should

---

*Coomb or coombe, from the English *Coomb*, a low valley. This term is peculiarly descriptive of the curved hollows which are scooped out in the sides of our Devonshire hills, especially in the sandstone formation.

fail in identifying any Druidical relic in this rocky labyrinth, the smiling coomb of Lustleigh below, contrasted with the stern magnificence of the moorland heights above, will abundantly repay the trouble of the explorer; and some will think the picturesque masses of rock with shrubs and foliage springing up from their fissures in the evergreen crofts of the little hamlet of Hammerslake just below, are more worthy of notice and admiration than the more conspicious and celebrated Cleave itself.

Returning through Lustleigh to the turnpike road, we shall leave it at a place called Slade, where a lane on the left mounts the hill eastward. On reaching the hill, by turning to the right, and proceeding along the crest of the eminence, we shall reach Bottor Rock, a conspicuous tor,* at the extremity of the headland which rises above the valley of the Teign and Bovey Heathfield.† The huge block on the highest part of the tor tradition says was formerly worshipped as a rock-idol. Some vestiges of antient remains have been discovered in the immediate vicinity, which were described long ago by the late W. C. Radley, of Newton Abbot. About three hundred yards S.W., in a large field called Brady Park, two rock-circles, concentric, one within the other, may still, in part, be seen, the one, measuring from the centre of the inner circle on either hand, thirty-eight feet and a half, to the verge of the outer circle, gives a diameter of seventy-seven feet, divided thus : outer wall four feet thick, then a circular space eighteen feet wide to the inner circle. The second wall is four and a half to five feet in thickness, and the diameter of the area within is twenty-four feet. It had been hollowed out to a lower depth than the surrounding ground. Both walls are neatly formed without cement, of rough unchiselled blocks of sienitic rock, the smooth faces being placed within, and without having the central part filled up with the smaller fragments, as stone walls are at present made.‡ From Bottor Rock which presents a noble panorama of varied interest, bounded by Haldon, the heights of Dartmoor and the coast, we shall bid farewell to the Teign, which has so long been the companion of our wanderings. We shall mark its course along the deep vale on the

---

*Bottor may be easily visited from Chudleigh, from which it is scarcely three miles distant.

†Bottor, near Hennock, has oak trees growing in its clefts, and at its feet are hollows, like caverns, lined with *byssus aurea*, which, according to De Luc, at particular spots, and in certain lights, displays a very glittering appearance, of a greenish hue.—*Notes to* Carrington's *Dartmoor.*

‡Letter by W. C. Radley, *in Woolmer's Exeter Gazette, Nov.*, 1841.

left, with the pleasant town of Chudleigh and its characteristic cliff, on the eastern bank. Below Chudleigh Bridge, it sweeps in front of the stately groves of Ugbrook Park and loses the character of a moorland stream. Leaving the narrow vales and deep glens through which it has hitherto pursued its devious way, it now enters upon the wide alluvial plains of Teigngrace and Kingsteignton, and through meadow, copse, and pasture, meanders, in gentler mood, along a gravelly channel to its estuary at Teignmouth.

Leaving with reluctance this pleasing scene of alternate softness and grandeur, and descending the hill by another lane, with the church-town of Bovey Tracey on the left, we shall cross the valley to the banks of its neighbouring tributary stream, by some called the West Teign, but described by Risdon, as the Bovey. Here we shall strike upon a road skirting the common below Yarnour Wood, and following the direction of a guide-post, pointing to Manaton, shall proceed to Becky* Fall—a considerable cascade on the Becky, a branch of the Bovey river, which we shall find by turning out of the road on the right, and repairing to the stream in the wood, nearly opposite to Lustleigh Cleave, about a mile from Manaton. When the river is not diminished by summer draughts, nor impoverished to furnish water-power for some adjacent works, it rolls down in a fine foamy volume, over a succession of rock stages, about seventy-five feet in height, from top to bottom. The fall is thickly overshadowed with foliage, and the general effect is pleasing, and characteristic of a moorland torrent. But if the tourist should be disappointed in his expectations, and find an insignificant rivulet trickling down through the moss-covered rocks, he should remember that the most celebrated waterfalls in the lake country are subject to the same contingency. Lodore, at the head of Derwentwater, whose " splashing and flashing and dashing and crashing," has been sung in echoing numbers by a laureate, will often be visited, when in the tamed and diminished stream, the sanguine admirer of Southey would be at utter fault in discovering " how the water " comes down from Lodore," in all the thundering magnificence of wintry streams or summer torrents, as faithfully represented in the simulative strains of the sportive muse.

Leaving Becky Fall, and proceeding up the hill side, S.W.,

---

*Beck, in the North of England, is the common term for a mountain rivulet. May we not here trace the etymology of *Becky* ?

F.J.Widgery.Pinx.　　　　　　　　　　　　　　　　　W.L.Colls.Ph.Sc.

BOWERMAN'S NOSE.

we shall notice a dilapidated cairn, with a trackway, bearing in some places the appearance of an imperfect avenue, or parallelithon, coming upwards N.E. from the valley, and ending, after a course which can be traced two hundred and forty yards, in the cairn above. We shall here find ourselves on a moorland road leading from Heytor to Manaton, and returning towards the latter place, we shall pass the small field on the right hand, where the singular elliptical circumvallation, before mentioned (p. 60) was formerly to be found but which no longer, unfortunately, attracts the attention of the antiquary and the tourist.

Our road will now lead us through Manaton church-town, screened from the north by a rugged tor, which rises immediately behind it. The steeple is of less sturdy appearance than some of our moorland towers, but in the western front, it has a massive two centred pointed granite doorway, of almost cyclopean character, but which is fifteenth century work. We shall notice with satisfaction, in passing, the simple rural churchyard, with its well-kept turf, and venerable yew, and the village green adjoining, a pleasing accompaniment, which one would rejoice to see connected with every hamlet in the kingdom.

Following the road to North Bovey, we shall pass below East Down, a detached pyramidal hill, forming a conspicuous object to all the country round. We shall be disappointed in our search for any antiquities on this eminence, although it is plentifully strewed with masses of the natural rock. Polwhele records the existence of a logan, formerly on this common, called the Whooping Rock, but which had been wantonly moved from its balance, some years before that author wrote his account. He describes it as " evidently a Druidical logan-stone," and says it " has been " venerated by the superstitious neighbourhood as an enchanted " rock, from the time of the Druids to the present day."

North Bovey, at the foot of the hill, is a village of similar character to Manaton (having also its well-planted green, or playstow, in front of the church), but with more picturesque accompaniments in the meanderings of the beautiful stream below, which we shall cross in our return to Moreton.

Our next excursion will cause us to retrace our steps to North Bovey, on our way to Bowerman's Nose, but when about a quarter of a mile from Manaton, leaving that village on the left, and crossing a tributary of the Bovey, we shall mount the hill by a moor-tract passing over Heighen or Hayne Down, in front of that remarkable pile. Bowerman's Nose,* as it is popularly called, rises from the brow of the headland which projects from Heytor and the hilly track, between the dale of Widecombe and those of Manaton and North Bovey. It is seen to greatest advantage when approached from the north by the road we are now traversing; and is found, on examination, to consist of five layers of granite blocks piled by the hand of nature—some of them severed into two distinct masses; the topmost stone (where we presume the nasal resemblance is traced), being a single block. Polwhele seems to have been mistaken in calculating the height at fifty feet; it is rather less than forty above the clatter from which it rises conspicuous from its position, and remarkable for its form, it is easy to conceive that this fantastic production of nature, might have been pointed out to an ignorant and deluded people as the object of worship; nor is it unworthy of remark that, viewed from below, it strongly resembles the rude colossal idols, found by our navigators when they visited Easter Island, in the Southern Pacific; and when seen from the south, on the higher ground, it presents the appearance of a Hindoo idol, in a sitting posture.

It is only on the spot that we can duly appreciate Carrington's graphic and faithful description,

> "On the very edge
> Of the vast moorland, startling every eye
> A shape enormous rises! High it towers
> Above the hill's bold brow, and seen from far,
> Assumes the human form; a granite god—
> To whom, in days long flown, the suppliant knee
> In trembling homage bow'd. The hamlets near,
> Have legends rude connected with the spot
> (Wild swept by every wind), on which he stands
> The giant of the moor."

Among the unnumbered shapes, which, as our poet so truly sings,

> " By Nature strangely form'd—fantastic, vast,
> The silent desert throng."—

Bowerman's tor will always occupy a position of highest rank,

---

*The cognomen of Bowerman. In his notes to Carrington's Dartmoor, ed. 1826, p. 193, Burt says—"It is generally considered as a rock idol, and bears the name of "Bowerman's Nose, of which name there was a person in the Conqueror's time, "who lived at Houn Tor or Houndtor in Manaton." The Editor is unable to verify this.

HOUND TOR WITH CIRCLE.

for its singular natural conformation, and for the legendary
recollections with which it is associated.

Among the numerous masses by which the hill-side is plentifully strewn, may be observed one, so well suited for the purposes
of a logan-stone, that very little artificial adaptation would be
required to impart to it considerable vibratory motion. A trackline connects the tor with another tor, southward, on the same
hill.  From this headland we look down upon Manaton.

Leaving the height, and proceeding southward, we shall soon
enter the Ashburton road, and passing through a moor gate, shall
not fail to remark a lofty tor on the left, the north front of which
presents the appearance of a mimic castellated building with two
bold projecting bastions.  On closer examination we shall find it
to be Houndtor, one of the most interesting of the tors on the moor.
The top of the hill is flanked by two colossal walls, piled up of huge
granite masses, sixty, eighty, and in some places probably a
hundred feet high, with an open space between forming an
esplanade where Titan sentinels might have paced along, or rebel
giants might have held a council of war.  Returning from Houndtor about a furlong south we shall pass the kistvaen described
above (p. 43) and follow the Ashburton road, until at the foot of
Rippon Tor, where the road diverges to the left, bringing us very
soon to Heytor—which from its commanding position on the
south-eastern frontier of the moor—at the head of a wide
expanse of declivities sloping directly down to the level country
(through which the great mail-roads from Exeter to Plymouth
passed, by Totnes and Ashburton, in full view of the tor for many
miles) is probably more generally known and admired than any of
its granite kindred of the waste.  Heytor rises from the brow of the
hill with sombre grandeur in two distinct piles, and when viewed
from the neighbourhood of Kingsteignton, and other adjacent
lowlands, under the influence of a sullen and cloudy sky, presents a
singularly accurate resemblance to a ruined castle, the massive
keep of which is represented by the eastern pile.  On the top is
a rock-basin, two feet and a half in diameter, but much less perfect
than Mistor Pan and many others.

We shall now find ourselves amidst "the sights and sounds"
so eloquently described by William Howitt.  And if our visit can
be so timed, we may even realize the characteristic accidents
which will not fail to enhance the intrinsic loveliness of the scene.
Here are "the wild thickets and half-shrouded faces of rock ;—the

" tors standing in the blue air in sublime silence, the heather and
" bilberry on either hand showing that cultivation has never
" disturbed the soil they grew in ; " and here, too, perchance, "one
" sole woodlark from the far-ascending forest on the right, filling the
" wild solitude with his wild autumnal note." We shall look with
eager interest for that "one large solitary house in the valley
" beneath the woods," which he has commemorated; and,
contemplating the manifold variety before us, of rock and
mountain, flood and fell, wood and meadow, busy towns and silent
wastes, the level flat of Bovey Heathfield and the beetling steeps
of Dartmoor, the placid estuary of the Teign, and the wide
expanse of ocean seen over the rock-bound coast stretching far
away to the misty verge of the southern horizon—shall enter into
the feelings which he has thus enthusiastically recorded, " So
" fair, so silent, save for the woodlark's note and the moaning
" river, so unearthly did the whole scene seem, that my
" imagination delighted to look upon it as fairy land."*

At the foot of the western pile of this conspicuous tor, we shall
observe a trackway, running from south-east to north-west,
intersected at the extremity by another, tending to the converse
points of the compass, and discernible to the extent of two
hundred and forty yards. The adjacent commons abound with
similar remains of trackways and tracklines. One of these, of very
marked character, comes down the hill from Rippon Tor, and
crossing both the Bovey and the Ashburton road, may be traced
about two miles. We shall also notice many hut-circles, and other
vestiges of aborginal occupancy. One of the circles may be
specified, consisting of eighteen stones closely placed, forming a
circumference of seventy-five feet. A large circumvallation
seventy-five feet in diameter is to be seen on the slope of Heytor
about W. N. W. of the western pile of rocks standing alone, to which
attention was first drawn, by the late Thomas Kelly, of Yealmpton,
Following the winding course of the trackline mentioned above,
we shall find ourselves on the high road to Chagford, which we
shall follow, retracing our steps to the moor-gate near Houndtor
and leaving Bowerman's Nose on the right, shall return towards
Moreton below East Down on the western side, and passing
Beetor Cross,—(the time-worn cross itself stands in an adjoining
field)—shall enter the town by the Plymouth and Tavistock road.

Our next excursion will lead us along that road until we reach

*HOWITT. *Rural Life of England*, vol. ii., p. 379.

the fifth mile-stone from Moreton. Here a group of interesting remains will attract our attention. One of the most prominent is a circle, or pound, two hundred and forty yards in circumference, inclosing two hut-circles. Three branches of trackways will be observed in connexion with this inclosure. One may be traced S.S.W., passing from the circumvallation to the valley below. Another beginning at the circle, is lost in the boggy hollows beneath, but reappears on the opposite hill, and crosses the turn-pike. Nearly parallel with the last, another line proceeds also from the circle and is lost on the opposite slope, after crossing the high road, about a furlong west of the former. We have now returned to a point where we have the means of ascertaining the course of the antient Perambulation. We have arrived at the bounds of the East Quarter which joins the North at Wotesbrook Lake foot, described in the original Perambulation as falling into the Teign, and which was thought by the Perambulators, who made their survey in the reign of James I.,* to be the same as the stream then called Whoodelake. There they accounted the North Quarter to end, one mile from Hingstone, or Highstone, near Fernworthy Hedges.† As the boundary proceeds from thence, in a straight line to the stream which rises below the cairn-crested hill called King's Oven, where it makes an angle, and then holds on in a direct line to King's Oven, we have in that well-known spot, and in Fernworthy, two ascertained points, between which we shall be able to trace the bounds of the East Quarter without danger of material error. In Broadmoor Mires we shall probably find the "turbary of Aberheve."‡ or Aberheeved, "the fennye place, now "called Turfehill," by the aforesaid Perambulators, and in "King's "Oven" on the hill above, Surt§ Regis (which seems to be a strange misprint for Furnum Regis), in Risdon's copy of the original document.

But we must again forsake the guidance of the Perambulators, and return to the scene of our recent investigations, with Warren Tor on the right. Diverging from the high road, and mounting

---

*6 Jac. I. August 16, A.D., 1608.

†Called by the Perambulators Fernworthie Hedges. The inclosures of Fern-worthie have therefore been evidently of long standing.

‡In the root of this word, we have an instance of the antient British prefix Aber, so rare with us, but so common in Wales and Scotland.

§Anerion in RISDON. Survey, p. 222, ed. 1811. The F is transcribed as if it was a long S, and the last letter, as if it was a *t*, instead of *n*, with the mark of abbrevia-tion, to show the omission of the letters, *um*.

the hill southward, we shall notice many other vestiges of hut-circles and tracklines, in our way over Shapeley Common. Passing the tor on the summit, we shall turn to observe the fine expanse of country which lies behind us, stretching away to the Exmoor range on the north. Taking the tors for our landmarks, we shall now keep a southward course, and make for Hooknor,* the nearest tor in that direction, as this will probably be our best guide for finding Grimspound, (which will be our next object) should our means of locomotion enable us to disregard the accommodation of roads. But if otherwise, the tourist will find it more convenient to proceed by the turnpike (instead of leaving it as above) to Vitifer mine, near a small inn by the way side, about six miles from Moreton. Here, at the Warren House Inn, a carriage may be put up, and he will find himself about two miles from the object of his search, which appears on the slope of the lofty ridge, terminating the prospect eastward. A tolerable road to the stamping mills in the valley below, will be our best course from this point. In the angle between this road and the turnpike, we shall notice an antient granite cross, locally known as Bennett's Cross, near the boundary of the parishes of Lydford and Chagford, standing erect in its original position, but time-worn and weather-beaten with the storms of centuries. The modern letters W. B. are graven on the shaft.

Leaving this venerable relic of mediæval times on the left we proceed eastward and cross the springs of the West Webburn near the source. The water-power thus furnished is rendered subservient to the mining operations in the valley below South-stone Common. A path east from the mine leads us still eastward over Challacombe Down where we shall notice many deep excavations and other remains of antient mines. On the saddle of Challacombe Down, with Grimspound immediately opposite, we shall cross at right angles an important parallelithon, or stone row† running north and south, much wider than those at Longstone and Merivale, although the stones are of the same size and character. But unlike those the Challacombe or Headland row has a third line of stones, so that instead of a single aisle a double one is formed. There are also remains of five other lines parallel to the three. These latter, however, are by some considered as the remains of a circle. At the southern end is a

---

*Hookney in the Ordnance Map.

†First noticed by the late John Prideaux in 1828.

triangular menhir. The line of avenue may be traced clearly to the extent of eighty yards, terminating towards Birch Tor, on the south, and on the north, lost in an old stream-work. This row has received careful attention at the hands of the Rev. S. Baring Gould, and the stones have been re-erected.

By a steep descent, we shall reach the vale of Challacombe, where the origin of the local designation will be observed at a glance, and its significance manifested in this secluded nook, hollowed out of the acclivities of surrounding hills. This coombe, which opens pleasantly to the south, is watered by another spring of the West Webburn, and presents a pleasing proof of successful cultivation, under favourable circumstances, in the heart of the moor. But Grimspound is now before us, as we mount the southern slope below Hooknor tor. A general description has been already given in Chapter iv., p. 59, of this remarkable specimen of a primitive town, fortified by a strong wall, and containing numerous remains of antient dwellings within its cyclopean bulwark. A large stone on the eastern side of the circle, marks the spot where the spring rises, and from whence, beneath the foundations of the wall, as already described, it flows, under the name of Grimslake, to join the Webburn. After a dry spring, and a whole month of continuous hot weather immediately preceding, we have found at Midsummer a clear and copious stream issuing from the source,* so that it would appear, under ordinary circumstances, those using the enclosure would have been always sufficiently supplied with pure and wholesome water. The classical investigator will probably be disappointed at not finding in Grimspound the characteristics of an antient British town, as it has been considered by Sir Gardner Wilkinson and others, defended by woods, swamps, and thickets, as described by Cæsar, in his account of the fortified post occupied by Cassivelaunus, where a large body of persons and herds of cattle might be congregated in security. But without raising the question whether, when Grimspound was originally built, these naked declivities might not have been clothed with wood, as some suppose, it has been contended that it presents all the features of a strong-hold, and that the present natural circumstances might suffice to account for

---

*It was, however, quite dry at the end of June, 1873, and we have found it so in subsequent years. Mr. Ormerod doubted whether it was anything more than surface water, but it is a stream which flows under the wall of the enclosure, and passing through it, renders the northern extremity somewhat boggy.

K

the different kind of castrametation exhibited in the stronghold of that valiant British prince.* The eastern Britons, on the banks of the Thames, had not the same advantage, in point of materials, as their Danmonian compatriots possessed, in the granite blocks and boulders of Dartmoor, from which an effectual circumvallation could be speedily formed; to which these aboriginal engineers appear to have deemed it unnecessary to add the further protection of a fosse, since Grimspound is totally unprovided with any kind of ditch, or additional outwork, beyond its single rampart. This, it is contended, is a feature of much significance, and should be duly regarded in our endeavours to ascertain the period of the erection of this rude but venerable fortress. The rampart is doubtless much lower than it was originally built, but unlike many of the valla of our hill-forts and earth-works, it has not been tampered with, nor the original design altered by successive occupants. Sir R. C. Hoare furnishes us with an important axiom in archæology, which may be legitimately applied in determining with proximate accuracy at least, the era of the erection of Grimspound. "In examining those earth-works, "we must endeavour to discriminate the work of the people who "constructed them; and wherever we find very strong and "elevated ramparts, and deep ditches with advanced outworks, "such as Bratton, Battlesbury, Scratchbury, Yarnbury, Chidbury "Barbury, Oldbury, etc., we may, without hesitation, attribute "these camps to the Belgic or Saxon era; for neither the Britons "nor Romans had recourse to strong ramparts."†

But to whatever conclusion the investigator may be led, as to the people by whom this marvel of the Moor was constructed, or the objects contemplated in its erection, he will not return from his examination of Grimspound, without being convinced that he has inspected one of the oldest monuments of our island; whilst the mystery in which its origin is shrouded, and the appearance of hoar antiquity, with which its gigantic rampart is invested, will add interest to his speculations, and deepen his recollections of this extraordinary, if not unique, relic of aboriginal times.

The late G. W. Ormerod, in his paper, "What is Grimspound"‡ discusses all the theories that have been advanced as to the use

---

*FOSBROOKE, misled by LYSONS, describes "Grimspound, in Devonshire, as a " circular inclosure, situate *in a marsh.*" *Ency. Antiq.*, p. 100, *ed.*. 1843.

†Ant. Wilts. Vol. ii., p, 108.

‡*Devon Assoc. Trans., vol. v., p.* 41.

GRIMSPOUND.

of this great enclosure and concludes,—" in the days when " Grimspound was built, there were doubtless wolves on " Dartmoor, and, if legends are true, there were bands of " robbers, to whom cattle would also be a great temptation. " For the protection of cattle from these, and in the severe " winters of Dartmoor, I think that Grimspound, Dunnabridge— " now used as the pound for the cattle straying in the forest— " and other smaller pounds were erected, and that the huts " were the dwellings of the owners or herdsmen." The work of the pick and spade, under the direction of the Rev. S. Baring Gould and Mr. R. Burnard, however, reveals the true history of Grimspound, and although it may have been used in later years as a pound for cattle, and the huts utilized by a mining population, it had its origin in pre-historic times, and was the fortified dwelling place of man in the Neolithic age.[*]

But no isolated examination of Grimspound, or speculation on its origin and purposes, will be satisfactory or complete, without reference to the other remains of primitive antiquity, existing in the immediate neighbourhood, and without due consideration of their probable bearings upon the question.

Cairns are numerous on the adjacent downs and hills. We shall find them on King Tor, north, and Hameldon Tor, east of Grimspound. Hameldon, the saddleback of Devonshire, rises majestically above the stronghold, in a long bold ridge, and on its lofty eminence we shall observe Hameldon beacon, commanding a vast extent of country in all directions, and admirably adapted for the conspicuous site of a signal-flame to alarm the country.

On Hameldon beacon, one of the most important finds on Dartmoor, was made by C. Spence Bate, in 1872. He opened a barrow, known as Two Barrows, which was about forty feet in diameter, and about four feet and a half high, and mixed up with the bones of the interment, under a stone, was found an amber ornament, inlaid with gold pins, which had formed probably the handle of a dagger, and the blade of a dagger of bronze.[†] Another barrow near, was also opened subsequently, a detailed of which will be found in the proceedings of the County Society which account is however not quite correct.[‡] The

---

*For a full account of the explorations here and at Broadun, see Trans. Dev. Assoc. 1894. Vol. xxvi., p. 101.

†Trans. Devon Assoc. vol. v., 1872, p. 549.

‡Trans. Devon Assoc., vol. vi., 1873, p. 272.

height of this barrow was three feet six inches, and roughly about sixty-six feet in diameter. A wall of loose stones was found, which indicated the original size of the barrow, the larger circumference having arisen we suppose, from the washing down of the covering earth. Almost in the centre of the barrow was found a beautifully built up cairn, of small flat stones —a perfect little beehive hut in fact—about three feet high. There was nothing inside, and to all appearance there had never been anything enclosed in it. The ground had never been disturbed in any way, and there was nothing but the natural surface soil, without any admixture of ash of any kind. The large flat stone mentioned, was nothing more than a surface one, and it rested upon the calm, and the same remark applies to the other flat stones outside the enclosing wall. The interment proper—indicated by a mass of comminuted bone and charcoal, among which was the palatal fang of a human upper molar tooth, evidently the remains of a cremated body—was far away from the centre, close upon the inner edge of the stone circle enclosing the mound. It really looked as if the cairn was placed only to mislead any possible disturber of the barrow. With the remains was found a thin square shaped flint implement. In general character the two barrows, the one first described and this one, were similar.

Mounting the hill, we shall come upon the great Central Trackway before mentioned, p. 62, and from this elevated position shall have an opportunity of observing the direction it takes, and the probable relation which such constructions have to the antient mining works in the neighbourhood, and to those of the Moor generally. In the general description of this trackway, reference has been made to the authority of the late Rev. James Holman Mason, formerly vicar of Widecombe, a cautious and practical antiquary, whose long and intimate acquaintance with the topography, history and traditions of the Moor entitle his views to the greatest respect, whatever difference of opinion may exist, as to his conclusions, from the facts which he has industriously collected. When therefore, he inclines rather to regard these curious vestiges of antiquity as boundaries than as roads, we are anxious to preserve his observations on a subject of much local and antiquarian interest, as invaluable data, which might otherwise be lost to those who would gladly have recourse to the testimony of a competent observer, in endeavouring to solve an archæological problem of no little difficulty.

The point in our perambulation at which we have now arrived, is peculiarly suitable for investigating the subject under consideration. Hameldon and its immediate neighbourhood, having been the principal scene of examination, with immediate reference to the trackways and tracklines, or rather, division lines, as they are termed by an antiquarian friend of Mr. Mason's,* who had referred to him on the subject, and to whom he replies in a communication which appeared in a provincial paper. " There is " no chance," writes Mr. Mason "of my being able to ascertain " the height of the boundary lines; they are now, I fear, in every " part, razed to the ground. I have reason to believe, from the " inquiries I have since made, that one of the boundary lines you " saw (that on Hamel Down) went to Crockern Tor, and from " thence on to the common adjoining Roborough Down ; if so, it " divided Dartmoor, and must have extended from twelve to " fourteen miles. There is a barrow on Peek hill, near Walk- " hampton, where the boundary-line is now to be traced." On this, Mr. Northmore remarks, " the whole line being from E.N.E. " to S.W., and Dartmoor being thus divided into two almost " equal parts, the north and south divisions,"—a distinction still traditionally recognised, as has been already noticed in a former chapter.

In the same correspondence, occur the following remarks by the Rev. John Pike Jones.† " The dykes, or trackways, have " been traced through the uncultivated parts of the parishes of " Manaton‡ and Widecombe, over Hameldon, and from thence " across Dartmoor. They generally run in a straight direction, " nearly parallel, and are from four to seven feet in breadth. " They are formed of large stones, and are raised above the level " of the ground, and are frequently lost in bogs. In the inclosed " country they cannot be traced, the stones having been removed. " Two of these dykes have been traced out; one terminates at " Crockern Tor, and the other about two miles distant, at

---

*This was Mr. Thomas Northmore, who, in a correspondence in the year 1825, addressed to the Editor of *Besley's Exeter News*, treats, at some length, of these division lines, and refers to the researches of Mr. Mason and others.

†At that time, curate of the neighbouring parish of North Bovey, a gentleman who had abundant opportunities for examining this quarter of the Moor, and who was well-known in the scientific world, for his publications on the Botany of Dartmoor and the vicinity.

‡One of these is probably the trackline before described, where the mural character was so striking, that, at a distance, it might be easily mistaken for a dilapidated new-take wall.

" Waydon [?] Tor, on Dartmoor.   They extend for about ten miles.
" On Hameldon, they are not above half a mile from each other,
"and in the neighbourhood, are several cairns, barrows, and
" circles."

" In tracing the northernmost *reave** from Hameldon," writes
Mr. Mason " we lost it in a tin-work.   The western end was,
" some time after, discovered towards Newhouse, emerging as it
" were, from a wall, the boundary of the Courtenay property."
Mr. Mason adds a suggestion of great pertinence.   "Are not
" these *reaves*, as they are called, the work of the tinners?  *Omne*
" *ignotum pro magnifico*.   Tin bounds have been brought down
"from an early period, and claimed by working tinners over
" property belonging to others.   The estate of Fernworthy, has in
" my recollection, taken in a very large track, according to an
" antient tin-bound, admitted at Lydford Castle, in the reign of
" Elizabeth.   In the neighbourhood of Gidleigh, similar reaves of
" stones were taken to be the boundary, of a grant from the
" Crown, of a considerable portion of the Forest, to Giles de
" Gidleigh, and the question at issue was thereby decided."†

Nothing can be more satisfactory or conclusive, than the
evidence thus adduced in favour of the existence of antient
boundary-lines on Dartmoor, constructed for marking the limits of
commons, grants, tin-bounds, and other like purposes.   But if a
corollary be thence deduced, that such boundary-lines comprehend
all constructions of this kind, we cannot but venture to question,
however deferentially, a conclusion which would militate against
the distinction drawn in the former part of this work, between
tracklines and trackways—the latter being regarded as causeways,
or means of communication; the former, boundary-banks, dykes,
or defensive lines.   This distinction is fortified by the opinion of
Sir R. C. Hoare, as it has been already observed, who remarks
that by following these trackways on the Wiltshire downs, in

---

*This is the term by which these lines are universally known among the moor-
men.   *Reave* is a vernacular term commonly used in Devonshire, to describe rows
or courses of stones, earth, or other substance, raised in any ridge-like shape,
sometimes it takes the form of *roave*, which expresses the same thing.   *Wind-reaves*
or *roaves*, are rows of hay, barley or oats, raked together in ridges in harvest
operations.   This is probably a remnant of our antient Teutonic language.   *Reef* in
Icelandic is *Roof*, and in the ridge, or roof-like form of these lines, may possibly be
traced the original idea conveyed in the vernacular term *reave*.   A reef of rocks is
probably derived from the same source.   It may not be inaptly remarked that the
old word *reaver* (Anglo-Saxon *reafere*) and the modern rover, are identical  so that
from *reave* to *roave* appears an ordinary transition.

†Letter from Rev. J. H. MASON, to the author.

more than one instance, he has been led directly into a British village. There seems no adequate reason for supposing that the Belgæ of Wiltshire enjoyed conveniences of this kind, which were not possessed by their Danmonian countrymen, and that which would be legitimately inferred from the nature of the case, seems clearly demonstrated by existing monuments. While the boundary or tracklines vary from three or four to seven feet in breadth, trackways are found fifteen and even twenty feet broad ; and while the former are seen to partake more or less of the mound, or vallum character, where not razed to the foundations, the trackways are totally destitute of all such appearance, and are merely causeways, constructed of stone rudely laid in the soil, and slightly raised above the natural level of the country. We can scarcely imagine that a line of pavement (however rude) twenty, or even fifteen feet wide, and of considerable length, could ever have been constructed for the mere purposes of demarkation. That roads, or *ridge-ways*, have served as boundaries, has already been shown, whilst the very etymology of the word, demonstrates the original design of the ridge too obviously, to admit of question.

The period when these works were constructed, is a point of far greater difficulty. Mr. Mason connects them with antient mining operations, justly remarking that " the earliest trade from " this country was in tin ; the tinners were the most numerous " class of working people. That they inhabited Dartmoor and its " purlieus, their extensive works, fallen enclosures, and remains of " hovels, evidently attest." Mr. Northmore thinks the dykes, or division-lines, may be of high antiquity, and originally constructed for a defence against beasts, as well as borderers ; but he adds, " I " am sometimes inclined to think them of later construction, having " relation to the Normans, and feudal rights and customs," and assigns as his reason for inclining to the latter opinion, a communication he had received from Dr. Oliver, with an extract from King John's Charter, *de libertatibus Devoniæ*, in which Mr. Northmore thinks there is evident reference to these division lines of Dartmoor, " within which the people of Devon could not make " their deer-leaps or enclosures." See Chapter xiii..

Having carefully examined these interesting monuments, we shall have no difficulty in concluding that they may have been connected with mining operations, and yet belong to the British period of our history. But without pursuing these speculations further, and leaving the opinions which have been advanced, to be brought to the test of existing remains by the practical antiquary, we shall now descend the north-east declivity of Hameldon, below the tor and notice a circular inclosure, called Berry Pound, much overgrown with fern and heather, but of similar construction to those already described in other parts of the moor.  Here a salient ridge projecting from the flank of Hameldon throws the drainage on one side to the tributaries of the Teign, and on the other side to those of the Dart and the Webburn.  By following the latter, we shall soon strike upon a lane that enters the head of the Widecombe vale, along which we shall now proceed, with the ridge of Hameldon high on the right, forming, for a considerable distance, the stupendous rampart of the valley on the western side.  Here the tourist will observe the most perfect counterpart in our western peninsula of one of the lovely dales of Westmorland or Cumberland, and the antiquary will find two logan-rocks as he proceeds, within half a mile of Widecombe churchtown.  The Ruggelstone, as it is called in the neighbourhood, is an immense oblong rock, of which the computed weight is one hundred and fifteen tons.  The length is about twenty two feet, by a breadth of about sixteen and a half feet, the sides being respectively, twenty, nineteen, twelve, and sixteen and a half feet.  The mean thickness is five and a half feet, and it contains one thousand five hundred and fifty cubic feet.  This huge mass rests on the supporting rocks beneath, so as to give the appearance of a huge cromlech.  It is said to be movable with the aid of the large key of the parish church, but those who are not able to procure this, may impart a very perceptible rocking motion by the application of a stout walking stick as a lever.  The other logan is a flat stone, about eleven feet in length by nine in breadth, but not more than fourteen or sixteen inches thick; which could formerly be set in motion by the pressure of the foot, but it has been mischievously deprived, in some way, of its logging power, of late years.

The dale expands about midway to make room for the pleasant knoll, on which the village and church are built, the " cynosure of " neighbouring eyes."  The lofty granite tower is finely proportioned, embattled, and finished with crocketted pinnacles.  The name of this sequestered sanctuary is permanently associated in local history with one of the most awful and sublime, and at the same time, characteristic accompaniments of moorland scenery—the thunder-storm.  Moreton has been called the land of thunder, and such terrific storms as those which sometimes occur when the greatest alarm is occasioned and considerable damage frequently done by the lightning, abundantly justify the appellation.  But the skirts of the moor generally, from their mountainous character, are subject to these terrific " skiey influences ; " and Widecombe, with the mighty ridge of Hameldon on one side, and the lofty crest of Rippon Tor on the other, to gather and arrest the thunder-cloud must be peculiarly exposed to such occasional visitations. Hence, probably the appalling outbreak of that awful storm, the terrors of which are traditionally recorded after the lapse of more than two centuries and a half.

> " Oft the swain,
> When deeply falls the winter night, narrates
> To his own rustic circle, seated near
> The peat pil'd hearth, how in th' involving cloud
> Tremendous, flashing forth unusual fires,
> Was wrapt the House of Prayer ;—thy sacred fane,
> Romantic Widecombe !  The village bard
> In simple verse that time has kindly spared,
> Has sung it ; and in style uncouth,
> The pious rural annalist has penn'd
> The fearful story."

The village bard, and the pious rural annalist thus commemorated, were Richard Hill, schoolmaster, and the Rev. George Lyde, vicar of the parish, " a laborious preacher and a " prudent pastor," as we learn from Prince, author of the Worthies of Devon, who, in his memoir of Mr. Lyde, embodies an account of this awful tempest (" the chief ground," he observes " of my inserting him here ") in the quaint and characteristic style of the age.  " In the year of our Lord, 1638, October 21, being " Sunday, and the congregation being gathered together in the " parish church of Wydecombe, in the afternoon, in service time, " there happened a very great darkness, which still increased to " that degree, that they could not see to read ; soon after, a " terrible and fearful thunder was heard, like the noise of so many " great guns ; accompanied with dreadful lightning, to the great " amazement of the people ; the darkness still increasing, that " they could not see each other, when there presently came such " an extraordinary flame of lightning, as filled the church with " fire, smoak, and a loathsome smell, like brimstone ; a ball of fire " came in likewise at the window, and passed thro' the church,

"which so affrighted the congregation, that most of them fell
"down in their seats; some upon their knees, others on their
"faces, and some one upon another, crying out of burning and
"scalding, and all giving themselves up for dead.  There were in
"all, four persons killed, and sixty-two hurt, divers of them
"having their linen burnt, tho' their outward garments were not
"so much as singed. . . . The church itself was much torn and
"defaced with the thunder and lightning; a beam whereof,
"breaking in the midst, fell down between the minister and clerk,
"and hurt neither.  The steeple was much wrent; and it was
"observed where the church was most torn, there the least hurt
"was done among the people.  There were none hurted with the
"timber or stone, but one man, who it was judged was killed by
"the fall of a stone; which might easily happen, since stones
"were thrown down from the steeple as fast as if it had been by
"a hundred men."*

The "village bard's" commemorative verses, inscribed "on a
"votive tablet, for that purpose ordained" in the church, also
contained, according to the same authority, "a brief history of
"what then happened, in large verse, consisting of seven feet; too
"too tedious to be here inserted, though they thus begun:"—

"In token of our thanks to God, this table is erected,
Who, in a dreadful thunder-storm, our persons here protected."†

One of the legends connected with the storm at Widecombe,
used to rivet the attention, and to excite the terrors of our child-
hood.  The tale passed current, that either a thunderbolt or a
terrific minister of wrath in an unearthly form, was sent to inflict
condign vengeance on one who was presumptuously playing at
cards in his pew, by dashing him against the moor-stone pillar,
where the bloody evidence of his guilt and punishment, as it was
believed, remained for a considerable period.  The original of this
legend seems to be recorded by Prince.  "Another man had his
"head cloven, his skull wrent into three pieces, and his brains
"thrown upon the ground whole; but the hair of his head, through
"the violence of the blow, stuck fast to a pillar near him, where
"it remained a woeful spectacle a long while after."  The Wide-

---

*JOHN PRINCE. *Worthies of Devon*, folio, p. 447. London. 1701; 4to ed. 1810, p. 569.

†These lines will be found *in extenso* in "Things, New and Old, concerning the
"parish of Widecombe-in-the-Moor, and its neighbourhood," by R. DYMOND, 1876.

combe storm is an important incident in Mr. Blackmore's fine
novel " Christowell."

With Rembrandt touch Carrington has skilfully heightened the
effect of his graphic delination of this fearful catastrophe, by
bringing into striking, but natural contrast the calm and security
of a rural sabbath day—with the sudden burst of the lowering
cloud, gathering blackness and standing out in sublimer terrors,
from the light and loveliness of the preceding scene.

> " Far o'er hill and dale
> Their summons glad the sabbath bells had flung ;
> From hill and dale obedient they had sped
> Who heard the holy welcoming ; and now
> They stood above the venerable dead
> Of centuries, and bow'd where they had bow'd
> Who slept below.   The simple touching tones
> Of England's psalmody upswell'd, and all
> With lip and heart united, loudly sang
> The praises of the Highest.   But anon
> Harsh mingling with that minstrelsy, was heard
> The fitful blast :—the pictur'd windows shook—
> Around the aged tower the rising gale
> Shrill whistled ; and the antient massive doors
> Swung on their jarring hinges.   Then—at once—
> Fell an unnatural calm, and with it came
> A fearful gloom, deep'ning and deep'ning till
> 'Twas dark as night's meridian ; for the cloud
> Descending had within its bosom wrapt
> The fated dome.   At first a herald flash
> Just chas'd the darkness, and the thunder spake,
> Breaking the strange tranquility.   But soon
> Pale horror reign'd—the mighty tempest burst
> In wrath appalling ; forth the lightning sprang
> And death came with it, and the living writh'd
> In that dread flame-sheet."

But the curious antiquary will endeavour with no little interest to trace, at the antient manor-house of North Hall, adjoining the church-yard, evidences of the accuracy of the rural chronicler's faithfulness of description, in such vestiges of its former importance as time and change may have spared; bearing in mind, as Prince quaintly remarks of Hill, that his "history may be good "though his poetry be but indifferent." And since there are not many villages that can boast the honours of local minstrelsy, we make no apology for inserting the metrical description of this venerable moor-land mansion, with its means and appliances for defence and delectation, traces of which still remain.

The messuage there, which antiently was chief or capital,
Tho' much decay'd, remaining still, is called yet North-hall:
Whereas the houses, courtlages, with gardens, orchards, and
A stately grove of trees within that place did sometime stand,
Were all enclosed round about with moats of standing water,
So that no thieves or enemies could enter in to batter
The houses, walls, roofs, windows, or what else besides was there;
The moats or trenches being fed with streams of water clear,
Wherein good store of fish was bred, as antient men did say;
The ruin'd banks whereof remain unto this very day.
And when the family within, would walk into the town,
Or else return, a draw-bridge firm they presently let down;
And at their pleasure drew it up to keep the household safe.
This house did antiently belong to Raph, the son of Raph,
So is he named in a deed of much antiquity,
Which bears no date, for at that time was less iniquity.

Between Whittaborough and Toptor—in the vernacular of the moormen, Taptor—on land belonging to the representatives of the late Robert Dymond, is a very fine kistvaen, perhaps the most perfect on the Moor. It was formerly covered with a cairn, and on Whittaborough close by, is a large cairn. The view of the valley from the hill above on the west is a beautiful one.

Leaving Widecombe—a smiling oasis in the desert—with all its natural attractions and olden associations, we shall proceed eastward by a road which mounts the hill in the direction of Heytor and Rippon Tor, where we shall again find ourselves among the ruder monuments of unrecorded antiquity, on the slopes of Thornhill or Toptor.  This is the hill, which is described above, as having its eastern declivity partitioned into antient rectangular inclosures, by tracklines or boundary-lines.  Circular inclosures also occur on the Widecombe side.

From Torrhill, in our way to Rippon Tor, we shall cross the high road to Ashburton, and notice near the trackway, or boundary-line already described, two hut circles, one thirty feet in diameter, and the other eighteen.  Within the latter are stones, having the appearance of a dilapidated kistvaen—but which Col. Hamilton Smith thought might have been a sort of storeplace for domestic purposes—within a circular foundation, whose dimensions would admit of a super-structure with a roof; this would seem therefore to have been erected, not as a fence to inclose a sepulchre of the dead, but as a house for the abode of the living.

We shall now scale the rocky summit of Rippon Tor, which according to the Ordnance Survey, rises to the height of fifteen hundred and sixty-three feet, but which, from its frontier position has been often supposed to approach more nearly to an equality with the loftiest points of the Dartmoor range.  The prospect, taking in the greater part of the South Hams, as well as a considerable extent to the eastward, and a fine sweep of hill country northward, is magnificent, but embraces so much that has been already viewed from Heytor, as not to call for more specific detail. The Tor itself has nothing sufficiently remarkable to detain us, after we are satisfied with the charms of the landscape; we shall therefore turn westwards, and following the sloping crest of the hill, shall find ourselves, about a quarter of a mile from the top, in the midst of a number of scattered moorstone masses, among which a logan-rock forms a prominent and curious object.  This logan is popularly known by the name of the Nutcrackers.  It measures about fifteen feet in length, about four feet in thickness, and about three and a half feet wide in the middle, tapering towards each end.  It contains about one hundred and eighty-seven cubic feet, and its estimated weight is rather less than fourteen tons.  It is extremely difficult to imagine the position of the superincumbent mass to have been purely accidental, although it might possibly have been thus singularly placed by a diluvian convulsion.  It can be still easily moved by the application of a suitable lever.

Returning to the road, the careful observer will find, on and near Rippon Tor, several fine cairns. We shall follow the highway, and soon enter the inclosed country with Buckland beacon on the right, and next notice the rugged crest of Auswell (not Answell as in the Ordnance map) Rock above the plantations, also on the right, with which, should we have time to climb the summit, we shall be much interested, looking directly down, as it does, upon the sylvan magnificence of Holne Chase. We shall retire from this glimpse of some of the loveliest woodland scenery in the west, with a full determination to return for a more leisurely inspection, and proceed to Ashburton, where the tourist will find every accommodation he may require.

# CHAPTER VII.

## The Perambulation Continued, Ashburton to Plympton.

In leaving Ashburton for our next excursion, on the right-hand side of North Street, in an old house, may be noticed a good arched doorway of timber in the Perpendicular style, with the square flower in the hollow, all round the arch. We shall proceed by the Holne road, as far as Holne Bridge (which here crosses the Dart in the midst of beautiful wood scenery) and leaving it on the left, shall trace the course of the river upwards, by a charming drive, which will take us immediately below Auswell Rock, and through a succession of fine woods and plantations, belonging to Mr. Baldwin. J. P. Bastard, of Buckland Court, with Holne Chase full in view on the opposite side of the Dart. The ancestor of the present owner—the late Col. Bastard—early in this century, purchased Auswell Manor, and planted the waste lands with fir, larch, and other forest trees, on so extensive a scale, that the thanks of the House of Commons were given him for what was designated, his patriotism.    The banks of the river, in many parts, rise in steep acclivities—bold cliffs occasionally project from amidst the rich and varied foliage, with which the sides of the hills are fringed, and the windings of the stream present successive points of wood, rock, and river scenery, often grand, and always charming.    The little rural church of Buckland-in-the-Moor stands high on the eastern bank.    Below, the two branches of the Webburn form one united stream at the southern extremity of the vale of Widecombe, which running between Buckland and Spitchwick—the seat of the late Lord Ashburton, falls into the Dart, in Holne Chase, about a mile below Newbridge, in sight of which we shall diverge from the riverside and follow the road to the moors, with Leigh Tor on the right. On entering again on the commons, the road passes very near Beltor, which presents no object worthy of particular remark. Sharpitor, or Sharptor, rises grandly above the river, and will well repay a visit to its craggy summit, but our attention here will be chiefly directed to a group of aboriginal relics, which will be noticed near a moorland farm called Rowbrook.    On the right of the road, on the western slope of the hill, is a remarkably perfect hut-circle, twenty-four feet in diameter, with the door-jamb erect, three feet high.    From this circle, a trackline or boundary bank, is carried down the hill, and connects the hut with the foundation of a rectangular inclosure, forty-two feet by eleven, formed of the same materials, and in the same manner as the hut-circle; but whilst the circular form is found in every part of the moor, the rectangular is of exceedingly rare occurrence.    Below the road, and nearer the river, just above the Eastcombe cottage, is a very fine circular foundation, of large dimensions, and of a very interesting description, being at least, thirty-eight feet in diameter, and having walls six feet in thickness.    The door-jamb is of unusual size, five feet high and six feet wide; and the whole ruin is in much finer preservation than any of the smaller hut-circles.

Yartor is one of the tors which should not be passed by without a visit, presenting as it does, the appearance of a hill, fortified by the engineering of Nature herself. On the north and south, are two courses, or walls, of natural rock. The western side has a low, rude fence formed of granite blocks, and the eastern, has a similar breast-work, though less perfect, and somewhat in advance of the parallel courses on the other sides of the tor. The whole conformation presents a rude but grand inclosure, suggesting the idea of a Cyclopean hill-fort, or of a natural temple admirably adapted to the wild and mystic rites of a dark, superstitious religion. The remains of some hut-circles, and the ruins of a kistvaen, the cover-stone of which is about five feet by three, will be observed N.E. from the tor.

In the vale below, the East Dart will be seen sweeping round the foot of Yartor Hill, in its progress to join the western branch of the river at Dartmeet, where the confluence takes place, and where also is the junction of the three parishes of Widecombe, Holne, and Lydford. Here we also meet again the Forest bounds, and find them well-defined by the watercourses of the Wallabrook and the Dart. The last point noticed in the line of perambulation was King's Oven (p. 143). From thence an imaginary line marked the boundary of the East Quarter to Wallabrook, or Wellabroke Head, "and soe along by Wallebrooke," say the Perambulators, "until it fall into Easter Dart," at a short distance north of Yartor foot. The East Dart then becomes the limit of the Forest, and of the parish of Lydford to the confluence, at Dartmeet. The scenery here is varied and interesting ; the fine reach of the Dart—the noble slope and mural crown of Yartor— the wildness of the moor contrasted with the plantations and inclosures of Brimpts, rising immediately above the bridge—all combine to attract and arrest the tourist's attention. An aboriginal Cyclopean bridge similar to that at Post-bridge, which formerly spanned the stream was thrown down many years since, by an inundation of the Dart, but was re-erected in 1888, by the Committee of the Dartmoor Preservation Association.

Crossing the bridge, we shall proceed by the turnpike road, leaving the line of perambulation, which follows the course of the West Dart up the valley. Below Huckaby Tor (which presents nothing remarkable) we shall diverge from the main road leading to Two Bridges, and proceed by the Holne road on the left, which winds down through the little moorland hamlet of Huckaby, to the river's bank again, in the midst of interesting border scenery. Here we cross the Dart at Hexworthy Bridge, and wind up the

L

hill on the opposite side.   Looking back over the valley of the
Dart, we shall observe the river making a fine sweep round the
common, rising boldly from the brink.   We follow the road about
a mile, and just before reaching Saddle Bridge, which crosses a
rivulet called Oldbrook, or Wobrook, flowing from Skaur Gut,
shall notice a group of trackline inclosures on the slope of the
hill, immediately above the road on the right.   Here we again
touch the Forest bounds, at the point of junction of the East and
South quarters.   Having crossed Saddle Bridge, and advanced on
the road about one hundred yards, we shall notice on the right
the remains of a building, constructed of materials like the circular
inclosures in other parts of the moor, and presenting a similar
appearance, but rectangular in form.   Ruins of the wall, to the
height of five feet remain, where the ground declines towards the
rivulet.   At a short distance above, on the same declivity, will be
observed the remains of a large pound-like inclosure, in good
preservation.   The stones of which the fence is constructed are
large, and are piled up more like walls than those which are
generally seen.   This is particularly observable at the entrance,
where, in most examples, granite slabs form the jambs ; but in the
present case, the sides of the doorway are built up.   This doorway
is on the east side, and the wall remains in some parts not less
than three feet high.   Skirting along the hollow above Oldbrook,
various remains of extensive stream-works will be noticed, with
which the buildings below were no doubt connected.   The whole
of this neighbourhood abounds with the traces of the old men—as
the natives call the miners of former days—ruins of blowing-
houses, moulds, mortars and mill-stones, are to be found.

Returning to the Holne road we shall soon reach Combeston
or Cumsdon Tor, on the left, standing on high ground, above the
valley of the Dart, and opposite Sharp Tor.   Here we shall
probably seek for a reputed logan-stone in vain, nor, although we
scale the highest pile of the tor, shall we find any rock-basins to
repay our search.   But we gain a commanding view of Dartmeet
Bridge, and of the windings of the river at some of the most
interesting points of its moorland course.

Crossing the road, and taking a course southward from
Combeston Tor, we shall proceed by a gentle ascent, over a wide
extent of common, towards Peter's Boundstone.   On this extensive track, we shall find very few monumental relics ; while those
that occur, such as a cairn near Combeston Tor, another about half

a mile south, and an inclosure fifty yards in circumference, at no great distance from the latter, present nothing worthy of particular remark. Cairns also are found on the eminences at Holne Ridge and Peter's Boundstone. Returning over Holne Lee, (a wide extent of monotonous moor country) we shall pass through Holne church-town, without observing anything of especial mark to detain us at that moorland village, except the " frugal fare " for man and horse, which may be there obtained, and will scarcely fail to be needed after so long an excursion over the breezy downs.

From hence our course will continue through Shuttaford to the road which traverses the ridge above the deep glen of the Dart, with Hembury Wood on the left. This will soon bring us to Hembury, or Henbury Castle, a hill-fort of an oblong irregular form, in the northern part of the parish of Buckfastleigh. Lysons computes the area inclosed by the ramparts at about seven acres, and adds, " at the north end* is a prætorium, forty-four feet by "seventeen." From Henry Woollcombe's examination of it, it appears to have remained in the same state as when we first visited it. Hembury occupies a commanding position on the wooded ridge which forms the western bank of the Dart, between Holne Bridge and Buckfast Abbey. Woollcombe's description gives the following particulars. " The ramparts are all very "entire, and the ditches on the south, west, and part of the north "sides are still deep, having been forty feet in width. On the "north and east the ground sinks so precipitously, as to form a "natural fence. These sides are now clothed with coppice, and "may perhaps have been always wooded." Hence this observant antiquary justly infers, that Hembury may have been one of the antient British towns, surrounded by thick woods. " The "prætorium," our old friend continues, "I imagine to be of "more modern construction, and it is so completely a mound of "earth, as to lead me to think it might have been raised there in "pre-Norman times. If I conclude it to have been occupied by the "Romans, and then to have had this prætorium added to it, I do "not see why they should have possessed themselves of it, not "being connected with any road through the country."† The site

---

*Not at the north, but in the south-western corner.

†WOOLLCOMBE. *Fortified Hills in Devon, MSS.* He appends a note, quoting from Polwhele, to the following effect. " Some years since, a great number of oval "stones were dug up at Hembury. They were plano-convex bodies, about three "inches in diameter; no doubt they were the sling-stones of the antient Britons."

is commanding, and well-chosen for defence, as well as for observation—the vale of the Dart, Holne, Brent Beacon, Haldon, and the southern heights of Dartmoor are all in view. By the road which skirts the western side of the fort, we shall soon descend to Buckfast Abbey and Dart Bridge, and shall terminate our lengthened excursion at Buckfastleigh, a small market-town, the spire of whose church, conspicuously placed on the brow of an eminence which rises above the Dart, is an interesting object to the whole neighbourhood.

> " Whose finger points to heaven."

It will be observed that this is the only spire among all the border churches. All the others have towers.

Our next excursion will lead us along the great Plymouth road to Dean gate; from whence we shall branch off to the right, in search of the scene thus described by Polwhele. "About four " miles from Ashburton, in the parish of Dean Prior, the vale of " Dean-Burn unites the terrible and the graceful in so striking a " manner, that to enter this recess hath the effect of enchantment ; " whilst enormous rocks seem to close around us, amidst the " foliage of venerable trees, and the roar of torrents. And Dean- " Burn would yield a noble machinery for working on superstitious " minds under the direction of the Druids."

Leaving the inclosed country, and proceeding westward, we shall return to the extensive tract of common land,* which we left on bearing southwards to visit Hembury Castle. On the ridge, near a cairn, we shall find a moorland road coming up in a straight direction from Dean, and here dividing into two branches, one diverging to the left, towards Huntingdon (or, as it is in the old Ordnance Map, Buntington) Cross and the Abbot's Way, and the other proceeding by Puppers and Ryder's Hill, to Aune, or Avon Head. We shall remark that these moors, extending between the Avon and the Dart are remarkably deficient in tors, which so strikingly characterise the borders in other parts. The monu-

---

*These, and similar tracts of waste, are probably those referred to by the Perambulators of 1609, when they " present that the soyle of dyvers moores, "comons, and wastes, lyinge for the most parte, aboute the same forrest of " Dartmoore, and usuallie called by the name of Common of Devonsheere, is " parcel of the Dutchie of Cornwall: and that the fosters, and other officers of his " Matie, and his progenitors, Kings and Queens of England, have allwayes accus- "tomed to drive the said commons, and wast groundes and all the commons, " moores, and wastes of other men (lyinge in like manner about the said forest, " home to the corne hedges, and leape yeates rounde aboute the same Common and " forest), some few places onlie excepted."—*Presentment of the Perambulators*, 1609. See chapter, xiii.

mental relics are also comparatively few, and consist principally of cairns on the most conspicuous eminences.

We shall now return to the boundary of the South Quarter, in the midst of these monotonous moors, at Knattleburrow, about a mile to the eastward of the springs of the Avon. This is supposed by the Perambulators " to be the same that is called, in " the old records Gnatteshill," and by Risdon (apparently) Batshill, From the point where the South and east quarters meet at Wobrooke, or Oldbrook, as mentioned above in our last excursion, it is not easy to trace the Forest bounds, which are described as " from thence linyallie ascending to Drylake, alias Drywoorke, " and from thence ascending by Drylake into Crefield Ford or " Dryfield Ford, and from thence to Knattleburrow "*—but from this point, we shall again have the advantage of the satisfactory guidance of natural objects. From Knattleburrow, the boundary proceeds lineally to Western Wallabrook Head, following that stream, till it falls into the river Avon. From this point the boundary-line is carried to Western Whittaburrow,† or Peter's Cross, and from thence it proceeds in a straight direction to Redlake foot, a rivulet which rises about a mile north of Erme Pound, falling into the Erme and marking the boundary of the Forest at the latter place.

But we have again reached a tract, where the hills are crowned with tors, and the moors abound with objects of antiquarian interest. We shall therefore leave the Forest bounds, and explore the interesting district between the line of perambulation on the north ; the verge of the common lands on the south ; the Erme westward, and the Avon on the east. Proceeding eastward from Peter's Cross, and following the old road at the foot of Western Whittaburrow, called the Abbot's Way, we shall regain the banks of the Avon. Leaving Huntingdon Cross on the left, we trace its course below Eastern Whittaburrow, through a wild and waste hollow, to Shipley Bridge, noticing some vestiges of aboriginal circles on the declivity as we proceed. The channel is steep and rocky, and the river flows vigorously towards the inclosed country, through a narrow gorge, flanked on one side by Black

---

*See as to the identification of places referred to in the Perambulation, Spence Bate, On an old map of Dartmoor, *Trans. Devon Assoc.*, vol v., p, 510, and papers by Dr. Arthur B. Prowse, Trans. Devon Assoc., vol. xxi., p. 166, vol. xxii., p. 185, and the xxiv., p. 418 See also chapter xviii., for an account of the old map above referred to, and the copy of the Perambulation of 1240.

†The Perambulation says Eastern Whittaburrow, but it would appear incorrectly.

Tor, and on the other, by Shipley Hill. The single-arched moor-stone bridge—little verdant pasture-crofts won from the waste—a moor farm, scarcely sheltered from the upland storms by a few sycamores—peat stacks and granite boulders—furze brakes and heather banks—rugged moor-tracks winding up from the valley to the heights above—all combine to impart a pleasing character of border wildness to the scene.

Following the moor-track which leads from Shipley Bridge westwards, with Black Tor on the right and Redlake rivulet on the left, we shall trace the stream upwards to the bog below Three Barrow Tor, from whence it takes its rise. Ascending its slope on the northern side, we shall strike upon a fine trackway, coming up the hill from the north-west, sixteen feet wide in many parts, and ending in the large cairn on the crest of the height. This cairn is of enormous size, probably one of the very largest in Devonshire ; and with the two others immediately near it on the same eminence, and in a straight line, gives name to this conspicuous and well-known tor. The cairns appear to have been erected upon the line of the trackway which we shall trace from the north-western tumulus, through the centre, to the south-eastern, and from thence we shall follow it in that direction to the extent of a mile.

Proceeding towards Coryndon Ball, we shall observe an entrance gate opening upon the inclosed lands adjoining the common, through which a road leads to South Brent. Within a hundred yards of the gate will be noticed a congeries of massive stones, in which the observant investigator will have no difficulty in discovering unequivocal evidence of a dolmen, once standing on this spot, but now in ruins, and apparently overthrown by intentional violence, as we observe that the supporters are not crippled under an impost as if pressed down by the superincumbent mass, but are lying in situations where they could not have accidentally fallen. The third supporter stands erect in its original position, of a pyramidal form, only four feet high, and five feet wide in the broadest part. The impost, or quoit, is eleven feet long, five feet at the widest end, and fourteen inches in average thickness. There are no other stones scattered around, so as to lead to the supposition that these are only large masses of granite, among many others, naturally thrown into these positions. There is only one other large flat stone, of greater size than the impost, suggesting the notion of a covering for an

Arkite cell. The height of the supporters of the overthrown cromlech appears more adapted to the purposes of a kistvaen than of a cromlech, and it may also be observed that the monument stood at the verge of a large mound of stone and sod, sixty yards in circumference. A few score yards S. S. E. are the evident remains of a cairn, sacked doubtless to build the boundary wall adjoining. While thus far on our way to South Brent, we shall take advantage of the moor-road over Coryndon Ball, to visit some interesting objects in and about that little market town, which is situated on the Avon, at the foot of a lofty pyramidal hill, known by the name of Brent Beacon. Passing through the village, and going about half a mile along the old Exeter road (which winds over its eastern shoulder by a toilsome ascent) we shall find a pathway leading to the top of the hill. Here there are no remains of a cairn or beacon, and but few vestiges of the building which formerly stood on the summit. From hence an extensive view spreads before us in every direction. In front, the vale of the Avon and the South Hams; on the north and west, the bleak expanse of the moor; while to the east, the prospect extends to the heights of Haldon. Descending over the steep declivity, on the north-western side, we shall reach the banks of the Avon, above the village, and proceed to the bridge, which is a single lofty arch spanning the deep and narrow channel of the genuine mountain stream, that runs chafing and foaming over the granite masses below. A pretty cottage, redolent with roses, and a "trim garden," overhanging the torrent, give contrast and effect to the scene. Returning by the river-side, through a stately avenue of beech, in the vicarage lawn, we shall pass the church, which is bounded on one side by a thickly-wooded and steep bank, rising immediately above the river. There is a fine old yew in the centre, which, with the low machicolated and battlemented tower, —the chancel higher than the nave, externally—the remains of the screen, and the piers and arches in the interior,—will not fail to detain and interest the tourist.

Following the Plymouth road to Brent Bridge, and there diverging towards the commons, we shall pass by Glaze Meet, on our way to the Eastern Beacon, a hill which, rising immediately above the inclosed country, forms a conspicuous object on the southern border of the moor, and is crowned with a characteristic tor, the western pile of which is surrounded by a cairn-like agglomeration of stones. We shall observe that all the neigh-

bouring heights are crowned with cairns, as we proceed southward,
to Butterton Hill and the Western Beacon, which (if we may
regard the chain of hills which encircles Dartmoor, as a vast
natural circumvallation) we shall describe as a huge ravelin projecting into the South Hams and overawing the lowlands.   Of all
the views gained from the border-heights of Dartmoor, none is
more extensive, varied, and interesting, than that which greets the
eye from this the southermost point of the great Devonshire
moorlands.   The South Hams lie mapped out, at our feet, with
the iron-bound coast from Torbay to Plymouth Sound forming
the rugged boundary seaward.   Beyond, the blue expanse of the
English Channel stretches away far and wide from Portland, in
Dorset, to the Lizard Point in Cornwall.   Bays, headlands, and
estuaries diversify the sea-board scene, while mansions, churches,
villages and farms are plentifully interspersed among the corn
fields, pastures, orchards, and woodlands which occupy the whole
district, from the foot of the hills to the verge of the channel.
The estuary of the Yealm beyond Kitley, and the Lary estuary,
near Saltram, being apparently land-locked lakes, while the
steeples and forts of Plymouth, rising amidst the smoke and haze
of a populous and busy port, form a conspicuous and interesting
feature in the western distance.   Nor shall we fail to notice the
railway's mazy track, winding round the base of those rugged
hills, and marking by those works of almost more than Roman
daring (the viaducts at Glaze Brook, Ivybridge, Blachford and
Slade, in this immediate neighbourhood) the memorable era in
which we live.   In such a spot as this, the admirer of natural
beauty may be pardoned, if catching the enthusism of a Goldsmith,
he cannot refrain from apostrophising the varied objects of interest
which meet his delighted gaze,—claiming them as his own by the
very power of appreciating and enjoying their charms.

> " Ye glitt'ring towns, with wealth and splendour crown'd ;
> Ye fields, where summer spreads profusion round,
> Ye lakes, whose vessels catch the busy gale ;
> Ye swains, whose labours till the flowry vale,
> For me, your tributary stores combine,
> Creation's heir, the world, the world is mine."—

We have thus reached, as already observed, the southernmost
point of the great western waste, from whence with a trusty
guide, it is possible to traverse, without any other obstacles, than

those of bogs and morasses, tors and clatters, a distance of twenty-two miles over an uninterrupted succession of moorlands, to the fences of Okehampton Park, in the north. Bending our steps northwards, and skirting the western slope of the hill, we shall notice some remains of hut-circles, and observe below Black Tor, a large pond, which, in winter, might almost aspire to the distinction of a mountain tarn. On the common, above Lukesland Grove, are traces of a considerable circle, or ring, much dilapidated, which will not detain us from our inn, in the valley, to which we shall hasten through the moor-gate above Stowford, and crossing the line of the Great Western railway, in front of the viaducts, which here span the ravine at one hundred and fifteen feet above the waterway of the Erme, and appear suspended in mid-air,—shall soon reach the border village of Ivybridge and there close our excursion.

Ivybridge, situated at the foot of the southern heights of Dartmoor, on the banks of the Erme, has been long celebrated for the picturesque bridge, draperied with ivy, and overhung with luxuriant foliage, to which it owes its name. The great mail road from Plymouth to Exeter was here, in former years, carried over the deep rocky channel of the Erme ; but more recently a commodious bridge has been erected lower down, now superseded in its turn by the Great Western railway, whose viaducts we have observed spanning the deep glen above the village, between Hanger Down and Stowford.

> " Nil mortalibus arduum est,
> Cœlum ipsum petimus."

Passing below this aerial highway, we shall proceed up the sylvan dell of the Erme to Harford Bridge, and from thence by Harford church, a little rustic sanctuary on the verge of the moor, with its characteristic granite steeple, and well-planted green adjoining, shall enter upon the commons, through a moor-gate hard by. In our progress along the side of the hill, above the eastern bank of the Erme, we shall notice a kistvaen in considerable perfection, within a circle of nine stones still erect, one of which is a large slab, four feet six long, by three feet wide in the broadest part. The kistvaen itself, known as the Langcombe Kist, is four feet six inches by two feet four—the cover-stone appears to have been broken, and has fallen into the cavity, which is about eighteen inches deep. This antient relic will be discovered without difficulty by a practised eye, as the surrounding common is remarkably free from natural rocks, furze, and heather. The lower part of the common towards the river, is inclosed by a new-take wall, within which we shall observe a group of singular inclosures, which the antiquary will find it difficult to classify. Antient tracklines or boundary-banks are mingled with walls, of apparently, more recent construction, yet these are evidently not erected for the ordinary purposes of modern fences. There are also the foundations of several large circular inclosures, one of which has the jambs erect, and another looks like a dilapidated cairn. The most perfect of these inclosures is thirty-two yards in circumference, but there are no hut-circles of the usual size, indicating aboriginal population. Traces of antient excavations, might lead to the supposition that these appearances are referable to the mining operations of former days; but the most plausible conjecture will still leave much room for speculation. The Erme runs at the foot of the declivity, and the battlements of Harford church are seen peeping over the shoulder of the hill southward. Near the river, a little distance higher up, will be noticed a small wood of scrubby oaks—Pile's Wood, somewhat resembling Wistman's Wood, which Capt. S. P. Oliver considered was a planted one.*

Proceeding up the slope of the common, north east, we shall cross a line of bound-stones, tending towards the cairn on the summit of Sharp Tor. This cairn is about sixty yards in circumference and at least ten feet high. A mountain track, which it may be possible for turf-carts to traverse, passes below this tor, and skirting Three Barrow Tor, bears onward to Erme plains. We shall follow this track to Redlake, where we left the Forest bounds in our last excursion, and reach Erme Pound, near the river. South-east of Erme pound is one of the most remarkable monuments on or about Dartmoor, which has been referred to in chapter iii. We have before us a careful plan, made by the Rev. W. C. Lukis. in 1880. Starting from the sacred circle, the line of stones runs for about two thousand feet almost due north, then following the dip of the country it descends to the river Erme, reaching the bank at a distance of three thousand nine hundred and sixty-six feet from the circle; gradually rising from the other bank, and crossing a small tributary of the river, it again reaches the level, where it crosses the stream of a modern mine work, and pursues its way, crossing another tributary, until it

---

*Vide Gardener's Chronicle, 1873.

reaches the cisted cairn, eleven thousand two hundred and thirty-nine feet eight inches from the circle. We shall trace the Forest boundary along the river to Erme or Erme Head, which the Perambulators take to be a place named in the said (old) records Grimsgrove.* Hence we shall strike across a tract of unvaried morasses, or bog-lands, to Plym Head, following the guidance of the Forest boundary line, which is here drawn from point to point, —from the source of the Avon to the springs of the Plym. Here the south quarter ends, and the western takes its commencement ; and near this point, about a quarter of a mile west of Plym Head, in Langcombe Bottom, with Sheepstor looming boldly against the western sky, we shall observe one of the most perfect specimens of the antient Kistvaen in the whole of Dartmoor—Grimsgrave or Grimsgrove.† This aboriginal sarcophagus is formed of granite slabs, about a hand-breadth in thickness. The side stones of the sarcophagus are four feet nine in length ; the foot stone is two feet three inches—the breadth of the kistvaen in the clear. The depth is about two feet. The coverstone has fallen in, but in other respects this antient sepulchre is singularly perfect. It seems to have been constructed on an artificial mound, or tumulus, slightly elevated above the natural level. A circular inclosure, fourteen feet in diameter, surrounds the kistvaen ; the stones

---

*Some etymologists have traced the name of Graham, or Graeme, in Grimsgrove and Grimspound, and have thought that these appellations should be included in the same etymological category with Graham's dyke.

†The votaries of nature, no less than the sons of Nimrod, will cordially respond to the general sentiment of the following characteristic lines, which were obligingly brought under our notice, at Goodamoor—formerly the seat of the late Paul Ourry Treby, now of Gen. Phillipps Treby—by whom the attention of the author to this kistvaen was first directed, and cannot be more appositely inserted than in this place.

" Let Fashion exult in her giddy career,
And headlong her course through the universe steer ;
There's a land in the west never bowed to her throne,
Where Nature for ages has triumphed alone,
And Dian oft revels in wild ecstacy,
O'er gray granite tors, or soft mossy lea,
Where the fox loves to kennel, the buzzard to soar
All boundless and free o'er the rugged Dartmoor.
    *      *      *      *

Far removed be the day ere Fashion deface
The features and charms of this primitive place !
    *      *      *      *

The Freehold of Nature, though rugged it be,
Long, long may it flourish, unsullied and free ;
May the fox love to kennel, the buzzard to soar,
As tenants of Nature on rugged Dartmoor."

From the song "The Rugged Dartmoor" by the Rev. E. W. L. DAVIS. Since published in his volume, "*Dartmoor Days, or Scenes in the Forest.*" p. 109, 1863.

of which it is formed, nine in number, remain erect in their
original position.   The ground on all sides, is much overgrown with heather, and the antiquary without a guide may
have some difficulty in finding the object of his search, but by
crossing the boggy tableland from Yealm Head to Plym Head,
N. N. W., and by following one of the springs of the Plym, as it
flows down Langcombe Bottom, carefully examining the right-
hand banks as he proceeds, he will not fail to discover near it the
northern brink of the stream.   Or if he comes from the Sheepstor
side and traces the river upwards, he will find it conversely on the
left hand.   And whilst he will not grudge the trouble of pene-
trating these difficult and dreary moorlands, he will scarcely fail
to be struck with surprise, to find this primitive tomb in the midst
of the wilderness, so far remote from every vestige of the occupation of living inhabitants.[*]

Turning from the Forest boundary, and mounting the bank
opposite to the kistvaen, we shall traverse the morasses, and pass
a modern bound-stone marked on three faces L.B.P. in our way
to Yealm Head.   This river takes its rise on the southern verge
of the swampy table-land, which stretches to a wide extent above
the sources of the Avon, the Erme, the Plym, and the Yealm.
We shall follow the course of the latter stream, down a narrow
moorland glen, between Broadall Down, and Stalldon Moor.   As
we skirt along the western bank, we shall observe on the opposite
declivity of Stalldon Moor, what the late Mr. Thomas Kelly
describes as one of the largest and best specimens of the aboriginal
village, on the western side of the moor.

In this glen, about a mile from the source, below the Waterfall, will be found the ruins of a building which was conjectured
by Henry Woollcombe (who discovered it in 1844) to have
been a hermitage.   " Far in a wild, unknown to public view," it
certainly is, and thus might have met the wishes of the most
solitary anchorite.   Sooth to say, the recluse might have found
some difficulty in supplying his scrip with fruits and herbs, like
the " gentle hermit of the dale " of lyric fame, except when June
had ripened the purple whortleberry ; but a supply of water from
the spring, clear and abundant, the Yealm would furnish, as it
flowed close to the walls of the sequestered cell, in a succession

---

*Reference may be here made to two clever papers by Mr. R. HANSFORD WORTH,
"*The Moorland Plym,*" and " *The Erme, Yealm, and Torry.*"  In these the topography
of the country near these rivers, and the antiquities are fully described.   Trans.
Plym. Inst., vol. x., 1889-90, p. 289; vol. xi., 1891-2, p. 173.

of cheery little waterfalls. A narrow strip of level ground runs along the river's brink, backed by a rocky scarp on the east. Under the lee of this ledge, are the ruined walls of a small oblong building, which (it seems almost wrong to interfere with the poetical idea of the hermit's cell) was a smelting or blowing-house, inclosing an area about twenty-one feet by sixteen. The walls are formed of large stones, laid in earth; no mortar appears to have been used. The remains of the walls are from one foot to three in height. The door was in the north-east corner. A squared stone, much mutilated, will also be noticed, in which two oblong apertures have been made. In the eastern wall is a mould, which Woollcombe thought was a piscina. The late Thomas Kelly published an account in the Journal of the Royal Institution of Cornwall, of the Yealm blowing-houses and the moulds found in them. They have been illustrated by Mr. R. Hansford Worth, and have been examined by Mr. Baring-Gould and Mr. John D. Pode, but no discoveries of any importance were made.*

Leaving the banks of the Yealm, and crossing Broadall Down, W. by S., we shall reach one of the tributaries of that river, rising in the hill-side below Pen Beacon. On the ascent immediately above, we shall observe the remains of numerous hut-circles, and other vestiges of antient occupation, within a large irregular curvilinear inclosure. From hence, mounting the hill, N.W. by N., we shall make for the cairn on the summit, well-known by the name of Pen Beacon. From this cairn, a trackline proceeds directly along the ridge; this we shall follow in the direction of the neighbouring eminence, which we shall observe rising above Pen Beacon to the north. As we proceed, we find the trackline, which probably here served as a boundary, on its approach to Shell Top, diverging from the tor on the summit, a little to the east. Here, as on Whittaburrow, a cairn has been built round the tor, which is of small size, and consists of layers of native rock, rising like shelves above the surrounding aggregation of loose stones. Shell Top, or to adopt the more euphonious appellation of the moormen, Penshiel, rises to the height of sixteen hundred feet above the sea-level, and is one hundred and thirty feet higher than Pen Beacon. As frontier heights, these are both

---

*For a further account of these houses, and for full information as to mining on Dartmoor generally, we must refer our readers to the very valuable contributions of Mr. ROBERT BURNARD to the history of the subject, *vide* " On the Track of the Old Men, Dartmoor,' and " Antiquity of Mining on Dartmoor," in the *Transactions of the Plymouth Institution* for 1888, 1889 and 1891.

conspicuous objects from all the adjacent lowlands; whilst the prospect from their summit, comprehending the greater part of those objects seen from the Western Beacon, is still more exten-sive towards the north-west, where Mistor, Cockstor, and Stapletor are seen on the western borders, and Bellever is discernible in the very centre of the moor, peering over the line of table-land on the north-east. The lake-like appearance of the estuaries of our Devonshire rivers, is here even still more decisive. If acquainted with the country, we can almost trace by its wooded banks, a great part of the course of the Yealm :—

" Pride of our austral vales "

as Carrington styles it, from the point where we left it before, through the pleasant vale of Blachford (with the church and village of Cornwood on the western bank above) onwards to the estuary, where surrounded by the groves and heights of Kitley, Puslinch, and Wembury, we can discern its tidal waters "sleeping in sunshine" like an inland lake. The Lary (the estuary of the Plym) seen curving round Saltram point; the Lynher, or St. German's lake; and the Tamar between Beer Ferrers and Landulph, are all visible, presenting the appearance of inland sheets of water more or less extensive.

But we must leave this noble panorama, and descend the south-western slope of the hill to examine a considerable aboriginal village, where the hut-circles are of the usual description, but the circumvallation is rectangular instead of oval or circular, as is more generally seen. Lower down is Whithill Yeo, where the Torry, a considerable tributary of the Plym, takes its rise. Passing through a moor gate, we now proceed S. S. W., to Cholwich Town moor, where, on the lands of the Earl of Morley, near Tolch Gate, there is a single line of stones, placed at regular intervals, of precisely the same description as the double lines, or avenues, already noticed in other parts of the moor. This venerable monument of antiquity has been lamentably despoiled within the last few years, but the line can still be traced to the extent of upwards of seven hundred feet. The stones are placed erect, at intervals of from three to six feet; at the northern extremity is a sacred circle of five yards in diameter, formed of six stones. The line runs nearly north and south; the highest stone is about six feet. A much larger stone was removed a short time since; this is described as having been twelve feet high, and was therefore probably a menhir, similar to others on the moor.

Under any circumstances, such spoliation would be most justly censured; how much more, when the whole neighbourhood abounds with granite, in all respects adapted for the purposes of the railway contractors, so that there is not the slightest plea for the sacrificing of those monuments of past ages at the shrine of modern enterprise. In the lane leading to Cholwich Town Farm house, is an antient stone cross, doing duty as a gatepost.

Passing through Tolch moor-gate, in the direction of Brimedge or Brimage, we shall notice some traces of tracklines and hut-circles much obliterated. From hence we shall pass Goodamoor. Near here, in the course of draining operations in the grounds of Mr. John D. Pode, Slade Hall, was found in July, 1879, an ingot of tin. Its weight is fifty-one pounds and a half; on its upper surface it measured fourteen inches by eight and a half inches, and on the lower, eleven inches by seven inches, and it is about three inches in thickness. It was presented by Mr. Pode to the Museum of the Plymouth Institution. Here we follow the Plympton road through the village of Sparkwell, and passing Beechwood,* the seat of Lord Seaton, formerly of Col. Mudge, to whose Ordnance Map of Devon, the Dartmoor tourist is so much indebted. We here leave the Plympton road and turning to the right, shall skirt the eastern side of Hemerdon Ball, on which an encampment for troops was formed at the beginning of the present century, in prospect of a French invasion; and which was then a heath-covered common, but which has since been cultivated almost to the summit, by the judicious management of a former proprietor, the late Admiral Woollcombe, of Hemerdon.

From hence we shall soon enter upon a good road which passes from Ivybridge, through Cornwood towards Tavistock, and in the neighbourhood we have just left, and as we advance

---

*The Beech grows vigorously in many spots on our moorland borders. At Great Fulford, the fine old seat of F. D. Fulford, Esq., is a noble avenue, so widely spreading that Virgil might have placed Tityrus with perfect satisfaction under the shade of the least. The seat of Lord Seaton, on the south border, derives its name from a number of these stately trees, which adorn and characterise the spot. In antient times the numbers were probably far greater, and with the oak, might have been frequented by our Pagan ancestors for the purposes of worship; and if our excursion from the heights of Pensheil to Beechwood has been made under a cloudless sky, we shall fully enter into the feelings of the friend of Wilberforce, who thus felicitously describes the amenities of a beechen grove, and carries us back to Druidical associations. "O what a delicious oratory is a beech wood in a calm hot "day! Not a leaf stirring,—not a sound,—a sacred kind of steady light, with here "and there a straggling sunbeam, like the gleam of providential direction in the "dark concerns of life. I do not doubt that the Druidical influence arose from the "worship in woods. It must have been irresistibly imposing.

J. Stephens to W. Wilberforce.—*Life*, vol ii., pp, 463-4.

along the commons, shall notice china-clay works on the lands of
the Rev. G. L. Woollcombe, the Earl of Morley, and others.   By
the roadside, on the right, on Lee Moor, north of the buildings
connected with these works, is a rude, massive cross, known as
Blackaton, the Roman or St. Rumon's Cross, the shaft of
which appeared to have been broken off, was there as only enough
left to raise the cross slightly above the large block in which a
socket had been formed to receive it.   It has now, however, by
the care of the Earl of Morley, been restored to what is supposed
was its original height, about six feet.   Diverging from the road,
and proceeding to the westward of the Morley clay works, we
shall find, near the road from those works to Shaugh church-town,
a singular relic, known in the neighbourhood as the Roman Camp,
but which, it certainly is not; nor does it appear to be an
entrenchment belonging either to the British, Saxon, or Danish
periods.   In form, it is a parallelogram, measuring one hundred
and fifty feet by eighty-six; the ramparts, or artificial banks by
which it is surrounded, are from twenty-six to forty feet high in
some places, and have been evidently constructed with sod and
earth taken from the inside, and not from without, so as to form
a fosse for more effectual defence, as is usually done.   Since it
could not have been an entrenchment for defence, the conjecture
has been hazarded that this singular erection might have been for
the purpose of exhibiting games, or for other large assemblies of
people, but in all probability it is nothing more than a reservoir
for water, of comparatively modern construction.

Returning to the highway, we shall proceed to Cadaford
Bridge; and diverging to the right, along the banks of the Plym
—sometimes erroneously called the Cad—shall visit Trowlsworthy
Warren, for the purpose of examining a group of antient relics in
that neighbourhood.   One of the numerous Dartmoor streams
which bear the name of Blackabrook, here renders its tribute to
the Plym.   There are two important enclosures, pounds, or
fortifications, one near the eastern bank of the Lee Moor China
Clay Works leat, the other on the same side, further to the north-
east.   Within both are hut circles.   The entrances to these are of
much interest, as they are protected by cross-shaped walls.   Near
the Warren House are two circular pounds, one with two hut
circles, the other with one only, and there are other enclosures.
Here is a curious wall, built evidently for protection, and the ruins
of a square building of early date.   It is thirty-four feet long by

eighteen feet wide, the walls are of rough granite, three feet in thickness. There are two stone rows, one double, the other single. The former runs nearly north and south, and is about four hundred and twenty feet long : at the north is a circle which is perfect, twenty-three feet in diameter, formed of eight stones, and at the south end, not far from the termination of the row, is a single stone. The second, the single row, runs east and west, and is about two hundred and fifty feet long, with a circled cairn, ending with a pillar. This row was rescued from destruction, in 1859, by the Rev. W. I. Coppard, the then incumbent of St. Mary's, Plympton. He wrote, "a party of navvies were employed in "cutting a small ditch for a water-course. To save the trouble of "getting materials at a very trifling distance, the men were "carrying off some of the stones from the avenue, which was near "at hand, and had blasted some of them with gun-powder. "Fortunately, the work of destruction had only just begun. I "took upon myself to stop this mischievous proceeding, and "hastened to my friend, Admiral Woollcombe, of Hemerdon, the "owner of the property, who immediately despatched peremptory "orders to prevent any similar damage in future."

Returning to the banks of the Plym, we follow the course of the river through a deep border-glen, which, under the name of the valley of the Cad, is thus graphically described by one of the annotators of Carrington, the son of the poet, H. E. Carrington:— "The traveller will behold the valley of the Cad to the greatest "advantage, by descending the left bank of the river from Cadaford "Bridge. . . . . . The right bank rises to a dizzy "height covered with a beautiful profusion of young trees. It is "opposed, however, on the other side by a slope of very different "appearance. All there is dreary, yet magnificent—barrenness "without a bough to shade it, and at first sight without a vegetable "beauty to recommend it. Huge fragments of granite lie scattered "about in wildest confusion. Some masses appear as if they had "just been torn out of the bowels of the moor by some unearthly "power; others are on tiptoe to quit their precarious situations "and roll down to the flashing torrent." Allured by such a description to thread the rocky mazes of this sequestered glen, we shall proceed until the rugged crest of Dewerstone, sung by more than one native minstrel, is descried towering above the scene. "This huge mass of rock," continues the same writer, "rises "perpendicularly from the stream to an immense height. Its

M

" whole surface is jagged and seamed in the manner so peculiar to
" granite, which makes the beholder imagine that the stones are
" regularly piled on each other.   It is profusely overgrown with
" ivy and other creeping plants which spread their pleasing foliage
" over its shattered front, as if anxious to bind up the wounds that
" time and tempest have inflicted.   To add to the striking effect of
" its appearance, numerous hawks, ravens, &c.,* may be seen
" floating around its rugged crest, and filling the air with their
" hoarse screamings.   The rocks immediately beneath seem as if
" they had been struck at once by a thousand thunderbolts, and
" appear only prevented from bursting asunder by chains of ivy.
" A few wild flowers are sprinkled about in the crevices of the
" cliff; tufts of broom wave like golden banners in the passing
" breeze; and these, with here and there a mountain ash, clinging
" half-way down the precipice, impart a wild animation to the
" spot."

We wind down the glen to Shaugh Bridge, amidst the familiar
scenes upon which the muse of Carrington loved to dwell, where
from " Dartmoor's prolific bosom,"

> " Rolls the Plym,
> With murmuring course by Sheepstor's dark-brow'd rock,
> And Meavy's venerable oak, to meet
> The ever-brawling Cad.†   How oft, as noon,
> Unnotic'd, faded into eve, my feet
> Have linger'd near thy bridge, romantic Shaugh!
> While as the sister waters rush'd beneath,
> Tumultuous, haply glanc'd the setting beam
> Upon the crest of Dewerstone."

This river has been happily characterized by our bard, as " the

---

*We do not know what the writer may have seen, but the visitor to the Dewer-
stone will now look in vain for " *numerous hawks, ravens, &c.*"

†The late N. Howard, of Tamerton, near Plymouth, in his interesting local
poem, *Bickleigh Vale*, has sketched some points of this border scenery in flowing
numbers.
> " Hence the Cad, o'er rocks white flashing, roars,
>    To meet the lucid Plym."

But both poets seem to be mistaken in designating this stream by the name of Cad.
That it is properly the Plym is evident from Plym Head being known as the source,
and Plym Steps being also on the same branch, not far from the source.   The name
of Cadaford Bridge has probably given rise to the mistake—it having been inferred
that *Cadaford* must necessarily mean the ford of the river Cad.   But *Cad* is a *battle-
field*.   Hence it may be conjectured, on more satisfactory grounds, that this bridge
may have been so designated from some unrecorded conflict on the neighbouring
moors.   The western branch of the Plym which joins it above Shaugh Bridge, has
been by some called the Mew

D E W E R S T O N E .

"sylvan Plym."* At Shaugh Bridge this pleasing and characteristic feature begins to be decisively manifested. Here the stern
ruggedness of the upland ravine appears blended with the softer
lineaments of downs and woodlands. From Dewerstone to
Saltram Point, where its estuary widens into a tidal lake, the
banks of the Plym are, for the most part, clothed with woods,
chiefly of England's national tree, the noble oak. The bold
headland, from the eastern flank of which Dewerstone protrudes, is
mantled with copse down to the "margent" of the united streams.
Few spots in the west display a greater share of natural charms
" than this vale in whose bosom the dark waters meet;" and here
too the "accidents" of moorland scenery in the most sublime and
awful forms may be contemplated, under singularly favourable
circumstances, by those who fear not to woo Nature in her wintry
garb, and in her mountain seclusion. A low temperature and a
thick fall of snow, are not unfrequently in our variable climate
succeeded by a rapid thaw, accompanied by heavy and continuous
rain. Such a sudden thaw took place during the severe winter of
1823, on the night of the the 27th of January. The pouring rains
and the melting snow rushed together from a hundred hills into a
narrow glen of the Plym, and speedily swelled the stream to a
mighty river, which overspread the entire floor of the vale, and
swept along high up the slopes of the acclivities with resistless
force, until the adamantine barrier of Dewerstone checked for a
moment the impetuous torrent. But like a furious animal loosened
from its bonds, and maddened by resistance, the raging stream
dashed its turbid waves against the beetling cliff and threw the
foaming spray, as in triumph, over its loftiest crag, while the roar
of conflict was heard far along the echoing dales. The unbridled
flood came careering down the widened vale, and rushing amain
through the lofty arch of old Shaugh Bridge, filled it to the
key-stone, and directing the main force of its overflowing current
along the eastern bank, dislodged the huge masses which formed
the antient causeway to the mill, as though they had been pebbles.
This bridge has been replaced by the present substantial structure
of hewn granite.

Following the road along the line of this causeway, we shall
diverge from the river and mount the hill, eastward, on our way to

* Plym, says Baxter in his glossary, from *Pilim*, Erse or Celtic, to roll, but the
origin of the word is one of the puzzles of Devonian nomenclature. See Plympton
Castle, by J. BROOKING-ROWE, *Trans. Plym. Institution.* Vol: vi, pp. 247, 248.

Shaugh church-town, a straggling village of genuine moorland character. The rude simplicity of this hamlet, and the Alpine wildness of the whole surrounding scenery, (in the opinion of a noble lady of no mean authority on points of art and taste, the late Countess of Morley,) forcibly impress the travelled observer with their resemblance to some well-remembered scenes amidst the Swiss mountains. The village church, with its lofty, well proportioned moorstone steeple, forms a conspicuous and pleasing object as we ascend the breezy common. And should we be tempted to turn aside to examine more closely this simple but venerable moorland sanctuary, we shall doubtless hear from the sexton an account of the well-remembered thunder-storm, which occured in the same winter as the flood above recorded, and which would have been no less terrific in its results than that of Widecombe, had it not providentially happened on a weekday, instead of on Sunday, in service time, as in the former case. The lightning struck off one of the pinnacles of the tower level with the battlements; and hurled the fragments on the roof over the southern aisle, the western part of which was laid in ruins. About two hundred and thirty panes of glass were shivered, and among the few that escaped uninjured, was a small one, at the east end, of stained glass, the emblazonment of which intimated the antient dependance of Shaugh church upon the priory of Plympton. Stones of large size were flung into the neighbouring croft, at a considerable distance. The rural chronicler will perhaps " point "a moral," by telling us that a parish meeting for certain business, had been fixed to be held in that very part of the west end of the aisle where the pinnacle fell and where, had the parishioners met as intended, the loss of life must have been far more terrific than at Widecombe:—he will probably assure us that there were many who thought at the time that the thunder-storm was intended to admonish against such a profanation of the house of God in future.

" rubente
Dextera sacras jaculatus arces."

On Shaugh Common, east of the village, we shall notice many remains of hut-circles, as well as some larger inclosures. Proceeding along the slope of the common, above the road from Shaugh to Plympton, we shall observe an interesting relic of the dolmen kind, but to which Polwhele denies the honour, for reasons, which on examination of the object itself, will immediately appear inapplicable and groundless. The impost-stone is doubtless supported in an unusual manner, resting partly on a ledge of rock which forms also a natural wall on one side of the area covered by the quoit, but artificially supported on the other side. The impost apparently, stands in its original position, and is similar in appearance to those which belong to undisputed dolmens.

Returning to the road, we pass through the moor-gate on the south, and following the highway towards Plympton, shall observe on the high ground south of Brixton Farm (originally known as Heath Down, but now inclosed) the vestiges of a camp, fort, or entrenchment. The site is of great strength, and standing five hundred feet above the sea, it commands the Plym estuary, and the valleys through which the streams running into it flow, and Plymouth Sound is clearly seen some seven miles away. It is known as Boringdon camp, sometimes, but not often, Castle Ring.* It has a circumference of five hundred yards, enclosing an area of about four acres. There is a single rampart and a ditch, the former in fair condition and easily traced ; the latter, except in one part, is destroyed. An engineer officer pointed out to us the fact, that this camp is in a direct line to Plympton Castle, and he thought that the people who raised the earthworks of the southern fortification, constructed the more distant one of Boringdon. The Buri-ton—for Boringdon is a late corruption of the original name—"was the fortified house and courtyard " of the mighty man, the king, the magistrate and the noble," as Bishop Stubbs says.—In Plympton, we have besides the burh, the township, the little knot of houses which clustered round the stronghold for shelter and protection, in times when life and property were not so safe as in our more happy days.

From hence we soon reach a sylvan lane which descends the hill between Newnham Park on the left, and the grounds of Elfordleigh on the right, and conducts us to the vale of the Torry, at Loughtor Mill, where we cross the stream, amidst scenery of much interest. Still journeying southwards, within two miles we shall arrive at the village of Ridgeway, where the name of the antient Roman road is still preserved in the modern appellation,

---

*This is the name commonly applied to the mound, with the masonry wall upon it, of Plympton Castle.

and where, in all probability, it will be found that the line of the antient highway is indicated, for some distance at least, by the present mail-road from Plymouth to Exeter.   At Plympton, in the vale below, as a stannary town, and as a place where the antiquary will not fail to find many objects of sufficient interest to excite inquiry and to repay examination, we shall terminate our excursion.

# CHAPTER VIII.

## The Perambulation Continued and Concluded,
## Plympton to Tavistock and Okehampton.

At the two Plymptons,— ecclesiastically St. Mary, and St. Maurice—we shall find within the circuit of about half a mile, an undoubted Roman road, the very complete mound and earthworks of a Pre-Norman fortress, the remains of the massive walls of the keep of a Norman baronial castle— with the base court, moat, and barbican clearly defined; the site and vestiges of a once wealthy and important priory; two churches of hewn stone, both, especially that of St. Mary, full of architectural interest, and a large school-house, raised on arches, with high-pitched roof, mullioned windows, and a spacious piazza below, and both indicating their proximity to the moorland district by the granite of which they are constructed.   Plympton St. Maurice, otherwise Plympton Comitis, Plympton Earl—the Earl being Baldwin, Earl of Devon, who gave the inhabitants in 1242, their first charter—was a borough town, and until 1832 returned two members to parliament, and the well-known couplet, current in the neighbourhood, alludes to the comparatively recent origin of its prosperous daughter town of Plymouth.

> " Plympton was a borough town,
> When Plymouth was a vuzzy down."

A respectable looking Guildhall, of the latter part of the seventeenth century, built on arches and projecting into the street according to the prevailing fashion, stands, as a monument of departed municipal honours.   The castle, once the possession of the powerful family of Redvers, earls of Devon, which overawed and protected their subject town, nestled in its pleasant valley under its formidable bulwarks.   The church was originally a chapel, served by the canons of Plympton Priory, adjoining. The Grammar school—the foundation of Elizeus Hele—is celebrated as the place where Sir Joshua Reynolds was born and received the rudiments of his education, under his father, then the master of the school.   Plympton, although not larger than many villages, is a complete town in miniature, with its continuous lines of houses, paved streets, and public buildings ; and with him, who like the author, cannot revisit its well-remembered purlieus, without a crowd of pleasing associations with by-gone years, the Donjon keep, the old penthouse, the venerable school, and the Great House—formerly the seat of the Trebys, now a private lunatic asylum—will remain indelibly impressed upon the memory as the characteristic features of the miniature municipality. From the ruined walls of the keep, or the loftier vantage ground of the tor-capt eminence, which rises boldly above the town on the south-west, all the varied and pleasing objects of the renowned and cheerful vale of Plympton, bounded on the north by the Dartmoor range, will be full in view, nor will he fail to recall with personal application, the appropriate lines of the great master of the English lyre:—

> " I feel the gales that from ye blow,
>  A momentary bliss bestow,
>    As waving fresh, with gladsome wing,
>  My weary soul they seem to sooth,
>  And redolent of joy and youth,
>    To breathe a second spring."

Coming down from the hill—Dorsmouth or Dartmouth—by a steep lane which enters the road at the west of Plympton, we shall proceed on our next excursion through Dark Street lane. In the significant appellation of *street*, most antiquaries detect good evidence of the existence of an old Roman road *(strata via)* and the proximity of the Ridge-way, to which we again return at the end of Dark Street lane, in the present instance, greatly favours the hypothesis.

Beyond the western extremity of the village of Ridgeway, in a low situation,* near the banks of the Torry Brook, a tributary of the Plym, we shall obtain a nearer view of the fine old parish church of Plympton St. Mary. The lofty granite tower, embattled, pinnacled, and crocketted; north and south porches, and the south aisle, also embattled; and the five roofs are the external features of this interesting specimen of Perpendicular architecture which will immediately strike the antiquarian observer. Nor will he be disappointed in the interior, where the

---

*A legend (similar to one found in other parts) connected with the building of this church, is called into requisition to account for its erection in a situation which originally must have been little better than a marsh. The site fixed upon (certainly a more central and dry one than the present) is said to have been Crownhay Castle, about a mile to the eastward, near the present Chaddlewood lodge, and there, accordingly, materials for the future church were deposited. But, to the astonishment of the workmen, the stone and timber collected there by day, were regularly and pertinaciously removed, by the Enemy at night; until at length, wearied by repeated attempts to build on the original site, the architect was constrained to erect his church where it now stands, some four or five miles from the eastern extremity of the parish. Those, however, who connect this legend with Plympton, forget the history of the church, and the topographical changes that have taken place. The church was built for the parishioners by the canons of Plympton, in the cemetery of the priory. The waters of the estuary flowed up close to the western side of the priory precincts, which side was protected from the incursions of the sea, by a massive masonry wall, in which were landing places for those persons who might arrive by barge or boat. After the dissolution no care was taken to keep this wall up, and it became a ruin, and much silting in consequence, took place, as will be seen from the condition of the tower of the church, the lower part of the buttresses, which should be visible, being buried. Important embanking operations undertaken early in this century, by the ancestors of the Earl of Morley, and alterations effected by the present Earl, have done very much to improve the condition of St. Mary's Churchyard and its surroundings.

eastern window in particular, the sedilia, the Courtenay and Strode monuments, the chapels, and the four arcades, will not fail to attract his attention.   Until recently, considerable remains of the once flourishing priory might have been observed on the south side of the church, but new buildings on the site have now reduced them to a few meagre relics.   On the south east the priory mill still exists.

At Plympton St. Mary bridge, we diverge from the Plymouth turnpike, and follow the road by which, from early times, an intercourse was kept up between the antient towns of Plympton and Tavistock.   Passing over the saddle of the hill, it skirts Boringdon Park—at one time the seat of the Parker's—ancestors of the Earls of Morley, who abandoned it in the middle of last century for the present residence, Saltram—and dropping into the well-wooded vale of the Plym, crosses that river at Plym Bridge, near which, beneath the trees on the right of the road, will be observed the scanty remains of an antient ruined chapel or cell.   We cross the bridge and mount the opposite hill to the Plymouth and Dartmoor railway—now only used for the conveyance of clay from the Lee Moor works—which follows the frequent sinuosities of the declivities, along which it is carried, and thus discloses, in succession, the justly celebrated charms of Bickleigh Vale, nor could a pleasure drive through a lordly domain, have been more felicitously laid out for the enjoyment of the scenery, than the line of railway between Leigham and the village of Jump, now called Roborough, where it skirts the Tavistock turnpike at the southern extremity of Roborough Down.   Here we look down upon the village and well-proportioned granite church-tower of Bickleigh, with Shaugh and the Dewerstone among the purple heights eastwards.

We pass over a breezy tract of open country, bounded by the ground of Maristow on one side, and the western branch of the Plym, or Mew, on the other, to the eastern verge of Roborough Down, at Hoo Meavy Bridge.   Here we cross the river and proceed to the village of Meavy (which appears to take its name from the neighbouring stream) where we shall pause to examine the simple rural church, with the venerable oak in front, coeval perhaps with the sacred structure itself.   The tree is of no great height, but spreads widely, and the trunk is of large circumference. Completely hollowed out as it is, it yet bears its leafy honours aloft, and presents an object of much interest and picturesque beauty. The village chronicles relate that nine persons once dined within the hollow trunk, where a peat-stack may now be frequently seen, piled up as winter fuel. The village cross, hard by, of which for a long time the base only remained intact, has been restored to its former condition, a former Vicar, the Rev. W. A. G. Gray having, with praiseworthy industry, sought out and recovered the stones belonging to it, which were scattered in various places about the parish, and added a newly carved head. Marchant's or Merchant's Cross, a very fine one, on the other side of the stream, we shall notice as we leave Meavy and trace the course of the river upwards to the adjoining parish of Sheepstor or Shitestor, noticing the waterfall as we proceed. The village church, with its moorstone tower, stands at the foot of the strange-shaped rugged tor, which rises boldly above, and gives name to the parish. We climb the hill, and soon find ourselves in a wilderness of scattered moorstone masses, with which the whole southern slope is profusely covered. In the midst of the *clatter* we shall discover the cave, or Pisky House, as it is popularly called, in which it is said, that one of the family of Elford once found a secure asylum in the troublous times of the civil wars. The opening, which is exceedingly difficult to find without a guide, is under an overhanging mass of moorstone. The passage proceeds at first in a straight direction, but suddenly turns, and terminates in a sort of recess, where two or three persons might lie concealed. The notion that this cave is the resort of the piskies or pixies, appears still to be extant in the neighbourhood.

Almost due east from Sheepstor the moorlands rise into a high ridge, the loftiest point of which is at Eylesburrow, where we once more meet the Forest boundary, coming hither in a direct line from Plym Head. From Eylesburrow we trace the bounds by an imaginary line to Siward's or Nun's Cross, which has inscribed on one face of the stone, the words Crux Siwardi, and on the other it has been thought the word Roolande, but Mr. W. Crossing has, we think, satisfactorily shewn that the latter word is not as stated, but Bocland, which is carved on the western face of the cross, the side on which the lands of the Monks of Buckland Abbey lay.* It appears that in the year 1846, by some means never satisfactorily ascertained, this antient cross was overthrown

---

*See Antient Crosses of Dartmoor, W. CROSSING. pp, 30, 31, and for the boundaries of the Abbey lands, J. BROOKING ROWE, *The Cistercian Houses of Devon*. p. 29.

and broken.  That a monument so interesting has not been irrecoverably lost, is owing to the timely care of the late Sir Ralph Lopes, who caused it to be repaired and replaced in its former position.

The remains of another cross in this quarter of the moor has been supposed to point out the spot where Childe, of Plymstock, was benighted and perished with intense cold, but this may be mere conjecture.  If Risdon's account is to be credited, the place where " the luckless hunter," near Fox Tor, met his death was marked by some kind of sepulchral monument.  This our quaint topographer describes as the second of the three remarkable things in the Forest.  " The second is Childe's of Plimstock's " tomb, of the manner of whose death mention is already made, " in Plimstock, which is to be seen in the moor, where he was " frozen to death."  The story of his slaying and disembowelling his horse to shelter himself from the biting blasts of the moor, and of his leaving a couplet to the following effect, which contained his last will and testament, written with his own blood, has been often told as well as sung.*

> The fyrste that fyndes and brings me to my grave,
> The lands of Plymstoke they shall have.

" Now whatever," observes Mrs. Bray, " modern critics may " think of the rhyme, it soon appeared that the monks of Tavistock " found there was reason in it, and good reason too, that they " should constitute themselves heirs of old Childe; for soon " hearing that he was frozen to death, somewhere near Crockern " Tor, they set their wits and hands to work to give him as speedily " as possible an honourable sepulchre.

" But as the heirship was thus left vague and open to competi- " tion, there were others who thought themselves quite as much, " if not more, entitled to succeed than the friars, and these were " the good people of Plymstock, in whose parish the lands in " question had their standing; and though not invited to the " funeral, yet out of respect to the old gentleman, or more " probably to his acres, they not only determined to invite them- " selves, but also to try how far club-law might settle the heirship

---

*CARRINGTON has sung the fate of the ill-starred sportsman in a spirited ballad, entitled *Childe the Hunter*, which concludes in the following stanzas :—

> " Yet one dear wish—one tender thought,
>   Came o'er that hunter brave,
> To sleep at last in hallow'd ground,
>   And find a Christian grave."

" in their favour ; and so taking post at a certain bridge, over
" which they conceived the corpse must of necessity be carried
" they came to the resolution to arrest the body out of the hands of
" the holy men by force, if no better settlement of the matter
" could be affected.

" The friars however were men of peace, and had no mind,
" may be to take up any weapon sharper than their wits ; since as
" Dr. Fuller says when speaking of this adventure, ' they must
" ' rise betimes, or rather not go to bed at all, that will overreach
" ' the monks in matter of profit ; ' for these cunning brothers,
" apprehensive of losing their precious relics, cast a slight bridge
" over the river at another place, and thus crossing with the
" corpse, they left the men of Plymstock the privilege of becoming
" very sincerely the chief mourners, whilst they interred old Childe
" in their own abbey church, and according to his last will took
" possession of his lands. ' In memory whereof' says Risdon,
" ' the bridge beareth the name of Guile Bridge to this day ; ' but
" according to Mrs. Bray, is now more commonly known by the
" name of the Abbey Bridge," which crosses the Tavy at the
south entrance of the town by the old Plymouth road. As the
Childe was buried at Tavistock, his monument in the Forest wilds
must have been a cenotaph. It is said to have existed till within
the beginning of this century, and then to have been destroyed by
the grantee of a new-take. Some of the stones which composed it
have been found, and the monument re-erected in 1890, under the
direction of Mr. E. Fearnley Tanner. The restorer, however, is not
satisfied with the result, stones being missing, and it being found
so difficult to maintain the original character of the monument.
There are many difficulties and discrepancies in the current
accounts of Childe and his fate, which it is difficult to reconcile ;
yet the story claims insertion, as one of the characteristic traditions
of the moor, where from time to time many benighted and be-
wildered wanderers have lost their lives on the bleak and trackless
waste.

We shall proceed from Siward's Cross in our return to the
tributaries of the Mew, or western branch of the Plym in search
of Clacy Well or Crazy Well Pool. A rough moor-track comes
up the valley from Sheepstor and Leather Tor, and on the right of
this road, as we advance westward, we shall observe a miniature
ravine in the common, down which runs a noisy rivulet. By
following this stream upwards from the road we shall soon reach

the pool south-east of Stanlake, south-west of Cramber Tor, and within a short distance of the Devonport leat. Clacy, Clazy, or Crazy Well is a large pool, or sheet of water, which covers about an acre of ground. It has been dug out of the southern part of the hill and along the verge of the banks on the top, the measurement is three hundred and forty-six yards. From this part, which is level with the adjacent common, the banks slope rapidly down to the margin of the pool. On the east side the bank is almost perpendicular, and is nearly one hundred feet high. At the lowest part it is, at least, thirty, except on the south where the water finds an outlet. All the banks are covered with heather and other moor plants, like the neighbouring common; but there can be little doubt that the greater part of the hollow is an artificial excavation, and that the moormen's notion of it is probably correct in the main, that it was "an old antient mining pit." They will also relate that the pit has no bottom, because the bell-ropes of Wakington—Walkhampton—church tower were once tied together and let down to try the depth, but no bottom could be found. But unfortunately for this legend, its credit has been much damaged in hot summers, when the pool has been nearly drained dry, to supply the deficiencies of the neighbouring leat.

In our progress from Siward's Cross we shall probably not have deviated materially from the course of the Perambulation. The boundary is described as running lineally to Little Hisworthie, that is Hessary Tor. But we have now reached a tract rich in antiquities, and must not pass onwards without a careful examination of those which will be found at one of the head springs of the Mew, near Black Tor, which rises about twelve furlongs south-west of Hessary.

The tor itself on a near approach, forms a striking object. An immense block, resting slightly on the main pile, has much of the appearance of a logan stone. On the edge of this mass, is a rock-basin, of an irregular oval form, two feet eight inches by one foot ten inches. Nearly a furlong from the tor in the glen below, on the eastern bank of the stream, are a pair of rows which are only forty feet apart, and run parallel to each other, east and west. They are formed of stones two feet and a half high, and each is terminated at the east end by a circle, thirty-six feet in diameter, consisting of fifteen stones, inclosing a cairn. A stream forms the western termination of both these rows; the southern can be traced about two hundred feet, and the northern, which is more

perfect and distinct, upwards of four hundred feet.   The stones at
the head of the avenues are of larger dimensions than the others,
as in other examples.    Between the northern avenue and the
stream is a cairn.   Another will be observed at the extremity of
the southern, but very imperfect.    It is somewhat remarkable
that these avenues have escaped entire demolition, as they are
intersected diagonally by an old stream-work.

On the slope of an adjacent hill is a Pound, or circumvallation,
of an irregular form, three hundred and sixty yards in circumference, inclosing nine hut circles of the ordinary description.
Nearly opposite Stanlake Farm, on the same hill, fronting westward, is another Pound of similar character, but not more than
two-thirds the size of the former.    Within and without the fence
are many hut-circles.    On the eastern side flows a brooklet, which
appears to have been diverted from the natural channel below the
Pound.

Proceeding northwards towards Hessary, we shall reach the
high road from Plymouth to Prince Town.    In the immediate
neighbourhood of an antient stream-work, we shall observe a
number of hut-circles, close to the highway.    There are many
others on the slope of the opposite hill eastward, the foundation
slabs are very perfect, with the door jambs standing.    North-west
of these is a cairn containing a dilapidated kistvaen.    Following
the road from hence, we shall soon arrive at Prince Town, where,
or at Two Bridges, distant scarcely two miles, we shall find
accommodation for the night, and a central position from which a
great number of interesting objects can be conveniently visited.

Foremost amongst these is Crockern Tor, which we shall reach
by proceeding from Two Bridges along the Moreton turnpike-
road, from which town it is distant about eleven miles.    This tor
has long been celebrated as one of the wonders of the Forest,
although there are numerous other objects, of far greater interest
in reality, which have been passed without notice by those who
have commemorated the antient Parliament Rock.    Yet, if
Polwhele's conjecture deserves any credit, faint as are the existing
vestiges of bygone ages which will repay the antiquary's investigations at Crockern Tor, the charm of association will not be
wanting to impart interest to the scene.    Our provincial historian
having fixed the seat of judicature for his cantred of Durius, at
Grimspound, assigns Crockern Tor as the site of the supreme
court of the cantred of Tamara.    To these antient courts of

justice, if such there were, Polwhele traces the origin of the stannary parliaments of Devon and Cornwall, which he affirms "were similar in every point of resemblance to the old British "courts." He observes that "Crockern Tor, from its situation "in the middle of Dartmoor Forest, is undoubtedly a very strange "place for holding meetings of any kind. Exposed as it is to the "severities of the weather, and distant as it always has been, "within our own times and the memory of man, from every "human habitation, we might well be surprised that it should "have been chosen for the spot on which our laws were to be "framed, unless some peculiar sanctity had been attached to it, "in consequence of its appropriation to legal or judicial purposes, "from the earliest antiquity. Besides, there is no other instance "that I recollect, within our own times, of such a court, in so "exposed and so remote a place. On this tor, not long since, was "the warden's or president's chair, seats for the jurors, a high "corner stone for the crier of the court, and a table—all rudely "hewn out of the rough moorstone of the tor, together with a "cavern which, for the convenience of our modern courts, was "used in these latter ages, as a repository for wine. Notwith- "standing this provision, indeed, Crockern Tor was too cold and "dreary a place for our legislators of the last generation, who after "opening their commissions and swearing the jurors on this spot, "merely to keep up the old formalities, usually adjourned the "court to one of the stannary towns."

That Crockern Tor was long the place where the hardy stannators of the moorlands held their conventions must be received as an established historical fact, whatever may be thought of our author's hypothesis of the original choice of the spot for judicial purposes. Our older topographers notice the circumstance. Prince, who wrote in the year 1697, records that Crockern Tor in the Forest of Dartmoor, was the place "where the "parliament is wont to be held for stannary causes ; unto which "the four principal stannary towns, Tavistock, Plympton, Ash- "burton, and Chagford, send each twenty-four burgesses, who are "summoned thither, when the Lord Warden of the Stannaries, "sees occasion, where they enact statutes, laws, and ordinances, "which, ratified by the Warden aforesaid, are in full force in all "matters between tinner and tinner, life and limb excepted. This "memorable place is only a great rock of moorstone, out of which "a table and seats are hewn, open to all the weather, storms, and

"tempests, having neither house nor refuge near it by divers
"miles. The borough of Tavistock is said to be the nearest, and
"yet that is distant ten miles off."

It would, perhaps, be incorrect to say that no traces whatever
of this celebrated hypæthral court can now be detected; but on
careful examination they will be found to be lamentably slight, if
not decidedly equivocal. The common report that the most
remarkable objects, such as the table and seats, were removed and
destroyed by the workmen of Sir Francis Buller, then the owner
of the neighbouring estate of Prince Hall, has been condemned by
the annotators on Carrington's "Dartmoor," as a calumny,
although the Rev. E. Bray affirms that the allegation is so far
confirmed by the fact of his finding at Dunnabridge (the place
whither the stannary tables is reported to have been carried) a
tabular moorstone, eight feet long by nearly six wide, which the
farmer at Dunnabridge stated, from his own knowledge, to have
been there fifty years; and that he had heard it was brought from
Crockern Tor about eighty years ago. In the first volume of
Mrs. Bray's Letters,* is an amusing account of Mr. Bray's
pursuit of the lost relic in 1831, and of its alleged discovery at
Dunnabridge Farm, near the well-known drift-pound of that name
on the banks of the West Dart. In 1835, some information was
obtained by the author, from a moorland patriarch near the spot,
who stated that he had lived on the moor sixty years, and had
been in the service of Judge Buller. He remembered, perfectly
well, when there was a chair, or stone seat, at Crockern Tor, with
four or five steps to go up to it, and that overhead there was a
large flat thinnish stone. These were all by degrees removed for
building, the last of them having been taken away, as well as he
could remember, about twenty years before that time.

With these recollections in our mind, let us descend from
Crockern Tor, and strike across the common over Cherrybrook
to Dunnabridge Pound, on the Ashburton road. Immediately
within the entrance is a stone seat, which, if our aged informant's
account of the judge's stannary chair be accurate, would present
an appearance greatly similar to that venerable relic before it was
demolished. Although others may be unable to discover in Dunnabridge those unequivocal evidences of aboriginal antiquity, which
were so satisfactory to Mr. Bray, the conclusions to which a

---

*Borders of Tamar and Tavy. Letter vii., 1st ed. vol. i., p, 109; 2nd. ed. vol. i.,
p. 103.

N

practised observer was led, on personal examination, will not fail
to be interesting.   " Had I any doubt before that the pound was
" erected on the base of an antient British, or rather Celtic circle,
" I could not entertain it now, for I have not the slightest doubt of
" the high antiquity of this massy chair."   After speaking of the
Reeve (the probable despoiler of Crockern Tor), he adds, " but I am
" fully convinced that it was originally designed for a much greater
" personage; no less perhaps than an Archdruid or President of
" some court of judicature."*   Dunnabridge Pound occupies a
large area, inclosed by a rough moorstone wall.   It is now used
for the forest drifts, and is capable of containing vast numbers of
cattle.

Dunnabridge adjoins the Ashburton road, which we shall
follow, until we cross a tributary of the Dart.   Near this rivulet
on the common, east of the road is an aboriginal village enclosure,
but without any remains of hut-circles within the area.   We have
now again approached the Forest bounds, at the junction of the
east and south Quarters on the West Dart.   We therefore return
over the common near the rivulet above mentioned, with Loughtor
about half a mile north.   From hence we can make our way
through a succession of enclosed common lands, to Bellever—
that is Bellaford—Tor, below which on the S. S. W., is a huge
moorstone slab, raised about nine inches above the natural rock
on which it stands, so as to be made to vibrate easily.   This is
probably one of the many similar masses on the moor, which has
fortuitously assumed the logan character.   Should we search for
rock-basins on this conspicuous tor, we shall be disappointed, but
the venerable pile affords a fine central station, from whence a
noble panoramic view of the moor is obtained.   Holne Lee, southward; Hessary, Great Mistor, Longaford Tor, west; Sittaford,
north; Hameldon, Houndtor and Rippon Tor, east; with
Buckland Beacon, Corndon† Down, and Yartor, south-west; and
a vast extent of waste are the characteristic objects by which, on
all sides, we are surrounded.   In the name of Bellever, as well as
Belstone and Beltor, many with Polwhele have imagined that they
can discover traces of the idol-worship of the antient Britons, and

---

*Tamar and Tavy, 1st ed., vol. i., p. 134, 2nd ed., vol. i., p. 103.   From Mr. BRAY'S
Journal, published in this work in 1833, it appears that his recorded observations
extend as far back as 1802.

†In the Ordnance Map Quarnion, a most remarkable error.   Probably it is Cairn
or Carn Down, so named from the cairns thereabout.

proofs of the eastern origin of their religion, supposing these places to have been so designated, from the celebrated oriental deity, Bel, or Baal.

Descending from the tor, northward, we cross a moor-road leading from the turnpike to Bellever Farm.  Crossing this road to the common opposite, we shall find many aboriginal relics on Lakehead Hill.  On the higher part of the eminence is a congeries of stones, possibly the ruins of a very large kistvaen, one of the side stones being about six feet in length.  At the east end, the stone is fallen, and the cover is also displaced.  On the same hill, about a furlong N.W., is a kistvaen in great perfection, the sides which are about four feet four inches long, by one foot nine inches, and stand fifteen inches above the ground.  Another kistvaen, at no great distance, will be observed in connexion with a cairn, as in other places.  We return to the rough moor-road, and having noticed, on the descent opposite Bellever, a circle, twenty yards in circumference, shall proceed by Bellever Farm (one of the oldest moor-farms in the Forest) to Bellever Bridge adjoining.  Below the modern structure over the East Dart, are the remains of an aboriginal Cyclopean bridge of three openings.  The rude piers and abutments still remain, and one massive granite slab still spans each of the eastern and western openings; but the centre stone has been displaced, and no trace of it appears in the stream below.  This primitive bridge is similar to that at Post Bridge, higher up the stream, but the stones which span the waterway are not so large, measuring only twelve feet six inches in length.

From hence, passing over Redridge Down, where we shall notice a circular inclosure in a very imperfect state, we shall proceed to the Wallabrook, above which Corndon Tor rises on the south-east.  In this direction we shall observe many cairns, but none sufficiently remarkable to detain us from our progress up the Wallabrook, for the purpose of tracing the line of perambulation from hence to King's Oven, where we left it in our former excursion.  The original *Furnum Regis*, the King's Oven, the tin smelting place, was destroyed probably some time during the last century, and was reduced to further ruin by the removal of stones, or the construction of the buildings of Bush Down Mine, which are hard by, but the site is still indicated by a pile of stones, in the midst of a pound that is nearly circular.  There are the remains of a rectangular building, on the south-west side of the pound, and there are also traces of a circle, enclosing

a cairn, and a kistvaen in the centre.    Having exercised our
ingenuity,* as others have done, in endeavouring to find
some relics which would account for this curious designation,
we shall direct our course westward, and leaving Merripit
Hill on the right, shall proceed to Post Bridge, on the East
Dart.    The aboriginal bridge has been already described ;
but when we observe that this is the scene of considerable
agricultural improvements, and that many dwellings have
been erected in the immediate neighbourhood, we shall be as
much surprised as pleased, to find that this venerable relic of
primitive times has escaped demolition, and has been preserved to
a period when a more enlightened appreciation of national
antiquities extensively prevails.    We shall remark that the
antient structure bears more east and west than the modern bridge,
and probably thus points to the great central trackway which
passes over Chittaford Down.†

At Archerton, on the East Dart, just above Post Bridge, Mr.
J. N. Bennett, of Plymouth, under grants from the Duchy, has
enclosed considerable tracts of land, in the centre of which he has
built a good dwelling house.    On the slope in front of the
house are some antiquities of great interest, which are now
carefully protected within a fence.    The remains of a singularly
formed elliptical inclosure can be traced, with an entrance
on the south-east, where the oval outline, instead of being
continuous is bent into two circular sweeps, between which,
apparently, was the original entrance to the inclosure.    Within
are vestiges of tracklines and the ruins of an aboriginal
hut, where not only the formation, but the remains of the
walls are still to be seen.    The planting of trees, the growth
of vegetation, and the gradual accumulation of what in time makes
soil, has obscured the main features of this enclosure.    At one
time the hut presented the most perfect specimen of an aboriginal
dwelling, of more solid construction than those generally found
remaining on the moor.    It appeared to have been constructed of
stone, the interstices being filled with sod, and to have had a roof
of the bee-hive, or domical form.    Within the inclosure are other

---

*Furnum Regis* must always have been a spot of mark.    For the results of a
recent examination of the site, see the account in the Second Report of the Dartmoor Exploration Committee.    *Vide* Trans. Devon. Assoc. 1895, Vol. xxvi.

†This as before mentioned, is not so.    The trackway crossed the Dart at Still
Pool, upwards of five hundred yards above this bridge.

P.J Widgery Pinx.

W.L.Colls Ph.Sc.

CYCLOPEAN BRIDGE, (POST BRIDGE.)

antiquities, and in the immediate vicinity, remains of kistvaens, more or less perfect.   One of these primitive sepulchres may be particularly noticed, as it is surrounded by an external circle eight feet in diameter.   The kistvaen itself measures four feet six inches by four feet three inches.   We have only mentioned a few of the remains hereabout, but in the neighbourhood of Post Bridge, was, as there is little doubt, an important settlement of prehistoric man. Dr. Arthur B. Prowse calls it the ancient Metropolis of the Moor, and he mentions fourteen pounds, containing at least one hundred hut-circles, and concludes that these were occupied by a population of about four hundred persons.   The great central trackway, the antient road modified and utilised by the Romans, runs through the middle of this settlement.*   Broadun is close by, and the careful investigations made here by Mr. Robert Burnard, confirm the previously expressed opinions of Dr. Arthur B. Prowse.†
The largest kistvaen found on Dartmoor was discovered by Mr. Robert Burnard, in 1893, at Roundy Park, about a mile N.N.W. of the Clapper Bridge.   In the bottom it is six feet six inches long, and three feet nine inches wide.   In it were found two flints—an arrow point (?) and a scraper and some bone charcoal.‡

Between the boundary of Mr. Bennett's estate and the Dart, a moor-track runs north towards Hamlyn's New-take, where we shall notice several hut-circles.   Still proceeding along the high ground, above the valley of the Dart, we shall observe in Templer's New-take, opposite Hartland Tor, and about a mile above Post Bridge, a Cyclopean circumvallation, which deserves the name of a miniature Grimspound ; but, unfortunately, its rampart is much less perfect, having been demolished on the N.W., and partially built upon for the purpose of forming a modern fence, which intersects the area on this side.   A large segment of the circular inclosure, however, still remains, forming a sweep below the new-take wall, two hundred and twenty-four yards in length.   The original base of the wall, or rampart, appears to have been about twelve feet wide ; in some parts of the circumvallation, it has more the appearance of a wall than usual, as the stones are piled upon each other instead of being heaped up promiscuously.   On the north side, the rampart re-appears beyond the new-take wall, but here the spoliation has been

*Trans. Devon Assoc.   Vol. xxiii., 1891, p. 307.

†Trans. Devon Assoc.   Vol. xxvi. 1894, p. 185.

‡Burnard.   Dartmoor Pictorial Records.   Vol. iv., p. 55.

lamentable.  We shall notice a large hut-circle with others of
smaller dimensions ; and the whole forms one of the most striking
and interesting objects in the Forest.    The pound in the six-inch
Ordnance Map (Sheet xcix., N.W.) is called a camp.

Passing over Broad Down or Broadun,* and Ladehill, we shall
notice several cairns on the heights, and, turning southwards,
shall cross Chittaford Down beyond the inclosed lands of
Archerton.   Here we shall trace without difficulty, the trackway
already described,† as it passes from the East Dart westward,
over the common, to Waydown Tor.   From hence we shall scale
the steep acclivity of the long ridge which runs between Cherrybrook and the West Dart, and terminates in an inland promontory
at Crockern Tor.   This ridge is fortified by a range of tors in
succession, of which the most conspicuous are Longaford, Beetor,
and White, or Whitten Tor.   On some are rock-basins, and, near
Longford, a hut-circle.   Of these relics, we shall observe many
more groups, and a pound, of irregular form, on the western slope
of the hill, above the narrow vale of the West Dart, and near the
" lonely wood of Wistman."

Wistman's, or Whistman's, Wood is the third of Risdon's
"three remarkable things " in the Forest of Dartmoor.   By him
it is described as consisting of " some acres of wood and trees
" that are a fathom about, and yet no taller than a man may touch
" the top with his hands."   The general description of this third
wonder of Dartmoor is in sufficient accordance with its present
condition to warrant the conclusion that the lapse of  more than
two centuries and a  half  has not materially changed its aspect,
and that probably for a much longer period it has presented the
same singular appearance as now.   The traditionary account that
the wood was planted by Isabella de Fortibus, Countess of Devon
and Albemarle, in the thirteenth century, has been related by
some authors ;  but there is no reason for supposing that this is a
planted wood.   Nor can there be any reasonable doubt that here
we behold the poor relics of those sylvan honours, which we may
reasonably conclude once graced many of the moorland  vales and
acclivities, without contending that the entire district—the granite

---

*On Broadun Down and at Broadun Ring, on its southern slope, many hut-circles
have been examined by Mr. Robert Burnard, and distinct evidences of their
permanent occupation by Neolithic people, obtained.  *Vide Devon Trans. Assoc.,*
1894, vol. xxvi., pp. 185-196.

†R. BURNARD.  The Great Central Trackway.  Trans. Devon Assoc. vol. xxi.,
pp. 431-436.

soil of which is unfavourable to the growth of trees—was at any
period one continuous forest in the ordinary acceptation of the
term.   Risdon, Bray, and other writers, report a Perambulation
made immediately after the Conquest, to prove that Wistman's
Wood was even at that remote period much the same as it now
appears.   We can trace no such document.   The earliest perambulation was in 1240, and there is no reference in it to this wood.

The whole world cannot boast, probably, a greater curiosity,
in sylvan archæology, than this solitary grove in the Devonshire
wilderness.   Wordsworth has celebrated the characteristic yews
of the Lakelands, in his description of the " Fraternal Four of
" Borrowdale ; " but whilst venerable yews may be found in a
thousand English sanctuaries, the antient storm-stricken oaks of
Wistman are without recorded parallel.   Viewed from the
opposite steep, when sullen clouds have lowered down upon
Longaford Tor, and shut out all surrounding objects—when mist-
wreaths half shroud and half reveal their hoary branches and
moss-covered trunks—there is something almost unearthly in their
aspect.   Our native bard has however chosen the profound sunlit
repose of a moorland noon (and it is only in the shelterless
solitudes of the moor, amidst the quivering rack of a heated
atmosphere, that the truthfulness and beauty of his imagery can
be appreciated) as most perfectly in keeping with the old
mysterious grove which had lived perhaps more than a thousand
years, but had not grown for centuries.

> " How heavily
> That old wood sleeps in the sunshine ;—not a leaf
> Is twinkling, not a wing is seen to move
> Within it ;—but, below a mountain-stream,
> Conflicting with the rocks, is ever heard,
> Cheering the drowsy noon.
>                     of this grove,
> This pigmy grove, not one has climb'd the air
> So emulously that its loftiest branch
> May brush the traveller's brow.   The twisted roots
> Have clasp'd, in search of nourishment, the rocks,
> And straggled wide, and pierced the stony soil :—
> In vain, denied maternal succour, here
> A dwarfish race has risen.   Round the boughs,
> Hoary and feeble, and around the trunks,

> With grasp destructive, feeding on the life
> That lingers yet, the ivy winds, and moss
> Of growth enormous.  E'en the dull vile weed
> Has fixed itself upon the very crown
> Of many an antient oak ; and thus refused
> By Nature kindly aid—dishonoured—old—
> Dreary in aspect—silently decays
> The lonely Wood of Wistman."

To add to this sketch, faithful and graphic as it is, would be superfluous and impertinent.  It will be only necessary to state that the account of the stature of the trees must be taken with due allowance for poetical license.  Ten feet might be more correctly given as the average height of the trees.  A botanical writer says :—" The trees are all dwarfs, apparently of the same " age, and growing on a singularly unfavourable site.  They " owe their preservation to an effectual defence in the shape of a " number of large stones which cover the site on which they " grow, and amid which the venerable dwarfs lift their branches. " The trunks of the trees are about the height of a common stool, " such as clerks sit upon, and I sat down on the crown of one in " passing, and leaned upon the main limbs.  The bole of this tree " was about three feet high, and its total height to the topmost " branches, fifteen feet.  The trunk was hollow, but still full of " life. Its circumference was six feet. It was at its prime, probably " about the height of an average oak : this must have been at the " period of the Norman Conquest, and it is still as tough a dwarf " for a tree, as the notorious Quilp was for a man.  Time-worn as " the stems and trunks are, they are well covered by their spread- " ing and flattened heads.  Seen at a distance in August, a sheet " of green seems spread upon the hillside.  I do not remember " oaks more uniform in the character of their umbrella like heads, " or with foliage of a brighter green.  Whether the trees were " planted by man or by nature, their security is due to the shelter- " ing blocks of granite, amid which they stand, and to the " moss-covered props and slabs on which the branches rest." Although it is probable that these trees have not increased in height for many an age, yet these dwarf patriarchs of the Forest produce bud and leaf in their season, but no acorns are at present borne, and the emitted roots are weak, in consequence of even the smallest branches being too old, hard and tough.  When therefore the old trees crumble, a thousand years hence, they will leave no successors.* The trees, which are in three clumps or divisions, separate from each other, extend for about a third of a mile, along the rocky declivity. In the widest part, neither group of trees is more than one hundred feet.

In this new edition we have indicated freely our disbelief in many of the speculations contained in the former issues of this book. Here in Wistman's Wood, the old antiquaries ran riot and found a sacred grove, dedicated to the rites of Druidism, and did not hesitate to advance theories, and to write in the following imaginative strain. If in other spots, led by the evidence of the pillared circle, the lustral basin, or the oracular logan, we are carried back in imagination to the age and ceremonial of a mysterious and sanguinary ritual—surely this antient oaken grove, whose age outdates tradition and history, and which is such an anomaly in physiology as to baffle scientific calculation, might have itself been a favourite resort of the hierophants of Druidism, and might have sheltered the last of the Danmonian priesthood, who, in these secluded wilds of the west might have found an asylum from the vengeance of the exasperated Roman. But it is not a little curious that among the aboriginal relics in the immediate neighbourhood, no sacred circle, no avenue, no logan, is to be observed. Nor among all the parasitical plants which crowd the branches of these venerable oaks—the most sacred tree of Druidism—has the far-famed mistletoe ever been discovered.† Yet would this consideration not be sufficient to detract from the claims of Wistman to be regarded as the remnant of a Druidical grove, especially since we learn, from an antient contemporary writer,‡ that the mistletoe, even then was scarce, and seldom to be met with, on the oak in particular. Hence when found, they gather it with great devotion and many ceremonies. But the same author informs us that whatever the Druids found growing on the oak, parasitically,

---

*Journal of Forestry, vol 5, p. 421.

†Although the mistletoe is plentifully produced on the apple tree, in the neighbouring county of Somerset, it is remarkable that in Devonshire, it is scarcely known as an indigenous plant. In the Floras of the county it is recorded as having been found at Holcombe Regis, near Plymouth, on an apple tree in the orchard at Higher Fordton, Crediton, Harford, Larkbere, near Otterton, and in an orchard at Ilsham. See Keys. Flora Devon and Cornwall, sub Viscum album. The mistletoe which thrives in Siberia, in certain situations, does not climb in England higher than five or six hundred feet above the level of the sea, and Wistman's Wood is not much less than one thousand feet above the sea level. Our Druidical friends must therefore like their predecessors for their flints, have gone some distance for their mistletoe.

‡Pliny, Nat. Hist., lib. xvi., 14.

whether mistletoe or other plants, they esteemed as a Divine gift, and as a token that their god had made that tree his peculiar choice.   If, then, the Wistman oaks were draperied with the same exoteric garniture as at present, they must have been regarded by the Druids with peculiar veneration.   Nor can "imagination body "forth" a place more congenial to the sights and sounds of dark and blood-stained rites, than this dreary, narrow, rock-strewn glen of the Dart.   We can imagine the appointed Druid, on the natural watch tower, afforded by the neighbouring tor, carefully marking the moment when the moon has completed the sixth day of her age—when haply a mistletoe has been found in the grove below ;—we follow him to the tree, and there see him clothed in his robe of pure white ; and bearing the golden hook, reverently ascend the oak and cut the plant, which is received by the assistant priests below with every demonstration of gladness and awe.   Wistman's Wood is just such a place as the holy prophet of the Most High describes as one of the scenes of the idolatrous orgies of the Israelites.   Here are the oaks—here "the valleys "under the clifts of the rocks" where they sacrificed their children—here "the smooth stones of the stream among which "was their portico."   In this spot too, might the Roman bard have found his original of the grove, which he depicts as conse-crated to the mystic ceremonies of Druidism.

> " Lucus erat longo nunquam violatus ab ævo,
>    Obscurum cingens connexis aera ramis,
>    Et gelidas alte summotis solibus umbras.
>    Hunc non ruricolæ Panes, nemorumque potentes
>    Silvani Nymphæ que tenent, sed barbara ritu
>    Sacra Deum, structæ sacris feralibus aræ
>    Omnis et humanis lustrata cruoribus arbos."*—
>
> > LUCAN, Pharsalia, Book iii.

---

*" Not far away for ages past had stood
   An old unviolated sacred wood ;
   Whose gloomy boughs, thick interwoven, made
   A chilly, chearless, everlasting shade ;
   There, not the rustick gods nor satyrs sport,
   Nor Fauns and Sylvans with the Nymphs resort ;
   But barbarous priests some dreadful Power adore,
   And lustrate every tree with human gore."—

Lucan's Pharsalia, translated into English verse by Nicholas Rowe, Esq., Servant to His Majesty. fol. 1718, p. 107. Nicholas Rowe, the translator of Lucan, was a son of Francis Rowe, of Lamerton, Serjeant-at-Law, with whom the author and editor of this work claim affinity. His version of this classic description of a Druidical grove, as that of a Devonshire poet, may be read with additional interest.

The explorer of Wistman's Wood should tread its rocky labyrinth with some caution in summer lest he should encounter somewhat unpleasant testimony to the accuracy of the resemblance in another particular noticed by the bard of the Pharsalia :—

" Roboraque amplexos circumfluxisse dracones."

Like many other sheltered glens strewn with moorstone, Wistman's Wood has an evil reputation among the country people, as abounding with noxious reptiles.† It was accordingly represented to Mrs. Bray by a neighbouring moor farmer in the genuine vernacular, as "a whist old place sure enough, and as full of adders "as can be." The notion of rendering these reptiles harmless by charming them with an ashen wand, which still obtains among our peasantry, is pronounced, by this lady, as "nothing less than "a vestige of the customs of Druid antiquity." We have already noticed the evident connexion between Druidism and the Ophite rites, as traced in the Dracontia, or serpent-temples, and in other particulars, and have seen that these were probably corruptions of the purer forms of Arkite worship. The celebrated *anguinum*, or serpent's egg, may also be mentioned, as bearing upon the subject, since it is alleged by Davies, to have reference to Arkite mysteries. The rock-strewn glen—the dwarfish, mysterious looking grove, its growth as if suddenly paralyzed by some malignant spell—the dark river flowing beneath—the hut circles, pillars, and cairns on

---

The late Mr. T. R. A. Briggs furnished us with the following list of plants he had found in and about Wistman's Wood :—

*Corydalis Claviculata*, Climbing Coridalis ; *Viola Sylvatica*, Dog Violet ; *Polygala vulgaris*, var *depressa*, Common Milkwort (Moors around) ; *Stellaria Holostea*, Greater Stitchwort ; *Geranium Robertianum*, Herb Robert ; *Oxalis Acetosella*, Wood Sorrel ; *Ilex Aquifolium*, Holly ; *Ulex Europœus*, Common Furze (Moors around) ; *Ulex Galii*, Planchon's Furze (Moors around) ; *Rubus*, various species ; *Pyrus Acuparia*, Mountain A-h ; *Sedum Anglicum*, English Stonecrop ; *Hedera Helix*, Ivy ; *Lonicera Periclymenum*, Honeysuckle ; *Galium saxatile*, Heath Bedstraw ; *Vaccinium Myrtillus*, Common Bilberry ; *Teucrium Scorodonia*, Wood Germander ; *Digitalis purpurea*, Fox glove ; *Rumex Acetosella*, Sheep's Sorrel :(?) *Corylus Avellana*, Hazel ; *Salix aurita*, Wrinkle Leaved sallow ; *Scilla nutans*, Blue Bell (close to the Wood) ; *Luzula sylvatica*, Great Woodrush ; *Juncus Sp.* *Carex, Sp. Anthoxanthum Odoratum*, Sweet-scented Vernal Grass ; *Aira Flexuosa*, Heath Hair Grass ; *Aira prœcox*, Early Hair Grass ; *Festuca Ovina*, Sheep's Fescue Grass (on Moors around) ; *Hymenophyllum Tunbridgense*, Tunbridge Filmy Fern ; *Hymenophyllum Unilaterale*, Wilson's Filmy Fern ; *Pteris Aquilina*, Bracken ; *Lomaria Spicant*, Hard Fern (close to the Wood) ; *Athyrium Filix-fœmina*, Lady Fern ; *Nephrodium Filix-mas*, Male Fern ; *Nephrodium dilatatum*, Broad Pricklytoothed Fern ; *Polypodium vulgare*, Common Polypody.

†It has been supposed by some that this is an error, and that the place is too damp for these reptiles. But the common belief is well founded, and the alternations of damp in some parts of the year and heat in others, seem as elsewhere to suit these " dragons."

the neighbouring heights—all forcibly lead to the conclusion that we are wandering amidst scenes congenial to the spirit of Druidism, and polluted of old by the sanguinary rites of that mystic and terrible superstition.    In July, 1888, by accident or mischief, the centre portion of the wood was set on fire.    The flames were seen from Prince Town, and Mr. Barrington, the Duchy Steward, and others hastened to the spot, and succeeded in extinguishing the fire.    As it proved, fortunately but little damage was done.

From Wistman's Wood, we return by a path along the eastern bank of the Dart, to the inn at Two Bridges, and there close our excursion through the central parts of the Forest.

On setting out for our next excursion northwards, we shall pass the little river Cowsic at its confluence with the Dart, immediately below Bairdown Hill, a long ridge of high ground with a series of tors, along the summit, known by the names of Bairdown Tor, Lidford and Devil Tor.    There is nothing of particular mark or interest in these tors, nor on the neighbouring common, except the Bairdown Man, a rude granite obelisk (similar to those already described), eleven feet in height and eight feet in girth.    In this popular designation of the rock-pillar, we shall doubtless discover the original term Maen, and shall find in Bairdown Man another specimen of the Menhir, or Long Upright Stone.    Bairdown Hill is peninsulated by the Dart on the east, and by the Cowsic on the west.    On the latter stream, near the confluence, we shall observe thriving plantations, showing the agricultural capabilities of the more sheltered parts of the moorlands.    To the improvements at Bairdown Farm, commenced by the late Mr. Bray, may be attributed much that has been done to reclaim portions of the moor; but it must be admitted that the sheltered dell, on the western side of the down, presented facilities which are not to be met with in less favoured situations.    The farm was afterwards in the possession of the late Mr. George Frean, who was for a considerable time successfully engaged in agricultural improvements, in this part of the Forest.

But the tourist will find "metal more attractive" in tracing the course of the Cowsic stream, as it foams along amidst the huge blocks of granite, with which its channel is studded, until he comes to the antient bridge, by which it is crossed in the dell below Bairdown Farm.    It was in excellent preservation until in 1873, a flood swept the massive stones, of which it was composed, into the stream.    They were replaced, but again in 1890 a deluge of rain flooded the rivers, and, besides doing much other mischief, swept away the impost of the bridge. It has been re-erected by the Committee of the Dartmoor Preservation Association. Though the clapper is on a smaller scale than some others, it is not the less interesting. It consists of five openings; thirty-seven feet in length, and somewhat less than four feet in average breadth. The roadway is scarcely three feet and a half from the water under ordinary circumstances.

We leave the vale of the Cowsic and proceed over the common westward to a clam, or single-stone bridge thrown over the Blackabrook, a stream which rises below Great Mistor, and falls into the West Dart between Two Bridges and Prince Hall. At a short distance from this primitive bridge, in a rushy swamp, is a structure of mediæval antiquity which has excited some speculation and no little discussion, as to the date which should be assigned for its erection. This is Fice's Well, thus commemorated by a writer in Blackwood's Magazine. " What a strange little " edifice ! Interior and sides of granite. Inscription (which must " be a lie) 1168." The inscription which has given rise to the supposition that the well was erected in the twelfth century, is on the front edge of the cover-stone; but whilst an unpractised observer might have misread the second figure of the date for 1, it is difficult to imagine how anyone who had been conversant with similar inscriptions could have been so misled. The letters are in low relief, inscribed in a kind of panel on the face of the stone above the well, and there is no doubt that the true date is 1568. Mr. Bray, justly remarks that the date would appear more or less distinct, according as it might happen to be viewed in full sunshine or in shadow. The cover-stone is three feet nine by three feet three, the opening about two feet square, and the well scarcely three feet in depth. This author assigns good reasons for supposing that the true designation is Fitz's, and not Fice's Well. " I " think it most likely that Fitz's Well was constructed by John " Fitz, the old lawyer and astrologer of Fitzford, whose traffic " with the stars, in foretelling the fate of his only son, is still the " theme of tradition." In addition to the evidence adduced by Mr. Bray, from old records, in confirmation of this conjecture, Mrs. Bray records the following legend of the origin of Fice's Well, which is too interesting to be omitted. " John Fitz the astrologer " and his lady, were once *pixy-led*, whilst riding on Dartmoor. " After long wandering in the vain effort to find the right path,

"they felt so fatigued and thirsty, that it was with extreme delight
"they discovered a spring of water, whose powers seemed to be
"miraculous ; for no sooner had they satisfied their thirst, than
"they were enabled to find their way through the moor towards
"home, without the least difficulty.   In gratitude for this deliver-
"ance, and the benefit they had received from the water, old
"John Fitz caused the stone memorial in question, bearing the
"date of the year, to be placed over the spring, for the advantage
"of all pixy-led travellers.   It is still considered to possess many
"healing virtues."   The well is now surrounded by a circular
stone wall, which has been erected for its protection.   The moor
around it has been brought into cultivation by prison labour, and
the care taken of this little building is commendable.   Except
when prisoners are at work in the immediate neighbourhood, it
can be easily approached by a new road.

Following the course of the Blackabrook* downwards to
Oakery Cottage, we shall observe close below the modern bridge
carrying the Plymouth road, near Prince Town, an old clapper
Bridge of two openings of smaller dimensions, but of similar
character to those already described.   Should the tourist be
anxious to examine the improvements commenced by Sir
Thomas Tyrwhitt, at Tor Royal, a short walk will bring him
there.   He will also have an opportunity of visiting the Prisons at
Prince Town, as well as the extensive granite quarries at
Fogginton, through which the Prince Town Railway passes.
But the antiquary, following the Tavistock road to Rendlestone,
will proceed along the highway to examine the large and
interesting group of aboriginal relics near Merivale Bridge, at the
spot popularly known in the neighbourhood as the Plague Market.
Here, it is traditionally reported, during a pestilence which prevailed at Tavistock—supposed by Mr. Bray to have been in 1625,
when the burials in the parish register amounted to five hundred
and twenty-two, or was it earlier when the Black Death was such
a scourge—provisions were brought for sale from the neighbouring
country, at a safe distance from the infected precincts of the town.
But to whatever purpose these venerable monuments might have
been applied, there can be no doubt that originally they were
erected by some of the earliest inhabitants of our island, and that
here will be found the remains of one of the most important

---

*The stranger must not attempt this now, as he will be considered a trespasser
upon the enclosed cultivated lands of the Prisons.

aboriginal settlements in the west.   In addition to the rows or
avenues, are to be found parallelithons, circles, and specimens of
almost all the other monuments of aboriginal antiquity.   The
town, or village, is within half a mile of the river Walkham,
which is crossed by Merivale Bridge in the valley below.   Its site
is on the slope of the common, inclining to the south-west, and
the ground, over which the circular foundations of houses are
scattered, is of considerable extent.

But among all other relics, the rows which will be noticed on
the south side of the road as we ascend the hill, from Merivale
Bridge towards Prince Town, will immediately strike the observer
as the characteristic feature of the place.   By the learned explorer
of Carnac, they would be described as undoubted parts of a
Dracontium, or serpent-temple ; but whether their presumed Ophite
character be admitted or not, there can be little doubt that they
were constructed by our Pagan forefathers for the purposes of
religious worship.   Their direction is towards the river, and they
are in immediate connexion with sacred circles ; the northern
terminating in one circle, and the southern having another at mid-
length.   It will also be observed that they are in apparent
relative connexion with a large sacred circle and lofty menhir.
From these circumstances, the avenues will afford the best central
station for describing the position of the several objects which
will engage the attention of the antiquary.

These avenues run east and west parallel to each other, one
hundred and five feet apart ; the longest, eleven hundred and forty-
three feet, the other upwards of eight hundred.   The former has the
circle in the centre, and at either extremity a stone of larger dimensions than those in the lines.   The western half of this parallelithon
is divided at mid-length by a higher stone, and ends with two
stones which have been thrown down.   About twenty-four yards
from the south avenue is a small dilapidated cairn ; with a line of
stones running in a south westerly direction from it, and one
hundred yards south, a circle sixty-seven feet in diameter, consisting of ten stones.   Near this is a fine specimen of the menhir,
maen, or rock-pillar, and near the avenues the ruins of a kistvaen.
N.E. by N. of the avenues is an inclosure, or pound, differing essentially from Grimspound and others, in the construction of the wall ;
this consisting chiefly, though not entirely, of upright stones, while
in many other examples they are rudely piled together.   Advantage
has been taken of the natural position of some huge blocks in

forming this singular fence, the form of which approaches, though imperfectly, to a circle, the diameter of which is one hundred and seventy-five feet.　At the upper or east end, is a vast block, large enough to form one of the sides of an interior rectangular inclosure; having remains of walls at right angles.　Thirty feet from this inclosure, a large quoit-like stone, sixteen feet by nine feet eight inches, and three others have all the appearance of supporters, and, with their impost, give the idea of a Cromlech, but this is deceptive, the supposed impost being a discarded mill stone. There are hut-circles within and immediately without the inclosure, which are of a large size, as well as many others throughout the town.　Although a little repetition is unavoidable, the results of the latest investigations at Merivale Bridge may be stated as follows —the so-called cromlech—which as above mentioned is a kistvaen —was wrecked by a man named Harding, about 1860, who cut two gate-posts out of the cap-stone, and split one of the side stones in half; then quartered one half, and carried off one quarter.　On taking off the broken capstone, the monument revealed itself as a kistvaen—interior measurement seven feet by two feet nine inches at the head of the cist, and two feet at the bottom.　It runs N. and S., and was composed of five supporters, whereof the largest measured seven feet, the height of all being three feet six inches.　This was on the west side : on the east, two stones, one four feet ten inches, and to fill the gap, there was a small stone set on a step and removable, so that access to the interior could be had by removing it.　It measured only two feet four inches in height, about one foot of step was below it.　The capstone originally measured nine feet three inches by four feet nine inches.　In the cist, near the head, was found a good flint scraper, a flint flake, and a polishing stone.

One of the most curious discoveries was, that near the sacred circle, are several pits from which large stones—some perhaps of the size of the menhir—have been removed for building the new-take wall below.　In these the trigger pieces remain, and out of one, a flint core was taken.　Near the menhir are two small cairns, from one, a small row of upright stones starts, but it consists of five only, and never had more, as no pits were found. These stones run south.　To the east of the menhir is another cairn, with a tall upright stone, six feet six inches high, and with indications of a circle around it.　To the south of this cairn is a pit from which an upright stone has been removed.　Near the great pair of rows, west of the circle, that interrupts the south pair of lines, but west of it is a small cairn, formerly marked* as a fallen cromlech. It probably contained a kistvaen, now destroyed. From this runs a line of stones of small size, nearly due south, this was first observed and planned by Lukis.† The large cairn shown in the plan of 1830‡ has been destroyed since 1851, when Mr. Baring-Gould made a drawing of it. It contained then an inner circle of stones, and indications of an outer one as well. Some of the hut-circles in the immediate neighbourhood were also examined, with the result that it seemed they had been overhauled, probably for stone for road making. But charcoal was found, and the hearths, and two flint flakes.

The whole of the Merivale Bridge remains are now being carefully planned under the direction of the Dartmoor exploration Committee of the Devonshire Association.

The ruins extend about a mile along the side of the hill, from the highest point of which Great Mistor majestically overlooks the whole, and may therefore with perfect propriety claim the right of giving name to this curious and interesting monument of the aboriginal occupancy of our island, as the Mistor town, or village, since the perambulators also described this part of the Forest as Mistor moor. "*From thence linyallie to another* "*Histworthie, and so from thence linyallie through the midst of* "*Mistor moore, to a rock called Mistor Pann..*"—*Perambulation*, 1609.

As we have again reached the line of Perambulation let us follow its direction as it passes from North Hessary Tor to Mistor Pan. The designation thus employed by the perambulators was evidently adopted by them from popular usage. Hence it is clear that the singularly perfect rock basin on the summit of Mistor has existed in its present state for centuries, and has been regarded as the characteristic feature of the tor, from time immemorial. It can therefore scarcely be deemed a forced inference, if, taking into account the existence of other relics, we conclude that Mistor Pan is an artificial excavation of high antiquity, and, unlike some others of its kind, can scarcely be attributed to the action of the elements, and the disintegration of the granite block, in this particular part of the tor. The basin is in a remarkably perfect state, three feet

---

*Trans. Plym. Inst., 1830, plan ii., p. 187.

†LUKIS. Soc. Ant. Plan No. 10.

‡Trans. Plym. Inst., 1830, plan I.

O

in diameter, eight inches deep, and with its perpendicular sides and flat bottom, suggesting to the moormen the idea of one of their dairy milk-pans, hewn out of the massive rock.

In our ascent to the top of Great Mistor, we shall pass an antient stream-work on the side of the hill of considerable extent. We shall also observe in our progress, Little Mistor, which may be noticed for its presenting a rude resemblance to a vase of colossal magnitude. On reaching Mistor summit, we shall command a magnificent prospect, along the western border; perhaps the finest from any part of the Moor, but among the many interesting objects which open to the view, Vixen Tor and the vale of the Walkham immediately below, will not fail to arrest the attention. Looking down the woodland gorge, between Walkhampton and Sampford Spiney, the eye at length rests upon that part of the noble estuary of the Tamar above Saltash, where it expands into a broad lake at the confluence of the Tavy with its waters, near Beer Ferrers. To the voyager up the Tamar, when he arrives abreast of Warleigh Point, and opens Maristow, Mistor rises with all the grandeur of a genuine mountain in the purple distance; nor could a more favourable point of view perhaps be chosen for giving a stranger a just impression of the elevation of our Dartmoor hills than this part of the Tamar estuary, or the Cornish bank of the river on the north precincts of the town of Saltash.

Leaving the summit of Mistor, on our way due south, we shall pass Greenaball, and its three mutilated tumuli on the right hand as we descend the steep slope to the Walkham river, and reaching the bank take our way across its rocky channel. Scaling the opposite side we shall find ourselves on Langstone Moor (on the Ordnance Map, Launceston), so called from the menhir which stands upon it, and which has been recently re-erected by the Duke of Bedford under the direction of Mr. Baring-Gould. Here, as well as on the western slope of Mistor as before-mentioned, are a large number of hut circles. Some of these—there are upwards of thirty—are surrounded by a pound-wall of the usual character. So far as they have been examined, these huts are similar to those at Grimspound and Broadun. The hearths and the beds, and charcoal and flint have been found, but no pot-boilers, and not a vestige of pottery. Mr. Robert Burnard is of opinion that if a hut is that of, or has been used by, a miner, pottery ought to be discovered. Ascending the hill still further we shall find a sacred circle of much interest. It was discovered in 1894 by the Rev. G.

SACRED CIRCLE ON LANGSTONE MOOR.

B. Berry, who drew the attention of the Exploration Committee to it. There was not a stone erect, but none had been mutilated or taken away. Willing permission having been granted by the owner of the land, the Duke of Bedford, and ready help having been furnished by his steward, Mr. Rundle, under the superintendence of the Rev. S. Baring-Gould, the stones, sixteen in number, have been once more placed upright, and in their proper places, there being no difficulty in ascertaining their original positions, and thus a very fine and perfect monument has been preserved. Two of the stones composing it are of a different character from the rest, which are ordinary moor-stone. These appear to be a fine sandstone. It would seem that there was another circle outside this one, but three stones only on the western side remain. We know no other instance on Dartmoor of a circle within a circle. The diameter of the Langstone Circle is about fifty-six feet. Approaching it from the north, with the pile of Great Mistor forming a grand back ground, the appearance of this antient monument—more especially as the day is closing—is weird and solemn in the extreme. About a third of a mile from here, southwestwards is the menhir before referred to.

Retracing our steps we return to the river, and reaching its bank much lower down, where it runs due north, at a point just opposite Little Mistor, we shall climb the ridge on which, in a line parallel to the course of the river, rise a series of conspicuous and remarkable tors. The northernmost of these is Rolls Tor, or Roose Tor, next to which is Great Stapletor ; Middle Stapletor is farther south, and Little Stapletor is on the declivity near an antient stream-work of large extent. Seen from Roborough Down and some other points southward, these tors have a strong resemblance to castellated ruins, and on a nearer examination will be found to present many features of much interest. Some of the component masses are granite slabs bearing the appearance of a cromlech quoit, or impost. Other blocks appear to be so marvellously poised as to be ready to be toppled down by the impulse of the first upland storm; and one has been thought to be a tolmen.* On the N.W. pile of Great Stapletor is a rock-basin, sixteen inches in diameter, and on Little Stapletor, near the edge of the highest and largest block, is another, two feet in diameter.

Continuing our southward course, we shall cross the road from

---

*Bray.  Tamar and Tavy.  1st Ed.  Vol. i., p. 242.

Tavistock to Two Bridges, leaving Merivale Bridge in the valley
on the left.   From hence we shall observe Vixen Tor, not forming
the crest of an eminence, as is more frequently the case, but
rising majestically from the common, near the steep banks of the
Walkham, about a mile below Merivale Bridge.   On a nearer
approach, we shall remark the resemblance which it bears to the
Egyptian Sphynx, when beheld from a particular point of view.
Fronting the river, the huge masses of which the tor is composed,
·are piled up, tier after tier, in a rude, but noble facade, divided
into three compartments by perpendicular fissures, through which
an ascent to the summit can be effected, whereon appearances of
rock-basins will be observed.   The river-front faces directly south,
and this lofty rock is traditionally reported to have been resorted
to in past times for astronomical purposes.   Vixen Tor, whether
considered in itself, or with reference to the striking scenery of
which it forms the central object, is one of the most interesting in
the moorland district.   The vale of the Walkham presents a long-
drawn mountain defile, stretching away to the south.   On the
acclivity beyond Merivale Bridge eastward, is the aboriginal town,
above described, where the admirer of Scott's truthful pictures of
natural scenery may trace the main features of the Black Dwarf's
forlorn retreat on Mucklestane Moor.   There is "the huge
"column of unhewn granite, raising its massy head on a knoll
"near the centre of the heath, and the ground strewed, or rather
"encumbered, with many huge fragments of stone of the same
"consistence with the column, which, as they lay scattered over
"the waste, were popularly called the Grey Geese of Mucklestane
"Moor."   And down the stream southward, near Ward Bridge
and Huckworthy Bridge, the river, rock, and wood scenery is of
the most fascinating description.   Should the tourist recross the
Walkham, and follow the windings of the Prince Town railway,
as it sweeps round the opposite hill by King Tor and Crip Tor
and Foggingtor, he will be abundantly repaid by a succession of
views of wide extent and varied interest.   Near the point where the
railway crosses the Plymouth and Prince Town road, he will be
struck with the peculiarly fine grouping of the tors, as he looks
towards the N.E., with the lofty tower of Walkhampton rising
conspicuously from the acclivity in the foreground.   The railway
station at Prince Town is about five thousand four hundred feet
above sea level.   From the junction at Yelverton the distance to
Prince Town, as the crow flies, is about six miles, but to reach it

VIXEN TOR.

and overcome the steep ascent, the railway winds for nearly
eleven miles, the gradient being one in sixty-five.   Returning by
Walkhampton, we shall leave the steep lane leading to the church,
and crossing a fine old moorstone stile, shall find a pathway along
the fields, which commands the vale of the Walkham at some of
the most picturesque points.   Far inferior as the accompanying
mountain elevations confessedly are, yet, in all other respects, the
scenery of this lovely glen may dispute the palm with the most
celebrated spots of North Wales or the Lakelands.   This conviction will be deepened by every step we take in the direction of
Ward Bridge, by which we shall cross the river, and having made
a detour N.E. over the common, to notice the rude time-worn
cross, called Beckamoor Cross, also known as the "Windy-post"
or "Windy-stone," near a rivulet on the plain, shall mount the
hill half-a-mile north of Sampford Spiney church, to visit Pewtor
Rock, a frontier eminence, and one of the most interesting of all
the moorland tors.

Pewtor was traditionally regarded as a Druidical court of
judicature, probably from the peculiar conformation of the granite
masses whereof it is composed.   Formed by the hand of nature
these masses form two divisions, that on the east consists of four
piles of rock, standing at the four cardinal points, like huge
bastions, connected on the eastern and western sides by a rude
breastwork or curtain, but open to the north and south.   On the
north-west pile is a series of rock-basins irregularly disposed over
the surface of the granite mass.   One on its northern margin is
complete, and is furnished with a lip or spout, calculated to pour
the water over the edge.   This basin communicates with a second,
much broken, which has a like communication with the third, of
a more oval figure, and is placed east of the second, on the verge
of the rock.   Near the western edge of the same mass, but
detached from the others, is a fourth basin, two feet in diameter,
and eleven inches deep.   Standing in the area of this hypæthral
judgment court, and looking southward, the natural piles of mimic
masonry form the frame of the landscape of great extent and
beauty, comprehending the bold uplands of Roborough, the confluence of the Tavy and Tamar, and the Cornish hills on the west.
From hence a pleasant walk of two miles and a half over Whitchurch Down will bring us to Tavistock, where we shall close our
excursion at the Bedford Hotel, in one of the most interesting
country towns in the West of England.

The explorer of Dartmoor will not forget that Tavistock is one
of the stannary towns, and that perhaps on the very spot where he
now "takes his ease in his inn," the earliest printed copy of the
stannary laws was struck off, a printing press having been established in Tavistock Abbey soon after the introduction of the art
of typography into England.    The inn is built within the antient
precincts of the monastery ; nor will the antiquary depart on his
next moorland excursion without examining the existing remains
of the largest and most magnificent abbey in Devonshire.    The
noble gate-house and adjacent buildings on the north-east—" the
" ivied abbey wall along the very brink of the Tavy, with ramparts,
" battlements, and parapets—the still-house tower, and the turret
" known as Betsy Grimbal's tower, within the vicarage premises,
" —are among the most interesting vestiges of the antient grandeur
" of this once famous monastery, which continued to advance in
" wealth and dignity until its abbots took their place among the
" mitred peers of the realm."    The spacious church, with its lofty
tower, under which will be observed the unusual feature of an
open arched passage, will also attract the traveller's attention.

At the western extremity of the town, just above the site of the
antient mansion of Fitzford, the tourist will obtain a most pleasing
view of Tavistock and its immediate neighbourhood.    The town,
with the church and abbey buildings, and some felicitously grouped
trees, form conspicuous objects in front ; on the right, the Tavy
flows vigorously down the vale, while a circling range of hills and
tors form a noble background.    As a central point for visiting the
various objects of picturesque and antiquarian interest with which
this part of Devonshire abounds, Tavistock cannot be surpassed.
Many of the antiquities of Dartmoor in the Western Quarter, the
moorland villages of Marytavy and Petertavy, the glens of the
Walkham, Denham Bridge, Buckland Abbey, the picturesque
hamlet of Milton, Maristow on the Tavy, Morwell Grange, Morwell Rocks, Calstock Church, the Weir Head, Newbridge and
Endsleigh on the Tamar, Brentor Church, Lydford Bridge,
Waterfalls, and Castle, are all within a circle of five or six miles
radius.

As a more detailed description of this interesting town and
neighbourhood would be incompatible with our plan, so it might
be deemed supererogatory if not presumptuous, by those who are
aware how elaborately the subject has been treated by Mrs. Bray,
the talented and lamented authoress of the " Letters to the

" Laureate," and of many popular tales founded on the legendary lore, and descriptive of the romantic scenery of the west. In the former work are embodied many valuable contributions on antiquarian subjects, by the late Rev E. A. Bray, a gentleman, who, as vicar of the parish, displayed a laudable zeal for the preservation of the antiquities of his native town.

Tavistock and the vicinity are replete with deeply-interesting associations of the olden time, and of poetic lore. Mason has placed the scene of his " Elfrida " at Harewood, on the banks of the Tamar, but the accuracy of his poetic venue has been questioned in the Letters to Southey, where it is contended that Prince* is

*PRINCE. Worthies of Devon, ed. 1810, p. 616.

correct in stating that Æthelwold was killed at Wilverley (since Warlwood) in Dartmoor and that therefore the memorable hunt took place in that Forest, where there is still a place called Willsworthy, not far from Tavistock. But another fair authoress, to whom the " green lawns and mantling woods and winding river " of Harewood, on the Tamar, are endeared as the home of her youth, thus modestly advances its claims.

> " Yet haply judged they rightly who here placed
> In this remote peninsular retreat
> The scene of Edgar's hidden loves, where dwelt
> The beauteous, yet unlovely, dame, whose false
> Aspiring heart betrayed to death her lord."

But admonished by her timely strain, let us turn from Earl Orgar and the gigantic Ordulph—from the ambitious Elfrida and the ill-starred Æthelwold, to our main object, for as she aptly proceeds—

> " Yonder ridge
> Of Dartmoor's pinnacles afar descried,
> And towering high into the azure air,
> Recalls the mind from scenes of human strife,
> And guilt and warfare, and each lowly thought
> Creeping along the littleness of life,
> To rove upon the vast and boundless range
> Of the eternal hills."*

*Scenes and Sketches in Cornwall.—Tavistock, 1844.

Passing forth from the town, along the pleasant causeway, between the embattled abbey-wall and the river, and leaving Guile Bridge, already commemorated, on the right, we shall depart from the town eastward, by the Okehampton road, through the valley of the Tavy.   In a neighbouring vale of much beauty —Inescombe, or Inscoombe, or Ina's Coombe—we shall be interested in tracing the resemblance to the original sketch by William Browne, the poet, who was born about—not earlier than—1591, at Tavistock—and commenced his education at the Grammar School there.

> There lies a vale extended to the north
> Of Tavy's stream, which (prodigal) sends forth
> In autumn, more rare fruits than have been spent
> In any greater plot of fruitful Kent.
> Two high-brow'd rocks on either side begin,
> As with an arch to close the valley in :
> Upon their rugged fronts, short writhen oaks
> Untouched of any feller's baneful strokes :
> The ivy, twisting round their barks, hath fed
> Past time, wild goats, which no man followed.
> Low in the valley some small herds of deer,
> For head and footmanship withouten peer,
> Feed undisturbed.   The swains that thereby thriv'd
> By the tradition from their sires deriv'd,
> Called it sweet Ina's Coombe.*

The description occurs in his principal work, Britannia's Pastorals, where the Wallabrook, a neighbouring tributary of the Tavy, is also celebrated in Arcadian allegories, characteristic of the pedantic euphuism of the age.   Browne is better known by his caustic description of Lydford, and its jurisprudence, a well known poem, which graphically illustrates the manners and sentiments of our Devonshire ancestors.

But we hasten onwards to the more immediate objects of our excursion, with the well-wooded grounds of Mount Tavy bounded by the river, on our right.   Crossing the stream at Harford Bridge, we shall make for Cock's Tor, a lofty frontier hill of trap-rock, where we shall notice several hut-circles.   A

---

*WILLIAM BROWNE.  Britannia's Pastorals.  Book II.  song 3,  lines,  1103-1117.  Vol. i., p. 303.  MR. GORDON GOODWIN'S edition, 1894.

rugged road at its foot will lead us to Petertavy, which, with its simple rustic church below, the fine bold brow of Smearidge, its picturesque mill, mountain torrent, and brawling cascades, will amply repay a visit. From hence by an upland road, through Cudliptown, with the Tavy murmuring along the hollow below, we reach White Tor, on the summit of which we shall find some very extraordinary masses of ruined fortifications which have never been properly investigated or described. The summit has apparently a double row of stones, which have been roughly but carefully placed one upon the other, forming a strong defence, now unfortunately much dilapidated. On the south is another pile, which looks as if it had originally formed a turret. These remains ought to be carefully examined and planned. East of White Tor is a kistvaen, first described by Dr. Arthur B. Prowse, and still further north-east, on Cock's Tor, are to be found traces of cairns and rows. From Cock's Tor, we proceed to Stannaton Down, a hill strewn with granite masses, and marked by a cairn, and turning south we shall traverse, not without difficulty, a tract of boggy land to Lints Tor, near the source of the Walkham, where are some imperfectly-defined traces of a trackway. Here, we presume, we again meet the Forest boundary, which we last marked at Mistor Pan, from thence it crosses the Walkham at the Hanging Rock, to Deadlake Head, which the Perambulators "think to be the next bound, called in the old records "Newborough." But, whatever difficulty there may be in identifying the last-named bound-place, we shall have no hesitation in fixing the next (described in the Perambulation as Lintsburrow) at South Lints Tor, to which the boundary line next advances.*

Leaving Lints Tor, and the Forest bounds, we proceed northwards to Furtor, in the North Quarter. We shall find that by a gradual ascent from the Tavy, we have here attained one of the loftiest points on the moor, the approximate height of Furtor, above the sea-level being given as no less than 1,877 feet. We have also penetrated to the most secluded and inaccessible parts of our western desert. Vast tracks of morass, bog, and heath, stretch away on every side. Besides Furtor, few tors appear to break

---

*Dr. ARTHUR B. PROWSE, however, for reasons which he gives, and which are no doubt of much weight, considers that the Forest boundary passed from Great Mistor north-west to White Tor, then in a north north-easterly direction past Bagga Tor, at the foot of South Lints Tor, and on over the east side of Stannon or Standon Hill, to the junction of the Rattlebrook with the Tavy. *Vide* Trans. Devon Assoc., vol. xxi. p. 170. But it must not be forgotten that White Tor belongs to the manor of Cudliptown, and therefore was probably never a part of the Forest.

"the deep-felt monotony" of the dreary wilds around. Not a
sheep-path or peat-stack gives token of the presence of man or
beast; and the heath-fowl which may occasionally be sprung
from the heather, only prove that this, one of their last retreats, is
seldom invaded by the sportsman. Furtor is "a sort of island
"of firm ground in the midst of a sea of peat-bogs. The district
"in which Furtor rises is to the rest of Dartmoor much that
"Dartmoor itself is to Devonshire. It is the very heart of the
"wilderness, of which it forms the highest ground—the water-
"shed, where the chief rivers rise, and from which they flow, the
"Dart to the south, the Taw and Torridge to the North." "Furtor
"is the most isolated of the Dartmoor heights, and to signify the
"'far' tor, is appropriate enough for a summit and its name,
"which seems to retain the old English '_feor_,' which is the most
"remote and the most difficult of access of any on Dartmoor.
"The peat moors which surround it, represent the decay of past
"ages—silent, dreary, lifeless—rarely visited during the greater
"part of the year, but by a wandering hill fox—the true 'deysart of
"'Dertymore,' as the natives call it. The climate, owing to the
"elevation of the district, is unusually damp, even for Dartmoor—
"so damp that filmy ferns grow on the open summit of Furtor.
"The evaporation from the great mass of peat never allows the
"atmosphere to become even warm, and thus plants have
"lingered here, survivors of a glacial period, the distance of
"which, from our own age, we are altogether unable to measure.
"Neither the Cowberry (_Vaccinium Vitis-Idæa_) and the Crow-
"berry (_Empetrum nigrum_) is found nearer to Dartmoor than the
"central parts of Wales, Shropshire and Derbyshire."* But, haply
twenty centuries ago, this solitary spot would seem to have been
occupied by man. Perhaps a Druid recluse (if such there were) here
found a place of studious retirement and meditation, where, at least,
he would have enjoyed ample opportunities for pursuing one of the
favourite sciences of his order, in the wide expanse of the starry
heavens, commanded from the brow of Furtor.† The foundation of
the structure is similar to that of the hut-circles in other parts, but
in form it is elliptical, about fifty feet in circumference. This
aboriginal dwelling stands alone on the brink of one of the tributaries of the Tavy. No vestige of any other antient remains is

---

*RICHARD JOHN KING. Dartmoor. Quarterly Review. vol. cxxxv., p. 144.

†Multa præterea de sideribus, atque eorum motu, de mundi ac terrarum magni-
tudine de rerum natura, de deorum immortalium.—CÆSAR. _Bell. Gall._, lib. vi., cap. 14.

Tavy Cleave.

near, except a cromlech in ruins, near the head of the river, about a furlong from its western bank. Although surrounded by many scattered blocks of granite, there can be little doubt as to the original intention of these four remarkable stones, which an experienced observer will readily distinguish from the surrounding masses lying in their natural position. The quoit, or impost, is about the ordinary dimensions, thirteen feet by five, and has fallen with its longest side in the ground. It is retained in a slanting position by the three original supporters, which appear to have yielded to the pressure of the superincumbent mass.

We now follow the stream of the Tavy downwards to Watern Oak and Western Redlake, a natural boundary, specified in the Perambulation, to which the line comes from Lints Tor. Between these two latter points according to the Perambulators, the Western and Northern Quarters meet. Near the same point a considerable stream from Amicombe Hill called Rattlebrook, falls into the Tavy, and forms the Forest boundary northward for some distance, to its head. Still following the course of the Tavy downwards, we shall soon reach Tavy Cleave, a magnificent range of castellated tors with which nature appears to have fortified this fine peninsular hill, while the rapid stream sweeps round the headland, and forms an effective moat to the Titanic citadel above. These tors range in succession along the precipitous sides of a rock-strewn declivity. There are five principal piles, of which the third is the loftiest and most majestic, and the whole cliff presents a remarkable resemblance to the dilapidated walls of a time-worn edifice. Even on a nearer approach, the illusion is kept up by the whortle, heath, and other plants flourishing in the interstices, so that the aspect of this mimic castle is novel and peculiar. Imagination, too, with little effort, may figure a natural outwork, or barbican, in the lower pile, on the southern glacis, guarding the approach, and thus fortifying this inland promontory almost to the river's brink. The whole declivity being overspread with scattered masses of granite, stands in bold contrast with the grassy common on the opposite bank.

The bed of the Tavy presents in general, the usual rocky characteristics of the Dartmoor rivers, but immediately below the Cleave, the stream flows for some distance over a solid granite floor. The view down the moorland glen, with far off glimpses of the cultivated country beyond, will abundantly repay the tourist for scaling these natural ramparts on his way to the neighbouring heights, along which we shall proceed westward to Gertor, or Great Tor, which crowns a bold eminence beetling over the Tavy, and is remarkable for its stratified character, as contrasted with Tavy Cleave.   If rock-basins are always to be ascribed to natural agencies, few tors would be more favourable to the production of such cavities, but none are to be found on any part of the rock. Between Tavy Cleave and Gertor we shall notice a hut-circle, with the jambs erect, and the doorway facing the river.   A track-line appears in connection with this ruined dwelling.   From hence, passing Great Tor, with the river for our guide, we shall wend our way to Marytavy, another rural church, amidst scenery pleasingly varied by homely objects, and the bolder features of the moorland border, and returning to the turnpike road, shall close our excursion at Tavistock.

Leaving the town by the old Okehampton road for our next excursion, we shall soon discern, high on an insulated hill before us, the church and steeple of Brentor,* four miles from Tavistock, on the northern verge of Heathfield Down.   Unlike the Dartmoor tors, Brentor is a volcanic eminence rising abruptly from the surrounding country.   The church which crowns the summit, is said to owe its erection to the pious gratitude of one of those "who "occupy their business in the great waters," in commemoration of his deliverance from the dangers of the stormy deep, and in fulfilment of a vow, which in the time of peril he had made, to build a church on the first land he might discover, should he be permitted to reach the shore in safety.   This is said to have been Brentor, and here accordingly the votive shrine was erected by the grateful merchant.   There is however a popular legend current in the neighbourhood, which reports that the church was intended to have occupied a more convenient site, but the design was frustrated by Satanic devices.

Of the existence of a church at Brentor, there is a record so early as 1283,† when it was known as St. Michael de Rupe; such lofty insulated sites being considered as peculiarly appropriate to

*Brent is supposed by many authors to be derived from the German *brennen*, or the English *byrnan*, to burn.   No doubt in former times this conspicuous eminence was used as a beacon, and that here, as on many other similar heights, signal fires were kindled, as a ready mode of telegraphic communication.

†The parish Church is referred to as that of Brintetorre in the deed of Deposition of John Chubbe, Abbot of Tavistock, by Bishop Bronescombe, in 1269.   The church was dedicated 4 Dec., 1319, by Bishop Stapeldon, but from Bishop Bronescombe's Register it is clear there was a church there before this.   The record, referred to in the text, of 1283, we have not been able to find.

churches dedicated to St. Michael the Archangel. The structure, built on the verge of the precipice, is small and low, but solid and durable, well calculated to brave the storms which so frequently and fiercely beat upon this rock-founded house of prayer. The roof is open, the exterior battlemented, and some traces of Early English architecture will be detected by the archæologist. Probably at the same period that the beacon flamed from its heights, Brentor was fortified, and there are some appearances of earthworks on the upper part of the hill. In surveying the varied panorama which this lofty eminence commands, the eye, glancing southward over the grove-crowned heights of Mount Edgcumbe and Maker, will rest on the expanse of the distant Channel, in search of the spot from whence land so anxiously sought for, could be descried by the storm-stricken mariner.

Returning to the highway, we shall reach the banks of the Lyd, at about three miles distance from Brentor, and find ourselves in the midst of scenery, characteristic of the immediate neighbourhood, and in many respects peculiar to this part of the moorland border. Through a rural homestead we pass onward to the copse, and by a steep zigzag pedestrian path, descend to the celebrated Lydford Fall. The stream, a tributary to the Lyd, turns the neighbouring mill, and falls over a slaty precipice, about one hundred and ten feet in height. Midway, a ledge of rock opposes a temporary obstacle to the headlong stream, and enhances the picturesque effect. In one of the happiest of his outdoor sketches, Carrington thus graphically paints the scene.

> "At once the stream, all light and music, springs
> From the bold bank. Yet not in one broad sheet
> It leaps the dark majestic cliff—a rock
> Divides it, and the bright and broken flood
> Impetuous, descends in graceful curves,
> To mingle with the foaming world below,
> While, sparkling in the midday beam, a shower
> Of spray, for ever hovering, baths the plants
> That love the mountain and the stream."*

To view, however, this cascade with advantage, it must be visited in winter, or after a summer storm, as the stream is

---

*N. T. CARRINGTON. Dartmoor, vol. i,, p. 75, ed. 1834.

inconsiderable at other times.   But the accompanying features of
the scene will never disappoint.   The spot is one of calm woodland seclusion, at the confluence of four deep and narrow glens, so
that when we stand at the foot of the waterfall, we are surrounded
by "insuperable height of loftiest shade."   Leaving this fascinating scene, we thread our adventurous way along a tangled and
"bosky" defile, guided by the darkly-flowing Lyd; but before we
reach Lydford Bridge, shall find it necessary to climb the
precipitous bank, as the channel there is formed in a narrow
ravine, through which the river struggles with a fretful murmuring
sound.   The rocky sides of the chasm are connected by the arch
which is thrown over the river, at the height of sixty or seventy
feet from the water.   The similarity observed in "the rifted banks
"of the Lyd" has given rise to the supposition that the ground
has been rent asunder by some terrible convulsion of nature;
whether this conjecture be well-founded or not, the scene at
Lydford Bridge is one of great singularity and uncommon interest.
Unlike other rivers, which glide through open plains or sunny
valleys, the Lyd forces its darkling way at the bottom of a deep
rocky fissure.   We have only to substitute the name of Lyd for
Tees, and Scott's vivid description of the northern stream will
apply, with striking accuracy, to our own.

> "Where Tees full many a fathom low
> Wears with his rage, no common foe;
> For pebbly bank, nor sand-bed here,
> Nor clay mound, checks his fierce career;
> Condemn'd to mine a channell'd way
> O'er solid sheets of marble grey."

The tourist who contents himself with the view from the
parapet, without venturing to explore the ravine below, as well as
above the bridge, will not duly appreciate the singular impressive-
ness of this romantic scene, the Devil's Bridge of Devon.   An
author* unbiassed by local predilections, thus warmly but faithfully
describes the scenery which greets the eye on the banks of the
Lyd.   "At a little distance below the arch the fissure gradually
"spreads its rocky jaws; the bottom opens and instead of the dark
"precipices, which have hitherto overhung and obscured the

---

*WARNER.  Walks through the Western Counties.

" struggling river, it now emerges into day and rolls its murmuring
" current through a winding valley, confined within magnificent
" banks, darkened with woods, which swell into bold promontories,
" or fall back into sweeping recesses till they are lost to the eye in
" the distance.  Thickly shaded by trees, which shoot out from the
" rent, the scene at Lydford Bridge is not so terrific as would
" have been, had a little light been let in upon the abyss, just
" sufficient to produce 'a darkness visible.'  As it is, however,
" the chasm cannot be regarded without shuddering, nor will the
" stoutest heart meditate unappalled upon the dreadful anecdotes
" connected with the spot."

A gentleman from the neighbourhood of Exeter, ruined by
gambling, is said to have crossed the moor on horseback to this
place, where dismounting, madly bent on self destruction, he
leaped down the terrific chasm.  In the deep pool above the
bridge, a maniac is also said to have drowned himself.  But the
scene is also associated with an incident to which the mind gladly
turns from the contemplation of madness and crime.  In our
present excursion we have traversed the old highway leading
from Plymouth, through Tavistock and Okehampton.  A benighted horseman once travelling this road, amid the din and fury
of a moorland tempest, on approaching Lydford, found as he
pressed briskly forward, that his horse made a sudden leap, for
which he could not account, as there was no apparent obstacle in
the way.  In the morning, however, all was explained, when he
heard with astonishment, and it may be hoped with thankfulness
also, that the bridge having been swept away by the raging
torrent during the previous night, had not his horse gallantly
cleared the chasm at a bound, he must inevitably have perished
in the yawning abyss.

Clambering along the bank above the bridge, and following
the course of the river upwards, about a mile, we shall reach
Kate's Fall, where the Lyd, fresh from the neighbouring moor,
bursting through a rocky fissure, and rushing down a steep descent,
forms a cascade, in some respects finer than the more celebrated
Lydford waterfall.  We cross the stream, above the cascade, and
through a lane on the opposite side shall soon reach the once
important borough of Lydford, the principal vestiges of whose
former greatness will be found in the keep of the antient castle,
which rises conspicuously on the west side of the present church-
town.

But Lydford appears to have been a place of importance even before the date of its castle.* " Yea, doubtless," writes Risdon, " in the Saxton Heptarchy, it was a town of some note, that felt " the furious rage of the merciless Danes," by whom it was plundered and burnt in the same expedition when Tavistock Abbey was destroyed by these marauding invaders. The castle was built subsequently to the Conquest, and by a charter of Edward I., Lydford was appointed as a stannary prison, where alone all offenders against the stannary laws were to be incarcerated. Here, accordingly, Richard Strode, member of parliament for Plympton, an ancestor of the Strodes, of Newnham Park, was imprisoned in 1512, as he states for his exertions in Parliament in procuring an act to prevent injury to harbours by mining operations.† He was summoned before the Stannators at their court at Crockern Tor, and having had, in his absence, a heavy fine inflicted upon him, was arrested, and, according to their sentence, confined in Lydford Castle. The sufferings of this gentleman (who, however, appears to have been condemned by due course of law, for interfering with certain tinners) and of other victims of these arbitrary enactments, in such a " heinous, contagious and detestable place " as this dungeon was commonly reported to be, must have been great. Both the jurisprudence and the prison, appear to have obtained an unenviable notoriety about this period. A proverb, in " Ray's Collection," doubtless embodied the popular opinion.

> " First hang and draw,
> Then hear the cause, is Lydford law."

Browne, our Tavistock poet, has described the castle and borough of Lydford " very exactly and facetely in running " metre " as old Westcote phrases it ; for which see chapter xviii. The expense incurred by Prince Charles, as Duke of Cornwall, in repairing the castle, appears to have done little to retard the ruin to which it seems to have been doomed in Browne's time. A survey of the Borough of Lydford gives an interesting, but lamentable account of its dilapidated state in 1650. Matters have

---

*We have an impression from a leaden seal, found in part of the ruins which was in the possession of the late Mr. Savile. It is very rude in design and execution, and represents a buttressed, battlemented, castle gateway. Only a part of the inscription can be made out,.. SIGILLUM—BURGV .. LIDE .., circular, two and a quarter inches in diameter.

†*Vide* 4 Hen. viii., c. 8.

not improved since that time. Indeed the condition of the Castle is "lamentable. A place of repute before the Norman Conquest "and for centuries afterwards, it was the terror of the West, from "the severity of the Stannary Laws and the noisomeness of its "dungeon; the rival of Exeter; the possessor of a mint that "coined its own money; the capital of the largest parish in Great "Britain, where even so recently as the time of George IV., the "Manor and Stannary Courts were held—Lydford is now a "desolate ruin. The fate of this place is more to be deplored, as "its destruction has been wanton and intentional. When the "business of the Court was removed to Prince Town, the cover-"ing, the floors, and the removable parts were purposely pulled "down, or left for the elements to work their will upon, and the "bell consigned to ruin.*

The castle, on the north and west sides, is defended by a deep hollow, with precipitous banks winding down to the glen of the Lyd. On the eastern side stands "the little church" commemorated by Browne, where there is a curious font, of such antique simplicity that it may have been coeval with the departed glories of Lydford, in Saxon-times.

Leaving Lydford, we shall direct our course to the mail road from Tavistock to Okehampton, and find sufficient accommodation for the night. Or, if disposed to pursue his researches, the traveller will cross the high road, and entering the commons, will pass over Highdown eastward, to meet the Lyd once more, as it comes foaming down from Noddon. On the brink of the river, in the vale below Doetor, which bears almost due east, is the ruined foundation of an antient hut, peculiar both in form and construction. The form is rectangular, and the stones of which the basement is composed, instead of being fixed erect in the ground, edge to edge, are set face to face, and in the present ruined condition of the building, have declined from their original erect position. The hut is twenty-six feet long by thirteen feet wide, and it stands apart from any other antient remains.

Having crossed the Lyd, we shall mount the opposite hill; and find ourselves in the midst of a fine group of tors. Between the Lyd and a tributary rivulet, Little Lints Tor, Armstor, Brator and Doetor form a range, in a line almost north and south. East

---

*P. O. Hutchinson. *Proc. Soc. Ant.*, *N.S.* Vol. viii.. p. 484. *Vid:* also R. N. Worth. Lydford and its Castle.

P

of the rivulet, Links Tor, Dannagoat, Clatter, Sharp Tor and
Hare Tor, form another series almost parallel to the former, and
fortify the ridge which ends in the promontory at Tavy Cleave.  At
the foot of this ridge on the east, the Rattlebrook pursues its
noisy way to the Tavy, and tracing its course upwards, we shall
once more return to the Forest bounds, which proceed northwards
from the head of Rattlebrook to Stengator, or Steincator, with
the lofty dorsal ridge of Amicombe high on the right.  Passing
over its northern extremity, we shall notice Brandscomb's Loaf,
Shelstone Tor, and Sourton Tor, the latter rising above the little
border church of that name.   In our progress over this part of
the moor, we shall meet with few antient monuments except
some cairns on the surrounding heights.

From Stengator the boundary goes straight to the vale of the
West Ockment, which it crosses at Sandyford, called also in the
Perambulation, Longaford.  From hence the boundary proceeds
in a straight line to High Wilhays, or Willinghayes, and from
thence to West Miltor, skirting the eastern flank of Yestor*
Here we deviate from the line to scale its lofty peak, the elevation
of which is just two thousand and thirty feet, and it has been
supposed to be the highest point on the moor.  But Yes Tor
must give way to another adjacent point, Wilhayes, just mentioned,
the centre bench mark of which is 2039·4 feet, and consequently is
the loftiest peak in the whole south of England.  From Yestor,
the whole of the western and north-western districts of Devon, and a
large extent of East Cornwall, lie mapped out before us.   Towards
the north-east we look over the broad shoulder of Cosdon, to Raddon
top and the higher points of country between Crediton and Tiverton;
whilst in the south-west, we descry the bold eminence of Hingston
Down, above Callington; and in front, stretch our gaze over
Broadbury, towards Holsworthy, Bude, and the Bristol Channel.

We shall find nothing worthy of special note at Miltor, and
shall therefore leave the guidance of the Perambulators, to follow
the course of a rivulet, which flowing down the hollow between
Yestor and Miltor, falls into the West Ockment below Blackdown.
The whole of this part of the moor is remarkably destitute of
antient remains; and eastward of Yestor is of the same dreary
monotonous character as the vicinity of Cranmere Pool to which

---

*Probably *East* tor is more correct.  The change of E or H into Y, is common in
the Devonshire vernacular.  Thus we have Yeaffield for Heathfield, and Yeffer for
Heifer, and Yaffull for handful.

F. V. Wedgery. Phot.

W. L. Colls. Ph. Sc.

OKEHAMPTON CASTLE.

it extends. The scenery on the West Ockment, in the deep glen at the foot of Black Tor, is grand and impressive, but will not long detain us from tracing the course of the river onwards till it sweeps below the venerable ruins of Okehampton Castle, which occupy the summit and declivity of a rocky mound, about half-a-mile from the western entrance of the town, and full in view of the main road into Cornwall. Above this eminence, thickly clothed with foliage, the massy walls of the keep are seen to rise, with the most picturesque and happy effect. One lofty fragment appears ready to topple down headlong, at the first assault of the blustering tempests from the neighbouring wilds of Dartmoor; but from the durable qualities of the cement, it has withstood the fury of the elements and may, we trust, long remain to add interest and beauty to this charming scene. The antiquary, with his thoughts reverting to the lordly barons who once here held sway, the Baldwins of the Norman era, and the Courtenays of Plantagenet times, will enter from the east, and trace the remains of the castle gate and the moat, the base court and the chapel, and reach the square keep on the western side by a pathway overhung with trees. Embosomed in foliage—its mouldering walls mantled with iyy, and surrounded by hills of varied form and hue, Okehampton Castle, in sunshine or in shower, "at "morn or dewy eve," will be always an object of pleasing interest; but like Melrose and other celebrated ruins, to see it in perfection the tourist should "visit it by the pale moonlight."

To facilitate this object, we shall take up our quarters for the night at Okehampton, and before proceeding next morning on our final excursion, shall visit the most prominent objects of interest in this antient borough, which we shall observe is situated on the very verge of our moorland district, nestling beneath the bold brow of the once celebrated park, on a pleasant little plain, watered by the twin streams of the Ockment, which peninsulate a large portion of its site, and unite their waters just below the town. The two bridges in the main street, the chantry chapel, dedicated to St. James, near the east bridge, with its embattled steeple, and some old gabled dwellings, will not fail to attract our attention; nor shall we grudge our walk to the church of All Saints, which occupies a commanding situation on the hill that rises above the town on the western side. This, the parish church of Okehampton, a spacious structure with a lofty pinnacled tower, forms a conspicuous and pleasing object amidst the surrounding scenery.

The old church was accidentally destroyed by fire a few years since, but it has since been re-built.

Returning to the town by a road in front of the vicarage lawn, we shall pass the entrance to Okelands, the charming grounds of which are enlivened and adorned by the Ockment, which here flows onward to render its tribute to the Torridge, through picturesque banks overhung with luxuriant foliage. It has been conjectured by some writers that a Roman road ran in and near Okehampton, on its way from Exeter to Holsworthy and Stratton. One circumstance on which this supposition has been grounded is the camp, which it is suggested is Roman, on Bradbury* Common, about five miles N.N.W. of Okehampton, in the line which such a road would probably have taken. But the traces of a fortified post and of a Roman road, which have been supposed to exist in the park near Halstock, cannot safely be adduced in evidence, as we shall find in our progress in that direction. Proceeding southward from the town, between the two Ockments, we shall enter the park by a rough road, which, as we ascend the hill, soon degenerates into a steep moor-track, chiefly used for bringing turf down from the commons, and for driving cattle to pasture. A few veteran hollies of large growth, on the northern and western declivities, are almost the sole remains 'of the sylvan honours of of the antient park of Okehampton, which was disafforested by Henry VIII. in 1589, at the same time that the castle was demolished. On this spot we are also reminded of the wild legend connected with Lady Howard's oak, still current in this part of Devonshire, and embodied in Mrs. Bray's tale of Fitz of Fitzford; nor is it improbable that there are some still, whose superstitious fancy figures to them the doomed spectre of the once proud heiress, in her coach of bones, preceded by her skeleton hound, driving through the streets of Tavistock, at midnight, to bring a blade of grass from Okehampton Park to the gateway of Fitzford. Nor shall we omit to notice Fitz's Well, a spring on the ridge of the hill, which, according to the statement of the author of a concise but interesting account of the history and antiquities of Okehampton, "it was a custom, till within a late period, for young persons

---

*It is the strong opinion of some, that Bradbury is a specimen of a Roman Summer Camp, on an extensive tract of table-land, in the parish of North Lew. The form is an oblong square, two hundred and sixty feet, by two hundred and thirty-six feet, and the vallum is not more than eighteen feet in the highest part, on the outer slope. The names of Chester Moor, Scob-Chester, and Wickchester, which occur in the immediate neighbourhood, appear to indicate the presence of the Romans.

" to visit on the morning of Easter-day."* From this commanding spot we shall gain varied and favourable views of the town in the valley, the church on the eminence above, the mansion and groves of Okelands, the course of the Ockments, and the picturesque ruins of the castle. We shall here also appreciate the extent of the park, which, stretching from the banks of the West Ockment in front of the castle, reaches to the channel of the eastern river, and forms the extreme northern foreland of the great Dartmoor waste which we have been perambulating.

Passing over the brow of the hill to Blackdown, we reach the Forest boundary once more, beyond the verge of the park, at Rowtor, or Roughtor, to which eminence it comes in a direct line from West Miltor, the spot at which we left it in our last excursion. The line of perambulation then goes down the north-eastern declivity of Rowtor to Chapel Ford, at the confluence of the Blackaven water with the East Ockment, called by the Perambulators "the ford which lieth in the east side of St. Michael's chapel " of Holstock." Scarcely a vestige of this antient sanctuary now remains. " The storms of six centuries," says the author above cited, "have wrought their work in its destruction. Excepting the " line of its foundations, now covered like the rest with green sward, " and a path leading to the spot from Belstone, with its crossing- "place over the East Ockment, still called the Chapelford, there " is little left to point where our forefathers worshipped."

The course of the river through this secluded glen presents a succession of scenes of romantic grandeur and wild magnificence. The river comes foaming down from the moors over a solid granite bed, in some places sufficiently steep to form a succession of waterfalls, and makes its way through a deep mountain-gorge to Belstone Cleave, where it sweeps round the bold acclivity which forms the eastern boundary of the park. The hanging woods clothing the steep bank on the Okehampton side, are strikingly contrasted with the bare and rock-strewn declivity which confronts them. Nor will the tourist reach this, the last definite bound-mark of the Forest, without confessing that in his whole perambulation, he has seen no spot where the peculiar features of our moorland scenery are more felicitously combined than in this the lonely glen of St. Michael of Halstock.

---

*W. B. BRIDGES. Account of the Barony and Town of Okehampton. This book was compiled by an enthusiast who ended his days in poverty. It was unfinished, but a second edition, published in 1889, contains the complete work.

Crossing the river, we shall mount the steep ascent towards Belstone Tor, and within a quarter of a mile on its western slope, we shall observe the circle called in the neighbourhood, Nine Stones, but which in reality consists of seventeen stones, erect, the highest of which is not more than two feet and a half from the ground. We shall climb the hill, and having noticed the fine series of tors which rise from the rock-strewn ridge, between the watercourses of the Ockment and the Taw, shall mark the direction of the line of perambulation, from the Chapel Ford in a line to Cosdon beacon, the Hoga de Cossdonne of the Perambulators.

Having thus reached once more the point at which we commenced our wanderings round the Forest bounds, on the banks of the Taw, we shall return towards Okehampton, and pass in our way the moorland village of Belstone, with its simple church and low sturdy tower, built as if to resist the fiercest onslaught of the mountain tempest. We shall regain the vale of the East Ockment, in front of Belstone Cleave, and the sombre gorge through which that river pours down into the valley on the north side of the park, and again crossing the stream, shall skirt the south bank in our return to Okehampton, and there terminate our last excursion.

# CHAPTER IX.

## Geology, Petrology, and Mineralogy of the Moor.[*]

### I.—Geology.

To the geologist, the word "Dartmoor" is associated with the idea of granite, for although other rocks of Lower Carboniferous and of Devonian age occur within the topographical limits of the Moor, these strata are confined to its borders, seldom encroaching far upon the higher slopes, and have nowhere been recognized in the central region, which is exclusively composed of granite.

Dartmoor forms the most easterly extremity of a chain of granite masses, appearing at intervals, among the slates or "Killas" of Cornwall, and in the Scilly Isles. Of these masses, Dartmoor is by far the largest, occupying an area of two hundred and twenty-five square miles. The Dartmoor granite forms a very irregularly shaped mass, its longer

*For the contents of this chapter, the Editor is greatly indebted to his two friends, Mr. W. A. E. Ussher, F.G.S., of the Geological Survey of the United Kingdom, who has written the part relating to Geology, and Mr. R. N. Worth, F.G.S., who has furnished the second part, Petrology and Mineralogy.

axis from near Okehampton to Ivybridge, N. and S., is twenty-two miles, and its greatest breadth from east to west is eighteen miles on the latitude of Bridford, whilst at its southern extremity and on the latitude of Meavy its breadth is only seven miles.*

The granite of Dartmoor is for the most part, a coarsely porphyritic rock, containing large prisms of Orthoclase felspar, colorless quartz and white mica, but on its outskirts it often becomes finer in texture, and veins or seams of fine grained granite are visible here and there, in places simulating interstratified beds in the coarser material.    A good example of this may be seen in the joint cleft which intersects Hell Tor.

The irregular weathering of the summit masses, which has produced the numerous Tors, with which Dartmoor is studded, has been facilitated by perpendicular or inclined joints, traversing more or less horizontal lines, which on a cursory glance, resemble bedding, but on nearer inspection are never found to be individually continuous for any distance in the same plane.    This pseudo bedded structure is rendered very distinct by the weathering of the rock, but in fresh quarried surfaces it is not always so apparent. The various shapes exhibited by the Tors are due to the local predominance of these structural lines of vertical and inclined joints, and more or less horizontal pseudo bedding.    Where the joints are vertical and numerous, such masses as Lustleigh Cleave have resulted, where they are inclined, as well as vertical, such Tors as Vixen Tor are the result.    Where the pseudo bedding lines are close and well developed and vertical joints rare, such masses as Kestor are found, and where the pseudo bedding is developed at considerable intervals, and vertical jointing is infrequent, we find great cake-like masses such as Hell Tor, Heytor, and Blackingstone Rock.

Tors which have been eaten away to the condition of pinnacles are exemplified in Bowerman's Nose near Manaton, and in the familiar example of the Cheesewring on the granite mass of Bodmin Moors, in East Cornwall.    In both these examples the horizontal structure is very apparent, but the difference in shape is no doubt due to the presence of close vertical joints in the original mass, of which Bowerman's Nose is the relic, and their absence in the other instance.    The late Mr. G. W. Ormerod

---

*Vide Chapter i., p. 2.

(Quart. Journ. Geol. Soc., for Aug. 1869, pp. 273-280; Rep. Brit. Assoc. for 1869.) described numerous instances of inclination or dip in the pseudo stratification of the granite, and the influence of N.N.W. to S.S.E., and nearly E. and W. joints, on the production of the Tors. Mr. Ormerod also drew attention to the occasional presence of spheroidal structure in the granite, and figured a good example near Lustleigh Station. The Dartmoor granite is frequently schorlaceous on and near its borders, and schorl or tourmaline, is also met with here and there, in more central regions. Commenting on this, De la Beche (Report on the Geol. of Corn. Devon and W. Somerset) points out the possibility of such occurrences being near the original granite surface, which, owing to the processes of denudation can now only be determined on the outskirts, where the granite passes beneath the Culm Measures and Devonian rocks.

The granite is of very unequal hardness, its constituent crystals being frequently separated, by the action of rain and frost, into an incoherent fine gravel, or coarse sand (the growan of Cornwall). This is more especially the case in depressions of the surface, where the rain would be likely to pond and filter downward. Upon such water-logged, gravelly surfaces, peaty growth has frequently taken place, giving rise to quagmires: or the ponded water forms little lakelets, such as Cranmere and Dozmare Pool,* and Clacywell Pool which is said to exceed ninety fathoms in depth. The large blocks of granite studding the surface, on the slopes and in the valleys, attest the unequal durability of the rock. The morasses of Dartmoor form natural reservoirs, from which, in contiguous sources, spring the East and West Okement, tributaries of the Torridge, the Taw, the Teign, and the Dart.

The Torquay water supply was obtained by the clearing out of a waterlogged depression near Hennock, and its conversion into a storage reservoir by regulating the escape of the natural drainage by sluices.

Another form of the decomposition of granite is illustrated in the china clay Works, between Cornwood and Princetown, near Cadover Bridge, and on Lee Moor. In this case the felspars have decomposed to koalin, and the fine clay is disengaged from the unaltered quartz and mica by washing.

---

*In the Parish of Alternon, Cornwall.

As a whole, the granite of Dartmoor is a coarse-grained brown grey rock, composed of large crystals of orthoclase felspar, quartz, and black or white mica, but there are very many divergencies from this general type—although unfortunately, except where exposed in quarries, or in the sides and clefts of the tors, the variations in the granite are rather unsatisfactorily indicated by surface stones.  Mr. R. N. Worth, F.G.S., who has given considerable attention to this subject, gives a long list of specimens, with their microscopic characters, obtained by him from various parts of Dartmoor, and from the beds of most of the streams descending from the Moor.*   Beside the ordinary coarse porphyritic granite, these include fine grained granites, felsites, pegmatites (quartz and felspar), greisen (quartz mica rocks), luxulyanites (felspar schorl rocks).   The granite varies in color from red to grey and yellow grey.   Many of the finer varieties occur in veins in the coarse granite, in dykes, called elvans, intersecting it, and also appearing in the surrounding slates in places, and on or near the margin of the mass.

The rocks of Dartmoor and its neighbourhood are extensively employed for economical purposes.   They are used as building stones with great profit, though much care is required in the selection, as the "free stones," so called from the facility of working them, are the soonest to decay.   "The most "beautiful red granite of Devon " says Mr. Worth, is supplied "by Trowlesworthy, and there is no richer red to be found "anywhere than its darker varieties."†   Mr. Worth also records "pink schorlaceous rock at Leather Tor," and a "fine-grained "dark grey granite" with black mica, at Sheepstor.   White granitoid rock occurs on the borders of the granite, near Meldon Viaduct, Okehampton, and near Bickley, in Cann Quarry, these rocks are called aplites, they belong to the elvans.

The junction between the granites and the rocks bordering it, is invariably a sharp one ; nowhere, is a passage observable.

For about half a mile outward from the granite boundary, the surrounding rocks are more or less highly altered, beyond this the alteration becomes slight, except where the granite border is sinuous, as west of Bovey Tracey, at Cornwood, and Meavy.   The alteration takes various forms, dependent on the

---

*See materials for a Census of Devonian Granites and Felsites.   R. N. WORTH Trans. Devon Assoc., vol xxiv, 1892, p. 182.

†The Rocks of Plymouth.  Trans. Plymouth Institution, vol. ix., p. 234.

original nature of the sediments affected.   Certain dark shales or slates, presumably belonging to the basement beds of the Culm Measures, exhibit well marked crystals of chiastolite, as near Ivybridge and Bovey Tracey, close to the granite boundary. Diabases and dolerites near the granite, become very hornblendic. Mr. Rutley notes the alteration of gabbro to amphibolite at Waspworthy and near Brazen Tor, where it is in contact with the granite.

Very hard fine grained banded rocks occur here and there round the granite, from Ivybridge by Okehampton to Lydford, possibly suggestive of the cherty rocks of the Lower Culm Measures.   Near Horrabridge, Yelverton, Cornwood, and Ivybridge, the grey slates of the Upper Devonian are spotted ; nearer to the granite, these seem to pass into andalusite slates and mica schist.   The granite also, near its borders, exhibits reciprocal alteration, a development of schorl or tourmaline being very general.   Mr. Rutley* speaking of the junction between amphibolite and granite at Brazen Tor says "the granite close to "the contact is very fine grained and felstone like, loose blocks "showing black nests and segregations of schorl, it becomes more "and more porphyritic toward the Tor itself."   Very often as to the east of Ivybridge, the granite on the border is a coarsely crystalline red, whitish and grey rock.

The actual junction of the granite and bordering rocks is visible in the bed of the River Erme above Ivybridge, in the branch railway between Lustleigh and Bovey Tracey, and in a quarry near Bovey Tracey.   As a rule however, the junction is effectually masked by a thick soil studded with granite boulders and consisting of disintegrated granite or growan, which has been washed down the slopes from higher ground.   Where well exposed near its border, as in the quarries worked by the G.W.R. Company, east of Ivybridge, on its eastern border, near Canonteign (Waterfall Valley), and in the gorge of the River Taw, above Belstone, the granite, through the inclination of its lateral or pseudo bedding joints, has an appearance of dipping under the bordering rocks.

Near Bickleigh the slate rocks bordering the granite may be of Middle Devonian age, but toward Walkhampton they probably belong to the Upper Devonian, and also toward Ivybridge, from

---

*F. RUTLEY.   The Eruptive Rocks of Brent Tor, etc., p. 26, 1878.

Walkhampton northwards to Lydford, and from Ivybridge towards Bovey Tracey, the contact rocks seem to belong to the Lower Culm Measures and to the Upper Devonian. The geological structure of Devon is complicated by the strain, compression, and crushing to which the originally horizontal beds of sand, clay, and limestone, which form the palæozoic surface, have been subjected since their deposition, and to the wearing away of the surface through long ages of denudation.

To the first of these causes—contraction of the crust—the distribution of the Carboniferous rocks or Culm Measures, in a shallow basin with its northern border, along a line from Barnstaple to Dulverton, and its irregular southern margin from Boscastle by Tavistock to Lydford, and from Dean Church by Ashburton and Bickington is due, as well as the appearance of the older or Devonian formation in North and South Devon.

To the latter—denudation—is to be ascribed the concealment of the older rocks, by secondary rocks (New Red Sandstone, of the older geologists) of Triassic and probably of Permian age, in the eastern part of the county.

The encroachment of these more modern sediments upon the Carboniferous and Devonian rocks is irregular, a long tongue extending westward from Exeter and Upton Pyne, past Crediton to Jacobstow, and a shorter tongue projecting westward from Tiverton junction by Tiverton and Washfield to Holmead. The presence of detached fragments of these secondary rocks at Hatherleigh, Highhampton and Stoodley Beacon, prove that they had a still further extension over the Palæozoic formations. Still newer formations of Tertiary age form an old lacustrine deposit of clays, sands and gravels, with bands of lignite in the Bovey valley, from whence they extend over the lowlands to Newton Abbot, and are found in stratified gravel masses, on Wolborough Hill and Milber Down. The more recent deposits, such as alluvia and old river gravels do not call for any special mention; they are to be found in most of the stream valleys, and, where the gradient is gentle, often form tracts of fairly considerable breadth. No true signs of glacial action have been recorded in Devon, if we except the large granite boulder embedded in consolidated raised beach on the rock platform, on which it rests, near Croyde, in North Devon, which may have been stranded by floating ice during the raised beach period.

As far as is certainly known, the oldest rocks in Devon belong to the Devonian formation; they occur in North Devon, to the north of a line connecting Barnstaple and Morebath near Dulverton, and reappear in South Devon, occupying the area south of Tavistock, Cornwood, Ivybridge, Ashburton, and Bickington, near Newton Abbot. These areas of Devonian rocks are separated by a great extension of carboniferous strata, which, from the occasional presence of anthracite seams near Bideford, Alverdiscot and Mornacot, near South Molton, are called Culm Measures. The Culm Measures form a carboniferous type which has its analogues in Westphalia, Thuringia, and other parts of Germany.

De la Beche and Phillips, about fifty years ago, showed that certain impersistent dark limestones containing the shell *Posidonomya Becheri*, occurred at intervals in the lower beds of the formation, near its northern and southern borders, whilst in the central regions these horizons were not met with. The correspondence of the lower beds of the Culm Measures, near their north and south margins, and the appearance of the older Devonian formation to the north and south, proved the existence of a trough or basin, occupied by Carboniferous rocks with Devonian rocks emerging from beneath them on the north and south. The type of the North Devon Devonian is, however, different from that of South Devon, and this led to the idea entertained by the late Dr. Holl and other geologists of eminence, that there was an irregular interval in time, between the deposition of the latest Devonian and earliest Culm Measure sediments, or in other words, that whilst the basement beds of the Culm Measures correspond in character on their north and south margins, the underlying Devonian beds exhibited no exact correspondence. A comparison of the Devonian types of North and South Devon, with those of France and Germany, shows, however, that the absence of exact correspondence is due to different conditions of deposit. The North Devon rocks afford evidence of shallower water conditions, by the presence of great masses of sandstone at intervals throughout their sequence, whilst in South Devon, arenaceous rocks are confined to the lower beds, and limestones are much more abundant. The presence of great masses of limestone, and of considerable developments of contemporaneous igneous rocks, give to the geology of South Devon, a much greater local variety than is met with in North Devon, where the strata consists of interstratified or alternating masses of slate, grit, and sandstone.

The following is a general table of the palæozoic strata of Devon :—

CULM MEASURES. Upper—Eggesford Grits.

> Middle—Morchard sandstones, grits, slates, and shales, and Exeter shales and grits.

> Lower—Dark shales, Chert beds* and impersistent limestones, containing *Posidonomya Becheri, etc.*

### DEVONIAN.

| N. Devon type. | S. Devon type. |
|---|---|
| Upper—Pilton beds, slates. | Slates, occasionally calcareous. |
| Baggy beds, sandstone with *Cucullæa* | Slates, red and grey, *Entomis*. |
| Slates with *Lingula*. | Slates with calcareous nodules. |
| Pickwell Down grits and slates. | Limestone beds, local. |
| Middle—Morte slates. | Volcanic developments, local. |
| Ilfracombe slates, with limestone and grit beds towards the base. | |
| Lower—Hangman grits and slates. | Limestone developments, local. Slates, with occasional limestone beds and volcanic rocks. |
| Lynton beds, even grits, and irregular, more or less calcareous slates. | |
| Foreland grits. | Slates, grits and sandstones. Staddon, Cockington, &c. |

The South Devon rocks are characterized by the presence of both contemporaneous and intrusive igneous materials. Dolerites occur in the Culm Measures, near Tavistock, and on the east of Dartmoor, between Bovey Tracey and Dunsford. Diabases and schalsteins attain a considerable development, near Totnes, where they constitute the Ashprington series, and from thence extend in dwindling force to the shores of Plymouth Sound, near Mount Batten.

---

*In specimens from the Lower Culm Measure Chert beds—supplied by Mr. Fox, Mr. Hamling, and the author—Dr. Hinde discovered *Radiolaria*.

Viewed apart from its surroundings, or at least without regard to the disposition of the rocks surrounding it, the age of the granite of Dartmoor has very generally been regarded as post Carboniferous, because rocks of Carboniferous age exhibit an alteration in their mineral characteristics on its borders, decreasing outward in intensity, and seldom extending to beyond half a mile.

De la Beche treats of the question of the age and relation of the Dartmoor and Cornish granites to their surroundings, in many passages in his Report on the geology of Cornwall and Devon. He considered a subterranean connection between all the large granite masses, from Dartmoor to the Land's End, at no very great depth beneath the surface, as highly probable. This great granitic backbone is supposed to have been upheaved under and through the palæozoic strata in post, Carboniferous and probably pre-Triassic times, and to have been in a molten condition, at the time of upheaval.

The inadequacy of this theory to explain the distribution of the Culm Measures and Devonian rocks around Dartmoor led to the suggestion of the intrusion of the Dartmoor granite as a laccolite, but a subsequent study of the palæozoic rocks in detail, and of the arguments of De la Beche led to the entire abandonment of the laccolitic theory, by its proposer, the subterranean connection of the granite, as advocated by De la Beche, seeming too strong a probability to be ignored. Mr. R. N. Worth propounded the theory that the granite of Dartmoor formed the stump of a post Carboniferous volcano, the erupted portions of which had been denuded away, and were partly accounted for by the varieties of granitoid and other igneous rocks met with in the New Red breccias of Teignmouth, Exeter and Crediton. This theory is open to the objection of ignoring the stratigraphy of the area, as well as to the absence of necessity for a volcanic excrescence to account for igneous fragments in the New Red rocks, which are very similar in character to those met with in parts of the German Permian.

From an examination of the fluid inclusions of the Dartmoor granites, Mr. A. R. Hunt* has been led to the conclusion that the Dartmoor rock is for the greater part an ancient, and probably Archœan granite, much modified in post carboniferous times by a

---

*See Brit. Assoc. Reports, 1889, p. 569, and 1890, p. 815.

partial reheating in the presence of salt water. Every slice examined of the Dartmoor rock contains chlorides, while all the crystalline rocks trawled in the English channel, and the quartz veins in the Start and Bolt District, are apparently free from saline inclusions. A quartz vein in the culm rocks bordering the granite near Lustleigh Cleave, contains unmistakeable salt.

The writer, after carefully working up the palæozoic and granite chapters of De la Beche's Report, was led to regard the subterranean connection of the granite masses, at no very great depth, as propounded by him, as too probable to admit of the explanations of an erupted granite mass, or of a laccolitic origin. Supplementing some considerable knowledge of the stratigraphy of Devon, by the observations of De la Beche, regarding the granites, elvans, and palæozoic rocks of Cornwall, he found that the distributions and relations of the palæozoic rocks and the granites seemed to favour the view of the greater antiquity of the latter as propounded by Mr. Hunt. In discussing the relations of the Culm Measures to the granites, the following sequence of events was maintained :

1. Deflections of strike and production of cleavage.
2. Contact Metamorphism.

Firstly, as the former were found to bear an exact relationship to the granite masses, it seemed incredible that this appearance should have been illusory, but that the granites occupied their present sites as rigid masses during the production of the strikes by the North and South movements.

Secondly, as the contact metamorphism was shown on petrological grounds to have taken place after the production of cleavage, this effect would appear to have been due to the yielding of the rigid masses, not *en masse*, but locally, at a time when the elvans prove a rise in the isogeotherms to have taken place.

Considerable misapprehension seems to have arisen as to the object and scope of this theory, put forward merely to account for insuperable stratigraphical difficulties that are quite inexplicable on the old post Carboniferous eruptive hypothesis. In a recent communication to the Geological Society entitled " Notes on " Dartmoor," General McMahon, without entering into or reviewing the chain of evidence upon which the foregoing hypothesis was based, maintains the post carboniferous eruptive hypothesis.

HILL BRIDGE.

He says* " There certainly seems no escape from the conclusion
" that the metamorphism of the fringing-zone is due to the thermal
" contact-action of an uncooled, unconsolidated granite.    The
" fringing-rocks exhibit in the mineral changes set up in them, such
" as the production of chiastolite in beds rich in carbonaceous
" material, evidence of the contact-action of heated granite."

" Now the material point is, that directly we get beyond this
" fringing metamorphic zone—that is to say, when we get a mile
" or a mile and a half, from the boundary of the Granite and the
" Culm Measures—we pass into unaltered rocks.    Is it possible
" that a stupendous north-and-south squeeze exerted on the whole
" region, and capable of fusing a rigid rock, covering an area of
" two hundred and twenty-five square miles, would have left
" these beds untouched ?"

" The best locality for studying the two types of granite, that
" I have seen, is in the valley of the Tavy, in the neighbourhood
" of Hill Bridge, between Hill Town and White Tor.    The
" passage from the fine, even-grained type to the porphyritic
" normal type is rapid.    In the bed of the river, owing to a long
" period of dry weather, I was fortunate enough to reach a mass
" of granite *in situ*, worn smooth on the surface by the water that
" showed the actual blending of the two types.    About fifty yards
" from where the slates first crop out, a mixture of the porphyritic
" and fine-grained varieties may be seen.    Masses of porphyritic
" rock containing rectangular crystals of felspar, from two and a
" half to three inches in length, are included in the fine-grained
" variety.    They have not the appearance of blocks of a coarse-
" grained granite, included in another eruptive rock, but look like
" aggregations of porphyritic crystals, in a fine grained non-
" porphyritic base.    The whole suggests the idea of an imperfectly
" stirred plum-pudding, in which the plums have got together in
" a lump.    We have here, I take it, evidence of the imperfect
" mixing of two portions of the granitic magma in different
" conditions of fluidity.    Students of quartz-porphyries and
" similar rocks, are well aware that when a relief of pressure takes
" place, and a partially crystallized deep-seated rock is moved
" toward the surface, a partial remelting of the already-formed
" crystals takes place.    The relief of pressure in this case, is
" believed to give increased potency to the solvent action of the

---

*McMAHON.   Notes on Dartmoor.   Quart. Journ. Geol. Soc.   Vol. xlix., p. 389.

" heated liquid in which the crystals are suspended.   It seems to
" me, that a similar result would be produced, if the pressure
" remained constant, and the heat were locally increased.   And
" the explanation I would suggest, is that, as the partially
" crystallized granite was moved upwards, the traction and friction
" against the sides of the vent, broke up the larger crystals and
" increased the heat, and consequent fluidity, of the marginal
" portions of the mass, so that we have a margin of fine grained
" granite around the normal porphyritic rock, and an imperfect
" blending of the two along the line of junction.   The loss of heat
" during cooling, would have been more rapid along the margin,
" than in the central portions, and although it evidently was
" sufficiently slow to enable both portions to set up a holocrys-
" talline structure, it was not slow enough to enable the marginal
" portion to develop porphyritic crystals."[*]

He adds " It is evident that a strong solvent action has been
" set up by the acid magma on the crystal of first consolidation.
" The biotites have been eaten into internally, and around their
" edges; similarly the felspars are eaten into, and riddled with
" granules of quartz.   Some are dappled over with numerous
" microscopic crystals of a colourless mica, such as one often sees
" in quartz-porphyries and granites.   There is nothing whatever
" to suggest that any of the above peculiarities have been set up
" by dynamic agencies after the consolidation of the granite.
" There is not a trace of parallelism of structure, or of strain-
" shadows, and lines of liquid inclusions in the quartz have no
" connexion with those in neighbouring grains.   The neighbouring
" porphyritic granite gives evidence of similar conditions, and
" exhibits similar phenomena, but they are not so prominent as in
" the marginal fine grained rock."

General Mc Mahon attributes the pseudo bedding and jointing
of the granite to subaerial agencies, and quotes a passage from
Sterry Hunt's " Mineral Physiology, and Physiography, p. 273.

---

[*] *Op cit.* pp. 392-393.

## II.—Petrology and Mineralogy.

The two most interesting features of the petrology of Dartmoor are the almost infinite variety of its felstones (or elvans), granites, and allied rocks; and the very noteworthy series produced by the action of the great granitic mass on its bordering zone of contact metamorphism.

Upwards of four hundred varieties of felstones and granites and their kin, have been noted and described from the Dartmoor area, and the total is by no means exhausted. They range from a wholly undifferentiated massive felstone of cherty aspect, which may almost be called a vitrophyre; or from a finely granular felsite, which to the uninitiated might well appear a grit; or from a rough quartzose mass—through all possible intermediate stages—to a thoroughly typical, even-textured granite, or to such a well-marked porphyritic form as that of Heytor, largely worked for the material of London Bridge. But all these rocks are essentially the product of the same original granitic magma, their present character depending, in the main, upon the conditions under which they solidified—chiefly the rate at which they cooled, and the extent and method of the pressure to which they were then subjected. Hence, widely as these rocks in their extreme forms may now seem to differ from each other, it is really not possible, so far as Dartmoor is concerned, to suggest any condition or gradation of felsitic material, in composition, structure, colour, or metamorphism, that is not represented, or that is not linked by intermediate phases to all the rest. What we attempt to distinguish as separate rocks in this connection, are in fact, nothing more than stages, the differentiation between them pathological and not generic. Their condition and appearance vary with their history, but at bottom they are essentially one and the same, and nowhere in the series can any hard and fast line be drawn.

How great a change in the direction thus indicated may be produced in a very small area, is excellently illustrated by the Shillamill elvan dyke, which is cut by the London and South-Western railway, between Tavistock and Berealston. In the centre, this elvan is granitoid and porphyritic; the outer portions are quartzose; the intermediate varyingly even-grained and felspathic. Different examples from this one dyke might well be taken to represent half-a-dozen distinct felsites, varying in texture as described, and in colour from warm buff, through shades of brown and cream, to plain and greenish grey.

What is perhaps a still more remarkable illustration of change of physical conditions within a very small range, is supplied by an igneous dyke at Withnoe, in Whitsand Bay, which passes within less than a dozen feet from a compact typical pitchstone to a loose-textured trachyte, essentially a porphyritic quartz-felsite, hardly to be distinguished from a form of Dartmoor elvan. There is also a dyke of quartz-porphyry, at Horswell, North Milton, which with equal certainty passes into an andesite. These points have a direct bearing upon the hypothetical petrology of the moorland from an historical point of view, as well as upon its general varietal conditions.

The most important series of changes in the condition of the granites and felsites of Dartmoor, since their original consolidation, are those which have been connected with the development of schorl or tourmaline, mainly in the outer area, where the granite is generally schorlaceous, the process of metamorphism being at times carried to such an extent, as to obliterate all suggestions of original character. This is particularly seen in the local luxulyanites (essentially felspar and schorl) in one of which the felspars are pink and in the other white. It is still more remarkably shown in the very beautiful rock called trowlesworthite, hitherto found only on Trowlesworthy Tor, and which consists of red felspar, black schorl, and violet fluor. Next to this development of schorl, the most important series of changes in the aspect of the granite is connected with the modification of the felspars into kaolin, and the development of beds of china-clay, as at Lee Moor, Cadover, and Hanger Down. Whether this decay of the felspars is caused from above or from below ; by acid-charged waters descending, or mineral solutions ascending, is still an open question ; but it is very noteworthy that schorl and kaolin are often close associates.

The granitoid rocks of Dartmoor may, on a general view, be classed as granites ; felsites, rocks with a felsitic matrix ; aplites or pegmatites, quartz-felspar rocks ; and greisens, quartz-mica rocks. A very distinctive variety of aplite is found at Meldon, which is commonly called granulite, and sometimes white granite.

There are detrital deposits in the valleys and low-lying parts of Dartmoor which, in addition to the rocks found at present *in situ*, yield, here and there, fragments of others, not now known to exist in place, which have evidently disappeared in the course of the enormous denudation to which Dartmoor has been subjected. Among these have occurred specimens of a distinctly volcanic character, which may fairly be held to indicate, in the opinion of the writer, apart from other considerations, that the igneous activities concerned in the creation of what has become Dartmoor, at some point or points reached the surface. Evidence of precisely the same character is supplied by many of the igneous fragments in the Permian breccias of the east coast of Devon; where, associated with examples of undoubted Dartmoor assign-. ment, are to be found others of more distinctly volcanic type— rhyolites, andesites, and basalts to a large extent, so little rounded as to show that they have travelled but a short distance from their points of origin to their present resting places. Andesites and volcanic rocks of a type no longer existing in the county have been found also in detritus at Cattedown, with unmistakeable Dartmoor material; and some of the beaches near the mouths of several of the Dartmoor rivers are particularly fruitful in felsites and porphyries—the Yealm, the Erme, Slapton Sands, and Rockham Bay, near Morthoe, being chiefly noteworthy.

The metamorphosed rocks on the verge of the Dartmoor granite afford abundant material for investigation. The varying course and nature of the changes depend apparently less upon the course and activity of the metamorphising agency, than upon the constitution of the rocks altered—the Carboniferous slates and shales taking a different aspect upon them as a rule to the Devonian. It is, however, in the latter rocks, probably because they were the most deeply seated, that the alteration is most marked. Thus near Shaugh, the Devonian clay-slate at a third of a mile from the granite assumes a slightly unctuous or silky character; then becomes sericitic, with a very fine fibrous silky texture; next andalusite appears in the form of spots, which increase and spread until the rock becomes an andalusite slate; and the development of mica in the andalusite spots and nodules, in its turn, leads the way to the production of a well-characterized mica schist, either touching or in immediate proximity to the granite. But there are deviations from this method. In some localities chiastolite is produced instead of the andalusitic form. This is well seen at Ivybridge, and is indeed apparently a tendency in the Carboniferous rocks. Sometimes the mica schist passes into a very deceptive well-foliated gneiss, as at Meavy. Occasionally, as at Shaugh, the slate next the granite has been fused into a hornfels—a distinct felstone, but never absolutely to the obliteration of all trace of origin, or to incorporation with the granite.

Elsewhere the effect of the granite—possibly where pressure had a larger share in the production of the change—is mainly one of induration.    Grits are changed into quartzites—at times, when the contact agency is also strong, with the development of tourmaline; slates into compact rocks, with semi-conchoidal fracture.   The combination of shearing action with ordinary pressure upon a gritty slate, near Okehampton, has led to the production of a series of evenly-dotted glossy spots, which suggest augite, but are merely the result of the uneven texture of the original rock, under this peculiar form of slipping pressure. Carboniferous slate in the vicinity of Lydford, may be seen porcellanised in bands: and on the other side of the Moor, near Ugborough, there are beds of what has been termed " green " jasper."   The original rock has been silicified, the green colour being due to the development of actinolite, forming a kind of prase.   This has no doubt resulted from the action of the granite on hornblende; for a similar development of actinolite is obser- vable in connexion with the hornblendic rocks near Mary Tavy. It seems as if these Ugborough rocks may have been originally massive dolerites, rendered schistose before the final change. One of the most interesting points connected with the production of contact minerals, is the formation of garnet.   This is specially to be seen at Belstone Consols and at Meldon, where green and brown garnet, massive and crystallised, abound.     Here the change is clearly dependent on original constitution.

The most singular occurrence of garnet in connection with Dartmoor is, however, near Leather Tor.   Here we have a laminated rock, one set of the lamina consisting of massive brown garnet; while the other set have resulted from the change, by pressure largely, of a Carboniferous shale.   The garnet may have come of the metamorphism of a dolerite or eclogite, though how it should have been injected so regularly as to give several alterna- tions in the space of an inch, it is difficult to see.   This is one of the many petrological problems of Dartmoor that await final solution.

The mineralogy of Dartmoor, like its petrology, would supply material for a treatise in itself.   The most important

VALLEY OF ROCKS.

metallic mineral connected with the Moor, is the oxide of tin, or cassiterite, detrital deposits of which have been worked in the moorland valleys from before the dawn of history. The existing tin lodes on Dartmoor are small, though often rich; and an enormous quantity of rock must have been removed and reduced by denudation ere such extensive deposits of tin stone could have been retained, as a consequence of their superior weight, in the river beds. In fact no better index could be supplied of the extent of this denudation, than the formation of deposits of stream tin which kept the tinners of Devon at work for centuries, and are not wholly exhausted even now, though all the more recent operations have been by mining proper and not by streaming. Next in importance to the tin lodes of the district, are the copper, but these were very little worked upon until within a century or so ago; and at the present moment all the copper mines are abandoned and tin mining has only a precarious existence, though the Dartmoor tin ore is the richest and most valuable in the world. The chief mining centres in and around the Moor, have been Sheepstor, Mary Tavy, Okehampton, Belstone, Sticklepath, North Bovey, Ilsington, Ashburton, Buckfastleigh; and most of the mines have yielded various ores of iron, though not of commercial value, lead, and occasionally silver. Gold was frequently found by the old tin streamers, in small grains, in the beds of the moorland streams; and it is probable that it occurs, or has occurred, more or less in the beds of all the larger rivers, the debris of the tin streamers in which, by the way, has been occasionally taken for moraines. The most important commercial mineral of the Moor at the present day is china-clay, already referred to, the works at Lee Moor being the largest in the kingdom. The subject of Mining in Dartmoor and its precincts, is further treated of in Chapter xi.

The more noteworthy minerals of Dartmoor, with special localities past and present, are :—Allophane (near Tavistock), actinolite, achroite, amethyst, andalusite, antimonite (Hennock), apatite (Bovey), arragonite (Buckfastleigh), axinite (Brent, Okehampton), barytes, beryl (Lustleigh), blende, calcedony (agate, jasper, prase, etc.), calcite, cassiterite, chiastolite (Ivybridge), celestite (Wh. Friendship), cerrusite, chalcocite, chalcopyrite, chalybite (Wh. Friendship), chessylite, childrenite, chlorite, chloropal, chrysocolla, copper, cuprite, diallogite (Bovey), epidote, erythrite, fahlerz, fluor, galena, garnet (Meldon, Lustleigh,

Haytor, Okehampton), goethite, gold, haytorite, hematite, ilmenite, kaolin, kupfernickel, lepidolite, limonite (ochre, umber, etc.), lithomarge, magnetite, malachite, manganite, murchisonite, marcasite, melaconite, mispickel, muscovite, olivenite, opal, ( Heytor, Lustleigh), orthoclase, psilomelane, pryrophyllite (Buckfastleigh), pyrites, pyrolusite, pyroxene (in various forms), pyrrhotite, (Meldon) rock crystal, rhodonite, scheelite (Wh. Friendship), silver (and various silver ores), scapolite (Chagford), serpentine (chrysotile), smaltite (Sampford Spiney), specular iron (Vitifer), staurolite, topaz (Meldon), torbernite (Lee Moor), tourmaline (Bovey), rubellite (Meldon), green tourmaline (ditto), vivianite (Wh. Friendship), wolfram (Wh. Friendship), wolframite (Wh. Friendship).

There are excellent opportunities of collecting minerals, and not unfrequently rare and choice specimens, by turning over some of the old mining heaps or burrows, and those at Wheal Friendship and Vitifer, may be specially recommended, though the really ardent mineralogist should by no means ignore the mine heaps of even insignificant ventures.

# CHAPTER X.

## SOIL AND AGRICULTURE.*

FARMING on Dartmoor has been for a long period a very debateable subject, and the efforts which have been occasionally made to render this barren spot productive, have been considered, in most instances, unsuccessful; and it is from this, that the prevailing opinion among the moormen arises, that it is incapable of cultivation. Still, when the difficulties to be surmounted are considered, the question arises, is, whether the defect is to be attributed to the climate, the elevation, or the soil. Much, no doubt, is owing to the exposure,† the snow-drifts in winter, and the long-continued rains in autumn; but this is nothing more than occurs in all Alpine countries, and is not wholly destructive of vegetation in Scotland or Switzerland. The right of common enjoyed by the inhabitants of the parishes surrounding the moor, which is a great drawback to improvement within the Forest boundary, may have some influence on the opinion, and also the application of plants to the soil, which it is not physically calculated to sustain, may be taken into account, and which the late improvements in chemistry may enable us to surmount; we will endeavour to illustrate this as we proceed.

It is scarcely to be expected that the debris of the granite rocks should support such a luxuriant vegetation as the more favoured spots resting on the schists and trap-rocks of the surrounding districts; still it may be a question whether much of the barren appearance, be not chiefly owing to a want of adequate shelter from the cold and high winds, which the more elevated localities are exposed to, since throughout the moor many of the dells and ravines, between the tors and in the neighbourhood of

---

* The earlier part of this chapter was written for the first edition, by the late Edward Moore, M.D., and although it is not perhaps now up to date, I have thought it desirable to retain it, with some slight alterations, as the information it contains is of value, and the necessary corrections can be easily made by the reader.

†The Rev. J. H. Mason wrote:—" I attended Mr. Vancouver, when he viewed " the moor, previously to his publishing his ' Survey of Devon'; and he imagined " that the blights the lowlands are subjected to, were occasioned by winds which " blew across the mass of peat. At Lydford, the S.E. wind, and at Widecombe, " the N.W. wind was injurious."

the rivers, present much fertility.    Wistman's Wood, whose
gnarled and stunted appearance is always quoted as an instance
of want of congeniality of climate, may as readily be adduced
as an indication of what Nature can perform there, in spite of
the obstacles which exist.    One of the necessary ingredients for
successful cultivation, water, is presented in the numerous rivers
and smaller streams which diversify the surface of the moor.

The soil of Dartmoor at the surface is chiefly peat, which for
ages has been accumulating in the bottoms between the tors, so
as to be occasionally found from one to twenty-five feet* in thickness, lessening in depth as we ascend the higher grounds, where
it is not above a few inches thick.    The subsoil is fine sand, which
is revealed beneath the peat in the numerous pits made to obtain
gravel for the various roadways.    The depth of this is uncertain,
probably filling up all the inequalities between the different granite
peaks.    The present state of the moor indicates less a want of
fertility than of luxuriance.    It is not deficient in grass, and the
whole forms a fine pasture for cattle, sheep and horses.    At
Bairdown Farm, near Two Bridges, very good plantations, have
long flourished.    The efforts of Sir Thomas Tyrwhitt, to be referred
to presently, though at first successful, have not been followed up
with equal energy, yet much benefit may be expected from recent
facilities of conveyance.    A granite soil is not in itself wholly
unproductive, since in low situations, the growans of Cornwall are
not deficient in that particular ;† and it has long been known
that the neighbourhood of Penzance supplies abundance of
potatoes to the London and Plymouth markets, and those of
Exeter are chiefly furnished from the neighbourhood of Moreton
itself.    De la Beche observes‡ that oaks, ash and sycamore, grow
well in growan, or granite soils, in sheltered situations, and though
from their readiness to part with their moisture, these soils are
less calculated for the support of fibrous than of bulbous roots,
yet on Dartmoor the great quantity of moisture which exists,
will compensate for this defective quality.    Sir Humphry Davy
observes,§ in a moist climate, a "siliceous sandy soil is much
"more productive than in dry districts."    And the same author
states, that a sandy or gravelly sub-soil, such as exists on

---

*Near Row Tor it is thirty feet deep.

†See Dr. BOASE, "Transactions of Geological Society of Cornwall." vol. iv,, p. 365.

‡" Report on Geology of Devon and Cornwall," p. 475.

§" Agricultural Chemistry," p. 165.

Dartmoor, " often corrects the imperfections of too great a degree " of absorbent power in the true soil." " A soil," says Liebig, " formed by the action of the weather on the component parts of " of granite, etc., will become a magazine of alkalies, in a " condition favourable for their assimilation by the roots of " plants."

In order to display the qualities of Dartmoor soil, in a more particular manner, let us make a few observations on soils in general, and their action on plants during vegetation.

Soils are compounds of earths, silica, alumina, lime, magnesia, oxides of iron and manganese, animal and vegetable matters in a decomposing state, and saline or alkaline combinations (*Davy*, p. 134) ; and the best natural soils are those of which the materials have been derived from different strata, intimately blended together. A soil may be considered a magazine of inorganic matters, which are prepared by the plant to suit the purposes destined for them in its nutrition.

The ultimate constituents of plants are those of organic matter in general, viz., carbon, hydrogen, nitrogen, and oxygen. These are united in various ways : in one, to form woody fibre, starch, gum, and sugar ; in another, for the organic acids ; in a third manner, to form volatile and fixed oils, wax, and resins ; and in a fourth, to produce albumen and gluten. A plant, therefore, requires for its development, the presence of substances containing carbon and nitrogen ; of the elements of water (viz., oxygen and hydrogen) and also of the soil, to furnish the inorganic matters essential to its vitality.

Acids and alkalies are the most important division of inorganic substances, both having a tendency to unite together and form neutral salts ; then alkaline earths, metallic oxides, &c. They vary according to the soil, and are obtained by chemical forces, guided by the vital principle acting on the ingredients in solution, which are absorbed by the roots, and the substances thus conveyed to plants are retained in greater or less quantity, or entirely separated, when not suited for assimilation. Sea plants require metallic iodides for their growth, and alkalies and alkaline earths (found in their ashes) are necessary for the development of land plants.

In spring, when the organs of plants, which nature has appointed for the assumption of nourishment from the atmosphere, are absent, the component substance of the seeds is exclusively

employed in the formation of the roots, which perform the functions of leaves from the first moment of their formation; they
extract from the soil their proper nourishment, viz., the carbonic
acid, generated by the *humus*.* (Bulbs and tubers do not require
food from the soil, and this class of plants is ranked amongst
those which do not exhaust a soil). By loosening the ground, we
favour the production of carbonic acid. The plant, as it increases,
itself effects this change, and receiving food, both by its roots
below and other organs above ground, rapidly advances to
maturity; and when the leaves, by which it obtains food from the
atmosphere, are fully formed, the carbonic acid of the soil is no
longer required. When the food of a plant is in greater quantity
than its organs require, the superfluous nourishment is employed in
the formation of new organs. The functions of leaves are to
absorb carbonic acid, and with the aid of light and moisture, to
appropriate its carbon, which serves for all the solid matters of the
plant. They also now produce sugar, starch and acids. When
woody fibre is produced to a certain extent, the supply of
nourishment takes a new direction, and blossoms are produced.
The functions of the leaves cease upon the ripening of the fruit,
and these now yielding to the chemical influence of the oxygen of
the air, decay, change colour, and fall off. Thus, in the earlier
stages, the carbon is derived from the humus, or decayed vegetable
matter in the soil, which is not taken up unaltered, but presents a
slow and lasting source of carbonic acid, which, acting in the same
manner in a soil permeable to the air, as in the air itself, is
absorbed by the roots. In a more mature state of the plant, the
carbon is derived from the carbonic acid of the atmosphere
(composed of oxygen, nitrogen, carbonic acid, and ammonia)
which plants decompose, and appropriating the carbon for their
own use, give out the oxygen again as soon as the direct or indirect
rays of the sun strike them.

The fertility of a soil is much influenced by its physical
properties of porosity, colour, attraction for moisture, and state of
disintegration; but independently of these, fertility also depends
on the chemical constituents of which it is composed. Alkalies,
earths, and phosphates, found in the ashes of plants, are
indispensible for their development. All the different families of
plants are distinguished by containing certain acids, in combination of earthy or alkaline bases. Thus, the vine contains tartaric;

---

*Woody fibre in a state of decay is the substance called *humus*.—Liebig, p. 48.

the sorrels, oxalic; and corn plants, silicic acid, extracted from the soil. There are also malic and citric acids, etc. The generation of these acids is prevented, when alkalies are absent from the soil in which they grow; potash, soda, lime, and magnesia, are thus as indispensible for the existence of plants as the carbon from which their organic acids are formed. Thus, the salts necessary for the support of the vital functions, if wanting in the soil, or if the bases are absent, cannot be formed, and the juice, leaves, and fruit, cannot be matured. Different plants require different acids and akalies; soda is found in saline plants; lime and potash, in corn plants, etc. Upon the correct knowledge of the bases and salts required for each plant, and on the composition of the soil on which it grows, depends the proper application of manures, and indeed the whole system of a rational theory of agriculture. Now in reference to Dartmoor, a pure sandy soil is generally barren; but in the disintegration of common granite (which consists of quartz, felspar, and mica) certain chemical constituents are found, which form useful components. Quartz is chiefly silica. Felspar, according to Bucholz and Vauquelin, contains sixty per cent of silica, twenty per cent of alumina, fourteen per cent of potash, and a little lime. Liebig states that it contains seventeen and three-quarters per cent of potash, and that albite (pure felspar) yields in addition 11.43 of soda. China-clay, or porcelain earth, is decomposed felspar. Mica, according to Klaproth, yields by analysis, silica forty-seven per cent, alumina twenty-two per cent, oxide of iron fifteen and a half per cent, potash fourteen and a half per cent, and a little manganese. Liebig says it contains only three to five per cent of potash; and according to Wallace, when binaxal, potash, the alkali lithia, and fluoric acid. When uniaxal, it contains magnesia, but no lime.

In the Dartmoor granite, we find an abundance of schorl, some times with, and sometimes replacing the mica. This species of tourmaline contains thirty-six per cent of silica, thirty-four and a half per cent of alumina, twenty-one per cent of oxide of iron, with a little potash, magnesia, and manganese, together with a large portion of boracic acid. The chief want, therefore, in the granitic debris of Dartmoor is a greater proportion of the alkaline earths, magnesia and lime, but these may be obtained in the neighbourhood. Limestones occur all round the moor; and hornblende, which is a component of the various trap-rocks, abounds in magnesia and lime. Hence we find nearly all the chemical ingredients necessary for vegetation in the various rocks of this district.

Again, the earthy matter of peat soils is uniformly analagous to that of the stratum on which they repose; therefore different peats on granite soils have always yielded ashes principally siliceous, but other important ingredients occur in them. A barren heath, near Brunswick, according to Liebig, yielded—

| | |
|---|---:|
| Silica, with sand ... ... ... ... ... | 92.651 |
| Alumina ... ... ... ... ... ... | 1.342 |
| Oxides of iron and manganese ... ... ... | 2.324 |
| Lime, with sulphuric and phosphoric acid ... | 0.929 |
| Magnesia, with sulphuric acid ... ... ... | 0.283 |
| Potash and soda, as sulphates and phosphates | 0.564 |
| Phosphoric acid, with lime ... ... ... | 0.250 |
| Sulphuric acid, with potash, soda, and lime ... | 1.620 |
| Chlorine in common salt... ... ... ... | 0.037 |
| | 100.000 |

This heath was rendered fertile by manuring with lime, marl, cow-dung, and the ashes of the heaths which grew upon it. The peat, then, besides furnishing these different salts, contributes also to form the vegetable mould, or humus, necessary for the support of vegetable life.

It will not be necessary to enter farther into the chemical changes which take place in plants. It is presumed that enough has been stated to point out that the soil of Dartmoor possesses qualities sufficient to warrant a fair prospect of profitable returns, when submitted to the ordinary processes of agriculture. The application of manures, whether animal or vegetable, must be determined by the necessities of the particular plants requiring to be cultivated, which if not found in the soil, must be externally supplied, for it is certain that the soil must gradually lose those of its constituents, which are removed in the seeds, roots, and leaves of plants reared upon it. Now in Dartmoor the great quantity of silica will afford one of the necessary ingredients for all the gramineous plants, and this is shown in the luxuriance sometimes observed in corn grown on the Moor. Mr. Frean informed us, that some of his fields have yielded stalks of corn-plants six feet in height.

In 1808, the Report of Charles Vancouver to the Board of Agriculture, was published, but in it no reference is made to any efforts which had been made to bring parts of the Moor into cultivation. But as early as 1780, a Mr. Gullet enclosed land at Prince Hall, and erected farm-buildings on the site of the antient tenement, and about the same time, Mr. Edward Bray, solicitor, of Tavistock, and steward to the Duke of Bedford, commenced the reclaiming of land at Bairdown. In 1785, Sir Thomas, then Mr. Tyrwhitt, who had been appointed Lord Warden of the Stannaries, entered upon that work which has proved of so much benefit to Dartmoor. By a judicious expenditure in draining and sowing grass seeds, he quickly converted the place he named Tor Royal, into a productive estate, and in 1798, the house with its fields, plantations, and gardens was completed, with its means of access by road from Prince Town. Mr. Tyrwhitt also undertook the formation of a road from Prince Town to Tavistock, and was instrumental in the formation of those other fine roads which now cross the Moor in various directions. To the energy and foresight of Sir Thomas Tyrwhitt, the various improvements on Dartmoor for the past century, are directly or indirectly owing, and he well deserved the eulogy which will be found on the memorial tablet in the church at Prince Town:—"*His name and Memory are* "*inseparable from all the Great Works in Dartmoor, and cannot* "*cease to be honoured in this District.*"*

Much enclosing and planting and cultivation was done by the Rev. James Mason, the Rev. Mr. Vollans, Mr. Sanders—who, like Sir Thomas Tyrwhitt, attempted to grow flax, and with some success, for he received a medal from the Bath Agricultural

---

*The full inscription is as follows :—

SIR THOMAS TYRWHITT, KNT.,
LATE OF TOR ROYAL,
LORD WARDEN OF THE STANNARIES
AND MANY YEARS USHER OF THE BLACK ROD,
DIED FEB. 24TH, 1833,
AGED 71.
HIS NAME AND MEMORY
ARE INSEPARABLE FROM ALL THE GREAT WORKS IN
DARTMOOR
AND CANNOT CEASE TO BE HONOURED
IN THIS DISTRICT.

Society for his efforts—and Messrs. Thomas and John Hullett, who built Post Bridge, their land being in that neighbourhood, this was afterwards sold to the Rev. Mr. Vollans. Later Mr. George Frean and Mr. John Nicholas Bennett made further enclosures between Two Bridges and Post Bridge, and the former established the powder manufactory now carried on by Mr. C. F. Williams.

Mr. Justice Buller bought Prince Hall of Mr. Gullet and continued the improvements, extended the enclosures, and added to the house, and he built the public-house at Two Bridges—the Saracen's Head—the crest of the judge. Some notes upon the system of cultivation adopted at Prince Hall, will be found in the Annals of Agriculture, vol. xxix., pp. 569-78 ; vol. xxx., pp. 297-8. Sir Francis Buller died in 1800.

In the Report of James Fraser, to the Board of Agriculture, printed in 1794, is an interesting account of the work of Sir Francis Buller at Two Bridges and the neighbourhood. It says that the judge "finding his health was greatly improved by the "purity of the air . . . . he sought for exercise and amusement "in the praiseworthy and rational pleasures, of endeavouring to "introduce cultivation into this neglected and almost desert "country. To the little colony he had assembled around him, "he behaves like a parent and a friend. Having no place of "Divine worship in the whole of this extensive tract, he assembles "them for that purpose, every Sunday at his own house ; "he settles all their little differences more like a friend than a "judge, and his advice and protection are always ready at their "call. To the stranger, whom curiosity, or love of the rural "arts, induce to visit this sequestered spot, the hospitalities of "Prince Hall are always open, and exercised with that affability "and politeness, which excite the highest veneration towards the "learned owner, and reflect honour on the illustrious personage, "whose name this hospitable mansion bears. While the learned "judge is in the country, his house is the constant resort of men "of enterprise and experience in the science of agriculture from "every part of the Kingdom. Dartmoor has by this means "become known to men accustomed to speculate on the improve-"ment of waste lands, and the judge spares no expense in making "experiments to meliorate the soil and pasture, and in procuring "such breeds of cattle and sheep as may be thought more likely "than the native breeds of Devon, to answer in this mountainous "part of the county. He has lately introduced the South Down "sheep, and the small Scotch breed of cattle." "He has been "very unsuccessful in his first endeavours in planting. Nearly "forty thousand trees consisting of larch and firs intermixed with "other trees, which he planted near Prince Hall, have almost "wholly perished."*

In 1846, the Prince Hall property was purchased by Mr. G. W. Fowler. He brought a large portion of the estate into a very high state of cultivation, and succeeded in growing excellent crops.† Under tillage, the land was made to bear very heavy crops, but at too great an expense, and it is the opinion of well-qualified judges, that the same good might have been attained at one-tenth of the cost. In course of time, Mr. Fowler came to the conclusion that Dartmoor was not a corn-growing country, and he determined to lay the land down to grass. His successor, Mr. Lamb, introduced Scotch sheep and cattle, and did very well with them, and had he lived a few years longer, so as to complete the perfecting of the breeds, he would have had a grand stock, and a paying one, and have set an example to Moorland farmers, which they would be wise to follow. The fact is, that Dartmoor is essentially a stock-rearing district, and extensive tillage will not pay, for the reasons that the lime is wanting, and the expense of obtaining it, heavy, and that in most seasons, the cereals will not attain maturity. The man who has his land fairly dry, and uses a little cake and corn in the grazing season will be able to send good cattle and sheep off the moor in the autumn, and at the same time improve his pasture. As an open common, Dartmoor is of most value when worked in connexion with in country farms, the great drawback being, that unless for a very hardy stock, the place is so very exposed, and the winters so long. Wherever a sheltered valley can be got for the home enclosures, a practical farmer can always do well. As instances, may be mentioned Dartmeet, Sherburton, Grendon, Cator Court, and on a wider scale, the Widecombe Valley.‡ But the most important agricultural operations on Dartmoor, are those which now for several years past have been carried on in connexion with the Convict

---

*ROBERT FRASER   General View of the County of Devon, with observations on the means of its improvement.   4to., 1794.

†HENRY TANNER.   The Cultivation of Dartmoor, pp. 15-16.

‡*Ex rel.* Mr. ALEXANDER WATT, F.S.I., late farm bailiff at the Prisons, to whom the editor is greatly indebted for valuable help in writing this chapter.

R

Prisons at Prince Town. The following account is epitomised from a report recently published in the Journal of the Royal Agricultural Society.*

The farm comprises in all, two thousand acres, the whole of which was, prior to 1850, mere common or unenclosed waste land. The reclamation has now extended to—the quantity is greater now —thirteen hundred acres, and is being continued at the rate of twenty-five acres yearly. The land is divided into square fields, of from fifteen to twenty acres, by high stone walls, built of granite boulders, raised in the prison quarries, or from the land, as the work of reclamation proceeds. Broad and excellent roads have been made, intersecting the farm where needed, and are being extended as required. The land is first trenched two, to two and a half feet deep, the lower layer being merely turned over, and not brought to the surface, whilst the surface sod is buried about a foot in depth. Where necessary, stone drains are put in, at three feet or deeper, according to the nature of the ground in which they have to be placed, and at intervals of from thirty to forty feet. The first crop is usually rape or rye (according to the time of year at which the land is ready). This is fed off by sheep, and a crop of swedes taken, which is again fed off by sheep, getting also cake and corn. Seeds are then sown for a short term, two or three years, and afterwards broken up, preparatory to the land being cropped under a short rotation, and ultimately laid down to permanent pasture. Swedes are the first crop in this rotation, and are followed by barley, with which are sown the seeds for per-manent grass. The mixture for the latter, which is found to answer best is as follows:—Perennial rye-grass, eight pounds; Italian rye-grass, four pounds; cocksfoot, cow-grass, white clover, and trefoil, three pounds each; meadow-grass, timothy and meadow fox-tail, two pounds each; various fiscues and alsike clover one pound each; in all, from thirty-four to thirty-six pounds per acre. If the herbage fails, or becomes unsatisfactory, the land is again dug up and put through a similar rotation; but so good has been the management, and so careful and judicious the selection of seeds in the past, that the greater portion of the pastures laid within the last fifteen to twenty years, are now in far too good a condition to require re-breaking. One field which twenty years ago was mostly rushes, is now able to carry a bullock per acre, through summer. No cleaner or purer pastures

---

*Vide Report, Directors Convict Prisons, 1890-91.

are to be found anywhere than those laid down on this farm,
within the last few years. Sixty-seven acres of meadow land
have been laid out for irrigation and utilization of the sewage from
the prison establishment, which, at times, numbers upwards of
one thousand persons. The sewage is precipitated in two settling
tanks by the aid of sulphate of alumina placed in the main sewer,
about two hundred yards above the tanks, in a large box, with a
perforated bottom, over which a water tap is fitted, so as to
regulate the quantity consumed at different times of the day.
Milk of lime is also used at the entrance to the tanks. The
effluent water is used for irrigation, the solids from the tanks
being applied to the land above the level of the carriers. Hay
and silage are both made from the crops of this land. Thirty acres
are devoted to the growth of garden vegetables, and are divided into
square plots of an acre each, by high hedges of elder, which grows
and thrives well here, and provides much shelter from spring frosts.
All kinds of vegetables are grown, and much success has been obtained in the growth of celery and cucumbers, of which latter, as
as many seven hundred have been raised and sold in a season. One
hundred and twenty thousand plants of cabbages and winter
greens are raised and planted out yearly. A dairy herd of forty-
five cows is kept, and all the calves are reared. Any additional
" bullocks" (which term in this county, means cattle of both
sexes and all ages) required, are purchased, and then fed off. The
animals selected, are, on account of the altitude, mainly North
Devons; but as dairy properties are here of almost as much
importance as hardihood, it is not surprising to find in many of
the cattle, a dash of other blood, and an occasional cross of some
more prolific milking breed. The dairy is managed on the ordinary
or raw cream process. A flock of four hundred sheep—" Improved
Dartmoors"—is kept, and has frequently been successful
in the local show-yards. The wool for so high a district, is
remarkably good, and of long staple, and at the present time,* is
expected to realise 7½d. to 8d. per pound. One ram seen, had
just clipped twenty-seven pounds, and the hogs averaged fourteen
to fifteen pounds per fleece. Thirty-five pony mares and their
produce, run on some of the fields, and in addition about fifty
mares—Dartmoor and Exmoor ponies—are taken in for a summer's
run, and stinted to selected sires. One of the latter now in use, is
a grandson of the celebrated " Sir George," whilst another won

---

*This Report is dated 1891.

first prize in its class, at the Royal Show at Plymouth. Seventeen cart mares, chiefly Clydesdales, are kept for the carting, and are mostly bred from. The nine foals bred this year, are by a Clydesdale stallion, bought at the Ayr Show. Much of the produce is sold to and consumed in the prison establishment; the rest is sold off either to residents in the district, or sent to Plymouth. Annual auctions of surplus live stock are held, at which, £1,400 or £1,500 worth are often sold. Private sales of ponies, sheep, and pigs, are also made. The whole of the work is done by the convicts without the aid of horses, except for carting.

The Dartmoor ponies are born on the Moor, and generally remain there until they are brought to the market town for sale. They have no shelter except of a casual nature, no hay or any food, but what they find on the Moor and commons. In time of snow, they can go for five days without food, without injury. They will scrape away the snow to browse upon the heather. Sheep also, shut up in the snow, will live five days under it without food.

# CHAPTER XI.

## HISTORICAL VIEW OF MINING IN DARTMOOR,
## AND THE PRECINCTS.

IN the course of the foregoing Perambulation, we have been led to make frequent reference to the mines and tin trade of Britain in the earliest ages, in connexion with the vestiges of antient stream-works still existing in our moorland district. Many particulars of great interest are preserved by the Greek writers; but although there can be no doubt that mining operations were carried on by the Romans, subsequently to those which had been successively undertaken in the times of the Phœnicians and Massilian Greeks, the information to be gathered from Latin authors on these interesting subjects is of limited extent and incidental character.

Cicero (who appears to have been misinformed) observes that no silver is produced in Britain. Cæsar, as we have already seen, confines himself to a notice of the *plumbum album*, raised in the interior, and the iron, which, in small quantities *(exigua copia)* was found near the coast. Even so late as the time of the Spanish geographer, Pomponius Mela (who wrote about A.D. 45) it would appear that little information could then be gleaned, since he indulges a hope that many more particulars would be obtained concerning the nature of the country, and its productions, than had yet transpired, *qualis sit qualesque progenerat, mox certiora et magis explorata dicentur.* Still, the reputation of the tin islands was firmly established; and the same author describes Britain, as abounding in wood and water, and in its estuaries, producing gems and pearls. *Fert nemora, saltusque, ac prægrandia flumina, alternis motibus, modo in pelagum, modo retro fluentia, et quœdam gemmas, margaritasque generantia.** With regard to the pearls and gems, we have no certain information, but the other particulars apply with much exactness to the district contiguous to Dartmoor, and to the rivers which issue from its heights, and flow through

---

*POMPONIUS MELA, De situ Orbis, lib. iii., cap. 8.

the tin districts to the sea, such as the Tavy, the Tamar, and the
Plym.  Nor can we imagine that so powerful and enterprising a
nation as the Romans would have failed to employ their supremacy
in Britain, to the obvious purpose of sharing in that branch of
commerce, for which the Cassiterides had been so long celebrated,
and which had been so eagerly pursued for so many ages by the
Phœnicians and Greeks in succession.    Norden, accordingly,
explicitly affirms that " the Romans also took their turn to searche
" for this commoditie, as is supposed by certain of their monies
" which have been found in some old workes renewed."*    They
seem not only to have engrossed the whole of the tin trade, but
to have improved the mining system by various inventions and
processes, which taught the Britons to apply to their domestic
purposes a metal that had before been only useful to them as an
article of commerce.

Nothing material is recorded of the history of mining operations in the west, during the Saxon period.    The miseries of
barbarian invasion, which affected the whole province, after the
withdrawal of the Roman legions, extended to Devonshire.    And
long after the eastern parts of south Britain had enjoyed comparative tranquility, under the Saxon sovereigns, the braver
inhabitants of the west, still contending for their independence,
and resisting the Saxon yoke, experienced the miseries which
must ever attend those countries which are made the seat of war.
This was peculiarly the case with the south-western parts of
Devon ; perpetual battles and skirmishes took place between the
British and the Saxons, who had overrun the country west of
Exeter, but had never conquered it.    Nor was it until the reign
of Athelstan, that the Tamar became the acknowledged boundary
between the invaders and the antient possessors of the soil,
although the Danmonian peninsula had been previously divided
into the counties of Devon and Cornwall, and nominally included
in the kingdom of Wessex.    Under such circumstances we need
not wonder at the absence of all notice of mining operations or
commercial enterprise ; as the unsettled state of public affairs
would necessarily affect the peaceful pursuits of trade and commerce in the most prejudicial manner.    To the incursions of the
Saxons, succeeded the piratical forays of the Danish freebooters,
who found ready access to the heart of the country by the navigable rivers, Tamar and Tavy—as when they destroyed the

*NORDEN.  "Cornwall."  Lond. 1728, p. 12.

monastery of Tavistock and the town of Lydford, in 997, and carried fire and sword through the stannary districts of Devon. These constant alarms must have materially injured the tin trade, as well as all other branches of commerce; yet it is thought that there must have been a large demand for tin in the sixth and following centuries, from the general use of bells in churches, which began to prevail from that period throughout Europe; and which, it is well known, are cast in a mixed metal, into which tin enters largely as an indispensible ingredient.

Under the firmer rule of the Norman conquerer, mining operations in the west once more revived. The works appear to have been chiefly in the hands of Jews, whose ancestors, it is supposed by Carew and other authors, had been thus employed from the time of the Romans downwards, having been brought hither as captives after the overthrow of Jerusalem, or else having found their way into those remote lands in consequence of the general dispersion which took place after that calamitous event. Traces of the outcasts of Israel, thus dispersed to the ends of the earth, under the ban of Almighty vengeance, are still to be observed in the mining district of the west, especially in Cornwall. From the Norman conquest to the reign of John,[*] the Jews engrossed the tin which was raised, and which, according to Borlase, was inconsiderable in Cornwall, the whole tin farm in that county being only one hundred marks, while the tin of Devon was at the same time farmed for £100.[†] In the reign of Henry III., the tin mines were worked by the same people, with increased effect; but upon the banishment of that oppressed race, by Edward I., mining affairs became neglected. "Afterwards," says

---

[*]This monarch granted a charter to the tinners of Devon and Cornwall, (3rd John, 29th October, 1201) a *fac-simile* of which is given in DE LA BECHE'S "Report," p. 627, and we also give a copy in chapter xiii.

[†]De la Beche gives from the Red Book, in the Exchequer, a copy of the Regulations for the Stannaries ix. Ric. I., 1197 (*Liber Rubeus, Capitula de Stannatoribus*), These regulations prove, as Mr. Joseph Jacobs states, the existence of Jews in Cornwall, and makes it probable that the "Jew's tin" and "Jew's Houses" connected with Cornwall to-day, preserve some traces of the Jewish buyers and storehouses of tin referred to in the ordinances. Camden, in his *Britannia* (ed. Gough, 1836, Danmonii, p. 10) remarks of the tinneries, "However their product "was very inconsiderable in the time of King John, the right of working them "being wholly in the King, as Earl of Cornwall, and the mines farmed by the Jews "for one hundred marks, and, according to this proportion, the tenth of it, viz:— "£6 13s. 4d. is at this day paid by the crown to the Bishop of Exeter." Unfortunately Camden (or Gough?) does not give his authority, but the details are too minute to have been invented. If the Jews had the whole of the tin market in their hands, it is not so improbable that survivals of their influence should remain even down to the present day.—JOSEPH JACOBS. The Jews of Angevin England, 1893, pp. 187-8.

Carew, "certain gentlemen, being lords of seven tithings,
"Blackmoore, whose grounds were best stored with this
"mineral (tin) grew desirous to renew this benefit; and so
"upon suit made to Edmond, Earl of Cornwall, son to
"Richard, king of the Romans, they obtained from him a
"charter, with sundry privileges, amongst which it was
"granted them to keep a court, and hold plea of all actions
"(life, limb, and land excepted) in consideration whereof
"the said lords accorded to pay the Earl a halfpenny for
"every pound of tin which should be wrought."* This charter
applied to the whole duchy, and therefore included Dartmoor
and the Devon mines in general. It also directed that certain
places should be appointed as stannary towns, and authorised
the holding of stannary parliaments. It was confirmed together
with that of King John, by the charter of Edward I., in the
thirty-third year of his reign. From this time the peculiar laws
and customs relating to the stannaries are chiefly to be dated;
many of which are still in force, though not to such an extent,
as in former times, when, with respect to tinners, the stannary
courts exercised an exclusive jurisdiction.†

From this period also the tinners of Devon and Cornwall, who
previously formed but one body, (meeting on Hingston Hill, near
Callington, every seventh or eighth year, to concert their common
interest) became divided, and formed distinct bodies of men.‡
Five coinage towns for Cornwall were then appointed, and three
for Devon, and each tinner was permitted to sell his own tin,
after being duly assayed at one of the said towns, unless the king
insisted on buying it himself, as stated in the said charter.

The Devonshire stannary towns were Tavistock, Ashburton
(Asperton) and Chagford, to which Plympton§ was added in the
reign of Edward III.,** and Lydford was exclusively appointed
as the stannary prison.††

---

*RICHARD CAREW. Survey of Cornwall, ed. 1811, p. 53.

†They now take cognizance of all causes relative to tin mines, and have still
considerable jurisdiction and peculiar privileges, but are—like so many other
things at the present time interfered with by uncalled for meddling—threatened
with extinction.

‡From this time also, probably, the Devonshire stannators began to hold their
stannary parliaments at Crockern Tor, in the centre of Dartmoor.

§These towns, it will be observed, are all situated along the verge of the Moor.

**In 1328, LYSONS. Devon, pp. 12, 96. and 408.

††Et si qui stannatorum prædictorum, in aliquo deliquerint, per quod incarcerari
debeant, per custodum prædictum arestentur, et in prisona nostra de Lydeford, et
non alibi, custodiantur et detineantur. Rot. Chart. 33 Edw. I.

It would appear from a petition to parliament in the first year of Edward III., a copy of which is also given in De la Beche's Report (p. 628) that the tinners of Devon exercised the privileges thus granted in a most arbitrary, undue, and oppressive manner, exceeding alike the bounds of their jurisdiction, and the powers with which they were vested. They claimed the whole county of Devon as their " stannary," whereas the petitioners alleged their permission to dig for tin "in every place of " waste and moor, where they believe tin can be found within the "said county," was confined to the Forest of Dartmoor only. They complained " that the said tinners do daily dig and claim to " dig in every species of land, as well in tilled as in other lands, " and destroy houses, meadows, and woods, and divert and turn " the course of waters running as well to mills as elsewhere, "throughout the whole county, to the great destruction and " dishersion of the said commonalty." This crying grievance seems not to have been effectually redressed for the next half century, as a petition to the same effect was presented to the king in parliament (50 Edward III., 1377) " when it was directed that "the customs and usages of the tinners should be diligently "enquired into, and that the warden of the stannaries should not " suffer any of them to dig in the meadows, fell the woods, and " knock down the houses of others out of malice."* That such extraordinary privileges appear to have been claimed with no little pertinacity, appears from Carew's account, from whom we learn that though, about the year 1600, the Cornish tinners only claimed to work without permission of the lord or owner of the land, " upon wastes or in wastrall," those of Devon still claimed the right to " digge for tynne in any man's ground, inclosed or " uninclosed, without license, tribute, or satisfaction."†

Grants for working mines in the county of Devon were made in the reigns of Edward III., Richard II., Henry IV., and Henry VI. The mines continued to be protected by the crown, and particularly by Henry VII., and Edward VI., when they were neglected, and in the reign of Queen Mary, they fell into decay. When Elizabeth succeeded to the crown, the mines of the kingdom partook of the fostering care which this renowned Queen extended to every object which might enlarge the resources, or contribute

---

*DE LA BECHE. Report on the Geology of Cornwall, Devon, etc., 1839, p. 629.

†CAREW. Survey of Cornwall, p. 13.

to the greatness of her government. As skilful miners were probably not then to be found in England, from the interruption which had taken place in carrying on works of this sort, she invited over Germans to open mines in different parts of the kingdom.* It is generally believed that the lead and silver mines at Beer Ferrers and Combe Martin, were extensively worked in this reign, although these mines are not noticed by any contemporary writers on the subject.†

The impulse given by the illustrious Elizabeth to these mining operations, seems to have reached to the succeeding reigns at least, since Risdon, who began his survey in 1605, and completed it in 1630, gives an account of the mining labourers, which leads to the conclusion that they must have then formed an extensive class among the inhabitants of the county. "There are also "labourers that serve for daily wages, whereof be two sorts: the "one is called a spadiard,‡ a daily labourer in tin works, with "whom there is no labourer in hardness of life to be compared— "for his apparel is coarse, his diet slender, his lodging hard, his "drink water, and for lack of a cup, he commonly drinketh out of "his spade or shovel, or some such thing, without curiosity in "satisfying nature. His life most commonly is in pits under the "ground, and in great danger, because the earth above his head "is in sundry places crossed over with timber to keep the same "from falling."§

At the close of the seventeenth century, as stated by the editors of Risdon, the tin mines of Devon appear to have been productive. Webster,** who wrote a treatise on metals in the year 1671, gives particulars of some situate on the hills above Plympton, which he had from one Thomas Creber of that place, "who was one," as he says, "that had wrought the tin mines, and all his ancestors "before him."

A century after, Chapple, in his Review of Risdon, in alluding to the above account, writes as if mining in Devon had hardly any existence. This however must have arisen from want of

---

*It has been remarked, that Crowndale, near Tavistock, so unlike the names of places in that neighbourhood, points its origin to these German miners, as it is very like the names of mines in Germany.

†Risdon. Introduction to Survey, edit. 1811. p. 13-19.

‡Why should not this expressive word be revived for "excavators," instead of the barbarious solecism of "*navigators*," certainly, a *non navigando!*

§Risdon. Survey, edit. 1811, p. 12.

**John Webster. Metallographia, or a History of Metals, 1676.

information on his part, since although mining has languished at various intervals, it has never entirely ceased in our district : or his observations might refer to stream-works for tin, which have been long declining and are not now found in Devon.  " The last " stream-work," says De la Beche, " of which we can obtain " information, seems to have been that carried on near Plympton " St. Mary, about the year 1808."*

Considerable improvements must have taken place in mining affairs, between the time to which Chapple refers, and the beginning of the present century.  The introduction to the modern edition of Risdon's Survey states the metallic produce of Devon (for a period of ten years, from 1801 to 1810, inclusive) to be as follows :—

|        |     |     | £       | s. | d.  |
|--------|-----|-----|---------|----|-----|
| Copper | ... | ... | 326,612 | 3  | 6½  |
| Tin... | ... | ... | 30,000  | 0  | 0   |
| Lead   | ... | ... | 12,874  | 1  | 6   |

The bulk of this produce was from the immediate vicinity of Dartmoor—from the two parishes of Mary Tavy and Tavistock; the mines in Mary Tavy having made returns equal in amount to £204,070 19s. 11¾d., and those of the parish of Tavistock being equal to £129,290 12s. 0½d.† From this comparative statement it will be evident that the copper mines had become by far the most productive at the period in question; but although, from the Report above quoted, it would appear that copper was raised in Devon early in the last century, it was not until the commencement of the present, that the copper mines in this country became important.  These, with the tin and lead mines, continued to be worked until somewhat recently.

The following historical notices are collected from De la Beche's Report, as an authority on which the fullest reliance may be placed.  " After being smelted, the tin for more than six " centuries paid a tax to the earls and dukes of Cornwall. Having " been cast into blocks, it was taken to the respective towns " already enumerated—examined by the duchy officers—stamped, " when found to be of proper quality, with the duchy seal—and " the dues duly paid, the blocks were then permitted to be sold. In " the sixteenth century the *coinages*, as they are called, took place

---

*DE LA BECHE'S " Report, etc." p. 647.
†RISDON.  Introduction to Survey, p 22.

" only twice a year, about Midsummer and Michælmas, but after-
" wards became quarterly. According to the charter of Edmund,
" Earl of Cornwall, the tin paid a duty of a halfpenny for every
" pound weight, when *coined*. In the reign of Edward I., the duty
" was fixed at four shillings for every hundred weight of coined tin,
" at which amount it has since continued. The duchy dues upon
" the tin coined in Devon have been long less than those imposed
" upon that of Cornwall, having been only at the rate of 1s 6½d.
" per cwt. By the act of William IV. (16th August 1836) the duties
" payable on the coinage of tin in Devon and Cornwall were
" abolished, and a compensation in lieu of them granted to the
" duchy, and fixed at 15s. per cwt. for tin, and at 10s. for tin ore.

    " In 1213, the duty on tin, payable to the Earl of Cornwall,
" was farmed for 200 marks for Cornwall, and £200 for Devon, by
" which it is evident that the mines of the latter county were then
" the more valuable. In 1337, the year in which the Black Prince
" was created Duke of Cornwall, the profits of the coinage of Devon
" were £273 19s. 5¾d. In 1471, the quantity of tin raised was
" 242,624*lbs*., the profits of the duchy in our county being
" £190 17s. 11½d., at the rate of 1s. 6¾d. per cwt. In 1479, the
" amount of the coinage dues was £166 9s. 5½d. In 1524, 424 tinners
" of Devon paid, in addition to the coinage, 8d, per annum for
" *white rent* to the duchy. In 1602 (44 Eliz.) the tin coinage
" amounted to £102 17s. 9¾d. The annual amount of tin raised
" in both counties, in the reigns of James I. and Charles I., is given
" from 1,400 to 1,600 tons, but the proportion for Devon is not
" specified. In the time of Charles II., the tin revenues were much
" reduced, probably owing to the disturbances of the great rebellion.
" Accordingly, in more tranquil times, under Queen Anne and
" George I., they had again risen to about 1,600 tons in the whole
" duchy. About 1742, the average produce for several years is
" reported at about 2,100 tons. At the close of the eighteenth and
" the beginning of the nineteenth century, the tin revenues of the
" duchy are stated at about £9,620 per annum; in 1814, about
" £8,500, and in 1820, about £11,125. From that year to the
" abolition of the coinage in 1838, the average has been commonly
" estimated at about £11,000 and £12,000 for the whole duchy."

    For some years past, the mining industry in Devon has been
declining, and on Dartmoor and its precincts it is practically
extinct, even as compared with the number of mines worked so
lately as 1861. A Mining Directory of that date, compiled by

J. Williams, gives a list of seventy-two mines in South Devon, and two in North Devon. The greater part of these have been since abandoned. Proceeding from Okehampton eastward round Dartmoor, the mines mentioned occur as follows:—

East Wheal Maria, Okehampton.—Copper.
Fursdon, and South Zeal Consols, South Tawton.—Copper.
Ivey Tor, South Tawton and Belstone.—Copper.
Exmouth, and North Wheal Exmouth, Christow.—Copper and Silver lead.
Frank Mills, Christow, and South Exmouth, Hennock.—Silver lead.
East Birch Tor, Chagford and North Bovey.—Tin.
Yarner, Bovey Tracey.—Copper and Mundic.
Atlas Mines, Ilsington.—Tin and Iron.
Sigford Consols, Ilsington.—Copper and Tin.
Ashburton Consols.—Copper.
Ashburton United.—Tin and Copper.
Devon Great Wheal Ellen, Ashburton.—Copper and Tin.
Devon New Copper Mines, Ashburton.—Copper.
Smith's Wood, Ashburton.—Tin.
West Ashburton, Ashburton.—Copper and Tin.
United Dart Mines, Ashburton and Buckfastleigh.—Copper.
Brookwood, Wheal Emma, Buckfastleigh.—Copper.
Bottle Hill, Plympton.—Tin and Copper.
Wheal Sidney, Plympton.—Tin.
Buller and Bertha, Buckland.—Copper.
Devon Poldice, Buckland.—Tin and Copper.
Devon Wheal Buller, Buckland.—Copper.
East Bertha Consols, Buckland.—Copper.
Furze Hill Wood Consols, Buckland.—Copper and Tin.
Lady Bertha, Buckland.—Copper.
South Lady Bertha, Buckland.—Copper.
Wheal France, Buckland.—Copper.
Virtuous Lady, Buckland.—Copper and Mundic.
Bickley Vale Wheal Phœnix, Bickley.—Copper and Tin.
Queen of Tamar, Beer Ferrers.—Copper and Lead.
Tamar Consols, Beer Ferrers.—Silver lead.
Huckworthy Bridge, Sampford Spiney and Walkhampton.—Copper.
North Wheal Robert, Sampford Spiney.—Copper.

New Birch Tor and Vitifer Consols.—Tin and Copper.
Devon and Courtney, Whitchurch.—Copper and Mundic.
Sortridge Consols, Whitchurch.—Copper.
United Mines, Tavistock and Whitchurch.—Tin and Copper.
Bedford Consols, Bedford United, Tavistock.—Copper.
Crelake Mine, Tavistock.—Copper and Lead.
Devon and Cornwall United, Tavistock.—Copper.
Devon Great Consols, Tavistock.—Copper and Mundic.
East Gunnislake and South Bedford, Tavistock.—Copper.
East Devon Great Consols.—Copper.
East Wheal Russel, Tavistock.—Copper.
Gawton's United, Tavistock.—Copper.
Tavy Consols, Tavistock.—Copper.
West Crebor, Tavistock.—Copper.
Wheal Russel, Tavistock.—Copper.
Concord, South Sydenham.—Silver lead and Copper.
Chillaton, Milton Abbot.—Manganese.
Peter Tavy and Mary Tavy Consols.—Copper.
Devon Wheal Union, Mary Tavy.—Copper.
North Wheal Friendship, Mary Tavy.—Copper and Lead.
South Wheal Betsy, Mary Tavy.—Copper and Lead.
Wheal Friendship, Mary Tavy.—Copper.
West Wheal Friendship, Brent Tor.—Copper.
Dippertown, Marystow.—Manganese.
Heale, Lifton.—Manganese.
Wheal Harris, Lifton.—Silver lead.
Wheal Henry, Lifton.—Manganese.
Callacombe, Lamerton.—Copper and Blende.
East Callacombe, Lamerton.—Copper.
West Maria and Fortescue Consols, Lamerton.—Copper and
　　Lead.
Lidford Consols, Lidford.—Tin.
Wheal Frederick, Lidford.—Tin.
Wheal Mary Emma, Lidford.—Tin.
Leco Wood and Furze Park, Lew Trenchard.—Manganese.

The great out-put of tin in former years has now, as we
learn from the Blue Book of 1893, dwindled down for the whole
of the county, to fifty-two tons, of the value of £2,779, and of
this, Hexworthy Mine, near Prince Town, produced more than
half—thirty tons, which sold for £1,709. The procuring of man-

ganese was an important commercial enterprise, and it was obtained from various mines on and about Dartmoor, but the only mine now working is that of Chillaton, Milton Abbot, which produced in 1893, three hundred and twenty-five tons of ore.

Dartmoor possesses the unique advantage of containing within its boundaries—natural, if not parochial—the two great constituents of fine earthenware, such as is produced in Staffordshire, viz: ball clay and china clay, and there is no other district so far as we know where these two forms of feldspathic clays are thus found in close juxta position.

Some years since, in 1834, an industry, which has now become of much importance, was started at Lee Moor, in the parish of Shaugh, by the late Mr. John Phillips, who was the first to open up China clay working combined with tin. Some few years after, the first fire bricks were made at the Lee Moor works, and subsequently salt glaze sanitary pipes. Fire bricks are now made extensively in both Devon and Cornwall, and sanitary ware in North and South Devon. China clay is now worked in various places, on the S. W. slope of the Moor, Cornwood, Hemerdon, and the neighbourhood, and is known to exist in many other parts, as in the Lydford district, at Haytor, and elsewhere.

For further information as to the archæological history of this interesting subject, we must refer our readers to the very full and valuable account given by Mr. Robert Burnard, in his papers, "On the track of the 'Old Men' of Dartmoor." Trans. Plymouth Institution, vol. x., p. 95, do., do., p. 223, and "Antiquity of Mining on Dartmoor," do., do., vol. xi., p. 85.

# CHAPTER XII.

## The Prisons.

FEW circumstances have had greater influence upon the present condition of the Moor than the formation, at the commencement of this century, of an extensive depôt for prisoners of war, in the centre of the Western Quarter. It is intended to give in this chapter a sketch of that important establishment, unique in its character and remarkable for its situation, as well of the Convict prisons which have succeeded it.

When the first decisive check had been given by Nelson, at Trafalgar, to the whirlwind career and gigantic designs of Napoleon, when France was to experience in her turn, the reverses of defeat, and the miseries of war which she had so long inflicted upon other countries—when the tide of victory gradually rolled back, and England numbered the captives of her prowess by thousands, it became necessary to provide ampler accommodation for the unfortunate exiles, than could be afforded in the crowded and unhealthy buildings, or prison ships, appropriated for that purpose at Plymouth. The late Sir Thomas Tyrwhitt, who held the office of Lord Warden of the Stannaries, under the Prince of Wales, afterwards George IV., and who had already distinguished himself as one of the earliest and most successful cultivators of Dartmoor, by his improvements at Tor Royal, suggested the erection of the necessary buildings at a spot about a mile from the scene of his own agricultural enterprise. Surveys were accordingly made by order of government, and the result of the investigation entered into was so favourable, that the place recommended was decided upon, as the site of a war prison establishment, on a scale suited to the exigences of the case, and worthy of the humanity and renown of Great Britain.

The ground required for the site was granted by the Prince, as Duke of Cornwall, and Lord of the Forest of Dartmoor. The foundation stone was laid by the Lord Warden, on the twentieth March, 1806, and the buildings were speedily raised, after the design, and under the superintendence of the architect, Mr.

Daniel Alexander. The following details are selected from the account given by the late Mr. Burt, in his Notes to Carrington's Dartmoor, and from a statement published about the time of the erection of the prison in the 1811 edition of Risdon's Survey of Devon, from personal observation, and from other sources.

"Granite taken from the moor," says Mr. Burt, "is the "principal material; and the whole, including some later addi- "tions, cost about £127,000, with the boundary walls, about "£130,000." "Two of the prisons, a row of houses for subor- "dinate officers, the walls of the chapel, and the parsonage house, "were erected by the French, and the interior of the chapel fitted "up by American prisoners, who received a daily gratuity for "their trouble; government, with a sympathy for these unhappy "victims of ruthless war, which deserves the highest praise, "kindly permitting them by this, and other modes of employment, "both in and outside the walls, to alleviate the tedium of their "captivity, and to increase their private comforts."*

The author of the additions to Risdon, published in 1811, gives the following description of the Prison, which had then been lately completed. "It is probably the finest thing of its kind. "An outer-wall encloses a circle of about thirty acres; within this "is another wall, which encloses the area in which the prisons "stand; this area is a smaller circle with a segment cut off. The "prisons are five large rectangular buildings, each capable of "containing more than fifteen hundred men; they have each "two floors, where is arranged a double tier of hammocks, slung "on cast-iron pillars; and a third floor in the roof, which is used "as a promenade in wet weather. There are, besides, two other "spacious buildings; one of which is a large hospital, and the other "is appropriated to the petty officers, who are judiciously "separated from the men. In the area, likewise, are sheds, or "open buildings, for recreation in bad weather. The space "between the walls forms a fine military road† round the whole "where the guard parades, and the sentinels being posted on "platforms overlooking the inner-wall, have a complete command of "the prison without intermixing with the prisoners. The segment "cut off from the inner circle, contains the governor's house, "and the other buildings necessary for the civil establishment;

---

*BURT. Carrington's "Dartmoor," p. 140.

†Nearly a mile in length.

S

" and into this part of the ground the country people are admitted,
" who resort to a daily market with vegetables, and such other
" things as the prisoners purchase to add to the fare that is
" provided for them, and which they buy at lower rates, than they
" can generally be procured for at the market towns.   The
" barracks for the troops form a detached building, and are
" distant from the prison above a quarter of a mile.   The number
" of prisoners that have been lodged here have been from five to
" seven thousand,* and the troops employed to guard them not
" more than from three to five hundred."†

The great gateway on the western side is arched over with
immense blocks of granite, bearing the appropriate inscription, in
Roman capitals, PARCERE SUBJECTIS.   Immediately opposite is
the ample reservoir, from whence the whole establishment was
served with copious supplies of purest water.   Indeed the
abundance and purity of this most essential article of daily life
was one of the causes which influenced the decision of government
in selecting the spot, which was incontrovertibly proved to be
remarkably healthy, notwithstanding the acknowledged severity of
the climate.   This statement is made on high professional
authority, that of the late Sir George Magrath, M.D., the
physician who presided over the medical department, from 1814
until the close of the war.   From official returns, it appeared that
the mortality among the prisoners was less in proportion than in
any town in England with an equal population.

Sir George Magrath wrote :—" From personal correspondence
" with other establishments similar to Dartmoor, I presume the
" statistical record of that great tomb of the living (embosomed
" as it is in a desert and desolate waste of wild, and, in the winter
" time, terrible scenery, exhibiting the sublimity and grandeur
" occasionally of elemental strife, but never partaking of the
" beautiful of nature,‡ its climate, too, cheerless and hyperborean)

---

*Subsequently as many as nine thousand six hundred were congregated within
the walls at one time.

†RISDON.   Survey of Devon, ed., 1811, p. 410.

‡The *gentler* beauties of nature are certainly not to be sought for in this
particular neighbourhood; and the effects of the wild scenery on the unhappy
captives, has been feelingly and faithfully noted by the moorland muse.

" O ! who that drags
A captive's chain, would feel his soul refresh'd,
Though scenes like those of Eden should arise
Around his hated cage !   But here green youth
Lost all its freshness, manhood all its prime,

"with all its disadvantages, will show that the health of its
"incarcerated tenants, in a general way, equalled if not surpassed,
"any war prison in England or Scotland. This might be con-
"sidered an anomaly in sanitary history, when we reflect how
"ungenially it might be supposed to act on southern constitutions;
"for it was not unusual in the months of December and January,
"for the thermometer to stand at from thirty-three to thirty-five
"degrees below freezing, indicating cold almost too intense to
"support animal life. But the density of the congregated numbers
"in the prison created an artificial climate, which counteracted
"the torpifying effect of the Russian climate without. Like most
"climates of extreme heat or cold, the new comers required a
"seasoning, to assimilate their constitution to its peculiarities,
"in the progress of which, indispositions, incidental to low
"temperature, assailed them; and it was an every day occurrence,
"among the reprobate and incorrigible classes of the prisoners,
"who gambled away their clothing and rations, for individuals to
"be brought up to the receiving room in a state of suspended
"animation, from which they were usually resuscitated by the
"process resorted to in like circumstances in frigid regions. I
"believe one death only took place during my sojourn at Dartmoor,
"from torpor induced by cold, and the profligate part of the
"French were the only sufferers. As soon as the system became
"acclimated to the region in which they lived, health was seldom
"disturbed.

"During my service there, malignant measles and small pox
"were imported from other contaminated sources. These diseases
"attained to great virulence among the Americans, chiefly arising
"from habits of indulgence from the ample pecuniary resources
"they possessed, and the facilities of obtaining spirits, and sump-
"tuous articles of diet from the market people, which no vigilance
"on the part of the authorities could suppress or obviate. The
"latter disease degenerated into an exasperated species of peri-
"pneumonia, accompanied by low typhoid symptoms, which
"became very unmanageable and destructive. Independently of
"these contagious epidemics (for they became so) the depôt may
"be said to have been surprisingly healthy.

And age sank to the tomb, ere peace her trump,
Exulting, blew; and still upon the eye,
In dread monotony, at morn, noon, eve,
Arose the moor—the moor!"—*Carrington.*

" I possess no register of the condition of health or disease
" obtaining in other war prisons, so as to enable me to draw an
" accurate parallel, but Dartmoor was generally considered equal,
" if not superior, to any depôt where the same numbers of men
" were confined in so narrow a compass; but it must be borne in
" mind, that after the closing of Mill-Bay Prison, Dartmoor
" received men from the colonies, long shut up in transports, and
" often landed with the seeds of infection generated among them,
" and predisposed, by privations and a vitiated atmosphere, to
" disease, while none were sent to the prisons in the interior, but
" men selected on purpose, in perfect health. The capacity of
" accommodation at Dartmoor was on a very extensive scale, and
" far beyond any other prison; a greater number of men was
" consequently congregated there, than elsewhere, which propor-
" tionately diminished its means of health, as it was calculated to
" contain nine thousand. Nor should it be forgotten that a state
" of confinement invokes moral and physical impressions dele-
" terious to mental as well as bodily health."

The foregoing observations refer particularly to the period
when the depôt was under the medical superintendence of Sir
George Magrath, viz., from his appointment to that important
office, in 1814, to the close of the establishment, in 1816, during
which time the diseases of the American prisoners, above specified,
came under his professional notice and care. Were it compatible
with the plan of this work, the subject might be further eluci-
dated, by reference to a testimonial, presented to him by the
prisoners, and transmitted to the President of the United States,
demonstrative of their regard, and expressive of the high sense
they entertained of his humane exertions and well-directed skill,
in alleviating, as far as possible, the sufferings and maladies to
which they were exposed in their place of durance. It may,
however, be remarked that independently of the state of foreign
prisoners, sufficient and most satisfactory proofs of the healthiness
of the general climate of the Moor, as well as of this particular
spot, may be adduced without difficulty. Situated at about
fourteen hundred feet above the level of the sea, and exposed to
the bleakest winds, Prince Town must necessarily often experience
great severity of weather; and accordingly there are very few days
in the year, when the cheerful peat-fire on the hearth, so characteristic of the district, would not form a most agreeable adjunct to
domestic comfort. But the free mountain air, an abundant supply

of water of the purest quality, and every facility for the most perfect drainage, would more than counterbalance, for many purposes, the coldness of the situation. Epidemic diseases are by no means so common in the moorlands, as in less elevated tracts, and the inhabitants generally, are remarkable for vigour of constitution, a green old age and length of life, and many of the most eminent medical practitioners of Plymouth and other neighbouring towns, have sent their patients for change of air to the Moor, with great success. The tourist, coming from the more genial clime of the lowlands into the bleak and cloudy regions "of the mountain "and the flood," may be inclined to commiserate the hardy countryman, whose life is spent amid the snows and mists, and the rocks and wastes of Dartmoor; but he, like other mountaineers, is little disposed to exchange the home of his youth, and the freedom of the Moor, for more circumscribed, though sunnier, spots, and from habit and early association, he is enabled to find subsistence and comfort, where a passing observer might imagine nothing but poverty, hardship, and wretchedness.

> " Dear is that shed to which his soul conforms,
> And dear that hill which lifts him to the storms,
> And as a child, when scaring sounds molest,
> Clings close and closer to the mother's breast,
> So the loud torrent, and the whirlwinds roar,
> But bind him to his native mountains more."
> —GOLDSMITH, The Traveller.

A substantial chapel with a tower, which forms a conspicuous object amidst the surrounding waste, was built for the accommodation of the officers of the depôt, the troops, and the inhabitants of the busy little town, which had rapidly sprung up in the immediate neighbourhood of the prison establishment, under the name of Prince Town, in honour of the royal lord of the soil. " Sir Thomas Tyrwhitt," remarks Mr. Burt, " with his wonted "regard for the welfare of Dartmoor, procured the privileges of "holding a market and a fair. The chapel and parsonage-house "lie a little way apart from the front of the prison. The former "is sixty feet long by forty wide, and was first opened for divine "service, in 1815, the parish church of Lydford being twelve or "thirteen miles distant. It is capable of accommodating five "hundred persons."

But the bustle and activity of this busy mart in the midst of the desert, were brought to an early, and, in the opinion of many, to an unexpected close. War had continued so long, that many feared, and some hoped that it would still be prolonged, even after the duration of a quarter of a century. But the period had arrived when the nations of the world were to be taught the instructive lesson that the mightiest conqueror is but an instrument in the hands of the King of kings. And thus the subjugator of a continent, for whose ambitious schemes, Europe was too narrow, was hurled from that portentous throne, which he had reared on the ruins of vanquished nations, and cemented with torrents of blood, and cast aside, when his work was done like " a " despised broken idol." When England, in the strength of a righteous cause, had chained the disturber of Europe, peace at length once more returned to bless the harassed and exhausted nations. The French, and subsequently the American prisoners, were restored to their native lands ; the troops stationed at the prison to guard them, were removed, and the vast establishment gradually broken up. Hope, though long deferred, came at last to incarcerated thousands, with joyful realization. Prince Town soon presented the forlorn spectacle of grass-grown highways and ruinous habitations ; shops and houses were shut up ; the once busy mill at Blackabrook, was still and silent, the moorland stream ran freely and uninterrupted in its antient channel ; while the prison itself, in the desolate stillness of its spacious courts and apartments, afforded a striking contrast to the ceaseless hum of the multitudinous human swarm previously hived together within the walls. Carrington alludes to the change with his usual felicity :—

" Silent now,—
How silent that grand pile, where England held
Within her victor gripe the vanquished foe ;
O here, full many a blooming cheek was blenched :
O here, full many a gallant heart was quelled
By stern captivity : protracted, till
Hope almost ceased to bless the drooping brave."

Various projects were from time to time suggested for the useful occupation of these spacious and commodious premises. A very early suggestion was to utilise the building for the reception of convicts. In Flinder's Western Luminary of 27th April, 1818, we find the following paragraph:—"The arrival of Sir Thomas "Tyrwhitt, last week at Dartmoor, gave rise to the report that the "plan so long talked of for converting the great war prison, thereon, "into a depôt for convicts, was to be carried into execution at "once."—Then a penitentiary—a school of industry and asylum for destitute children, rescued from the streets of the metropolis— a peat gas manufactory, &c., all which were abandoned in succession.

The scheme for a school of industry was an ambitious one: it received the patronage of Royalty, and excited considerable attention at the time. It was proposed to collect a large number of orphan children from the streets of the metropolis and to place them at Prince Town under a system of religious, moral and industrial training, which it was confidently hoped, would tend to reclaim them from habits of vice and immorality, and render them useful members of society. At a public meeting, held in London, in 1820, it was announced that his majesty, George IV. had headed the subscription for the accomplishment of these objects, by a princely donation of £1,000, and had further offered to grant part of the neighbouring moor for the same benevolent purpose. But unexpected difficulties intervened, and the resolutions of the meeting were never carried into effect.

Another proposal was to check the flow of emigration. Those who would otherwise have gone to the colonies were to have occupied the buildings, and the waste lands of the moor were to be reclaimed and brought into cultivation. A company having for its objects the extraction of naptha from peat, had possession of the buildings for some little time, but this speculation failed, and the works came to a standstill.

The late Prince Consort in 1846, visited the Duchy estates, and among them Dartmoor, and the question of making use of the old prisons came under his notice, more especially in connection with the anti-emigration project. He saw immediately, it is stated, that this was a place which private enterprise could not deal with, and it is presumed that it was under the advice of his Royal Highness, that the old plan of using the place as a convict establishment was reverted to and carried into effect. In 1850, preparations were made for the formation of a convict settlement. Two hundred convicts were sent to alter the buildings, and convert them into prisons, arranged upon the single cell system, so that every prisoner should, after the work of the day was completed, be isolated.

About two thousand acres of common or unenclosed waste land was granted by the Duchy to the prison authorities, and farming operations commenced. Considerable additions to the buildings, have been made from time to time. In the Prisons in 1893-4 were accommodated one thousand and seventy-five convicts. "The criminals received at this establishment, are men "who have been sentenced to penal servitude, and none less than "five years, some for life. A large proportion of those sent to "Dartmoor are convicts, who, having some malady or malforma- "tion, are rendered unfit for the severe labour at other stations, "but who, when employed here, upon work to which they are "accustomed, are capable of producing satisfactory results in all "branches of industry. Many are sent to Dartmoor for their "health's sake, for in the early stages of chest complaint, the "climate is most efficacious. The medical officers have from "time to time, recorded their opinion of the great advantages "which are to be derived by phthisical patients, from a residence "at such an altitude above the sea-level, and the improved "condition of the men removed from London and the large "manufacturing towns, goes far to prove the correctness of their "views."*

From the last Report of the Directors of Convict Prisons (1894) we find that the amount realized during the preceding year, for farm produce sold and transferred for prison use, was £2,486 15s. 5d. a considerable increase over the receipts of former years, and the total value of the work done by the convicts was £21,738 6s. 1d. On the farm are bred horses, ponies, bullocks, pigs and sheep. There is a large kitchen garden and dairy, the produce of both of which is used in the prison. At the September Prince Town Fair, horses, ponies, bullocks and pigs are sold by auction, and generally fetch good prices. Further information as to this Government farm, will be found in Chapter x., on the Agriculture of the Moor.

*Capt. VERNON HARRIS, late Governor of the Prisons, "*Dartmoor Prison, Past and Present*" p. 48. This little work contains an interesting and full account of the Prison and its inmates, from 1808 to 1816.

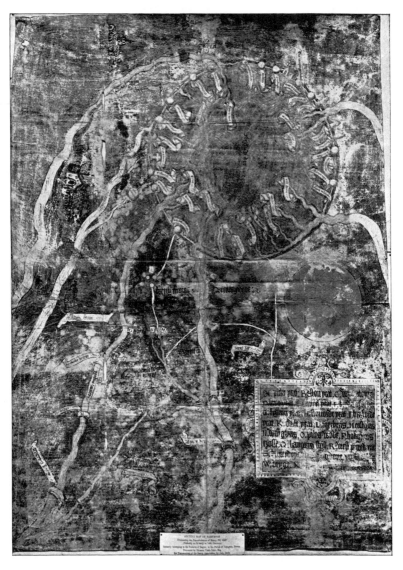

ANCIENT MAP OF DARTMOOR.

# CHAPTER XIII.

## HISTORICAL DOCUMENTS.

COPIES of some of the following documents were obtained by the late Mr. Pitman Jones, of Exeter, and handed to the author. The introduction, and the greater part of the notes, were written by the late Sir Edward (then Mr.) Smirke, Deputy Warden of the Stannaries. Additions have been made, and the documents printed by Mr. Dymond (Trans. Devon Assoc. 1879, vol. xi., p. 370) have also been included.

Nowhere are the vestiges of Norman rule, more distinctly traceable than in the county and confines of Devonshire. Exeter attempted to maintain against the Conqueror, the same independent spirit, which she had asserted against the Saxon sovereign,* and the sullen obedience of that antient metropolis and the surrounding territory, required to be insured by at least ten castles, of a date not long subsequent to the Conquest. The rivers which opened an access to the interior of the county, were guarded by the fortresses of Exeter, Totnes, Plympton, Trematon, and Barnstaple; while the inland passes and vulnerable points were secured by the castles of Launceston, Okehampton, Tiverton, Berry, and Lydford. To the same, or a not much later period, we may perhaps assign castles, of which few traces can now be found;

---

*Angliæ regi nisi ad libitum suum, famulari sub rege Edwardi aliisque prioribus olim despexerat. ORDERICUS VITALIS, Lib. iv., Cap 4.

namely those of Bradninch, Torrington, Bampton, Winkleigh, and Gidleigh. The Domesday Survey is silent as to any of these castles, except Okehampton and Trematon ; yet we know from unexceptionable historical evidence, that one at least of the others was erected immediately after the capture of Exeter,* and their surviving ruins carry intrinsic evidence of the early date of some of the rest.

Lydford is named in Domesday, yet it is clear that nothing but the borough is there noticed. The Royal Castle and Manor, with the Forest which has been immemorially appended to them, are nowhere to be found in that record : nor is this at all surprising. Until the property was granted to a subject, in a subsequent reign, it was in the king's hands, and could not have been liable to the payment of any of those taxes, which, under the name of hidage carrucage, etc., were chiefly in view when the Survey was made. A tract of land like Dartmoor, was under no circumstances likely to find its way into the enumeration of lands in Domesday, for it is very evident that the land intended to be included in it, and to which alone the description of *hides* and *carrucates* can strictly apply, was land under tillage, or some other form of profitable management, yielding an annual revenue to its owner, and therefore the fit subject of a land-tax. For the same reason the silence of the Survey as to tin mines, or their produce, both in Devon and Cornwall, cannot be relied upon as the slightest evidence that they had ceased to be worked. Public records of undoubted authority show that those mines were in full activity in the twelfth century.†

" It is probable, from the first document which we give, that the Forest was occasionally under grant to members of the royal family during the twelfth century ; but the first distinct notice of any transfer of the Castle, Manor, and Forest by the crown to a subject, is the grant by Henry III.,‡ to his brother Richard, Earl of Cornwall, commonly called the King of the Romans, or of Germany. From that date, the property has been from time to time under grant from the crown ; and since 1337, has been permanently annexed to the Duchy of Cornwall.

---

*" *Locum intra mœnia Exoniæ ad extruendum castellum delegit.*" [*Rex Willelmus*] ORDERICUS VITALIS, Lib. iv., Cap 4.

†" Pipe Roll.," 2 Hen. II., etc.

‡" Rot. Cart.," 23 Hen. III. m.I.

It has been justly observed that the technical meaning of the term *Forest* does not necessarily imply that there should be more timber or herbage than may be sufficient to supply food and shelter for the wild animals that range over it. It is indeed possible that there formerly existed more wood on Dartmoor than is now to be found, and that the tinners, who certainly were allowed to supply themselves with fuel, for the fusion of the ore, have laid waste the surface; but it is more probable that the granitic table-land of the forest was never covered with any thing entitled to the name of timber, and that it was reserved as a mere hunting ground. Nor is it to be assumed that diversion was the main object of these appropriations of land. It is very certain that our ancestors (excluding of course, those who were obliged to be satisfied with humble fare) relied upon their deer parks, chases, and warrens for the supply of their larders ; and that cured venison was an important article of food in royal households.*

Yet we know that the princely owners of Dartmoor have always provided for the contingency of their personal presence in the field. Lymstone manor was held by the tenure of furnishing two arrows and an oaten loaf to the Lord of Lydford, when he came to hunt on Dartmoor. The Lord of Kingdon, Shiredon, and Hockneton, was bound to present three arrows on the like occasion ; and the Lord of Druscombe held his land by the sergeantry of bearing a bow and three arrows to the King's use, when he hunted on Dartmoor. These tenures are set forth in the Hundred Rolls, and the Records of the Knight's Fees in the Exchequer :† from which we also learn that if the Lord of Dartmoor should pursue the chase over the neighbouring waste of Exmoor, there are lands at Braunton that are bound to drag the Taw or the Torridge to supply the table of the Prince with one of the best salmon that can be found there. Nor is this all : if the Prince should avail himself of the hunting season at Dartmoor, to visit his antient castle of Launceston, the lord of the manor of Cabilia will infallibly subject his land to the peril of forfeiture, unless he stations himself at Poulston bridge, ready to receive His Royal Highness, and to present to him "*unam*

---

*It was packed and salted, and sent from distant parts of the country to the king's larders. "Prefatory Observations on Wardrobe Accounts," 28 Ed. I., ed. 1787.

†*I. Hund. Rot.*, 3 Edw. I,, print ed.. pp. 66-81-85-86. *Testa de Nevil*, printed ed., p. 197.

"*capam griseam,*" or "*de grisauco,*"* a service, the more perilous, inasmuch as he will have to consult the Society of Antiquaries, from whom he will probably only learn that the "*capa grisea*" may mean either a grey mantle, or a fur cape, and that the word "*grisauco*" is not to be found in the glossaries at all.

Let us now turn to the documents, and shortly notice their contents.

The conversion of large tracts of land into royal forest was the subject of frequent complaint against the early Norman princes, and some relief appears to have been promised in the Charters of Henry I., 1101, and of Stephen, 1136.

The great Charter of John, promulgated 1215, contained a promise to disafforest all forests of recent creation, and in that year writs were issued to the officers of the forest with a view to ascertain and redress the grievances alluded to in this Charter.† There was, however, no Forest charter, distinct from the Great Charter of liberties, until the following reign.

In the second year of Henry III., 1217, we have the first authentic evidence of the promulgation of a distinct charter on the subject of the royal forests. The writ is still extant which directs the sheriffs of the different counties of England, to summon the knights, who were to choose twelve others to perambulate between the old and new forest lands,‡ and the charter itself, which had escaped the search of Sir W. Blackstone, was found in Durham cathedral, in 1806.§

In the ninth year of the same king, another charter of the Forest, not materially varying from the last, was published, a copy of which is usually prefixed to the common editions of the statutes at large. One of the most important provisions of this charter, was to disafforest lands which had been converted into forests by Henry II., Richard I., and John.

This Charter was followed by general perambulations, made in all the forest counties, under royal commissions or writs,** which were repeated in this and the following reigns.

---

*Blount. Tenures, ed. 1784. p. 63, ed. 1874, p. 56. Lysons. Cornwall, p. 246.
†Patent Roll. 17 John.
‡"Rot. Pat." 2 Hen. III.
§It is prefixed to the last edition of the Statutes at Large.
**See Blackstone. "Introduction to the Great Charter," pp. 78, 107, (8vo. edit.)

The first document is a charter of John, Earl of Morton (i.e., Mortaigne, in Normandy) who was Earl of Cornwall during the life of his brother Richard I., and afterwards became king. It professes to grant certain immunities to free tenants, out of the Regard of the forest, which were in fact little more than mere declarations of their common law rights.

The original, under the seal of the Earl, is in the possession of the Dean and Chapter of Exeter. It must have been granted before 27th May, 1199, on which day, John was crowned king.

### I.—Carta Johannis Comitis Moreton de Foresta Devoniæ.

Johannes Comes Moreton omnibus hominibus et amicis suis Francie et Anglie presentibus et futuris Salutem. Sciatis me concessisse redidisse et hac carta mea confirmasse comitibus baronibus militibus et omnibus libere tenentibus clericis et laicis in Devenesir' libertates suas foreste quas habuerunt tempore Henrici Regis proavi mei. Tenendas et habendas illis et heredibus suis de me et heredibus meis. Et nominatim quod habeant arcus et pharetras et sagittas in terris suis deferendas extra reguardum foreste mee et quod canes sui vel hominum suorum non sint espaltati extra reguardum foreste et quod habeant canes suos et alias libertates sicut melius et liberius illas habuerunt tempore ejusdem Henrici Regis et reisellos suos et quod capiant capreolam vulpem cattum lupum leporem lutrum ubicunque illa invenerint extra reguardum foreste mee. Et ideo vobis firmiter precipio quod nullus eis de hiis vel aliis libertatibus suis molestiam inferat vel gravamen. Hiis testibus. Willelmo Marescall. Willelmo Comite Sarisbir'. Willelmo Comite de Vern'. Stephano Ridell Cancellario meo. Willelmo de Wenn'. Hamon de Valoin'. Rogero de Novoburgo. Ingelr' de Pratell. Roberto de Mortem. Waltero Maltravers'. Radulpho Morin. Waltero de Cautelo. Fulcon' fratre suo, Gileberto Morin' et multis aliis.

The second document contains a copy of a charter by the same person when king. It disafforests all lands in Devonshire except the antient Regards of the Forests of Dartmoor and Exmoor, and bears date the 18th May, *anno regni* 5 (1203 or 1204) eleven or twelve years before the date of Magna Charta.

### II.—Carta Regis Johannis de Comitatu Devoniæ deafforestando.

Johannes Dei gratia Rex Anglie Dominus Hibernie Dux Normannie et Aquitanie Comes Andegavie archiepiscopis episcopis abbatibus comitibus baronibus justiciariis forestariis vicecomitibus prepositis ministris et omnibus baillivis et fidelibus suis salutem. Sciatis nos deafforestasse totam Devoniam de omnibus que ad forestam et ad forestarios pertinent usque ad metas antiquorum regardorum de Dertemora et Exemora que regarda fuerunt tempore regis Henrici primi : ita quod tota Devonia et homines in ea manentes et heredes eorum sint deafforestati omnino et quieti et soluti de nobis et heredibus nostris imperpetuum de omnibus que ad forestam et ad forestarios pertinent exceptis duabus moris prenominatis scilicet Dertemora et Exemora per predictas metas. Volumus eciam et concedimus quod predicti homines de Devonia et heredes eorum habeant consuetudines intra regarda morarum illarum sicut habere consueverant tempore predicti regis Henrici faciendo inde consuetudines quas inde facere tunc consueverant et debuerant. Et quod liceat eis qui voluerint extra predictas metas essartare, parcos facere, omnimodam venationem capere, canes arcus et sagittas et alia omnimoda arma habere, et saltatoria facere, nisi in divisis predictarum morarum ubi non poterunt saltatoria vel haias facere. Et si canes eorum excurrerint in forestam nostram volumus quod ipsi inde deducantur sicut et alii barones et milites inde deducuntur qui sunt deafforestati et qui marchiant alibi foreste nostre. Et volumus quod unus turnus vicecomitis tantum fiat per annum in comitatu Devonie et ille turnus fiat post festum Sancti Michaelis ad inquirendum placita corone et alia que ad coronam pertinent sine occasionibus alicui faciendis, et quod plures turnos non faciat nisi pro placitis corone cum evenerint attachiandis cum coronatoribus et propter pacem assecurandam ; ita quidem quod in itinere illo nichil capiat ad opus suum. De prisonibus vero qui capti fuerint in comitatu Devonie de quibus vicecomes habeat potestatem eos replegiandi et quorum plegiagium comes Devonie voluerit super se capere, volu *mus et* concedimus quod per consilium eorum replegientur ; ita quod per odium vel occasionem vicecomitis ulterius in prisona non detineantur. Et si vicecomes injuste gravaverit predictos homines Devonie et inde convictus fuerit incidet in misericordiam nostram et nos de eo misericordiam capiemus et alium vicecomitem eis substituemus qui eos bene et legaliter tractabit. Teste Domino Hereberto Sarum Episcopo. Galfrido filio Petri Comite Essex. Baldewino Comite Albemarlie. Willelmo Comite de Fferariis. Henrico Comite Hereford. Willelmo de Braos'. Hugone de Nevill. Willelmo Briwer. Simone de Pateshull. Data per manum Domini Simonsis Cicestriensis electi apud Wynton decimo octavo Die Maii anno regni nostri quinto. [18 May, 5 John, 1204.]

Charter Roll. 5 John p. 132.

This charter, with the confirmation of Henry III., was kept in Tavistock Abbey. Walter de Stapeldon, Bishop of Exeter, whilst in London, during the autumn of 1320, was anxious to examine the original charter of John, and applied to the Abbot, Robert Champeaux, to send it to him. The Abbot entrusted it to a careful messenger, Thomas Newbegyn, and the Bishop conceived it to be of such importance that he caused it to be copied into his Register, *ad pleniorem memoriam futurorum*. Prebendary Hingeston-Randolph, in his Register of Stapeldon, gives this confirmation as it is therein copied, pp. 139-148. It appears under the head of *Carta de Libertatibus Devonie.*

Memorandum quod Carta Originalis Regis Anglie de Libertatibus Comitatus Devonie remanet in custodia Abbatis et Conventus Tavistochie; sub hac forma.—

Henricus, Dei gracia Rex Anglie, Dominus Hibernie, Dux Normannie, Aquitanie, et Comes Andegavie, Archiepiscopis, Episcopis, Abbatibus, Prioribus, Comitibus, Baronibus, Justiciariis, Forestariis, Vicecomitibus, Prepositis, Ministris, et omnibus Ballivis et Fidelibus suis, salutem.—Inspeximus Cartam quam Dominus Johannes Rex, Pater noster, fecit omnibus Hominibus de tota Devonia, in hec verba,—Johannes Dei gracia, etc. . . . . Archiepiscopis, Episcopis, etc. . . . . salutem.

Then follows John's Charter as above.

The charter then proceeds:—Nos, autem, concessiones predictas ratas habentes et gratas, eas pro nobis et heredibus nostris concedimus et confirmamus, sicut Carta predicti Domini Johannis Regis, Patris nostri, plenius et liberius testatur; hiis testibus,— Venerabili Patre, Waltero, Eboracensi Archiepiscopo, Anglie Primate; Petro de Sabaudia; Magistro Willellmo de Kilkenny, Archidiacono Conventrensi; Bertramo de Criolle; Ricardo de Grei; Johanne de Grei; Roberto de Muscegros; Gilberto de Segrave; Roberto Wallerand; Bartholomeo Pecche; Roberto le Noreis; Willelmo de Cheemy (*sic*); Johanne de Gerres; et aliis.— Datum, per manum nostram, apud Wyndeleshoure, vicesimo quinto die Aprilis, Anno Regni nostri, tricesimo sexto [1252].

Et nos, Walterus, permissione Divina Exoniensis Episcopus, existentes Londoniis, et videntes dictam Originalem Cartam in manibus cujusdam Thome Neubegyn, clerici dicti Abbatis, cum ipsa Originali per Fratrem Robertum Champeaux, tunc Abbatem Tavistochie, Londonias, ut dicebatur, missi, Transcriptum seu Copiam ipsius, ut suprascribitur, nobis fieri fecimus viij die mensis Octobris, Anno Domini Millesimo CCC$^{mo}$ vicesimo, et Regni Regis Edwardi, Filii Regis Edwardi, quartodecimo, et in hoc nostro Registro rescribi, ad pleniorem memoriam futurorum.

The third document is an instruction or mandate to the bailiffs of Lydford, probably the governing officers of the borough, to permit the king's tinners (as indeed at this time all the tinners in Devon and Cornwall were called) to take coal, that is peat, from Dartmoor for the use of the stannary; no doubt for the fusion of the ore.

### III.—*Royal Writ, directing the Bailiffs of Lydford to permit the Tinners of Devon to take fuel from the Moor.*

Rex baillivis de Ledeford salutem. Precipimus vobis quod permittatis stagnarios nostros Devonie capere et habere carbonem in mora nostra de Dertemore ad stagnariam nostram sicut habere consueverint tempore domini Johannis patris nostri et nostro, nec eis inde faciatis vel fieri permittatis molestiam vel impedimentum. Teste apud Turrim London. 18 die Julii. (6 Hen. III., 1222.)

Close Roll. printed ed. p. 505.

The next document is a grant by Henry III. of the tithe of the herbage of Dartmoor, to the Chaplain of Lydford. Tithe is not due of common right from royal forests, hence the necessity of this special concession, by which the tithe of agistment was assigned to the church of Lydford.

### IV.—*Pro decima herbagii Dertemoræ ecclesiæ Sancti Petrochi de Ludeford concessa.*

Rex dedit et concessit Deo et ecclesie Sancti Petrochi de Ludeford et capellano ministrando in eadem ecclesia ad sustentationem suam quicumque pro tempore ibidem capellanus fuerit decimam herbagii more de Dertemor'. In cujus Rei &c. Teste Rege apud Wudestok. 12 die Julii.

Et mandatum est Herberto filio Mathei quod persone ejusdem ecclesie decimas predictas haberi faciat. Teste ut supra.

Patent Roll. 21 Hen. III., 1236, m. 6.

No. V. is a writ, A.D. 1240, from Henry III., directing the Sheriff of Devon to summon a jury for twelve knights to determine, by perambulation, the boundary of the Forest of Dartmoor. It will be observed that where the word *linealiter* is used in the perambulation, the boundary is not necessarily represented by a *straight* line, although that construction may possibly be put

upon the word.  Nor should it be overlooked that, according to
the Forest law, the object which forms the boundary, if it be a
road, river, etc., is wholly included within the franchise of the
forest.*

The official return to this writ has not been found, but there
are several copies extant of various dates, none of which exactly
agree.  A copy of one of these forms the sixth document.

*V.—Writ directing a Perambulation of the Forest of Dartmoor.*

Rex vicecomiti Devonie Salutem.  Sciatis quod dilectus frater
noster Ricardus Comes Pictavie et Cornubie pro parte sua et
Henricus de Mereton, Hamelinus de Eudon, Robertus de Halyun,
et Willelmus le Pruz, pro parte militum et libere tenencium
habencium terras et feoda juxta forestam ejusdem comitatus de
Dertemore posuerunt se coram nobis in perambulacionem inter
terras eorum et predictam forestam ejusdem comitatus faciendam
et ideo tibi precipimus quod si alii de comitatu tuo habentes terras
Juxta forestam predictam cognoverint coram te et coram custodibus
placitorum corone nostre quod predicti quatuor milites de consensu
aliorum omnium posuerint se in perambulationem illam pro
omnibus aliis tunc assumptis tecum duodecim legalibus militibus
de comitatu tuo in propria persona tua accedas ad forestam et
terras predictas et per eorum sacramenta fieri faciatis perambulationem inter predictam forestam et terras predictas; ita quod
perambulatio illa fiat per certas metas et divisas.  Et scire nobis
facias ubicumque fueruis distincte et aperte sub sigillo tuo et per
quatuor milites ex illis qui perambulationi illi interfuerint per quas
metas et divisas perambulatio facta fuerit et habeas ibi nomina
militum et hoc breve.  Teste Rege apud Westmonasterium die
Junii.

Close Roll., 24 Hen. III., 1240, m. 11.

In No. VI. we give between brackets and in italics, the
various readings in other copies and suggested identifications.
For further information as to this Perambulation, Writ, and
Return, see C. Spence Bate on The Map of the Forest of
Dartmoor, etc., Trans. Devon Assoc. vol. v., p. 510.  R. Dymond,
Historical Documents relating to Dartmoor, vol. xi., p. 370.  Also
Risdon's Survey, ed. 1714, p. 283 ; edit. 1811, p. 221.

---

*Coke, Institutes, 4 p. 318,

T

*VI.—Perambulation of the Boundaries of Dartmoor Forest, made under the above commission, No. V. 24 Henry III.*, 1240.

Hec est Perambulatio facta et ordinata per commune consilium Ricardi Comitis Cornubie et Pictavie et militum et libere tenentium in comitatu Devon per preceptum domini Regis Henrici filii Johannis anno coronationis dicti Henrici vicesimo quarto in vigilia Sancti Jacobi apostoli per sacramentum militum subscriptorum, scilicet, Willielmi de la Brewer, Guidonis de Bretevyle, Willielmi de Wydeworthy, Hugonis de Bollay [*Bellay*] Ricardi Gyffard', Odonis de Treverbyn, Henrici filii Henrici, Willielmi Trenchard, Philippi Parrer [*Parre, Perer*] Nicholai de Heamton [*Heamden, Heamton*] Willielmi de Moreleghe, et Durantis filii Botonis [*Boton*] qui incipiunt perambulationem ad hogam de Cossdonne et inde linealiter usque ad parvam hogam que vocatur parva Hundetorre, et inde linealiter usque ad Thurlestone, et inde linealiter usque ad Wotesbrokelakesfote que cadit in Tyng, et inde linealiter usque ad Heigheston [*Hengheston*] et inde linealiter usque ad Langestone [*Yessetone*] et inde linealiter usque per mediam turbariam de Alberysheved [*Aberesheved*] et sic in longum Wallebroke et inde linealiter usque ad Furnum regis et inde linealiter usque ad Wallebrokeshede et sic in longum Wallebroke usque cadit in Dertam, et sic per Dertam usque ad aliam Dertam, et sic per aliam Dertam ascendendo usque Okebrokysfote, et sic ascendendo Okebroke usque ad la Dryeworke, et ita ascendendo usque ad la Dryfeld ford, et sic inde linealiter usque ad Battyshull [*Cattyshill, Gnattishull*] et inde linealiter usque ad caput de Wester Wellabroke et sic per Wester Wellabroke usque cadit in Avenam, et inde linealiter usque ad Ester Whyteburghe et inde linealiter usque ad la Redelake [*Rodelake*] que cadit in Erme et inde linealiter usque ad Grymsgrove et inde linealiter usque ad Elysburghe et sic linealiter usque at crucem Sywardi et inde usque ad Ysfother et sic per aliam Ysfother et inde per mediam Mystor [*Mistmore*] usque ad Mewyburghe et inde usque ad Lullingesfote [*Hullingssete*] et inde usque ad Rakernesbrokysfote, et sic ad caput ejusdem aque et deinde usque ad la Westsolle et inde linealiter usque ad Ernestorre et inde linealiter usque at vadum proximum in orientali parte capelle Sancti Michaelis de Halgestoke et inde linealiter usque ad predictum hogam de Cossdonne in orientali parte.

The seventh document is an interesting ecclesiastical instrument by which the Bishop of Exeter, 1260, transferred the villages of Balbenny and Pushyll to the Parish of Widecombe from from Lydford, for the convenience of their inhabitants. The

transfer is only partial. For some purposes they were to remain
parcel of the mother parish of Lydford. The arrangement is
believed to be still in force.

*VII.—Extract from the Register of Bishop Walter Bronescombe.*
13 *Kalends of September,* [20 *of August* 1260.] *Exeter*
*Episcopal Registers.   Folio* 16, *b.*

Exivit littera universis &c. Episcopus &c. Fide dignorum
assertione intelligentes quod quidam parochiani ecclesie de Lideford
villulas que dicuntur Balbenye et Pushyll inhabitantes adeo distant
ab eorum ecclesia matrice predicta, quod cum pre nimia distantia
nullo modo visitare possunt quocies eis fuerit opportunum, dilecto
filio officiali archidiaconi Totton nostris litteris dedimus in
mandatis, ut facta inquisitione solemni in pleno capitulo ejusdem
loci, nos literatorie reddet certiores, ad homines predicti ad
erectionem sufficerint oratorii ; item que parochialis ecclesia villulis
ipsis vicinior existat ; necnon iidem homines sine prejudicio juris
alieni audire divina et ecclesiastica percipere valeant sacramenta ;
et quanto eadem villule distant a matrice ecclesia predicta ; et si
tempestatibus et inundationibus aquarum exortis, parochianis ipsis
matricem ecclesiam predictam visitare volentibus via longior
debeatur.    Cumque per certificationem officialis memorati invene-
rimus, quod incolis ipsis ad constructionem oratorii minime
sufficientibus, parochialis ecclesia de Wydecombe locis ipsis plus
aliis omnibus est vicina, et quod loca predicta a matrice ecclesia
de Lideford sereno tempore per octo, et tempestatibus exortis in
circuitu per quindecim, distant miliaria ; salutem animarum sicut
non debemus negligere ulla ratione volentes, ecclesiarum ipsarum
rectores ad nostram fecimus presentiam evocari : rectoribus igitur
predictis coram nobis constitutis, et exposito eisdem hujuscemodi
periculo, ac de expresso consensu utriusque ecclesie patronorum,
ordinationi nostre se supponentibus, promittentibusque bona fide
voluntati nostre parere in hac parte ac nostram ordinationem
predictam observare in perpetuum, de consilio prudentium virorum
nobis assistentium taliter ordinavimus, videlicet, quod predictorum
et adjacentium locorum incolis sic in unitate sue parochialis ecclesie
de Lideford perpetuo remanentibus, in ecclesia de Wydecombe
imposterum divina audiant et omnia in vita et morte ecclesiastica
percipiant sacramenta.    In coopertura et fabrica ecclesie de
Wydecombe, clausura cemeterii, subsidio luminarium et deferendo
pane benedicto cum ipsis ecclesie parochialis contribuant : consuetudines ipsius ecclesie in visitationibus infirmorum, benedictionibus
nubentium, in purgationibus post partum, in baptismatibus
parvulorum, in mortuariis et sepulturis morientium observent :
Offerant quoque ibidem solemniter ter in anno et decimam nihil-
ominus agnorum eidem ecclesie cum integritate persolvant.    In

signum vero subjectionis et agnitionem juris parochialis, quilibet incola dictorum locorum terram tenens semel in anno, videlicet die sancti Petroci, in ecclesia de Lideford solemniter offerat et omnes decimas et obventiones majores et minores, hiis duntaxat exceptis que superius enunciantur, matrici ecclesie sue de Lideford sine qualibet diminutione et contradictione persolvant. In cujus, &c.

The extract, No. VIII., sufficiently explains itself. The original, which we believe is in the Duchy office, is in latin, and is much more voluminous. It is an account rendered in 1297 to the Earl of Cornwall, to whose father the castle, manor, borough and forest had been granted; and the items are arranged under the heads of Lydford (i.e. the borough) and its fee-farm rent; the Manor, including the profits arising from the mill, fairs, toll-tin, stray cattle, etc.; and the Forest, the profits of which arose at that time from a water-mill—from mortgable (probably acknowledgments paid for the use of dead wood found on the moor)—the fines of vills, now called the Venville rents—pasturage and folding of cattle—payments made by peat diggers—agistment of the cattle of out-lying tenants—rents paid by the censers, and the pannage, or feed of pigs. Some of these sources of revenue would seem to indicate the existence of more timber than is now to be seen within the present supposed limits of the forest. The Lydford and Dartmoor courts were probably held, as now, together; and the long list of fines on various law proceedings, shows an amount of litigation, to which the pacific inhabitants of the Moor' have happily long been strangers. The reader may recognise among the names of litigants or offenders, some that are still familiar in the neighbourhood.

It will be observed that neither this nor any other Dartmoor account, notices the profit accruing to the Earl or the Duchy, from the stannaries. The dues paid by tinners working in the demesne land, whether manor or forest, and called toll-tin, are mentioned; but the far larger revenue, arising from coinage and and pre-emption of tin is not included. There can be no reasonable doubt that the Stannaries of Devon in the twelfth century, were more productive than those of Cornwall, for the fixed sum paid to the Bishops of Exeter for the last seven centuries and a half, as the tithe of the royalty or farm of tin, is greater for Devon than for Cornwall. In Devon too, as in Cornwall, four courts have immemorially settled all ordinary suits and quarrels, in which tinners are parties: and the records of their proceedings, still extant in great abundance, from the reign of Edward III., bear witness to an enormous amount of petty litigation, which for some centuries yielded to the crown, the prince or their officers, an income by no means contemptible. The scene of these mining operations was the moor and its confines: for although the warden and stewards of the stannaries claimed all Devon as stannary ground, and Exeter itself could not secure the defendant from an involuntary visit to Lydford castle, under the escort of a tin bailiff, it is as certain as any geological fact can be, that Dartmoor alone has hitherto been the centre and source of all the tin stream works in the country. The authentic annals of the tin revenues must be sought for not in the Dartmoor rentals, but in the coinage rolls: a series quite distinct from the rentals or bailiffs' accounts of Lydford or Dartmoor forest.

*VIII.—Extracts from an account rendered by the Ministers of Edmund, Earl of Cornwall, 25 Edw. I., 1296-7.*

LYDFORD.

*Rents of Assize.*—The same (Accountant) renders account of 50s. 5¼d. of assized rent this year.

Sum, £2 10s. 5¼d.

*Issues of the Manor.*—The same renders account of 30s. for a water-mill let to farm; of 3s. 5½d. for toll of the fairs this year; of toll of tin* on the waste of Lydeford nil that year; of 12s. 9d. from amercements of the borough this year; of 21s. from stray colts and bullocks this year; of 2s. 2d. from censarii for having liberty.†

Sum, £3 9s. 4½d.

*Fines.*—The same renders account of 6s. 8d. from Richard Smith, of Lydeford, for iron carried away from the Earl's castle.

Sum 6s. 8d.

Sum total, £6 6s. 5¾d.

DERTEMORE.

*Rents of Assize.*—The same renders account of 75s. of assized rent per annum.

Sum, £3 15s. od.

*Issues of the Forest.*—The same renders account of 34s. 4d. from the farm of a water-mill there this year; of 14s. 6d. from

---

*In original "tollon' stagm,'" i.e. tolloneum or tollnetum stagminis.

†"De cens' pro libertate habenda." Whether this was a census paid for enjoying certain immunities or privileges, or was a capitage paid in respect of exemption from personal servitude is not clear:—a class of tenants was always called censers, or censarii, and are still so named in some of the drift warrants.

mortgable;* of £4 1s. 8d. from the fines of vills† for having pasture for their cattle; of 15s. 10d. from 96 folds this year, viz. from each fold 2d.; of 11s. 3d. from 27 colliers‡ this year, viz. from each collier 5d.; of 15s. 6½d. from 2442 cattle agisted and attended by the shepherds of the Lord Earl there this year, viz. for each head of cattle 1½d.; of 33s. 3d. from 399 cattle at farm near Okehampton this year; of 8s. for the farm of the said cattle as demised by the bailiff this year; of £15 17s. 7½d. from 2141 cattle returning to fold§ this year, viz. from each head of cattle 1½d.; of £4 14s. from 487 horses feeding there this year, viz. for each horse 2d.; of 3s. from 36 folds of Lydeforde and and Waterfalle near Lydeforde this year; of 8d. from the rent of censarii for having the advowson**; of 2s. 3d. from pannage of pigs this year.

Sum £45 3s. 1d.

*Perquisites* (of Courts).—The same renders account of 2s. 6d. from Richard Rys and three others,†† for trespass; of 18s. from William Batoshelle and two others, for the same; of 2s. from William rector of Beleston and two others for default and trespass; of 12d. from the same William for false claim; of 12d. from Ralph de Combe for having had his dog in the forest in fence time;‡‡ of 12d. from Antone Martin for horses not entered in writing;§§ of 12d. from Antony de Foddreford for oxen not entered; of 12d. from Richard of the same place for the like cause; of 12d. from the parson of Beleston for the like; of 12d. from Jordan de Lukesmore because he whom he vouched to warranty was not forthcoming;$ of 2s. from John Luccok and three others for cattle not entered; of 12d. from William parson of Beleston for oxen not entered; of 5d. from John Wagheberd and six others for divers trespasses; of 2s. 2d. from John Attewode for the same; of 2s. 5d. from John Adam and five others for the same; of 4s. from Michael Cole and three others for the same; of 12d. from John de la Torre for foolish delivery; of 12d. from

---

*" De mortuo gabulo," called mortgable or more-gable in later records, probably payments for dead wood.

†" De finibus villarum.

‡" De carbonariis," explained in later accounts to mean diggers of turf or peat, for fuel.

§Averiis redeuntibus ad faldam.

**It should seem that at this time the advowson of Lydford parish was on farm to certain tenants paying census or rent.

††" Ric Rys et tribus sociis suis." In these accounts " socii " only mean co-defendants.

‡‡" In tempore prohibito."

§§" Pro equis non scriptis." The usage has always been to enter cattle in the books of the clerk of the forest before they are turned on the forest.

$" Quia non habuit quam vocavit ad warrantiam."

William the carpenter for cattle not entered; of 2s. from John de la Torre for trespass; of 6s. from Joel Kyr and three others for trespass in the wood; of 2s. from Geoffry de la Woghebye for concealment; * of 6s. 8d. from Elyas de Cristenestowe because he was found in the forest in fence time; of 3s. 9d. for the heriot of Richard le Sopere; of 6s. 8d. from the same Richard for ingress;† of 2s. of William Lutereford and another for trespass; of 2s. from Henry de la Hurne for many defaults; of 2s. from the same Henry for foolish delivery of cattle;‡ of 6s. 8d. from Richard le Syneger and two others for ingress; of 3s. 9d. from the same parties for reliefs; of 5s. from Henry Penystrang and Adam de Cadetun for trespass; of 2s. from William de Hevytru for contempt; of 2s. from Robert Atteheved for twenty oxen not entered; of 5s. from Roger Repe and nine others for horses and cattle not entered; of 6s. 8d. from William Attewelle for cattle not entered.

Sum 102s. 5d.
Sum total £54 os. 6d.

*Allowances.*—The same accounts in tithe paid to the parson of Lydeford 60s.; in the stipends and "poutura"§ of the foresters per annum 42s.; in their expences in fence month 22s.; in peutura of twelve shepherds tending the agisted cattle from the Feast of the Invention of the Holy Cross (3rd May) till the Assumption (15 Aug.) 52s. 6d.; in stipends of the same 24s.

Sum £9 18s. 6d.
Debet (or clear balance) £44 2s. od.

The next contains extracts from the Hundred Rolls of 1275, so far as they relate to the Hundreds of Roborough and Plympton, and Dartmoor.

### IX.—*Extracts from Hundred Roll*, 1275.

#### DEVON.

Hundredum de Rouberg pro Rege Dominica Que eciam maneria esse solent &c. Dicunt quod manerium de Lideford cum Foresta de Dertemor solet esse in manu Henrici Regis Patris Domini Regis nunc pertinens ad coronam suam et idem Henricus Rex Predictum Manerium cum Foresta tradidit Ricardo Fratri suo Comiti Cornubie ad feodi firmam scilicet decem libras per

---

*That is for not presenting offences at the lord's court.

†"Pro ingressu." i.e. for admittance on alienation or descent to a customary tenement.

‡" Pro fatua deliberatione averiorum," meaning possibly an amerciament for unadvisedly releasing cattle from the pound before payment.

§Probably *potura*, or drink provided for the shepherds, also spelt *peutura*.

annum dicto Domino Henrico Regi Reddendo quibus terris ignorant et similiter quo waranto a tempore triginta annorum elapsorum quod quidem Manerium Edmundus filius predicti Ricardi nunc Comes Cornubie tenet et valet per annum quadraginta libras et amplius. Item dicunt quod idem Edmundus tenet modo filium aque de Thaini usque Meweston per occupacionem. Dicunt eciam quod Osbertus Giffard habit Warrenam apud Heckeboclond Comton et Havetnolle de novo per cartam Domini Regis Henrici Patris Domini Regis nunc. Item dicunt quod Willelmus de Engelfeld tunc vicecomes cepit de Elia de Blacaston unam marcam pro respectu habendo quod miles non esset jam viginti annorum elapsorum Et Thomas de Pyn dum fuit in vicecomes cepit de eodem Elia per eodem decem solidis uno anno elapso.

### Hundredum de Plimton.

Juratores illius Hundredi dicunt quod Lideford et Dertemore tempore Domini Henrici Regis Patris Domini Regis nunc fuerunt in manu sua pertinentia ad coronam suam et nunc sunt in manu comitis Cornubie et prills fuerunt in manu Regis Alemanie per tempus triginta annorum sed ignorant quo waranto. Item dicunt quod Isabella de Fortibus Comitissa Insule tenet placita de Namio vetito sed ignorant a quo tempore et quo Waranto similiter habet libertatis regias ut furcam et assisam panis et cervicie sed ignorant quo waranto vel a quo tempore Item dicunt quod eadem Isabella habet warrenam in Dominicis suis apud Plimpton sed ignorant quo waranto et a quo tempore Item dicunt quod Thomas Pipard fuit in custodia Domini Regis et maritatus est per magistrum Ricardum de Clifford.

### Hund. Rolls, 4 Ed. I., 1275.

No. X is the very interesting account of Thomas Sherrigge, Bailiff in the early part of the fourteenth century. Compare this with No. VIII., of a little earlier date.

### X.—*Account of Thomas de Sherrigge, Custos of the Bailwick of Dartmoor.*

Facto visu compoti Thome de Sherrigge de exitibus Ballive de Dertemor de annis Regni Regis Edwardi Filii Regis Edwardi Septimo Octavo nono et primo Dimidio anno Decimo. Idem Thomas onerat se de liij$^s$ iiij$^d$ quadrante de Redditu assiso Burgi de Ludeford de toto anno septimo. Et de triginta solidis de firma unius Molendini aquatici ibidem de eodem anno et de octo solidis octo Denariis de Placitis et perquisitis Curiarum ibidem per idem tempus. Et de viginti duobus denariis obola de

perquisitis duarum nundinarum ibidem de eodem anno. Et de
tribus solidis de censura hominum que vocatur advocacio. Et de
centum undecim solidis duobus Denariis de Redditu Assiso
tenencium Regis de Dertemor de eodem anno Septimo. Et de
Trisdecem solidis sex Denariis de mortuo gabulo ibidem de eodem
anno. Et de tribus libris octo solidis duobus Denariis de Finibus
Villarum ibidem de eodem anno. Et de viginti sex solidis octo
denariis de firma unius Molendini aquatici ibidem. Et de sexdecim
solidis octo Denariis de centum faldis ibidem eodem anno videlicit
pro falda duobus denarios. Et de tribus solidis de triginta sex
Faldis de Ludeford et waterualle videlicit pro qualibet Falda de
certa consuetudine uno denario. Et de undecem solidis octo
denariis de redditu viginti octo carbonariorum facientium carbones
in mora de Dertemor eodem anno. Et de quatuor libris quindecem
solidis de placitis et perquisitis curiarum ibidem eodem anno. Et de
sexaginta uno solidis quatuor denariis de tres centum sexaginta
octo equis agistatis in Foresta hoc anno. Et de xii$^{li}$ vi$^s$ MM. dcviij
bobus agistatis in eadem foresta ad quatuor predictas Terminos
videlicit pro Bovi uno Denario obulo. Et de ix$^{li}$ xviij$^s$ receptis de
md$^{ƚ}$ iiij$^{xx}$ iiij$^{or}$ Bobus rediuntibus ad Faldas agistatis ibidem
eodem anno. Et de xl$^{li}$ xix$^s$ iij$^d$ q$^a$ de consimilibus exitibus Burgi
de Ludeford et foreste de Dertemor de toto anno viij$^o$. Et de xlix$^{li}$
xv$^s$ iij$^d$ q$^a$ de consimilibus exitibus Burgi de Ludeford et Foreste
de Dertemor de toto anno nono. Et de vi$^{li}$ o$^s$ viij$^d$ de consimilibus
exitibus eorundem Burgi et Foreste de primo Dimidio anno x$^o$. Et
de vii$^{li}$ xvij$^s$ x$^d$ de exitibus stannariarum de toto anno septimo. Et
de ix$^{li}$ xiiij$^s$ viij$^d$ de consimilibus exitibus de toto anno viij$^o$. Et de
ix$^{li}$ xiiij$^s$ vi$^d$ de consimilibus exitibus stannariarum de toto anno
nono. Et non plus de eisdem annis de exitibus [coignagii *interlined*]
Stannariarum pro eo quod coignagium fuit signatum sub sigillo
Antonii de Pessaigne cui Dominus rex commisit emptionem
Stanni ibidem qui quidem Antonius nullum stannum coigniari
permisserit tempore predicto ut idem Thomas dicit. Et de cxxxv$^{li}$
xvj$^s$ viij$^d$ denariis qua de exitibus Stannariarum et coignagii ibidem
de predicto primo dimidio anno x$^o$.

Summa totius Receptionis cccxj$^{li}$ vi$^s$ xj$^d$ ob.

De quibus ponuntur ei in visu usque super compotum suum ix$^s$
pro decima soluta persone Ecclesie de Ludeford pro averiis agistatis
in predicta Foresta de Dertemor predicto anno septimo et xlij$^s$
pro potura et stipendiis sex forestariorum custodiencium Forestam
per idem tempus videlicit cuilibet eorum vii$^s$ [per annum *interlined*] et xx$^s$ pro expensis eorundem tempore Fennacionis*
videlicit cuilibet eorum iij$^s$ iiij$^d$. Et lj$^s$ pro vadiis et stipendiis octo
pastorum custodiencium averia agistata in foresta predicta, a Festo
Invencionis Sancte Crucis usque in Crastinum Assumptionis Beate

---

*Fanning time. E.S.

Marie per quindecim septimanas videlicet cuilibet eorum pro vadiis suis per septimanam iij$^d$ ob. et pro Stipendiis ij$^s$ per idem tempus. Et xiij$^s$ iiij$^d$ in emendacione et reparacione domorum Regis de Pushull. Et viij$^{li}$ xiij$^s$ pro stipendiis et potura Fo [restariorum ut supra et aliis *interlined*] misis et expensis factis apud Ludeford et Dertemor anno viij°. et viij$^{li}$ xiij$^s$ de consimilibus misis et expensis factis ibidem toto anno ix°. Et xxj$^s$ in stipendiis sex forestariorum custodencium forestam predictam predicto primo dimidio anno x°. Et x$^{li}$ pro decima soluta Episcopo Exonie de exitibus coignagii Stannarie pro ultimo [dimidio *interlined*] anno nono et predicto primo dimidio anno x°. Et xxj$^{li}$ v$^s$ x$^d$ pro vadiis predicti custodis per totum tempus predictum capientis [*captum*] per diem iiij$^d$ sicut allocatum Thome de Sweynes nuper costodi ibidem.

Summa expensarum lviij$^{li}$ xix$^s$ ij$^d$. Et debitorum cciij$^{li}$ vii$^s$ ix$^d$ ob°. De quibus solvit cxvi$^{li}$ xiij$^s$ iiij$^d$ per quatuor tallias de Scaccario quos ostendit et debit cxxxv$^{li}$ xiiij$^s$ v$^d$ ob. De quibus solvit Nicholas de Ceriolo Mercatori de Janua* [cc marcas *interlined*] per breve Regis et literam ipsius Nicholai recepcionem dictarum ducentarum marcarum testificantem et debit xlvij$^s$ ix$^d$ ob.

Indorsed, Visus compotus Thome de Sherrigg de mora de Dertemor facti per J. de Foxle.

Augmentation Office. Misc. Records, late Queen's Remembrancer, 7, 8, 9, and 10, Edw. II., 1314-17.

Number XI is a writ and return to the same in the 12 year of Richard II., 1388, respecting rights of pasture in and about the Forest. The enquiry was held at Chagford.

*XI.—Writ directing an enquiry with respect to depasturing cattle in and about Dartmoor Forest.*

Rex dilectis et fidelibus suis Johanni di Rentwode chivalier et Johanni Copleston Senescallo nostro in comitatu Devon. Salutem, Monstravit nobis dilectus et fidelis noster Ricardus de Abberbury Chivaler, qui propiua herbagii Foreste de Dertemor in Comitatu predicto percepit et a longo tempore perceperit quod cum antiquitus consuetum fuisset quod quilibet homo extra Forestam predictam commorans qui boves vaccas seu alia animalia in Foresta predicta depascentia optinebat pro quolibet hujus-modi animali unum denarium et obolum solveret ac postmodum per covinam Forestariorum ibidem propter eorum singulare commodum et

---

*? Genoa.

emolumentum fuisset ordinatum quod quilibet hujus-modi homo
pro omnibus animalibus suis in Foresta predicta depascentibus
tres denarios per annum solvere deberet unde nos duos denarios
inde et Forestarius ibidem tercium denarium qui faldagium
nuncupatur habueremus quorum quidem trium denariorum solucio
per tempus non modicum continuata fuit, quousque Johannes
Debernon et alii Ministri nostri dampnum et exhereditacionem
que in hac parte sustinere deberemus in futuro plenius propicientes
[? pro *perspicientes*] hujus usum penitus amoverunt et in priori
antiqua consuetudine posuerunt ac jam pro eo quod auditores
nostri ac compotum ibidem nomine nostro audiendum deputati
faldagium predictum in libris compotorum ibidem invenerunt,
ministros ipsius Ricardi ad computandum coram eis de tribus
denariis predictis pro quolibet faldagio ibidem indebite onerarunt
in ipsius Ricardi dampnum et dispendium manifesta, unde nobis
supplicavit sibi per nos de remedio congruo provideri. Nos volentes
super veritate et certitudine materie predicte per vos plenius
cerciorari assignavimus vos ad inquirendum per sacramentum
proborum et legalium hominum de comitatu predicto tam infra
libertates quam extra per quos rei veritas melius sciri poterit de
omnibus et singulis premissis ac aliis articulis et circumstanciis ea
qualiter cumque concernentibus plenius veritatem et ideo vobis
mandamus quod ad certos dies et loca quos ad hoc provideritis
super premissis diligentem faciatis inquisitionem et eam distincte
et aperte factam nobis in cancellariam nostram sub sigillis vestris
et sigillis eorum per quos facta fuerit citra quindecim Festi Sancti
Michaelis proximi futuri mittatis et hoc breve. Mandavimus
enim vicecomito nostro commitatus predicti quod at certos &c.,
quos ei scire faciatas venire faciatis coram vobis tot &c., de
Balliva sua tam infra libertates quam extra per quos &c., et
inquiri. In cujus &c., Teste Rege apud Westmonasterium 25 Die
Junii [1388].

Inquisitio capta apud Chaggeford die mercurii proxima ante
Festum Sancti Michaelis anno Regni Regis Ricardi secundi
duodecimo coram Johanne Rentwode Chivaler et Johanne
Copleston Senescallo Domini Regis in Comitatu Devon virtute
cujusdam commissionis Domini eis directi per sacramentum
Johannis Yunglyng Willielmi Clonaburgh Johannis Gorsenne
Radulphi Durg Thome Pytton, Johannis Ayss.........Willielmi
Walwyn Willielmi Smythe Stephani Corvyng Roberti.........
Thome Carneslegh et Johannis Thomas Qui dicunt per sacramentum suam quod antiquitus consuetum fuisset et adhuc est talis
consuetudo quod omnes homines in Foresta de Dertemore boves
vaccas boviculos sue alia animalia depascentia habentes et extra
dictam Forestam et certas villatas prope et circa eandem commorantes unum denarium et obolum pro quolibet hujus-modi animali

per annum reddere deberent et adhuc reddent et dicunt quod omnes illi homines commorantes in villatis predictis certos annuales redditus vocatos Fyn de Vile semper reddere consueverunt et adhuc reddunt pro averiis suis in predicta Foresta inter solis ortum et occasum depascentibus et ultra in eadem non commorantibus noctu. Item dicunt quod quondam fuit talis consuetudo quod quilibet homo commorans prope dictam Forestam extra Villatas predictas et juxta eandum Forestam faldam habens et animalia provenientia in falda sua et per diem vel dies in dicta Foresta depascentia pro pastura hujus-modi animalium duos denarios Domino Regi aut Domino dicte Foreste qui pro tempore fuisset annuatim redderet quod adtunc faldagium dicebatur Et quod videbatur Johanni Dobernoun nuper Senescallo Domini Edwardi nuper Principes Walli et Ducis Cornubie Patris Domini Regis nunc adtunc Domini dicte Foreste maximum dampnum et exhereditacionem prefato Domino suo et heredibus suis in salutione et recuperatione dictorum duorum denariorum pro pastura hujus-modi animalium de faldis predictis sic depascentium in Foresta predicta habendum pro majori utilitate predicti Domini sui et heredum suorum statuit et ordinavit quod hujus-modi homines talia animalia et faldas habentes redderent per annum pro quolibet animali unum denarium et obulum sicut ceteri hominum et illos exoneravit de solucione dictorum duorum denariorum et adhuc inde exonerati existunt ut dicunt super sacramentum suum In cujus rei testimonium predicti juratores huic Inquisitioni sigilla sua opposuerunt.

Patent Roll, 12 Ric. II.. Part I., Memb. 35 *in dorso.*

The Charter, an extract from which forms No. XII contains a grant by the King in 1466, to the tinners of Cornwall, of the liberty of taking peat on Dartmoor for melting their tin. The recital shows that at this date, the timber or fuel in Cornwall had been so much destroyed, that there no longer existed in that county sufficient materials for supplying the furnaces of the blowing-houses. It was confirmed by Letters Patent of succeeding sovereigns.

XII.—*Extract from Patent Roll, 5 Edw. IV., containing an additional grant to the tinners of Cornwall of turbary and pasturage in Dartmoor Forest.*

[After reciting that the moors and woods of the county of Cornwall had been so much wasted, that fuel for melting tin could not be obtained in sufficient quantities, or at reasonable prices, and that the coinage had consequently fallen off three hundred marks and more, the King proceeds to grant, for himself and his successors, to the tinners for the time being now or hereafter.]

Quod ipsi et servientes sui infra forestam nostram de Dartemore in comitatu Devon ad libitum suum ingredi et intrare et turbas in eadem foresta in quocumque loco sibi placuerit fodere et succindere, et carbones inde facere, et eos sic factos ab inde in comitatu Cornubie ad hujus-modi stannum suum ibidem fundendum in carrettis sive summagiis vel aliter ad libitum suum, tociens quociens eis placuerit, cariare, abducere et asportare valeant licite et impune absque impeticione * * * * unacum pastura ad ani-malia sua in eadem foresta pascendum tempore cariationis, abduc-tionis et asportationis hujusmodi ibidem existentis : proviso semper quod stannatores predicti solvant pro hujusmodi turbis fodiendis et succidendis et pastura prout stannatores, sive alique alie persone forestam predictam in casu consimili occupantes, solve-runt et solvere solebant, et non aliter nec alio modo in futuro. T. 7 Feb. [1466.]

Article No. XIII is a copious analysis of an account rendered by the reeves and foresters of Lydford and Dartmoor in the reign of Henry VII. In this document all the heads in the former account, already referred to, are repeated with greater detail and more instructive particularity. The old division of the forest into four quarters, or bailiwicks, is here distinctly apparent.

This article is followed by some extracts, No. XIV., from court rolls, relating to the forest. They appear to be selected from the rolls of the leet or law court of the forest, and chiefly concern offences committed by encroaching on the forest or venville commons, neglecting to repair fences, and other delinquencies.

*XIII.—Abstract of Minister's accounts rendered anno regni regis* 18 *Henrici Septimi*, 1502-3. *(Translated from the original in the Augmentation Office.)*

LYDEFORD BOROUGH.—Account of the Reeve there.
*Rents of Assize.*—Of free tenants (i.e. freeholders)...    32s. 11d.
   From lands and tenements without the borough...    25s.   1d.
   A customary payment called " Foldepeny." pay-
     able at Michaelmas    ...    ...    ...    ...    2s.
   Increased rent for the pasture round the castle as
     contained in the court roll, 23 Edw. III., 1349    12d.

*Farm of the Mill* ... ... ... ... ... 22s.

*Issues of Fairs.*—From the fair on the feast of St.
　　Petrock and St. Bartholomew, Apostle, *nil*, this
　　year. In the reign of Edw. III., it produced
　　13s. 11d.

*Perquisites of Courts.*—Pleas and perquisites of courts
　　this year 18d. as appears by the court rolls.

　　　　　　　Sum total of receipts. £4 3s. 0d.
　　Out of which was paid to the Rector of the church
　　　　for tithe of agistment there and throughout
　　　　the Forest of Dartmore ... ... ... £3 0s. 0d.
　　　　　　　　　　Clear receipts £1 3s. 0d.

LYDEFORD MANOR :—Account of the Reeve.

*Rents of Assize* ... ... ... ... ... ... £7 15s. 5¼d.
　　New rent of John Peccombe ... ... ... 9d.
　　New rent of the hamlet of William de Bibraugh
　　　　and Richard Druru for two acres of waste
　　　　inclosed ... ... ... ... ... ... 3d.
　　Similar new rents of small portions of land de-
　　　　mised, chiefly at will, by court roll in the
　　　　following places :—in Wellbrokeland, Dun-
　　　　briggeford (for life), Pillardeswell, Ledtorre,
　　　　Leddercombe, Shirbonescrofte, Driablake,
　　　　Shirlyng, Ordehall, Brodemede, Pollades-
　　　　wallen', Redegripp', Dert, Bromehill.

*Farm of the Mill.*—Demised to the whole homage ... 20s.

*Gable Rent* (redditus gabuli).—For the custom called
　　" More gabull " payable at Easter and Michaelmas 13s. 4d.
　　For a parcel of land in the waste of the lord of
　　　　Polleshill ... ... ... ... ... 4d.

*Perquisites of Courts.*—None here, because the forester
　　of East [Quarter] has accounted for them ; nor is
　　there any account rendered here of moneys arising
　　from censar' (censaria ?) of certain men dwelling
　　within the precinct of the Lordship, because the
　　same forester has accounted for them in the court
　　roll of the East [Quarter]

　　　　　　　　　　　　　　　£9 15s. 1d.

EAST.—Account of the Forester there (that is of the
　　East Quarter)

　　　　　　　　　　　　　　　s. d.
*Arrears* ... ... ... ... ... ... ... 0 2
*Foreign Rents.*—For rent called " Fines Villarum,"
　　22s. 11d. per annum, payable at the Feast of
　　St. John the Baptist, that is to say :—

|                                                                          | s. | d. |
|--------------------------------------------------------------------------|----|----|
| The vill (villata) of Chagford ... ... ...                               | 1  | 0  |
| The hamlet of Tenkenhamhorne ... ... ...                                 | 4  | 0  |
| The vill of Hereston ... ... ... ...                                     | 1  | 8  |
| The vill of Litterford, in the parish of North Bovey ... ... ... ... ... | 0  | 4  |
| The hamlet of Hokyn, the same ... ... ...                                | 0  | 4  |
| The hamlet of Kyndon ... ... ... ...                                     | 0  | 1  |
| The hamlet of North Werthiehed, in the parish of Whitecole (Widdecombe?) ... ... ... | 0 | 4½ |
| Another hamlet in the same parish (not named)...                         | 3  | 0  |
| The vill of Shirwyll, in the same ... ... ...                            | 0  | 3  |
| The hamlet of North Catrowe, in the same ...                             | 1  | 6  |
| The vill of Higher Catrowe, in the same ...                              | 3  | 7  |
| The vill of Grendon, in the same ... ... ...                             | 1  | 0  |
| The vill of Fenne, in the parish of Chagford ...                         | 0  | 4½ |
| The vill of Jurston (Jesson?) the same ... ...                           | 0  | 8  |
| The vill of Willuhede, the same ... ... ...                              | 0  | 5  |
| The vill of Edworthie ... ... ... ...                                    | 0  | 6  |
| The vill of Higher Jurston... ... ... ...                                | 0  | 3  |
| The vill of Chalnecombe, in the parish of Manaton                        | 0  | 6  |

*New Rents.*—New rent of two acres of moorland in the forest of the Lord at Childrest, as demised to Lawrence Hanneworthy to hold in the name of *Launde-bote,* according to the custom of the forest, as appears in the court roll, 9 Hen. VI., (1430-1) 3d.

(Then follows a series of similar new takes in the forest, chiefly of single acres; among them is the following).

The new rent of 3d. from John Wille, of Hille, for the watercourse of the Teynge within the forest beyond the land of the forest, and at the end of the lane, to the mill of the said John at Southill, within the parish of Chagford, to have to him, and his heirs according to the custom of the forest, rendering yearly 7d. as appears in the Court roll, 11 Henry VII. (1495-6.)

|                                                                          | £  | s. | d. |
|--------------------------------------------------------------------------|----|----|----|
| *Agistment within the Forest.*—For agistment of 1785 beasts agisted in this bailiwick going to fold without the forest,* viz. from each head 1d. ... ... | 11 | 15 | 7½ |
| For agistment of two heifers at 2d. a head ...                           | 0  | 0  | 4  |

*In older records the words stand thus:—" agistamentum averiorum agistatorum infra forestam euntium ad faldum *extra* forestam in eadem balliva, et averiorum agistatorum in eadem balliva euntium ad faldum *infra* forestam," Compot. 29 Edw. III.

|  | £ | s. | d. |
|---|---|---|---|
| Customary payment of 5d. a head | | | |
| For 36 Colliers digging turves to make coal for sale | 0 | 15 | 0 |
| For agistment of 60 sheep at ¾qr. a pair*...　　... | 0 | 1 | 10½ |
| For attachment of 39 men trespassing with their cattle within the bailiwick, from each 3d., by custom, as shown by a bill of record in the King's Exchequer at Lostwithiel　...　　... | 0 | 9 | 9 |
| *Issues of the Manor.*—"Censar" of 22 men dwelling within the forest of Dartmore for having the liberty of it, scilicet, from each 2d. by ancient custom†... | 0 | 3 | 4 |
| *Perquisites of Courts.*—Pleas and perquisites of two courts leet, and eleven other courts, this year, including estrays kept beyond a year　...　　... | 3 | 2 | 8 |

Sum total £18　15　7½

*Deductions.*

*Fees and Wages.*—Stipends of two foresters; of a "præhurdarius"‡ to keep the cattle at the prey [præda] of Dunnabridge; of the clerk writing down the particulars of cattle agisted on the moor, and assisting the foresters at the said drift over the whole moor on divers occasions.

　　This part of the account is closed by particulars of money paid over to the proper officer of the Duchy, and of fines respited.


WEST.—Account of the forester there (i.e. of the West Quarter.)

| *Foreign Rents.*—The fines of vills§　...　　...　　... | 0 | 11 | 11½ |
|---|---|---|---|
| that is to say, the vill of Shawe**　...　　...　　... | 0 | 0 | 7 |
| The vill of Brighteworth in the parish of Mewe†† | 0 | 2 | 0 |
| The hamlet of Lonnington, the same　...　　... | 0 | 0 | 2 |
| The vill of Godemewe,‡‡ the same　　...　　... | 0 | 0 | 2 |
| The vill of Mewey,§§ the same　...　　...　　... | 0 | 0 | 2 |
| The parish of Shidford$　...　　...　　...　　... | 0 | 3 | 0 |

---

*7½d. per score in modern presentments.

†This perhaps explains the Lydford account 25 Edward I. ante. No. viii.　In some early accounts this census is treated as a capitation tax on residents, not having land of the lord.

‡This seems to be the person now called the *prior*, i.e. chief herdsman.

§The name of the vills vary in some of the records.

**Shaugh.

††Meavy.

‡‡Goodameavy.

§§Meavy.

$Sheepstor.

|  | £ | s. | d. |
|---|---|---|---|
| The vill of Dennecumbe, in the parish of Walkhampton ... ... ... ... ... ... | 0 | 1 | 6 |
| The parish of Sampford Spanley (Spiney) ... | 0 | 1 | 0 |
| The parish of Whitechurch ... ... ... | 0 | 1 | 0 |
| The parish of Petarsetavie* ... ... ... | 0 | 0 | 5 |
| The vill of Chodlype† ... ... ... ... | 0 | 0 | 5 |
| The vill of Twyste, in the parish of Tavistocke... | 0 | 0 | 2½ |
| The vills of Raddyche and Pytcheclyff ... ... | 0 | 0 | 3 |
| The vill of Margaret Land, in the same parish ... | 0 | 0 | 2 |
| The new rent of one acre of land within the forest, near Plympstapers‡ leased by court roll, 12 May, 14 Henry VII. ... ... ... | 0 | 0 | 1½ |

*Agistment within the Forest.*—For the agistment of 999 cattle agisted within the Bailiwick, going from the fold without the forest, etc. [Then follows a series of entries like those of the East Quarter, and under the same heads, differing only in the number of colliers or cattle].

*Perquisites of Courts.*—Similar to those in the East Quarter.

|  | £ | s. | d. |
|---|---|---|---|
| Sum | 9 | 12 | 2 |

Deductions for wages of Foresters and " Præhurdarius " and for payments as in the East Quarter."

SOUTH.—Account of the Forester of the South Quarter.

*Foreign Rents*—For certain rent called Fines of vills, that is to say ...

|  | £ | s. | d. |
|---|---|---|---|
| that is to say ... ... ... ... ... ... | 1 | 16 | 0 |
| The ville of Helle ... ... ... ... ... | 0 | 18 | 0 |
| The hamlet of Stouton, in Buckfastleigh parish... | 0 | 17 | 0 |
| The vill of Skyridon,§ in the parish of Dene ... | 0 | 0 | 7 |
| The vill of Ugbirough ... ... ... ... | 0 | 0 | 5 |

New rents under this head are various new grants of small customary tenements, as in the East Quarter.

| Agistment within the forest Agistment of 1,830 beasts going from fold without the forest ... | 11 | 8 | 9 |
|---|---|---|---|

(Under this head are other entries like those in the East and West Quarters).

| Perquisites of Courts ... ... ... ... ... | 3 | 15 | 10 |
|---|---|---|---|
| Sum total £17 | 8 | 10¾ |

*Petertavy.
†Cudliptown.
‡Plymsteps.
§Skyridon or Shiredon.

U

£   s.   d.

Deductions and payments follow, as in the other Quarters : at the foot of the account occurs the following entry of some importance as regards the commons adjacent to the forest, formerly known as the Commons of Devon.

" Afterwards he (the forester) is charged with " 1½d. being new rent of Thomas Rawe, John Beare " and others for one acre of land on the common " of Devon, lying neare to Yerme between Erme " Pound and Quyocke Bemefote,* to hold to them " according to the custom of the forest of Dartmore, " as appears by the court roll there of 16 Henry " VII., and with 1½d. of new rent of Thomas " Hanneworthie, John Cole and others for one acre " of land on the common of Devon, lying in the " east part of the Erme between Hortelake and " Whitepytte, to hold to them according to the " custom of the manor and forest, as appears by " the court roll aforesaid."

NORTH.—Account of the forester there (i.e. of the North Quarter).

*Foreign Rents.*—22s. 10½d. for fines of vills, viz.—

| | £ | s. | d. |
|---|---|---|---|
| The vill of Throulegh ... ... ... ... | 0 | 2 | 6 |
| The vill of Collerowe, in the parish of Chagford | 0 | 0 | 7½ |
| The parish of South Tawton ... ... ... | 0 | 7 | 4½ |
| The vill of Sele* ... ... ... ... ... | 0 | 0 | 6½ |
| The parish of Belston ... ... ... ... | 0 | 3 | 0 |
| The vill of Hallestoke ... ... ... ... | 0 | 2 | 6 |
| The parish of Sourton ... ... ... ... | 0 | 0 | 4½ |
| The parish of Briddestowe... ... ... ... | 0 | 2 | 0 |
| The vill of Willesworth ... ... ... ... | 0 | 2 | 0 |

*Agistment within the Forest.*—Agistment of 1397 beasts going from the fold within the forest ...   8  13  7½
(The other entries are similar to those in the other quarters.)

*Perquisites of Courts* ...   ...   ...   ...   ...   1  15  3
Sum total £13  14  0½
The deductions are as in the preceding Accounts.

*Quickbeamfoot.
†South Zeal.

*XIV.—Sundry Miscellaneous extracts from Court Rolls of the
Manor of Lydford and Forest of Dartmoor.*

*West Dartmore.*—Law Court of the Manor and Forest, held
on Monday next before the Feast of St. Luke, 8 Edw. IV.
[1468].

The bailiffs are amerced for default in not distraining Reginald
Cole and others to answer to the Lord the King for enclosing,
emparking, and appropriating two hundred acres of land of the
common pasture of Devon, at Sodilburghill and Dastame Hill,
between the rivers Erme and Aune, to the great damage, &c.

Walter Bradmore amerced for entering on the King's Moor
without License, and digging for turves and coal for eight years
last past, and selling the same and carrying it off from the moor
to places without Venville.

Bailiffs amerced for not distraining Thomas Thurusldon to
answer for keeping eight beasts in the Forest and Common of
Devon for seven years without license, etc.

*West Dartmore.*—Law Court at Lydford, 18 Edw. IV., 1479.

The homage present Walter Abbot and another for permitting
the gate of the Moor at Staledon [*Stalldon between* the rivers
Erme and Yealm] called the Abbot's Gate, to be ruinous, to the
nuisance of the country and they are amerced accordingly.

There are numerous presentments in all the rolls for not
keeping up the fences against the forest and commons.

John Billock, Vicar of Walkhampton, is attached to answer
the Lord for disturbing the Prince's tenants, by suing them in the
Spiritual Court for tithes of cattle depastured in the common of
Devon, near and around the Forest of Dartmore, contrary to the
liberties and customs of the said common and to the prejudice of
the Prince.

*West Lidford.*—Law Court of the Manor and Forest, 16 May,
2 Jas. I., 1604.

The homage present Richard Richards for cutting turves in
the forest, for one inhabiting out of Venville, against the custom
and to the destruction of the land of the forest : He is fined 1s. 6d.

The same 21 Sept., 6 Jas. I., 1608.

Presentment of the inhabitants of Wapsworthie for permitting
Wapsworthie hedge, near the forest, to be in decay :—also of
divers persons not inhabiting within Venville, for depasturing
sheep in the forest.


No. XV. in the series is one of considerable interest, which
was first published in this work. The earliest printed statutes

of the Stannary Parliaments are of the reign of Henry VIII.,
and were amongst the first productions of the press of this
country, having been printed at Tavistock, within the precincts
of the abbey, in the year 1510.   These statutes, or ordinances
were passed at a Crockern Tor convocation, or Parliament of
Tinners, in the year 1494, assembled by authority of Prince
Arthur, then Duke of Cornwall, held in the presence of his
officers, and subsequently ratified by him.   Each of the stannary
towns, Chagford, Ashburton, Tavistock, and Plympton, sent
twenty-four tinners to represent the general body of Devonshire
stannators, and to consult for the common interest and welfare of
the stannaries of that county.

The chief provisions of the statutes are made for the purpose
of regulating the enjoyment of tinworks, that is of tinbounds, as
they are now called, and the blowing or smelting of tin ore.   On
the first head, the most remarkable enactment is one which forbids
anyone to become the owner of tinworks, who possesses landed
property worth more than £10 per annum, excepting those who
claim them in their own freehold.

To what extent such a bye-law, affecting all ranks of the
king's subjects, and not merely the tinners, by whom, or whose
representatives, the law was made, may well be doubted, and it
is questionable whether it has ever been enforced.   But it very
clearly indicates the class of persons who were at this time considered to be alone entitled to the antient franchises claimed by
the tinners, viz :—working or labouring tinners, who pitched their
tinbounds for the purpose of effectually extracting the ore and
supplying the blowing houses.

The provisions for entering a description of the bounds at the
Stannary Courts, and for using certain marks to distinguish the
quality and ownership of the smelted tin, are reasonable, and have
long been in operation in Cornwall.

The exclusion of professional legal advisers from practising in
any Stannary Court is also peculiar to this Parliament, and
entitles it to the name of the *Parliamentum indoctum*, assigned
to a Parliament once held in this country.   It is also a law which
has probbably never been enforced.

*XV.—Ordres and decres set downe anno* 10 *Henrici VII. for the
Tynne Works, A.D.* 1494.

Ad magnam curiam Stannariorum tentam ad Crockerntor

undecimo die mensis Septembris anno Regni metuendissimi Domini nostri regis Henrici septimi decimo coram magistro Johanne Arundell, clerico, prepotentissimi principis domini Arthuri Christiantissimi Regis predicti primogeniti Principis Walliæ Ducis Cornubiæ, Comitis Cestri et Flynt, cancellario, Magistro Roberto Frost elemosinario, Willielmo Uvedale milite, cameræ ejusdem Principis Thesaurario, magistro Hugone Oldom, clerico, et sociis suis commissionariis dicti Principis in Comitatu Devoniæ deputatis ac coram Johanne Sapcote milite, deputato custodis sive gardiani Stannariorum in comitatu predicto. Quæ-dam actus, statuta, et ordinaciones pro bono commodo, utilitate, et tranquillitate Stannariorum in Comitatu Devoniæ predicto per viginti quatuor Juratores de Chaggeford, viginti quatuor Juratores de Aysshperton, viginti quatuor Juratores de Tavistock, et viginti quatuor Juratores de Plympton, quorum nomina, unacum dictis actibus, statutis et ordinationibus, inferius inscribuntur, inactitata edita, stabilata, et auctoritate dictæ curiæ constructa et approbata in forma sequenti.

[Here follow the names of 24 Jurors for each Stannary Town.]

Qui quidem Juratores dicunt presentant et inactitant prout sequitur:

Be it enacted and establysshed by the hole body of the Stayniery in the high Court of Crockerntorr That no person neyther persones having possession of londes and tenements above the yerly value of X£ nor noone other to theyr use be owners of eny Tynwork or parcel of eny Tynworke. But suche as have Tynneworkes or parcell of Tynnworkes by inheritaunce from their auncesters or such as have now any Tynworkes in peasible possession by lawfull title or hereafter shall have within their owne frehold.

Also that no abbot, priour, neyther ony spirituall person nor noone other to their use be owner of eny Tynneworke or parcell of eny Tynneworke but as be or hereafter shal be in their owne freholde other then suche as they have now in peasible possession by lawfull title.

Also that no warden of Staynierey, underwarden, steward, neither understeward ne clerke of the court of the Staynierey, bailyff or underbailyff of Staynierey, neither no forster ne under forster of the More nor none other to their use be awner of eny Tynworke or parcell of eny Tynneworke but such as have the saide tynneworke or parcell of a Tynneworke by inheritaunce from their auncestors or suche as have now eny Tynnworke in peasible possession by lawfull title.

Also yf ony person or persones be owners of eny Tynneworke
or parcell of ony Tynworkes contrary to theyes foresaide acts
after Mighelmasse cometh twelvemoneth, that then he or they
shall forfaite to the Prynce for every Tynnework that he or they
beth so owners of XX£, and the said tynworke or parcell of ony
suche tynworke be forfaited to the said Prince.

Also that from hensforth every Tynner that herafter shal pithe
ony tynworke that at the next lawe court after such pithe made,
the same pither shal entre the hole bondes of the same tynworke
in the same court and the name therof and as well to put in the
names of all those that such pither hath named owners in the
same worke and this uppon payne of XL shillings to be forfaited
to the Prince ; and whosoever pithe contrarie to this that then his
pithe be voide.   And that for eny such entre of ony such bondes
no payment be made therfor to warden, steward, steward's clerke
or ony oder.

Also that th' owners of everye blowing howse shall bryng a
certen marke of his blowing howse to the court of the stayniery
within the precinct wher the said blowing howse is sett byfore
that ony tynne shall be marked withall, to the entent that al suche
markes may be drawen in a boke which shall remayne in the same
court And all tynne to be blown in the same howse to bere the
same marke and the marke of the owner.   And if it shall happen
from hensforth ony marchaunt to bye eny false tynne and so to be
disseyved, that yf he bring to the court the marke of the blowyng
howse and of the owner in metall, let him come theder with
sufficiant evidans and prove that the tynne wheruppon the said
marke was sett was false and untruly medelyd, that they [then]
incontinently the Prince's officers for the tyme being shal make
serche by the said boke who be owners of thoes markes and geve
notice of their names to the warden or his deputie at the cunage
in opyn court, and he forthwith shal committ theym to warde
that oweth the markes and the blowers, and to compell theym to
satisfye the marchaunt of al suche hurt ard damage as he hath
take by such false tynne, and then the blower to remayne in ward
and make fyne as shall be thought resonable by the Prince and
his councill.   And that no money be payed for entre of ony marke
in to the said boke to warden, steward, or steward's clerke or ony
oder.

Also that every owner of tynne that shal bring tynne into any
blowing howse to be blowen and fyned shal bryng a certen marke
in to the said court ther to be put in a boke, as is afore rehersed,
upon payne of X£ to be forfaited to the Prince, without ony payment makyng therfor as is afore said.

Also that no suche owners shal chenge their marke soo ones
marked and emprynted in suche a boke, neyder use eny oder
markes without a reasonable cause shewed and approved by the

warden or his deputie at the cunage in opyn court, and also that
the new markes as they entend to use to be entred and marked in
the same boke withouten ony money paying.  And yf ony tynne
be founde having no markes or marked with ony oder marke then
is comprised in the said boke, that then all suche tynne be forfaited to the Prynce.

Also that no man from hensforth make no synder tynne after
that it is wartered, be it allayed with oder tynne or not allaide, or
eny oder manner of harde tynne without it be marked with this
letter H as well as with the markes of the owners and blowing
howses, uppon payne of forfaitour thereof, th' one half to the
Prince and th' oder half to the ffynder.

Also yf ony man from hensforth shall arreare and make eny
new or chaunge his blowing howse, or ony new man entre into
ony suche howse, that then he shall not occupie the saide howse
unto tyme he hath browght his marke to be drawen in a boke at
the next court as is before rehersed without eny thyng paying,
uppon payne of X£ to be forfaited to the Prince.

Also that from hensforth ther shal no man learned in the lawes
spiritualle or temporalle plede nor be a counsell to make bylle,
plee or answer in ony court of the Stayniery uppon payne of XX£
to be forfaited th' on half to the Prince and th' oder half to them
that wille sue the same.

Also be it enacted that no Tynner nor Tynners be in no wise
reteyned with no maner man of what degre or condicion he be of
by othe, promise, signe, token, liverey or fee, then suche as be
menyall servaunts according to the lawes as is permitted, what-
somever he be shall forfaite unto the Prince every moneth XX
shillings and the receyver XL shillings.

Provided allewey that it be lawfull to every person, what
possession he be of, to pithe, occupie, and enjoye ony tynnework
or tynneworkes within their owne frehold, ony acte or actes above
rehersed or made notwithstondyng.

Et nos Princeps prescriptus omnia et singula actus statuta et
ordinaciones predicta jure prerogativæ nostræ ac cum matura
deliberacione et advisamento consilii nostri ratificamus appro-
bamus et confirmamus ac ab omnibus et singulis stannatoribus et
aliis hominibus nostris firmiter observari in forma suprascripta
volumus et præcipimus sub pena incumbente.   Mandantes insuper
gardiano custodi sive senescallo Stannariæ nostræ predictæ et
omnibus aliis officiariis nostris ac eorum deputatis quod omnia et
singula actus statuta et ordinaciones prescripta observant et
observari faciant et execucioni demandent sicut decet.   In cujus
rei testimonium presentibus sigillum nostrum apponi fecimus.
Datum apud castrum nostrum de Ludlowe tercio die mensis
Aprillis anno supradicto.

This is the earliest order and decree extant.   Later ones in the reigns of Henry VIII., Edward VI., and Elizabeth, are given in Pearce's *Laws and Customs of the Stannaries in the Counties of Cornwall and Devon*, fol., 1725.

No. XVI. is a presentment or finding by a jury summoned in 1609, to enquire respecting the boundaries of the forest, and other matters relating to Dartmoor.   The open commons in the parishes and places adjoining the forest are here called " the Commons of " Devonshire."   It is believed that they are not now familiarly known by that name, though it was certainly long in use, both before and since this presentment, and the term is now coming into use again.   This is printed from a copy certified by the Keeper of the Records at the Duchy Office.

*XVI.—The presentment of the Jury at a Survey Court for the Forest of Dartmore, A.D. 1609.*

At a courte of Survey holden at Okehampton in the countie of Devon the xvith daye of August in the sixth yere of the raigne of our most gratious Sov'raigne Lord James by the grace of God of England France and Ireland Kinge Defender of the fayth, &c., and of Scotland the forty second, before Sr. Willm. Strode Knight, Richard Connocke Esquire Auditor of the Dutchie of Cornwall, Robt. Moore Esquire and Robt. Paddon Gent., Com'issioners by virtue of a com'ission from his said Matie. to them and others directed bearing date the       day of       in the ffyvth yere of his said Maties. most happie Raigne concerninge the Survey of divers honors castles mannors messuages lands tenemts fforestes chases parks and other proffits belonging to the said Dutchie of Cornwall as by the said Com'ission under the great seale of England more at lardge doth and maye appere ;   The jurors then and ther retourned scilt. Edward Skirrett, Walter Hele, Roger Cole, Henrie Burges, Richard Edmond, Gregory Gaye, John Bickford, Hugh Elford, John Masye, Roger Drake, Walter Lillicrappe, John Chubbe, Stephen Taverner, Andrew Haywood, Roger Wickett, Willm. Searell, Robt. Hannaford, John Willes, John Hele, Walter Tookerman, Willm. Mudge, William Ilbert, Thomas Turges, Ellies Harryes and John Parnell, all wch. being sworn to enquire of the boundes and limitts of the Forrest of Dartmoore and of all such pson. and psons. as have interest of com'on there and wth. what beastes and at what tymes and seasons and what other com'odities the same pson. and psons. may usuallie have and take wth. in the said fforest and mannor of Lidford and what proffits and com'odities doe from them yerelie come unto his matie. and to the Lord Prince for the same—And lykewyse what other landes and tenemts. royalties rightes estrayes and proffitts do belong unto his said matie. and Lord Prince lyinge adjoininge and nere to the said Forrest and what right title or occupacon anie pson. or psons. do clayme or ought to have of and in the same, and what yearlie proffitts do arrise and growe out of the said landes and lykewyse what offences trespasses and misdemeanures are com'itted and donne wth. in the said Forrest and landes and by whom : The said jurors uppon good testymonie showed them witnesses sworne, and uppon their own knowledges do p'sent upon the'r oathes as followeth ; FFIRST they p'sent that the bounds of the fforest of Dartmoore as they the said jurors do fynde partlie by the coppies of auncient recordes ptlie. upon the evidence of other p'sons and ptlie. upon their owne knowledge but especiallie as the boundes have been and are used and accustomed to be these as follows.— Beginning at a high hill lying in the north quarter of the said fforest called at this day Cosdon, al's Cosson, and in the old records written Hoga de Costdonne and from thence lineallie eastward by estimacon one mile or more unto little houndetorr wch. in the said records is called (hogna de parva houndetorr) and from thence lineallie to a place named in the said records Thurleston, now as they suppose called Waterdontorr being about three quarters of a myle from Houndtorr aforesaid, and from thence near a myle to Wotesbrookelake foote wch. falleth into Teynge and wch. lake they thincke to be the same wch. is now called Whoodelake, att wch. place they accompt the North Quarter to end ; and from thence nere one mile to Hingeston, al's Highstone, in the east quarter lyinge near ffernworthie hedges, and from thence lineallie nere one mile to Yeston, al's Geston, now com'onlie called Hethstone, and from thence lineallie through a fennye place now called Turfehill, but named in the old records per mediam tubariam de Albereeheved, to a place called Kinge's Oven and in the said record namely Furnum Regis, and from thence to Wallebrookeheade and so alonge by Wallebrooke until it fall into easter Dart, and so downwards by the said easter Dart to another Dart called wester Dart and from thence ascendinge by the said west Dart unto Wobrookefoote wher the east quarter endeth ; and from thence linyallie ascendinge to Drylake, al's Dryewoorke, and from thence ascendinge by Drylake unto Crefeild fford or Dryefeild ford and from thence to Knattleburroughe, wch. they take to be the same that is called in the old records Gnatteshill, and so from thence descending linyallie to Wester Wellebrooke headd and so by the same Wester Wellebrooke until it falleth into Owne, al's Aven, and from thence linyallie to Easter Whitaburrowe and from thence liniallie to Redlake foote whir it falleth into Erme, and from thence liniallie ascendinge unto Arme

headd, wch. they take to be a place named in the same records
Grimsgrove; and from thence to Plimheadd, where the South
quarter endeth ; and from thence linyallie to Elisboroughe and
from thence linyallie to Seward's Crosse and from thence linyallie
to little Hisworthie and so from thence linyallie to another
Hisworthie and so from thence linyallie through the midst of
Mistorr moore to a rocke called Mistorpann, and from thence
linyallie to Dedlakeheadd wch. the thincke to be the next bound
wch. is called in the old records Meuborough, and from thence
linyallie northwardes to Luntesborowe, wch. they think to be the
same that is called in the records Lullingesete, and from thence
linyallie to Wester Redlake between wch. said two bounds the
wester quarter endeth ; and from thence northward to Rattlebrooke
foote and soe from thence to the headd of the same Rattlebrooke,
and so from thence linyallie unto Steinegtorr and from thence
linyallie to Langaford, al's Sandyford, and so from thence linyallie
to the ford wch lyeth in the east syde of the chapple of Halstocke
and so from thence linyallye unto the said hill called Cosdon, al's
Cosson, wher they did begin.

2. Itm. they do also present. that the soyle of dyvers moores,
com'ons, and wastes, lyinge for the most parte aboute the same
forrest of Dartmoore and usuallie called by the name of the
Common of Devonsheere, is parcell of the Dutchie of Cornwall,
and that the ffosters and other officers of his matie. and his
progenitors Kinges and Queens of England have alwayes accustomed to drive the said commons and waste growndes and all the
commons, moores and wasts of other men (lyinge in lyke manner
about the said fforest) home to the corne hedges and leape yeates
round about the same Common and fforest, some few places onlie
exempted, and that the said ffosters and officers have taken and
gathered to his matie's. use at the tymes of dryft within the same
commons such proffitts and other duties as they have and ought
to do within the said fforest ; how be it they intend not herebye
to prejudice the particular rightes wch. anie persons do clayme for
themselves or their ten'nts in anie commons or sev'all growndes in
or adjoyninge to the said common or fforest, but do leave the same
to judgment of the lawe and to the justnesse of their tytles wch.
they make to the same.

3. Itm. more they do present that all the Kinge's ten'nts wch. are
Venvill have accustomed and used to have and take tyme out of
minde in and uppon the forrest of Dartmoore all thinges that
maye doe them good, savinge vert (whch. they take to be green
oke) and venson, payinge for the same their Venvill rents and
other dues as hath been tyme out of mynde accustomed, and
doinge their suits and services to his maties. courtes of the
mannor and forreste of Dartmoore aforesaid, and also excepting
night rest, for the wch. everie one of them have of long tyme out

of mynde yerelie payde or ought to paye iiid., commonlye called
a *grasewait*, and also to have and take tyme out of mynde common
of pasture for all manner their beastes, shepe, and cattle in and
upon all the moores, wastes, and com'ons, usuallie called the
Common of Devonshere, and also turves, vagges, heath, stone,
cole and other thinges according to their custombes, payinge
nothinge for the same but the renttes dues and services aforesaid,
neverthelesse their meaninge is that the Venvill men ought not to
turne or put into the said fforest or common at anie tyme or tymes
anie more or other beastes and cattell then they can or maye
usuallie winter in and upon their tenements and growndes lyinge
within Venvill.

4. Itm. further they present that no stranger ought to turne or
put to pasture into the said forrest of Dartmoor anie sheepe, or
pigges, and that such strangers as have donne so have been
usuallie presented at Lidford for the same, and that the owners of
such pigges as have subverted and spoyled the soyle of the said
forest are often presented for the same at Lidford and so are to be
fyned by the steward there. And as touchinge the dryftes made
yerelie in the said fforest and commons adjoyninge for his Matie.
they referre it to the forrest men being also ten'nts of the forrest
and manor aforesaid wch. have presented the same, wth. the
orders and custombes thereof.

5. Itm. they do present that one Edward Ashe in the sommer
tyme 1607 was at Sampford within venvill (by his own confession)
at the rowsinge of a stagge and was at huntinge of the same dere
with houndes till he was kild about Blanchdon, wch. was not
lawful to be donne without license.

6. Itm. further also they do present that Willm. Chastie (by
his owne confessyon) kild a stagge wth. a pece or gun nere a
month since about Blacktorrebeare (wch. is part in the fforest of
Dartmoore and part in Venville) and that he did it for Sir Thomas
Wys . . . . and delivered the same to the said Sir Thomas at his
house at Sidnham, at wch. tyme he told him that he had killed the
same dere in the fforest.

7. Itm. also they present that all the waste growndes, moores
and commons wch. have bene heretofore claymed by the ancestors
of Gamaliel Slanninge Esquire and are scituate lyinge in the west
parte of the boundes aforesaid, that is to saye, from Elisboroughe
unto Seaward's Crosse from thence to little Hisworthie, from
thence to great Hisworthie and from thence to Mistorpan and
from thence extendinge towards the auncient corneditches, are
parcell of the Dutchie of Cornwall; without wch. auncyent corne
ditches, that is to saie towards the forrest, the auncestors of the
said Gamaliel Slanninge have caused to be erected certayne howses
and have enclosed some parcells of the said wast grownde, and
that he or his tenants do now use and occupie the same to his or

their own use ; the whole contayninge by estimacion ten thowsand acres as it is specyfied in the exemplificacion of a judgmt. geven against Nicholas Slanninge Esquire ancestor of the said Gamaliel for the same wastes and moores in the ixth yere of the raigne of Queen Elizabeth.

No. xvii. is a Survey, or part of a Survey, of the castle and borough of Lydford (but not of the manor or forest) made by direction of the Commonwealth Parliament under the act or ordinance passed for the sale of lands belonging to the royal family.  It is apparent that the castle was at this time in a state little less ruinous than its present condition.   In the reign of Edward III., the Commons complained that tinners confined there for debt were so well entertained, that they never troubled themselves to pay their creditors [2 Parl. Rolls, 344]. Latterly, the castle lost its character as a place of pleasant retirement for insolvent debtors, and was pronounced one of " the most hanious, " contagious, and detestable places in the realm.   Lyson's Devon, "vol. II., p. 414."

*XVII.—Extract from the Parliamentary Survey of the Borough of Lydford, made 27th August, 1650.*

A survey of the Borough of Lidford, with the rights members and appurtenances situate lying and being in the Co. of Devon part of the Duchy there and parcel of the possessions of Charles Stewart late Duke of Cornwall but now settled in trustees for the use of the Commonwealth, held as of the manor of East Greenwich in free and common Soccage by Fealty only—taken by Edward Hore, George Crompton, George Gentleman, Gabriel Taylor and George Goodman and by them returned the 27 Day of August 1650.

LIDFORD CASTLE.—The said castle is very much in decay and almost totally ruined.  The walls are built of lime and stone within the compass of which wall there is four little roomes whereof to are above stairs, the flore of which is all broken divers of the chiefest beames being fallen to the ground and all the rest is following, only the roof of the said castle (being lately repaired by the Prince and covered with lead) is more substantial than the other parts.

The scite of the said castle with the ditches and courte contain half an acre of land of which the borough of Lidford holdeth the court at the will of the Lord for which they pay the yearly rent of twelve pence.  The said scite is valued to be worth at an improvement besides the aforesaid rent per ann. 5s. The stones about the castle are not worth the taking down, but there are divers parcels of old timber which we value to be worth de claro 6£. There is one part of the tower leaded containing 1445 square feet, every foot containeth (by weight) nine pounds, in all thirteen thousand eight hundred and ninety five pounds which at a penny halfpenny a pound cometh to eighty six pounds sixteen shillings and tenpence halfpenny, but consideration being had to the taking it down and the portage, we reprise, six pounds sixteene shillings tenpence halfpenny, so then it amounteth to, de claro, £80.

*Rents of Assize.*—The Quit Rents or Rents of Assize of the said Boroughe doe amonte to yearly the sum of £3 : 1 : 4 part of which said rents (viz £3) is paid to the Rector of the parish of Lidford in lieu of all the tithes of the Forest of Dartmoore so y$^t$ y$^e$ cleare rent accruing to the Lord amounteth to the yearly rent of one shilling and four pence  1s : 4.

*Rent of the Faire.*—The said Borrough doth pay to the Lord for the faire that is yearly held there viz. at the Feast of St. Bartholomew, the sum of one shilling and sixpence per ann. 1s. : 6.

*Ale Rents.*—There is also paid by the said Borough for Ale waights the sum of twelve pence per annum.  1s.

So that the whole rent which the said Borough payeth to the Lord, with the one shilling for the Castle greene, amounteth to per annum £0 4s. 10d.

No. XVIII. is a Terrier of Lydford parish, from the Records of the See of Exeter.

### XVIII.—*Terrier of the Parish of Lydford,* 1727.

The inhabitants within the Manor of Lidford pay their Tithe Lambs and all the surplice fees and mortuaries to the Vicar of Withycombe. All their other tithe is due and payable in kind to the Rector of Lidford excepting the Tithe herbage of barren cattle kept and depastured in the reputed forest or waste of Dartmoor for which the sum of three pounds is yearly paid at Michaelmas to the said Rector out of the Prince's high rents issuing out of the Borough of Lidford, 4 May, 1727.

THOMAS BURNAFORD, *Rector.*
Stephen Maddaford, Churchwarden.
Valentine Phillips, Side Man.

No. XIX. in this series of Dartmoor documents is a presentment of the Jurors in 1786, which shows *inter alia* the metes and bounds of the Forest, and which is interesting for comparison with the older perambulations.

### XIX.—The Manor of Lydford and Forest of Dartmoor.

At a Court of Survey holden at Lidford Castle in the county of Devon the 13 Day of October in the year of our Lord 1786.

The jurors then and there returned viz., Mr. John Hooper, George Furnis, &c., &c.

To enquire of the rights customs and boundaries of the Manor of Lidford and Forest of Dartmoor belonging to his Royal Highness the Prince of Wales, being parcel of the possessions of the Duchy of Cornwall; and of all such person and persons as have interest or common there and with what beasts and at what times and seasons and what other commodities the same person and persons may usually have and take within the said Forest and Manor of Lidford and what profits and commodities do from them yearly come unto the Lord Prince for the same and likewise what other Lands and Tenements, Royalties, rights, estrayes and profits do belong to the said Lord Prince, lying, adjoining and near to the said Forest and what right title or occupation any person or persons do claim or ought to have of in and to the same and what yearly profits do arise and grow out of the said Lands; and likewise what offences trespasses and misdemeanours are committed and done within the said Forest and Lands and by whom the said Jurors and Homages upon good testimony showed them and upon their own knowledges do present upon their oaths as followeth.

First they present that the bounds of the said Forest have been used and accustomed to these as follows.

Beginning at a hill lying on the North quarter of the said Forest called Cawson Hill and from thence to Hound-torr from thence to Whodelake foot where it falls into the Teigne, at which place the North quarter ends, and from thence by Whodelake to Heighstone or Langstone near the corner of Fernworthy Hedge, and from thence to Hethstone, from thence to King's Oven, from thence to Wallbrook, and so down Wallbrook till it falls into East Dart and then down East Dart till it joins West Dart at a place called Dartsmeet, and from thence up West Dart to Wobrook foot, where the East quarter ends, and from thence up to Wobrook Head, thence to Drylake and Dryfield ford, from thence to Knatteshill, from thence to West Wellebrook head and so down the said brook till it falleth into the Owne or Aven by Huntingdon's Cross, from thence to East Whittaborough, from thence to Redlake foot where it falls into the Erme, and thence up to Erme Head, from thence to Plym Head where the South quarter ends; and from thence to Ellisborough, thence to Sewards Cross, thence to South Hisworthy, thence to North Hisworthy, thence to Mistor Pan, and from thence to Deadlake head, from thence to Steynkaton Huntsborough, thence to West Redlake between which last two bounds the West quarter ends, and from thence to Rattlebrook foot, and so up to Rattlebrook head, from thence to Sourton Torr or Steynkatorr, thence to Laudiford, thence to Milltorr, thence to Rowtor, thence to Chapel Ford at Halstock, and from thence again to Cawson Hill.

Item they present that there are thirty-five copyhold estates of Inheritance and that the copy holders are Tenants by the Verge to them and to their heirs according to the custom of this manor.

Item they present that they take the land in the open court by Surrender to the Steward by the delivery of a mote in the presence of the Reeve and of thence to the Homagers, whereupon the Steward doth grant the same again by the redelivery of the same mote.

Item they present that upon the death or surrender of every Tenant the Lord Prince is to have a Relief viz. one year's Rent.

Item they present that upon warning given by the Forester to the Reeve and by the Reeve to the Tenants they are bound by the custom of this manor to assist all the Foresters of the East, South and West Quarters of the Forest of Dartmore to make as well one Winter Drift for the Colts at their own charge from Ladyday to St. George's Day old stile, and to drive them to Dunnabridge Pound and keep them there in the pound by the space of two days and three nights next after the s⁴ Drift at their own charge and from thence to drive them to Lydford to the Prince's Pound there at their own charge likewise taking of the Forester only one half penny white loalf of bread a piece, as also three several drifts of cattle in the summer time between Midsummer and Lammas Old Stile, commonly called the Summer Drifts, and bring the beasts to the said Dunnabridge and Lydford Pounds at their own charge as is aforesaid taking also of the said Foresters for each of them one half penny loaf of white bread, and for every default herein by any of the said Tenants or of some other sufficient person for him to do this service every tenant making default herein doth forfeit to the Prince the sum of six shillings and eight pence of lawful money of England.

Item they present that if two or more estrayed Colts or Horses do remain at the Surrender day, which is the next Court yearly held after Roodmas [3 May] that the best of such colts or horses the steward takes always for his fee, and the second the Reeve and Tenants do take as their fee, the residue of such estrayes are the Lords of this Manor and are to be sold and accounted for at the next audit.

Item they present that of the estrayed Bullocks the Steward of the Manor hath the first to his own use and the Lord the residue.

Item they present that every estrayed beast as well as horses as bullocks are to remain two days and three nights in Dunnabridge Pound and from thence are to be driven to Lydford Pound, there to remain eight days at the least before the Surrender day, being the Sixteenth day of August Old Stile, and if none come to claim them within that time then they are to be surrendered as is aforesaid.

Item if any Cattle be taken unmarked above the age of one year and one day they are to be seized to the Lords use.

Item they do present that the Foresters ought not make their Summer drifts before they be appointed by the Steward a day certain for every of their several drifts, and that the Steward of Lydford or some deputy for him ought to be at the Pound of Dunnabridge to take and set down in writing the number of the Cattle for which the Steward hath an yearly fee, provided the Forest is in hand.

Item they do present that there are divers Towns or Villages abutting upon the Forest and within the Purlieu thereof and because their Cattle did daily escape into the Forest were at a certain Fine, which being turned into a Rent was called Fines Villarum, and those which dwell within those liberties and pay those rents are called Venvill men.

Item they present that the Venvill men in regard of this rent which they pay do claim common for as many Cattle as they may winter upon their tenements and to cut turf for their own use. If they keep more Cattle upon the Forest than they can winter upon their tenements they are to pay as Strangers for the overplus.

Item they present the ancient custom to be that no man is to put any Cattle into the Forest before he has entered them with the clerk of the Forest when the Forest is not leased.

Item they present that there is a mill on the Scite of a mill within the Forest called Babenny Mill, belonging to the Lord Prince.

The next documents, Nos. XX., XXI., XXII., XXIII., and XXIV., relate to Mining on Dartmoor, and it has been thought well to include them in this chapter for reference, although some of them have been printed in De la Beche's Report, and in the Appendix to Smirke's Report of the Case in the Stannary Court of Cornwall, " Vice *versus* Thomas."

The first—No. XX., is the grant of King John, 29 October, 1201, referred to in Chapter XI.

The second—No. XXI., is the grant of the tithe of the ferm of Tin, by the King to the Bishop of Exeter and his successors— the gift of John not long before his death. Notwithstanding this is called a tithe, it does not seem that anything more than a fixed payment was ever made, which appears to have been a tenth of the whole ferm in the two counties in the reign of King John, the sum being then £16 13s. 4d., as it has been in recent times.

Nos. XXII. and XXIII., are the Charters to the Tinners of Devon and Cornwall, from the Charter Roll, 33 Edw. I. We are obliged to give both, as the greater part of the Cornish charter is, in the enrolment, made to do duty for Devon also.

### XX.—*Charter granted by* KING JOHN, 1201.

JOHANNES, Die gratia, Rex Angliæ, etc. Sciatis nos concessisse quod omnes Stammatores nostri in Cornubia et Devonia sint liberi et quieti de placitis nativorum, dum operantur ad commodum firme nostre vel commodum marcarum novi redditus nostri. Quia stammariæ sunt nostra dominica. Et quod possint omni tempore libere et quiete absque alicujus hominis vexatione fodere stammum et turbas ad stammum fundendum ubique in moris et feodis episcoporum et abbatum comitum sicut solebant et consueverunt et emere buscam ad funturam stammi sine vasto in regardis forestarum et divertere aquas ad operationem eorum in stammariis sicut de antiqua consuetudine consueverunt. Et quod non recedant ab operationibus suis pro alicujus summonicione nisi per summonicionem capitalis custodis stammariarum vel baillivorum ejus. Concessimus etiam quod capitalis custos stammariarum et bailivi ejus per eum habeant super predictos stammatores plenarium potestatem ad eos justificandos et ad rectum producendos et quod ab eis in carceribus nostris recipiantur si contigerit quod aliquis prædictorum stammatorum debeat capi vel incarcerari pro aliquo retto. Et si contigerit quod aliquis eorum fuerit fugitivus vel udlugatus quod catella eorum nobis reddantur per manum custodis stammariarum nostrarum, quia stammatores firmarii nostri sunt et semper in debito* nostro. Præterea concessimus thesaurariis et ponderatoribus nostris ut sint fideliores et intentiores ad utilitatem nostram in receptione et custodia thesauri nostri per villas marcandas quod sint quieti in villis ubi manent de auxiliis et taillagiis dum fuerint in servito nostra thesaurarii et pondera-tores nostri quia nihil habent aliud vel habere possunt per annum pro predicto servicio nostro. Testibus Wilielmo Comite Sarres-

---

*Or dominico.

V

buriæ, Petro de Stokes, Warino filio Geroldi.   Data per manum
S. Wellensis Archidiaconi apud Bonam Villam super Tokam
vicesimo nono die Octobris anno regni nostri tertio.

CARTÆ ANTIQUÆ K. 5. 29 Oct., 1201, 3 John.   [Confirmed by
Inspeximus, 36 Henry III., Rot Cart. m. 18.]


*XXI.—Grant and Confirmation of the Tithe of the Ferm of Tin
to the Bishop of Exeter and his successors, 18 John, 1216.*

Johannes etc.   Sciatis quod, intuitu Dei et pro Salute anime
nostre et antecessorum et successorum nostrorum, concessimus et
presenti carta nostra confirmavimus Deo et Ecclesie Beati Petri
Exon et venerabili patri nostro domino S.* Exon episcopo, et
successoribus suis Exon' episcopis in perpetuum decimam de
firma stangni in comitatibus Devonie et Cornubie habendam sibi
et successoribus suis Exon episcopis de nobis et heredibus notris
in liberam, puram, et perpetuum eleemosynam bene et in pace,
libere et quiete, integre et plenarie, cum omnibus libertatibus etc.
Volumus etiam quod predictus S. Exon episcopus et successores
sui in perpetuum percipiant predictam decimam in eisdem
comitatibus sine aliqua difficultate, etc., per manus illius vel
illorum sui Stangnarium habuerint in custodia.   Quare volumus,
etc., quod predicta ecclesia Beati Petri Exon' et S. Exon' episcopus
et successores sui habeant in perpetuum predictam decimam de
antiqua firma stangni in Com Devonie et Cornubie de nobis et
heredibus nostris in liberam, puram, etc.   Sicut predictum est.
T. 13 Junii. 1216.

Charter Roll. 18 John.

From the Patent Rolls. 10 Edw. II., it appears that the then
Bishop, Walter de Stapledon, successfully claimed the full and
true tithe of the profit and coinage of the Stannaries in Devon and
Cornwall, alleging that the above Charter was only a confirmation
of a previous right that the farm of the Stannary of Devon was
then £100, and that of Cornwall 100 marks, but that he was now
entitled to a larger sum.


*XXII.—Charter of Edward I.*

Rex Archiepiscopis, &c., salutem.   Sciatis nos ad emendationem Stannariarum nostrarum in comitatu Cornubiæ et ad
tranquillitatem et utilitatem Stannatorum nostrorum earundem

---

*This was Simon de Apulia, Bishop of Exeter, from 14 Oct. 1214, to 9 Sept.
1223.

concessisse pro nobis et heredibus nostris. Quod omnes stannatores predicti operantes in Stannariis illis quæ sunt dominica nostra dum operantur in eisdem stannariis sint liberi et quieti de placitis nativorum et de omnibus placitis et querelis curiam nostram et heredum nostrorum quoquo modo tangentibus, ita quod non respondeant coram aliquibus justiciariis vel ministris nostris seu-heredum nostrorum de aliquo placito seu querela infra predictas stannarias emergente nisi coram custode nostro stannariarum nostrorum prædictarum qui pro tempore fuerit, exceptis placitis terre, et vite, et membrorum ; nec recedant ab operationibus suis per summonicionem alicujus ministrorum nostrorum seu heredum nostrorum nisi per summonicionem dicti custodis nostri. Et quod quieti sint de omnibus talliagiis theoloniis stallagiis auxiliis, et aliis custumis quibuscunque in villis, portubus, feriis, et mercatis infra comitatum prædictam de bonis suis propriis. Concessimus etiam eisdem stannatoribus quod fodere possint stannum et turbas ad stannum fundendum ubique in terris moris et vastis nostris et aliorum quorumcumque in comitatu predicto et aquas et cursus aquarum ad operationes stannariarum predictarum divertere ubi et quociens opus fuerit, et emere buscam ad funturum stanni sicut antiquibus fieri consuevit. Sine impedimento nostri vel hæredum nostrorum, episcoporum abbatum, priorum comitum baronum seu aliorum quorumcumque. Et quod custos noster predictus vel ejus locum tenens teneat omnia placita inter stannatores predictos emergentia, et etiam inter ipsos et alios forinsecos de omnibus transgressionibus querelis et contractibus factis in locis in quibus operantur infra stannarias predictas similiter emergentia, et quod idem custos habeat plenam potestatem ad stannarios predictos et alios forensecos in hujus-modi placitis justiciandos et partibus justiciam faciendam prout justum et hactenus in stannariis illis fuerit usitatum. Et si qui stannariorum predic-torum in aliquo deliquerint per quod incarcerari debeant, per custodem predictum arrestentur et in prisona nostra de Lostwythiel et non alibi custodiantur et detineantur quousque secundum legem et consuetudinem regni nostri deliberentur. Et si aliqui stannatorium predictorum super aliquo facto infra comitatum predictum, non tangente stannarias predictas, se posuerint in inquisitionem patriæ una medietas juratorum inquisicionis hujus-modi sit de stannatoribus predictis et alia medietas de forensecis ; et de facto totaliter tangente stannarias predictas fiant inquisitiones sicut hactenus fieri consueverunt. Et si quis eorundem stanna-torum fugitivis fuerit vel utlagatus vel aliquod delictum fecerit pro quo catalla sua amittere debeat, catalla illa per custodem præd ctum et coronatorem nostrum comitatus prædicti apprecientur et per ipsos proximis villatis liberentur ad respondendum inde nobis et heredibus nostris coram justitiariis itinerantibus in comitatu predicto. Volumus insuper et firmiter precipimus quod totum stannum tam album quam nigrum, ubicumque inventum et operatum fuerit in comitatu predicto ponderetur apud Lostwithiel, Bodmynyan, Liskiriet, Treueru vel Helleston per pondera nostra ad hoc ordinata et signata, sub forisfactura totius stanni predicto et quod totum illud stannum coignietur in eisdem villis singulis coram custodo predicto ante diem Sancti Michaelis in Septembre sub forisfactura predicta. Et concessimus pro nobis et heredibus nostris quod omnes stannatores nostri predicti totum stannum suum sic ponderatum licite vendere possint quicunque voluerint in villis predictis faciendo inde nobis et heredibus nostris coignagium et alias consuetudines debitas et usitatas, nisi nos vel heredes nostri stannum illud emere voluerimus. Quare volumus et fermiter precipimus pro nobis et heredibus nostris quod stannatores nostri predicti habeant omnes libertates, liberas consuetudines, et quietancias supra-scriptas, et quod eis sine occasione vel impedimento nostri vel heredum nostrorum, justiciariorum escatorum vicecomitum aut aliorum ballivorum seu ministrorum nostrorum quorumcunque rationabiliter gaudeant et utantur in forma predicta.

Hiis testibus venerabilibus patribus W. Coventrensi et Lychfeldensi, S. Sarum, J. Karliolensi Episcopus. Henrico de Lacy, Comite Lincolniæ. Radulpho de Monte Hemerii comite Gloucestriæ et Herefordiæ. Humfrido de Bolum comite Herefordiæ et Essexiæ. Adomaro de Valencia, Hugone Le Despenser. Johanne de Hastinges, et aliis.

Data per manum nostram apud Westmonasterium decimo die Aprilis.

### XXIII.—*Pro Stannatoribus in Comitatu Devoniæ.*

Rex Archiepiscopis, &c., Salutem. Sciatis nos ad emendationem Stanniarum nostrarum in comitatu Devoniæ ed ad tranquillatem et utilitatem stannatorum nostrorum earundem concessisse &c. [*ut supra*]. Et si qui stannatorum predictorum in aliquo deliquerint per quod incarcerari debeant per custodem predictum arestentur et in prisona nostra de Lydeford et non alibi custodiantur et delineantur quousque secundem legem, &c. [*ut supra*]. Volumus insuper et fermiter præcipimus quod totum stannum tam album quam nigrum ubicunque inventum et operatum fuerit in comitatu prædicto ponderetur apud Tavystok, Asperton vel Chaggeford per pondera nostra ad hoc ordinata et signata sub forisfactura &c. [*ut supra*]. Quare volumus, &c. [*ut supra*]. Hiis testibus, &c. [*ut supra*]. Data [*ut supra*].

Charter Roll., 33 Edw. I., memb. 8.

XXIV.—The next is an extract from the Charter 17 March, 11 Edw. III., 1337, to Prince Edward, the first Duke of Cornwall, granting him the Stannaries of Devon and Cornwall. At the time of this grant the custody of the Stannary of Devon was out on a grant for life to Thomas West, at the ferm of £100 per annum. On the 3rd of October, 11 Edw. III., the King by his letters patent, stating that he had forgotten this outstanding grant when he made the new grant to his first-born son, directed that West should be attendant on the Prince for his rent, and declared that the Stannary should revert to the Prince at the death of West. Rot. Pat. 11 Edw. III. [EDWARD SMIRKE.]

Rex archiepiscopis etc., salutem, etc. Dedimus et concessimus pro nobis et heredibus nostris, et hac presenti carta confirmavimus eidem filio nostro sub nomine et honore ducis dicti loci [i.e. *Cornubie.*] castra, maneria, terras et tenementa et alia subscripta, videlicet . . . . Stannariam nostram in eodem comitatu Cornubie una cum cunagio ejusdem Stannarie, et cum omnibus exitibus et proficuis inde provenientibus, ac etiam expletiis proficuis et perquisitis cur [*iarum*] Stannarie, et minere in eodem comitatu . . . . ac etiam Stannarium nostram in comitatu Devonie cum cunagio et omnibus exitibus et proficuis ejusdem ac etiam expletiis proficuis, et perquisitis cur' ejusdem Stannarie . . . . habend' et tenend' eidem duci et ipsius et heredum suorum, regum Anglie, filiis primogenitis et dicti loci ducibus in regno Anglie hereditarie successuris, una cum omnibus libertatibus, liberis consuetudinibus . . . . et omnibus aliis . . . . ad predicta . . . . stannarias et cunagia . . . . qualitercunque et ubicunque spectantibus, de nobis et heredibus nostris in perpetuum . . . . Que quidem stannarias et cunagia . . . . predicto ducatui presenti carta nostra pro nobis et heredibus nostris annectimus et unimus eidem in perpetuum remansura, ita quod ab eodem ducatu aliquo tempore nullatenus separentur nec alicui seu aliquibus aliis quam dicti loci ducibus per nos vel heredes nostros donentur, sen quomodolibet concedantur, &c.

Per ipsum regem et totum consilium in Parliamento.

Charter Roll. 3 Edw. III.

We have referred to the imprisonment of Richard Strode, page 224. The following is the Act which he succeeded in having passed for his protection.

### XXV.—Anno Quarto Henrici Octavi, Cap. 8.

### An acte concernying Richard Strode.

Lamentablie complaineth and showeth vnto your moste discrete wisedoms in this present parliamêt assembled, Richard Strode gent. of the countie of Devonshyre, one of the burgeis of this honorable house, for the burgh of Plimton in the countie aforesaide, that where the said Richard condescended and greed with others of this house, to put forth certain billes in this present parliament against certain persons, named tynners in the countie forsaid, for the reformacion of the perishing, hurting, and distroy-ing of divers portes, hauens and crekes, and other billes for the common weale of the said countie, the whiche here in this high Court of parliament shoulde and oughte to be communed and treated of.

¶And for because the saide Richard is a tynner, for the causes and maters afore rehersed, one John Furse, tynner, understewarde of the Steimerie in the said countie, in and at foure courtes of the said Steimerie at diuers places and times before hym seuerally holden in the saide countie, he and other have condempned the said Richard in the somme of clx$^{li.}$   That is to wete at euery court day xl$^{li.}$ and that by the procurement of the said John Furse at the said foure severall courtes and law daies in the said Steimerie by him holden, in this maner published and saide, that the same Richard in the last parliament holden at Westminster, wolde auoided and vtterly distroied all liberties, privileges and grannates concerning the Steimerie: by reason whereof the saide Richard, vpon four billes had and made thereof by the said John Furse and others, caused the saide Richard was presented and founden giltie of the premises in euerye of the same courtes in xl$^{li.}$ to be loste and forfaite by hym, by reason of an acte and ordinance by tynners, made and had at a place in the said countie called Crockentor: the tenour of the which acte appereth in a Cedule to this bill annexed; to the which the said Richard was neuer warned nor called to make answere to the premisses, contrarie to all lawes, right, reason and good conscience. And for the execucion of the same one John Agwilliam vpon a surmise by him made to the Kynges highnes of the said con-dempnacion to be to his grace forfaite, thereof attained a bill assigned of xx$^{li.}$ parcell of the said clx$^{li.}$ to be to him granted by the said Kynges highnes; wherevpon the said John Agwilliam and other caused the said Richard was taken and imprisoned in a dungeon and a depe pitte under the grounde in the Castell of Lidforde in the said countie, and there and elles where remained by the space of thre wekes and more, vnto suche time he was deliuered by a writte of privilege out of the kinges exchequere at Westminster, for that he was one of collectors in the said countie

for the first of the two quindecins granted at and in this present
parliament; the which prison is one of the moste annoyous,
côtagious and detestable places within this realme: so that by
reason of the same imprisonment he was put in great parell and
ieoperdie of his life, and the said Richard so beying in prison
and the said John Agwilliam seying the same cruell imprisonment
of the said Richard, entreated and instantly desired one Phillippe
Furse (then beynge keper of the said prison) straitly to kepe the
said Richard in prison, and to put irons vpon him to his more
greater peine and ieoperdie, and to geue him but bread and water
onely, to the extent to cause the said Richard to be faine to
content and paie him the said xx$^{li.}$ And for the same promised
the saide keeper four markes of money; for the which foure
markes the saide Richard for to be eased of his yrons and peinful
imprisonment aforesaid (for sauegard of his life) promised and
graunted to paie the said keeper foure marke: whereof he paied
the saide keper in hande xiii.s. iiii.d. And ouer that the saide
Richard for to be eased of his saide peinfull imprisonment, was
also of necessitee driuen to be bounden to Thomas Denis, deputie
vnto Syr Henry Marney, knight, warden of the said Steimerie, in
an obligacion of the somme of c$^{li.}$ upon condicion whereof partie
is as hereafter foloweth; that is to saie that if the above bounden
Richard Strode, defende and saue harmles the saide Thomas
Denis, and to vse hym selfe as a true prisoner during the time it
shall please the Kynge to have hym prisoner in the Castell of
Lidforde, and also to do nothyng, whereby he shall in the lawe be
deemed out of prison, and other articles comprised in the said
condicion, the whiche the said Richard perfetiy remêbreth not:
wherefore the premises by your great wisdoms tenderly considered,
the said Richard humblye praieth that it maie be ordeined,
established, and enacted, by the Kynge our soveraine lorde, and
by the lordes spirituall and temporall and the commons in this
present parliament assembled, and by auctoritee of the same that
the saide condemnacion and condemnacions of the said cxl$^{li.}$ and
every parcell therof and iudgementes and execucions had or to be
had for the premises or any of them, to be utterly voide against
the said Richarde and of none effecte.

¶And ouer that it be enacted by the saide auctoritee, that all
suites, accusementes, condemnacions, execucions, fines, amerce-
mentes, punisshmentes, corrections, grauntes, charges, and
impositions put or had, or hereafter to be put or had vnto or vpon
the said Richard, and to euery other of the person or persons afore
specified, that now he of this present parliament, or that of any
parliament hereafter shall be, for any bill, spekying, reasonyng or
declaryng of any matter or matters concernyng the parliament to
be communed and treated of, be vtterly voide and of none effecte.

¶And ouer that be it enacted by the said auctoritee, that if the said Richard Strode, or any of all the saide other person or persons, hereafter to be vexed, troubled, or otherwise charged for any causes, as is aforesaide, that then he or they and euery of them so vexed or troubled, of and for the same, to haue action upon the case agaynst euery such person or persones, so vexyng or troublyng any contrarie to this ordinaunce and prouision, in the whiche action the partie greued shall recouer treble damages and costes. And that no protection, essonie, nor wager of lawe in the saide action in any wise be admitted nor received.

Be it enquered for our Soueraigne lorde the kynge, that where as at the parliament holden at Crokerenton, before Thomas Denis, deputie to Syr Henry Marney, knight, warden of the Steimerie, the xiiii. daie of September the seconde yere of the reigne of kynge Henry the VIII. It was ordeined, stablisshed, and enacted that (from the day aforesaide) it shal be lawfull for euery man to digge tynne within the countie of Deuonshire in all places whereas tynne maie be founden. And also to carie the water to their workes without any let or trouble of any person or persons according to our vsages and confirmacions of our charter, and accordyng to our custome out of mynde. And if any person or persons lette trouble, or vexe any man to digge tynne, or to carie water for the same contrary to our olde custom and vsage, and if it be fonden by verdite of xii. men at the lawe daie, he that so letteth, vexeth or troubleth any suche person or persons, shall fall in the penaltee of xl$^{li.}$ as ofte as he so vexeth or troubleth; the one halfe to my lorde prince, and the other halfe to hym that was so letted, vexed, or troubled. And a fieri facias to be warded, as well for my lord prince as for the partie, if one Richard Strode of Plymton, tynner, at the parliament holden at Westminster the fourth day of February last paste, letted, vexed, and troubled one William Rede the yonger and Elis Elforde tynner, and all other tynners in the same parliament for diggyng of tynne in the severall soile of the saide Richard and other persons contrarie to this our acte made.

In thus bringing to a close this chapter of documents we may direct the attention of our readers to the first volume of the publications of the Dartmoor Preservation Association, 1890, in which are printed other valuable Charters, Inquisitions, Extracts from Court Rolls, and accounts, relating to the Forest and Manor.

# CHAPTER XIV.

## THE WILD QUADRUPEDS OF THE MOOR.*

ALTHOUGH little, if any, direct evidence as to what quadrupeds in antient days had their habitat on the high lands of Dartmoor, is obtainable from the fact that much of the outskirts of the Moor, and some of the boglands were, as we have in former chapters shown, timbered with the oak, the alder, the beech, the birch, and the holly (and the existing woods—of which Buckland Woods, Moreton Woods, and the Abbey Ford Woods, at Okehampton, are instances—and the many remains met with in the various bogs by peat-cutters—prove this) and from the fact that among the flint arrow heads and flakes found scattered over all parts of the Moor, many from their size adapted only for hunting or killing smaller beasts or birds and not for warlike operations, it would appear that the wild moorland in days of old as now, was regarded as a happy hunting ground for sportsmen. The numerous flint thumb-stones and scrapers, found all

*I am much indebted to Mr. J. D. Prickman, and Mr. W. P. Stark, for valuable assistance in completing this chapter. I have taken the generic and specific names om LYDEKKER. *Handbook British Mammalia*, 1895. Collections of the Mammalia of Devon—and in them specimens of quadrupeds from the Moor—will be found in the Albert Museum, at Exeter, and in the Museum at the Athenæum of the Plymouth Institution, and there are private collections.

over the Moor, would further seem to indicate the existence there, at all events, in the Neolithic period, animals valuable for their skins. The large collection of Dartmoor flint arrow heads belonging to Mr. F. N. Budd, of Batworthy, the smaller one of Mr. J. D. Prickman, of Okehampton, and those of Mr. R. Burnard, Mr. Francis Brent, and the Albert Museum, Exeter, are all worth inspection.

GREAT HORSE-SHOE BAT.—*Rhinolophus ferrum-equinum.*

This species has never to our knowledge been found on the Moor, although in the first edition of this work, Dr. Edward Moore includes it in his list. We have, however, captured specimens on the borders, and have met with it several times at Plympton. It has inhabited Kent's Cavern, Torquay, apparently continuously, since the age of the Mammoth.

LONG-EARED BAT.—*Plecotus auritus.*

This is a common animal in the county and is frequently noticed upon Dartmoor, its shrill cry, not heard by some, being the certain test for determining the species.

BARBASTELLE.—*Synotus Barbastellus.*

This is a rare species, first noticed by the Devonshire naturalist, Montagu, at Milton, on the borders of Dartmoor, as well as near his own residence at Kingsbridge. We have obtained specimens, as have others, not far from the forest boundary.

NOCTULE OR GREAT BAT.—*Vesperugo noctula.*

Generally common from May to October, but in some years, either not observed at all, or is very scarce. It is our largest species, sometimes measuring sixteen inches from tip to tip of wing.

PIPISTRELLE, COMMON BAT OR FLITTER MOUSE.—*Vesperugo pipistrellus.*

As in other parts of the County, this bat is common upon Dartmoor and its borders.

HEDGEHOG.—*Erinaceus Europæus.*

Common as elsewhere in Devon.

MOLE.—*Talpa Europœa.*

Common—varieties in colour occur.

COMMON SHREW.—*Sorex araneus (vulgaris).*

Common in the lowlands, but Mr. Stark has found this species as well as the Water Shrew, *(Crossopus fodiens)* on the edge of the Moor, over eight hundred feet above the sea-level.

LESSER SHREW.—*Sorex minutus (pygmæus).*

The Rev. R. Douglas, rector of Manadon, was the first to record the occurrence of this species in Devon, in the year 1877, at Manadon. Mr. W. B. Stark has also taken specimens on the borders of the Moor, between eight hundred and nine hundred feet above the sea-level. There are specimens in the Museums at Exeter and Torquay.

WATER SHREW.—*Crossopus fodiens.*

This shrew—the largest of the genus in Britain, is scarce in Devon, but has been observed on the borders of the Moor. As stated above, Mr. Stark has met with it over eight hundred feet above the sea-level. Its habits are very retiring, and the slightest fright sends it to cover, which accounts probably for its apparent rarity.

COMMON FOX.—*Canis vulpes.*

The Fox maintains its existence only by the efforts of sportsmen. If by any chance fox-hunting ceased, in a very short time there would not be a fox throughout the length and breadth of the county.

The necessity for travelling long distances and the rough climate, has led, by the survival of the fittest, in the matter of foxes, to the formation of almost a special breed in the Dartmoor Highlands, having distinct peculiarities. This special fox, known among hunting men as the " Dartmoor Greyhound," from his superior length of limb, his massive head and grey neck, is still to be found, but like his cousin the Broadbury Tiger—the inhabitant of the Broadbury ridge (a spur of Dartmoor, running North-west, and breaking away hard by Sourton, and then running North almost to Holsworthy) is fast being improved off the country.— He is found however, with blood unblemished, on the Moor, from Tavy Cleave in the West, all around the Northern side to Widecombe on the East, and his strong form is in great contrast to the fox on the Southern side—the regions of Ivybridge to Huntingdon Warren. The body of this last named fox is smaller than the other, the face is shorter, the colour more red, and it is said, and we believe with truth, that it is of Continental extraction.

There are four packs of Foxhounds hunting Dartmoor.— " The Dartmoor," of which Mr. Coryton is master, hunting the Southern portion of the Moor :—Mr. Sperling's pack hunting the Western side :—" The Mid Devon," of which Mr. Hayter-Hames and Mr. Windham H. Holley are joint-masters, hunting that portion which is bounded on the West by the Okement river, on the South by Cut Lane to Post Bridge, and from thence on the East by the Prince Town and Moreton Road;—and "The South "Devon," which hunts the Eastern portion of the Moor.

Foxes are found all over the Moor, but the great holding places are Tavy Cleave, Blacka Tor, Teign Head, Fur Tor, Bengay Tor, Woodholes, and the various other collections of granite rocks—clitters—which lie scattered about.

PINE MARTEN.—*Mustela martes.*

MARTEN.—*Mustela foina.*

No doubt both the martens, if we can claim two species, were formerly denizens of the woods of Dartmoor and its borders. We have, however, no information as to their having been observed in the neighbourhood for many years. Specimens said, and no doubt correctly, to be from Dartmoor, are in the Museum of the Plymouth Institution.

POLE CAT.—*Mustela putorius.*

The Pole Cat, Fitchet, Fitchet Weasel, Fitchew, or Foumart, is now almost extinct. The last specimen we have had any intelligence of, was killed in 1887, in the upper part of the Taw valley, between Hanging Stone Hill and Cranmere, by Mr. Williams, of Rewe, and Mr. J. D. Prickman.

STOAT.—*Mustela erminea.*

The Stoat or Ermine, is found all over the Moor and its adjacent lands, but as might be expected, plentifully in the neighbourhood of rabbit-warrens.

WEASEL.—*Mustela vulgaris.*

This is also common in all parts.

BADGER.—*Meles taxus.*

The Badger, Brock or Grey, as he is called, the last of the bear species in our country, is found in many places on the borders of the Moor. Badgers are frequently taken out of their strong holds by the help of small terriers, who mark them to ground either in the rocks or in their earths. They are nearly always found near the cultivated lands, and of course the food question generally determines their locality. Their favourite food is a beetle, found in stale horse dung. From this—coupled with the fact that they are not adapted for long distance journeys, they are rarely if ever found in the central strong-holds of the Moor, but rather in the roughly enclosed fields adjoining the moorland, where the grass struggles with the rocky boulders, and where the moor ponies provide food for the beetles, who in their turn furnish food for the badger. Adjoining these fields—possibly in the banks, or on the hill sides, or in the clitter or Tor, near at hand, Badgers have their home. Near Manadon, where moorland or rough pasture join hand in hand, they are numerous, and have been since the earliest days. Grey Tor, Haytor Down, most probably derives its name from the Badger, as even now they are found in considerable numbers amid the rocky fortresses. At Chagford and at Gidleigh, at Okehampton and at Lydford they are to be found, as well as at Dartmeet, and on the more Southern side, at Dinnicombe, the coverts of the Misses Carew, at South Brent; but at all these places not on the open Moor, but on its borders, where the coverts or the green fields run up in spurs to the Moor.

OTTER.—*Lutra vulgaris.*

The otter is found in all the Dartmoor streams, but as a rule, chiefly in the early part of the year, seeking the deeper waters down stream as the summer draws near. Nowhere can otters be said to be abundant, in fact, to use an Americanism, "he does'nt "plentify," although nearly all the rivers rising on the Moor, have generally one or two in their sea-ward course. The principal packs of hounds are Mr. Cheriton's, from Morchard Bishop, which, under Mr. Budgett, hunt the Teign and the Taw and the combined waters of the Okement and Torridge; Mr. Calmady's which hunt the Okement; and the Dartmoor Otter Hounds which under Major Green, hunt the Dart, the Plym, the Avon, the Tavy, and the southern streams. On one occasion, an almost white, or rather cream coloured otter, was killed on the Dart by the foxhounds.

SQUIRREL.—*Sciurus vulgaris.*

Numerous in woods and plantations on the borders of the Moor.

DORMOUSE.—*Muscardinus avellanarius.*

Also common in the wooded districts about and around the Moor.

HARVEST MOUSE.—*Mus minutus.*

Sometimes found in suitable localities.

MEADOW MOUSE.—*Mus sylvaticus.*

The long-tailed Field Mouse, Meadow or Field Mouse, as it is commonly called, is abundant not only in fields but in thickets

and hedges, and it visits barns and corn-stacks. Mr. Lydekker
suggests that it should be called the Wood Mouse, to distinguish
it from the Field Vole, which is generally known as the Short-
tailed Field Mouse.

COMMON MOUSE.—*Mus musculus.*

BROWN OR NORWAY RAT.—*Mus decumanus.*

Both these are, it is needless to say, common. They both
wander from the ordinary shelter of houses, and Mr. Stark has
found the Brown Rat some distance up the streams on the Moor
in summer time.

COMMON FIELD VOLE.—*Microtus agrestis.*

This, the Short-tailed Field Mouse, like some other mammals,
has been with us for a long time, its fossil remains having been
found in Kent's Cavern, Torquay. It is common, but although not
hitherto a plague here, it may become so at any time if Buzzards,
Hawks, Owls, and others of its enemies are so persistently
destroyed by game-keepers and warreners.

BANK VOLE.—*Microtus glareolus.*

This species we have never met with, although it is said to
have been found on Dartmoor.

WATER VOLE.—*Microtus amphibius.*

Generally but incorrectly called the Water Rat. Common.
Mr. W. P. Stark has met with it during the past winter, 1894-95,
upon the Moor, as well as the preceding species.

HARE.—*Lepus Europæus.*

The hare is becoming scarcer and scarcer every year. It is
found on the outlying borders. In size the Dartmoor hare is
rather smaller than that found in the in-country, probably the food
is not so nutritious, and the climate too austere; be that as it may,
he rarely exceeds six pounds in weight, whilst occasionally a
" Jack " does not weigh more than four, or four and a half pounds.
There are several packs of harriers hunting Dartmoor and the
neighbourhood. Mr. Sperling's hunting Dartmoor and the
adjacent country; Mr. Bragg's the Chagford district; while the
Dart Vale and Mr. Netherton's hunt the southern side. The two
last named packs have an annual Spring meeting for what is
known as " The Bellever Tor Week," and which is of world-wide
celebrity. The Friday's Meet, known as the Lady's Day, resolves
itself into a large picnic on the top of the Tor, and attracts numbers of visitors to the Moor on foot and horseback. In 1893, it
was estimated that there were upwards of two hundred horses,

and nearly one thousand persons on foot or with carriages, were present. This year (1895) there were upwards of one hundred and fifty carriages, besides five hundred persons on foot, and four hundred on horse-back. The Dart Vale Harriers, of which Mr. Skidmore is the Master, hunted with fifteen and a half couples of hounds.

RABBIT.—*Lepus cuniculus.*

Rabbits are numerous upon Dartmoor and its borders, and are preserved in Warrens. Ditsworthy and Trowlsworthy, Huntingdon and Headland—Challacombe—cover considerable areas. Headland has extended greatly during the past few years, and we believe it now joins the adjacent warren of Soussons.

Albinos of most of the smaller mammals are frequently found. The white or cream coloured mole is constantly met with, as well as white hares, rabbits, and rats, and a white otter we have mentioned.

RED DEER.—*Cervus elaphus.*

The bordering districts of Dartmoor contain many evidences of Deer parks. That Okehampton park was a Deer park, and that there were Deer parks in the parishes of Inwardleigh, Lydford, Gidleigh and Chagford, and at Whyddon, and that they were associated with the long line of castles on the northern side —at Winkleigh, at Milsom Castle near Bondleigh, Okehampton, Lydford and Launceston Castles—there can be no doubt.

The Wild Red Deer, in the old days, inhabited these parts, and undoubtedly roamed over the Dartmoor and Cornish hills, in the same way as their descendants in these latter days have their home on Exmoor and the Quantocks. Towards the end of the last century Red Deer were very plentiful upon Dartmoor, so much so, that in consequence of the complaints of the farmers, they were exterminated by the staghounds of the Duke of Bedford, sent down from Woburn for the purpose. Tavistock was so glutted with venison that only the haunches of the animals killed were saved, the rest being given to the hounds* It is a curious fact that scarcely a year passes but that Red Deer, from Exmoor, though it is distant more than forty miles, are seen either on Dartmoor or in the adjacent lands or woods. For the past three years, 1892-3-4, Red Deer have harboured in Buckland Woods. In 1893, a stag was seen several

---

*MRS. BRAY, Tamar and Tavy, 1 ed.. vol. 1., p. 340., 2 ed., vol. 1., p. 294.

times in the covers in the neighbourhood of Sampford Courtenay, and a stag and two hinds were roused on two or three occasions on the South side of Cosdon, and were heard of down the valley of the Teign, in Moreton Woods, afterwards over Hameldon and in the Buckland Woods.  Mr. C. F. Burnard while fishing recently came across a fine stag, near Swincombe, which, obligingly took a flying leap over a six foot wall full in his sight.  In the autumn of 1892, there were two Red Deer in Hembury, and at the same time a stag, two hinds and a fawn took up their abode in Buckland Woods, much to the annoyance of the neighbouring farmers.  Mr. Baldwin J. P. Bastard was asked to have them destroyed, but he, as might have been expected, refused.  In the month of December, the Dart Vale Harriers, by invitation of the squire, came to try to move the deer.  After drawing the woods for about three quarters of an hour, the two hinds and the fawn were found lying under Auswell Rock.  The dogs hit the line, and were off in an instant over the fence into Auswell Common, back into the woods, running close to the wall towards Buckland Village, across the road over the wire fencing on to the Beacon.  Reaching the wall by Birches, the fawn turned back into the wood again, where the pack divided, causing considerable delay to the riders.  Getting on the common, over Redacleave, about six couple of hounds were seen sailing over the bog, below New-House.  Crossing, they dashed over Tanhill Rocks, then to Bonehill.  The two deer were then viewed running abreast, topping Honeybag, about a quarter of a mile ahead of the hounds.  They then turned against the wind, and crossed the Widecombe Valley above Isaford farm. Hameldon was then the point.  Galloping to the iron gate into Blackadon New-take, the valley to Challacombe was crossed, when it was found that one hind had gone up the valley towards Grimspound, and the other, with about five couple of hounds, was pointing towards Grendon.  Racing across Soussons to Grendon, she was left to herself in the plantation, after a smart run of over ten miles.*

Some persons attribute these wanderings of the Red Deer, to their having been harassed on Exmoor, either by the swaleings— as the periodical burnings of the furze and heather upon Dartmoor and Exmoor are called—or to their being driven away by

---

*Western Morning News.  20 Dec., 1892.

the hunting which goes on over that wild moorland, or to the natural wanderings of the male in search of companions, but these reasons do not sufficiently account for them. The wanderings take place at all times of the year, in winter as well as summer, and during periods other than the rutting season, and the wanderers are as often hinds as stags, and sometimes there are two or three together. It is difficult to give an altogether satisfactory reason, but possibly it may be these very deer are descendants of those which formerly inhabited Dartmoor, and it is inherited instinct which takes them so far from their birth-place to the land they "wot "not of." This is of course only speculation, but be it as it may, certain it is the wanderings exist.

It was a stag which gave rise to the saying that "*the "Devil died of the cold in the Parish of North Lew*" which is an outlying parish, some ten miles west of Okehampton. The explanation of the saying is, that a stag was run by the hounds in that direction, that it escaped its pursuers, but wandering down the valley of the Lewer—a small tributary of the Ockment—got into the bogs. Weakened and frightened after its long chase, it was unable to resist the effects of cold and wet, and could not extricate itself, and so perished miserably. Some little time after, a farmer of North Lew discovered the dead body. He thought at first that it was a donkey, but on turning it over, to his great alarm, found its horns, and afterwards its cloven feet. Never having seen a stag, but having an idea of what Satan ought to be like—the possessor of horns and hoofs—he concluded he had come across the corpse of the Evil One, and proclaimed his discovery to his friends and neighbours, who received the tidings with much dismay. The inhabitants of North Lew, it is said, do not now care to hear of this story.

Stag hunting on Exmoor is one of the most popular sports of the day. The late Mr. Fenwick-Bissett did much to raise its general tone, and his successors down to the present—Col. Hornby—have all contributed their quota with the same object. The kennels are at present at Exford, a small village about twelve miles north of South Molton. The opening meet is at Cloutsham—not far from Porlock— early in August. Stags are run from August to the end

w

of October, and hinds afterwards. The pack consists of large fox hounds—being the largest hounds drafted from nearly all the fox-hound packs in England. We may refer our readers for further information upon this interesting subject, to Collyn's Chase of the Wild Red Deer in Devon and Somerset, and Fortescue's Hunting the Red Deer, &c., and in fiction to Whyte Melville's Katerfelto.

# CHAPTER XV.

THE catalogue of Dartmoor birds will be found of a much more limited character than the wildness of its aspect would lead us to expect. The preservation of game, induces a watchful scrutiny of the district, and no sooner does one of the elegant falcon tribe make its appearance, than, under the name of vermin, it becomes a sacrifice to the merciless gin or the gun of the gamekeeper. The progress of cultivation, also, has tended to drive away the antient denizens of the Forest, and the eagle, the bustard, the crane and the kite are never now to be met with. Though the ring-ouzel still clings to the locality, yet it may not be long ere the extension of civilized life may deprive it of its resting-place. The chronicler of the day, however, must take nature as he finds it, and be content to register the changes which time in its progress may effect. The present state of the Moor still exhibits that dreary character, which excites the admiration of the poet, and the explorer of nature will yet discover many a spot where he may fancy himself to be far removed from the busy haunts of men, where the view is bounded by the surrounding tors and sky, and the awful silence which reigns around, will afford ample scope for sublime contemplation, only interrupted perhaps by the sudden flight of the ring-ouzel, scared by his presence from its nest; or he may occasionally be startled from his reverie by the scream of the curlew, or the shrill whistle of the lapwing or golden plover.

The aerial visitants of the moor itself are generally those whose wild nature precludes their descending into the lower grounds; but the greater cultivation on its eastward side has occasioned its ornithology to be there of a mixed character; while around its borders, where good shelter occurs, we shall find most of the rarer specimens belonging to the climate. The frequenters of the uncultivated parts are now chiefly the sparrow-hawk, the hen-harrier, and the buzzard. In the neighbourhood of the solitary turf cottage, may be often found the blackbird, thrush, the redbreast, sparrow, chaffinch, and wren, and occasionally the swallow and martin. Near the water courses are the wagtails, the kingfisher, and the water ouzel. On the open downs and heaths are the skylark, titlark, wheatear, mountain linnet, black grouse, quail, golden, great and grey plovers, lapwing, dotterel, curlew, whimbrel, snipe, purre and sanderling. Gulls are occasional visitants, and the ring-ouzel remains the greater part of the year.

It must be understood that the birds mentioned in the following list are to be found not exclusively on the Moor itself, but there, and in the parts of the country immediately adjacent to it. The letter (*b*) after the name of the species shows that it breeds with us.

Nearly the whole of the private ornithological collections mentioned by Dr. Moore in the Appendix to the first edition of this work have been dispersed. The only ones remaining, I believe, are those of The Right Honble. the Earl of Morley, The Right Honble. the Earl of Mount Edgecumbe, the late Rev. C. T. Collins-Trelawny, and my late father's, with which my own has been incorporated. The collections of the Plymouth Institution, and of the Devon and Cornwall Natural History Society have been amalgamated for many years past, and are now at the Athenæum, and have been recently greatly added to.

For the ornithology of Dartmoor, and of the county generally, the very capital work of Messrs. D'Urban and Mathew, " The " Birds of Devon," 8vo., 1892, must be consulted.

TURDIDÆ.

*Turdus viscivorus.*—Mistle Thrush (*b*). The common name given in Devon to this species—Holme Screech—is derived from its feeding on the berries of the Holly or Holm. Common.

*Turdus musicus.*—Song Thrush (*b*). Common.

*Turdus iliacus.*—Redwing. Common in winter.

*Turdus pilaris.*—Fieldfare. Common in winter. Earlier on Dartmoor than in other parts.

*Turdus varius.*—White's Thrush. One in January, 1881, near Ashburton.

*Turdus merula.*—Blackbird (*b*). Common.

*Turdus torquatus.*—Ring Ouzel (*b*). Common on all parts of the Moor from April to October.

*Saxicola œnanthe.*—Wheatear (*b*). Common.

*Pratincola rubetra.*—Whinchat (*b*). Common.

*Pratincola rubicola.*—Stonechat (*b*). Common.

*Ruticilla phœnicurus.*—Redstart (*b*). Common on the Eastern and Northern borders of the Moor.

*Erithacus rubecula.*—Redbreast (*b*). Common.

*Sylvia cinerea.*—Whitethroat (*b*). Common.

*Sylvia atricapilla.*—Blackcap (*b*). Common.

*Sylvia hortensis.*—Garden Warbler (*b*). Common on the Southern border.

*Mezophilus nudatus.*—Dartford Warbler. Formerly frequently seen in furzebrakes, but we have not seen, or heard of anyone seeing, this interesting little bird for a long time.

*Regulus cristatus.*—Golden crested Wren (*b*). Common.

*Phylloscopus rufus.*—Chiffchaff, Lesser Pettychaps (*b*). Common.

*Phylloscopus trochilus.*—Willow Wren (*b*). Common.

*Phylloscopus sibilatrix.*—Wood Wren (*b*). Common in suitable localities.

*Acrocephalus phragmitis.*—Sedge Warbler (*b*). Occasionally found on the borders, but not so common as nearer the south coast of the county.

*Accentor modularis.*—Hedge Sparrow (*b*). Common.

CINCLIDÆ.

*Cinclus aquaticus.*—Dipper (*b*). Common.

PARIDÆ.

*Parus major.*—Great Tit. Hickymaul (*b*). Common.

*Parus Britannicus.*—Coal Tit (*b*). In the south. Common.

*Parus palustris.*—Marsh Tit (*b*). Common.

*Parus cœruleus.*—Blue Tit (*b*). Common.

SITTIDÆ.

*Sitta cæsia*—Nuthatch (*b*). Scarce.

TROGLODYTIDÆ.
   *Troglodites parvulus.*—Wren (*b*).   Common.

MOTACILLIDÆ.
   *Motacilla alba.*—White Wagtail (*b*).   Scarce.
   *Motacilla lugubris.*—Pied Wagtail, Dishwasher, (*b*). Common.
   *Motacilla melanope.*—Grey Wagtail (*b*).   Common.
   *Motacilla Raii.*—Yellow Wagtail (*b*).   Rare.
   *Anthus pratensis.*—Meadow Pipit.   Titlark (*b*).   Common.
   *Anthus trivialis.*—Tree Pipit (*b*).   Common.

ORIOLIDÆ.
   *Oriolus galbula.*—Golden Oriole (*b*).   Occasionally on the
borders.

LANIDÆ.
   *Lanius excubitor.*   Great Grey Strike.   Has occurred.

MUSCICAPIDÆ.
   *Muscicapa grisola.*—Spotted Flycatcher (*b*).   Common.

HIRUNDINIDÆ.
   *Hirundo rustica.*—Swallow (*b*).   Common.
   *Chelidon urbica.*—Martin (*b*).   Common.
   *Cotile riparia.*—Sand Martin (*b*).   Breeds in a few suitable
places.
   Swallows and Martins after leaving the nest, roost in
large flocks in the low brushwood on the borders of the Moor.

CERTHIIDÆ.
   *Certhia familiaris.*—Creeper (*b*).   Woods and plantations on
the borders.

FRINGILLIDÆ.
   *Carduelis elegans.*—Goldfinch (*b*).   Now very scarce.
   *Ligurinus chloris.*—Greenfinch (*b*).   Common.
   *Passer domesticus.*—Sparrow (*b*).   Abundant.   It has been
said that sparrows are never seen in some Moorland villages—
Sheepstor and Widecombe being mentioned, but there is no doubt
that these places have these birds as occasional visitors.
   *Fringilla cœlebs.*—Chaffinch, Copper Finch (*b*).   Abundant.

*Fringilla montifringilla.* — Brambling.   In some winters common.

*Linota cannabina.*—Linnet (*b*).   Common.

*Pyrrhula europœa.* — Bullfinch.   Hoop. ( *b* ).   Common. Commoner in some years than in others.   Much persecuted by gardeners.

*Emberiza miliaria.*—Corn Bunting (*b*).   Scarce.

*Emberiza citrinella.*—Yellow hammer, Gladdy (*b*).   Abundant.

*Emberiza cirlus.*—Cirl Bunting (*b*).   More frequently seen in some years than others.

*Emberiza schœniclus.*—Reed   Bunting  ( *b* ).   Occasionally found.

*Plectrophenax nivalis.*—Snow  Bunting.   I have a specimen from Roborough Down, killed in October, 1851, and it is sometimes observed on or near the Moor, in autumn and winter.

STURNIDÆ.

*Sturnus vulgaris.*—Starling (*b*).   Common.

CORVIDÆ.

*Garrulus glandarius.*—Jay (*b*).   Becoming scarce.

*Pica rustica.*—Magpie (*b*).   Common.

*Corvus monedula.*—Jackdaw (*b*).   Common.

*Corvus corone.*—Carrion Crow (*b*).   Frequent.

*Corvus frugilegus.*—Rook (*b*).   Common.

*Corvus corax.*—Raven (*b*).   Now scarce, but it breeds still in some unfrequented parts of the Moor.

ALAUDIDÆ.

*Alauda arvensis.*—Skylark (*b*).   Common.

*Alauda arborea.*—Woodlark (*b*).   Common.

CYPSELIDÆ.

*Cypselus apus.*—Swift (*b*).   Common.

CAPRIMULGIDÆ.

*Caprimulgus europœus.*—Nightjar (*b*).   Frequent.

PICIDÆ.

*Dendrocopus major.*—Great Spotted Woodpecker (*b*).   More common then is generally thought.

*Dendrocopus minor.*—Lesser Spotted Woodpecker (*b*). The remark upon the preceding species applied to this one also.

*Gecinus viridis.*—Green Woodpecker, Woodwall (*b*). Frequently met with.

*Iynx torquilla.*—Wryneck (*b*). This too, is a more common bird then is supposed. In 1886 I found a nest in the bank of a running stream in my garden, very near the house, at Plympton.

### Alcedinidæ.

*Alcedo ispida.*—Kingfisher (*b*). Much persecuted, but still frequently met with in the lower parts of the Dartmoor rivers.

*Upupa epops.*—Hoopoe. A rare visitor.

*Cuculus canorus.*—Cuckoo (*b*). Common.

### Strigidæ.

*Strix flammea.*—Barn Owl (*b*). Common.

*Asio otus.*—Long-eared Owl. Occasionally met with.

*Asio brachyotus.*—Short-eared Owl. Infrequent.

*Syrnum aluco.*—Tawny or Brown Owl (*b*). Common.

*Nyctea scandiaca.*—Snowy Owl. The last recorded specimen in this county, of this fine bird, was killed at Ditsworthy Warren, in March, 1876.

## ACCIPITRES.

### Falconidæ.

*Circus æruginosus.*—Moor Buzzard. Formerly frequently observed on and in the neighbourhood of the Moor, but we have not heard of any having been seen for many years.

*Circus cyaneus.*—Hen Harrier (*b*). Formerly a common bird but now seldom seen. I saw a fine male near the Lee Moor China Clay Works, on Easter Monday, 1893.

*Circus cineraceus.*—Montagu's Harrier (*b*). Not uncommon. Old birds seldom seen, but young ones often noticed.

*Buteo vulgaris.*—Buzzard (*b*). Like all other birds of prey, becoming scarce. It was the commonest of the family on Dartmoor and the borders, in former years.

*Archibuteo lagopus.*—Rough-legged Buzzard. Specimens have been obtained from time to time.

*Aquila chrysaetos.*—Golden Eagle.

*Haliaëtus albicilla.*—White tailed Eagle. In the first edition of this work, Dr. Moore says "that the Golden Eagle is associated "traditionally with Dartmoor. The late Mr. Gosling, of Leigham, "who was well acquainted with the subject, informed me that "there was an old standing report that its nest was formerly "known on the Dewerstone." It is very probable that the Dewerstone eagles were *H. albicilla*, of which species, straggling specimens have been noticed, and some killed, on the Moor. Very recently a White-tailed Eagle was seen in the neighbourhood of Ashburton, in July, 1895.

*Accipiter nisus.*—Sparrow Hawk (*b*). Common.

*Milvus ictinus.*—Kite (*b*). Formerly a common bird, and nested on the borders of the Moor; several specimens have been obtained in the county from time to time in recent years.

*Falco peregrinus.*—Peregrine (*b*.) Not often seen on the Moor.

*Falco subbuteo.*—Hobby (*b*). Nests in woods on the borders, but like all its congeners, scarce now.

*Falco æsalon.*—Merlin. Specimens have been occasionally obtained.

*Tinnunculus alaudarius.* Kestrel (*b*). Common.

## COLUMBIDÆ.

*Columba pulumbus.*—Wood Pigeon (*b*). Common in woods on borders of the Moor.

*Columba ænas.*—Stock Dove (*b*). I have been told that Stock Doves breed in some gullies on the Moor, but I am unable to verify the statement.

## GALLINÆ.

*Perdix cinerea.*—Partridge (*b*). Common in parts where shelter is to be had.

*Tetrao tetrix.*—Black Grouse, Heath Poult (*b*). Some still remain in spite of much persecution. Sir Robert Torrens for some time preserved this fine bird. It would be a very good thing if the Duchy authorities would make a charge for a game license, and devote the money thus raised to the payment of two or three keepers, to protect the game. There is a great deal of poaching, and too many lurchers are kept in the Moorland villages just now.

## RALLIDÆ.

*Rallus aquaticus.*—Water Rail (*b*). Common.

*Crex pratensis.*—Land Rail, Corn Crake, (*b*). Common.

*Gallinula chloropus.*—Moor Hen, Water Hen (*b*). Common.
*Fulica atra.*—Coot (*b*). Occasionally on the lower parts of the rivers in winter.

GRUIDÆ.
*Grus communis.*—Crane. A male killed at Buckland Monachorum in 1826. Now in the collection of the late E. H. Rodd, at Trebartha Hall.

LIMICOLÆ.
*Œdicnemus scolopax.*—Stone Curlew, Thick-knee. Occasionally.

CHARADRIIDÆ.
*Charadrius pluvialis.*—Golden Plover (*b*). Formerly more plentiful in summer than at present. It is now an autumn and winter visitant mainly.
*Squatarola helvetica.*—Grey Plover. Occasionally met with, but not common.
*Ægialites hiaticula.*—Ringed Plover, Ringed Dotterel (*b*). Sometimes met with far from the shore.
*Eudromias morinellus.*—Dotterel. Rare now, but has been frequently observed.
*Vanellus vulgaris.*—Lapwing, Green Plover (*b*). Common in all parts of the year.

SCOLOPACIDÆ.
*Scolopax rusticula.*—Woodcock (*b*). Breeds in small numbers, but mainly an autumn and winter visitor.
*Gallinago cœlestis.*—Common Snipe (*b*). Breeds on the Moor, but not in any number; as a winter visitor it is plentiful.
*Limnocryptes gallinula.*—Jack Snipe. A winter visitor. Common.
*Tringa alpina.*—Dunlin. Sanderling. Purre (*b*). "Probably "breeding in small numbers on Dartmoor."—D'Urban and Mathew.
*Tringoides hypoleucus.*—Common Sandpiper (*b*). Breeds. Not often met with now.
*Numenius arquata.*—Curlew (*b*). Breeds on the Moor.

PODICIPEDIDÆ.
*Tachybaptus fluviatilis.*—Little Grebe, Dabchick (*b*). Common. Breeds on the borders.

# CHAPTER XVI.

## Fishes of Dartmoor.*

Most of the streams of Dartmoor are so shallow, so rapid from the abrupt elevation of the ground, and so exposed to sudden freshets from heavy rains, as to be not well calculated for the resort of a large variety of fishes. The principal species are of the family *Salmonidæ;* and even these, from the depredations committed by netters and anglers, have but little opportunity of reaching their full growth—seldom, in the higher grounds, exceeding five or six inches in length, and not often acquiring half a pound in weight, although larger fish from two lbs. to four lbs. are sometimes obtained. They all pass under the name of trout, but in truth there are several other species among them. Mr. Spence was for some time occupied in investigating the progress of the growth of the young salmon, so as to test the assertion of Mr. Shaw,† that the parr is the young of the salmon, at one period of its growth; for this purpose he was supplied weekly with fresh fish from the neighbouring rivers, from February to August. Fishes were obtained distinctly retaining the characters of the parr, during the whole of the months of July and August, at which time it is generally understood that the young salmon of the previous year have lost those marks, have acquired their silvery coats, and gone down to the sea as smolts; at the same time the pinks of the year are increasing in size,

---

*By the late Edward Moore, M.D., F.L.S., revised.

†" Edinburgh New Philosophical Journal," July, 1836, and Jan., 1838.

being in August about five inches long, assuming the smolt dress, while the parrs are mostly eight inches long, retaining their lateral markings, and instead of being silvery, are yellowish in colour like the trout, hence it follows that that this is a distinct fish from the salmon; in this case an opinion opposed to that of Mr. Shaw, would seem to be a necessary consequence.*

The following fishes are found in the rivers of the moor, chiefly in the young state.

### Order, MALACOPTERGII ABDOMINALES—Fam. SALMONIDÆ.

The Salmon—*Salmo salar.* Abundant as salmon-pink (three inches long) and as they become larger, they are found lower down the rivers (until the spring of their second year, says Mr. Shaw) when changing to salmon-smolt, they migrate to the sea. We are not aware that any have been obtained on the Moor as Salmon-peal or Grilse,† which perhaps from the impediments of weirs, hutches, and fishermen, is scarcely to be expected, but occasionally a full-grown salmon has been seen.

Bull-trout, or Roundtail—*Salmo eriox.* The Gray Trout of Pennant. The young is the Whitling of the Tweed; it is found in the Plym and Tavy, whence Mr. Spence obtained specimens: it is also sometimes termed a Truffe.

Salmon-trout—*Salmo trutta.* The White-fish of Devonshire —Sea-trout of Pennant—found in the Dartmoor rivers. Mr. Spence, however, imagined that this had been mistaken for the young of the former.

Par, or Samlet—*Salmo salmulus.* Termed Brandling, or Fingerling; Skegger, on the Thames; Hepper, on the Dart. Very numerous in the Plym and Tavy.

Trout—*Salmo fario.* Also numerous. These fish are some-times obtained by tickling; we have seen half-a-dozen in an hour caught by a farmer's boy in this manner, by wading into the river under shady banks or small bridges.

The very difficult family of the Salmonidæ has been carefully

---

*See Mr. Yarrell's " British Fishes," vol. II., p. 43, 3rd edition, vol I, p. 172, *et seq.*, and " Treatise on the Growth of Salmon in fresh water."

†Young salmon, if under two pounds weight, are termed Salmon-peal, if above that, Grilse. The Bull-trout and Salmon-trout are often erroneously called Salmon-peal.

examined by the late Francis Day, in the second volume of his
work, on the Fishes of Great Britain and Ireland, vol. II., pp.
52-138, 1880-84.

The species given above are those found in our rivers, and the
names given are those by which they are commonly known, but
in strictness they require further examination and discrimination,
before it can be said that they are entitled to the scientific names
applied to them.

### Order, MALACOPTERGII APODES—FAM. MURÆNIDÆ.

Sharp-nosed Eel—*Anguilla vulgaris.* These are found in
great plenty, and are frequently caught by a ground line, baited
with worm, in sheltered nooks during freshets.

The Snig—*Anguilla mediorostris.* At Mr. Spence's, from
the Plym.

Another eel has been obtained by Mr. Spence, which Mr.
Yarrell thinks to be a distinct species.

Francis Day states that the eel is subject to so many variations depending upon local causes, that he does not think we
possess more than one fresh-water species in these Islands, and
which is almost cosmopolitan in its range. See Day, *op. cit.*, vol.
II., p. 242.

### Order, CHONDROPTERYGII—FAM. PETROMYZIDÆ.

River Lamprey—*Petromyzon fluviatilis.* Found in the
Dartmoor rivers, according to Polwhele, but we doubt very much
whether any are found so high up.

# CHAPTER XVII.

## The Botany of Dartmoor and its Borders.*

Dartmoor proper, consists almost entirely of granite, its Tors and Downs rising, in some instances, to a height of 2,000 feet above the sea —the slopes of its hills covered with blocks of broken stone, and its downs with bogs of peat, or scanty pastures of rough grass and sedges. Scarcely a tree is to be met with, except where planted, near farms or buildings, or, as at Wistman's Wood, where a few hundreds of stunted oaks grow from amongst the clitter of the Tors;—or except in the deep and sheltered valleys, through which rush rapid and broken streams.

Its borders however, are composed of other rocks than the granite on which they lie, and slope upwards to a considerable height. These rocks, where broken up and decomposed, form, in some places, a fertile soil; and in the fields, heaths, and meadows on the surface, many flowering plants, some rare, are to be met with—and the Flora is probably not to be excelled by any other district of the like extent, in Devonshire.

If Dartmoor cannot boast of many, or rare flowering plants, not so with the cryptogamous plants—the very circumstances of

*The Botanical Appendix in the first edition of this work was written by Dr. Edward Moore. Mr. Francis Brent has been good enough to furnish the Editcr with the lists contained in this chapter, and to write the introductory portion.

rocks, peat, barren downs, and moist climate, which are unfavourable to the first, are exactly such as many of the latter rejoice in, the moor-stones on the hill sides, the boulders in the rivers, the stunted bushes that fringe the borders of the rushing streams are covered with lichens and mosses, and rare ferns haunt the recesses of the rocks in the sheltered vales.

But Dartmoor has never been thoroughly explored, and there are many portions thereof, especially in the centre, and towards the north and north-east, from which scarcely a record exists of plants that have been met with; doubtless the number might be considerably increased, were this efficiently done. Its borders, however, have been fairly well hunted up, especially towards the west and south, and the records are nearly all that can be required.

The plants of Devonshire, as recorded in the Flora Devoniensis, number about 1,440, of these 774 species, comprised in 71 natural orders and 343 Genera, belong to the Phanerogamous, or Flowering plants, and 660 species, comprised in 157 genera, belong to the Cryptogamous, or flower-less plants.

The plants of Dartmoor and its borders, as recorded in the Flora Devoniensis and other more recent accounts, number about 1,052; of these 546 species, comprised in 70 natural orders, and 296 genera, belong to the Flowering plants, and 506 comprised in 147 genera are Cryptogamous plants, but a comparison is of little use, inasmuch as about 300 species of the plants of the Flora Devoniensis consist of Marine Algæ, the saltmarsh plants of the estuaries, which of course are not to be met with on the high lands of Dartmoor and its borders, or of the smaller Fungi and Gastromyci—but few of which are recorded for the moor— deducting these from the Devonshire plants, their number is reduced to 1,140—which exceeds the Dartmoor plants (1,052) by about nine per cent. only. This comparison must not however be taken as accurate, as during late years many plants have been recorded, especially amongst the Lichens and Mosses, which are not noticed in the Flora Devoniensis.

No separate account of the Dartmoor plants has been published, and in preparing the accompanying lists much difficulty has been encountered, which it is feared has not, in all cases been overcome, so as to render the list perfectly correct, as many plants, known to occur on Dartmoor, have not been recorded as such, or only in such a general way as to leave a doubt as to

whether they have been met with or not. Still it is to be hoped
that these lists are fairly correct.

Of late years the solitude of our grand old moor has been
encroached upon, and the silence of its granite tors and peaceful
vales has been rudely broken. The railway now runs to some of
its border towns, and even almost to the heart of the moor itself.
Cheap trains and coaches carry hundreds of tourists who are
spread over the hills where once were peace and quiet. Some of
these ruthlessly destroy the antiquities—or tear from their
resting places the rare flowers, or still rarer ferns; encouraged by
purchasers, strolling fern-hunters have almost annihilated some
of the few habitats, and after all nearly to no purpose, as few of
our beautiful plants, when taken from their pure native air,
survive their transport to the smoke of the towns—most of them
lingering on perhaps for a few months—ultimately dwindle away
and perish. The so-called Botanical Field Clubs do even more
harm ; to offer rewards for the greatest number of rare plants,
cannot but cause the extremest mischief.

Few of us, accustomed to wander on our moor and take an
interest in its Flora, can have failed to notice the diminution,
it may be said destruction, of some of our rarer Ferns. *Osmunda
regalis* has been utterly eradicated from near Cornwood where it
once grew with fronds six feet high ; *Lastrea Fœnisecii* has been
reduced to a few plants at Shaugh ; the two *Hymenophylla*, once
so abundant in the valley of the Cad, and on the rocks near the
Meavy, can now scarcely be met with, and the little oak fern,
always extremely rare, is entirely gone. *Asplenium lanceolatum*,
ophioglossum and the moonwort, still linger on, the difficulty in
finding them has conduced to their preservation, and it is to be
hoped that those who are acquainted with their habitats, will
hesitate to divulge their localities to others than those who will
carefully protect them. A few years since might be seen, in the
streets of Plymouth, itinerant fern collectors who were exposing
for sale, large mats of hymenophyllum, torn ruthlessly from their
rocks, the scars on which remain in the Meavy and Cornwood
valleys to the present day. A few years since *Meconopis
cambrica* could be found at Lydford Falls, but has not been met
with there for some time.

But some plants have been found for the first time, or re-dis-
covered during the last years. Amongst these may be mentioned
*Pyrus communis*, var, *Briggsii*, found by the late Mr. T. R. A.

Briggs, near Egg Buckland, and amongst mosses *Glyphomitrium Daviesii* has been rediscovered on Cocks Tor. *Atrichum laxifolium*, found on rocks in the Rattle Brook; *Pogonatum alpinum*, on Great Mis Tor and Tavy Cleave, *Tortula papillosa*, on trees near Tavistock, and others might be added.

The following works have been consulted :—

WEST DEVON AND CORNWALL FLORA, Rev. J. Jacob, 1836.
THE PLYMOUTH AND DEVONPORT FLORA, George Banks, 1830.
BOTANY OF SOUTH DEVON, W. S. M. D'Urban, in BESLEY'S ROUTE BOOK OF DEVON, ? 1870.
FLORA DEVONIENSIS, Rev. J. P. Jones and J. F. Kingston, 1829.
FLORA OF PLYMOUTH, T. R. Archer Briggs, 1880. FLORA OF DEVON AND CORNWALL, Isaiah W. N. Keys. MOSSES OF DEVON AND CORNWALL, E. M. Holmes and Francis Brent. SCALE MOSSES, LIVERWORTS AND LICHENS OF DEVON AND CORNWALL, E. M. Holmes. MOSS FLORA OF DEVONSHIRE, Edward Parfitt. IN TRANSACTIONS PLYMOUTH INSTITUTION AND DEVON AND CORNWALL NATURAL HISTORY SOCIETY, vol. II., 1865-69.
LICHEN FLORA OF DEVONSHIRE, Edward Parfitt, in TRANSACTIONS OF THE DEVONSHIRE ASSOCIATION, vols. XV. and XVI. IN ROWE'S PERAMBULATION OF DARTMOOR, 1st ed., 1848. BOTANY OF DARTMOOR, Edward Moore, M.D.
FLOWERING PLANTS AND FERNS, GROWING WILD IN THE COUNTY OF DEVON, Thomas F. Ravenshaw, 1869, and Supplement 1872.

## PHANEROGAMIA—DICOTYLEDONES.

### RANUNCULACEÆ.

| ENGLISH NAMES. | LATIN NAMES. | LOCALITY. |
|---|---|---|
| Traveller's Joy. ...... | Clematis Vitalba ... | Elfordleigh, Yelverton. |
| Wood Anemone...... | Anemone nemorosa | Harford, Bickleigh. |
| Shield Crowfoot...... | Ranunculus peltatus | Yealm Bridge |
| Water Crowfoot...... | R. Aquatilis ......... | Bovey Heathfield |
| Lenormands' Water Crowfoot | R. Lenormandi...... | Shaugh. |
| Lesser Spearwort ... | R. Flammula......... | Dartmoor, Bickleigh. |

x

| ENGLISH NAMES. | LATIN NAMES. | LOCALITY. |
|---|---|---|
| Golden Cup............ | R. Acris............... | Dartmoor. |
| Creeping Crowfoot... | R. repens ............ | Dartmoor. |
| Small Flowered ...... Crowfoot | R. parviflorus ...... | Chudleigh. Ringmore. |
| Corn Crowfoot ...... | R. arvensis............ | Bickleigh. |
| Lesser Celandine, Pilewort... | R. Ficaria ............ | Dartmoor. |
| Wood Crowfoot...... | R. auricomus......... | Chudleigh. |
| Marsh Marigold...... | Caltha palustris...... | Ugborough. |
| Green Hellebore ... | Helleborus viridis... | Ilsington |
| Columbine ............ | Aquilegia vulgaris... | Holne Chase. |
| Monk's Hood......... | Aconitum Napellus | Banks of the Dart, Ilsington. |

BERBERIDACEÆ.

| | | |
|---|---|---|
| Barberry ............... | Berberis vulgaris ... | Chudleigh, Ilsington. |

NYMPHÆACEÆ.

| | | |
|---|---|---|
| Yellow Water Lily... | Nuphar lutea......... | Dartmoor. |

PAPAVERACEÆ.

| | | |
|---|---|---|
| Common Red Poppy | Papaver Rhœas ... | Cornfields. |
| Long prickly-headed Poppy... | P. Argemone......... | North Bovey. |
| Long smooth-headed Poppy... | P. dubium ............ | North Bovey. |
| Welsh Poppy......... | Meconopsis cambrica... | Lydford (Hooker) |
| Celandine ............ | Chelidonium majus | Ivybridge, Shaugh |

FUMARIACEÆ.

| | | |
|---|---|---|
| White climbing Corydalis... | Corydalis claviculata ... | Wistman's Wood, Ilsington. |
| Rampant Fumitory | Fumaria confusa ... | Cornwood, Manaton. |
| Common Fumitory | F. officinalis ......... | Fields. |

CRUCIFERÆ.

| | | |
|---|---|---|
| Charlock ............... | Sinapis arvensis...... | Cornfields. |
| White Mustard ...... | S. alba ............... | Cornwood. |
| Black Mustard ...... | S. nigra ............... | Cornfields. |
| Hedge Mustard ...... | Sisymbrium officinale ... | Common. |

| ENGLISH NAMES. | LATIN NAMES. | LOCALITY. |
| --- | --- | --- |
| Garlic. Hedge Mustard...... | S. Alliaria ............ | Common. |
| Treacle Hedge Mustard ... | Erysimum cheiranthoides ... | Shaugh, Moreton. |
| Wallflower ............ | Cheiranthus cheiri... | Oldwalls, Ashburton. |
| Coleseed .............. | Brassica Napus...... | Moreton. |
| Wild Navew ......... | B. campestris ...... | North Bovey. |
| Meadow Lady's Smock, Cuckoo Flower... | Cardamine pratensis ... | Common. |
| Early Winter Cress | Barbarea prœcox ... | Bovey Tracey. |
| Hairy Wall Cress... | Arabis hirsuta ...... | Ilsington. |
| Watercress ............ | Nasturtium officinale ... | Common. |
| Creeping Nasturtium | N. sylvestre ......... | Maristow. |
| Common Whitlow-grass... | Draba verna ......... | Common. |
| Gold of pleasure...... | Camelina sativa...... | Egg Buckland. |
| Field Pennycress ... | Thlaspi arvense...... | Chudleigh, North Bovey. |
| Naked stalked Teesdalia ... | Teesdalia nudicaulis ... | Cadover Bridge. Widecombe. |
| Treacle hedge-mustard ... | Erysimum cheiranthoides ... | Moreton. |
| Shepherd's Purse ... | Capsella Bursa-pastoris ... | Common. |
| Mithridate Pepper-wort... | Lepidium campestre | Egg Buckland. |
| Smooth Field Pepperwort ... | L. Smithii ............ | Cornwood. |
| Lesser Wart Cress | Senebiera didyma... | Cornwood. |
| Common Wart Cress... | S. Coronopus ...... | Ivybridge. |

### RESEDACEÆ.

| | | |
| --- | --- | --- |
| Wild Dyer's-Weed | Reseda luteola ...... | Ivybridge, Chudleigh. |

### VIOLACEÆ.

| | | |
| --- | --- | --- |
| Marsh Violet ......... | Viola palustris ...... | Swamps, Dartmoor. |
| Hairy Violet ......... | V. hirta .............. | Ilsington, Chudleigh. |
| Dog Violet ............ | V. sylvatica ......... | Ugborough. |

| ENGLISH NAMES. | LATIN NAMES. | LOCALITY. |
|---|---|---|
| Dillenius's Dog Violet | V. canina ............ | Bickleigh Down. |
| Smith's Dog Violet | V. lactea.............. | Bickleigh, Wigford. |
| Heartsease ............ | V. tricolor ............ | Common in fields. |

### DROSERACEÆ.

| | | |
|---|---|---|
| Round leaved Sundew | Drosera rotundifolia | Shaugh, Sheepstor Chagford. |
| Lesser long-leaved... Sundew | D. intermedia ...... | Lee Moor Clay-Works, Dartmoor |

### POLYGALACEÆ.

| | | |
|---|---|---|
| Common Milkwort | Polygala vulgaris ... | Ringmoor, Dartmoor. |

### CARYOPHYLLACEÆ.

| | | |
|---|---|---|
| Deptford Pink ...... | Dianthus Armeria... | Bovey Tracey. |
| Soapwort.............. | Saponaria officinalis | Shaugh. |
| Bladder Campion ... | Silene inflata......... | Ivybridge. |
| English Catchfly ... | S. anglica ............ | Shaugh, Lustleigh |
| Night flowering...... Catchfly | S. noctiflora ......... | Goodamoor, Ivybridge. |
| White Campion...... | Lychnis vespertina | Ivybridge. |
| Red Campion......... | L. diurna      ... | Common, Dartmoor. |
| Ragged Robin ...... | L. flos-cuculi    ... | Bogs, common. |
| Corn Cockle ......... | L. Githago     ... | Fields, Dartmoor. |
| Upright Mœnchia ... | Mœnchia erecta   ... | Moreton, North Bovey. |
| Great Chickweed ... | Cerastium ............ aquaticum | Totnes, Banks of Dart. |
| Mouse-ear Chickweed | Cerastium triviale | Ringmoor Down. |
| Wood Stitchwort ... | Stellaria nemorum | Chudleigh. |
| Common Chickweed | S. media .............. | Dartmoor. |
| Milkmaids ............ | S. Holostea ......... | Common. |
| Glacous Marsh Stitchwort... | S. glauca ............ | North Bovey. |
| Lesser Stitchwort ... | S. graminea ......... | Dartmoor, Bickleigh. |
| Bog Stitchwort ...... | S. uliginosa ......... | Bogs, Dartmoor, Bickleigh. |
| Sandwort.............. | Arenaria trinervis... | Sheepstor. |
| Thyme-leaved Sandwort ... | A. serpyllifolia ...... | Ivybridge. |

| ENGLISH NAMES | LATIN NAMES. | LOCALITY. |
|---|---|---|
| Small-flowered Pearlwort ... | Sagina apetala ...... | Ivybridge |
| Procumbent Pearlwort... | S. procumbens ...... | Dartmoor. |
| Awl-shaped Spurrey | S. subulata............ | Cadover Bridge. |
| Corn Spurrey ......... | Spergula arvensis ... | Dartmoor. |
| Knotted Spurrey ... | S. nodosa .......... . | Ivybridge. |
| Field Sandwort-Spurrey... | Spergularia rubra... | Ringmoor Down. |

ILLECEBRACEÆ.

| | | |
|---|---|---|
| Annual Knawell...... | Scleranthus annua ... | Roborough Down |

PORTULACEÆ.

| | | |
|---|---|---|
| Water Blinks ......... | Montia fontana ...... | Ringmoor Down. |

HYPERICACEÆ.

| | | |
|---|---|---|
| Tutsan.................. | Hypericum Androsæmum ...... | Cornwood, Bickleigh. |
| Dotted leaved St. John's Wort | H. perforatum ...... | Common. |
| Waved leaved......... St. John's Wort | H. bœticum ......... | Egg Buckland, |
| Trailing St. John's Wort | H. humifusum ...... | Shaugh,Ivybridge |
| Small upright St. John's Wort | H. pulchrum ......... | Dartmoor. |
| Hairy St. John's Wort | H. hirsutum ......... | Chudleigh. |
| Marsh St. John's Wort | H. elodes ............ | Bogs, Dartmoor. |

MALVACEÆ.

| | | |
|---|---|---|
| Musk Mallow......... | Malva moschata ... | Tavistock, Chagford. |
| Dwarf Mallow ...... | M. rotundifolia ...... | N. Bovey, Ilsington. |
| Common Mallow ... | M. sylvestris ......... | Common. |

TILIACEÆ.

| | | |
|---|---|---|
| Small leaved Lime | Tilia parvifolia ...... | Buckland, Ashburton. |

## LINACEÆ.

| ENGLISH NAMES. | LATIN NAMES. | LOCALITY. |
| --- | --- | --- |
| Flax Seed ............ | Radiola millegrana | Crownhill Down, Bickleigh. |
| Purging Flax ......... | Linum catharticum | Dartmoor. |
| Narrow leaved Flax | L. angustifolium ... | Bickleigh. |

## GERANIACEÆ.

| | | |
| --- | --- | --- |
| Dusky Crane's Bill | Geranium phœum | Cornwood, Becky Fall. |
| Bloody Crane's Bill | G. sanguineum ...... | Dartmoor. |
| Soft Crane's Bill ... | G. molle............... | Common. |
| Small flowered Crane's Bill | G. pusillum ......... | Cornwood. |
| Jagged Crane's Bill | G. dissectum......... | Dartmoor, Bickleigh. |
| Long stalked Crane's Bill | G. columbinum...... | Bickleigh. |
| Shining Crane's Bill | G. lucidum............ | Peter Tavy. |
| Herb Robert ......... | G. Robertianum ... | Cornwood. |
| Stork's Bill ............ | Erodium cicutarium | Moreton. |

## OXALIDEÆ.

| | | |
| --- | --- | --- |
| Wood Sorrel ......... | Oxalis acetosella ... | Sheepstor. |

## ILICACEÆ.

| | | |
| --- | --- | --- |
| Holly. Holm ...... | Ilex Aquifolium ... | Vale below Crownhill Down. |

## EMPETREÆ.

| | | |
| --- | --- | --- |
| Crowberry ............ | Empetrum nigrum | Dartmoor, Furtor, |

## THYMELEACEÆ.

| | | |
| --- | --- | --- |
| Spurge Laurel ...... | Daphne Laureola... | Harford Bridge, |

## CELASTRACEÆ.

| | | |
| --- | --- | --- |
| Spindle Tree ......... | Euonymus Europæus ... | Bickleigh. |

## RHAMNACEÆ.

| | | |
| --- | --- | --- |
| Buckthorn ............ | Rhamnus Frangula | Shaugh, Ilsington |

## SAPINDACEÆ.

| ENGLISH NAMES. | LATIN NAMES. | LOCALITY. |
|---|---|---|
| Common Maple ...... | Acer campestre ...... | Ivybridge, Cornwood. |

## LEGUMINIFERÆ.

| | | |
|---|---|---|
| Furze ................... | Ulex Europæus ... | Dartmoor |
| Planchons' Furze... | U. Gallii.............. | Dartmoor. |
| Needle Furze......... | Genista Anglica ... | Widecombe, Bovey, Heathfield |
| Common Broom...... | Sarothamnus ......... scoparius | Bickleigh, Meavy. |
| Rest Harrow ......... | Ononis arvensis...... | Cornwood. |
| Black Medick......... | Medicago lupulina | Common. |
| Spotted Medick ...... | M. maculata ......... | Chudleigh. |
| Yellow Melilot ...... | Melilotus officinalis | Chudleigh. |
| Zigzag Clover ...... | Trifolium medium... | Yannaton Down. |
| Purple Clover......... | T. pratense............ | Dartmoor. |
| Dutch Clover......... | T. repens ............ | Dartmoor. |
| Hare's Foot Trefoil | T. arvense ............ | Ilsington. |
| Hop Trefoil ......... | T. procumbens ...... | Common. |
| Lesser Yellow Trefoil | T. minus.............. | Common. |
| Bird's-foot Trefoil ... | Lotus corniculatus | Dartmoor. |
| Least Bird's-foot ... | Ornithopus perpusillus... | Shaugh Hill, Brent Tor |
| Tufted Vetch ......... | Vicia cracca ......... | Dartmoor. |
| Bush Vetch ......... | V. sepium ............ | Common. |
| Common Wild Vetch | V. angustifolia ...... | Bickleigh Bridge. |
| Meadow Vetching ... | Lathyrus pratensis | Dartmoor. |
| Tuberous Bitter Vetch... | Orobus tuberosus ... | Bickleigh. |

## ROSACEÆ.

| | | |
|---|---|---|
| Blackthorn ............ | Prunus spinosa ...... | Hedges, Dartmoor |
| Bullace ............... | P. insititia ............ | Cornwood |
| Wild Plum ............ | P. domestica ......... | Shaugh |
| Wild Cherry ......... | P. Avium ............ | Cornwood, Bickleigh. |
| Dwarf Cherry......... | P. Cerasus ............ | Chudleigh. |
| Meadow Sweet ...... | Spiræa Ulmaria...... | Common. |
| Agrimony.............. | Agrimonia Eupatoria ... | Common, Shaugh |
| Great Burnet ......... | Poterium ............ officinalis ... | Cadover Bridge, Mistor. |
| Salad Burnet ......... | P. Sanguisorba ...... | Bickleigh, Chudleigh. |

| ENGLISH NAMES. | LATIN NAMES. | LOCALITY. |
| --- | --- | --- |
| Field Lady's Mantle | Alchemilla ............ arvensis... | Very common, Walkhampton, Widecombe. |
| Common Lady's Mantle... | A. vulgaris............ | Cadover Bridge. |
| Barren Strawberry | Potentilla Fragariastrum...... | Very common. |
| Common Tormentil | P. Tormentilla ...... | Sheepstor. |
| Creeping Cinquefoil | P. reptans ............ | Shaugh. |
| Silver Weed ......... | P. anserina............ | Common. |
| Wild Strawberry ... | Fragaria vesca ...... | Common. |
| Raspberry ............ | Rubus Idæus......... | Dewerstone, Lydford. |
| Sub-erect Bramble... | R. suberectus ...... | Copse, Shaugh Hill. |
| Common Bramble... | R. discolor............ | Very Common. |
| Roseflowered Bramble... | R. rosaceus ......... | Ivybridge, Harford. |
| Dewberry ............ | R. cæsius ............ | Chudleigh. |
| Wood Avens ......... | Geum urbanum...... | Common. |
| Water Avens ......... | G. rivale.............. | Lydford Fall. |
| Burnet Rose ......... | Rosa spinosissima | Moreton, Okehampton. |
| Downy leaved Rose | R. tomentosa......... | Hemerdon, North Bovey. |
| Common Sweet Briar | R. rubiginosa......... | Lustleigh, Bickleigh. |
| Small flowered Sweet Briar ... | R. micrantha......... | Bickleigh. |
| Dog rose ............... | R. canina ............ | Common. |
| Columnar-styled...... Dog rose | R. systyla ............ | Chudleigh, Bickleigh. |
| White flowered Trailing Rose... | R. arvensis............ | Bickleigh, Chudleigh. |
| White Thorn ......... | Cratægus Oxyacantha ... | Common. |
| Medlar.................. | Mespilus germanica...... | Chudleigh. |
| Wild Service Tree... | Pyrus torminalis ... | Ilsington, Boringdon. |
| Broad-leaved White Beam | P. latifolia ............ | Wigvor Down, Meavy. |
| Mountain Ash ...... | P. Aucuparia......... | Wistman's Wood, Dewer-stone. |
| Wild Pear ............ | P. communis c Briggsii... | Egg Buckland. |

| ENGLISH NAMES. | LATIN NAMES. | LOCALITY. |
|---|---|---|
| Crab Apple............ | P. Malus............... | Dewerstone, Chudleigh. |
| | LYTHRACEÆ. | |
| Water Purslane ...... | Peplis Portula ...... | Wigvor Down, Shaugh. |
| | ONAGRACEÆ. | |
| Broad-leaved Willow-Herb... | Epilobium montanum... | Very common. |
| Great Hairy Willow-Herb... | E. hirsutum ......... | Bickleigh Vale. |
| Small-flowered Hairy Willow-Herb... | E. parviflorum ...... | Ilsington, Bovey-Heathfield. |
| Short-podded Square-stalked Willow Herb | E. palustre............ | Leathertor, Dartmoor, Tory Brook. |
| Enchanter's, Nightshade ... | Circæa lutetiana ... | Cann Quarry. |
| | HALORAGIACEÆ. | |
| Spiked Water Milfoil | Myriophyllum ...... spicatum | Yealm, Cornwood, River Bovey, at N. Bovey. |
| Large-fruited Water Starwort... | Callitriche stagnalis | Pool, Cadover-Bridge. |
| Mare's-tail ............ | Hippuris vulgaris... | Dartmoor. |
| | GROSSULARIACEÆ. | |
| Red Currant ......... | Ribes rubrum   ... | Widecombe, N. Bovey. |
| Black Currant ...... | Ribes nigrum......... | Plym Bridge. |
| | CRASSULACEÆ. | |
| Mossy Tillœa......... | Tillæa muscosa...... | Egg Buckland, Cann Quarry. |
| Everlasting Orpine | Sedum telephium ... | Cornwood, Chudleigh. |
| English Stonecrop... | S. Anglicum ......... | Dartmoor, Sheepstor. |
| Biting Stonecrop ... | S. acre ............... | Dartmoor. |
| Navel Wort, Penny Pies | Cotyledon umbilicus | Dartmoor, Common. |

## SAXIFRAGACEÆ.

| ENGLISH NAMES. | LATIN NAMES. | LOCALITY. |
|---|---|---|
| Rue-leaved Saxifrage | Saxifraga tridactylites...... | Cornwood. |
| Opposite leaved-...... | Chrysosplenium ... | Bickleigh. |
| Golden Saxifrage ... | oppositifolium ...... | Cornwood. |

## UMBELLIFERÆ.

| | | |
|---|---|---|
| Marsh Pennywort ... | Hydrocotyle vulgaris... | Ringmoor Down, Chudleigh. |
| Sanicle.................. | Sanicula Europæa | Common, Chudleigh. |
| Procumbent Water Parsnip | Heliosciadium ...... nodiflorum | Cornwood, Chudleigh. |
| Corn Parsley ......... | Petroselinum......... segetum | Ashburton, Ilsington. |
| Stonewort ............ | Sison amomum...... | Buckfastleigh. |
| Common Goutweed | Ægopodium Podagraria... | Moreton. |
| Pig-nut ............... | Bunium flexuosum | Bickleigh, Chudleigh. |
| Common Burnet...... Saxifrage | Pimpinella saxifraga | Common, Shaugh. |
| Great Burnet Saxifrage... | P. magna ............ | Shaugh. |
| Water Drop-wort ... | Œnanthe fistulosa | Ilsington |
| Hemlock Water...... Dropwort | Œ. crocata............ | Chudleigh, Moreton. |
| Fools' Parsley ...... | Æthusa Cynapium | Common, Buckfastleigh, Tavistock. |
| Fennel ................. | Fœniculum vulgare... | Chudleigh Rock. |
| Wild Angelica ...... | Angelica sylvestris | Common, Chudleigh. |
| Cow Parsnip ......... | Heracleum............ Spondylium | Common, Shaugh, Chudleigh. |
| Wild Carrot ......... | Daucus Carota ...... | Common, Chudleigh. |
| Upright Hedge-Parsley... | Torilis Authriscus... | Buckfastleigh. |
| Knotted Hedge-Parsley... | T. nodosa ............ | Chudleigh. |
| Spreading Hedge-Parsley... | T. infesta ............ | Ilsington. |

| ENGLISH NAMES. | LATIN NAMES. | LOCALITY. |
|---|---|---|
| Rough Chervil ...... | Chærophyllum temulum... | Common. |
| Common Venus-comb | Scandix Pecten- ... Veneris | Common, Cornwood. |
| Chervil................. | Anthriscus sylvestris... | Chudleigh. |
| Hemlock .............. | Conium maculatum | Lydford. |
| Alexanders ........... | Smyrnium ............ Olusatrum | Peter Tavy, Chudleigh. |

### ARALIACEÆ.

| | | |
|---|---|---|
| Common Ivy ......... | Hedera Helix ...... | Common. |

### CORNACEÆ.

| | | |
|---|---|---|
| Dogwood.............. | Cornus sanguinea... | Egg Buckland, Hemerdon. |

### CAPRIFOLIACEÆ.

| | | |
|---|---|---|
| Moschatel ........... | Adoxa................. Moschatellina | Tavistock, Lustleigh. |
| Elder ................. | Sambucus nigra ... | Dartmoor. |
| Dwarf Elder ......... | S. Ebulus ............ | Cann Quarry. |
| Wayfaring Tree...... | Viburnum Lantana | Chudleigh, Ashburton. |
| Common Guelder Rose | V. Opulus ............ | Bickleigh, Ashburton. |
| Woodbine, Honeysuckle... | Lonicera Pericly-menum... | Hedges, Common |

### RUBIACEÆ.

| | | |
|---|---|---|
| Wild Madder ......... | Rubia peregrina ... | Ilsington. |
| Crosswort ............ | Galium cruciatum | Chudleigh. |
| Yellow Bedstraw ... | G. verum ............ | Ivybridge, Chudleigh. |
| Common Great Bedstraw... | G. mollugo............ | Common. |
| Heath Bedstraw ... | G. saxatile..... ...... | Sheepstor, Chagford. |
| Rough Marsh Bedstraw... | G. uliginosum ...... | Gidleigh. |
| Marsh Bedstraw ... | G. palustre ......... | Meavy, Sheepstor |
| Goose-Grass ......... | G. aparine............ | Very common. |
| Rough Corn Bedstraw... | G. tricorne............ | Goodamoor. |

| ENGLISH NAMES. | LATIN NAMES. | LOCALITY. |
|---|---|---|
| Woodruff ............ | Asperula odorata ... | Lidford, Lustleigh. |
| Blue Field Madder | Sherardia arvensis | Very common. |

### VALERIANACEÆ.

| | | |
|---|---|---|
| Great Valerian ...... | Valeriana ............ officinalis | Cornwood, Ugborough. |
| Lamb's Lettuce, Corn Salad | Valerianella Olitoria | Very common. |
| Narrow Fruited Lamb's Lettuce | V. dentata ............ | Shaugh, Moreton. |

### DIPSACEÆ.

| | | |
|---|---|---|
| Wild Teasel ......... | Dipsacus sylvestris | Ringmore, Chudleigh. |
| Devil's-bit Scabious | Scabiosa succisa ... | Very common, Chudleigh. |

### COMPOSITÆ.

| | | |
|---|---|---|
| Milk Thistle ......... | Silybum Marianum | Bovey-Heathfield. |
| Musk Thistle ......... | Carduus nutans...... | Egg Buckland, Chudleigh. |
| Spear Thistle ......... | C. lanceolatus ...... | Common, Dartmoor, Chudleigh |
| Marsh Thistle......... | C. palustris ......... | Common, Bickleigh, Chudleigh. |
| Creeping Plume...... Thistle | C. arvensis............ | Common, Walkhampton, Chudleigh. |
| Carline Thistle ...... | Carlina vulgaris ... | Shaugh, Chudleigh. |
| Lesser Burdock ...... | Arctium minus ...... | Tavistock. |
| Saw Wort ............ | Serratula tinctoria | Shaugh Moor, Holne Chase. |
| Black Knapweed ... | Centaurea nigra ... | Common, Ivybridge. |
| Corn Blue Bottle ... | C. Cyanus ............ | Chudleigh. |
| Greater Knapweed | C. Scabiosa ......... | Egg Buckland, Chudleigh. |
| Corn Marigold ...... | Chrysanthemum segetum... | Cornwood. |

| ENGLISH NAMES. | LATIN NAMES. | LOCALITY. |
|---|---|---|
| Great White Ox-eye | C. Leucanthemum | Very common. |
| Common Feverfew | Matricaria ... Parthenium... | Lydford, Ilsington. |
| Scentless Feverfew | M. inodora............ | Ivybridge. |
| Wild Chamomile ... | M. Chamomilla...... | Bovey-Heathfield |
| Common Tansy ...... | Tanacetum vulgare | Petertavy, Moreton. |
| Stinking Mayweed... | Anthemis Cotula ... | Shaugh Bridge, Chudleigh. |
| Corn Chamomile ... | A. arvensis............ | Moreton, Ilsington. |
| Common Chamomile | A. nobilis ............ | Shaugh, Bovey-Heathfield, Cornwood. |
| Yarrow................... | Achillea millefolium | Very common. |
| Sneezewort ............ | A. Ptarmica ......... | Sheepstor, Moreton, Okehampton. |
| Wormwood............ | Artemisia ............ Absinthium | Petertavy, Cornwood. |
| Mugwort ..... ......... | A. vulgaris............ | Chudleigh. |
| Common Cudweed | Filago germanica ... | Bickleigh, Chudleigh. |
| Slender Cudweed ... | F. minima ............ | Chagford, Widecombe. |
| Marsh Cudweed ...... | Gnaphalium uliginosum... | Shaugh. |
| Upright Cudweed ... | G. sylvaticum ...... | Shaugh, Chagford |
| Mountain Cudweed | G. dioicum............ | Dartmoor Roborough. |
| Groundsel ............ | Senecio vulgaris ... | Common. |
| Common Ragwort... | S. Jacobæa............ | Common. |
| Marsh Ragwort ...... | S. aquaticus ......... | Ringmore, Chudleigh. |
| Ploughman's ......... Spikenard | Inula Conyza......... | Crownhill, Chudleigh. |
| Fleabane .............. | I. dysenterica......... | Common. |
| Trifid Bur Marigold | Bidens tripartita ... | Chudleigh. |
| The Daisy ............ | Bellis perennis ...... | Common. |
| Golden Rod............ | Solidago Virga-aurea ... | Sheepstor. |
| Coltsfoot ... .......... | Tussilago farfara ... | Common. |
| Common Butter Bur | Petasites vulgaris ... | Chudleigh. |
| Hemp Agrimony ... | Eupatorium ......... cannabinum | Common, Chudleigh. |
| Wild Succory ...... | Cichorium Intybus | Ilsington. |

| ENGLISH NAMES. | LATIN NAMES. | LOCALITY. |
|---|---|---|
| Common Nipplewort | Lapsana communis | Common, Bickleigh. |
| Long-rooted Cat's-ear | Hypochœris radicata | Common. |
| Yellow Goat's-beard | Tragopogon pratensis... | Chudleigh. |
| Dandelion ............ | Taraxacum officinale... | Common. |
| Ox-tongue ............ | Helminthia echioides... | Ilsington. |
| Sowthistle ............ | Sonchus oleraceus... | Common. |
| Rough Sowthistle ... | S. asper ............... | Common. |
| Corn Sowthistle ...... | S. arvensis............ | Tavy valley. |
| Hawk'sBeard ......... | Crepis virens......... | Common. |
| Hawkweed ............ | Hieracium pilosella | Common. |
| Wall Hawkweed ... | H. murorum ......... | Hey Tor Rocks |
| Wood Hawkweed ... | H. vulgatum ......... | Chagford |
| Narrow-leaved ...... Hawkweed | H. umbellatum ...... | Cornwood, Holne Chase. |
| Broad-leaved Hawkweed... | H. boreale............. | North Bovey. |

## CAMPANULACEÆ.

| | | |
|---|---|---|
| Sheeps' Bit ............ | Iasione montana ... | Horrabridge, Ivybridge. |
| Bell Flower ........... | Campanula ... rotundifolia | Dartmoor, Ilsington. |
| Ivy-leaved Bellflower | Wahlenburgia ...... hederacea | Plaster Down, Holne Chase, Cornwood, Bovey |

## ERICACEÆ.

| | | |
|---|---|---|
| Whortle Berry ...... | Vaccinium............ Myrtillus | Dartmoor, Cornwood. |
| Cowberry............... | V. Vitis Idæa ...... | Dartmoor, Furtor. |
| Crossleaved Heath... | Erica tetralix......... | Sheepstor, Bovey Tracey. |
| Fine-leaved Heath... | E. cinerea ............ | Bickleigh Down, Chudleigh. |
| Ling, Heather......... | Calluna vulgaris ... | Dartmoor. |

## JASMINACEÆ.

| | | |
|---|---|---|
| Common Ash ......... | Fraxinus excelsior | Common. |
| Privet .................. | Ligustrum vulgare | Egg Buckland. |

## Apocynaceæ.

| ENGLISH NAMES. | LATIN NAMES. | LOCALITY. |
| --- | --- | --- |
| Greater Periwinkle | Vinca major ......... | Ivybridge. |
| Lesser Periwinkle ... | V. minor............... | Shaugh, Bickleigh |

## Gentianaceæ.

| | | |
| --- | --- | --- |
| Centaury ............... | Erythrœa pulchella | Bovey-Heathfield. |
| Common Centaury... | E. Centaurium ...... | Shaugh, Chudleigh. |
| Field Gentian ... ... | Gentiana compestris | Bickleigh Down. |
| Buckbean ............ | Menyanthes ......... trifoliata | Bogs, Trowlsworthy, White Tor. |

## Convolvulaceæ.

| | | |
| --- | --- | --- |
| Small Bindweed...... | Convolvulus arvensis... | Very common. |
| White Smock ......... | C. sepium ............ | Common, Bovey Tracy. |
| Lesser Dodder ...... | Cuscuta Epithymum... | Shaugh Hill. |
| Clover Dodder ...... | C. Trifolii ............ | Egg Buckland, Chudleigh. |

## Solanaceæ.

| | | |
| --- | --- | --- |
| Woody Nightshade | Solanum Dulcamara... | Bickleigh. |
| Black Nightshade ... | S. nigrum ............ | Chudleigh. |
| Henbane ............... | Hyoscyamus niger | Chudleigh. |

## Scrophulariaceæ.

| | | |
| --- | --- | --- |
| Great Mullein ......... | Verbascum Thapsus... | Ringmoor Down. |
| Moth Mullein ......... | V. Blattaria ......... | Ashburton, Lustleigh. |
| Large Flowered Mullein... | V. virgatum ......... | Ringmoor Down, Bovey Heathfield. |
| Common Water Betony... | Scrophularia Balbisii ...... | Common. |
| Knotty-rooted Figwort | S. nodosa ............ | Very common. |
| Foxglove ............... | Digitalis purpurea... | Common. |
| Snapdragon............ | Antirrhinum majus | Chudleigh. |
| Corn Snapdragon ... | A. Orontium ......... | Chagford. |

| ENGLISH NAMES. | LATIN NAMES. | LOCALITY. |
|---|---|---|
| Mother of Millions | Linaria Cymbalaria | Very common, Ivybridge. |
| Sharp-leaved Fluellen... | L. Elatine ............ | Ivybridge, Chudleigh. |
| Yellow Toadflax...... | L.vulgaris ............ | Common. |
| Least Toadflax ...... | L. minor.............. | Ilsington. |
| Cornish Moneywort | Sibthorpia Europœa | Shaugh Bridge, Holne Chase. |
| Ivy-leaved Speedwell | Veronica hederifolia | Common. |
| Grey procumbent Speedwell... | V. polita.............. | Common, Tavistock. |
| Green procumbent Speedwell... | V. Agrestis ......... | Common. |
| Buxbaum's Speedwell... | V. Buxbaumii ...... | Roborough. |
| Germander Speedwell... | V. Chamœdris ...... | Very common. |
| Mountain Speedwell | V. montana ......... | Bickleigh, Ilsington. |
| Common Speedwell | V. officinalis ......... | Shaugh, Ivybridge |
| Marsh Speedwell ... | V. scutellata......... | Dartmoor Hanger Down. |
| Water Speedwell ... | V. Anagallis ......... | Bickleigh Vale |
| Brooklime ............ | V. Beccabunga...... | Very common. |
| Common Eyebright | Euphrasia officinalis | Dartmoor. |
| Red Bartsia............ | Bartsia Odontites... | Cornwood. |
| Yellow Bartsia ...... | B. viscosa ............ | Shaugh, Ivybridge |
| Upright Lousewort | Pedicularis palustris | Vixen Tor, Chudleigh. |
| Procumbent Lousewort... | P. sylvatica ........ | Sampford Spiney. |
| Yellow Rattle ......... | Rhinanthus ......... Christa-galli | Sheepstor, Shell Top. |
| Cow wheat ............ | Melampyrum ...... pratense | Lidford Falls, Bickleigh. |

OROBANCHACEÆ:

| | | |
|---|---|---|
| Greater Broomrape | Orobanche major... | Sampford Spiney, Lustleigh Cleave. |
| Lesser Broomrape... | O. minor ............ | Shaugh, Moreton, |
| Toothwort ............ | Lathræa squamaria | Wood, Chudleigh |

VERBENACEÆ.

| | | |
|---|---|---|
| Common Vervain .. | Verbena officinalis | Cornwood. |

## LABIATÆ.

| ENGLISH NAMES. | LATIN NAMES. | LOCALITY. |
| --- | --- | --- |
| Gipsy Wort ......... | Lycopus Europæus | Bickleigh, Drewsteignton |
| Round-leaved Mint... | Mentha rotundifolia | Ringmoor, Ilsington. |
| Peppermint............ | M. piperita ......... | Egg Buckland, Chudleigh. |
| Hairy Water Mint... | M. hirsuta............ | Common, Ivybridge. |
| Marsh Whorled Mint | M. sativa ............ | Bickleigh Vale. |
| Corn Mint ............ | M. arvensis ......... | Bickleigh, Chudleigh. |
| Wild Thyme ......... | Thymus Serpyllum | Dartmoor, Chudleigh. |
| Marjoram ............ | Origanum vulgare | Bickleigh, Moreton. |
| Wild Basil ............ | Calamintha, Clinopodium... | Ivybridge. |
| Basil Thyme ......... | C. Acinos ............ | Egg Buckland, Chudleigh. |
| Calamint .............. | C. menthifolia ...... | Shaugh,Ivybridge Lustleigh. |
| Catmint ............... | Nepeta Cataria...... | Ilsington, Lustleigh. |
| Ground Ivy............ | N. Glechoma ...... | Common. |
| Self Heal... ... ........ | Prunella vulgaris ... | Common, Bickleigh. |
| Common Skullcap ... | Scutellaria............ galericulata | Fingle Bridge. |
| Lesser Skullcap ...... | S. minor ............ | Dartmoor,Shaugh, Bovey. |
| Bastard Balm......... | Melittis .............. Melissophyllum | Bickleigh Vale, Holne Chase. |
| Marsh Woundwort... | Stachys palustris ... | Common. |
| Hedge Woundwort... | S. sylvatica ......... | Common. |
| Corn Woundwort ... | S. arvensis ......... | Common. |
| Betony . ..... ......... | S. Betonica ......... | Common. |
| Red Hemp Nettle ... | Galeopsis Ladanum | Dartmoor, Chudleigh. |
| Common Hemp Nettle... | G. Tetrahit ......... | Very common. |
| Red Dead Nettle ... | Lamium purpureum | Very common. |
| White Dead Nettle... | L. album ............ | Bickleigh, Walkhampton. |
| Yellow Archangel ... | L. Galeobdolon...... | Chudleigh. |

Y

| ENGLISH NAMES. | LATIN NAMES. | LOCALITY. |
|---|---|---|
| Common Bugle ... | Ajuga reptans ...... | Common. |
| Wood Germander ... | Teucrium Scorodonia... | Common. |
| Motherwort............ | Leonurus Cardiaca | Chudleigh, Lustleigh. |

### BORAGINACEÆ.

| | | |
|---|---|---|
| Common Gromwell | Lithospermum officinale... | Ilsington. |
| Corn Gromwell ...... | L. arvense ......... | Chudleigh. |
| Scorpion Grass ...... | Myosotis palustris | Ivybridge, Chudleigh. |
| Creeping Water ...... Forget-me-not | M. repens ............ | Wigvor Down, Cornwood. |
| Field Forget-me-not | M. arvensis ......... | Common. |
| Yellow and blue Forget-me-not... | M. versicolor......... | Shaugh, Ivybridge |
| Evergreen Alkanet... | Anchusa sempervirens... | Ilsington. |
| Bugloss .............. | Lycopsis arvensis... | North Bovey. |
| Borage................. | Borago officinalis... | Chagford. |
| Comfrey .............. | Symphytum officinale... | Bovey. |
| Common Hounds ... Tongue | Cynoglossum officinale... | Chudleigh. |

### PINGUICULACEÆ.

| | | |
|---|---|---|
| Pale Butterwort...... | Pinguicula lusitanica... | Cocks Tor, Sheepstor, Harford |

### PRIMULACEÆ.

| | | |
|---|---|---|
| Primrose .............. | Primula vulgaris ... | Very common. |
| Cowslip, Paigle ...... | P. veris .............. | Tor Royal Dartmoor, Chudleigh. |
| Loosestrife ............ | Lysimachia ......... vulgaris | Buckfastleigh. |
| Yellow Pimpernel ... | L. nemorum ......... | Bickleigh, Cornwood. |
| Scarlet Pimpernel ... | Anagallis arvensis | Common. |
| Bog Pimpernel ...... | A. tenella ............ | Shaugh, Dartmoor |
| Bastard Pimpernel... | Centunculus ......... minimus... | Bovey Heathfield. |

## PLANTAGINACEÆ.

| ENGLISH NAMES. | LATIN NAMES. | LOCALITY. |
|---|---|---|
| Greater Plantain ... | Plantago major ... | Common. |
| Honey Plantain ... | P. media ............ | Ivybridge. |
| Rib Grass, Hard-head | P. lanceolata ...... | Common. |
| Buck's Horn Plantain | P. Coronopus ...... | Harford. |
| Plantain Shore Weed | Littorella lacustris | Widecombe |
| | | Bovey Heathfield. |

## CHENOPODIACEÆ.

| | | |
|---|---|---|
| Many-seeded ......... Goosefoot | Chenopodium ...... polyspermum | Ivybridge. |
| White Goosefoot ... | C. album ............ | Ivybridge. |
| Stinking Goosefoot... | C. olidum ............ | Chudleigh. |
| Allgood ............... | C. Bonus-Henricus | Ilsington, Wide- combe. |
| Narrow-leaved Orache... | Atriplex angustifolia | Common. |
| Spear-leaved Orache | A. erecta ............ | Cornwood. |

## POLYGONACEÆ.

| | | |
|---|---|---|
| Sharp Dock............ | Rumex conglomeratus... | Very common. |
| Bloody-veined Dock | R. sanguineus ...... | Ilsington. |
| Fiddle Dock ......... | R. pulcher ......... | Chudleigh. |
| Broad-leaved Dock | R. obtusifolius ...... | Common. |
| Curled Dock ......... | R. crispus ............ | Common. |
| Sour Sabs, Sorrel ... | R. Acetosa ......... | Common. |
| Sheeps' Sorrel ...... | R. Acetosella ...... | Common. |
| Climbing Buckwheat | Polygonum convolvulus... | Common. |
| Common Knot-grass | P. aviculare ......... | Very common. |
| Water Pepper ...... | P. Hydropiper ...... | Common. |
| Common Persicary | P. Persicaria ...... | Common. |
| Glandular Persicary | P. lapathifolium ... | Chudleigh. |
| Common Bistort...... | P. bistorta............ | Widecombe. |

## THYMELEACEÆ.

| | | |
|---|---|---|
| Spurge Laurel ...... | Daphne Laureola... | Harford Bridge. |

## EUPHORBIACEÆ.

| | | |
|---|---|---|
| Wood Spurge......... | Euphorbia amygdaloides... | Colebrook. |

| ENGLISH NAMES. | LATIN NAMES. | LOCALITY. |
|---|---|---|
| Petty Spurge .... ... | E. Peplus ............ | Common. |
| Dwarf Spurge......... | E. exigua ............ | Walkhampton, Cornwood. |
| Perennial Dog's Mercury.... | Mercurialis perennis | Common. |

### URTICACEÆ.

| | | |
|---|---|---|
| Pellitory of the Wall | Parietaria diffusa ... | Common. |
| Common Nettle ...... | Urtica dioica......... | Common. |
| Small Nettle ......... | U. urens ............ | Colebrook. |
| Common Hop......... | Humulus Lupulus | Chudleigh. |
| Common Elm......... | Ulmus suberosa ... | Common, Ivybridge. |
| Broad-leaved Elm ... | U. montana ......... | Ivybridge. |

### AMENTIFERÆ.

| | | |
|---|---|---|
| Common Oak ......... | Quercus Robur...... | Common. |
| Sweet Chestnut ...... | Castanea vulgaris... | Bickleigh. |
| Hazel .................. | Corylus Avellana . . | Common. |
| Hornbeam ............ | Carpinus Betulus... | Shaugh. |
| Alder .................. | Alnus glutinosa ... | Shaugh, Fingle Bridge. |
| White Birch ......... | Betula alba ......... | Harford,Bickleigh |
| Bog Myrtle............ | Myrica Gale ......... | Cornwood, Chagford. |
| Aspen .................. | Populus tremula ... | Chudleigh. |
| Crack Willow......... | Salix fragilis......... | Ivybridge, Chagford. |
| Common Osier ...... | S. viminalis ......... | Ivybridge. |
| Ferruginous Osier | S. ferruginea......... | Ivybridge. |
| Common Sallow...... | S. cinerea ............ | Ivybridge. |
| Wrinkled-leaved...... Sallow | S aurita.............. | Yannaton Down, Chudleigh. |
| Great Sallow ......... | S. caprea ............ | Common. |
| Dwarf Willow ...... | S. repens ............ | Chudleigh. |

### PHANEROGAMIA—MONOCOTYLEDONES.

### TYPHACEÆ.

| | | |
|---|---|---|
| Common Cat's Tail | Typha latifolia ...... | Chudleigh. |

### ARACEÆ.

| | | |
|---|---|---|
| Cuckoo pint ......... | Arum maculatum... | Common. |

## LEMNACEÆ.

| ENGLISH NAMES. | LATIN NAMES. | LOCALITY. |
|---|---|---|
| Lesser Duckweed ... | Lemna minor ...... | Common. |

## NAIADACEÆ.

| | | |
|---|---|---|
| Floating Pondweed | Potamogeton natans | Shaugh Bridge, Wigvor Down. |
| Oblong-leaved Pondweed... | P. polygonifolius ... | Ivybridge. |
| Plantain-leaved Pondweed... | P. plantagineus ... | Dartmoor. |

## ALISMACEÆ.

| | | |
|---|---|---|
| Greater Water ...... Plantain | Alisma Plantago ... | Ivybridge, Ilsington. |

## ORCHIDACEÆ.

| | | |
|---|---|---|
| Pyramidal Orchis ... | Orchis pyramidalis | Ilsington, Chudleigh. |
| Broad-leaved Marsh Orchis | O. latifolia............ | Horrabridge, Chudleigh. |
| Early Purple Orchis | O. mascula ......... | Common. |
| Spotted Palmate Orchis... | O. maculata ......... | Shaugh Wood. |
| Dwarf Orchis ......... | O. ustulata ......... | Shaugh Vale. |
| Fragrant Orchis...... | Gymnadenia ......... conopsea | Cann Wood, Roborough. |
| Frog Orchis ......... | Habenaria viridis... | Smear Down, Chudleigh. |
| Lesser Butterfly...... Orchis | H. bifolia ............ | Cadover Bridge, Lustleigh. |
| Greater Butterfly ... Orchis | H. Chlorantha ...... | Bickleigh, Harford. |
| Autumnal Ladies' Tresses... | Spiranthes autumnalis... | Hemerdon, Bickleigh. |
| Common Twayblade | Listera ovata ...... | Hemerdon, Chudleigh. |
| Bird's nest ............ | Neottia nidus-avis | Haldon. |
| Broad-leaved Helleborine... | Epipactis latifolia... | Bickleigh. |
| Marsh Bog Orchis... | Malaxis paludosa... | Dartmoor, S. Tawton. |

## IRIDACEÆ.

| | | |
|---|---|---|
| Yellow Water Iris ... | Iris Pseudacorus ... | Dartmoor |
| Fœtid Iris ............ | I. fœtidissima ...... | Chudleigh, Ilsington. |

## AMARYLLIDACEÆ.

| ENGLISH NAMES. | LATIN NAMES. | LOCALITY. |
|---|---|---|
| Common Daffodil Lent Lily... | Narcissus Pseudo- Narcissus... | Egg Buckland. |
| Whit-sundays ...... | N. biflorus............ | Bickleigh, Ilsington. |
| Snowdrop ............ | Galanthus nivalis... | Meavy, Becky Falls. |

## DIOSCOREACEÆ.

| | | |
|---|---|---|
| Black Briony ........... | Tamus communis... | Common. |

## LILIACEÆ.

| | | |
|---|---|---|
| Lily of the Valley ... | Convallaria majalis | North Wood, Shaugh. |
| Blue Bell............... | Scilla nutans......... | Common. |
| Ramsons ............... | Allium ursinum ... | Bickleigh, Hemerdon. |
| Star of Bethlehem ... | Ornithogalum ...... umbellatum... | Orchards at Ilsington. |

## JUNCACEÆ.

| | | |
|---|---|---|
| Lancashire Asphodel | Narthecium ......... ossifragum | Yestor, Crockern- Tor, Shaugh. |
| Narrow-leaved hairy Woodrush | Luzula Forsteri ... | Bickleigh, Ilsington |
| Broad-leaved hairy Woodrush | L. pilosa ............ | Egg Buckland, Chudleigh. |
| Great Woodrush ... | L. sylvatica ......... | Blackystone Rocks. |
| Field Woodrush...... | L. campestris ...... | Common. |
| Many-headed Woodrush... | L. multiflora......... | Hemerdon. |
| Common Rush ...... | Juncus con- glomeratus... | Shaugh. |
| Soft Rush ............ | J. effusus ............ | Ivybridge, Chudleigh. |
| Hard Rush ............ | J. glaucus ............ | Chudleigh. |
| Lesser-jointed Rush | J. supinus ............ | Shaugh,Cornwood |
| Toad Rush ............ | J. bufonius ......... | Dartmoor. |
| Heath Rush ......... | J. squarrosus......... | Shaugh,Chudleigh |
| Sharp-flowered Rush | J. acutiflorus... ..... | Chudleigh. |
| Round-fruited Rush | J. compressus ...... | Bovey Heathfield |

## CYPERACEÆ.

| | | |
|---|---|---|
| White beaked Sedge | Rhyncospora alba... | Dartmoor,Shaugh. Bovey Heathfield. |

| ENGLISH NAMES. | LATIN NAMES. | LOCALITY. |
|---|---|---|
| Black Bog rush ...... | Schænus nigricans | Bovey Heathfield, |
| Many stemmed club rush... | Scirpus multicaulis | Leathertor. |
| Bullrush ............... | S. lacustris ......... | Chudleigh. |
| Scaly stemmed club rush... | S. cæspitosus ...... | Staldon Barrow, Dartmoor. |
| Floating Club rush | S. fluitans ......... | Sheepstor, Torey Brook. |
| Savi's, Club rush ... | S. Savii ............... | Borders of Dartmoor, Bickleigh Vale. |
| Bristle-like Club...... rush | S. setaeus ............ | Cornwood, Harford. |
| Hare's Tail Cotton Grass... | Eriophorum vaginatum... | Swamps, Dartmoor, Ivybridge. |
| Common Cotton Grass... | E. angustifolium... | Dartmoor. |
| Prickly Twig-rush... | Cladium mariscus... | Dartmoor. |
| Flea Sedge ............ | Carex pulicaris ..... | Moreton. Ilsington. |
| Soft Brown Sedge ... | C. disticha............ | Chudleigh, Bovey Heathfield. |
| Greater Panicled Sedge... | C. paniculata ...... | Ivybridge. |
| Great Sedge ......... | C. vulpina ............ | Dartmoor, Chudleigh. |
| Greater Prickly Sedge... | C. muricata ......... | Chudleigh, Dartmoor. |
| Grey Sedge ............ | C. divulsa ............ | Chudleigh. |
| Little Prickly Sedge | C. stellulata ......... | Sheepstor. |
| Distant Spiked Sedge | C. remota ............ | Egg Buckland. |
| Oval Spiked Sedge.. | C. ovalis............ ... | Shaugh, Haldon. |
| Common Sedge ...... | C. vulgaris ......... | Shaugh, Wigvor Down. |
| Glaucous Heath ...... Sedge | C. glauca ............ | Ilsington, Common. |
| Round-headed Sedge | C. pilulifera ......... | Ringmoor Down. |
| Pale Sedge ............ | C. pallescens......... | Bickleigh. |
| Pink-leaved Sedge ... | C. panicea............ | Sheepstor. |
| Great Pendulous Sedge... | C. pendula........... | Moreton, Widecombe. |
| Pendulous Wood Sedge... | C. sylvatica ......... | Hemerdon, Ivybridge. |
| Smooth-stalkedSedge | C. lœvigata ......... | Shaugh, Trowlesworthy. |
| Green-ribbed Sedge | C. binervis ......... | Cadover Bridge. |

| ENGLISH NAMES. | LATIN NAMES. | LOCALITY. |
|---|---|---|
| Distant Spiked Sedge | C. distans ............ | Chudleigh, Haldon. |
| Hammer Sedge .. ... | C. hirta ............... | Below Ringmoor. |
| Bottle Sedge ......... | C. ampullacea ...... | Chagford, below Shell Top. |

## GRAMINA.

| | | |
|---|---|---|
| Sweet-scented Vernal Grass... | Anthoxanthemum odoratum... | Dartmoor. |
| Ribbon Grass......... | Digraphis arundinacea... | Cornwood. |
| Floating Foxtail Grass... | Alopecurus geniculatus... | Buckfastleigh. |
| Meadow Foxtail Grass... | A. pratenis ......... | Cornwood, Ivybridge. |
| Slender Foxtail Grass | A. agrestis............ | Chudleigh. |
| Timothy Grass ... .. | Phleum pratense ... | Very common. |
| Bristle-leaved Bent Grass | Agrostis setacea ... | Ivybridge, Holne Chase. |
| Brown Bent Grass... | A. canina ............ | Ugborough Beacon, Bickleigh. |
| Common Bent Grass | A. vulgaris ......... | Dartmoor, common. |
| Marsh Bent Grass... | A. Alba ............ | Buckland Monachorum. |
| Wood Millet Grass... | Milium effusum ... | Ivybridge. |
| Tufted Hair Grass... | Aira cœspitosa ...... | Sheepstor. |
| Heath Hair Grass ... | A. flexuosa ......... | Shaugh, Sheepstor. |
| Silvery Hair Grass... | A. caryophyllea ... | Roborough, Bickleigh. |
| Early Hair Grass ... | A. prœcox............ | Cadover Bridge. |
| Yellow Oat Grass ... | Avena flavescens ... | Chudleigh Ivybridge. |
| Wild Oat............... | A. fatua........... ... | Ilsington. |
| Narrow-leaved Perennial Oat... | A. pratensis ......... | Chudleigh. |
| Creeping Soft Grass | Holcns mollis ...... | Bickleigh. |
| Yorkshire Fog......... | H. lanatus............ | Ivybridge. |
| Decumbent Heath Grass... | Triodia decumbens | Hey Tor, Sheepstor. |
| Crested Hair Grass... | Kœleria cristata ... | Ilsington. |
| Purple Hair Grass... | Molinia cærulea ... | Lee Moor, Sheepstor. |
| Wood Melic Grass... | Melica uniflora...... | Bickleigh, Lustleigh Cleave. |

| ENGLISH NAMES. | LATIN NAMES. | LOCALITY. |
|---|---|---|
| Annual Meadow Grass... | Poa annua............ | Common. |
| Smooth Meadow Grass... | P. pratensis ........ | Common. |
| Rough Meadow Grass... | P. trivialis............ | Common, Dartmoor. |
| Flat-stemmed Meadow Grass... | P. compressa ...... | Ilsington. |
| Water-Whorl Grass | Catabrosa aquatica | Dartmoor. |
| Floating Meadow Grass... | Glyceria fluitans ... | Dartmoor. |
| Hard Meadow Grass | Sclerochloa rigida | Common. |
| Common Quaking Grass... | Briza media ......... | Chudleigh. |
| Small Quaking Grass | B. minor ............ | Chagford. |
| Crested Dogs-tail Grass... | Cynosurus cristatus | Common. |
| Rough Cocks-foot Grass... | Dactylis glomerata | Common. |
| Wall Fescue Grass... | Festuca Pseudo-myurus... | Ilsington, Bovey. |
| Barren Fescue Grass | F. Sciuroides ...... | Ilsington. |
| Sheeps' Fescue Grass | F. ovina... ............ | Dartmoor. |
| Hard Fescue Grass | F. rubra............... | Common. |
| Tall Fescue Grass ... | F. elatior .......... | Colebrook, Chudleigh. |
| Meadow Fescue Grass... | F. pratensis ......... | Ivybridge. |
| Barren Brome-grass | Bromus sterilis ... | Very common. |
| Upright Brome-grass | B. erectus............ | Chudleigh. |
| Racemose Brome-grass... | B. racemosus ...... | Horrabridge. |
| Rough Brome-grass | B. asper ............ | Chudleigh. |
| Soft Brome-grass ... | B. mollis .. ......... | Common. |
| False Wood Brome-grass... | Brachypodium sylvaticum... | Common, Chudleigh. |
| Spiked Wood Brome-grass ... | B. pinnatum......... | Bovey Tracy |
| Couch-grass ........ | Triticum repens ... | Very common. |
| Perennial Rye-grass | Lolium perenne ... | Very common. |
| Wall Barley ......... | Hordeum murinum | Common. |
| Meadow Barley ...... | H. pratense ......... | Chudleigh. |
| Mat-grass ............ | Nardus strictus...... | Ringmoor Down, Sheepstor. |

## CRYPTOGAMIA. ACOTYLEDONES.

### FILICES.

| ENGLISH NAMES. | LATIN NAMES. | LOCALITY. |
| --- | --- | --- |
| Tunbridge Filmy Fern... | Hymenophyllum Tunbridgense... | Sheepstor, Shaugh. |
| Wilson's Filmy Fern... | H. unilaterale ...... | Dewerstone, Ivybridge, Mis Tor |
| Bracken ............... | Pteris aquilina ...... | Dartmoor Common. |
| Hard Fern ............ | Lomaria spicant ... | Sheepstor, Cornwood. |
| Rue leaved Spleenwort ... | Asplenium Ruta- muraria... | Shaugh, Ivybridge. |
| Common Spleenwort | A. Trichomanes ... | Shaugh, Cornwood. |
| Lanceolate Spleenwort | A. lanceolatum...... | Shaugh, Peter Tavy. |
| Black Spleenwort ... | A. Adiantum nigrum... | Dartmoor, Shaugh. |
| Lady Fern .. ......... | Athyrium Filix fœmina... | Cornwood, Shaugh. |
| Scaly Spleenwort ... | Ceterach officinarum... | Ivybridge, Buckfastleigh. |
| Hart's Tongue ...... | Scolopendrium vulgare... | Common. |
| Common Prickly Shield Fern... | Aspidium aculeatum... | Ilsington. |
| Angular lobed Shield Fern... | A. angulare ......... | Horrabridge. |
| Bladder Fern ......... | Cystopteris fragilis... | Bickleigh Vale |
| Male Fern ........... | Nephrodium Filix mas... | Dartmoor. |
| Narrow Prickly-toothed Fern... | N. Spinulostum ... | Bickleigh Vale, Fingle Bridge. |
| Broad Prickly-toothed Fern... | N. dilatatum......... | Dartmoor, Wistman's Wood. |
| Recurved Fern ...... | N. æmulum ......... | Shaugh, Cadover Bridge, Ivybridge. |
| Sweet Mountain Fern. | N. Oreopteris ...... | Cornwood, Shaugh. |
| Common Polypody... | Polypodium vulgare... | Cornwood, Ivybridge. |
| Beech Polypody...... | P. Phegopteris ... | Brent, Meavy, Harter Tor. |

| ENGLISH NAMES. | LATIN NAMES. | LOCALITY. |
|---|---|---|
| Oak Polypody......... | P. Dryopteris ...... | Two Bridges, Harford. |
| Royal Flowering Fern... | Osmunda regalis ... | Plym Bridge, Ivy-bridge, Cornwood, |
| Adder's Tongue ...... | Ophioglossum vulgatum... | Meadow near Baggy Tor. |
| Moonwort ............ | Botrychium Lunaria... | Meadow, Baggy Tor (with O. vulgatum) Cadover Bridge, Cocks Tor. |

## MARSILEACEÆ.

| | | |
|---|---|---|
| Pillwort .............. | Pilularia globulifera | Blackdown. |

## LYCOPODIACEÆ.

| | | |
|---|---|---|
| Common Clubmoss | Lycopodium clavatum .. | Near Cadover Bridge. |
| Fir Clubmoss ...... .. | L. Selago ............ | Great Mis Tor. |
| Marsh Clubmoss ... | L. inundatum ...... | Bovey Heathfield. |

## EQUISETACEÆ.

| | | |
|---|---|---|
| Cornfield Horsetail | Equisetum arvense | Very common. |
| Water Horsetail...... | E. maximum ...... | Chudleigh. Ilsington. |
| Marsh Horsetail...... | E. palustre ......... | Colebrook, Ilsington. |
| Smooth naked Horsetail... | E. limosum ......... | Near Tavistock, Chudleigh. |

## CHARACEÆ.

| | | |
|---|---|---|
| Flexile Chara ......... | Chara flexilis ...... | Bovey Heathfield. |
| Fetid Chara............ | C fœtida ........... | Bovey Heathfield. |

## MUSCI.

## SPHAGNACEÆ.

| | | |
|---|---|---|
| Blunt-leaved Bog Moss... | Sphagnum cymbifolium... | Tavy Cleave |
| Compact Bog Moss... | S. compactum ...... | Dartmoor. |
| Pale dwarf Bog Moss | S. molluscum ...... | Nuns Cross. |
| Red dwarf Bog Moss | S. rubellum ......... | Fox Tor. |
| Slender Bog Moss ... | S. acutifolium ...... | Dartmoor. |
| Fringe-leaved Bog Moss... | S. fimbriatum ...... | Dartmoor. |

| ENGLISH NAMES. | LATIN NAMES. | LOCALITY. |
|---|---|---|
| Wavy-leaved Bog Moss... | S. cuspidatum ...... | Dartmoor. |
| Black-stemmed Bog Moss... | S. contortum .... | Cocks Tor. |
| Spreading-leaved Bog Moss... | S. squarrosum ...... | Dartmoor. Sheepstor. |

### ANDREÆACEÆ.

| | | |
|---|---|---|
| Rock Andreæa ...... | Andreæa petrophila... | Cock's Tor. |
| Black falcate Andreæa... | A rupestris ........ | Dartmoor, Hey Tor. |

### TETRAPHIDACEÆ.

| | | |
|---|---|---|
| Pellucid four-toothed Moss... | Tetraphis pellucida | Lydford. |
| Brown's four-toothed Moss... | Tetradontium Brownianum... | Cornwood, Cascade, Fox Tor. |

### BUXBAUMÎACEÆ.

| | | |
|---|---|---|
| Leafy Buxbaumia ... | Diphyscium foliosum... | Shaugh, Tavy Cleave, Holne. |

### POLYTRÎCHACEÆ.

| | | |
|---|---|---|
| Soft-leaved Hair Moss... | Atrichum laxifolium | Banks of Rattle-Brook, |
| Wavy-leaved Hair Moss... | A undulatum ...... | Dartmoor. |
| Dwarf Hair Moss ... | Pogonatum nanum... | Dartmoor. |
| Aloe-leaved Hair Moss... | P. aloides ............ | Dartmoor. |
| Urn-fruited Hair Moss... | P. urnigerum ...... | Hooe Meavy. |
| Alpine Hair Moss .. | P. alpinum . ...... | Great Mis Tor, Tavy Cleave. |
| Slender-hair Moss ... | Polytrichum gracile... | Trowlesworthy Bog. |
| Beautiful hair Moss | P. formosum........ | Tavy Cleave. |
| Juniper-leaved Hair Moss... | P. juniperinum ...... | Dartmoor. |
| Brittle-pointed hair Moss... | P. piliferum ......... | Dartmoor, Holne Chase. |
| Common hair Moss | P. commune ......... | Bogs, Dartmoor. |

## LEUCOBRYACEÆ.

| ENGLISH NAMES | LATIN NAMES. | LOCALITY. |
|---|---|---|
| White-leaved Fork Moss... | Leucobryum glaucum ............ | Heytor Down. |

## DICRANACEÆ.

| | | |
|---|---|---|
| Long-leaved Earth Moss... | Pleuridium alternifolium ......... | Shaugh, Ilsington. |
| Awl-leaved Fork Moss... | Dicranella subulata | Ilsington. |
| Spur-necked Fork Moss... | D. cerviculata ...... | Dartmoor. |
| Drooping-leaved Fork Moss... | D. squarrosa ...... | Tavy Cleave, Whitetor, Vitifer. |
| Curved-leaved Didymodon... | Ditrichum homomallum... | Dartmoor. |
| Bent-leaved Didymodon... | Leptodontium flexifolium... | Yes Tor, Vixen Tor. |
| Acute-leaved Blindia | Blindia acuta ...... | Yanaton Down. |
| Dr. Scott's Fork Moss... | Dicranum Scottianum... | Shaugh, Cornwood. |
| Broom Fork Moss... | D. scoparium ...... | Cornwood. |
| Tall Fork Moss ...... | D. majus ..... ...... | Cornwood. |
| Wide-leaved Fork Moss... | D. spurium ......... | Roborough Down. |
| Rusty Swan-necked Moss... | Campylopus flexuosus... | Dartmoor. |
| Pale Swan-necked Moss... | C. fragilis ............ | Plym Bridge, Sheepstor. |
| Dwarf Swan-necked Moss... | C. torfaceus ......... | Fox Tor, Great Mis Tor, Lydford. |
| Bristly Swan-necked Moss... | C. longipilus ......... | Dartmoor. |
| Compact Swan-necked Moss... | C. brevipilus... ..... | Trowlesworthy, Shaugh. |

## TRICHOSTOMACEÆ.

| | | |
|---|---|---|
| Small-mouthed Beardless Moss... | Weissia microstoma... | Hooe Meavy. |
| Dwarf Streak Moss | Rhabdoweissia fugax... | Sheepstor, Tavy Cleave. |
| Brunton's Fork-Moss... | Cynodontium Bruntoni... | Higher parts of Dartmoor. |
| Green Spur-footed Fork-Moss... | C. virens ............ | Dartmoor, near Prisons. |

| ENGLISH NAMES. | LATIN NAMES. | LOCALITY. |
| --- | --- | --- |
| Many Fruited Fork-Moss... | C. polycarpum ...... | Dartmoor, near Prisons. |
| Transparent Fork-Moss... | Dichodontium pellucidum... | Lydford. |
| Mougeot's Yoke-Moss... | Cylicocarpus Mougeotii... | Lydford, Bickleigh. |
| Spiral-fruited Extinguisher Moss | Encalypta streptocarpa... | On Shaugh Bridge. |
| Common dwarf Earth Moss... | Phascum muticum | Ilsington. |
| Swan-necked Earth Moss... | P. curvicollum ...... | Ilsington. |
| Curly-leaved Trichostomum... | Trichostomum crispulum... | Buckfastleigh. |
| Bluntish-leaved Trichostomum ... | T. tophaceum ...... | Ashburton. |
| Wedge-leaved Screw Moss... | Tortula cuneifolia... | Ilsington. |
| Wall Screw Moss ... | T. muralis............ | Common. |
| Convolute Screw Moss | T. convoluta ......... | Common, Moreton. |
| Revolute Screw Moss | T. revoluta ......... | North Bovey. |
| Fallacious Screw Moss... | T. fallax ............ | North Bovey. |
| Soft-tufted Screw Moss... | T. insulana ......... | Manadon, Lydford. |
| Great hairy Screw Moss... | T. ruralis .......... .. | Common. |
| Roughest-leaved Screw Moss .. | Tortula papillosa ... | Tavistock. |
| Broken-leaved Screw Moss... | T. nitida ............ | Dartmoor. |
| Awl-leaved Screw Moss... | T. subulata ......... | Prince Town, Moreton. |
| Curley-leaved Srew Moss... | T. tortuosa............ | Chudleigh, Dartmoor. |
| Purple Fork-Moss ... | Ceratodon purpureus... | Dartmoor, Common. |

## GRIMMIACEÆ.

| | | |
| --- | --- | --- |
| Smaller Water Screw-Moss... | Cinclidotus fontinaloides... | River Dart, Totnes. |
| Larger Water Screw-Moss... | C. riparius ......... | Chudleigh Waterfall. |

| ENGLISH NAMES | LATIN NAMES. | LOCALITY. |
|---|---|---|
| Sessile Grimmia ... | Schistidium | Common. |
| River Grimmia ...... | S. rivulare | |
| | apocarpum... | Fingle Bridge, |
| Grey cushioned | Grimmia | |
| Grimmia... | pulvinata... | Common. |
| Schultz's Grimmia ... | G. Schultzii ......... | On the Plym. |
| | | Dewerstone, |
| | | Vixen Tor. |
| Hair-pointed | G. trichophylla ...... | Lustleigh Cleave, |
| Grimmia... | | Shaugh. |
| Oval-fruited | | |
| Grimmia... | G. ovata ............ | Hey Tor, |
| Hoary Grimmia ...... | G. leucophœa ...... | Holne Chase |
| Tall Alpine Grimmia | Racomitrium | Sheepstor. |
| | patens... | |
| Dark Mountain | R. aciculare ......... | Dartmoor, Tavy |
| Fringe Moss... | | Cleave. |
| Narrow-leaved | | Tavy Cleave. |
| Mountain Fringe | R. protensum......... | Tavy Cleave. |
| Moss... | | |
| Slender Mountain | R. sudeticum ...... | Great Mis Tor, |
| Fringe Moss... | | Sheepstor. |
| Bristly Mountain | R. heterostichum... | Shaugh, |
| Fringe Moss ... | | Yannaton. |
| Green Mountain | R. fasciculare ...... | Dewerstone. |
| Fringe Moss... | | |
| Woolly Fringe Moss | R. lanuginosum ... | Dartmoor, |
| | | Common. |
| Small-fruited | | |
| Mountain Fringe | | |
| Moss... | R. microcarpon ... | Lustleigh. |
| Hoary Fringe Moss | R. canescens......... | Bickleigh Vale. |
| Hoary branched | Hedwigia ciliata ... | Dartmoor, |
| beardless Moss... | | Dewerstone. |
| Davies's Veil Moss... | Glyphomitrium | Cock's Tor, |
| | Daviesii... | Dartmoor. |
| Many-leaved Fringe | Ptychomitrium | Rocks, Dartmoor, |
| Moss... | polyphyllum... | common. |

ORTHOTRICHACEÆ.

| | | |
|---|---|---|
| Lesser Yoke Moss... | Zygodon conoideus | Lydford. |
| Green-tufted Yoke | | |
| Moss... | Z. viridissimus ...... | Colebrook. |
| Miss Hutchins' | | |
| Bristle Moss... | Ulota Hutchinsiœ | Rocks, Shaugh. |

| ENGLISH NAMES. | LATIN NAMES. | LOCALITY. |
|---|---|---|
| Curled Bristle Moss | U. crispa ............ | Trees, Dartmoor. |
| Frizzled Bristle Moss | U. phyllantha ...... | Tavistock. |
| Single-fringed sessile Bristle Moss... | Orthotricum cupulatum... | Ilsington, Okehampton. |
| Common Wood Bristle Moss... | O. affine............... | Common. |
| Rock Bristle Moss | O. rupestre ......... | North Bovey. |
| River Bristle Moss... | O. rivulare............ | Fingle Bridge. |
| White-tipped Bristle Moss... | O. diaphanum ..... | Common. |
| Elegant Bristle Moss | O. pulchellum ...... | North Bovey, Lydford. |
| Smooth-fruited Bristle Moss... | O. leiocarpum . ... | Bickleigh. |
| Lyell's Bristle Moss | O. Lyellii ............ | Lustleigh Cleave, Cornwood, Okehampton. |

### SPLACHNACEÆ.

| | | |
|---|---|---|
| Flagon-fruited Collar Moss... | Splachnum ampullaceum... | Eylesbarrow, Hey Tor. |
| Round-fruited Collar Moss... | S. sphœricum ...... | Nun's Cross, Great Mistor. |

### FUNARIACEÆ.

| | | |
|---|---|---|
| Templeton's Cord Moss... | Entostodon Templetoni ... | Fingle Bridge, Hood Bridge. |
| Common Cord Moss | Funaria hygrometrica... | Common. |
| Muhlenberg's Cord Moss... | F. Muhlenbergii ... | Ilsington. |
| Calcareous Cord Moss... | F. calcarea ......... | Ilsington. |

### BRYACEÆ.

| | | |
|---|---|---|
| Long-fruited Thread Moss... | Lamprophyllum elongatum... | Yannaton Down, Great Mis Tor, Wild Tor. |
| Silky pendulous Thread Moss... | L. nutans ............ | Great Mis Tor, Eylesbarrow. |
| Alpine glaucous Thread Moss... | L. crudum ......... | Great Links Tor. |
| Wahlenberg's Thread Moss... | L. albicans ......... | Bickleigh, Lydford. |
| Wall Thread Moss... | L. murale ..... ...... | Ilsington. |

| ENGLISH NAMES | LATIN NAMES. | LOCALITY. |
|---|---|---|
| Dark purple Thread Moss... | L. atropurpureum | Cornwood. |
| Alpine Thread Moss | L. alpinum ......... | Dartmoor, Heytor. |
| Obconical Thread Moss... | L. obconicum ...... | Shaugh Bridge. |
| Alpine-Bog Thread Moss... | L. pseudotri- quetrum... | Lydford. |
| Pale-leaved Thread Moss... | L. pallens ............ | Heytor, Trowlesworthy. |
| Pear-fruited Thread Moss... | L. turbinatum ...... | Heytor Bog. |
| Rosaceus Thyme Thread Moss... | L. roseum ............ | Lydford, Shaugh. |
| Silvery Thread Moss | L. argenteum ...... | Common. |
| Slender-branched Thread Moss... | L. julaceum ......... | Lydford. |
| Tozer's Thread Moss | Epipterygium Tozeri... | Buckfastleigh. |

### MNIACEÆ.

| | | |
|---|---|---|
| Many-fruited Thyme Thread Moss .. | Mnium affine ...... | Trowlesworthy Bog. |
| Pointed Thyme Thread Moss... | M. cuspidatum...... | Manaton. |
| Bog-leaved Thyme Thread Moss... | M. undulatum ...... | Lydford, Horrabridge. |
| Long-beaked Thyme Thread Moss... | M. rostratum ...... | Lydford. |
| Swan-necked Thyme Thread Moss. . | M. hornum ......... | Common. |
| Serrated Thyme Thread Moss... | M. serratum ......... | Meavy, |
| Star-leaved Thyme Thread Moss | M. stellare............ | Lydford, Buckfastleigh. |
| Dotted Thyme Thread Moss... | M. punctatum . ... | Lydford, Common. |
| Round-fruited Thyme Thread Moss... | M. subglobosum ... | Ivybridge. |

### BARTRAMIACEÆ.

| | | |
|---|---|---|
| Marsh Thread Moss | Gymnocybe palustris... | Dartmoor. |
| Fountain Apple Moss... | Philonotis fontana | Trowlesworthy. |

z

| ENGLISH NAMES. | LATIN NAMES. | LOCALITY. |
|---|---|---|
| Curve-stalked Apple Moss... | Breutelia arcuata... | Lydford, Tavy, Cleave. |
| Common Apple Moss | Bartramia pomiformis... | Dartmoor, Common. |
| Straight-leaved Apple Moss... | B. ithyphylla ...... | Shaugh, Yannaton. |

SCHISTOSTEGACEÆ

| | | |
|---|---|---|
| Cavern Moss .... .... | Schistostega osmundacea... | Leather Tor, Yannaton. |

FISSIDENTACEÆ.

| | | |
|---|---|---|
| Alpine flat Fork Moss .. | Fissidens osmundoides... | Lydford. |
| Fern-like Fork Moss | F. polyphyllus ...... | Holne Bridge. |
| Common flat Fork Moss... | F. bryoides ........ | Banks of Tavy. |

HOOKERIACEÆ.

| | | |
|---|---|---|
| Shining Hookeria ... | Pterogophyllum lucens... | Lydford, Common. |

FONTINALACEÆ.

| | | |
|---|---|---|
| Greater Water Moss | Fontinalis antipyretica... | Streams, Ilsington. |
| Alpine Water Moss | F. squamosa........ | Streams, Dartmoor. |

NECKERACEÆ.

| | | |
|---|---|---|
| Lateral Cryphæa ... | Cryphæa heteromalla... | Blackingstone Rock. |
| Squirrel-tailed Leucodon... | Leucodon sciuroides | Lustleigh. |
| Pendulous Wing-Moss... | Antitrichia curtipendula... | Wistman's Wood. |
| Dwarf Neckera ..... | Neckera pumila ... | Lustleigh Cleave, Burrow Tor. |
| Crisped Neckera...... | N. crispa ........... | Lydford, Chudleigh. |
| Flat-leaved Neckera | N. complanata ...... | Fingle Pridge, Chagford. |
| Blunt fern-like Feather Moss... | Homalia trichomanoides... | Lydford Fall. |

## LESKEACEÆ.

| ENGLISH NAMES | LATIN NAMES. | LOCALITY. |
|---|---|---|
| Slender Wing Moss | Pterogonium gracile... | Trees, Shaugh Bridge. |
| Many-fruited Leskea | Leskea polycarpa... | Fingle Bridge. |
| Tall Anomodon ...... | Anomodon viticulosus... | Meavy. |
| Wry-leaved Feather Moss... | Heterocladium heteropterum... | Dartmoor. |
| Tamarisk Feather Moss... | Thuidium tamariscinum... | Woods, Cornwood. |
| Habrodon ............ | Habrodon Notarisii | Ashburton. |

## HYPNACEÆ.

| | | |
|---|---|---|
| Marsh Tree Moss ... | Climacium dendroides... | Banks of Tavy |
| Blunt-leaved Frond Moss... | Isothecium myurum | Trees, Dartmoor. |
| Silky Leskea ......... | Homolothecium sericeum... | Trees, Dartmoor. |
| Velvet Feather Moss | Brachythecium velutinum... | Tavistock. |
| Larger Streaky Feather Moss... | B. glareosum......... | Buckfastleigh. |
| Common Rough-stalked Feather Moss | B. rutabulum ...... | Common. |
| River Rough-stalked Feather Moss... | B. rivulare ......... | Dartmoor, Streams, Fingle Bridge. |
| Matted Feather Moss | B. populeum... ..... | Common. |
| Rusty Feather Moss | B. plumosum ...... | Common, Ilsington. |
| Acute-leaved Frond Moss... | Eurynchium myosuroides... | Common. |
| Hair-pointed Feather Moss... | E. piliferum ......... | Lydford, Ilsington. |
| Prolonged Feather Moss... | E. prœlongum ... | Lydford. |
| Streaked Feather Moss... | E. striatum ......... | Wistman's Wood. |
| Long-branched Feather Moss... | Hyocomium flagellare... | Burrow Tor— Waterfall, Lydford. |

| ENGLISH NAMES. | LATIN NAMES. | LOCALITY. |
|---|---|---|
| Tender Awl-leaved Feather Moss... | Rhyncostegium tenellum... | Common. |
| Water Feather Moss | R. fluviatile ......... | Lustleigh Cleave. |
| Depressed Feather Moss... | R. depressum ...... | Lydford |
| Clustered Feather Moss... | R. confertum ...... | Common, Ilsington. |
| Wall Feather Moss | R. murale ............ | Cornwood. |
| Long-beaked Water Feather Moss... | R. rusciforme ...... | Streams, Dartmoor. |
| Foxtailed Feather Moss... | Thamnium alopecurum... | Lydford Falls. |
| Neat Mountain Feather Moss... | Plagiothecium pulchellum . | Ilsington. |
| Sharp flat-leaved Feather Moss... | P. denticulatum ... | Great Mistor. |
| Wood Feather Moss | P. sylvaticum ...... | Bickleigh Vale. |
| Elegant Feather Moss... | P. elegans..... | Sheepstor, Great Mistor. |
| Waved Feather Moss .. | P. undulatum ...... | Lydford, Cornwood. |
| Dwarf Starry Feather Moss... | Hypnum Sommerfeltii... | Hood Bridge |
| Golden-leaved Feather Moss .. | H. chrysophyllum | Shaugh. |
| Yellow Starry Feather Moss... | H. stellatum ......... | Ilsington, Lydford, Cock's Tor. |
| Large Claw-leaved Bog Feather Moss | H. lycopodioides ... | Bogs, Dartmoor, Tory Brook. |
| Floating Feather Moss... | H. fluitans... ....... | Great Mistor, North Bovey. |
| Twirling Feather Moss... | H. revolvens......... | White-Tor, Cock's Tor. |
| Sickle-leaved Feather Moss... | H. uncinatum ...... | Shaugh Bridge, Cock's Tor. |
| Curled Fern Feather Moss... | H. commutatum ... | Shaugh Bridge, |
| Sendtner's Feather Moss... | H. Sendtneri ... .. | White Tor, Nun's Cross. |
| Cyprus-leaved Feather Moss... | H. cupressiforme ... | Dartmoor. |
| Upward- turned Feather Moss ... | H. resupinatum ... | Common. |
| Wet-meadow Feather Moss... | H. Lindbergii ...... | Bickleigh Down, Heytor. |

| ENGLISH NAMES. | LATIN NAMES. | LOCALITY. |
|---|---|---|
| Plumy-crested Feather Moss | H. molluscum ...... | Dartmoor, Common. |
| Yellow mountain-Rill Feather Moss... | H. ochraceum ...... | Dartmoor. |
| Neat-meadow Feather Moss... | H. purum ............ | Shaugh, Cornwood. |
| Straw-like Feather Moss... | H. stramineum...... | Cock's Tor, Nun's Cross. |
| Scorpion Feather Moss... | H. scorpioides ...... | White Tor, Tavy Cleave. |
| Schreber's Feather Moss... | Pleurozium Shreberi... | Dartmoor, Common. |
| Glittering Feather Moss... | P. splendens ...... .. | Lydford, Shaugh. |
| Short-beaked Feather Moss... | Hylocomium brevirostre... | Yannadon, Lydford. |
| Drooping-leaved Feather Moss... | H. squarrosum ...... | Prince Town, Vixen Tor. |
| Triangular-leaved Feather Moss... | H. triquetrum ...... | Shaugh Bridge, Lydford. |
| Rambling Mountain Feather Moss... | H. loreum ............ | Lydford, Vixen Tor. |

## Scale Mosses and Liverworts.

### Hepaticæ.

| LATIN NAMES. | LOCALITY. |
|---|---|
| Gymnomitrium crenulatum... | Great Mistor. |
| Sarcoscyphus Ehrhardti ...... | Bickleigh, Lydford Houndtor. |
| Alicularia scalaris ... | Bickleigh Vale, Fingle Bridge. |
| A. compressa ......... | Tavy Cleave. |
| Plagiochila spinulosa... | Holne Chase, Lydford. |
| Scapania compacta... | Blackingstone Rock Bagtor, Fingle Bridge. |
| S. æquiloba ......... | Dewerstone, Auswell Rock. |
| S. undulata ......... | Tavy Cleave. |
| S. irrigua ............ | Tavy Cleave. |
| S. nemorosa ......... | Tavy Cleave, Holne Chase. |

| LATIN NAMES. | LOCALITY. |
|---|---|
| S. umbrosa............ | Tavy Cleave, Lydford. |
| Jungermannia albicans... | Holne Chase. |
| J. crenulata ......... | Lydford Cascade, Buckfastleigh. |
| J. gracillima ......... | Lydford, Lustleigh. |
| J. nana ............ ... | Lydford. |
| J. sphœrocarpa ...... | Tavy Cleave. |
| J. obovata ............ | Cornwood Cascade. |
| J. hyalina ............ | Sheepstor Bridge, Fingle Bridge. |
| J. riparia ............ | Tavy Cleave. |
| J. inflata ............. | Ilsington. |
| J. ventricosa ......... | Shaugh Bridge. |
| J. intermedia ........ | Vixen Tor, Dewerstone. |
| J. barbata ............ | Becky Fall, Lydford Fall. |
| J. divaricata ........ | Buckfastleigh. |
| J. bicuspidata ...... | Shaugh, Lydford, Blackingstone Rock |
| J. connivens ... . ... | Dewerstone, Fingle Bridge. |
| J. julacea ............ | Castor Rock, Blackingstone Rock |
| Sphagnœcetis communis... | Vixen Tor, Shaugh. |
| Chiloscyphus polyanthus... | Fingle Bridge, Tavy Cleave. |
| Lophocolea bidentata... | Common. |
| L. heterophylla...... | Chudleigh. |
| Saccogyna viticulosa... | Dewerstone, Cornwood |
| Calypogeia trichomanes... | Lydford, Ilsington. |
| Lepidozia reptans... | Houndtor Wood. |
| L. cupressina.. ...... | Vixen Tor. |
| Mastigobryum trilobatum... | Dewerstone, Tavy Cleave. |
| Physiotium cochleariforme... | Dartmoor, Fingle Bridge. |

| LATIN NAMES. | LOCALITY. |
|---|---|
| Trichocolea tormentella... | Lydford, Ivy-bridge, Buckfastleigh. |
| Ptilidium ciliare...... | Shaugh,Sheepstor |
| Madotheca lœvigata | Lydford, Holne Chase. |
| M. rivularis ......... | On alder trees, Fingle Bridge. |
| Frullania Hutchinsiœ... | Lydford. |
| F. fragilifolia... ..... | Dartmoor. |
| Aneura pinguis ...... | Bogs, Dartmoor, Rippon Tor. |
| A. multifida ......... | Holne Chase, Lydford. |
| Phragmicoma Mackaii... | Lydford, Chudleigh Rocks. |
| Lejeunia serpyllifolia... | Tavy, Dartmoor. |

## MARCHANTIACEÆ.

| | |
|---|---|
| Marchantia polymorpha... | Common. |
| Dumortiera irrigua... | Dartmoor. |
| Reboulia hemisphœrica.. | Bickleigh Vale. |
| Targionia Michelii... | Ilsington. |
| Anthoceros punctatus... | Ilsington, Bovey Heathfield. |
| Lejeunia minutissima... | Shaugh Bridge, |

## EPIPHYTÆ.

| | |
|---|---|
| Cylindrosporium concentricum... | Ilsington. |

## GASTROMYCI.

| | |
|---|---|
| Tremella albida...... | Moreton. |
| Puccinia potentillæ | Rora Wood, Ilsington. |
| P. Heraclei ......... | Ilsington. |

| LATIN NAMES. | LOCALITY. |
| --- | --- |
| Uredo geranii ...... | Ilsington. |
| U. fabœ .............. | Ilsington. |
| U. candida ........... | Ilsington. |
| Æcidium pini......... | Hay's Wood, Meavy. |
| Æ. berberidis ..... | Ilsington. |
| Erineum acerinum | Ilsington. |
| E. pyrinum ......... | Meavy Parsonage. |
| E. griseum ........... | Meavy. |
| Lycogala miniata ... | Palmer's Wood, Meavy. |
| L. minuta ........... | Penn Wood, Ilsington. |
| Trichia ovata......... | Penn Wood, Ilsington. |
| Arscyria punicea ... | Ilsington. |
| Schleroderma verrucosum... | Rora Wood, Ilsington. |
| Bonista nigrescens | High Tor, Down. |
| Cyathus striatus ... | Houndtor Wood, Manaton. |
| C. crucibulum ...... | Court Wood, Ilsington. |
| C. olla .............. | Court Wood, Ilsington. |

## FUNGI.

| | |
| --- | --- |
| Amanita muscaria... | Rora Wood, Ilsington. |
| Agaricus procerus... | Penn Wood, Ilsington. |
| A. melleus ............ | Houndtor, Manaton |
| A. eburneus . ...... | Ilsington. |
| A. nitidus ......... .. | Houndtor and Bagtor Woods. |
| A. lactifluus ......... | Houndtor Woods. |
| A. piperatus ...... .. | Penn Wood, Ilsington. |
| A. gilvus............... | Bagtor, Ilsington. |
| A. odorus ............ | Rora Wood, Ilsington. |
| A. farinaceus ......... | Ilsington. |
| A. tuberosus ......... | Ilsington. |

| LATIN NAMES. | LOCALITY. |
|---|---|
| A. squamula ......... | Rora Wood, Ilsington. |
| A. sordidus ......... | Bagtor Wood, Ilsington. |
| A. violaceus ......... | Penn Wood, Ilsington. |
| A. cinnamomeus ... | Bagtor Wood, Ilsington. |
| A. floccus ........... | Ilsington. |
| A. tener .............. | High Tor Down. |
| A. hypnorum......... | High Tor Down. |
| A. campestris......... | Sheepstor. |
| Cantharellus cibarius .. | Bagtor Wood. |
| Polyporus perennis | Moreton. |
| Boletus bovinus ... | Bovey Tracey, Stover. |
| B. piperitus ......... | Houndtor Wood. |
| B. luridus .......... . | Rora Wood, Ilsington. |
| B. scaber ........... | Bagtor Wood. |
| Calvaria trichopus | Penn Wood. |
| Geoglossum hirsutum... | Ilsington. |
| Helvella mitra ...... | Ilsington. |
| Leotia lubrica ...... | Court Wood, Ilsington. |
| Phallus foetidus...... | Becky Fall, Bagtor. |
| Peziza repanda ...... | Bagtor Wood. |

## HYPOXALA.

| | |
|---|---|
| Stormatosphæria fusca... | Ilsington. |
| Cucurbitaria coccinea ... | Buckland Woods. |
| Cryptosphæria Taxi... | Ilsington. |
| Sphæria spermoides | Meavy. |
| S. aurea .............. | Rora Wood |
| Phacidium coronatum... | Buckland Wood. |
| Hysterium pulicare | Buckland Wood. |
| H. rubi .............. | Penn Wood, Ilsington, Shaugh Bridge. |

## LICHENES.

| LATIN NAMES. | LOCALITY. |
|---|---|
| Ephebe pubescens | Foxtor, Pewtor, Blackingstone. |
| Collema nigrescens | Holne Chase. |
| Leptogium muscicola... | Blackstone, Lustleigh Cleave. |
| L. tremelloides ...... | North Bren Tor. |
| L. Burgessii ......... | Lydford. |
| L. lacerum ......... | Buckfastleigh. |
| L. sinuatum ......... | Ashburton, Chagford. |
| Calicium trachelinum | Holne Chase. |
| C. quercinum ...... | Ilsington. |
| Sphærophoron compressum... | Dartmoor. |
| S. coralloides ..... ... | Sheepstor, Vixen Tor. |
| S. fragile ............ | Sheepstor, Vixen Tor. |
| Bæomyces rufus ... | Lustleigh Cleave. |
| B. roseus ............ | Bovey Heathfield. |
| Cladonia endiviœfolia... | Lustleigh Cleave, Heytor. |
| C. cervicornis ...... | Dartmoor, Heytor. |
| Cladonia delicata ... | Vixen Tor. |
| C. alcicornis ......... | Dartmoor. |
| C. gracilis ............ | Sheepstor, Blackingstone Rock |
| C. cornucopioides... | Dartmoor. |
| C. digitata ............ | North Bovey, Ilsington. |
| C. bellidiflora......... | Lustleigh Cleave. |
| Cladina sylvatica ... | Dartmoor. |
| C. uncialis ............ | Dartmoor. |
| C. turgescens......... | Great Tor. |
| Stereocaulon coralloides... | Leather Tor, Yestor. |
| S. paschale ......... | Blackingstone Rock, Vixen Tor. |
| S. denudatum......... | Crockern Tor. |
| Usnea barbata ...... | Bickleigh Vale. |
| U. hirta ............... | Ilsington. |
| Alectoria bicolor ... | Foxtor, Pewtor. |
| A. jubata ............ | Lustleigh Cleave. |

| LATIN NAMES. | LOCALITY. |
|---|---|
| Evernia furfuracea | Great Mistor. |
| Cetraria aculeata ... | Foxtor, Pewtor. |
| C. var, muricata...... | Pewtor. |
| Platysma triste ...... | Dartmoor. |
| P. sœpincola ......... | Vixen Tor. |
| P. Fahlunense ...... | Heytor. |
| P. glaucum............ | Dartmoor, Widecombe. |
| P. coralloides......... | Vixen Tor. |
| Nephromium lusitanicum... | Bickleigh, Ashburton. |
| N. lœvigatum......... | Chagford. |
| Peltigera aphthosa | Ilsington. |
| P. canina ............ | Common. |
| P. rufescens ......... | Lustleigh Cleave, North Bovey. |
| P. polydactyla ...... | Cornwood, Becky Fall. |
| P. scutata ........... | Lustleigh Cleave, Lydford, |
| P. horizontalis ...... | Ilsington, Dartmoor. |
| Strictina intricata. . | Heytor. |
| S. crocata ............ | Dartmoor. |
| S. limbata ............ | Shaugh, Dartmoor. |
| S. fuliginosa ......... | Dewerstone Rocks, Ivybridge. |
| S. sylvatica ......... | Dartmoor. |
| S. Dufourei ........ | Lydford. |
| S. scrobiculata ...... | Dewerstone. |
| Stricta pulmonacea | Lydford, Ivybridge. |
| Ricasolia amplissima... | Lustleigh Cleave, Bren Tor, Widecombe. |
| R. lœtevirens...... .. | Lydford, Ivybridge |
| Parmelia caperata... | Common. |
| P. olivacea ............ | Common. |
| P. exasperata......... | Shaugh Bridge. |
| P. lanata ............. | Dartmoor. |
| P. physodes ......... | Dewerstone. |
| P. cetrarioides ...... | Okehampton, Vixen Tor. |
| P. perlata ........... | Vixen Tor. |

| LATIN NAMES. | LOCALITY. |
|---|---|
| P. pertusa ............ | North Bovey. |
| P. tiliacea ............ | Holne Chase. |
| B. Borreri ...... ..... | North Bovey, Ilsington. |
| P. conspersa .. ...... | North Bovey, Ilsington. |
| P. saxatilis............ | Dartmoor, Common. |
| P. lœvigata ......... | Two Bridges. |
| Physcia aquila . .... | Dewerstone Rocks Lustleigh Cleave. |
| P. flavicans ......... | South Brent. |
| Umbilicaria pustulata... | Dartmoor, Heytor |
| U. polyphylla......... | Dartmoor. |
| U. monophylla ...... | Blackingstone Rock. |
| U· flocculosa ......... | Near Prison, Princetown. |
| U. erosa ........ ...... | Great Mistor. |
| U. polyrrhiza......... | Pew Tor, Houndtor. |
| U. proboscidea ...... | Blackingstone Rocks. |
| U. cylindrica ......... | Crockern Tor. |
| Pannaria rubiginosa | Lydford. |
| P. triptophylla ...... | Lydford. |
| P. carnosa ...... ... | South Brent. |
| Squamaria saxicola | Brent Tor. |
| Placodium candicans... | Okehampton, Chudleigh. |
| Lecanora squamulosa | Leather Tor. |
| L. f. simplex ......... | Buckfastleigh, |
| L. tartarea ............ | Lustleigh Cleave, Yestor. |
| L. parella ............ | Moreton. |
| L. rupestris ......... | Chudleigh Rocks. |
| L. calcarea............ | Chudleigh. |
| L. Dicksonii ....... . | Cranbrook Castle. |
| L. glaucoma ......... | Dartmoor. |
| L. anaurtiaca......... | Chudleigh. |
| L. epulotica ......... | Ashburton. |
| L. pyracea............ | Ilsington. |
| L. hœmatomma . | Whiddon Park. |
| L. rubra .............. | Moreton. |

| LATIN NAMES. | LOCALITY. |
|---|---|
| L. ventosa ............ | Pewtor, Dartmoor |
| Pertusaria dealbata... | Dartmoor. |
| P. ceuthocarpa ...... | Bagtor, Ilsington. |
| Lecidea sylvicola... | Buckfastleigh. |
| L. lucida............... | Cornwood. |
| L. decolorans......... | Great Links Tor. |
| L. lapicida ............ | Yestor. |
| L. rivulosa............ | Sheepstor, Lustleigh. |
| L. fusco-atra ...... .. | Dartmoor. |
| L. contigua ........ | Dartmoor. |
| L. confluens ......... | Chudleigh Rock. |
| L. calcivora ......... | Ashburton. |
| L. platycarpa ...... | Yestor. |
| L. canescens ......... | Chudleigh. |
| L. atro alba ......... | Chudleigh. |
| L. lutea ............... | Lydford. |
| L. pulverea ......... | Lydford. |
| L. citrinella ......... | Heytor, Dartmoor. |
| L. sphœroides ...... | Lustleigh Cleave. |
| L. carneola ......... | Ilsington, Blackingstone Rock. |
| L. geographica ...... | Dartmoor |
| L. petrœa .......... .. | Lustleigh. |
| L. Parmeliarum ... | Bovey Tracey. |
| Graphis elegans...... | Lydford, Ivybridge, |
| G. scripta ........ ... | Common. |
| G. dendritica ......... | Ivybridge. |
| G. betuligna ......... | Ilsington. |
| Opegrapha lentiginosa... | Lydford, Ivybridge. |
| O. herpetica ......... | Common. |
| O. atra ............... | Common. |
| Stigmatidium circumscriptum... | Lydford. |
| Arthonia lurida ...... | Okehampton, Lydford. |
| A. astroidea .. ...... | Bickleigh. |
| A. trachylioides .. .. | Chudleigh. |
| Normandina pulchella... | Lydford. |

| LATIN NAMES. | LOCALITY. |
|---|---|
| Endocarpon miniatum... | Chudleigh. |
| E. fluviatile ......... | Rivers Plym, Lyd, Teign. |
| E. rufescens ......... | Okehampton. |
| E. hepaticum ......... | Blackingstone Rock. |
| Verrucaria calciseda | Chudleigh Rock. |
| V. antesellens......... | Ivybridge, Lydford |

## ALGÆ.

| | |
|---|---|
| Palmella rosea ...... | Houndtor Wood, Manaton. |
| Nostoc verrucosum | Dartmoor. |
| Zygnema bipunctatum... | Ilsington. |
| Z. quiniuum ......... | Ashburton. |
| Z. inflatum............ | Haytor Down. |
| Conferva ericetorum... | Bovey Heathfield. |
| Ectocarpus aureus | Dartmoor, Ilsington. |
| Ulva bullosa ....... | Ilsington, Ashburton. |

YES TOR.

# CHAPTER XVIII.

## MISCELLANEOUS.

THE TORS, HILLS, EMINENCES AND ROCKS OF DARTMOOR AND THE
BORDERS—LIST OF THE KNOWN EXISTING STONE ROWS ON DART-
MOOR—FLINT AND BRONZE ON DARTMOOR—LUKIS' PLANS OF DART-
MOOR ANTIQUITIES—DARTMOOR AND STANNARY SEALS—FOLK-LORE OF
DARTMOOR—WILLIAM BROWNE'S LYDFORD JOURNEY—THE GUBBINS'
TRIBE—THE AMMIL ON DARTMOOR.

### LIST OF THE TORS, HILLS, EMINENCES, AND ROCKS OF DARTMOOR AND ITS BORDERS.*

AISH TOR.—South of the hamlet of Poundsgate, Widecombe.
108, S.W.

AMICOMBE HILL.—Bounded on the east by the West Okement,
on the west by the Rattlebrook. 88, N.E.

ARCH TOR.—Archeton, Post Bridge. 99, S.W.

ARMS TOR.—Lydford, 1411 ft. 88, S.W.

ASSYCOMBE HILL.—Midway between King's Oven and Fernworthy,
1500 ft. 99, N.E.

AUSEWELL OR ANSWELL ROCKS, OR HAZEL ROCK, OR TOR—
Buckland in the Moor, 1000 ft. 108, S.W.

BAG TOR.—Ilsington. 108, N.E.

BAGGA OR BOG TOR.—South of Standon Hill. 1219 ft. 98 N.E.

BAIR, OR BARE DOWN TOR AND HILL.—Two Bridges. 1681 ft.
99 S.W.

BARN HILL.—On the north side of the road from Tavistock to
Merivale Bridge. The road is 1080 ft. 96, N.W.

BEACON ROCKS.—Ugborough Beacon, north west of the
Wrangaton Railway Station. 1233 ft. 119 S.E.

BEL TOR.—North east of Widecombe, south of Sherberton
Common. 1208 ft. 108, S.W.

BEL TOR.—South of Honeybag Tor. 1319 ft. 100 S.W.

BELLEVER TOR. Between the Moreton and Ashburton Roads.
1456 ft. 107, N.E.

---

*The references are to the sheets of the six inch ordnance map. Where different
heights are shown on the map, the highest is here given.

BELSTONE TOR.—South of Belstone village, between the East Okement and Taw Rivers. The Ordnance Bench Mark near is 1568 ft. 77, S.W.

BENCH TOR, or BENGIE or BENJAY TOR,.—Between the Venford Brook and the Dart River, on the north-eastern part of Holne Moor. 108, S.W.

BIRCH TOR.—North of Headland Warren. 99, N.E.

BLACK DUNG HILL.—East of Great Mis Tor, above the source of the Blackabrook. 1615 ft. 98, S.E.

BLACK TOR.—There are three Black Tors on Dartmoor, as shown on the Ordnance Map. The first is near Brent, on the Avon, above Shipley Bridge. 119, N.E. The second is on Walkhampton Common, east of the road to Prince Town. 106, S.E. And the third, far away in the North quarter, on Okehampton Common, near the east bank of the Okement River, west of Yes Tor, and High Wilhayes. The highest point is 1646 ft. 88 N.E.

BLACKADON TOR.—Near Leusdon Hamlet, Widecombe. 108, N.W.

BLACK ALDER TOR.—Lee Moor. 118, N.E.

BLACK RIDGE.—West of Cranmere Pool, between Great and Little Kneeset. 1853 ft. 88, S.E.

BLACK DOWN.—The Down on the eastern side of the railway as the line approaches Lydford from Tavistock. Highest point, 1280 ft. 88, S.W.

BLACK DOWN HILL.—The high ground north of Yes Tor. Highest point 1345 ft. 76, S.E.

BLACK HILL.—North of Hey Tor Down, west of Yarner Wood. 1333 ft. 100, S.E.

BLACKINGSTONE ROCK.—East of Moreton Hampstead. 1033 ft. 90, S E.

BOTTOR ROCK.—Hemiock. 101, N.W.

BOWERMAN'S NOSE.—Hayne Down, Manadon, 100, N.E.

BONE HILL ROCKS.—North-east of Widecombe Village. 1227 ft. 100, S.W.

BOULTER'S TOR.—Above Peter Tavy. 1000 ft. 98, S.W.

BRA TOR.—See Broad Tor.

BRANSCOMBE'S LOAF AND CHEESE.—North of Bridestowe and Sourton Commons. 1744 ft. 88, N.E.

BRENT TOR.—St Michael's Church upon it. Four miles north of Tavistock. 97, N.E.

BRENT HILL.—Above South Brent. 120, N.W.

BRIM HILL TOR.— Mary Tavy. 98, S.W.

BROAD DOWN.—Otherwise Broadun, between the sources of the East and West Dart. 1738 ft. 99, N.W.

BROAD TOR, OR BRA TOR.—Between Arms Tor and Doe Tor, N.E. of Lydford. 1511 ft. The late Mr. Widgery, the well known artist and painter of Dartmoor scenery, erected upon this Tor, in 1887 as a Queen's Jubilee Memorial, a granite cross which is clearly seen from the railway by travellers to Lydford. 88, S.W.

BROWN HEATH.—Between the junction of Red Lake with the River Erme. At the foot is Erme pound. 1356 ft. 113, S.E.

BUCKLAND BEACON.—West of the village of Buckland in the Moor. 1282 ft. 108, S.W.

BUTTERDON HILL.—West of Harford, north of the Western Beacon. 1204 ft. 90, N.E.

BUTTERTON HILL.—Between Ugborough and Harford Moors. 1196 ft. 119 S.E.

BUTTERN HILL.—North of Gidleigh Common. 1357 ft. 89, N.E.

CALLISHAM TOR.—Meavy. 112, S.W.

CALVES-LAKE TOR.—South-west of Plym Head. 113, N.W.

CAWSAND BEACON, see COSDONNE HILL.

CASTOR ROCK.—On Chagford Common. 89, S.E.

CATER'S BEAM.—Above Plym Head. 1544 ft. 113, N.W.

CHAT TOR.—West of the Rattlebrook Stream. 1774 ft. 88, S.E.

CHINKWELL TOR.—South of Honey-Bag Tor, above Widecombe. 1463 ft, 100 S.W.

CLEAVE TOR, OR CLEAVE ROCKS.—West of Belstone, near Halstock Cleave. 77, N.W.

COCK'S HILL.—North-east of Langstone Moor, above the Walkham River. 1644 ft. 98, S.E.

COLLARD TOR.—Shaugh Moor. 118, N.E.

COMBESTONE TOR.—North of Holne Moor. The leat of the disused Wheal Emma Mine flows round its base. 107, S.E.

COMBESHEAD TOR.—North of Combshead farmhouse, above Ditsworthy. 112, N.E.

COOMBE TOR, GREAT. COOMBE TOR, LITTLE.—East of Peter Tavy. The Peter Tavy Brook runs between the two Tors. 98 S.W.

CONIES' DOWN TOR.—On Conies' Down, between the Cowsic and Walkham Rivers. 1668 ft. 98, S.E.

AA

CORNDON TOR.—On the North after leaving Dartmeet, on the Ashburton Road. 107, N.E.

COSDONNE HILL, OR CAWSAND BEACON.—1796 ft. 77, S.W.

COX TOR.—West of Great Staple Tor. 1414 ft. 106, N.W.

CRAMBER TOR.—South of Prince Town. 1426 ft. 106, S.E.

CROCKERN TOR.—Above Two Bridges. 1295 ft. 107, N.W.

CROW TOR.—West of the West Dart. 1646 ft. 99 S.W.

CROWNHILL TOR.—Crownhill Down, above Plympton. 118, N.E.

CUCKOO BALL.—East of Western Beacon. 119, S.E.

CUMSTON, OR COMBESTON TOR.—Overlooking the Dart, south of Dartmeet. 1156 ft. 107, S.E.

CUTHILL.—Between the higher waters of the Tavy and the East Dart. 1980 ft. 99, N.W.

DANAGOAT, OR DUNAGOAT TOR, HIGHER.—1845 ft.⎫
DANAGOAT, OR DUNAGOAT TOR, LOWER.—1832 ft.⎬ 88, S.E.
On Bridestowe and Sourton Common. ⎭

DEVIL'S TOR.—Near Bairdown Menhir. 1784 ft. 99, S.W.

DEWERSTONE ROCK.—Above Shaugh Bridge, on the Plym. 118, N.W.

DINGER TOR.—South of High Wilhayes, above the source of Brim Brook, a tributary of the West Okement. 1810 ft. 88, N.E.

DOE TOR.—On Doe Tor Common. East of Lydford, between the Doe Tor Brook and the Wallabrook. 88, S.W.

DOWN RIDGE.—The high ground east of the Swincombe River. South of Hexworthy. Highest elevation, 1398 ft. 107, S.E.

DOWN TOR.—On the western part of Walkhampton Common. 1201 ft, 112, N.E.

EASDON, OR EAST DOWN TOR, OR EASTDON.—West of North Bovey and Manadon villages. 1439 ft. 100 N.W.

EASDON HILL.—Is further east than the last mentioned tor.

EASTERN BEACON.—South of Ugborough Beacon, and Beacon Rocks. 119 S.E.

EAST HILL.—West of Halstock and Belstone. The heights are given as 1087 ft. and 1149 ft. 76, N.E.

EAST, OR EASTERN TOR.—Above the Warren House of Ditsworthy on the north. 76, S.W.

EYLES BARROW.—Walkhampton Common. 113, N.W.

FEATHER TOR.—West of Vixen Tor, called Feat Feather Tor in the 6 inch Ordnance map. 106, N.W.

FORESLAND LEDGE.—On the south west slope below High Willhayes. About 1980 ft. 88, N.E.

Fox Holes.—West Dart. 1473 ft. 99, S.W.

Fox Tor.—Mary Tavy. 98, S.W.

Fox Tor.—East of Nun's Cross. Below is Child's Tomb and Fox Tor Mire 113, N.W.

Fur Tor.—In the most dreary part of the Moor, near the sources of the Tavy. The height is 1877 ft. Cut Hill, on the east, rises to 1981 ft. 98, N.E.

Ger or Great Tor.—West of Tavy Cleave. 1250 ft. 98, N.W.

Giants' Hill.—Above the junction of the Plym and the Shavercombe Brook. 113, S.W.

Gidleigh Tor.—"Crowned with the ruins of a house, which a "Mr. Prinsep commenced to build upon it and never "completed, and in consequence known as Prinsep's Folly. "The tor is also generally referred to by this name." Wm. Crossing. 89, N.E.

Glasscombe Ball.—East of Harford. 1179 ft. 119, S.E.

Grea Tor.—On Heytor Down. 100, S.E.

Grea Tor Rocks.—West of Grea Tor, on the other side of the Becka Brook. Sometimes called Leighon Tor. 100, S.E.

Gradner Rocks.—Near Lustleigh Cleave. 529 ft. 100, N.E.

Green Hill.—South of Foxtor Mire, near the rise of the upper tributaries of the Erme. 113, N.W.

Green Tor.—South of Amicombe Hill, above the Rattlebrook. 1750 ft. 88, S.E.

Gren Tor.—On the southern part of the Common lands of the parishes of Sourton and Bridestowe. 1693 ft. 88, N.E.

Gut, or Gutter Tor.—North-west of Ditsworthy Warren House. The height is not given, but the Ordnance Bench mark on the high ground south is 1149 ft 112, S.E.

Hare Tor.—West of Watern Oak. 1740 ft. 88, S.E.

Harter Tor.—Walkhampton Common. 106, S.E.

Harter Tor, Higher.—⎫ Above Ditsworthy Warren. 113,
Harter Tor, Lower.—⎭ N.W.

Hameldown Beacon.—On Hamel Down, above Widecombe. 1695 ft. 100, S.W.

Hameldown Tor.—On Hamel Down, south of Grimspound. 100, N.W.

Hangershell Rock.—Eastward, above Harford. 1142 ft. 119, S.E.

Hawks Tor.—Shaugh Moor. 118, N.E.

HANGER DOWN.—A high Common extending from the Erme river to Cornwood. 715 ft. 119. S.W.

HANGING STONE HILL.—East of Taw Head. 1983 ft. 89. S.W.

HARTLAND TOR.—On the right bank of the East Dart, above Post Bridge. 1350 ft. 99, N.W.

HAWTHORN CLITTER.—Hew Down, Gidleigh. 89, S.W.

HAY TOR ROCKS.—On Hay Tor Down, north of Ilsington. 100, S.E.

HEMSTONE ROCKS.—Between Fernworthy and the Grey Wethers. 89, S.E,

HEMERDON BALL.—East of Plympton. 700 ft. 118, S.E.

HENLAKE DOWN.—The high ground immediately above Ivybridge Railway Station. 696 ft. 125, N.W.

HEN TOR.—Between the Plym, near Ditsworthy Warren House and Shatercombe Head. 113, S.W.

HESSARY TOR.—See Histworthy.

HICKATON HILL.—Dean Moor. 113, S.E.

HIGH TOR.—Mary Tavy. 98, S.W.

HIGHER TOR.—South of Belstone Tor, 77, S.W.

HIGH WILHAYES.—South of Okehampton. The highest point in the South of England. The central Bench Mark is 2039.4 ft. 88, N.E.

HISTWORTHY TOR, NORTH.} Prince Town, commonly called North
HISTWORTHY TOR, SOUTH. } and South Hessary Tors, 107, S.W.

HOCKINGTON TOR.—South of Mel Tor Wood, on the Dart, Widecombe. 108, S.W.

HOLNE RIDGE.—South of the village. 1555 ft. 113, N.E.

HOLLOW TOR.—North-east of Prince Town. 106, N.E.

HOLLOW TOR.—North of Tunhill Rock, Blackslade Down. 108. N.W.

HONEYBAG TOR.—North-east of Widecombe. 100, S.W.

HOLE ROCK.—Hay Tor Down. 100, S.E.

HOLWELL TOR.—On Hay Tor Down, above the Blackabrook. 100, S.E.

HOMERTON HILL.—West of Yes Tor. 76, S.E.

HOOKNEY TOR.—On Hookney Down, North of Grimspound. 100, N.W.

HOUND TOR.—On Hound Tor Down, Manadon. 100, S.E.

HOUND TOR.—Metheral Hill, south of Taw Marsh. 1622 ft. 89, N.W.

HUNT TOR —Above the buildings of the Rattlebrook Peat Works, on Bridestowe and Sourton Common. 1843 ft. 88, N.E.

HUNTS' TOR.—Piddledown Common, in the Fingle Valley, west of Whyddon Park, which is opposite. 78, S.W.

HUNTER'S TOR.—Lustleigh Cleave. 100, N.E.

HUCCABY TOR.—Between Dunnabridge Pound and Dartmeet, on the North. The Bench Mark in the road below is 1067 ft. 107, N.E.

HUCKEN TOR.—Above Merivale Bridge, to the South, near the Prince Town railway. On the other side of the railway is King Tor. 1083 ft. 106, N.E.

INGRA TOR.—On Walkhampton Common. North-east of Leedon Tor. 106, S.E.

IVY TOR.—Near Belstone, on the opposite side of the river. 77, N.W.

KENNON HILL.—Throwleigh Common. 1563 ft. 89, N.W.

KING TOR.—On Hookney Down. 100, N.W.

KING'S TOR.—On Walkhampton Common. The Prince Town railway winds round it. 106, N.E.

KITTY TOR OR KIT TOR.—On the northern slope of Amicombe Hill. 1920 ft. 88, N.E.

KNEESET GREAT.—North West of Black Ridge. 1835 ft. 88, S.E.

KNEESET LITTLE.—South of Great Kneeset. 1665 ft. 88, S.E.

KIT TOR.—See Kitty Tor.

LAUGHTER TOR.—North of Dunnabridge Pound. 107, N.E.

LEATHER TOR.—Walkhampton Common. 112, N.E.

LEEDEN TOR.—Walkhampton Common. 106, S.E.

LEGIS TOR.—Ringmoor Down. 112, S.E.

LEIGHON TOR.—See Grea Tor Rocks.

LEIGH TOR.—A long range of rocks running east and west, in Widecombe, west of Holne Chase, on the other side of the Dart. 108, S.W.

LYDFORD TOR.—Two Bridges. 1647 ft. 99, S.W.

LINK'S TOR, GREAT.—On Bridestowe and Sourton Common. 1908 ft. 88, N.E.

LINK'S TOR, LITTLE.—Bridestowe and Sourton Common. 1704 ft. 88, N.W.

LINTS TOR.—Between the West Ockment River and Brim Brook, 88, N.E.

LITTAFORD TORS.—South-east of Wistman's Wood. 152 ft. 1460 ft. 99, S.W.

LONGAFORD TOR.—The fine pile of rocks north-east of Wistman's Wood. Highest point 1595 ft. 99, S.W.

Lover's Leap.—A rock in Buckland Woods, above the Dart, with a legend.  108, S.W.

Lowery Tor.—Walkhampton Common, between the Prince Town railway Station and the road to Moreton Hampstead and the Devonport leat.  112, N.E.

Luckey Tor.—On the south part of Yar Tor Down, close to the Dart River.  107, S.E.

Long Timber Tor.—Near the river Tavy, south of Mary Tavy.  98, S.W.

Lynch Tor [or Lints Tor, on the old one inch Ordnance Map] South East of Stannon Hill.  98, N.E.

Maiden Hill.—East of the sources of the Walkham River. 1774 ft.  98, S.E.

Meldon Hill.—South of Chagford.  90, S.W.

Mel Tor.—Near Lower Torr, Widecombe.  108, S.W.

Merrypit Hill.—About a mile from the Warren House Inn, west of the road from Tavistock to Moretonhampstead. 99, N.E.

Metheral Hill.—South of Taw Marsh.  1500 ft.  77, S.W.

Middledown, Milldown or Meldon Hill.—South of Chagford. 90, S.W.

Middle Tor.—Chagford Common.  89, S.E.

Mill Tor East.—Black Down, Okehampton.  1683 ft. 77, S.W.

Mill Tor West.—Black Down, Okehampton.  76, S.E.

Mistor Great.—North-west of Prince Town.  98, S.E. 106, N.E.

Mistor Little.—South of Great Mistor.  106, N.E.

Nat Tor.—On Nattor Down, below Tavy Cleave.  98, N.W.

Nattadon Common.—South of Chagford.  90, N.W,

Nodden Great.—North of Bridestowe and Sourton Commons. 1430 ft.  88, N.W.

Okement Hill.  1850 ft.  89, N.W.

Oke Tor.—On the northern part of Belstone Common.  77, S.W.

Peek Hill.—Walkhampton Common.  1311 ft.  112 N.E.

Penn Beacon.—Cornwood.  1403 ft.  119 N.W.

Pew Tor.—Sampford Spiney.  958 ft.  106, S.W.

Puggie Stone.—A rock on the right above Holy Street Mill, Chagford.

Raven's Tor.—On the Lyd, below the Gorge.  88, S.W.

Raven Rock.—In Buckland Woods.  108. S.W.

Rendlestone Tor.—Prince Town.  106, N.E.

Rippon Tor.—Ashburton. 1531 ft. 108, N.E.

Roborough Rock.—On Roborough Down. In old maps Ulstor, or Ullestor Rock.

Rolls Tor.—106, N.W.

Rook Tor.—East of Cholwich Town, Cornwood. 119, N.W.

Rough Tor.—West of the West Dart, 1793 ft. 99, S.W.

Rough Tor.—Between the Moor Brook and the Blackavon Brook. East of Black Down. 76, S.E.

Royal Hill.—East of Prince Town, 1333 ft. 107, S.W.

Saddle Tor.—Bagtor Down. 108, N.E.

Scarey Tor.—Belstone Common, West. About 1200 ft. 77, S.W.

Shapeley Tor.—On Shapeley Common. 1597 ft. 108, N.W.

Sharp Tor.—On Piddledown Common,. Whyddon Wood is opposite. 78, S.W.

Sharpi Tor.—In Lustleigh Cleave. 100 N.E.

Sharp Tor.—On Yar Tor Down, south. 107, S.E.

Sharp Tor.—Rattlebrook Hill. 1701 ft. 88, S.E.

Sharpitor.—Walkhampton Common. 112, N.E.

Shavercombe Tor.—South West of the Shavercombe Brook, a tributary of the Plym. 113, S.W.

Sheepstor, or Shittistor.—Above Sheepstor village. 112, N.E.

Shell Top.—North of Penn Beacon, Cornwood. 1544 ft. 119, N.W.

Shilstone Tor.—Bridestowe and Sourton Common, north. 76, S.E.

Shilston Tor.—[Shellstone Hill] Throwleigh Common, east. 1029 ft. 77, S.E.

Sittaford Tor.—Near the Grey Wethers. 1764 ft. 99, N.W.

Skat Tor.—Above the Teign Valley, between Bridford and Christow. 91 S.W.

Slipper Stones.—On the West Okement. Opposite Black Tor Copse, which is on the eastern side of the river 88, N.E.

Sourton Tors.—Near Sourton Village. 76, S.W.

Stannon Tor and Stannon Hill.—West of the road from Prince Town to Moreton Hampstead. 99, N.E.

Stannon Hill.—Stannon Down, Peter Tavy. 98, N.E.

Staple Tor, Great. —⎫ Peter Tavy. The heights 106, N.W.
Staple Tor, Little. —⎬ are not given but they 106, N.W.
Staple Tor, Middle.—⎭ probably average 1400 feet. 106, N.W.

STEEPERTON TOR.—Between the small streams, sources of the River Taw. 1738 ft. 89, N.W.

STEWART'S HILL—Shaugh Moor. 118, N.E.

STINKA TOR.—On Bridestowe and Sourton Commons, east. The height is probably about 1900 ft. 88, N.E.

THORNWORTHY TOR.—Thornworthy Down. 89, S.E.

THREE BARROWS.—West of Hickley Plains, Ugborough, 1521 ft. 119, N.E.

TOP TOR.—Blackslade Down. 108, N.W.

TOR ROCKS.—Harford. 119, S.E.

TOR ROYAL, or South Hessary Tor. 107, S.W.

TROWLESWORTHY TOR, GREAT.—⎱ Lee Moor. 112, S.E.
TROWLESWORTHY TOR, LITTLE.—⎰ North of the latter. 112, S.E.

TUNHILL ROCKS.—Blackslade Down, Widecombe. 108, N.W.

UGBOROUGH BEACON.—1230 ft. See Beacon Rocks. 119, S.E.

VIXEN TOR.—Walkhampton. 106, N.W.

WALKHAM HEAD.—The high point between the sources of the Walkham and Tavy. 1762 ft. 98, N.E.

WATER HILL.—West of the Warren House Inn, 1605 ft. 99, N.E.

WATERN TOR.—1756 ft. 89, N.W.

WESTERN BEACON.—Ugborough, above Ivybridge. 119, S.E.

WETTERDON HILL.—Harford. 119, S.E.

WIND TOR.—Widecombe. 108, N.W.

WILLINGSTONE ROCK.—North of Moreton Hampstead. The Bench mark just below, gives a height of 1066 ft.

WHITE BARRON, EASTERN.—⎱ South Brent. 113, S.E.
WHITE BARRON, WESTERN.—⎰

WHITE HILL.—Black Down, Lydford, 1272 ft. 88, S.W.

WHITE HILL.—Taw Marsh, east. 77, S.W.

WHITE HILL TOR.—Lee Moor. 118, N.E.

WHITE HORSE HILL.—Above Dart Head, the source of the East Dart. 1936 ft.

WHITE TOR.—Cudliptown Down. 1529 ft. 98, S.W.

WHITE TOR, HIGHER.—Between the West Dart and the Cherry Brook. 1712 ft. 99, S.W.

WHITE TOR, LOWER.—Further north of the last. 1658 ft. 99, S.W.

WHITTEN KNOWLES ROCKS.—To the north of Ditsworthy Warren House. 112, S.E.

WILD TOR.—East of Okement Hill. 1741 ft. 89, N.W.

WINTER TOR.—On Belstone Common. 77, S.W.

WOODCOCK HILL.—Between Gren Tor and Hunt Tor, Bridestowe
   and Sourton Common.   88, N.E.

YANNADON.—A high Common, north of Meavy.   112 N.W.

YAR TOR.—Widecombe.   107, N.E.

YES TOR.—Formerly supposed to be the highest elevation on
   Dartmoor, but High Wilhays is now ascertained to exceed
   it by ten feet or thereabouts.   2029 ft.   76, S.E.

### LIST OF STONE ROWS ON DARTMOOR.†

Marked thus * are shewn in the six inch Ordnance Map.

| LOCALITY. | ORDNANCE MAP. | REMARKS. |
|---|---|---|
| *Cosdon | 77 S.W. | East of Cosdon ( or Cawsand ) Beacon, on South Tawton Common. A triple row of stones, starting from sepulchral circles at the west end, and kistvaen. Direction varies a little south of west to east. |
| *Batworthy and * Fernworthy | 89 S.E. | Five double rows of stones, connected with sepulchral remains. Sadly mutilated by newtake wall builders. |
| Langstone Moor, erroneously called Launceston Moor. | 98 S.E. | Single row leading from a dewpond ( ? an excavated cairn) to a menhir.   Direction N.N.E. and S.S.W., length 396 feet. A second single row not quite parallel, about 200 feet to W., now enclosed in old ruined wall, led from a cairn to a blocking stone at right angles, length 330 feet. Numerous sepulchral remains. |
| Conies Down. | 98 S.E. | Double row running almost north and south.   Slight traces of a small cairn 250 feet from south end of row.   Length 529 feet. |

†Furnished by Mr. ROBERT BURNARD.

| LOCALITY. | ORDNANCE MAP. | REMARKS. |
|---|---|---|
| Headland or Challacombe | 99 N.E. | Well defined triple row with remains of five others parallel to the three. Some observers consider that certain of the stones of the latter are the remains of a circle. The north end has been disturbed by mining operations, the south extremity is closed by a triangular menhir. There is a blocking stone near the north end, but the row is continued beyond this. Direction of row north and south. The length is 511 feet. |
| Assacombe. | 99 N.E. | Double row, starting from a sepulchral circle at the eastern end. Blocking stone, at west end, and menhir at east end. Direction, east and west |
| Watern Down. | 99 N.E. | Double row, starting from a wasted cairn and running from south-west to north-east. Menhir S.W. Blocking stone, N.E. Length 460 feet. |
| *Merivale | 106 N.E. | Two double rows, running almost east and west. The south row 849 feet long, the north row, 590 feet. In connection with sepulchral remains. There are traces of a third row connecting with the great menhir. Blocking stone to northern pair of rows at east end. |
| *Hartor | 106 S.E. | A double row and a single row, the latter not parallel with the former, and both starting from sepulchral circles at the eastern ends. Direction, about north-east to south-east. Length of double row, 460 feet, single row, 260 feet. |

| LOCALITY. | ORDNANCE MAP. | REMARKS. |
|---|---|---|
| Peek Hill. | 106 S.E. | Double row, 312 feet long. Twenty-four standing stones, many fallen. Another single row of small stones, parallel with the double, is 36 feet long. All the stones in both rows are very small and the whole is in a ruinous condition. The rows run E.N.E. to W.S.W. There are the remains of a small sepulchral circle, 245 feet E.N.E. of the E.N.E. end. It is possible that the row may have connected with this. These rows are exactly on the summit of Peek Hill, and just behind the dew pond which abuts the road to Prince Town. |
| Laugh Tor. | 107 N.E. | Double row, much pillaged for wall building. No definite sepulchral remains left, but a prostrate menhir closed the north-west end. Direction, south-east to north-west. |
| *Down Tor. | 112 N.E. | Single row starting from a sepulchral circle at the western end and pointing to a cairn east of the other end and distant about 200 yards. Direction south west to north east. There is a blocking stone at the eastern end, and a menhir at the west end of row. Length 1175 feet. |
| *Drizzlecombe. | 112 S.E. | Two single rows, and another which is double for a portion of its length only. Connected with fine sepulchral remains. Blocking stones and menhir to each. The directions of all these are nearly east and west. The row connected with the great Menhir is 260 feet long. |

| LOCALITY. | ORDNANCE MAP. | REMARKS. |
|---|---|---|
| *Trowlesworthy. | 112 S.E. | Single row. Direction east and west. |
| *Stalldon Moor. | 113 S.W. | Single row starting at south end from a large circle which is more of the sacred, than sepulchral type. This extraordinary row which runs south to north, not however in a strait line, can be clearly traced for a mile and a half. It is said to extend to 2¼ miles terminating in a kistvaen. |
| *Hook Lake. | 113 S.E. | Double row which starts from a circle at the north end. Associated with sepulchral remains. Direction north and south. |
| *Cholwich Town | 118 N.E. | Single row of large stones. Commences on the north with the remains of a sepulchral circle. Direction north east to south south-west. Length 710 feet. |
| *Trowlesworthy. | 118 N.E. | Remains of a double row, starting at the north end from a sepulchral circle with a second double row running in a somewhat different direction N. and S., one being 405 feet 6 inches long, and the other 252 feet 7 inches long. |
| Stalldon Barrow. | 119 N.W. | This very fine row of large stones, mostly prostrate, situated about 350 yards north-west of Stalldon Barrow, starts from sepulchral remains, at the north end and runs almost due south. Length 1400 feet. |
| Butterdon Hill. | 119 N.E. | Starts from a circle of fallen stones and runs a little east of north, terminating in a tall stone, to the south-east of Sharp Tor. |

| LOCALITY. | ORDNANCE MAP. | REMARKS. |
|---|---|---|
| Glazecombe | 119 N.E. | A row, with western end double, whilst towards the east it is single. Connected with sepulchral remains. Direction, S.W. to N.E. |
| Coryndon Ball. | 119 N.E. | Eight rows in all, parallel. Connected with sepulchral remains. Direction, S.W. to N.E. These and Glazecombe vary from 300 to 400 feet in length. |
| Tristis Rock. | 119 S.W. | Single row. Starting at south end, with a sepulchral circle, and running due north. Length, 1200 feet. |

Besides these, here mentioned, Mr. R. N. Worth has noted others recently, which are described in his papers, in the Transactions of the Devonshire Association, 1893, 1894 and 1895.

## List of Plans of Dartmoor Antiquities, by the Rev. W. C. Lukis, M.A.

In the Library of the Society of Antiquaries, Burlington House, London, is a portfolio of plans, drawn to scale, from careful surveys made by the Rev. William Collins Lukis, M.A., F.S.A. in the years 1879 and 1880, at the request of the Council, and at the cost of the Society. It is hoped that before long, arrangements may be made for publishing these plans, but examination shows that in many, revision is necessary, and it will not be wise to publish without careful verification of the measurements of Mr. Lukis.

The following is a list :—

1.—Ground plan of a hut circle on the north-west slope of Teigncomb Down. Castor.
2.—Elevation and section of the same hut circle.
3.—Ground plan, section and elevation of the Roundy Pound, Teigncomb Down.
4.—Ground plan, section and elevation on the south-east slope of Teigncomb Down.
5.—Holed stones in walls in lane near Teigncomb hamlet.

6.—Holed stone in North Hill Lane, near Teigncomb hamlet.

7.—South avenue, Merivale Bridge, with menhirs and cairn.

8.—Avenue leading to a ruined circle ?   Merivale Bridge.

9.—The Long Stone circle and barrow.   Merivale Bridge.

10.—Details of No. 7.

11.—Plans and elevations of four lines of stone row, Chilla-combe Down.

12.—Do.      do.

13.—Stone row No. 1.   Trowlesworthy ; about 400 feet long.

14.—Do.   No. 2.   do.

15.—Stone row on Castor.

16.—Stone row on Castor ; The Longstone Avenue.   See Journ. Brit. Arch. Assoc., 1860, vol. xvi., p. 113.

17.—Plan of stone row on Castor with cairn.

18.—Plan of stone row leading to cairn with four concentric circles. Between the row and the cairn are two fallen pillars, one 11 feet 7 inches long, the other 7 feet 3 inches long.   See 6-inch Ordnance Map, Sheet lxxxix., S.E.

19.—The menhir at end of stone row.   Castor.

20.—Stone rows.   Hickley Plain, Coryndon Ball.

21.—Plan of two monuments on the Moor outside Glazecombe Moor Wall, between the East and West Glazebrooks, Coryndon Ball.   Many of the stones of these rows are small, buried nearly to their tops and many are invisible, and were found by probing the ground.   In one row there are thirteen lines of stone connected with a cairn.   See Proc. Soc. Ant. 2 Ser., vol. viii., p. 477.

22.—Plan of row and small circle.   Cholwich Town Moor, Cornwood.

23.—Stone cross used as a gate-post in the lane leading to Cholwich Town Farm, Cornwood.

24.—Plan and elevation of row and circle, No. 22.

25.—Line of stone with cairn, on the Plym.   Drizzlecombe.

26.—Avenues at foot of Hartor, east of Black Tor, with two cairns.

27.—Details of row on Hartor, east of Black Tor, No. 26.

28.—Details of cairn and line on Hartor, east of Black Tor, below Prince Town.

29.—Plan of Drewsteignton Dolmen as re-erected.

30.—Plan of the Grey Wethers, Sittaford Tor.

31.—Plans and elevations of stones of south circle, Sittaford Tor.

32.—Plan of stone row leading to cairn, Hartor, Drizzlecombe, with menhir now re-erected.

33.—Plan and elevation of circle and barrows. Froggymead, Fernworthy.

34.—Plan of barrow with cist near junction of Upper Plym and Langcombe.

35.—Plan of Grimsgrave, in Langcombe Bottom.

35a.—Plan of cisted barrow near Brisworthy, north-east of Brisworthy circle.

36.—Plan of the Druid's Circle, Scaurhill, Gidleigh.

37.—Plan of Brisworthy Circle, and plan and elevation of stones of circle ; north of Trowlesworthy.

38.—Plan and section of Beehive hut on the north side of Stalldon Moor ; right bank of Erme.

39.—Plan of circle and part of line of stones on Stalldon Moor.

40.—Plans of stones of the Stalldon Moor monument for a distance of 842 feet from the circle.

41.—Plan of sacred circle and plan and elevation of stone row, south-east of Erme pound.

42.—Plan showing the deviation of line of stones on Stalldon Moor. 11,239 feet 8 inches from circle on south to cisted cairn.

43.—Holed stones in wall of land on right and left hand before arriving at French-bere Farm. Chagford.

44.—Holed stone used as a gate-post at the entrance of farm-yard, French-bere.

44a.—Holed stone lying on ground at entrance to field on the left of road by gate of French-bere Farm.

45.—Plan of oblong enclosure and of hut circles on French-bere.

46.—Plans and elevations of stones of oblong enclosure, French-bere.

47.—Plan and elevation of walls of hut circle on French-bere.

48.—Plan of remains of hut circle, French-bere, and section and elevation.

49.—Plan of circle and cairn, The Nine Maidens, Belstone.

50.—Holed stone on ground on the right hand of road up Middleton Hill, near the Ashburton Road. Split for gate-post.

50a.—Holed stone used as a gate-post at entranc to a field on the left hand at foot of hill, on the way from ddleton Hill towards Prince Town.

50b.—Holed stone in a ditch on right hand, in l...e leading from Chagford to Prince Town.

50c.—Holed stone in a wall at the end of lane leading from Chagford to Prince Town, near the edge of the down.

51.—Plan of stone row and cairns on Hingston Hill, east of Down Tor, from cairn to cairn, 1475 feet.

52.—Plans and elevations of stones of row, Hingston Hill, No. 51.

53.—Do.    do., continuation.

54.—Do.    do., plan, elevation and section of cairn and circle, west end of row.

55.—Plan, section and elevation of hut on Roundy Hill, Cramber Tor.

### FLINT IMPLEMENTS.

It was, we believe, Mr. Francis Brent who first drew attention to the fact that stone implements were to be found upon Dartmoor, and he, and the late C. Spence Bate obtained, not only arrow heads, scrapers, and flakes, but also two polished celts from the peat near the head of the Walkham. Other specimens of different kinds were met with from time to time in various parts of the Moor, and in 1887, flakes and nodules of flint in very considerable numbers were found by Mr. F. N. Budd, on his estate at Batworthy, near Chagford. The nearest point from which flint is obtainable, is upwards of twenty miles from Chagford Common, where Batworthy is situated. Up to 1889, Mr. Budd had found in three adjoining fields, covering an area of about nine acres, no less than five thousand two hundred specimens of flint and chert, and in the whole he had collected six thousand four hundred flakes and nodules, a large number of which had been more or less carefully worked. "With few "exceptions, the nodules, from which the flakes had been struck "off, were water-worn, sea-shore pebbles,* * * * and as many of "the specimens were of a chocolate-coloured chert, similar in "character to the chert pebbles which occur on the beach at "Sidmouth, and some of the Batworthy flints evidently came "from the chalk and not from the greensand, Mr. Budd was "inclined to look to the east of the Exe for the source from which "much of the material came."*

Large numbers of flint flakes aud other small implements have, as above mentioned, been procured by Mr. Brent, from various localities on the Moor, more especially from Yes Tor,

*Proceedings Teign Naturalists' Field Club, 1889, p. 9.

White Tor, and Cock's Tor Hill; from the cultivated land near the latter place he obtained several hundreds.*

From the neighbourhood of Okehampton, Mr. J. D. Prickman obtained arrow heads and flint flakes, which he presented to the Albert Museum, Exeter; and Mr. Robert Burnard and members of his family have, from time to time, found large numbers of flakes, scrapers, arrow heads, knives, cores and fragments, and from Brown Berry, upwards of four thousand specimens have been collected by them. Mr. Burnard has compiled a list of such stone implements as have hitherto been found upon Dartmoor, showing the locality, by whom collected, and in whose possession they now are.†

These discoveries afford further evidence, if such is needed, of the fact of there having been a large population upon Dartmoor, in Neolithic times.

### BRONZE.

While evidences of the Stone age are so abundant on Dartmoor, it is the reverse with the relics of the bronze using people, but it should be remembered, as Mr. Francis Brent observes, that "the recorded finds of bronze implements in Devon "and Cornwall are numerous in comparison with those in some "other counties," and he gives a long list of recorded examples.‡ As mentioned in another part of this volume a beautiful pommel of a dagger handle, and a part of a dagger blade were taken from a barrow, on Hameldon, in 1872.§ Many years ago, the date of which we cannot ascertain, but it was probably between 1840 and 1850, eight bronze celts were found at Bovey Tracey, four placed side by side, under a granite block—perhaps the coverstone of a kistvaen, or the capstone of a dolmen—the others scattered about. In 1851, in the parish of Hemiock, two stone moulds for casting bronze weapons were found. Several spear-heads were found in 1854, on the verge of Dartmoor, in the parish of South Brent, at a place called the Bloodypool,** and with them ferules for their shafts. Another ferule in the possession of Mr. Robert

---

*Trans. Devon Assoc., vol. xvii., pp, 70-77, Ibid. vol. xviii,. pp. 74-75

†Dartmoor Pictorial Records, Vol. iv., pp. 12-18.

‡Trans. Plymouth Inst. vol. ix., pp. 307-313.

§Ante p. 147.

**Archæological Journal, vol. ix., pp. 185-186. *Ibid.* vol. xii., pp. 84-85. *Ibid.* vol. xviii. pp. 160-161

Burnard, was found at Gawler Bottom, Post Bridge, in 1892, and Mr. H. P. Hearder, of Plymouth, has a bronze dagger, found by a moor-man, working in a peat bog at Broadhall, near Plym Head, also in the year 1892. These are the last recorded finds of articles of bronze upon Dartmoor or its borders.

### DUCHY AND STANNARY SEALS.

It may be desirable to describe such seals of the Duchy of Cornwall and the Stannary Courts as are known. Impressions of nearly all are in the British Museum.

#### I.—STANNARY SEAL.

A shield of arms with a carved scroll at each side: fifteen bezants in pile, five, four, three, two and one for the county of Cornwall. Above the shield, a duke's coronet of five strawberry leaves.

·PRO·STANNARIIS·IN·COMITAT·DEVO·

1¾ in., 16 cent.

#### II.—SEAL OF HENRY, PRINCE OF WALES, DUKE OF CORNWALL, AND EARL OF CHESTER, AFTERWARDS HENRY V. OFFICE OF THE COCKETT.

In a quadrilobe a shield of arms: quarterly 1, 4, France, modern; 2, 3, England; over all a label of three points, each indistinctly charged; Henry Prince of Wales. Between two ostrich feathers labelled; over the shield a swan rising.

S'HENRIC'PRINCIPIS WAL'DUC'CORNUB' COMIT'CESTR'DE'OFFICIO COCKETTI DUCATUS CORNUBIE.

2⅛ in. A.D., 1399-1413.

#### III.—SEAL OF CORPORATION OF STANNATORS OF THE STANNARIES.

On a platform two miners, to the left, working: the one on the right, has a spade with triangular blade and single shoulder, the other on the left, a mattock. In the centre a lion's face, the tongue protruded, back ground diapered lozengy, with a rose in each space.

S'COMVNITATIS·STANGNATORUM·CORNUBIE.

2 in., 13 cent.

### IV.—COCKETT SEAL OF DUCHY OF CORNWALL.

Bust of a king, with crown of three points fleury, drapery fastened on the breast with a fibula, between two sprigs of foliage.

SIGILLU·DE·COKETT·DUCAT·CORNUB'.

$1\frac{1}{16}$in.  14 cent.

### V.—SECRETARY'S LETTER SEAL.

Oval: an oval shield of the royal arms of Great Britain, with an escutcheon of Saxony and label of three points for difference, encircled with a garter inscribed with the motto of the order, and ensigned with a prince's crown and plume. Supporters of Great Britain, each with a label, and placed on a riband, bearing the motto, ICH DIEN, entwined with the rose, thistle, and shamrock.

Inscription in the field above:—

DUCHY OF CORNWALL.

Below on a plinth,

SECRETARY.

$1\frac{7}{8}$ in.  *cir.* 1842.

### VI.—SEAL OF SIR WALTER RALEGH, KNT.

Warden of the Stannaries of Cornwall and Devon ; Captain of the Royal Guard, and Governor of the Island of Jersey.

The Warden, in plate armour, with plumed helmet, sword and shield of arms, riding to the left, on a galloping horse, caparisoned and plumed. The armorial bearings of the shield and caparisons are, five lozenges in bend ; Ralegh.

Border of two concentric circles beaded.

Legend in two concentric circles :—

(1).  SIGILL·DNI·WALTERI:RALEGH:MILITIS:
GARDIAN:STANNAR:CORNVB:ET:DEVON.

(2).  CAPITAN:GARD:REG:ET:GVBERNATOR:INSVLÆ:
DE:JERSEY.

Outer border beaded.

$1\frac{3}{4}$in.  *cir.* 1600.

See Gent. Mag., vol. lvii., p. 459.

### VII.—LETTER SEAL OF ALBERT EDWARD, PRINCE OF WALES, K.G.

Rectangular, with rounded corners : an oval shield of the royal arms of Great Britain, with an escutcheon of Saxony, and label of three points for difference; Prince of Wales. The shield is enriched with a garter, inscribed with the motto of the order, and ensigned with a prince's crown and plume of three ostrich feathers. Supporters of Great Britain, each with a label as above, and placed on carved scrolls. In base a riband bearing the motto: ICH DIEN. The whole within a border bezantée, for Cornwall, inscribed in base:—

DUCHY OF CO[RNWALL.]

$1\frac{9}{10}$ in.  *cir.* 1842.

### VIII.—THE SEAL NOW IN USE AT THE DUCHY OFFICE FOR DEEDS, LEASES, ETC.

In a circle, a battlemented portcullised gateway, flanked by two battlemented towers. In front of the gate-way a lion, with mural crown, sejant gardant. Above, a shield of arms with fifteen bezants in pile, 5, 4, 3, 2 and 1, for the county of Cornwall. Above the shield a duke's coronet. In a circle around the legend:—

THE SEAL OF THE DUCHY OF CORNWALL.

As a crest upon the letter paper, used at the Duchy office is the towered gateway, lion and ducal crown; and the arms of the Prince of Wales are also used thus:

Quarterly 1 and 4, gu., three lions passant, gardant or, England; 2, or, a lion rampant within the royal tressure, gu, Scotland; 3 az. a harp or, stringed arg., Ireland; a label of three points arg. for difference, on an inescutcheon, barry of ten, or and sa, a rue crown in bend vert, Saxony. Crest; on the coronet of the Prince of Wales a plume of three ostrich feathers. Motto of the Garter. Supporters:—Dexter, a lion gardant or, crowned with the Prince of Wales' coronet. Sinister, an unicorn arg., gorged with a coronet, therefrom a chain reflexed over the back, or, each differenced as in the arms. Motto—Ich Dien.

### FOLK-LORE.

We can only touch this most interesting subject very briefly. There is much to be done with reference to it, and many facts are to be collected. Our loving and loved friend, Richard John King, used to say that he believed almost every form of superstition, or of superstitious observance condemned in the Penitential of Bartholomew, Bishop of Exeter—1161-1184, might be found sheltering itself under the Dartmoor Tors,* and yet no collection has been made of such beliefs. It is true that the Devonshire Association has a committee, which has printed twelve reports on the Folk-Lore of Devon, but the contents of these are very fragmentary, and, so far, no serious effort has been made to compile an account of the Folk-lore peculiar to Dartmoor and its borders, to say nothing of the wider area of the County—to deal with which would greatly extend the scope of the enquiry.

" Thor and Woden are mere names to us, but to trace them " back, in the Folk-Lore of Dartmoor, or elsewhere, to days when " they were mighty powers, ' felt in the blast and heard upon the " wind;' to follow up existing beliefs to the time when our first " English ancestors made their appearance on the skirts of " Cosdon, or of Hey Tor ; or to find in local names and traditions, " indications of the same obscure period, when the old creeds of " the opponent races, Briton or Englishman, were brought face to " face ; this is certainly no ' chasse aux blanches moines,' no idle " or unprofitable field for the exercise of true imagination."†

We are not aware that there is any item of Folk-lore, or an observance of any kind which is peculiar to Dartmoor. All seem to have their analogies elsewhere. We find the " black fire- " breathing hounds of Odin, in the pack of hell-dogs, led by their " dark hunter—a tall figure with a hunting poll—rushing headlong, " regardless of bog or river, in their wild chase, and the moor- " man shudders as he sees and hears the wish hounds." And well he may, for the sight and sound bring misfortune, especially if the day be a Sunday. With dogs and ferrets, certain men went rabbiting, on the first day of the week, an old moor-man narrates, and when in a wild glen above the Avon river, they heard the wish-hounds ; with a dismal noise the dogs fled homeward, and at the end of a fortnight, men, dogs, and ferrets were all dead. And there are many other weird stories of these hounds told with bated breath, by the dwellers on the Moor, and in spite of Mission Chapels and Board schools, with undoubting credulity. The black dog of the Moor is often seen, and James Perrott, the Chagford guide‡ firmly believed he had encountered it more than

---

*See also RICHARD JOHN KING. Sketches and Studies, 1874, p. 324-5.

†RICHARD JOHN KING. The Folk-lore of Devonshire. Fraser's Mag., vol. viii. NS. p. 774.

‡The death of this well-known fisherman and Dartmoor enthusiast is announced while this book is passing through the press. He was a guide, philosopher, and friend to many, who will regret the loss of so genial and original a companion.

once, and on one occasion he was bold enough to attack it, but without any result. This dog haunts the Dewerstone, the stone of Tiu—the Teutonic Deity, who still visits this rock, the traces of a naked human foot, and a cloven hoof being sometimes visible in the snow.

The great Dolmen of Drewsteignton and the stories connected with it have already been referred to. The Three Spinners still linger in the persons of three witches, who on a certain night in June pass through the air, dropping, or refraining from dropping, charms upon the bloom of the orchards, and in those in which the charms fall, there will be no fruit that year.

Rock and river worship have their survivals. The Stone Row (*Stan-ræwe*) dances at noon and at midnight, the Grey Wethers turn round in the sunshine, and the river Sprite of the Dart, claims its yearly victim :—

> " River of Dart, river of Dart,
> Every year thou claims't a heart."

Within the memory of the older generation, May fires were lighted, and milch cows were made to pass through them to make the animals fruitful, and to keep them from ill during the coming year.

The visit of the Evil one to Widecombe in 1638, followed by the great storm—before described and commemorated in prose and verse—may also be mentioned.

The belief in pixies is very strong, and the Dartmoor wanderer is frequently pixy-led, but the remedy for this is simple, the little folk are tidy and neat, and a derangement of some part of the traveller's attire, will restore him to his proper course. In the books of Mrs. Bray and Mr. Crossing, will be found a good deal of information with respect to these elves, who are to be conciliated but not defied.* They are not, however, so frequently seen as formerly, the reason given, being, that they object to the sound of the bells—*ding-dongs* the moor-men call them—now rung for the services at the Dartmeet and Post Bridge new Mission Chapels.

Richard John King, who as we have said, was always keenly interested in the subject, would repeat the story he had heard in the neighbourhood, of Knowles, the famous and prosperous weaver of Dean Coombe, who died and was buried, but the next

---

*MRS. BRAY. A Peep at the Pixies, or Legends of the West, 1854. WILLIAM CROSSING. Tales of the Dartmoor Pixies, 1890.

day he appeared sitting at the loom in his chamber, working diligently as when he was alive. His son applied to the parson, who went accordingly to the foot of the stairs, and heard the noise of the weaver's shuttle in the room above. "Knowles," he said, "come down, this is no place for thee." "I will," said the weaver "as soon as I have worked out my quill," *i.e.*, his shuttle full of wool. "Nay," said the vicar, "thou hast been long "enough at thy work, come down at once!" So when the spirit came down, the vicar took a handful of earth from the church yard, and threw it in its face, and in a moment it became a black hound. "Follow me," said the vicar, and it followed him to the gate of the wood. When they came there, it seemed as if all the trees in the wood were coming together, so great was the wind. Then the vicar took a nut-shell with a hole in it, and led the hound to the Pan pool, in the vale of Dean Burn, below the waterfall. "Take this shell," he said, "and when thou shalt "have dipped out the pool with it, thou mayest rest—not before." At mid-day or at midnight, the hound may still be heard at its work, and some have seen it.

Many old customs, charms, omens and beliefs linger yet upon and about the Moor, but for various reasons they are disappearing, and are not being handed down from parent to child as formerly. Will no one do for the Folk-lore of the West what has been done for its Songs?

### WILLIAM BROWNE'S LYDFORD JOURNEY.

Although it has been printed over and over again, we cannot omit from this volume the poem of Lydford Law, or Lydford Journey, by William Browne. This was first printed by Prince, in his Worthies of Devon, sixteen verses being given, and later in a more complete state, by Andrew Brice, in his Grand Gazetteer or Topographical Dictionary, 1759, in a note to the article on Lydford, page 828. Brice calls it a pretty old piece of humour, and says that he was "furnished with a true copy of "the original very Manuscript, by the Transcriber, late Mr. Hals, "of Cornwall's own Hand," and that Mr. Hals stated—"This Mr. "*Wm. Brown* (says he) A.D., 1644, coming to *Lydford* Castle to "visit his Friend, Lieut. Col. *James Hals* (Son of Sir *Nicholas* "*Hals*, late of *Fentongollen*, *Cornwal*, Knt.) then and there a "Prisoner of War, of the Parliament party, under the custody of "Sir *Richard Grenvill*, Knt., King Charles I.'s General in the

" *West*, and the said Mr. *Browne* (and his companions) having had
" a full View of this Town and Castle of *Lydford*, soon after his
" return to *Tavistock*, sent Mr. *Hals*, under his own MS. those
" now [*viz*. by Mr. *Prince*] printed Verses, with the MS.
" Additions of verse 9-10-11, of which Mr. *Prince* absolutely
" wanted knowledge."

Brice was, however mis-informed, for as Mr. Gordon Goodwin,
the latest editor of Browne's poems, points out, the verses must
have been written before 1644, for they are found in the manuscript of Westcote's *View of Devonshire*, the date of which is
1630—printed for the first time in 1845. The three verses
9-10-11, to which Brice refers as not having been known to Prince,
do not, however, as Mr. Goodwin thinks, appear in Westcote's
MS., at least, they are not in a manuscript copy in our possession,
nor in two other copies which we have examined, and we suppose
that Dr. Oliver and Pitman Jones took them from the Grand
Gazetteer to make the poem complete.

Law, as administered at Lydford, was in bad odour long before
the days of William Browne, for Wright in his Political Poems,
prints some verses,* the date of which he fixes as of the earlier
half of the month of September 1399, in which the following lines
occur :—

> Now be the law of Lydfford
> in londe ne in water,
> oughte evylle to thryve,
> thilke lewde ladde
> that hongith on his hippis
> More than he Wynneth,
> And doughteth no debte,
> so dukis hem preise,
> but beggeth and borwith
> of burgeis in townes
> ffurris of ffoyne
> and other ffelle whare,
> and not the better of a bene,
> though they born evere.

So that in the 14th century Lydford law had an evil reputation.
It is not unlikely that this reputation was acquired when the old

---

*THOMAS WRIGHT. Political Poems and Songs relating to English History, com-
posed during the period from the Accession of Edward III to that of Richard III,
vol. 1, p. 399.

Forest Courts existed and the Law of the Forest was administered with all its severity. The tradition was carried on when the Stannary Courts flourished, and, if what a German writer tells us is true as to the punishments inflicted by the latter, there was nothing to choose between the cruel penalties to life and limb inflicted by the Courts of the Forest, and those of the Tinners.

The poem, if such it can be called, of William Browne follows in its integrity.

> I oft have heard of Lydford law
> How in the morn they hang and draw
>     And sit in judgment after :
> At first I wondered at it much ;
> But soon I found the matter such
>     As it deserves no laughter.
>
>
> They have a castle on a hill ;
> I took it for some old wind-mill,
>     The vanes blown off by weather.
> Than lie therein one night 'tis guessed,
> 'Twere better to be stoned or pressed,
>     Or hanged, ere you come hither.
>
>
> Ten men less room within this cave
> Than five mice in a lanthorn have :
>     The keepers too are sly ones :
> If any could devise by art,
> To get it up into a cart.
>     'Twere fit to carry lions.
>
>
> When I beheld it, Lord ! thought I,
> What justice and what clemency
>     Hath Lydford castle's high hall !
> I know none gladly there would stay,
> But rather hang out of the way,
>     Than tarry for a trial.

Prince Charles* a hundred pounds hath sent
To mend the leads and planchings† rent
    Within this living tomb ;
Some forty-five pounds more had paid
The debts of all that shall be laid
    There till the day of doom.

One, lies there for a seam of malt,
Another, for two pecks of salt,
    Two, sureties for a noble.
If this be true, or else false news
You may go ask of Master Cruise,‡
    John Vaughan or John Doble.§

Near these poor men that lie in lurch,
See a dire bridge, a little church,
    Seven ashes and one oak ;
Three houses standing, and ten down ;
They say the rector hath a gown,
    But I saw ne'er a cloak :

Whereby you may consider well
That plain simplicity doth dwell
    At Lydford without bravery ;
And in that town, both young and grave
Do love the naked truth, and have,
    No cloaks to hide their knavery.

This town's enclosed with desert moors,
But where no bear nor lion roars,
    And nought can live but hogs :
For, all o'erturned by Noah's flood,
Of fourscore miles scarce one foot's good,
    And hills are wholly bogs.

---

*This would seem to fix approximately the date of the verses, viz., between 1612, the year of the death of Prince Henry, and 1625, the date of the accession of Charles.

†*Planchings*, *i.e.*, wooden floor. The word is still in use in the Devonshire verna-cular as meaning board of any wood of about an inch thick, *i.e.*, flooring board if thicker it is *plank*.

‡Steward of the Court.

§Attorneys of the Court. These notes appear in Westcote's MS., and the names are probably those of well-known persons.

And near hereto's the Gubbins' cave ;
A people that no knowledge have
    Of law, of GOD, or men :
Whom Cæsar never yet subdued ;
Who've lawless liv'd ; of manners rude ;
    All savage in their den.

By whom, if any pass that way,
He dares not the least time to stay,
    For presently they howl ;
Upon which signal they do muster
Their naked forces in a cluster,
    Led forth by Roger Rowle.

The people all within this clime
Are frozen in the winter time,
    Or drown'd with snow or rain ;
And when the summer is begun
They lie like silkworms in the sun,
    And come to life again.

'Twas told me, ' in King Cæsar's time
This town was built of stone and lime,'
    But sure the walls were clay ;
And these are fall'n for aught I see,
And since the houses have got free,
    The town is run away.

O Cæsar ! if thou there didst reign,
While one house stands, come there again,
    Come quickly, while there is one ;
For if thou stay'st one little fit,
But five years more, they will commit
    The whole town to a prison.

To see it thus, much grieved was I ;
The proverb saith " Sorrow be dry,"
    So was I at the matter ;
When by good luck, I know not how,
There thither came a strange stray cow.
    And we had milk and water.

Sure I believe it then did rain,
A cow or two from Charles his wain,
 For none alive did see :
Such kind of creatures there before,
Nor shall from hence for evermore
 Save pris'ners, geese and we.


To nine good stomachs with our whigg,
At last we got a tithen pig,
 This diet was our bounds ;
And this was just as if 'twere known
A pound of butter had been thrown
 Among a pack of hounds.


One glass of drink I got by chance,
'Twas claret when it was in France,
 But now from it much wider ;
I think a man might make as good
With green crabs* boil'd in Brazil wood
 And half-a-pint of cider.


I kiss'd the mayor's hand of the town,†
Who, though he wears no scarlet gown,
 Honours the rose and thistle.
A piece of coral to the mace,
Which there I saw to serve in place,
 Would make a good child's whistle.


At six o'clock I came away,
And pray'd for those that were to stay
 Within a place so arrant :
Wide and ope the winds so roar,
By God's grace I'll come there no more
 'Till forc'd by a tin-warrant.‡

---

*Green crabs, *i.e.*, the wild apple.

†The town ceased to return members to parliament in the reign of Edward III., but there was a mayor and corporation until the middle of the 18th century.

‡That is a warrant from the Stannary or Tinner's Court.

## THE GUBBINS' TRIBE.

The memorable journey of Amyas Leigh and Salvation Yeo
from Plymouth to Lydford, as narrated by Charles Kingsley, is of
course known to all our readers, and the fear of an encounter with
the Gubbings was an added peril to the expedition. The travellers
saw the tiny threads of blue smoke rising from the dens of these out-
laws, far away down the slopes below Brent Tor. Fuller hazards
the displeasure of his readers by adding the Gubbings to the list
of Wonders of the County of Devon, daring to call them so,
secured by distance as he says, which one of more valour durst
not do to their face, for fear their fury fall upon him. Fuller's
account, written very probably during his stay at Exeter, 1644-
1647, full of quaintness and quips, is worth quoting in full :—

"Yet, hitherto, have I met with none, who could render a
"reason of their Name. We call the *Shavings* of *Fish* (which are
"little worth) *Gubbings*, and sure it is they are sensible that the
"word importeth *shame* and *disgrace*. As for the suggestion of
"my worthy and learned Friend [*M. Joseph Maynard*] borrowed
"from Buxtorsius [*in his Talmundical Rabinical Dictionary*,
"*Verbo.*] that such who did *inhabitare Montes Gibbercsus*,
"were called Gubbins, such will *smile* at the Ingenuity, who
"dissent from the truth of the *Etymology*."

"I have read of an *England* beyond *Wales* : [See *Camden's*
"*Brit. in Pembrokeshire*] but the *Gubbings-Land* is a *Scythia*
"within *England*, and they pure heathens therein. It lyeth near
"*Brent-Tor* in the edge of *Dartmore*. It is reported that some two
"hundred years since, *two strumpets* being with child, fled hither
"to hide themselves, to whom certain lewd fellows resorted, and
"this was their first original. They are a *Peculiar* of their own
"making, exempt from *Bishop*, *Archdeacon*, and all Authority,
"either *ecclesiastical* or *civil*. They live in *Cotts* (rather *Holes* than
"*Houses*) like *Swine*, having all in common, *multiplied*, without
"*marriage*, into many *hundreds* : Their language is the *drosse* of
"the *dregs* of the *Vulgar* Devonian : and the more learned a man
"is, the worse he can understand them. During our Civil Wars,
"no *Souldiers* were *quartered* amongst them. Their wealth con-
"sisted in other *men's goods*, and they live by stealing the Sheep on
"the *More*, and vain it is for any to search their Houses, being a
"Work *beneath* the pains of a *Sheriff*, and *above* the *power* of
"any *constable*. Such their *Fleetness*, they will out-run many

" horses : *vivaciousnesse*, they outlive *most men*, living in the
" ignorance of luxury, the Extinguisher of Life, they hold
" together like *Burrs*, offend *One*, and *All* will revenge his
" Quarrel."

" But now I am informed, that they begin to be civilized, and
" tender their children to *Baptisme*; and return to be men, yea
" Christians again. I hope no *Civil people* amongst us will turn
" *Barbarians*, now these Barbarians begin to be civilized."*

Fuller, no doubt, heard of the Gubbings during the time he
was in Devonshire, and perhaps had met with William Browne's
poem " Lydford Journey," which was written apparently some
years before, from which we find at that time, the head of the
lawless gang was called Roger Rowle.

As far as we know these are the only contemporary references
to the Gubbins' tribe. There are no allusions to them in Risdon
or Westcote, and later writers are silent, so that we may conclude
that by the middle of the seventeenth century, these unsatisfactory
persons had ceased to be a terror. It is remarkable, that some
five and twenty years since, the inhabitants of a pleasant country
parish in this county, Nymet Rowland, should have been molested
by a family of squatters, who for a time, made things quite as
disagreeable, as did the Gubbins in their generation.


## THE AMMIL.

The Ammil is a well-known phenomenon on Dartmoor, but it
is one that is rarely seen. It consists of the formation of a body
of ice which envelopes every projecting object exposed to the open
air—every stem, spur, berry and leaf of trees and plants, every
blade and member of grass, down to the finest and most minute
particle; each particular stem, leaf, leaflet, blade or berry, bearing
its own separate ice pendant, taking the form of what it encircles,
the pendant of the leaf taking the form of the leaf, the whole leaf
being enclosed in a body of ice of about equal thickness throughout, the pendant of each blade of grass being in the form of the
blade—the deposit or course of ice being proportioned to the size
of the body that bears it, a stout leafless stem of a tree often bearing
a pendant of more than a foot in length and an inch or more in
thickness, whilst the smallest blade or particle of grass bears a
pendant so minute and fine, as to allow of its remaining suspended

---

*THOMAS FULLER. The Worthies of England, ed. 1662, p. 248.

in a bent form without being quite weighed down to the ground.

In January, 1868, this singular appearance was observed throughout the length and breadth of the Moor, and it was quickly announced by the Moor-dwellers that "the ammil was on." An account of the occurrence was written by Mr. J. N. Bennett, of Archeton, and we are quoting freely from him* as it is the only account we know of in print, describing this interesting atmospheric condition. The ammil continued for two nights and days. The effect of the sun shining upon this coating of ice, every point on which the eye could rest, giving forth prismatic colours, dancing and sparkling in the breeze, was beautiful beyond description. A holly tree, between Prince Town and Tor Royal, full of leaves and berries, was an object of wonder and delight to all who saw it.

An appearance similar to this, we are informed, is mentioned as being sometimes witnessed in the North of England, and also in Canada, but we have not been able to obtain any information with regard to it.

The word is curious. It is evidently, as Mr. Shelly points out, the old English word *ammel=enamel.* "Enamelling down to the "sixteenth century, was an art very much practised in England, "and it is curious to find the word surviving from the times when "the work was very familiar, and used still by people, to whom "it is of course, wholly unknown, and who employ the word in "ignorance of its meaning."

*J. N. BENNETT. *Trans. Plym. Inst.*, vol. v., p. 389.

# CHAPTER XIX.

## LYDFORD CHURCH
### AND THE
## CHURCHES OF THE MOORLAND BORDERS.

THE whole of the Forest of Dartmoor is included ecclesiastically in the Parish of Lydford, but it is surrounded on all sides by other parishes, and many of their churches are of interest, and contain monuments which for various reasons, are worthy of note. We propose, in this chapter, to give a short account of each church, drawing attention to what seems most important in connection with its architecture, history or contents. We begin with Lydford, and proceeding northwards, take the churches in order as they lie around the Moor.

**Lydford,**
ST. PETROCK.

This place, eight miles south-west from Okehampton, poor and desolate as it now is, was, as we have seen, in early days, a place of considerable importance. The church consists of a nave about fifty feet long by fourteen feet wide, chancel about eighteen feet long by ten feet wide, south aisle about forty-two feet long by nine feet wide, south porch, and low tower with battlements and crocketted pinnacles, containing five bells, all of one date, 1789, by Pennington, who re-cast them from an antient peal of three, adding fresh metal.

The building is mainly Perpendicular, fifteenth century, but there are earlier remains in the chancel. The open rood-loft staircase is of an unusual character, and the hagioscope which runs through the south pier of the chancel arch and the rood-loft staircase, is curious. The beautiful piscina in the south wall is Decorated, and the very interesting font is perhaps pre Norman.

On a floor stone is the following inscription, in which the reader is taken into confidence :—

Here lyeth the body of Mrs. Elizabeth Farington, the wife of Mr. Thomas Farington the son of Henry Farington of Wyzold in the county of Nottingham gent. There have been eight knights in that family. He died the 8 day of August in the year of our Lord God 1738 aged 94 years we think.

> In Oxford born, in Lydford dust I lie,
> Dont break my grave until ye judgment day,
> Then shall I rise in shining glory bright,
> To meet my Lord with comfort and delight.

The frequently quoted epitaph of George Routleigh, is in the churchyard :—

> Here lies in horizontal position
> the outside case of
> George Routleigh, Watch-maker,
> whose abilities in that line were an honour
> to his profession.

Integrity was the main-spring
and prudence, the regulator
of all the actions of his life.
Humane generous and liberal
his hand never stopped
till he had relieved distress.
So nicely regulated were all his motions
that he never went wrong
except when set a going
by people
who did not know
his key :
even then he was easily
set right again.
He had the art of disposing his time so well
that his hours glided away
in one continuous round
of pleasure and delight
till an unlucky minute put a period to
his existence.
He departed this life
Nov. 14, 1802,
aged 57
wound up
in hopes of being taken in hand
by his Maker
and of being thoroughly cleaned, repaired
and set agoing
in the world to come.

The parish of Lydford includes, as we have said, the whole of
Dartmoor—a parish, probably the largest in England—and in

former days every parishioner, however distant his dwelling might be, had to go for his sacraments to Lydford church, and there he had to take his dead for burial, There were, however, some episcopal relaxations, as in 1260, when the inhabitants of Babbeny and Pushill, had license granted them to attend Widecombe church for the Divine Offices, instead of going, eight miles in fine weather or fifteen in foul, to Lydford. See p. 120.

In connection with the prisons at Prince Town, a church was built by the French prisoners, and fitted up by the Americans, at the beginning of the century. It is dedicated to St. Michael and All Angels. It has a tower which is conspicuous from many parts of the Moor, and the surrounding neighbourhood, and from some parts of Plymouth—Prince Town itself being so elevated.— There is nothing of interest in the church except the pulpit—a Jacobean one—with figures of the the four Evangelists, which was formerly in St. Sidwell's Church, Exeter, and was sold to make room for a modern one.

On a slab fixed against the wall on the south side of Prince Town churchyard is the following inscription, rudely cut :—

> In Memory of
> Three valiant Soldiers
> of the 7th Royal Fusiliers
> Who died on Dartmoor in a
> Snow drift 12 Feby. 53. Corpl. Joseph
> Penton aged 26 years. Privt patk.
> Carlin 23. Geog. Driver 27 years.

The two privates marched from Plymouth to join their company which was stationed at Prince Town, and reaching Jump, now Roborough, were met by the corporal. On arriving at Dousland Barn, the landlord of the inn there, advised them not to go on, as snow was falling and the weather looking very bad. They said, however, they must obey orders, and started again. There were heavy snow-drifts on the road, but the men seem to have succeeded in getting through them, and in reaching the Devil's Bridge, about a mile from Prince Town. There, however, the snow was too much for them, and they appear to have retraced their steps, but they were soon enveloped in the snow and the two privates perished. The corporal somehow struggled back, and surmounting the difficulties at the Devil's Bridge, actually succeeded in reaching a spot within two hundred yards of the Duchy Hotel, Prince Town, where his body was found, when the weather permitted a search to be made.

There are two Mission Chapels, one dedicated to St. Gabriel, at Post Bridge, the other at Dartmeet, dedicated to St. Raphael, and at these, and at the parish church and the church at Prince Town, are provided frequent services for the worship of the dwellers on the Moor.

**Bridestowe,** St. Brigida. This place is situate six miles south-east of Oke-hampton. There have been three churches at different times in this parish. The first was built somewhere below the junction of the two rivulets which pass through the village. This church was destroyed, for what reason is not known, and another was erected near where the present church stands. Why this one was abandoned is a mystery, but it was, and eventually used as the poor-house, and divided up into separate tenements, and the present edifice erected for the worship of the people. In course of time the poor-house became a disgraceful habitation, and an eye-sore to the churchyard. After a long struggle the parishioners at length agreed to its removal, and a new poor-house was provided. In one of the tenements was the arch which now stands at the principal entrance of the

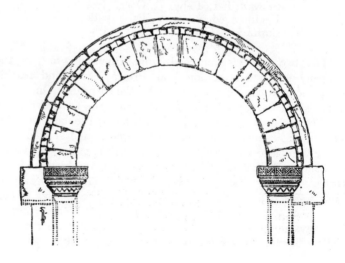

churchyard from the village, which was rescued from destruction and removed with great care. It divided the nave of the church from the chancel.

The nave of the present church (which was restored in 1860) is about forty-eight feet long by fifteen feet wide, chancel thirty feet long by twelve feet wide, north and south aisles; north and south porches; tower at the western end, battlemented, with four square turrets and crocketted pinnacles, with six bells, cast by Taylor, in 1828. The church is said to have been built in 1450, which is the date of the bulk of the edifice. The arcades between the nave and aisles are very good, as are the east window and one on the south. The chancel appears to be Early English. There was formerly a fine, well-proportioned rood screen, which has perished in the various vicissitudes this church has endured from plaster and cement loving custodians, but much has been done of late years to bring it somewhat nearer its original fair proportions.

There are monuments to members of the families of Calmady, 1663; Luxmoore; Wrey, 1576; Nosworthie, 1665; Wollocombe, 1814, and others; and there is a floor-slab with the date 1488, but the rest of the lettering is worn out. That to the Lady Honor Calmady, who died 17 Dec. 1663, has the following lines :—

> Eight fruitful branches still are springing found
> Though here the root lies dead within the ground
> Two husbands in their turns divided lie
> Who both did in the bed of Honor die
> But here the king of terrors—oh ! unjust
> At last has laid their Honor in the dust
> Till that which here is in dishonour sown
> Be raised in honor to a glorious throne.

On Jone Nosworthies' slab, 1665, is the following :—

> An Anagram.
> O none is worthye.
> Approach ye mourners of the sable traine
> Unsluce your sorrows—oh let run amaine
> Hartes swelling fludes of grief, command eache eye
> To melte into a dropping elegye,
> And in doleful language and sad stile
> Lets carve our sister's monumental pile
> Then pollishe it with kisses—that being done
> With an amazed silence let eache one
> Court Fate like Niobe—we may become
> Companion as in life so in the Tombe.

**Sourton,**
**St. Thomas**
**of**
**Canterbury.**
This church is on the north-western edge of the Moor, on a remote and barren down, but close to the line of the South Western Railway. It has chancel, nave, north aisle and tower of three stages, with five bells. The chancel is modern, having been rebuilt in 1848. The old chancel was twenty-four feet long, by ten feet six inches wide. It had a Decorated window of two lights, and another window still earlier. The nave is thirty-six feet long by fifteen feet wide, and the aisle is thirty-four feet six inches long by eight feet nine inches wide. The tower has been said to be Decorated, but Mr. James Hine is of opinion that it is—as is the whole of the rest of the church—Perpendicular, except the south porch, which is part of an earlier church and has a stoup.

There is not a single monumental inscription.

**Okehampton,**
**All Saints.**
The parish church of this pretty and interesting town was, with the exception of the tower, destroyed by fire in 1842, and the antient building and every monument in it perished.

The Chapel of St. James is in the town, the granite tower is Perpendicular, and there are some fragments of carved bench ends. It is the property of the Corporation, and is called the Mayor's Chapel.

**Belstone,**
**St. Mary.**
Two and a half miles south-east from Okehampton. The church consists of nave, about thirty feet long by fourteen feet wide; a chancel about fifteen feet long by fourteen feet wide; south aisle about forty-five feet long by nine feet wide; north porch, and a low square embattled, pinnacled tower, containing five bells, cast in 1751 by Pennington. The tower is Perpendicular, as is the nave, or rather what remains of the older work. There were formerly some remains of Norman and Decorated work. The church had been suffered to go into a miserable state of dilapidation, and in 1881, what amounted really to the re-building of the edifice, except the tower, was effected.

There are no monuments or inscriptions requiring our notice.

The two incised stones at Belstone ought to have careful attention, and a better examination than has been hitherto made, given them.

**South Tawton,** ST. ANDREW.  This, the most northern of the moorland border parishes, is situate about four miles and a half east of Okehampton. The church comprises a nave sixty-six feet long, by eighteen feet wide, a chancel about sixteen feet long by the same in width, with vestry on the north side, north and south aisles sixty-six feet long, the same length as the nave, and nine feet wide, a heavy embattled south porch and a lofty tower embattled and with pinnacled turrets, containing six bells, all except the second which was re-cast in 1837, dated 1744, and cast by Gooding. Against the south wall of the church is a large sun-dial, with the motto from Juvenal, *Obrepit non intellecta senectus.* The building is Perpendicular. There are some good bosses with heads and foliage, and some old glass with shields of arms. The pulpit is of the eighteenth century, of oak, with statuettes of the four evangelists, well carved in wood of a lightish colour.

There are many monumental inscriptions to the members of the Oxenhams, Weekes, Northmores, Whiddons, and other families.

There is a low altar tomb on which is the effigy of a man in armour, with a ruff around his neck, in an attitude of prayer, a bird at his feet, and a canopy over supported by Ionic columns ornamented with scrolls. There is no inscription, but in front is the date 1592, and at the back are two shields of arms; *three battle axes,* for Weekes; and, *in a lozenge, three fusils conjoined in fesse, with a crescent for difference,* for Giffard.

There is also a curious black marble tablet engraved with several figures : a man and a woman kneeling at a desk between them ; under the man, the initials R. B. [Robert Burgoyne] under the woman, the initials M. B. [M. Burgoyne] and a skull : behind the man figures of his sons kneeling, marked respectively G. P. F. and W., with a skull, and an infant in a shroud with the letter O : behind the woman is the figure of a daughter with the letter M. and a skull, and a child in a cradle marked E, also with a skull ; the skulls show that the children were dead. On the desk is the date, 1651. Over is a shield of arms containing a *talbot passant,* for Burgoyne, and *a chevron between three spear-*

*heads*, for Whiddon. The monument is to Robert Burgoyne and Margaret Whiddon his wife. The children indicated by the initials, are George, Phillip, Francis and William, and the infant in the shroud, Oliver, and Margaret, a daughter. The name of the child in the cradle we cannot trace.

**South Zeal.** This is a hamlet five miles south-east of Okehampton, in the parish of South Tawton. Towards the upper end stands a village cross raised from the ground by a base of masonry and four high steps. There is a chapel, dedicated to St. Mary the Virgin and St. Thomas of Canterbury, formerly occupied as a school house, but now restored and used for worship.

**Throwleigh.** This place is seven miles south-east of Okehampton. The church has a nave thirty-six feet long, by sixteen feet wide, chancel twenty-two feet long by thirteen feet wide, north aisle forty-six feet long by ten feet wide, south porch and lofty west tower (the highest on this side of the Moor) embattled with four pinnacles, containing five bells, by Pennington, dated 1763. The style is Perpendicular throughout. It was restored in 1862. The ribs and bosses of the roofs are carved with foliage, and are good. The pulpit, is apparently made up of old bench ends. The priest's door on the south side of the chancel is elaborate. The dedication of this church is not known.

In the north wall of the chancel is a tomb under a low arch, supported by rude heavy buttresses, all of granite, but there is no inscription, and there are no inscriptions of general interest in the church. There is a fifteenth century lichgate, and the priest's house or church house is of the same date.

**Gidleigh, HOLY TRINITY.** Gidleigh is a desolate looking village, but surrounded with wild and romantic scenery. The church consists of nave, about forty-two feet long by fifteen feet wide, chancel about eighteen feet long by twelve feet wide, south aisle about forty feet long by nine feet wide, small north porch and tower of two stages, battlemented, and with four square pinnacles containing four bells, the first, third, and tenor, being pre-reformation, the second cast in 1674. The building is in style, Perpendicular, the screen remains, gilded and coloured, but the loft and vaulting or groining is gone: in the lower panels are figures of saints. There are some fragments of stained glass. The priest's door in the chancel is on the north side. There are no monuments or any inscriptions of general interest.

The remains of Gidleigh Castle, the square tower forming a picturesque object, are of fourteenth century date.

**Drewsteignton.** In this parish is the famous Dolmen, two miles west of the church. The church consists of nave sixty feet long by eighteen feet wide, chancel eighteen feet long by fourteen feet wide, north and south aisles and lofty embattled and pinnacled west tower containing six bells by Pennington, 1784. The nave and tower are Perpendicular, but the latter has a Decorated window, presumably from the older church. The chancel is modern. The dedication is uncertain. Dr. Oliver gives it as the Holy Trinity, and afterwards says it is Allhallows, but it is mentioned in Brantyngham's Register as dedicated to St. Peter.

There are several slabs and tablets commemorating members of the families of Battishill, Pitts, Hill, Bragg, Hall, and others.

**Chagford.** The view eastward from the churchyard is a very fine one. The church consists of nave about **St. Michael.** sixty-two feet long by twenty feet wide, chancel twenty-seven feet long by eighteen feet wide, north and south aisles about seventy-six feet long by ten feet wide, a south porch, and a tower of three stages, with battlements, and containing six bells, re-cast in 1766, by the Bilbies, from an older peal of five.

The church was consecrated in 1261, but little remains of this earlier church. It must have been almost entirely re-built in the middle of the fifteenth century, when the Gorges family had much property in the parish, and the carved *whirlpool* or *gorges* in the bosses of the roof, show the connection between the family and the church.

There are two monuments of importance. Against the north wall of the chancel is a handsome stone altar tomb, with a canopy formed by two semi-circular arches, supported by four columns, with cornice above. There are two shields of arms. It commemorates Sir John Whiddon, of Whiddon Park, judge of the King's Bench, who died 27 January, 1575.

Another is to the memory of John Prouze, who died 19 May, 1664, with a latin inscription and three shields of arms. Other members of the Prouze family are buried here.

Here lyeth the body of ......... wife of Oliver Whiddon, esq., who died the xxxi. day of October, An. Dom. 164-.

> Reader wilt thou know who here is laid,
> Behold a matron, yett a maid,
> A modest look, a pious heart,
> A seekinge for the better part,
> But dry thine eies, why wilt thou weepe,
> Such damsells doe not die but sleepe.

**Moreton Hampstead,**
ST. ANDREW.

This church is beautifully placed in the midst of glorious scenery. Its architecture—Perpendicular throughout—is poor, but from its height, the general appearance is not altogether unsatisfactory, but the appointments —for example, the pulpit of wood painted to imitate granite—are wretched. The nave is about fifty-five feet long by seventeen feet wide, chancel about thirty-three feet long by fifteen feet wide, north and south aisles, south porch, and lofty square embattled tower with six bells re-cast from an ancient peal of five by the Penningtons in 1762. The original design of the late Gothic church has been much interfered with from time to time. The screen was a very good one, but only a few fragments have been preserved. There are some seventeenth and eighteenth century floor and other slabs. The granite memorial floor slabs with inscriptions, in this and neighbouring churches, in Manaton more especially, should be noticed.

Two epitaphs may be quoted: the first on the stone of Francis Whiddon, thirty-two years minister of the parish, 1656.

> Lo here the watchman fallen asleep,
> The pastor that the flock did keep,
> This Jacob's labours now are done,
> He's gone to take his rest thereon.
> Noe planet meteor falling light,
> His orb he shined, a star most bright ;
> Christ's hand did hold him while he went,

His circuit in this firmament.
Weep Moreton, think on't, don't forget,
Thy Cynosura now is sett,
Yet he's but changed, the saint not dies,
This day-star only sets to rise.

On a wooden tablet to the memory of Matthias Nosworthy,
1728.

> If time to come forget
>   How thou in youthful days,
> Remembered God, then let
>   These lines speak thy just praise.
> In sober conversation,
>   On earth did thee advance,
> Now hath made of salvation,
>   An heavenly inheritance.

In the yard on the south side :—

> Sacred to the memory of
> Charles Tozer late of Howten in this
> Parish who died the 27 of February 1813 in the
> 29 year of his Age, Also of two of his children.

A pining sickness gave the fatal blow,
The stroke was certain, but the effect was slow,
With wasting pain, Death found sore oppressed,
Pitied my sighs and kindly gave me rest.

The famous dancing tree of Moreton—an elm—is now sadly
dwindled from its former capacious dimensions, and to all
appearance will soon die.

**Bridford,**
St. Thomas,
of Canterbury.

Consists of nave, chancel, north aisle, south
porch and tower at the western end, embattled
and pinnacled at the corners.

The tower contains four bells, one, the
second, a pre-reformation bell, with the in-
scription, *ora pro nobis :* the tenor is dated 1639, the treble 1664,
and the third 1689.

The nave is about thirty-six feet long by sixteen feet wide,
the chancel about twenty-five feet long by fifteen feet wide, and the
north aisle including the chancel aisle, about fifty feet long by
twelve feet wide. The nave and chancel are separated from the

north aisle by an arcade of four low arches, resting on columns of four shafts, with mouldings between and plain circular moulded capitals.

The chancel has a granite ogee arched piscina, windows three and two light, Decorated, and a lancet. The windows of the north aisle are Perpendicular, one with some fine fragments of stained glass, and in the east window are some shields of arms, among them those of Champernowne and Courtenay.

The screen, without the loft, and despoiled of its groining—a very fine and rich one, said to be of the date 1508, which is confirmed by the badge of Catherine of Arragon being found among its enrichments, gilded and painted—crosses the church at the easternmost pier, and here the chancel ceiling stops without an arch of masonry. Above are mouldings of foliage, and the panels below are filled with figures of saints, bishops, and monks, carved in bold relief, standing in canopied niches. The pulpit has a large ogee domed canopy, and enriched in a manner so similar, and with figures partaking so much of the same character, that Mr. Ashworth thought it must have been made of fragments from the rood screen.

There are some old oak benches with the ends well carved.

There are no monuments, inscriptions, or tablets of any importance.

**North Bovey.**
St. John
the Baptist.

The church, close to the village green, has a nave forty-eight feet long by eighteen feet wide, chancel about twenty-six feet long by twelve feet wide, north and south aisles sixty feet long by nine feet wide, south porch, and embattled tower, containing six bells, all except the fifth, dated 1814, by Bilbie, The style is Perpendicular, but there are some remains of earlier work. The tower is of three stages, and it has the stair turret projecting from the southern face. Much of the rood screen remains, with figures in the lower panels, and also the parclose screens, some antient glass, and much of the original seating of the fifteenth century. There were formerly four old bells, but in 1813 the bishop granted a license for their being cast into a peal of six. The fifth has been recently re-cast by Mears and Stainbank.

The church is beautifully situated on the Hayne or Bovey stream, which is a tributary of the Teign.

This village is beautifully situated on the eastern
**Manaton,** edge of the Moor. The church, churchyard, and
St. Winnifred. the few houses with the green, form a very
pleasing picture. The church has nave about
forty-five feet long by fifteen feet wide, chancel twenty-four feet
long by fourteen feet wide, north and south aisles about fifteen
feet long by eight feet wide, north chapel, south porch with parvise chamber over, and tower one hundred and three feet high,
embattled, and containing four bells, the second, third and tenor
being pre-reformation. There are some fragments of old glass
remaining. The style is Perpendicular, and there are no remains
of an earlier church. The material of which the edifice is built, is
granite, and therefore, although the proportions are good, the
construction is somewhat rough and the details, as usual, coarse.
The south front, however, with porch and parvise chamber, and the
stair turret of the rood loft, is very well proportioned and striking
in its effect. There is a good rood screen, retaining much of its
original decoration, with figures of saints in the panels, disfigured,
as may be often observed in other churches; and the villagers
point out marks which they say were made by the Parliamentary

troops (who are made responsible for a great deal of mischief really wrought by others) in the seventeenth century.

Mr. Hine* points out a noticeable feature in some of the Moorland churches of the eastern border—a fifteenth century doorway formed of four immense granite stones—two arch-stones meeting at the point of the arch and two jamb stones. Here is a very characteristic example. The doorway, as has been mentioned before, p. 139, is of almost Cyclopean character. The arch is two-centred and pointed, the jamb and arch-stones are double-chamfered on the outer edge.

There are here many massive granite floor slabs, with inscriptions, of the seventeenth century.

**Lustleigh, St. John the Baptist.** Beautifully situated, this church presents many features of interest. It has nave about thirty-four feet long by sixteen feet wide, chancel about thirty feet long by fifteen feet wide, north aisle about forty-eight feet long by fifteen feet wide, and a transeptal chapel on the south, about fourteen feet square, south porch, and low embattled tower with four bells cast by Bilbie in 1799, to which, two have been recently added.

The style is Decorated and Perpendicular, with Early English work in the chancel, and the font is Norman, and was much mutilated but has been recently restored. There is a double arched piscina with one drain. The screen, crossing the nave and north aisle, has been restored, but without the loft or vaulting. The south porch is very long, of the same length as the south chapel. In the east wall of this porch are two openings or squints enabling persons in the porch to see the altar in the chapel.

There are effigies in the north aisle, of a knight in armour and his lady, of which Risdon says " another tomb there is arched " over, where some say the Lord Dinham† and his lady were " interred, whose pictures are to be seen, very glorious, in a glass " window having their armories between them and likewise on " their surcoats, escutcheons of arms."‡ These are probably of the date of Edward III., but as there is no heraldic blazonry left

---

*Notes on Moorland Churches, Part II., p. 4.

†Lord John Dinham, temp Edw. IV., had the custody of the Forest of Dartmoor, and Manor and Borough of Lydford.

‡RISDON. Survey of Devon, p. 134, *ed.* 1812.

now on statue or in window, it is not certain that members of the family of Dinham are here commemorated.

There is another effigy, about which there is not so much doubt, although, unfortunately, it does not occupy its proper position in the church. The south transept was built as a mortuary chapel for the Prouze family, and the figure was no doubt originally there, although it has been suggested that it came from under the low archway in the north wall of the chancel, where it has been now placed. It is the effigy of Sir William Prouze, to whom the Manor of Lustleigh belonged.* By his will, he directed that he should be buried with his ancestors at Lustleigh, but for some reason, his executors disregarded his instructions, and he was interred at Holbeton. Some time after, the wishes of her father having come to the knowledge of the Lady Alice Mules, wife of Sir Roger Mules, Baron of Cadbury, and finding that they had not been obeyed, she petitioned Grandisson, Bishop of Exeter, that the remains might be removed from Holbeton to Lustleigh, and her prayer was granted.†

There are no other monuments or tablets of any interest, but at the entrance forming the sill of the Decorated south door, is a long and large granite stone with a Romano-British inscription, the interpretation of which is doubtful, but which has been rendered as DAVID SON OF CONNINOC.

There are here also examples of the massive granite memorial floor slabs, and the west doorway is of the same form as that at Manadon, and built of four huge stones.

**South Bovey or Bovey Tracey, St. Thomas of Canterbury.** Bovey Tracey, the name by which this parish is generally known, is situated five miles north-west of Newton Abbot. The church consists of nave about fifty-six feet long by sixteen feet wide, chancel about thirty-three feet long by sixteen feet wide, north and south aisles about seventy feet long by twelve feet wide, south porch stone vaulted, with a central boss with four heads, and embattled tower, containing six bells, re-cast from an old peal of five, in 1818. It is Perpendicular throughout, but the tower is probably of the preceding style. The screen with rood loft is handsome, and in the lower panels, the figures of prophets and apostles

---

*There is, however, some doubt as to whether this is Sir William's effigy. It was placed in its present position, in the Easter Sepulchre niche, by the Rector, the Rev. Prebendary Tudor.

†Grandisson's Register, vol. ii., 1329, fol. 131 *b*.

are well preserved. The pulpit is stone, gilded and coloured, with figures of the four evangelists, and saints, somewhat rudely, but boldly carved. Some old glass and a good deal of the old wood-work remains.

The only monuments requiring mention are three. The first a mural monument of stone, richly carved, an altar tomb, with rich cornice and architrave, supported by two Corinthian columns, and adorned with angels, cherubs, scrolls and devices; on the top are three figures, apparently of Time, Justice, and Charity and her children. On the tomb is a whole length figure of a man in early seventeenth century costume. There is no inscription, but it commemorates Nicholas Eveleigh, fifth son of John Eveleigh, of Holcombe, whose mother was Joane Southcott, of Bovey Tracey, who married Alice Bray, and died in 1620. His widow married Elizeus Hele, whose monument of marble is also here. It is a tomb with two Corinthian columns supporting a pediment with a cornice and scrolls, ornamented with variously coloured marbles. On the tomb is the alabaster effigy of the generous Devonshire donor, who left the whole of his great property for the benefit of his native county, and whose benefactions to this day help to support so many valuable institutions. Below the tomb are three kneeling figures, two women in ruffs, and a young man with hands uplifted in prayer. There is no inscription. Hele was buried in Exeter Cathedral, and it is believed that these monuments were erected to her two husbands by their widow. The third monu-ment is to Sir John Stawell, who died in 1669.

**Widecombe in the Moor, St. Pancras.** The Cathedral of the Moor, as it has been called, comprises a nave and chancel, north and south chancel aisles, north and south aisles and south transept, south porch and fine tower containing six bells of varying dates, the earliest being 1632. The style is Perpendicular throughout, the eastern part early, the tower and aisles later. Some fragments in the transept may be of earlier date. Mr. Hine (from whose description* of the church we take this) gives the extreme internal length as nearly one hundred and four feet; the chancel is twenty-three feet long by fifteen and a half feet in width. The roof has many of the original bosses, carved and painted with heads, flowers and leaves, one has a figure of St. Catherine, and there are many

---

*Notes on Moorland Churches, part II., p. 9.

figures, R. J. King says, which obscurely shadow forth the learning of the alchemist, the church having, it is stated, been intimately connected with miners. On one of the bosses is the combination of three rabbits, each with a single ear which join in the centre, forming a triangle, a favourite alchemical symbol, called the hunt of Venus. The interesting wall-plates of the chancel with the badge of Richard II. the white hart, and heads and griffins were unfortunately destroyed. The priest's doorway is cut diagonally through the wall to leave space for the piscina, as may be seen as well in neighbouring churches. Parts of the rood-screen only remain, the panels contain paintings, among others, of Our Lord, saints, a bishop and doctors, and a king and queen, in very perfect condition. The bosses of the roofs of the aisles are well carved with flowers and fruit. The east window of the north chancel aisle is of three lights ; the label springs from two heads, and at the point of the arch is the head of Our Lady crowned ; in this window are fragments of ancient glass with the Courtenay arms and the cross of St. George.

" For beauty of proportion the tower has been compared to " that of Magdalen College, Oxford, and for sharpness and finish " of detail, it may probably rank first among the granite towers of " the west. It is in three stages, and from the plinth to the para- " pet is exceedingly bold and effective in style. It terminates at " the top with a fine battlement, and large and handsome " octagonal pinnacles, five feet in diameter, each crocketted and " surrounded with a cross." J. Hine, *op. cit.*

There are some memorials worth referring to ; among others, one to Roger Hill, who was killed by being dashed against the wall of the church during the great storm before mentioned, pp. 153-154.

John Elford, of Sheepstor, buried the third of his four wives, Mary Gale, here, and placed upon a slab, the following inscription, with anagram and chronogram, over her remains.

To THE MEMORIE OF
MARY THE THIRD WIFE OF JOHN ELFORD OF
SHITSTOR ESQR., WAS HEER INTERRED FEBY YE 16
Ao 1642 HAVING ISSUE AT A BIRTH MARY AND SARAH.

Wed poesie.
AS MARYE'S CHOYCE MADE JOHN REIOYCE below

DD

Soe was her losse his heauie crosse must know
Yet lost she is not sure but found aboue
Death gaue her life t'imbrace A dearer loue.

Anagr. { MARY ELFORD } FEAR MY LORD.

Then FEAR MY LORD whilst yet you moust on hold
That soe these armes that mee may thee infold
Neer twelue moneths day her maridge heer did pass
Her heauenly nuptiall consummated was
She fertile prou'd in soule and bodye both
In life good workes at death she twyns brought forth
And like A fruitfull tree with bearing dy'd
Yet Phœnix like for one there two suruiu'd
Which shortly posted their deare mother after
Least sins' contagion their poore soules might slaughter
Then cease your sad laments I am but gone
To reape aboue what I belowe haue sowne.

Ao ætat VIXIt ob IIt s V per Is
MarIa GaLe IohannIs E L for D V X or tertIa
{ heV ob IIt e X p Verp I o }
{ Erectum fuit Ao 1650 }

There are shields with the arms of Elford and Gale on each side of the tablet, and below is another, quartering Elford with Coplestone, Northcote, Gale and Woollcombe.

A floor stone, now decayed, had this inscription cut round the slab :—

Here lyeth Richard Langworthye
of Lysewill gent.   He was buried on the 17 daye
of July in the yeare of our Lord God, 1617
Vita vana vita.

In the centre of the stone were these lines :—
The man whose body heere doth lie
Begann to live when he did dye
God both in life and death he prou'd
And was of God and man belou'd   '
Now he liveth in heaven's joye
And never more to feele annoy.

To make the history of Widecombe Church more complete, we give the lines on the painted tablets in the church,

although they are to be found in Lysons* and in " Things New and
" Old,"† as these books may not be accessible to many of our
readers. The verses are said to be the composition of Hill, the
village schoolmaster, who also wrote the lines upon North Hall,
given at page 156.

" It is of the Lord's mercies that we are not consumed, because
his compassions fail not."—*Lam.* iii., 22.

" The merciful and gracious Lord hath so done his marvellous
works that they ought to be had in remembrance."—*Ps.* cxi., 4.

In token of our thanks to God these tables are erected
Who in a dreadful thunder storm our persons here protected
Within this church of Widecombe 'mongst many fearful signs
The manner of it is declared in these ensuing lines.

In sixteen hundred thirty-eight October twenty-first
On the Lord's day at afternoon when people were addrest
To their devotion in this church while singing here they were
A psalm, distrusting nothing of the danger then so near
A crack of thunder suddenly with lightening, hail and fire,
Fell on the church and tower here and ran into the choir
A sulphureous smell came with it and the tower strangely rent
The stones abroad into the air with violence were sent
Some broken small or dust, or sand, some whole as they came out
From off the building and here lay in places round about
Some fell upon the church, and brake the roof in many places
Men so perplexed were, they knew not one another's faces
They all or most were stupified with that so strange a smell
Or other force whate'er it was which at that time befell.
One man was struck dead, two wounded so that they died a few
       hours after
No father could think on his son, nor mother mind her daughter,
One man was scorched so that he lived but fourteen days and died,
Whose clothes were very little burnt, but many there beside
Were wounded, scorched and stupified in that so strange a storm,
Which who had seen would say 'twas hard to have preserved a
       worm.
The different affections of people then were such
That, touching some particulars, we have omitted much,
But what we here related have is truth in most men's mouths.

---

*LYSONS. Devon, vol. ii., p. 557.

†R. DYMOND. " Things New and Old," concerning the Parish of Widecombe in
the Moor, pp. 108-109.

Some had their skin all over scorched, yet no harm in their
    clothes :
One man had money in his purse, which melted was in part,
A key likewise, which hung thereto, and yet the purse not hurt,
Save only some black holes so small as with a needle made.
Lightening, some say, no scabbard hurts, but breaks and melts the
    blade,
One man there was sat on the bier that stood fast by the wall,
The bier was tore with stones that fell, he had no harm at all,
Not knowing how he thence came forth, nor how the bier was
    torn.
Thus in this doleful accident great numbers were forborne,
Among the rest a little child, which scarce knew good from ill,
Was seen to walk amidst the church, and yet preserved still.
The greatest admiration was that most men should be free,
Among so many dangers here which we did hear and see.
The church within so filled was with timber, stone and fire
That scarce a vacant place was seen in church or in the choir ;
Nor had we memory to strive from those things to be gone,
Which would have been but work in vain, all was so quickly done.
The wit of man could not cast down so much from off the steeple,
From off the churche's roof, and not destroy much of the people ;
But He who rules both air and fire and other forces all
Hast us preserved, blessed be His name in that most dreadful
    fall.
If ever people have cause to serve the Lord and pray,
For judgment and deliverance, then surely we are they :
Which that we may perform, by the assistance of His grace,
That we at last in time may have with Him a dwelling place,
All ye who look upon these lines of this so sad a story,
Remember who hath you preserved, ascribe unto His glory
The preservation of your lives, who might have lost your
    breath
When others did, if mercy had not step'd twixt you and death,
We hope that they were well prepared, although we know not
    how
'Twas then with them, its well with you if you are ready now.

*Amos* iv., 11.—Ye were as a fire brand pluck'd
out of the burning.
1786 Peter and Silvester Mann,
Churchwardens.

These were originally in black letter, but the boards on which
they were painted having become decayed, new ones which are
now against the interior south wall of the basement of the tower
were substituted in 1786. Recently a fragment of the original

board has been found in a Widecombe cottage, which has been preserved and is now placed on the opposite side of the tower wall.

The panels with paintings of Moses and Aaron, which during the eighteenth century, it was the fashion to place in churches, are preserved here.

**Bickington,**
ST. JAMES
OR
ST. KATHERINE.

This little village—the parish containing about two hundred and fifty inhabitants—is about four miles north-east of Ashburton. At the entrance to the churchyard is a 15th century lich-gate, and over it, as at Ilsington, a room which was formerly used for a school, reached by a flight of steps on one side. The church is Perpendicular, the nave about forty-six feet long by fifteen feet wide, chancel about twelve feet long by fifteen feet wide, north aisle forty-eight feet long by twelve feet wide, south porch, and western tower embattled, with projecting octagonal stair-turret on the south face, containing four bells, the third and tenor dated 1664, the second, formerly the treble, 1746 and the present treble, 1887.

The most antient inscription in the church is: Here lyeth Ralfe Woodley, Lord of this Manor, year of our Lord, 1593.

There is a tablet to William Woollcombe, fifty-eight years rector, and there are memorials to members of the Stawell, Bickford, Furzland and Savery families.

**Buckland**
**in**
**the Moor.**

We do not know the dedication of this church. It is situated three and a half miles north-west of Ashburton, and like many other border churches in the midst of delightful scenery. The little building has a nave about thirty-three feet long by fourteen feet wide, chancel about twenty feet long by fourteen feet wide, with north aisle about thirty-three feet by six feet, with small north transept, and low tower, containing five bells, all of the date 1759, cast by Bilbie. The tower is interesting, of Decorated work, with the projection of the stair turret on the southern face.

The font is Norman, the screen, which is said—on what authority we know not, to have been brought from Buckfastleigh church—is good, and goes across the chancel only, and has paintings of Saints in the lower panels, and also larger paintings in the panels facing east, which last are very curious; they are, one, a warrior in a helmet, with lance; two, a figure wearing a turban; three, a monk; four, a monk?; five, a canon? or king? in ermine tippet; six, a figure in an attitude of prayer, in apparently a girded alb. The vaulting is gone, but some parts of it are nailed against the spandrels of the screen. There are some early tiles in the pavement of the nave.

|  |  |
|---|---|
| **Holne.**<br>St. Mary. | A most picturesque village. The cottages on the left-hand side as it is entered, are charming, with their little gardens full of flowers, and the walls covered with roses. |

The church has a Decorated tower and the rest of the building is also late Decorated. It contains nave about forty-five feet long by twelve feet wide, chancel twenty-one feet long by twelve feet wide, north and south aisles and north and south transeptal chapels. The tower contains five bells dated 1743, by Gooding. The old font, cast forth at one time to make room for a more modern one, has been recovered and replaced in the church.

The screen remains in a very perfect condition with much of the original gilding and colouring, but the rood-loft and vaulting are gone. In the panels of the lower part of the screen are painted figures of saints, which have been identified and a list may be seen in the church. There are thirty-eight.

The pulpit is, like the screen, fifteenth century work, and similarly carved and ornamented, and there are also upon it shields of arms—Bouchier, Fitzwarren, Oldam (which probably fixes the date of the pulpit and screen, as he was Bishop of Exeter, 1504-1519) the Royal arms, and the armorial bearings of the Abbey of Buckfast.

Charles Kingsley was born in Holne Vicarage, his father being the vicar, and a stained glass window depicting the Adoration of the Magi has been placed in the north transept to commemorate his connection with this place.

In the churchyard:

> Here lies poor old Ned, on his last mattrass bed,
> During life he was honest and free;
> He knew well the chase, but has now run his race,
> And his name it was Colling, d'ye see.

He died December 28th, 1780, aged 77.

**Ilsington,**
St. Michael.

This church, five miles north of Ashburton, is spacious and lofty, containing nave fifty-seven feet long by eighteen feet wide, chancel twenty-seven feet long by sixteen feet wide, north and south aisles seventy-two feet long by ten feet wide, north and south transepts, south porch with parvise over, reached by a flight of steps in the south wall, lofty embattled tower, with a half octagon stair-turret projecting on the southern face, containing five bells, all but the second, having been cast by Bilbie, and dáted 1797. The building is for the most part Perpendicular, but the chancel is older, the east window and the window in the north wall of the chancel being late Early English or early Decorated, and in the former is some old glass; the east window of the north aisle is of the same date.

In the north transept is a tomb with effigy of a lady, supposed to be of the family of Dinham, long resident in this parish, benefactors to the church, and founders of the chantry in this transept, the date of which is 13th century. The south transept was a chapel of the Pomeroys, of Ingeston, which is now occupied as a farm house.

There are many remains of old woodwork in the church. The screen runs across the whole width of the nave and aisles, and is well carved with fruit and leaves. The paintings on the panels have been destroyed. Some of the bosses of the roof are worth notice, there are the heads of a king and queen, the three rabbits with ears conjoined, and others, and there are also upon corbels in the nave roof, eight figures of saints carved in oak.

The monumental inscriptions are not of much interest. In the south aisle, in the floor, is a slab, with the following :—

1610 Hic jacet corpus Thomæ Pomeroy de Engesdon
armigeri qui obiit decimo octavo Aprilis anno
salutis nostræ millessimo sexcentessimo decimo
anno vero ætatis suæ sexagessimo primo.
En tibi rex regum pomum regale dedisti
Pomeroy et carpis quid ne qui serit ille metat.

Vita quid ad morté via quid mors janua
vitæ qua vitam eripuit mors mihi vita fuit.

Members of the family of Ford, of Bagtor, are interred in the church and churchyard. John Ford, the dramatist, was born in this parish, perhaps at Bagtor, in 1586, and was baptised in the church, the 17th of April in that year. It is probable that he died and was buried at Ilsington, as his biographers state that having obtained a competency at the bar, he retired to Devonshire to end his days. In the yard is a tomb with the following inscription, the chronogram giving the date of the death, 1657.

THOMÆ FORDE DE SIDFORD GEN. QVI

DE POSITUM

CHRONOGRAMMA.

DORMIO ET VT SPERO CINERES

SINE LAVE RESVRGENT.

NONO DIE NOVEMBRIS.

OBIIT DECIMO

On the east and west sides of the churchyard are lych-gates. Over the west gate is a room long used as a school, and in connection with it, a story, thought at the time worthy of remembrance, is found in the register, written presumably by the then rector of the parish, Dr. Robert Dove, and which may be printed here :—

" To the everlastynge prayse of God in the memory of a most " wonderful deliverance."

September 17, 1639. Over the west gate of the churchyard here in Ilsington, there was a room antiently built, about ten feet from the ground, sixteen feet in length, and twelve feet in breadth, the east and west walls are about ten feet in height. The covering was of slatt or shingle-stone, layd uppon fayre timber raftere, about twelve feet in length. This room was lately converted to a school-house, whither there usually came neere to the number of thirty scholler boyes. But September 17, being Tuesday A° 1639, the morning was wett, wch with other avocations, kept some at home, others to the number of seventeene, were together at school with their schoolmaster, neere upon eleven of the clocke, at wch time the schollers were ready to dept for dinner. A woman passed underneath, and lett the gate, being heavy, fall too, as formerly it had done. Before she was gone to a house about six yards from the place, part of the south stone wall wch bare upp the timber worke of the roofe, slidd away, so that the whole roofe spread abroad, drove out both side walls, east and west, and fell downe upon the flower of the roome, not one stick, stone or pinn of the whole structure remaininge where it was formerly placed.

The schoole door w̄ch opened to the inside was shutt when the house begun to fall.

Fower of the scholler boyes fell downe into the churchyard with the east side wall, and escaped with little hurt.

One ran into the chymney, where he continued safe.

Some were stricken down with timber and stones w<sup>ch</sup> fell from over their hedde.

The timber lock'd one boy fast in the middle of the roome and when it was lifted up, he rose up and run away.

And w<sup>ch</sup> was yet more wonderful, another sweet child, called Humphrey Deyon, fell out with the east side wall into the street, where he was close covered and buried under the rubbish soe that noe pt of his body or clothes appeared, there he lay for a quarter of an hower's space or more. At length perceiving that child to be wanting, a stricter search was made among the lomber w<sup>ch</sup> fell into the roome, then searching among the rubbish which fell into the street, he was there happily found, and taken up for dead, in the judgment of all that beheld him. But heat was not utterly gone, the child recovered life, is healthy and well, and free from any griefe.

In this ancient and special demonstration of God's providence and goodness, in delivering from imminent danger, twelve had their heads cut and broken, so that they bledd, for it to mind them all of the danger they were in : but God with a guard of angels surround them, so that not a bone was broken, nor a joint displaced : their wounds are all healed, and there is not any member of them any way infected from doing its proper office as in former times. At the writing hereof they are all in health and so living to praise God for this deliverance.

" I will always give thanks to the Lord, His praise shall be
" always in my mouth. O praise the Lord with me, and let us
" magnify His name together. He hath preserved all our bones,
" so that not one of them is broken. The Lord delivereth the
" souls of His servants, and they that put their trust in Him shall
" not be forsaken."

In the margin is written :—

Present in the school when the house fell
Hannibal Corbin Schoolmaster
Scollers.

Then follow the names of the boys present, and of those absent who came usually to school.

**Ashburton, St. ANDREW.** This fine church—which of late years has had much attention paid to it, and has been carefully restored, suffered greatly in former years. There was at one time a great deal of painting on wall and panel, the beautiful chancel and parclose screen were torn down and cast forth from the church, and sold and used as firewood, and the brass eagle lectern was also considered useless, and was purchased by the parishioners of Bigbury, whose church it now adorns. The church stands in an elevated and commanding situation, at the upper end of the town. It consists of nave, chancel, eighteen feet square, north and south aisles, north and south transepts, north porch, and lofty buttressed battlemented and pinnacled tower at the west end ninety-two feet high, it had at one time a spire, which we believe was taken down some sixty or seventy years since. From the floor of the tower there is a descent into the church. At the east end, behind the altar (which it may be noted is a stone one, erected long before any controversy arose as to the material of which altars should be constructed) is a room now used as a vestry, but which was probably formerly a bone house. It was approached by a door on the north side of the altar, but alterations and additions have been recently made, and it is now approached through another vestry on the south side.

The tower contains eight bells—all except the two new trebles added in 1887, and the seventh re-cast by Pannell in 1844—cast by Lester, and dated 1740.

Among the monuments may be mentioned that to John Dunning, Lord Ashburton, who was born near the town, " who " by his private virtues, united with the exertion of rare and " excellent talents rose to that pre-eminence, which neither birth " nor title can bestow."

There is a great deal of stained glass, placed in the church in recent years.

On a tablet on the south wall :—

> Here lyeth the bodys of Thomas Crvse gent
> who was heere interred the 28 day of April 1642
> and George Crvse gent who was alsoe interred
> the 8 of January 1649.

Within this vrne two Brothers here confin'd
Though by death parted yet by death close joyn'd
The eldest of these two plac'd in his roome
Greeted the younger with a wellcome home,
They liv'd they lov'd and now they rest in tomb.
Togeather sleepinge in their mother's womb.

Thomas Harris, Farmer, died September, 1637.

Feare not to die
Learne this of me
No ills in death,
If good thou be.

Elizabeth Ireland died 1779,

Here I lie at the chancel door ;
Here I lie because I'm poor,
The further in the more you pay
Here lie I as warm as they.

This stone is now destroyed.

The chapel of the Guild of St. Laurence, in the town, is now used as the Grammar School. The Free Grammar School of Ashburton was founded by Walter Stapeldon, Bishop of Exeter, 1308-1327, and upon the members of the Guild, who undertook to carry out the Bishop's wishes, he bestowed this chapel. The tower, with buttresses, battlements, pinnacles, low spire and vane, alone remains ; the rest of the building is modern, having been rebuilt for the purposes of the school, still carried on as it has been for nearly six hundred years. Upon the walls are shields with the arms of Hayne, Gifford, Yonge, Williams, Colleton, Howard, Brotherton, and Warren.

**Buckfastleigh.**
Holy Trinity.
The church of this busy little town is indeed set upon a hill—one of limestone—reached by a flight of one hundred and forty steps, and is some little distance from the two villages, Buckfast and Buckfastleigh, which form the town. The churchyard is extensive, and is approached from the west by a lych-gate, near to which is an upping-stock for the convenience of equestrians. In the yard are two buildings, one near the south porch of the church,

a large square chamber with a projecting roof with a grated window, and door in the eastern side, the burial place of the Cabell family : the other, on the eastern side of the yard, a venerable ruin, overgrown with ivy, consisting of three walls with lancet windows east and south, and a doorway on the south, said to be the chancel of a church earlier than the present, but also stated to be a baptistry or chantry chapel.

The church consists of a Perpendicular nave about sixty-six feet long by twenty feet wide, a chancel about thirty feet long by sixteen feet wide, north and south aisles eighty feet long by twelve feet wide, north and south transepts, south porch and a lofty square early English tower at the west end ornamented by a corbel table resembling machicollations below the battlements, from which rises a tall spire surmounted by a cross, which is an object visible from great distances. There are six bells, the second, third, fifth and tenor dated 1793, the treble, 1794, all these by Bilbie, the fourth is dated 1844, and is by Hambling.

In the south wall of the chancel is a double piscina.

There is much modern stained glass by Beer, of Exeter.

There are no monuments or inscriptions of general interest.

**South Brent,** This church, containing features of much interest,
ST. PATRICK. has a chancel about thirty feet long by eighteen feet wide, north and south aisles, nave about eighty feet long by eighteen feet wide, north and

south aisles of the same length as the nave and nine feet wide, with a transept or chapel to each. It is for the most part Decorated and Perpendicular, but the west end—where is now the tower, which was originally the central tower of a cross church—Norman and Early English. The east window is late Decorated. Much of the chancel is new work, the old sedilia and piscina having been partially destroyed and blocked up with masonry. During the restoration, portions of a life-sized recumbent effigy, and high tomb, with much colour remaining upon them, were discovered. This is supposed to be the monument of a vicar murdered in the church about 1436, in which year Bishop Lacy reconciled it, dedicating three altars therein.

The tower is in four stages, late Norman, except the upper part and a window of later insertion, above the west door, these are Early English. On the south is what was the transept of the cross church, and doubtless there was one on the north side also.

The font is a beautiful one of Transitional Norman, of red sandstone, very similar to others in neighbouring churches.

The memory of Robert Herrick haunts this church **Dean Prior,** and neighbourhood. Here he, in 1629, came as ST. GEORGE. vicar, and remained until 1648, when Syms, the Puritan, ejected him. Syms receiving the income of the rightful owner, refused to pay to his predecessor the fifth of the revenue, which was the condition upon which he was enabled to thrust himself upon the parish. In 1660, Herrick returned to his vicarage, and in it, at the age of eighty-three, in 1674, he died. No stone marks the place of his burial in church or churchyard, but it is probable, his remains rest within the walls of the church in which he ministered.

The church in its general condition is, doubtless, very different from what it was in Herrick's time. It consists of tower, south porch, nave, north and south aisles, and chancel. The building has been much pulled about, a considerable amount of money having been injudiciously spent upon it in 1835; and again in 1868, it underwent much repair. The tower is Decorated, as was probably originally the rest of the church. The font of red sand-stone is Norman, and similar in character to those at South Brent, Rattery, Blackawton, and in other churches in this locality.

There is an Elizabethan or Jacobean monument said to be that of Sir Edward Gyles and his wife, but there is no inscription legible, and it is more probable that it commemorates John Gyles, father of Sir Edward and Agnes his wife, daughter of Sir Hugh Stukeley, and John Gyles their son, who died young. The epitaph—said to have been written by Herrick, and if so, doubt-less at the request of his friend and patron, Edward Gyles—is worth quoting :—

No trust to Metals, nor to Marbles, when
These have their Fate and wear away as men:
Times, Titles, Trophies, may be lost and spent :
But Vertue Rears th' eternal monument.
What more than these can Tombs or Tomb-Stones pay ?
But here's the Sun-set of a Tedious day :
These Two asleep are : I'll but be Vndrest
And so to Bed : Pray with us all Good Rest.

Until 1857. there was nothing in the church of Dean Prior to show to the casual visitor that Herrick the poet was ever connected with this remote neighbourhood. In that year however, the late William Perry Herrick, of Beau Manor Park, Leicester-

shire, a descendant of a kinsman of the poet, and the then head of
the family, placed on the north wall of the building a carved
memorial stone, with a brass plate containing the following
inscription :—

IN THIS CHURCH YARD LIE THE REMAINS OF
ROBERT HERRICK,
AUTHOR OF THE HESPERIDES AND OTHER POEMS,

OF AN ANCIENT FAMILY
IN LEICESTERSHIRE AND
BORN IN THE YEAR 1591
HE WAS EDUCATED AT ST.
JOHN'S COLL. AND TRI-
NITY HALL CAMBRIDGE.

PRESENTED TO THIS LIV-
ING BY KING CHARLES I.
IN THE YEAR 1629 EJECT-
ED DURING THE COMMON-
WEALTH AND RE-INSTATED
SOON AFTER YE RESTORA-
TION.

HE DIED VICAR OF THIS PARISH IN THE YEAR 1694.
THIS TABLET WAS ERECTED
TO HIS MEMORY BY HIS KINSMAN WILLIAM PERRY-
HERRICK OF BEAU MANOR PARK
LEICESTERSHIRE A.D. 1857.
VIRTUS OMNIA NOBILITAT.

OUR MORTAL PARTS MAY WRAPT IN SEARE CLOTHES LYE
THEIR SPIRITS NEVER WITH THEIR BODIES DIE.—*Hesperides.*

In the register will be found the entry of Herrick's burial:—

" Dean Prior.
The names of all those yt have been buried in ye same parish
from ye year of our Lord God 1561 and so forwards."
*Robert Herrick, Vicker, was buried ye 15 day of October* 1674.

There is, or was, a floor-stone with the following inscription :—

the 5th of December, 1595.
Time past is forgotten er men be aware,
Time present is thought on with wonderful care,
Time coming is feared and therefore we save,
Yet oft er it comes we be gone to the grave.

On another :—

Here was buried John Furse gent sone and heire
to Robert Furse of Morshed gent who died
the xvi of March anno 1609.
What is life—the way unto death,
What is death—the gate of life.
Death hath taken life from me
Which death is life unto me eternall.

In the tower are five bells, all, except the second, by John Pennington, and dated 1734, with the Yarde arms, *a chevron between three water bougets.* The second bell is dated 1836.

Dean Burn, the Vale of Dean Burn, or Dean Coombe, before referred to, is in this parish, and the description given by Polwhele (see page 164, *ante*) has served for all subsequent writers who have written of this romantic spot. It is a rock strewn glen, through which the Burn finds its way over a boulder-strewn bed, with, at the upper part some small but picturesque waterfalls. Herrick apostrophises this " Dean Bourn, a rude river, by which he some- " times lived," on his ejection from his vicarage, and under the circumstances he may be surely excused if he did not find at that time the softer influences of the scenery affect him.

> Dean Bourn fare well : I never look to see
> Deane, or thy warty incivility.
> Thy rockie bottome, that doth teare thy streams
> And makes them frantick, ev'n to all extremes :
> To my content, I never sho'd behold,
> Were thy streams silver, or thy rocks all gold.

Below the first waterfall is the Hound's Pool, or the Pan Pool, the scene of Knowle's labours (see p. 423) and where the noise of his shuttle, or the sound of the nut-shell against the sides of the pool, may be heard. That there is a strange noise many people affirm, but unbelievers say that the sound is made by stones in the bottom of the pool, rattled against each other by the falling water.

**Harford.**
ST. PATRICK.

The church of this little parish—population all told about one hundred and fifty—is apparently entirely Perpendicular, consisting of nave thirty-six feet long and fourteen feet wide, chancel twenty-six feet long and fourteen feet wide, south aisle about fifty feet long and fourteen feet wide, south porch, low embattled tower with pinnacles at the angles, with three bells, the tenor 1666, and the other two more antient, with latin inscriptions. There was a north transept or chapel now destroyed, and a new vestry now occupies its site. The east wall of the church is apparently older. Five feet from the original floor level, there have been placed recently, altar steps; in the south wall of the chancel, is a niche, and over it a small two-light square-headed window. Its object is not easy to suggest. The ribs of the roof and the wall-plates are well carved, in the latter I.H.S. several times repeated. On the wall-plate on the north side of the chancel is an inscription :—

I.H.S. helpe us. Amen Walter Hele p'son 1539. I.H.S. Salus.

and other letters. The church underwent restoration in 1879.

On the north side of the chancel is an altar tomb with brasses upon it, in memory of Thomas Williams, Speaker of the House of Commons, of the family of that name formerly resident at Stowford, in the parish. The first brass at the head contains the Williams' arms, *sa, three curlew's heads erased or.* On another brass is the following :—

> Here lyeth the corps of Thoms Willims esquier.
> Twise Reader he in Court appointed was
> Whose sacred minde to vertu did aspire
> Of parlament he Speaker hence did passe.
>
> The comen peace he studied to preserue
> And trew religion euer to maynteyne
> In place of Justyce where as he dyd serue
> And nowe in heaven with myghtie Jove doth Raigne.

Another brass contains the figure in armour, and on a small narrow plate at the foot :—

> Obiit primo die mensis Julii A° d'm M°CCCCC°LXVI°
> Etatis suæ anno quinquagesimo secundo.

The other monument requiring mention, is that to John and Agnes Prideaux, the father and mother of John Prideaux, Rector of Exeter College, Oxford, and Bishop of Worcester, by whom this very poor memorial was placed here. It is of metal—brass or copper—in a wooden frame. Above are John and Agnes Prideaux, kneeling on either side of a lectern : behind the former are also kneeling seven sons, and behind the wife three daughters. The doctor in his scarlet hood is very conspicuous in his place as fourth son, but outside the rank. There is a chequered lozengy pavement in front. Below is the following inscription :—

EE

Here rest the bodies of John Prideaux
of Stoford and Agnes his only wife the
parents of (7) sonnes and (3) daughters
to whom
John Prideaux their 4th Sonne Doctor of
Divinity and the King's Maiesties profes-
sovr thereof in the Vniversity of Oxford
Rector of Excester Colledge and Chap-
laine to Prince Henry King James the
First and King Charles the First
hath left this Fileall
Remembrance
Ivly 20. 1639.

**Cornwood.**
ST. MICHAEL.

A Perpendicular church, with Early English
chancel, about eighty feet long by fifteen feet
wide, north and south aisles about seventy feet
long by ten feet wide, north and south transepts,
south porch, and a low western tower—earlier than the church—
with six bells, all—except the treble which is dated 1835—by
Pennington, 1770.  The pulpit is seventeenth century.

There is little in the building requiring special attention.  The
reredos, the gift of the late Lord Blachford, of alabaster and
coloured marble, is handsome, but is hardly in keeping with the
architecture of the church.  There has been much restoration.

Some of the monuments and inscriptions are of interest.

There is a small monument of black marble, with the figures
of a man and woman kneeling at a desk with books and on a
tablet, the inscription—

Here lyeth the bodies of Robert Bellmaine late of Dallamoore
esqire, and Dorithy his wife who departed this life, shee on the
27 day of Aprill, he on the 9th day of May following, 1627.

Here's rest and peace
Within this graue,
Whitch wee in life
Could never haue.

With a shield of arms, quarterly of twenty.

An altar tomb with shields, two with the arms of Cole and
Williams, the others being illegible.  Over the tomb, against the
wall, is a stone monument, painted with the figures of a man and

woman in ruffs, kneeling at a table with books.  There is no inscription left, but above is a shield with the arms of Cole.  This is no doubt the memorial of the last of the Coles of Slade— Richard Cole—whose mother was Jane the daughter of Thomas Williams, of Stowford, and who married Radigon the daughter of Nicholas Boscowan.

Near this place lyeth the body of Mr. John Savery son of William Savery of Slade esq. by Prudence his wife, daughter of John Drake of Iveybridge esq. who departed this life the the 21st of Feb. 1696.

> This infant fled from our admiring sight
> His stay so short, so sudden was his flight
> That he has taught us by his hasting hence
> That th' earth's too vile for so much innocence
> Reader relent since thou noe more shall see
> This matchless childe but in his effigie.

The recumbent figure of the child represents him in a green mantle or  cloak edged with ermine ; beneath is an oval tablet of white marble, which bears the inscription just given.

There is another stone on the floor, in memory of this John Savery, with these lines :—

> His curious frame and pretty charming love
> Seraphin like prepar'd him for above.
> His change was glorious, his assent was braue,
> His soul's in heaven, triumphant ore the graue.

> John Savery son of William Savery of
> Slade esq., buried, 27 Feb 1696.

A tablet in the north aisle, to the Memory of Benjamin Burell who died 16 March 1715 in his 91st year.   He was a captain in the army of Charles I.

**Plympton Earl.**
**St. Maurice.**
Plympton Comitis, otherwise Earl's Plympton —the earls being those of Devon, the Redvers —ecclesiastically Plympton St. Thomas, otherwise Plympton St. Maurice, was as before said, one of the Stannary Towns.

The church, dedicated to St. Thomas of Canterbury, but more commonly known as St. Maurice, from the Chantry chapel in it founded by John Brackley at the close of the fourteenth century, is for the most part, Perpendicular. It consists of nave and chancel about seventy feet long by eighteen feet wide, south chapel—that of St. Maurice—with piscina of about the date 1380, north and south aisles, the former has been recently extended eastwards to form a vestry, south porch with parvise over, north door-way, and western tower, with eight bells—the tenor cast by Pennell in 1833, the third, fourth, fifth, sixth and seventh by Pennington, in 1768, the first and second by Mears and Stainbank, 1895. There are remains of Early English work in the south side of the chancel, and at the west end. When the church had no fixed seats, the pulpit was placed against the second column of the south aisle arcade, and the granite base and some steps still remain, an unusual ecclesiological feature. The tower is a very good one and well-proportioned, with stair turret in the north-east angle. The floor-slabs in memory of some members of the Spark family are worth notice. The chapel of St. Maurice, in the south aisle, founded by John Brackley, about 1380, is now restored and used for worship. The screen and rood loft have also been carefully restored, and the old portions which had been preserved, iucorporated. An image of St. Thomas of Canterbury is in a niche over the north door.

Writers of guide books are always confused as to the history of this church. It has always been a parish church, the early dedication of which is unknown. In the excess of devotion, inspired by the martyrdom of St. Thomas Becket, the antient dedication was, as in so many other instances, ignored, and the name of the then popular saint substituted. Of late years it has been the fashion to drop the name of St. Thomas, and use that of St. Maurice in connection with the church. Notwithstanding its being a parish church, it was served by the Canons of Plympton, and until the dissolution, was an appendant chapelry of the Priory.

This decayed but very interesting town was the birth-place of Sir Joshua Reynolds. The grammar school remains as the great painter knew it, but the master's house, the house in which his father and mother lived, had, from the badness of the material of which it was built and its construction, fallen into such a state of dilapidation that it was impossible to preserve it, and it was taken down a few years since and a new residence built. The castle is of much interest. The pre-Norman earthworks are almost perfect, but of the later Norman masonry, except the tottering walls of the keep, slighted by the parliamentary troops in the seventeenth century, nothing remains.

**Plympton.**
**ST. MARY.**

The church was built by the monks of Plympton in the cemetery of their conventual church for the parishioners, and was dedicated in 1311, by Bishop Stapeldon, but little remains of this edifice in the fine building which we now see, and which is almost entirely Perpendicular. It is a mistake to suppose that this church was the Priory church, the latter is further south, and is in ruins, but its foundations can be traced.

The church consists of nave about eighty-nine feet six inches long by twenty-one feet wide, the chancel is about forty-one feet long by nineteen feet wide, with ancient vestry on the north, north and south aisles one hundred and eight feet long by six feet wide, another aisle—the chapel of St. Katherine—on the north, and another on the south, the former is fifty-five feet long by fourteen feet six inches wide, and the latter about forty-four feet long by fifteen feet wide, north and south porches, over the latter, parvise of two stories, containing a library, and western tower about nineteen feet by sixteen feet and one hundred and eleven feet high, at each corner is an octagonal, embattled turret, from which rises a high crocketted pinnacle. There are eight bells, the fourth and tenor—this is a very fine bell—by Perdue, 1614, the third, fifth, sixth, and seventh by Pennington, 1725-1766, and the first and second added a few years since.

The chancel and north chapel are the most antient parts of the building, Early English and Decorated, the windows, piscina, and sedilia, are very good.

There are two monuments, one in the north chapel to Richard Strode, of Newnham, whose will is dated 12 Oct., 1464, a recumbent effigy in armour; and another in the south wall of the south aisle, to William Courtenay, of about the same date, also in armour, with the Courtenay shield and Hungerford badge, *three sickles conjoined.*

In the north aisle is a seventeenth century mural monument to Sir William Strode, of Newnham, and his two wives, with their effigies, below the figure of one of the wives in a tablet are the busts of ten children in bas relief, and below the other wife, Death, with his scythe, cutting down a flower which is caught by a hand issuing from a cloud. There are inscriptions in Latin and English.

The south porch, with the two chambers over, is a charming piece of architecture. It is under an embattled tower, which rises above the aisle roof. The vaulting of the groined roof is Roborough stone, divided into squares and diagonal lines with bosses, the centre one having a carving of the Crucifixion upon it, with a small figure under each arm of the Cross. Over the interior door are three niches, but the figures have disappeared. On the exterior face of the porch are three canopied niches; the centre one containing a figure representing the Blessed Trinity ;— The Almighty is seated, holding the Cross, but the Dove is gone : below two angels are holding drapery, upon which are four small figures, the idea being the presentation of purified souls : the two other niches contain figures of the Blessed Virgin, and the Angel of the Annunciation, Gabriel. The worn stone below contains the helmet and wreath of the Strodes, one of whom, no doubt, built this beautiful porch.

The few scanty remains of the once stately priory of Plympton may be discovered on the south of the church yard.

**Bickleigh.** This church is a modern one, rebuilt in 1838, with the exception of the tower. The ancient dedication is unknown. The old church consisted of nave and south aisle of Perpendicular work which took the place, it is stated as is probable, of a Decorated building. But there was a still older church on the site, for an antient font of polyphant was found during the rebuilding. The present edifice consists of nave and chancel about fifty feet long by twenty feet wide, with side aisles of the same length. The tower is buttressed and battlemented, with four pinnacles embattled and crocketted.

Some of the tablets and memorial stones in the old church, were re-erected in the present building, and among them portions of the interesting monument to Nicholas Slanning, who was killed by Sir John Fitz, which is the only one of any general interest.

John Fitz was born about 1575, and married Bridget, daughter of Sir William Courtenay. He appears to have been of a dissipated, quarrelsome disposition, and judging from what happened later, was a lunatic. He picked a quarrel with Nicholas Slanning, and unfairly slew him, in 1599. He succeeded in obtaining a pardon from Queen Elizabeth, and was knighted four years later by

James I.   In 1605, he was at Kingston-on-Thames, on his way to London, and wandering to Twickenham, took up his abode with one Daniel Allez.   In the morning he rose in a frenzied state, and meeting with Allez, killed him with his rapier, and then stabbed himself.

The monument in Bickleigh Church, is to the memory of Nicholas Slanning, the unfortunate gentleman who fell a victim to the anger of John Fitz.   It is but a small part of what was once a fine memorial of the dead, a full description of which will be found in the paper by the late Winslow Jones on the Slannings.*

In the yard is a low altar tomb, upon which is sculptured a cross with floriated arms, which may have covered the remains of "*Thomas Pontyngton, Pson ecclie de Bikelegh*, 1373."

**Shaugh Prior.**
**St. Edward.**
So called, from its having belonged to the Priory of Plympton, the gift to the Monks by Roger de Novant.   The church dedicated to St. Edward stands very high on the slope of the hill, and is a conspicuous object from many points of view.   It is mainly Perpendicular, consisting of nave about sixty-five feet long by eighteen feet wide, chancel about twelve feet long by fifteen feet wide, north and south aisles sixty-five feet long.   The tower is lofty, has battlements and a stair turret on the south face, with embattled and crocketted pinnacles at the corners.   There are six bells cast in 1769 by Pennington from an old peal of four larger ones.   The tenor, having met with an accident, was recast in 1886.

There is a beautiful font cover which some few years ago was ignominiously cast forth from the church, but which was fortunately discovered and rescued from destruction by a former vicar, the Rev. J. B. Strother, and having been put in order, now serves its legitimate purpose in the church.

In the church is a tablet to the memory of the poet of Dartmoor, placed there by his son, Mr. W. M. Carrington, in 1871, which bears the following inscription :—

Sacred
To the Memory of
N. T. Carrington
Author of " Dartmoor," " Banks of Tamar,"
" My Native Village," and other Poems.

---

*Trans. Dev. Assoc., vol. xix., 1887, p. 451.

He was born at Plymouth 19<sup>th</sup> July 1777
And died at Bath. 2<sup>nd</sup> September 1830
Aged 53 years
He lies buried in the church yard of Combehay
Near that City.
Distinguished by his literary works
He won the regard of his country men.
Mild and meek of nature his heart overflowed
" With the milk of human kindness,"
He lived and practised virtue
For its own pure sake, and, without show of formality
He was in spirit and in practice, a humble and an
Earnest Christian.

" Around his grave let sweetest flowers up-spring
" In memory of that fragrance which was once
" From his mild manners quietly exaled."

**Sheepstor.** On the border of the Moor, the neighbourhood of this little village is now very busy, the important new works in connection with the water supply of Plymouth, going on close by, and altering the face of the country by the damming up of a valley for the construction of a vast reservoir.

The strange shape of the tor marks it out from all the rest of the Dartmoor tors, and the Pixy Cave in the side, we have already referred to, p. 187. Indeed Sheepstor is the reputed home of the pixies who stored the precious metals which are said to be hidden here.

The church is a typical moorland one; the nave about forty feet long by fifteen feet wide, chancel about fifteen feet square, south aisle about thirty-four feet long by twelve feet wide, south porch and large square embattled tower with turrets at each corner, terminating in crocketted pinnacles. Above the porch is a curious stone, no doubt part of a sun-dial.

The tower contains a peal of five bells, cast in 1769 by Pennington, probably from an old one. The style throughout is Perpendicular. The dedication is not known.

There are monuments to the Elfords of Langstone, with a good deal of heraldry, and a very curious one to Elizabeth, daughter of John Copplestone, and wife of John Elford, representing her in a bed, with her daughter kneeling by it.

In the yard lies buried Sir James Brooke, Rájá of Saráwak, who died at Burrator in this parish, where he had retired in broken health in 1868.

It was in this church that the clergyman, non-resident then, and who only came into the parish once a week, was prevented from entering the pulpit by the clerk, being told that "th' "ould guse had bin a' settin a brude there all the week."

|  |  |
|---|---|
| **Meavy,** ST. PETER. | Consists of nave, chancel, south aisle, south transept, south chancel aisle—the Drake aisle—south porch, and tower with six bells, the fifth being the oldest, cast by Pennington in 1779, the rest were |

re-cast from the old peal in 1876 by Mears and Stainbank. The north respond of the chancel arch—which is banded in coloured stones, green Tavistockite, and a pink stone changing to yellow, probably an outcrop in the parish—is, together with the north, east, and part of the south wall of chancel, the oldest part of the building, and is Norman. The angle stones immediately under the plain capitals, have rude carvings of human faces with enlarged ears, and on the side facing west, a bishop's pastoral staff. The north wall of the nave is probably of the same date.

Over the south window of the transept, forming a frame-work
for a ledger tomb-stone, now built into the wall, which has on its
length a raised cross crosslet, are the stones which formed one of
the narrow round headed Saxon or Norman windows. The porch,
in which the stoup should be noticed, is transitional Norman or
very Early English.

In the east window of the chancel and in the east and south-
east windows of the chancel aisle, removed here from the south
chancel wall when the aisle was added, will be found the work of
the next period, about 1260; next in date the south transept, then
the south chancel aisle and Lady chapel, and then lastly, about
1430, the nave, south aisle and upper part of the tower.

There are wagon roofs throughout, except where the plaster
has been knocked away over the nave. There are some very
curious bosses in the roof over the Drake aisle, one represents
a women's head, with a mouse coming out of her ear; another, a
lion with curled tail; another a dying stag; and in the easternmost
rib of the roof is our Saviour's head, with a crown of thorns.

In 1874 the church was restored and re-seated, and the organ
chamber built. Dry rot destroyed the woodwork, and the seating
had to be renewed in 1879. The pulpit, reredos, clock and
chancel stalls have been added of late years.

In the churchyard is an epitaph, a variant of others found
elsewhere :—

> Our life is but a winter's day ;
> Some only breakfast, and away :
> Others to dinner stay, and are full fed,
> The oldest man but sups, and goes to bed.
> Large is his debt who lingers out the day :
> Who goes the soonest has the least to pay.

The point here is that the stone commemorates the members
of a family, who died at the ages respectively of 94 ,88, 29 and 16.

Outside the church is the Meavy oak, of song and tradition,
and the village Cross which has been lovingly re-erected by the Rev.
W. A. Gordon Gray, who collected the stones which had been
scattered about the parish, but fortunately not destroyed, and
put them in their proper places, as mentioned before, p. 187.

**Buckland Monachorum,**
St. Andrew.

This place is four and a half miles
south of Tavistock. The church, built
by the Cistercian monks of Buckland
for the parishioners, is one of the

most handsome and well-proportioned of Devonshire churches, and a very good specimen of Perpendicular work. The nave is about fifty-eight feet long by twenty-four feet wide, chancel about thirty-two feet long by twenty-four feet wide, north and south aisles, north and south transepts, south porch buttressed and embattled with pinnacles at the angles, western tower containing six bells, re-cast, like so many others, about the same time, by Pennington, in 1723.

The church was well restored in 1869. The wagon roofs are good, and there are many bosses at the intersection of the ribs, the central boss of the nave has carving representing the coronation of the Blessed Virgin. In the nave roof are also figures of angels holding instruments of music. The south chancel aisle is groined and ribbed in stone, the bosses roughly sculptured with foliage and human faces. In consequence of evident alterations and additions in the fifteenth century, and the removal of the roof loft, and interference with its supports, the chancel arch presents a very disfiguring appearance. The carved bench ends and poppy heads of the seats are good.

Sir Francis Drake became possessed of the lands of Buckland Abbey by grant and purchase in Elizabeth's reign, and many members of the family are here interred. Lord Heathfield, the defender of Gibraltar, married Anne Pollexfen, daughter of Sir Francis Henry Drake, and although he was buried at Heathfield, in Sussex, a monument by Bacon, was here erected to his memory in 1795. Elaborate as this is, its taste is not that of past ages or of the present, as the following description will show;—there is a base, with a lofty pyramid, on which is a medallion portrait, encircled by a laurel wreath, and a whole length figure of Fame, adding an honourable augmentation of the chief with its bearings, to the shield with the family arms of Elliott. At the foot of Fame is a cupid with a helmet on his head and the shield of Britannia by his side, holding a palm branch in one hand, and a key in the other. On and above the base, are panels sculptured in bas relief, representing a piece of ordnance—a furnace for heating cannon balls—the commander directing military operations —floating batteries on fire, with drowning sailors rescued from the waves. The inscription is :—

" Sacred to the memory of George Augustus Elliott, Baron " Heathfield, of Gibraltar, Knight of the Bath, General of His " Majesty's Forces, and Governor of Gibraltar. He was the

"seventh son of Sir Gilbert Elliott, Bart., of Stobs, in the county
"of Roxburgh, in Scotland. The University of Leyden enriched
"his mind with science, and formed his taste for literature and the
"polite arts. The bias of his genius soon inclined him to the
"profession of arms, in which he rose by regular gradations to the
"highest eminence, and at length closed a brilliant career with
"immortal glory. Germany beheld him in the war of seven years,
"discharging all the duties of a gallant officer. The British cavalry
"owed to him a system of discipline that made them the pride of
"their country. The Havannah, the metropolis of the Island of
"Cuba, saw him among the officers who levelled her boasted fortifi-
"cations and conquered by their valour. Gibraltar was reserved to
"crown him with unfading laurels. Though closely pressed during
"a siege that lasted three years without intermission, he remained
"invincible. The spectacle which he there exhibited to the eyes of
"France and Spain, and to an amphitheatre of princes who beheld
"the glorious scene, will be an eternal memorial of British courage
"and British humanity. General Elliott derived no hereditary
"honours from his ancestors. His titles were earned by services to
"his country * * * History will tell the rest. He died July 6,
"1790, aged 72 years."

There is also a monument to the second Baron, son of the
the former, who died in 1813. There is a good deal of heraldry
upon and about these monuments, which are in the south chancel
aisle, known as the Drake chapel.

There is a monument in white marble, by Westmacott, to the
memory of Eleanor, wife of Sir Thomas Trayton Fuller Elliott
Drake, who died 18 Sept. 1841.

In the church-yard are the base and shaft of a cross, and in the
village is the very large octagonal base of a cross, formed by four
high stone steps.

Not far from the village are the remains of the once important
Abbey, founded by Amicia, the mother of Isabella, wife of
William de Fortibus, Earl of Albemarle, in 1280, although lands
were acquired by her for the purposes of the foundation, several
years before. The present residence is really the monastic church,
divided into floors and fitted with staircases. The tower is perfect,
and there are portions of some of the antient buildings remaining,
more especially the great barn, more than one hundred feet long,
in much the same state as when the monks left it.*

---

*See J. BROOKING ROWE. Cistercian Houses of Devon, 1878.

The dedication of this church is not known.
**Walkhampton.** It is very conspicuous from many points, and from the Prince Town Railway.

It consists of nave about fifty-four feet long by eighteen feet wide, chancel about twenty-four feet long by eighteen feet wide, north aisle about fifty-four feet long by twelve feet wide, south aisle about seventy-six feet long by twelve feet wide, and lofty tower with stair turret in north-west angle, and containing six bells, the treble, second, third and fourth, being dated 1764, and the fifth and tenor, 1769.

The style throughout is Perpendicular, but the base of the tower is earlier, the corbels of the tower arch with human heads, should be noticed, and the west doorway is a very beautiful one.

There are no monuments or tablets of any importance, but the following epitaphs may be given.

Richard Attwell, 1674 :—

 Within this sacred dust doth lye
 A son of Adam born to dye,
 My state of life was sixty year,
 Which being done, you find me here,
 In Christ I died, you that survive,
 Must die in him to be alive.

John Cowbridge, vicar, 1642 :—

 Death is my night—life was my day
  My grave my bed of rest
 I did not falle, but down I lay
  By sleepe, not death, possest.

Richard Cole, 1779.

 Dear parents weep for me no more
  Nor brothers nor sisters shed a tear
 For I am gone but just before
  Unto my Saviour dear
 There I lay by my dear Aunt
  All covered with cold clay
 Hoping with joy to meet our Lord
  At the eternal day.
 Kind angels watch this sleeping dust
  Till Jesus come to raise the just
 Then may you wake with sweet surprise
  And in your Saviour's image rise.

The dedication of this church is not known.
**Sampford Spiney.** It consists of a nave about thirty feet long
by fifteen feet wide, chancel about twenty
feet long by fifteen feet wide, a south aisle about forty-two feet
long by twelve feet wide, and a north transept about twelve feet
square, now used as a vestry, south porch, and tower, with three
bells, the treble dated 1674, the second 1653, and the tenor 1764.
The tower is a fine one, Perpendicular, " with " as Mr. Ashworth
says " buttresses flushing their upper stage with the parapet, from
" the angles of which rise crocketted pinnacles." On the south face
on the west side of the central window is a carved stone, with the
arms of Plympton Priory, a shield with two keys across it.   The
chancel was Decorated, recently rebuilt ; the nave Perpendicular.
In the south aisle the windows are three light under a square label.
In the chapel is a piscina, and in the north wall a Decorated
canopied niche, in which, doubtless, there was at one time an effigy.

In the south aisle are two hatchments, now so seldom used or
preserved, for Hall of Manadon, and St. John.

The village cross stands on the green, west of the church.
The farm house close by was the Manor house of the Halls.

A mile and a half south-east of Tavistock, this
**Whitchurch,**   church and village form a pleasing object in the
St. Andrew.   view.   The church consists of nave about fifty-
seven feet long by eighteen feet wide, chancel
about twenty-four feet long by eighteen feet wide, a north aisle
about fifty-seven feet long by twelve feet wide, south transept,
south porch, western tower, with pinnacles and half octagonal
stair-turret on the north side, containing six bells, all cast by
Pennington in 1786, from an old peal of five.   The porch is good,
the roof vaulted, with ribs and bosses.

The style is Perpendicular.   There are fragments of the screen
in the north chancel aisle and in the reading desk.   There is a
seventeenth century monument, with figures, in memory of members of the Alleyn and Morringe families, on the north side of the
chancel, and others to Pengelly, Sowter, Jope, Spry, Drake, and
Courtenay of Walreddon.

The church is a large building, which was
**Tavistock.**   erected during the fifteenth and sixteenth
St. Eustachius.   centuries, taking the place of an earlier
building of Abbot Champeaux, which was

consecrated in 1318. The base of the tower is of this latter date, but there are no other remains of the Decorated period. The church has a nave eighty feet long by twenty feet wide, chancel about thirty feet long by twenty feet wide, north and south aisles about thirty feet long by fourteen feet wide, and a second south aisle eighty feet long by fifteen feet wide, porch covering the south door-way, vestry north of the chancel, and a tower one hundred and six feet high, by twenty-seven feet square, with buttresses, battlemented parapet pinnacles with vanes, and at the foot pierced with arches on all four sides, so that it stands upon piers. There are eight bells, all cast by Thomas Bilbie, of Collumpton, in 1769. The tower was completed by Abbot Cullyng, in 1380, having been commenced early in the same century. The additional south aisle is that of St. Thomas of Canterbury, erected by Constantia Coffin, Robert Bonefas, and Maurice Berd, in 1445, as a Guild chapel. It is now known as the Cloth-worker's aisle. The carving of the ribs and bosses of the roofs are good. At the east end of the church are exhibited some old documents connected with the church, and the seals with rush rings may be noticed. Besides the high altar, there were probably ten other altars in the church in the fifteenth century. The church underwent considerable alterations, and suffered many things in 1833, and 1845.

There are two monuments to be noticed. The first an altar tomb, with canopy supported by five Corinthian columns and a heavy pediment above. On the tomb are two whole length effigies of a knight and lady. The former is in armour, a ruff around his neck, his head resting on a pillow, a lion at his feet, and his hands in an attitude of prayer. The effigy of the lady represents her in a handsome dress and large ruff, a lamb at her foot. At the back against the wall is the figure of a youth kneeling at a desk with a book before him. The monument commemorates members of the Fitz family, probably Sir John Fitz, of Fitzford, who died 1589, and Mary his wife, daughter of Sir John Sydenham, of Brimpton, Somerset.

The other is the altar tomb of Sir John Glanville, the elder, an attorney of Tavistock, who was called to the bar in 1574, and made judge of the Common Pleas in June 1598, but he only sur-vived about two years, dying in July 1600. He built the mansion of Kilworthy. The effigy represents him in his scarlet robes of office. Below is the figure of his wife, Alice Skerret, in fardingale and ruff and golden chain, and in the front, at the bottom of the tomb, were the figures of their seven children, but some have now disappeared. Latin inscriptions on tablets give the names of parents and children.

In the church are preserved some human bones, belonging to a man of great stature, which, it is said, were found in a stone coffin, which is preserved, in the ruins of the abbey. The custodian will tell the visitor that they are the bones of Ordulf, founder of the abbey.

The Abbey Church and Conventual buildings, were on the south of the parish church. In the yard may be seen a relic of the wall arcading of the cloister—a beautiful piece of Early English work. Other remains of the abbey buildings will be found in the rear of the Bedford Hotel, and in the vicarage gardens; the Refectory is now the Unitarian Chapel, and the north gate-way and tower are on the opposite side of the square.

**St. Peter Tavy.** This church, three miles north east of Tavistock,
ST. PETER. consists of nave about thirty-three feet long oy fifteen feet wide, chancel about twenty-two feet long by twelve feet wide, north aisle about fifty-five feet long by twelve feet wide, south transept twelve feet square, south porch, and western tower sixteen feet six inches by twenty feet six inches at the bottom, with six bells, formerly five only, of which the treble, which was cracked, was recast in 1888, and a new treble added. The others were cast by the Cornish Penningtons, 1722-1790. The building is mainly Perpendicular, but the aisle is Decorated and was part of the earlier church. It underwent restoration in 1870—when the remains of the fine rood loft and screen were put on one side, and the wood-

work of the renaissance pews discarded.    In these border church-yards are frequently found tomb-stones of the seventeenth century, consisting of a massive granite slab, supported at each end by an up-right granite stone.   Mr. Hine considers them peculiar to this neighbourhood.   This is a very good one in the yard at Peter Tavy.

Some of the memorial inscriptions are of interest.

Here lye the bodies of five daughters of Richard Eveleigh, Rector of Peter Tavy, two Maries, two Elizabeths, and one Eleanor, all which died younge, ye longest and last liver being but a yeare old when she died, which was Sept. 13, 1632.

> Under this stone by nature's fatall doome
> Five sisters lie cropt in their tender bloome
> They breathed awhile and looked the world about
> And like new lighted candles soon went out
> Their sunne no sooner did arise, but set.
> Their journies' end at setting forth they met.
> They op'd their eyes, and in the world's disdaine
> Full quickly did they close them up againe.
> Their life was short, the less they did amisse,
> The shorter life the longer is their blisse.
>
> Five infant sisters from one wombe,
> Here lie together in one tombe :
> Their tide did ebb before full sea,
> Their welcome was their well away.
> Their parents have no cause to weepe,
> Sith they lie here, but in a sleepe.

Another on the memorial stone of Hannah Arthur :—

> Corruption, earth and worms,
>     Shall but refine her flesh
> Till her triumphant spirit comes
>     To put it on afresh.

**St. Mary Tavy.** This small, picturesquely situated church is in the immediate neighbourhood of the ST. MARY THE VIRGIN. remains of what was formerly one of the most important mines in the West of England—Great Wheal Friendship—now, like almost all the others, stopped, or as the miners say, knacked.  The stupendous machinery worked in connection with this mine, half a mile from the church, was, in the days of the mine's prosperity, a triumph of engineering,

FF

and there are many indications, in water courses, discarded iron-work and useless material, of the importance of the enterprise.

Outside the church-yard, in the street of the village, are the remains of the cross, the shaft, and its base on three high steps, the base has rude quatrefoils, circles, and mouldings.

The church is small, chancel, nave, south aisle, south porch, and tower.    It is for the most part Perpendicular.    There is a chapel at the east end of the aisle, with piscina in the south wall, formed in the jamb of one of the windows.    The church has been well restored, and is complete with rood and loft and other proper adjuncts.    The curious little pendants or drops to be seen in Meavy church, may be noticed here at the springing of the arch ribs of the nave.    At the feet of the ribs in the aisle, are small carved angels with outstretched wings, the intersection of the ribs being enriched with bosses of foliage and heads.

**Brent Tor.**
St. Michael. This church, built on "a high rocky place" as Risdon says, and visible from far and near, "a "mark to sailors who bear with Plymouth "haven."    The church stands "full bleak and "weather beaten, all alone, as it were forsaken, whose church-"yard doth hardly afford depth of earth to bury the dead : yet "doubtless, they rest as secure as in sumptuous St. Peter's, until "the day of dawn."

The church was built by the monks of Tavistock, and Mr. Hine says that most of the church is contemporaneous with the earliest existing remains of the Abbey—the very beautiful portions of the Early English arcade and arch in the church-yard at Tavistock.*    Erected in the thirteenth century, the edifice probably perpetuated and emphasised the purpose to which the hill, "a "famous sea mark," had been devoted—one of a line of Dartmoor beacons, from a remote time.

There are many traditions connected with the erection of this church, as there are of other churches in similar positions.    It is said that there was a church on this tor in 1283, and the church now visible is the original building with some few later insertions, and it dates back probably, half a century earlier than this.    Placed on the verge of what may be termed a precipice, 1130 feet above

---

*J. Hine.    St. Michael's, Brent Tor.    Trans. Dev. Assoc., vol. I., p. 116.
†Hine.    Op. cit., p. 119.

sea level, the western side only six feet from the edge, from which there is a prospect of vast extent, bounded on the east by the Tors of Dartmoor, on the south by the English Channel, on the west by the Cornish Hills, and on the remaining horizon by the hazy elevations of North Devon, the little building, consisting of a nave, chancel and western tower, with a porch covering the northern door, was dedicated in 1319, by Bishop Stapeldon. The measurement outside the walls is about forty-eight feet long by eighteen feet wide. The walls are very low, finished by low battlements, with a corbel table below. The tower also is embattled, and contained one bell with the inscription " *Gallus vocor ego, solus per omne sono*," but there are now three. The nave is thirty-seven feet six inches long and fourteen feet six inches wide, the tower opening to it, about eight feet square. The floor at the east is raised one step, but the screen marking the chancel is gone. There is a door-way on the south as well as on the north, and the church is lighted by two small Early English windows, only seven inches wide, and an east window. The walls are generally three feet in thickness. Granite has not been used in the building, the masonry is of dark brown stone, apparently iron stone, the dressings being of the green slate stone, from the neighbourhood of Tavistock, and the beautiful and simple lines and curves of Early English work have been, as Mr. Hine well points out, adopted in this lonely and unfrequented little church. From the floor to the ridge the building is between ten and eleven feet high, and had a massive moulded oak roof, covered with lead, the inclination from the walls to the ridge being about twelve inches. The tower, thirty-two feet high, has three small lights, one, that in the west face, an insertion of the fifteenth century. The altar, altar rails, pulpit and pews were of oak, and very rude. The font is an octagonal moor-stone basin, on a pedestal of the same form, without ornament of any kind. On the walls were some wooden tablets with scripture texts painted on them, and among them, " On this rock will I build my church and the gates of hell shall " not prevail against it."

Against the north wall is a stone tablet :—

Heare under this stone lyeth the bodie of John
Cole junr. of Litton who departed this life the 23rd
of Novemb. 1694 ætat 22. also Johan his sister
who was buried the 1st of February 1694 ætat 11.

If thou be sereous, friend peruse this stone,
If thou be not soe, pray let it alone,
Against death's person, vertue's the best art
When good men seeme to die they but depart.
Live well—then at the last with us thou'lt feele
Bare dying makes not death—but dying ill.

On the floor is a slab, of which the following words only can be read :—

this dear woman was buried
the      day of      A.D. 1688.

Against the north wall outside, is a stone with a rude attempt at an ornamental border with devices and the initials W.B. fancifully intertwined, and the inscription :—

Memontari mors.
Heare vnder this stone lyeth the body of
Walter Batten of Brinsabach who was buried
Aprill the sixth 1677 allso Alce his wife was
buried the therd of desember 1681.

In the yard is a stone with this inscription :—

In memory of Elizabeth Kinsman daughter
of John and Grace Kinsman of this parish who
departed this life May 16 1834 aged 2 years.

Happy infant early blest
Rest in peaceful slumber rest
Early rescued from the cares
Which increase with growing years.

The yard is full of graves, some of which have been cut out of the rock, and during the renovations in 1889-90, upwards of forty skeletons were found under the floor of the church. Standing in great need of repair, the church was substantially restored by Hastings, Duke of Bedford, and re-opened by the Bishop of Exeter, on Whit Tuesday, 1890. It now seats about fifty persons.

In the parish—at North Brent Tor—is another church, a modern building.

SAMUEL ROWE, M.A.

# CHAPTER XX.

## DARTMOOR LITERATURE.

THIS list of books and publications relating to Dartmoor and the neighbourhood—although probably not perfect—contains the title of every book, pamphlet, or paper of any importance, relating to the locality with which we are acquainted. Many of these are contributions to the Transactions of the County Society, and of the Plymouth Institution, and it will be readily seen how very much good work has been done since the publication of the first edition of this work. Mr. W. Crossing has kindly furnished us with several titles.

As to the Early Inhabitants and their migrations, see :—

*Forschungen im Gebiete der alten Völkerkunde.* Johan Gustav Cuno.

*Die Arier.* Theodor Pösche.

*Origines Ariacæ.* Karl Penka.

*Die Herkunft der Arier.* Karl Penka.

*Sprachvergleichung und Urgeschichte.* O. Schrader.

*Les Premier Habitants de l'Europe d'aprs les Ecrivains de l'Antiquité et les Travaux des Linguisètes.* Henri d'Arbois de Jubainville.

*The Origin of the Aryans.* Isaac Taylor.

Allen, Grant. An Ancient Lake Bottom. Longman's Magazine, June, 1884.

——From Moor to Sea. English Illustrated Mag. Dec. 1889.

——A Corner of Devon. Cornhill Magazine, November, 1882.

Amery, P. F. S. Dartmoor Forest, its Laws and Legends. Lecture, 1889,

——Stones found at Swincombe, probably connected with Ancient Mining there. Trans. Dev. Asso., vol. IV., 1870, p. 136.

Andrew, Thomas. Dartmoor, a paper read before the Exeter Naturalist's Society, 1872.

Andrews, Charles. The Prisoner's Memoirs, or Dartmoor Prison. History of Captivity of American Prisoners. New York, 1815. Another edition, 1852.

Appleton, Edward. Archæological Notes of Tavistock and Neighbourhood. Trans. Dev. Assoc. Vol. I., 1866, p. 122.

Baring-Gould, Rev. Sabine. Some Devon Monoliths. Trans. Dev. Assoc., vol. XX., 1888, p. 158.

────── and others. The Exploration of Grimspound. First Report Dartmoor Exploration Committee. Trans., Dev. Assoc. vol., XXVI., 1894, p. 100.

──────Second Report Dartmoor Exploration Committee. Trans. Dev. Assoc., vol., XXVII, 1895, p. 81.

──────Hut Circles at Tavy Cleave. Dev. Assoc. Trans., vol., XXVI., 1894, p. 196.

Baron, S. Botany of Dartmoor. Evans' Home Scenes, ed. 1846, p. 252.

Bate, C. Spence. Pre-historic Dartmoor. Trans. Plymouth Institution, vol. IV., p. 157.

──────Grimspound and its Associated Relics. Trans. Plymouth Institution, vol. V., p. 36.

──────Traces of the Scandinavian on Dartmoor. Trans. Plymouth Institution, vol. VI., p. 166.

──────Inscribed Stones and Ancient Crosses of Devon. Trans. Plymouth Institution, vol. V., p. 392 ; vol. VI., p. 154 ; vol. VIII., p. 142.

──────On the Pre-historic Antiquities of Dartmoor. Trans. Devon Assoc., vol. IV., 1871, p. 491.

──────A contribution towards determining the Etymology of Dartmoor names. Trans. Dev. Assoc., vol. IV., 1871, p. 520.

──────On the Clitter of the Tors of Dartmoor. Trans. Dev. Assoc., vol. IV., 1871, p. 517.

──────Pre-historic Antiquities of Dartmoor. Royal Cornwall Polytechnic Society, 40th Report, 1872.

──────Report on the Pre-historic Antiquities of Dartmoor. Journal Anthropological Institute, 1872 ?

──────On the Original Map of the Royal Forest of Dartmoor, illustrating the Perambulation of Henry III., 1240. Trans. Dev. Assoc., vol. V., 1871, p. 510.

──────Researches into some Ancient Tumuli on Dartmoor. Trans. Dev. Assoc., vol. V., 1872, p. 549.

Bate, C. Spence. Researches into some Ancient Tumuli on Dartmoor. Trans. Dev. Assoc., vol. VI., 1873, p. 272.

Bennett, John Nicholas. The Ammil on Dartmoor. Trans. Plymouth Institution, vol. V., p. 389.

Blizzard in the West, The. (9 March, 1891). 1891.

Bradford, John. Tales of the Moor, by Josias Homely. 1841.

Bray, Mrs. Anne Elizabeth. The Borders of the Tamar and Tavy, 3 vols, 1836. 2nd edition, 2 vols, 1879.

——A Peep at the Pixies, or Legends of the West. 1854.

Brent, Francis. On a Group of Pre-historic Remains on Dartmoor. Jour. Brit. Arch. Assoc , vol. XXXIX., 1883, p. 217.

——Flint Implements. Trans. Devon Assoc. vol. XVII., p. 70; vol. XVIII., p. 74.

Bridges, William B. Some Account of the Barony and Town of Okehampton, *cir.* 1839. New edition, 1889.

——Short Account of Dartmoor, in Description of Tour through West of England. Gentleman's Magazine, vol. LIX., p. 518.

Buckland, Rev. Wm., D.D. Notices of a series of specimens from the Granite Quarries at Prince Town. Report Brit. Assoc. 1841-1842.

Budd, F. N. Flint Implements, at Batworthy. Proceedings Teign Naturalists' Field Club, 1889, p. 9.

Burnard, Robert. Notes on Antiquities around Post Bridge, Dartmoor. Western Antiquary, vol. IX., p. 88.

——Flood of 17 July, 1870. Western Antiquary, vol. X., p. 16.

——The Great Central Trackway, Dartmoor. Trans. Dev. Assoc., vol. XXI, 1889, p. 431.

——Notes on Dartmoor Kistvaens. Trans. Dev. Assoc., vol. XXII., 1890, p. 200.

——On the Track of the Old Men of Dartmoor. Trans. Plym. Inst., vol. X., p. 95, do. p. 223.

——Antiquity of Mining on Dartmoor. Trans. Plym. Inst., vol. XI., p. 85.

——Dartmoor Pictorial Records, vols. 1, 2, 3 & 4, 1890-94.

——Exploration of the Hut Circles in Broadun Ring and Broadun. Trans. Dev. Assoc. vol. XXVI., 1894, p. 185.

——The Acquisition of the Forest of Dartmoor as a County Park, 1894.

Burt, William. Preface and Notes to Carrington's Dartmoor, first edition, 1826.

———The Plymouth and Dartmoor Railway. South Devon Museum, vol. VII., 1836.

Butcher, Rev. J. H. The Parish of Ashburton in the 15th and 16th centuries, 1870.

Carrington, Nicholas Toms. Dartmoor. A Poem. See also Burt, W., 1826. [*Several times reprinted without the Preface and Notes.*]

Catel, L. La Prison de Dartmoor, ou Récit Historique des Infortunes et Evasions des Prisonniers Français, 1809-1814, 2 vols, 1847.

Chagford on the Moor. David Carr. Pall Mall Gaz., 14 August 1885.

Chagford and Manadon, Recent Discoveries in the Parishes of. W. Pengelly. Trans. Dev. Assoc., vol. XII., 1888, pp. 365-379.

Chagford, The Parish of. G. W. Omerod. Trans. Dev. Assoc. vol. VIII., 1876, p. 62.

Chapple, William. Description and Exegesis of the Drewsteignton Cromlech, *cir.* 1779.

Chattock, R. S. Dartmoor. Aunt Judy's Magazine. Nov. 1882.

Childe the Hunter. The Childe. Article in Western Daily Standard, under the initials C.A.H., 23 Feb. 1870.

Chudleigh, John. Devonshire Antiquities, 1st. ed. 1891, 2nd. ed. 1893.

Cleghorn, J. On the Rock Basins of Dartmoor. Quart. Jour. Geol. Soc., vol. XIII., 1857.

Collier, William Frederick. Dartmoor. Trans. Dev. Assoc., vol. VIII., 1876, p. 370.

———Reports of the Committee on Dartmoor. Trans. Dev. Assoc., vol. IX., p. 120; vol. X., p. 110; vol. XI., p. 117; 1877, 1878, 1879

———The Duchy of Cornwall on Dartmoor. Trans. Dev. Assoc., XXI., 1889, p. 289.

———Fox Hunting on Dartmoor; Otter Hunting on Dartmoor. Reprinted from Saturday Review, in " A New Book of Sports," 1885.

———Venville Rights on Dartmoor. Trans. Dev. Assoc., vol. XIX., 1887, p. 377.

———Dartmoor and the County Council of Dartmoor. Trans. Devon Assoc., vol. XXVII., 1895, p. 213.

Colt-Drift, A.   Dartmoor, Saturday Review, 5th Sept., 1885.
Convict Prisons, Dartmoor.   Saturday Review, 23 Nov., 1889.
Coppard, Rev. W. I.   Preservation of Remains on Dartmoor.
    Archæological Journal, XVII., p. 70.
Cottle, Joseph.   Dartmoor and other Poems, with Notes, 1823.
Croker, J. G.   A Guide to the Eastern Escarpment of Dartmoor,
    1859.
————Dartmoor, its History and Antiquities.   A pamphlet of
    twenty pages, without author's name or date.
————See also Halle Fraser.
Crossing, William.   The Tors of Dartmoor.   The West Country
    Annual, 1894.
————The Land of Stream and Tor.   Privately printed, 1891.
————The Dartmoor Hills.   The West Country Annual, 1895.
————Tales of the Dartmoor Pixies, 1890.
————Amid Devonia's Alps, or Wanderings and Adventures on
    Dartmoor, 1888.
————Ancient Crosses of Dartmoor, 1884.
————    Do.    do. new and enlarged edition, 1887.
————Crockern Tor and the antient Stannary Parliament.
    Western Antiquary, vols. VIII and IX.
————The Old Stone Crosses of the Dartmoor Borders, 1892.
See also Okehampton.   Besides the works above mentioned,
    Mr. Crossing is the author of numerous contributions to the
    Western Antiquary, the West Country Annual, and other
    publications.
Dartmoor : Convict Life at.   Temple Bar, vol. XL. p. 348.
Dartmoor : R. J. King.   Western Daily Standard, 23 July 1873.
Dartmoor : R. J. King.   Standard (London) 24 July, 1873.
Dartmoor : Autumn and other Manœuvres on, by A. D. Tor
    [Miss Phillips] 1873.
Dartmoor : A Drive in Devonshire.   Holiday Rambles in Ordi-
    nary Places.   By a Wife with her Husband, 1880.
Dartmoor : Eclectic Review, vol. XXV.
Dartmoor : A Tramp through.   Belgravia, vol. XXI., p. 272.
Dartmoor : Quarterly Review, vol. CXXXV., p. 138.
Dartmoor : London Quarterly, vol. XXIV., p. 341.
Dartmoor : Edinburgh Review, 1835.
Dartmoor : Edinburgh Review, XXIV, 1855.
Dartmoor : A Poem.   Felicia D. Hemans, 1821.
Dartmoor : All the Year Round, vol. XXI., p. 283.

Dartmoor Preservation Association. Short History of the Rights of Common upon Dartmoor and the Commons of Devon, Publications, vol. I., 1890.

Dartmoor: Guide Books. Besley—Wood—Murray—Black—Ward and Lock—C. S. Ward and M. J. B. Baddeley, and others.

Dartmoor : Ten Days on. Guardian, 3 Oct, 1877.

Dartmoor: Guardian, 19 August, 1874.

Dartmoor: Gentleman's Magazine, July, 1871.

Dartmoor: Gentleman's Magazine, 1873.

Dartmoor: Gentleman's Magazine, 1874.

Dartmoor : Straight across. Temple Bar, XIX., p. 272.

Dartmoor : Saturday Review, 7 Sept. 1861 ; 6 July, 1889 ; 2 Nov. 1893.

Dartmoor : Colt-Drift. Saturday Review, 5 Sept. 1885.

Dartmoor Experiences. London Society, vol. XI., p. 516.

Dartmoor Prisons. The First Week at Dartmoor, by [late] 24 B. Devon and Exeter Gazette, 2 Oct. 1866.

Dartmoor Prison, as it was and as it is. Fraser's Mag, vol. XLVIII., p. 577.

Dartmoor: The South of Devon and. With a sketch of the Natural History of the District, by W. S. M. D'Urban. From Besley's Route Book of Devon, of which several editions have been published.

Dartmoor: Archæologia, vol. XXII., p. 429; XXV., pp. 53, 195; XXVIII., p. 450.

Dartmoor. Journal British Archæological Association, vol. XVIII., pp. 341-3.

Dartmoor Sketches, by A.Z., [said to be by Mrs. Prior] 1875 ?

Dartmoor Prisons. Democratic Review [N. Hawthorne] vol. XVIII., pp. 31, 457; vol. XIX., pp. 141, 209.

Dartmoor Prisons. Sharpe's Magazine, vol. XXXI., p. 134.

Dartmoor: Winter Days on. St. James' Magazine, vol. XXIII., p. 791.

Dartmoor Legends, and other Poems, by a Lady, 1857.

Dartmoor: Military Manœuvres and Convicts at. Temple Bar, vol. XL., p. 272.

Davidson, J. B. Some Anglo-Saxon Boundaries. Trans. Dev. Assoc., VIII., 1876.

Davies, Rev. E. W. L. Dartmoor Days, or Scenes in the Forest. 1863

Dawkins, W. Boyd. Early Man in Britain. 1886.

Deane, Rev. John Bathurst. Observations on Dracontia. Archæologia, vol. XXV., pp. 188-195, et seq.

Devonshire Sketches. A series of fourteen clever papers which appeared in the Plymouth Western Daily Standard, from July to October, 1869, said to have been written by Richard John King, but this is doubtful.

Dixon, Sophie. A Journal of Ten days Excursion on the Western and Northern Borders of Dartmoor, etc., 1830.

———A Journal of Eighteen Days' Excursion on the Eastern and Southern Borders of Dartmoor, etc., 1830.

Dymond, Robert. Things New and Old concerning the Parish of Widecombe in the Moor and its neighbourhood, 1876.

———Historical Documents relating to Dartmoor. Dev. Assoc., vol. XI., 1879, p. 371.

Eaton, Nathaniel. On some of the more remarkable British Monuments in Devon. Contained in the volume of Essays, by a Society of Gentlemen at Exeter, 1796, pp. 106-130.

Evans, Arthur J. Stone Circles, Stonehenge, &c. Archæological Review, vol. II., p. 312. See also Flinder Petries' Stonehenge.

Evans, John. The Ancient Stone Implements, Weapons, and Ornaments of Great Britain, 1872. *Contains references to finds on Dartmoor.*

Evans, John. The Ancient Bronze Implements, Weapons, and Ornaments of Great Britain and Ireland, 1881. *Contains references to finds on Dartmoor.*

Evans, Rachel. Home Scenes, or Tavistock and its Vicinity, 1846.

———Home Scenes, or Tavistock and its Vicinity, 2nd edition, 1875.

Fergusson, James. Rude Stone Monuments in all Countries, their age and uses, 1872.

Five Years Penal Servitude, by one who served it, 1877.

Forest of Dartmoor. R. J. King. Fortnightly Review, vol. VI., p. 300.

Fraser, Robert. General View of the County of Devon, with observations on the means of Impovement, 1794.

Gerrard, John, Curate of Withycombe in the Moor, Devon. Poems, 1769.

Gibbons, M. S. We Donkeys on Dartmoor, 1886.

Gosse, Phillip Henry. Dartmoor and the Dart. Intellectual Observer, vol. III., p. 318. Reprinted with engravings in the author's Sea and Land, p. 379, 1869.

Grimspound: the Exploration of. See Baring-Gould, Spence Bate, and Ormerod.

Halle, Fraser. Letters Historical and Botanical, relating chiefly to places in the Vale of Teign, etc. with Geological Notices by Dr. Croker, 1851.

Harford. A Moorland Church. Saturday Review, 27 Jan. 1877.

Harris, Capt. Vernon. Dartmoor Prison, Past and Present, *cir.* 1880.

Hawker, Rev. John Manley. River of Dart. Trans. Dev. Assoc., vol. XI., 1880, p. 274.

Hine, James. Notes on some Moorland and Border Churches in Devon. Trans. Plymouth Institution, vol. IV., p. 398, vol. V., p. 187.

——St. Michael's, Brent Tor. Trans. Dev. Assoc., vol. I., 1866, p. 116.

Hounsell, H. Strangway, M.D. Note on a Water-spout seen recently on Dartmoor. A paper read before the Torquay Natural History Society, 1881.

Hunt, Arthur Roope. On the Age of the Granites of Dartmoor and the English Channel. Trans. Dev. Assoc., vol. XXI., 1889.

Hunt, Robert. Dartmoor, its Tors and Tin Mines. Geological and Natural History Repertory, vol. I., 1865.

Hutchinson, P. O. State of Lydford and Okehampton Castles. Proceedings Soc. Ant., 2 Ser., vol. VIII., p. 484.

Johnson, W. On the Granite Quarries of Dartmoor, etc. Report Brit. Assoc., 1841.

Jones, John Pike. Observations on the Scenery and Antiquities of the Neighbourhood of Moreton Hampstead, and on the Forest of Dartmoor, 1823. New edition, 1830.

———A Guide to the Scenery in the Neighbourhood of Ashburton, 1823.

Kempe, Alfred John. Account of some Monuments conjectured to be British, still existing upon Dartmoor. Archæologia, vol. XXII., p. 429.

King, Richard John. The Forest of Dartmoor and its Borders. 1856.

——Folk Lore of Devonshire. Fraser's Magazine, Dec. 1873.

King, Richard John. The Forest of Dartmoor. Fortnightly Review, 15 Sept. 1866.

——Dartmoor. Quarterly Review, vol. 135.

——The Forest of Dartmoor. Fortnightly Review, vol. VI., p. 300.

Kingston, J. T. Account of the Iron Mine at Hey Tor. Philosophical Magazine, vol. III., 1828.

Kelly, Thomas. Timber on Dartmoor. Western Antiquary, vol. IV., p. 94.

——Celtic Remains on Dartmoor. Trans. Dev. Assoc., vol. I., 1866, p. 45. Also Journal Royal Inst. Cornwall, vol. II., 1866-7, p. 124.

Laskey, A. Ramble on Dartmoor. Gentleman's Magazine, vol. LXVI., 1796.

Lewis, A. L. Stone Circles of Britain. Jour. Royal Arch. Inst., vol. XLIX., 1892, p. 136.

——Stone Circles of England and Wales. Proceedings Society of Antiquaries, vol. XIV., 1892-3, p. 150.

——British Stone Circles. Science, 1893.

Lewis, F. C. Picturesque Scenery of the Devonshire Rivers. Various dates.

Lukis, Rev. W. C. Report on Pre-historic Monuments of Devon and Dartmoor. Proc. Soc. Ant. 2 Ser., vol. VIII., pp. 285-470.

——Report on the Monuments of Dartmoor, its Avenues, Large Circles, Burial Mounds, Hut Circles and Holed Stones, 1881. *From the Proceedings Soc. Ant.*

Lysons, Samuel. Account of Discoveries made in taking down the Old Bridge over the River Teign. Archæologia, vol. XIX, p. 308.

Mackenzie, H. P. Jottings at the Dartmoor Autumn Manœuvres. A series of lithographs, Torquay, 1873.

Manadon and Chagford: Recent Discoveries in the Parishes of. W. Pengelly. Trans. Devon Assoc., vol. XII., pp. 365-379.

McCarthy, R. H. A day on Dartmoor. English Illustrated Mag., July 1891.

Mitchell, Philip. A Dartmoor Celt. Trans. Plymouth Institution, vol. IV., p. 34.

Moore, Stuart A. Short History of the Rights of Common upon Dartmoor and the Commons of Devon. Dartmoor Pres. Assoc. Publications, vol. I., 1890.

Okehampton: The Commons and Park of. W. Crossing, in Bridges' Okehampton, 2nd ed. 1889, p. 192.

Ormerod, G. Waring. Account of certain supposed British and Druidical Remains in the Parishes of Chagford and Gidleigh, and the adjoining part of the Forest of Dartmoor. Transactions Plym. Institution, vol. I., 1858, p. 20.

——Rock Basins in the Granite of the Dartmoor District. Quarterly Jour. Geol. Soc., Feb. 1859. Other Geological Papers on Dartmoor by this author, will be found in the volumes of the Transactions of the Devonshire Association, and the Quarterly Journal of the Geological Society.

——Hut Circles on the Eastern side of Dartmoor. Journal Brit. Arch. Assoc., vol. XX., 1864, p. 229

——On the Traces of Tin Streaming, in the Vicinity of Chagford. Trans. Dev. Assoc., vol. I., 1866, p. 110.

——Account of the Wardens of Chagford, from 1480 to 1559. Report Teign Naturalists' Field Club, 1870.

——The Fall and Restoration of the Cromlech at Drewsteignton. Trans. Dev. Assoc., vol. IV., 1876, p. 409.

——What is Grimspound? Trans. Dev. Assoc., vol. V., 1872, p. 41.

——Notes of Pre-historic Remains, formerly existing near the Drewsteignton Cromlech, observed by the Rev. R. Polwhele, prior to 1793, and mapped by the Rev. William Grey, in 1838. Trans. Dev. Assoc., Vol. V., 1872, p. 73.

——On the Fall and Restoration of the Drewsteignton Cromlech. Journal Royal Archæol. Institute, vol. XXIX., 1873.

——Notes on Rude Stone remains situate on the easterly side of Dartmoor, 8vo, privately printed, 1873.

——Wayside Crosses in the District bordering the East of Dartmoor. Trans. Dev. Assoc., vol. VI., 1874, p. 387.

——Historical Sketch of the Parish of Chagford. Trans. Dev. Assoc., vol. VIII., 1876, p. 62.

Page, John Lloyd Warden. An Exploration of Dartmoor and its Antiquities, 1889.

——Okehampton, its Castle and the surrounding country, 1890.

——The Names of the Dartmoor Tors. West. Ant., vol. VII., 1887.

Pattison, R. S.   The Dwellings of the Celts.   Leisure Hour [?1865.]

Pearce, Thomas.   The Laws and Customs of the Stannaries in the Counties of Cornwall and Devon, 1725.

Pengelly, William.   The Extinct Lake of Bovey Tracey.   Trans. Plym. Inst., vol. IX., p. 188.

————On the Age of the Dartmoor Granite.   Trans. Devon Assoc., 1863.

———— and Rev. Oswald Heer.   The Lignite Formation of Bovey Tracey, 1863.

————See Manadon.

Pollock, Sir Frederick.   Dartmoor and the Walkham.   English Illustrated Magazine, January, 1884.

Polwhele, Richard.   Historical Views of Devonshire, vol., 1 (all published) 1793.

————The History of Devonshire, 3 vols, 1797.

Pony and Pegasus, or a Ride and a Rhyme about Dartmoor, 1862.

Prickman, J. D.   Okehampton, and what is to be seen there, 1895.

————[Pidgon.]   Rambles on Dartmoor.   Devon and Exeter Gazette, October, November, December, 1887, and January, 1888.

Prideaux, John.   Geological Sketch of the Country between the Rivers Plym and Tamar, from the Granite of Dartmoor, southward to the sea, 1828.

Princetown.   Its History and its Prisons.   Three articles in the Western Daily Mercury, April, 1869 [by H. S. Hill]

Prowse, Arthur B.   Notes on the Neighbourhood of White Tor, West Dartmoor.   Trans. Dev. Assoc., XXI., 1889, p. 166.

————Notes on the Neighbourhood of Taw Marsh, North Dartmoor.   Trans. Dev. Assoc., vol. XXII., 1890, p. 185.

————The Ancient Metropolis of Dartmoor.   Trans. Dev. Assoc., vol. XXIII., 1891, p. 307.

Radford, Daniel.   The Natural Storage of Water on Dartmoor. Trans. Dev. Assoc., vol. XXI., 1889, p. 205.

Radford, Mrs. G. H.   History of the Church at Lydford.   Trans. Dev. Assoc., vol. XXI., 1889, p. 71.

Rambles on Dartmoor.   See Prickman.

Richardson, Wm.   Essay on the Improvement of Dartmoor Forest, Bath, 1813.

Rowe, J. Brooking. The Cistercian Houses of Devon, 1878.
———Plympton Castle. Trans. Plymouth Institution, vol. VI., p. 246.
Rowe, Samuel. Antiquarian Investigations in the Forest of Dartmoor, Devon. Transactions Plymouth Institution, 1830, p. 179.
———A Perambulation of the Antient and Royal Forest of Dartmoor, and the Venville Precincts, 1848.
———Ditto, second edition, 1856.
Rowlands, Henry. Mona Antiqua Restaurata. An Archæological Discourse, etc., of the Isle of Anglesea, 1723, 2nd edition, 1766. Frequently quoted by the author in the first edition of this work.
Rutley, Frank. The Eruptive Rocks of Brent Tor and its Neighbourhood, 1878
Shelly, John. A plea for Dartmoor. Clack, 1865.
Spencer, Rev. E. A Few Remarks on Dartmoor, 1892.
Tanner, Henry. The Cultivation of Dartmoor, 1854.
Taylor, Isaac. Personal Recollections. Devonshire and Dartmoor. Good Words, 1864, p. 516.
Thompson, Mrs. E. P. A Guide to some Excursions around Dartmoor, 1883.
Tickler. (E. Tozer) Devonshire Sketches, Dartmoor and its Borders, 1869.
———Devonshire Sketches, Pixy Lore, etc., 1871.
Tumuli on Dartmoor, Notes on, with plan. Archæologia, vol. XXII., p. 429.
Tyrwhitt, Thomas. Substance of a statement made to the Chamber of Commerce concerning the Formation of a railroad from the Forest of Dartmoor, 1818.
Ussher, W. A. E. Physical Features of Devonshire. Trans. Dev. Assoc., vol. XI., 1888, p. 264. Other Geological papers by Mr. Ussher, will be found in the Transactions of the Devonshire Association, and the Quarterly Journal of the Geological Society.
Vancouver, Charles. General View of the Agriculture of the County of Devon, 1808.
Watt, Alexander. Breeding of Cobs and Ponies on Waste Hill Lands. 1886.
Waddington, Horace. Straight across Dartmoor. Temple Bar, 1867.
Watkins, M. G. A tramp through Dartmoor. Belgravia, vol. XXI.

Whale, Rev. T. W. Some remarks on the Bounds of the Forest of Dartmoor, with special reference to the Parishes of Throwleigh, Chagford and Gidleigh. Trans. Dev. Assoc., vol. XXV., 1893, p. 510.

Wilkins, John. A Chapter on the Stannaries. Gentleman's Magazine, April 1866.

Widecombe. A true Relation of those sad and lamentable accidents which happened in and about the Parish Church of Withycombe in the Dartmoores, in Devonshire the 21 of October last, 1638.

——A second and most exact relation of those sad and lamentable accidents which happened in and about the Parish Church of Wydecombe, neere the Dartmoores in Devonshire, on Sunday the 21 of October last, 1638. 1638.

Wilkinson, Sir J. G. On the Rock Basins of Dartmoor, and some British Remains in England. Journ. Brit. Arch. Assoc., vol. XVI., 1860, p. 101.

——British Remains on Dartmoor. Journ. Brit. Arch. Assoc., vol. XVIII., 1862, p. 22.

Wistman's Wood. Gardener's Chronicle, 1875, pp. 387, 522, 711, and 813.

Worth. Richard Hansford. The Moorland Plym. Trans. Plym. Inst., vol. X., p. 289.

——The Erme, Yealm and Torry. Trans. Plym. Inst., vol. XI., p. 173.

Worth, Richard Nicholls. The Ancient Stannary of Ashburton. Trans. Dev. Assoc., vol. VIII., 1876, p. 311.

——Lydford and Its Castle. Trans. Dev. Assoc., vol. XI., 1879, p. 282.

——Were there Druids in Devon? Trans. Dev. Assoc., vol. XI., 1880, p. 228.

——The Druidical Myth. Trans. Plymouth Institution, vol. VI., p. 224.

——Lydford and its Castle. Jour. Brit. Arch. Assoc., vol. XXXIX., 1883, p. 350.

——A Hut Cluster on Dartmoor. Trans. Dev. Assoc., vol. XXII., 1890, p. 237.

——The Rude Stone Monuments of Cornwall. Journal Royal Inst. of Cornwall, vol. XII., 1894.

Worth, Richard Nicholls. Notes upon some Dartmoor Antiquities.
    Notes and Gleanings, vol. II.
———The Stone Rows of Dartmoor. Trans. Dev. Assoc., vols.
    XXIV., XXV., XXVI., and XXVII., 1892-5,
Worthy, Charles.  Ashburton and its Neighbourhood, 1875.
———Devonshire Parishes, 2 vols.    1887.

# NOTES AND CORRECTIONS.

Page 43. Line 10 from top, the supposed Cromlech is a Kistvaen, see pp. 207-8

119. Line 14 from top of page, *for* notice, *read* noticed.

140. Line 12 from top, full stop after the word rises. The word Conspicuous, should begin a new sentence.

143. Line 1 in last foot note, *for* Anerion, *read* An error.

154. Line 21 from top of page, *omit* the word too.

165. First foot note, *omit* from XVIII to second *the* in the sentence, and insert, XIII, p. 290, for a. An account of the old map formerly in the possession of the Tothills of Bagtor and afterwards of Thomas Veale Lane, Esq., and presented by him to the Albert Museum, Exeter, of which we give a photographic reduction opposite page 165, wil be found in the Transactions of the Devonshire Association, Vol. V, p. 510.

182. Line 4 from top, *for* mail, *read* main.

200. Wistman's Wood. We may hope that the prediction of the writer in the Journal of Forestry—that in a thousand years hence the oaks of the wood having crumbled and no acorns having been borne by them they will have no successors—will not be fulfilled. If the production of acorns will preserve the wood it is safe, for acorns are to be found, sparingly it is true, upon the trees. In September last, after a long search in the hope of disputing the statement of this writer, a lady discovered two, besides a third of the previous year. These two acorns having been carefully sown, have germinated, and are now growing.

215. After line 12 from top the printer has placed the foot note, which should be at the bottom of the page.

Page 271. Since Chapter XI. was printed, the Blue Book containing the Mineral Statistics for 1894 has been issued. As in 1893, the only tin mines now being worked are Golden Dagger and Hexworthy, which together produced fifty tons of ore of the value of £1373. This shows a further decline. The once important manganese industry has now, too, dwindled down to very small proportions, thirty-one tons in 1894 only having been raised, as against three · hundred and seventy-five tons in 1893, the value of these thirty-one tons being only £12.

290. Line 1 from bottom, *omit* from.

312. This presentment, it is said cannot now be found at the Duchy Office. No doubt the certified copy was obtained by Sir Edward Smirke, and the original has been lost or mislaid, or there may be a mistake in the mention of its place of deposit.

383. Line 3 from top, *after* Schistidium, *insert* apocarpum, which specific name is in the wrong place below.
Last line, *for* Hutchinsiœ, *read* Hutchinsii.

391. After line 21 from top, *insert* Lejeunia minutissima, Shaugh Bridge, *wrongly inserted lower down the page under Marchantiaceœ.*

395. Line 25 from top, *for* Strictina, *read* Stictina.
Line 34 from top, *for* Stricta, *read* Sticta.
Line 37 from top, *for* Bren, *read* Brent.
Line 39 from top, *for* lœtevirens, *read* lœtivirens.

396. Line 5 from top, *for* B. Borreri, *read* P. Borreri.
Line 5 from bottom, *for* anaurtiaca, *read* aurantiaca.

397. Line 7 from top, the locality for P. ceuthocarpa is Sharpitor. P. globulifera has been omitted and should follow, the localities being Bagtor and Ilsington.

398. Line 8 from bottom, *for* Z-quiniuum, *read* Z. quininum.

435. Line 8 from top, *for* p. 120. *read* p. 290.

438. Line 2 from top, *for* down, *read* Down.

439. Line 16 from top, *for* Senectus, *read* Senectus.

443. Line 24 from top, *insert the word*, me—Death found me sore oppressed.

513. Line 2 and 3 from bottom, *for* Slamming *read* Slanning.

515. Line 3 from bottom, 1st col., *for* Teachwarp, *read* **Trackways.**

# INDEX.

W. J. SOUTHWOOD & CO., "DYNAMO" WORKS, EXETER.

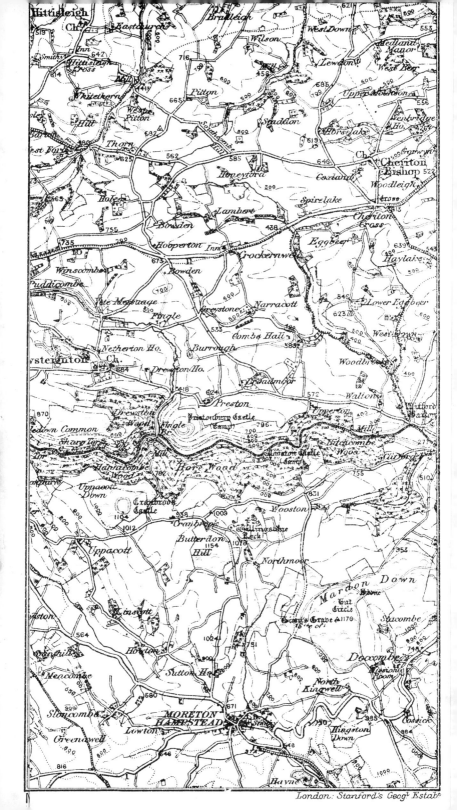